DOING COMPUTATIONAL SOCIAL SCIENCE

Sara Miller McCune founded SAGE Publishing in 1965 to support the dissemination of usable knowledge and educate a global community. SAGE publishes more than 1000 journals and over 800 new books each year, spanning a wide range of subject areas. Our growing selection of library products includes archives, data, case studies and video. SAGE remains majority owned by our founder and after her lifetime will become owned by a charitable trust that secures the company's continued independence.

Los Angeles | London | New Delhi | Singapore | Washington DC | Melbourne

DOING COMPUTATIONAL SOCIAL SCIENCE

A PRACTICAL INTRODUCTION

JOHN McLEVEY

Los Angeles | London | New Delhi
Singapore | Washington DC | Melbourne

Los Angeles | London | New Delhi
Singapore | Washington DC | Melbourne

SAGE Publications Ltd
1 Oliver's Yard
55 City Road
London EC1Y 1SP

SAGE Publications Inc.
2455 Teller Road
Thousand Oaks, California 91320

SAGE Publications India Pvt Ltd
B 1/I 1 Mohan Cooperative Industrial Area
Mathura Road
New Delhi 110 044

SAGE Publications Asia-Pacific Pte Ltd
3 Church Street
#10-04 Samsung Hub
Singapore 049483

Editor: Jai Seaman
Assistant editor: Charlotte Bush
Production editor: Ian Antcliff
Copyeditor: QuADS Prepress Pvt Ltd
Proofreader: Neville Hankins
Indexer: David Rudeforth
Marketing manager: Ben Griffin-Sherwood
Cover design: Shaun Mercier
Typeset by: C&M Digitals (P) Ltd, Chennai, India

Library of Congress Control Number: 2021937242

British Library Cataloguing in Publication data

A catalogue record for this book is available from the British Library

ISBN 978-1-5264-6819-2
ISBN 978-1-5264-6818-5 (pbk)

CONTENTS

DISCOVER YOUR ONLINE RESOURCES!

Doing Computational Social Science is accompanied by a wealth of online resources to support learning and teaching. Find them at: https://study.sagepub.com/mclevey

For students:

- **Screencast video tutorials** from author John McLevey demo step-by-step how to use Python so you can build your confidence navigating the software.
- Links to all the **datasets** used in the book help you develop your computational skills by applying what you've learned to real-world data.
- **Problem sets** for every chapter mean you can test what you've learned and check your understanding.
- A growing collection of **perspectives and practical advice** from computational social scientists and data scientists from around the globe give you expert insight into the field.
- **High resolution colour figures** from the book mean you can see data visualisation up close.
- Access to **dozens of language models** trained by John McLevey and Tyler Crick, along with instructions for how to download and use them, enable you to put your learning into practice with real computational models.

- A **virtual environment** for the book ensures you can use the packages John discusses no matter what operating system your computer is running.
- A **Python package** of functions that you will learn in the book helps you get to grips with different techniques and tasks.

For instructors:

- **HTML slides and Jupyter Notebooks** for each chapter of the book can be customized for use in your own lectures and presentations.
- A teaching guide including lesson plans, case studies and journal articles.
- **Multiple-choice questions** for each chapter that can be used in class, as homework or exams to test your students' understanding.
- An **answer key** to the student problem sets.

ACKNOWLEDGEMENTS

This book would not exist in its current form, or perhaps at all, without the support, advice, and contributions of a great many other people. I am extremely grateful to all of them.

First and foremost, thanks to my PhD students Pierson Browne, Tyler Crick, and Alexander (Sasha) Graham for their many contributions to this book, especially in the final 6 months of work, when all three made a series of invaluable contributions to the project. Pierson Browne constructed the datasets used in the Bayesian regression modelling chapters and was instrumental in the development of all Bayesian data analysis chapters. Similarly, Tyler Crick was instrumental in the development of the chapters on stochastic block models, generative topic models, word embeddings, and transformers. He also put considerable effort into cleaning the Enron communication network. Sasha Graham was instrumental in the development of the chapters on network analysis and research ethics, and helped track the many complex knowledge and skill dependencies that stretch across all 33 chapters. He also helped identify something on the order of 50,000 cuttable words as production deadlines loomed. Pierson, Tyler, and Sasha have improved this book immeasurably, and I am very grateful for it. Thanks to Laine Bourassa and Alec for tolerating the same sort of working-all-hours nonsense that my partner has tolerated for far too long, even though they should not have had to.

Secondly, thanks to Jillian Anderson for providing an extremely thorough technical review of the manuscript, especially given that the word count of the version she reviewed was closer to 300,000 than 200,000. She has improved the manuscript in many ways, including by sharing her thoughts on data science, machine learning, ethics, computation, and professional development in our many conversations over the years. I'm especially grateful for all the practical wisdom she shared while we were co-teaching at GESIS in Cologne in early 2020. Her experience and expertise have had a strong influence on how I've come to see the field.

I would like to thank the students who have worked in my research lab (Netlab) at the University of Waterloo over the years, and who have all been centrally involved in my own learning process in computational social science. In addition to Pierson, Tyler, Sasha, and Jillian (who is now a big data developer at Simon Fraser University), I'd like to thank Reid McIlroy-Young, Joel Becker, Mumtahin Monzoor, Tiffany Lin, Rachel Wood, Alex de Witt, Alexis Foss Hill, Steve McColl, Brittany Etmanski, and Evaleen Hellinga. Thanks also to 'honorary' members of the lab, Yasmin Koop-Monteiro, Adam Howe, and François Lapachelle from the University of British Columbia, and Yixi Yang from Memorial University.

Thank you to all the undergraduate and graduate students who have taken courses in computational social science with me at the University of Waterloo. There are far too many to name, but I am especially grateful to those students whose feedback and level of engagement have resulted in substantial improvements to the material in this book. Thanks especially to Michelle Ashburner, Silas Tsui, Sunny Luo, Zane Elias, Ben Ang, Cassidy Raynham, Stephanie Reimer Rempel, Jordan Klassen, David Borkenhagen, Emilie Caron, Khoa Tran, Tyler Kruger, Nate Flatch, and Terry Zhang. Similarly, I would like to thank participants in workshops I've taught with preliminary chapter drafts at the University of Waterloo, the University of British Columbia, and at GESIS Leibniz Institute for the Social Sciences in Cologne. In particular, I would like to thank Stijn Daenekindt, Jessica Herzing, Tina Kretshel, Janice Aurini, Ali Marin, Eugena Kwon, Xiaowei Li, and Soli Dubash.

Many colleagues and friends have improved the content in this book (sometimes even unwittingly) via conversation and in some cases directly commenting on chapter drafts. I am especially grateful to Allyson Stokes, Peter Carrington, Johan Koskinen, David Tindall, Anabel Quan-Haase, Lorien Jasny, Mario Diani, Tuomas Ylä-Anttila, Antti Gronow, Lasse Folke-Henriksen, Andrew Osmond, Ian Milligan, Igor Grossman, Howard Ramos, Marlene Mauk, Rochelle Terman, Jennifer Earl, Tina Fetner, Heather Douglas, Bernie Hogan, Raphael Heiberger, Jan Riebling, Alix Rule, Bonnie Erickson, Qiang Fu, Luka Kronegger, Deena Abul Fottouh, Harry Collins, Rob Evans, Martin Innes, Kate Duart, Alun Preece, Darrin Durant, Martin Weinel, Nicky Priaulx, Nina Kolleck, Marty Cooke, Owen Gallupe, Vanessa Schweizer, Rob Gorbet, Katie Plaisance, Ed Jernigan, Rob Nolan, Rashmee Singh, and John Scott. Thanks also to the anonymous reviewers who provided extremely helpful comments on draft chapters.

Thanks to my colleagues in the Faculty of Environment (ENV) at the University of Waterloo for providing an intellectual home where interdisciplinary research and teaching are encouraged and valued. I'm especially grateful to the faculty, staff, and students in Knowledge Integration, who have led by interdisciplinary example, curious open-mindedness, and a willingness to slow down and learn from people who do things differently. Thanks also to my ENV friends and colleagues for providing inspiration and support, and for keeping things in perspective.

At SAGE, I would like to thank Jai Seaman for believing in this project from the start and doing everything she could to support it, including during tough times when the work felt insurmountable. Jai's editorial experience, expertise, patience, and goodwill helped make a book out of a sprawling collection of chapters. Charlotte Bush similarly played a central role in making this project a reality, and I am thankful to her for her expertise and patience. Thanks to Ian Antcliff for expertly guiding the manuscript through the production process despite disruptions related to COVID-19, and to everyone who contributed to the production of the book despite the challenges of the pandemic.

Thanks to my endlessly patient and understanding partner Allyson Stokes. She has supported and improved this project in many ways over the years, both as a partner and intellectually as a fellow sociologist. Ally, thank you for everything. Thanks to Vincenza Etchegary, my music teacher of roughly a decade, for teaching me how to practice deliberately (long before I learned about deliberate practice from the research of cognitive scientists such as K. Anders Ericsson) and for imparting a deep love of the long road to mastery. Finally, thank you to my friends and family for all the support, love, and much-needed fun.

This book was written using a combination of markdown, LaTeX, and Python written using open source text editors and Jupyter Notebooks, with pandoc for document conversion, git for version control, and conda and Docker for virtualization. Thanks to the many people who develop and maintain these and other open source tools.

ABOUT THE AUTHOR

 John McLevey is an associate professor in the Department of Knowledge Integration at the University of Waterloo (Ontario, Canada). He is also appointed to the Departments of Sociology & Legal Studies and Geography and Environmental Management, is a Policy Fellow at the Balsillie School of International Affairs, and is a Member of the Cybersecurity and Privacy Institute at the University of Waterloo. His work is funded by research grants from the Social Science and Humanities Research Council of Canada and an Early Researcher Award from the Ontario Ministry of Research and Innovation. His current research project focuses on disinformation, censorship, and political deliberation in the public sphere across a wide variety of national contexts and political regimes. This book is written from his experiences as a researcher and advisor, as well as teaching courses in computational social science, data science, and research methods to students from diverse disciplinary backgrounds at the undergraduate and graduate levels.

INTRODUCTION: LEARNING TO DO COMPUTATIONAL SOCIAL SCIENCE

This book aims to show you how to do computational social science, and data science more generally, using the open source programming language Python and complex imperfect datasets of the kind you might actually work with in your own research working with messy real-world data. It differs from other books and learning materials in the field in many respects, the most salient three being the following:

- It is designed to accommodate researchers with widely varying intellectual and technical backgrounds
- It covers a very broad range of methods and models while still emphasizing deep understanding
- It does so in an unapologetically practical way. I've tried to write as if we were sitting down at a computer looking at data and fitting models together

I start with the very basics (setting up a scientific computing environment and typing your first line of Python code) and end with in-depth examples of developing a variety of models that are currently at the cutting edge of machine learning and statistics, network science, and natural language processing. The content is cumulative and carefully scaffolded, provided you start at the beginning and work through each chapter sequentially. If you already have a good foundation and are looking to go further in one area or another, you can safely read chapters out of sequence. If you are starting with little to no prior experience to build on, the early chapters will help lay a foundation that subsequent chapters can build on, brick by brick.

I've done my best to identify what you really need to know to go from a beginner to a highly skilled researcher with a good bit of breadth and depth. However, to learn effectively from this book – *to get the most from it* – you will need to honestly assess where you are and where you want to be, and plan your learning accordingly. Below, I'll outline some of the assumptions I make about what you already know. Then I'll offer some practical advice on how to learn to do computational social science from this book so that you can start using your new knowledge and skills in your own projects as quickly as possible.

0.1 Who Is This Book for?

I have tried to write this book for as broad and diverse a readership as possible, but even with 235,000 words, it can't cover everything, and it can't be a book for everyone. The type of person

I have primarily kept in mind is a scientific researcher – regardless of their specific disciplinary background or research interests – with little to no computational experience or expertise. I have no specific career stage in mind; rather than writing for students of a particular level, I have tried to write for anyone who is new, or relatively new, to computational social science. That could be as true for a tenured professor as for a graduate student or an advanced undergraduate student.

What do I mean by 'scientific researcher', or scientist? I use these terms a lot, and pretty casually, so it's worth taking a moment to clarify what I mean by them. I mean 'scientist' in a very general sense, inclusive of all the social, cognitive, and communication sciences; applied health sciences; environmental sciences; and interdisciplinary fields, like network science, that cut across nearly every branch of science. While it is easy to enumerate dozens of things that make sociologists different from epidemiologists, economists different from biologists, and everyone different from physicists, my preference in writing this book has been to emphasize what we have in common: we all engage in efforts to honestly and systematically advance the state of general knowledge in our fields using a combination of empirical data, theory, and models. Given that you are currently reading this book, I assume you are interested in furthering your ability to do so using computational approaches.

Assumed knowledge and skills

I assume that you have little to no previous experience with programming or scientific computing. The early chapters are intended to give you that foundation, which later chapters will build on.

In terms of methodological background, I assume that you have a basic familiarity with the core components of research design for observational and experimental research and some general knowledge of conventional quantitative research methods. I do not assume any specific experience or expertise in quantitative methods beyond what would be covered in an introductory undergraduate class in the social, physical, health, or environmental sciences:

- Knowledge of descriptive statistics
- Knowledge of how to interpret common statistical graphics (e.g. histograms and scatter plots)
- Knowledge of correlation and some familiarity with the basics of regression analysis

In some chapters, I also assume some familiarity with the basic logic of qualitative and historical methods, but – once again – my assumption is that you know about as much as one would after completing a generic undergraduate research methods class.

If you have not completed a research methods course of some kind, it's still possible to learn from this book, but you should know that I have allocated minimal space to these more introductory topics that are not unique to computational social science. While I would have preferred to cover them thoroughly as well, I had to make room for other introductory content that is almost never taught in existing courses, such as basic programming and scientific computing skills.

People come to computational social science from a broad variety of intellectual backgrounds. In my experience of teaching and advising, the most relevant differences seem to be in terms of previous experience with quantitative data analysis, programming, and open source computing. Before going further, I want to briefly share some thoughts about how some of these different backgrounds are likely to shape your learning process.

First, some good for the 'quants': previous experience with quantitative data analysis is a major asset when learning computational social science. If your knowledge is close to what you might find in a graduate-level quantitative methods class or higher, you probably have a very good foundation to build on. You will most likely find that you have an easier time grasping many of the more complex methods and models. The other advantages you have may be a bit less obvious, such as *general comfort* with probabilistic and model-based thinking.

However, if you are coming to computational social science with a more qualitative or interpretive background, *you also have many useful and relevant skills to build on*. They're just different from those of your more quantitatively minded peers. Many methods and models used in computational social science are useful precisely because they are well-aligned with theories that conventional quantitative approaches are poorly aligned with. As a result, there is a lot of exciting work happening in fields where researchers have long made use of text data (e.g. computational cultural sociology or computational political sociology/political science). The type of theory that has developed in these fields is not necessarily better or worse than what you see in fields that are more oriented towards linear models, but it's definitely *different*. Having some facility with the kind of theory used in these fields is a great asset. You can even translate your *theory* advantage into a *modelling* advantage once you get comfortable representing those abstract theoretical ideas as computational models. If you have some experience working with unstructured data in the form of text and images, then you also come to the table with some methodological advantages. Computational approaches to working with those kinds of data will probably be very foreign to you at first, but as I will argue later in the book, it is generally a very good idea to pair computational text analysis with qualitative analysis. The main point is this: your methodological experience matters. Whether quantitative or qualitative, you have existing intellectual strengths that will simplify or motivate various portions of the learning process.

Finally, there is the matter of learning to program in the first place. While some quantitative researchers may enjoy an advantage here, the benefits are not ubiquitous. Having to write at least some code does not mean professional quantitative researchers adhere to best programming or scientific computing practices. Most of the time, the scripts they write get the job done in ugly and inefficient ways because they have acquired what programming knowledge they have in quantitative methods courses and/or by trying to solve specific data analysis problems rather than starting from the basics. I speak from personal experience.

While problem-driven learning is excellent in general (it features heavily in this book), it can develop many bad habits that – all aesthetic judgements aside – are bad for science. Even the most impressive stats nerds tend to be pretty bad programmers and could benefit from learning some basics. This is not so easily done, though, because some things that are good practice in programming and software development are not necessarily good practice in science. While you don't have to become a professional programmer to do great computational social science, it is very important to fix bad habits.

Advice on using this book to learn computational social science efficiently

When you are first learning computational social science or data science, it can feel like you are drinking from a fire hose. If that's the case for you, I have a few pieces of general advice that might help.

First, I would recommend using a simplified version of Bloom's taxonomy of learning outcomes (just a web search away) to determine (1) where you are right now and (2) where you want to be. Don't skip steps in the taxonomy. If there are multiple steps between where you are and where you want to be, that's OK, but you need to take those steps one at a time. Work through the book slowly and deliberately. After each chapter, take stock of your cumulative knowledge. What have you learnt, and how does it relate to what you learnt previously? Can you *explain* what you've learnt in your own words? Can you *do* the things that are introduced in each chapter on your own? In doing this, you may find that you understand something when you see it on the page, but are unable to clearly explain that thing, or do that thing yourself. You are experiencing the fuzzy threshold between different levels of competence: understanding (level 1 of Bloom's taxonomy), explanation (level 2), and application (level 3). If you have no previous experience of any kind, then your learning goals should focus on understanding before all else. Just make sense of what's going on. Once you have acquired understanding, then you can work on being able to correctly and clearly explain. The third step is competent application of your new knowledge and skills.

The book supports this scaffolded approach to learning by design (inspired by Brown et al., 2014; Ericsson and Pool 2016; Doyle and Zakrajsek, 2018; Weinstein et al., 2018). I recommend you read each chapter twice. Read it the first time on its own. Focus on understanding the concepts and see how each part of the chapter fits together into a coherent whole. Read the code and take notes. If something is unclear to you, write a reminder about what you don't understand *but keep reading*. Once you get to the end of the chapter, stop. If you have time, sleep on it. Give your brain a chance to process everything you've exposed it to. Let it move some of that content from short-term memory to long-term memory overnight! Then, without letting too much time pass, go back to the start of the chapter, but this time, *make sure you are sitting in front of a computer*. Type out the code in the chapter as you go, changing little things here and there to see how things work. Then, try to work through the problems and online learning materials associated with the chapter (described below). Whenever you encounter a gap in your knowledge, (1) explicitly make note of it and (2) fill it by going back to the relevant part of the chapter or by searching online.

My second piece of advice is to consider your learning process in computational social science as a kind of enculturation process (even though computational social science has many different communities and cultures). This is very different from the learning-with-a-checklist mindset. Checklists are helpful when they break complex things down into small manageable chunks (which is why each chapter starts with a (check)list of learning objectives). That said, checklists make it easy to forget that the individual items themselves are not really the point. The way I present computational social science is heavily focused on the underlying principles and practices of the field, as well as the shared conceptual underpinnings of a wide variety of methods and models. The goal is to learn how to think and work like a professional computational social scientist.

Learning to do computational social science in line with these principles usually requires slowing down at first to unlearn some deeply ingrained habits and replace them with others. It's less about 'learning Python' or other specific skills than it is about enculturation into a culture of transparent, auditable, and reproducible scientific computing. To align yourself with these core principles, you must know how to write all of your data collection, cleaning, and analysis code in well-organized scripts or notebooks, managed using virtual environments and version control software, and executed from the command line. Knowing how to use each tool is just the first step; to subsume principle and practice is the end goal. Most social scientists are never taught this, and many well-intentioned efforts to share important 'how-to' knowledge have the unintended consequence of disorienting and overwhelming highly capable newcomers who, through no fault of their own, can't see the point of doing things in such a seemingly byzantine fashion.

My third piece of advice is to be kind to yourself. Regardless of how challenging you find the material, *there is a lot to learn,* and you can't learn it all at once. The knowledge and skills that are required to develop deep expertise are scattered throughout the entire book. Most of the foundational computational skills you need to know to get started with data analysis, however, are introduced in the earliest chapters. Everything else is about gradually layering more specific computing, data analysis, and modelling skills on top of the general foundation. As you progress, regularly and honestly assess the state of your knowledge: you will see progress over time.

0.2 Roadmap

This book is carefully scaffolded, so a complete newcomer can start at the beginning and work their way through it chapter by chapter. It's also possible to work through the book in a different sequence if you already have some experience to build on. Here's what you can expect in the pages that follow.

Part I is all about foundations. Chapters 1 through 8 get you set up, using Python, processing and exploring datasets, and creating simple visualizations. Chapter 8 ends this sequence by introducing one of the main themes of the book: latent variables.

Part II consists of Chapters 9 through 12 and introduces the fundamentals of text analysis. It covers many low-level natural language processing techniques that you will use often for cleaning and preparing your text data for downstream modelling tasks. Then we discuss iterative workflows for text analysis, followed by a couple of chapters on descriptive and exploratory text analysis and 'latent semantic analysis', where we connect back to some of the ideas introduced in Chapter 8 and start thinking about latent thematic content in text data.

Part III consists of Chapters 13 to 17, inclusive. It does for network analysis what Part II does for text analysis. Chapter 13 introduces network analysis and relational thinking and discusses some foundational concepts. Chapters 14 and 15 introduce essential knowledge on descriptive network analysis (community detection and centrality analysis), and Chapters 16 and 17 introduce diffusion models that simulate the spread of various types of contagions through networks.

Together, Parts I to III, a little over the first half of the book, provide a solid grounding in scientific computing and Python programming; data collection and processing; iterative workflows; doing exploratory and descriptive work with structured, relational, and text data; and get you started with modelling.

Chapter 18 introduces a series of ethical and political challenges in computational social science and marks a transition between the methods covered in Parts II and III and the machine learning methods and probabilistic models that feature heavily in the latter parts of the book.

Part IV shifts our attention towards various different types of machine learning. We'll start with a high-level overview of different types of machine learning (Chapter 19) followed by an introduction to developing 'supervised' machine learning models within the 'symbolic' paradigm (Chapters 20 and 21) and neural network models within the 'connectionist' paradigm (Chapters 22 and 23).

Part V expands the discussion of machine learning to include probabilistic programming, generative modelling, and Bayesian data analysis. As with other parts of the book, I've written this sequence of chapters on the assumption that you know about as much statistics as you would get in a typical undergraduate statistics class for (social) science students. Chapter 24 explains what probabilistic programming, generative modelling, and Bayesian data analysis are and how they relate to classical statistics. Chapter 25 is a general primer on probability theory (essential for the chapters that follow) and the logic of Bayesian statistical inference, and Chapter 26 introduces one of the most important computational methods for Bayesian inference, stochastic sampling, and introduces some special notation we will use for specifying probabilistic models.

Part VI builds directly on Part V by showing you, with end-to-end realistic examples, how to develop Bayesian models with structured data using linear and hierarchical linear regression models (Chapters 27 and 28), as well as latent variable models for text (generative topic models, Chapter 29) and networks (stochastic block models, Chapter 30).

Finally, Part VII rounds out the book by taking you right to the bleeding edge of computational text analysis. Chapter 31 introduces neural word embeddings and Chapter 32 introduces named entity recognition, transfer learning, and large-scale neural language models (specifically transformers and contextual embeddings) that are shattering performance records and really changing what's possible in text analysis.

Now, there's a good chance that the roadmap included names of things you've never heard of before, or which you have heard of but currently know little about. Good. That's a sign that you're holding the right book! By the time you're through with it, you'll know what all those things are and more.

0.3 Datasets Used in This Book

As I mentioned previously, the examples in this book are based around a variety of real-world datasets that are likely more similar to what you would work with on a daily basis than the convenient toy datasets that are often used in other learning materials. These datasets generally fall into one of three categories:

1   'Structured' datasets, for lack of a better term. If you've worked with real-world statistical data before, the format of these structured datasets is likely to be familiar to you: their rows represent observations (or cases), and their columns represent variables. We will make frequent use of four such datasets, each described in the subsection below.

    - Varieties of Democracy (VDEM)
    - European Values Study (EVS)
    - Freedom House 'Freedom on the Net'
    - US 2020 Election Dataset

2   Relational/network datasets. These are also 'structured' data, but they differ from the structured data listed above in that they describe meaningful relationships between entities (e.g. people). We will make frequent use of four relational datasets, also described below.

    - SocioPatterns friendship networks
    - The Copenhagen Networks Study data
    - The Enron email communication network
    - A series of networks constructed by parsing information from text data

3   Text datasets. We will make use of a number of text datasets throughout the book, but the two most important by far are datasets of millions of political speeches by Canadian and British politicians.

- The Canadian Hansards, 1867–2020
- The British Hansards, 1802–2020

Below, I provide a general overview of these datasets and explain where to go if you want to learn more about them. You may want to come back to these descriptions as you work through the book.

'Structured' datasets

The VDEM dataset (Coppedge et al., 2020) is the result of a massive project with collaborators from nearly every country in the world, headquartered out of the VDEM Institute at the University of Gothenburg, Sweden. It contains a dizzying array of data points that are, in aggregate, used to measure key aspects of political regimes for countries around the world along a continuum of democratic and autocratic, grounded in the five major theoretical traditions in political science, political sociology, and political theory and philosophy. The dataset includes more than 4000 variables per country-year, including a set of five high-level scales used to assess the extent of electoral, liberal, participatory, deliberative, and egalitarian democracy in a given country per year, stretching back to the 1800s. We will be using subsets of the larger VDEM dataset extensively, especially in the first half of the book. You can learn a lot about the VDEM project, and everything you would ever want to know about this dataset and more from Coppedge et al. (2020) and from the codebook for version 11 of the dataset (Coppedge et al., 2021).

The EVS (2017), housed at the Data Archive for the Social Sciences of GESIS – Leibniz Institute in Cologne, is a set of standardized surveys of participants across Europe on topics including religion, national identity, morality, politics, family, work, society, and the environment, among other things. Each survey dataset includes more than 400 variables spanning demographics and the aforementioned focal areas. They are administered in the context of 1-hour face-to-face interviews with an additional questionnaire. Participation in all EVS surveys is on the basis of informed consent and is completely voluntary. Participation in the study is confidential, all data is anonymized, and direct identifiers are never added to the EVS database.

The Freedom on the Net is a dataset created and maintained by Freedom House (2020), a US non-profit headquartered in Washington, DC. Unlike the two massive datasets preceding this one, the Freedom on the Net dataset consists of five substantive variables for each of the 65 countries included. Three of these variables are sector scores, tracking 'Obstacles to Access', 'Limits on Content', and 'Violations of User Rights'. The final two are an overall numerical score measuring internet freedom and a categorical label derived from the overall numerical score that labels countries as having either 'Free', 'Partly Free', or 'Not Free' access to the internet. We primarily use the Freedom House dataset as a companion to the VDEM dataset to see if it's possible to predict a country's internet freedoms using other (non-internet-related) democratic indices.

The final 'structured' dataset we will use in this book is a US 2020 Election Dataset, created by my PhD student Pierson Browne specifically for this book. The dataset was built from components of three different datasets:

- 'Individual Contributions', from the US Federal Election Commission (2020)
- The 2017 Cook Partisan Voting Index (Wasserman and Flinn, 2020)
- Raphael Fontes' 'US Election 2020' dataset, publicly available on Kaggle (Fontes, 2020)

The dataset covers Campaign Spending Differential, Vote Differential, Cook Partisan Voting Index, Republican Incumbency, and Democratic Incumbency, for each of the 435 Federal Congressional Districts electing Voting Representatives contested in the 2020 US General Election. We will use this dataset extensively throughout our chapters on Bayesian regression and Bayesian hierarchical linear regression.

Relational/network datasets

The Copenhagen Networks Study dataset was created by Piotr Sapiezynski et al. (2019). It consists of multiple relational datasets constructed from digital and face-to-face interactions between 700 undergraduate students from the Technical University of Denmark. We will use this dataset in the chapters that discuss diffusion dynamics on social networks. The data was primarily collected from questionnaires, Facebook, and participants' smartphones. It includes measures of digital interaction, physical proximity, and online 'friendship'. There are too many details to fully recount here but Sapiezynski et al. (2019) provide extensive details in their *Nature (Scientific Data)* article. All participants gave free and informed consent and were aware of their ability to withdraw from the study at any time and/or to have their data deleted. The authors took great pains to ensure participant privacy throughout. All of the automatically logged data was anonymized.

The Enron email communication network dataset was collated by my PhD student Tyler Crick specifically for this book, once again by doing extensive work cleaning and augmenting existing datasets. The base download of the data came from a version with corrections made by Arne Ruhe (2016). This version was later found to have inconsistencies with other available versions, such as the many available from EnronData.org under a Creative Commons Attribution 3.0 United States license. A significant number of job titles were still missing from these datasets, so thorough searches of LinkedIn, Google's web cache, and the Internet Archive were used to verify the identified job titles and correct missing or vague ones ('Employee', e.g. quite often was actually a trader). The data was used here only for social network analysis, so only the relational aspects (sender and receiver email address) were retained from the emails – no text content from the email bodies is reproduced here.

The SocioPatterns dataset (Mastrandrea et al., 2015) is the result of a collaborative research project run by the ISI Foundation in Turin, Italy; the Centre de Physique Théorique in Marseilles, France; and Bitmanufactory in Cambridge, United Kingdom. There are a number of datasets contained therein, but we will only use two:

- A directed self-reported friendship network between high school students in Marseilles, France, in December 2013
- A directed contact network constructed from students' contact diaries

All participants were older than 18 years of age at the time of study deployment and offered free and informed consent. The Commission Nationale de l'Informatique et des Libertés approved the study, including its privacy measures.

Text datasets

Nearly all of the text analysis we do in this book will focus on examples from two massive text datasets: The Canadian Commons Hansard and the British Commons Hansard. Both are very similar but are unique to their national contexts. The British Commons Hansard is created by the British Government (The UK Parliament, 2021) and contain transcripts (not verbatim, but close) of recorded speeches in the British Parliament, dating back to 1802. It consists of all of the speeches made by politicians in parliamentary sessions, recorded, transcribed, and entered into public record. Similarly, the Canadian Commons Hansard (The Canadian Parliament, 2021) is created by the Canadian government and consists of transcripts (not verbatim, but close) of recorded speeches in the Canadian Parliament, dating back to 1867.

There is, of course, much more to say about these datasets than what is included here, or in the specific chapters where we use these datasets. I encourage you to consult the citations for each dataset to learn more. There are also additional details available in the online supplementary materials (described below).

0.4 Learning Materials

Learning objectives, recommended content, and key points

Each chapter in this book follows a few conventions to help you learn. First, each chapter starts with a set of itemized learning objectives and ends with a bulleted set of key points in the chapter. Of course, these are not meant to cover *everything*. The learning objectives highlight some of the key things you should ensure you understand before moving on to the next chapter. The key points that conclude each chapter are intended to help connect the end of each chapter with the start of the next; note that they are not detailed enough to stand in for carefully working your way through the chapter (by design). Finally, each chapter also contains boxes that provide some additional advice and recommendation. Most of the time, I'll point you to other readings and resources that you can use to further develop your knowledge and skills.

Online supplementary learning materials

The central design decision that has guided all other decisions in the creation of this book – to show you how to do computational social science – means that many of the additional learning materials are not well-suited to the printed page. Every chapter in this book is accompanied by a wide variety of supplementary materials created by myself, Pierson Browne, Tyler Crick, Alexander Graham, Jillian Anderson, and a number of other computational social scientists and data scientists. These materials are all provided as an online supplement because (1) it makes them vastly more useful to you and (2) it frees up an astonishingly large number of words in the book that can be put to other uses, like teaching more methods and models and in greater depth than would otherwise be possible.

All of the supplementary learning materials for this book are provided in a git repository (which you will learn all about in the next chapter) available at github.com/UWNETLAB/ doing_computational_social_science. Among other things, you will find the following:

1. A set of carefully scaffolded problem sets accompanying each chapter in the book. These problem sets are much more extensively developed than what you would typically find at the end of each chapter in books such as this one. These are the problems that I use in my own classes at the University of Waterloo. An answer key for instructors is available upon request

2. Copies of the datasets we use in this book, though filtered and subsetted to include only the portions I actually use in each chapter. You will also find instructions to secure the full datasets if you wish

3 A set of perspectives and practical advice from other computational social scientists and data scientists. Many of these were initially part of the book manuscript itself, but the combination of life interrupted via COVID-19 (coronavirus disease 2019) and with more than 100,000 words to cut from the penultimate draft, they've been moved to the online materials. An unintended benefit of this change is that more perspectives can be included afterwards. Expect this part of the online materials to grow over time

4 High-resolution colour images of every one of the figures in this book, with filenames that are easily matched back to images in the book

5 Instructions on how to download and use dozens of large-scale pretrained language models that Tyler Crick and I developed at the University of Waterloo

6 A wealth of additional materials on scientific computing that will take you *well* beyond the basics introduced in Chapter 1

7 Short video lectures and screencasts covering key content from each chapter

8 A DCSS (*Doing Computational Social Science*) virtual environment (explained below and in Chapter 1)

9 and more . . .

These supplementary materials are intended to help you work interactively through every chapter of the book, to test your knowledge and practise your skills, to share important views and experiences other than my own, and to provide some additional chapter-specific material that is worthwhile but doesn't 'fit' in this version of the book for one reason or another.

Chapter 1 explains how to download these materials and get your scientific computing environment set up. Once you've done that, you'll be able to make extensive use of all of the accompanying materials as you work through the book.

The DCSS virtual environment and Python package

This book also ships with its very own virtual environment and Python package. If you don't know what these things are, you will soon! In short, the virtual environment ensures that you will be able to use all the exact packages (with the exact same versions) that are used in this book no matter which operating system you are using, and no matter what changes occur between the time this book goes to the printers and when you pick it up to read it. It will make your life a *lot* more convenient, not to mention that of instructors who may assign this book in a course while looking to spend less time on technical support. Everything you need to know about this carefully crafted environment, including how to access it and use it, is provided in the next chapter.

I've also created a Python package, appropriately called DCSS, to accompany this book. This is largely a collection of 'utility functions' for tasks that we do repeatedly, such as preprocessing and cleaning data, extracting specific pieces of information from highly nested data structures, and quickly constructing some more complex visualizations. This package is included in the installations managed by the virtual environment.

0.5 Conclusion

Now that you have a sense of what this book is about, how it's designed, and how you can get the most from it, it's time to start doing computational social science! We'll start by introducing you to some essential computing tools and setting up your scientific computing environment. Then we'll jump right into Python.

PART I

FOUNDATIONS

1

SETTING UP YOUR OPEN SOURCE SCIENTIFIC COMPUTING ENVIRONMENT

1.1 Learning Objectives

By the end of this chapter, you should be able to do the following:

- Know how to download, install, and use Python, Anaconda, `git`, a plain text editor, and a terminal emulator
- Execute basic shell commands to interact with a computer from the command line
- Create, configure, and activate virtual environments using `conda`
- Set up a new computing project
- Use `git` to track changes to your project and push those changes to a remote repository
- Download and get set up with the online supplementary learning materials for this book

1.2 Introduction

This chapter is devoted entirely to the practical knowledge you need to set up a scientific computing environment and get started with Python programming for computational social science. I'll start by introducing the command line, which is the most foundational tool upon which all others rest. Once I've explained the basics of interacting with your computer from the command line, I'll walk you through setting up a scientific computing environment with a good text editor and the Anaconda Python 3 distribution, which includes the Jupyter Notebook/Lab Integrated Development Environment (IDE) and a wide variety of packages for scientific computing with Python. Then I'll introduce 'version control' and 'virtualization' tools to round out the essential tools you'll need to do computational social science. To bring them all together, I'll explain how to use these tools to download and get started with the online supplementary learning materials.

1.3 Command Line Computing

Doing computational social science or data science requires interacting with computers using a command line interface (CLI). This may feel unfamiliar and inefficient in the age of mobile computing, beautifully designed graphical user interfaces (GUIs), and touchscreens, but it is what enables us to do computational research in the first place. A bit of knowledge unlocks a vast world of high-quality open source tools and enables us to benefit from the expertise and experience of many other researchers, scientists, and engineers around the world. Among a great many other things, command line computing also enables us to work on remote computers; to organize our software, data, and models according to best practices; to efficiently manage and track our research projects; and to make collaboration much easier, and transparency, accountability, and reproducibility possible. The command line is our common point of departure, regardless of which operating system you happen to be using. In what follows, I'll introduce some essentials of command line computing, starting with an introduction to 'the shell'.

The shell

When I talk about working 'on the command line' or 'in a terminal', what I really mean is that we tell our computer's operating system what we want it to do by interacting with a program called the shell. We interact with the shell by typing commands into a terminal emulator, or 'terminal'. Linux, macOS, and Windows all come with pre-installed terminal emulators, though (as you will soon see) these are not necessarily the ones you will want to use for doing computational social science. Still, take a moment to launch the default one on your system. You should be able to find what you're looking for by doing a search for 'terminal', or 'command prompt', depending on your operating system.

When you first open a terminal window, you will likely see a minimal black screen with white text. Things may differ slightly based on the machine you are on, but you should see `username@computername`, followed by `$`:

```
username@computer$
```

To interact with the shell – that is, to tell our computer what we want to do – we type commands on the command line and then hit the 'Return' key (i.e. Enter). To see how this works, type `cal` on the command line, and then hit 'Return':

```
cal
```

`cal` is a command line program installed on your computer; when you type the command `cal`, your computer executes that program and prints a calendar to the screen with the current day highlighted. Other commands we pass to the shell are also programs, and as we will see below, they tend to be most useful when we provide those programs with additional information about what we want. If you happen to issue a command that your computer does not recognize, nothing bad will happen. Your computer will just tell you that it doesn't understand what you want it to do. Go ahead and type something like `Hi, shell!` and hit 'Return'. We can do almost anything we want on the command line, but we have to use commands that our computer knows about.

The structure of shell commands

Generally, the commands you execute will have the same basic structure, though the components of a command may be called different things by different people. (Many use 'options' and 'arguments' interchangeably, for example.) The first word you type is the command itself, or the name of the program you are going to execute. Often, the default behaviour can be modified by using options, which can be specified using a 'short' version (a letter following a -, such as ls -l) or a long version (a word following --, such as ls --long). When using the short version, you can string multiple options together following a single -, such as ls -ltS. In addition to the command itself and the options that follow, commands may take arguments, such as the name of a file or directory that a command should act on. This may seem very abstract now, but if you follow along with the commands below in your terminal, it will become more concrete:

[COMMAND] + [-OPTION(S)] + [ARGUMENT(S)]

While there are different terminal applications available, they all do the same thing: interact with the shell. Unless you're using Linux as your primary operating system, you're probably going to end up running into the limitations of your default terminal emulator pretty quickly, so the first thing we need to do is get ourselves set up with a good terminal emulator and configure it to best meet our needs.

Unfortunately, I don't have the room in this chapter to cover the process of setting up a terminal emulator and package manager on each of the three major operating systems, but I've compiled some extensive guidelines for you in the online supplementary learning materials for this chapter (the link for which is provided at the end of this chapter in the subsection 'Getting and using the supplementary learning materials'). There you'll find everything you need to guide you through the process of installing and customizing a terminal emulator with an eye to creating a smooth, enjoyable, productive command line environment for you to work with.

For now, those of you working from a Linux installation will likely be in good stead working with your default terminal set-up (most likely Bash or similar). The same is true if you are using macOS, though you may wish to consider upgrading to the iTerm2 terminal emulator, which offers some nice additional functionality, and you'll need to download the Homebrew package manager. If you're using Windows, your operating system doesn't ship with a proper terminal emulator, so you'll need to install and familiarize yourself with one. There are a few good options; I'm not a Windows user, but the Cmder terminal emulator and the Chocolatey package manager are widely used.

Now that you're set up with a good terminal emulator, let's discuss a few very simple but essential actions for getting work done on the command line. We'll focus on a small subset of commands for navigating the file system and doing various things with directories and files.

Getting around the file system

The commands you will use the most frequently are those that enable you to navigate a computer's file system and perform basic operations for directories (i.e. 'folders') and files. Let's focus on those commands first. I recommend that you work through this chapter with your terminal open. You are likely to learn faster and more deeply if you execute these commands as you read, and if you take little breaks along the way to practise what you've learnt.

Directories and files

Although there are some differences across operating systems – chiefly between Windows and the *nix systems Linux and macOS – these operating systems all organize directories (or 'folders') as hierarchical trees. The `root` directory sits at the top of that tree; all files and subdirectories are contained within it. We call it 'root', but in most operating systems, it'll just look like a single forward slash (/). Most users navigate through this directory structure using a GUI, such as Finder on macOS or File Explorer on Windows.

This process works a little differently on the command line, of course, but ultimately we want to do the same thing: get 'into' the directories where our files are, as well as the directories above and below them in the file system. The directory we are 'in' at any given time is the current working directory. To see where we are in the file system, we can print the path to that directory by typing the command `pwd` (print working directory):

```
pwd
```

```
cd
```

The command `cd`, short for 'change directory,' is usually followed by an `argument`, which provides more information to the shell about where you want to go. For example, you could provide an absolute path, which starts with the root directory and goes to whatever directory you want to be in. For example, if I wanted to `cd` into a directory where I keep various files related to graduate supervision, I could type the absolute path:

```
cd /users/johnmclevey/Documents/supervision/grad_students/
```

The path is essentially an ordered list of the nested directories you would have clicked through if you were navigating the file system using a GUI like Finder or Files Explorer. Each step in the path is separated by a / on macOS and Linux, and by \ on Windows.

Because this path starts at the root directory, I can execute it regardless of where in the file system I currently am. Alternatively, I can provide `cd` with a relative path, which tells the shell where to go relative to the current working directory. For example, if my current working directory was `/users/johnmclevey/Documents/` and I wanted to get to `grad_students/`, I could use the following relative path:

```
cd supervision/grad_students/
```

In this case, the command worked because we were 'in' the Documents directory. But if `/users/johnmclevey/Dropbox/` was my current working directory and I typed the same command, the shell would tell me that there is no such file or directory. When using relative paths, you have to provide the path from the current working directory to the directory where you want to be.

To list the files in a directory, you can use the command `ls`. If we execute `ls` without any arguments, it will default to printing the files in the current working directory, but if provided with an absolute or relative path, it will list the contents of that directory instead. Below, for example, we list the contents of the current working directory's parent directory:

```
ls ..
```

We can provide `ls` with a number of options that modify what the program prints to screen. For example, we can print some metadata about our files – such as the access permission of a file, the name of the user who owns the file, the file size, the last time the file was modified, and so on – if we add the option `-l`, which is short for 'long output':

```
ls -l
```

We can string together a number of these short options to change the behaviour of the command. For example, adding the option `t` to our command (`ls -lt`) changes the order of the files printed to screen such that the most recently modified files are at the top of the list, whereas `ls -lS` prints them with the largest files on top. Using the `ls -a` will display 'hidden' files, some of which we will discuss below.

Creating files and directories

It is also possible to create new directories and files from the command line. For example, to make a new directory inside the current working directory, we can use the command `mkdir` followed by the name of the directory we want to create. Once created, we can move into it using `cd`:

```
mkdir learning_shell
```

To create a new file, we use the `touch` command followed by the name of the file we want to create. For example, we could create a simple text file called `test.txt`:

```
touch test.txt
```

`test.txt` is an empty file. If we wanted to quickly add text to it from the command line, we could use a built-in command line text editor, the most minimal of which is called `nano`. We can edit the file by calling `nano` and providing the name of the file we want to edit as an argument:

```
nano test.txt
```

Getting help

The commands we've just learnt, summarized in Table 1.1, are the ones that you will use the most often when working on the command line and are worth committing to memory. You can build out your knowledge from here on an as-needed basis. One way to do this is to look up information about any given command and the options and arguments it takes by pulling up its manual page using the `man` command. For example, to learn more about `ls`, you could type

```
man ls
```

You can then page through the results using your spacebar and return to the command line by pressing the letter `q`.

Table 1.1 Essential commands for working from the command line

Command	Action	Example
pwd	Print current working directory	pwd
cd	Change directory	cd ..
ls	List directory contents	ls -ltS
mkdir	Make new directory	mkdir figures tables
touch	Make a new text file	touch search_log.txt
rm	Remove file/directory	rm output
cp	Copy file/directory	cp manuscript_draft submitted_manuscripts
mv	Move file/directory	mv manuscript_draft submitted_manuscripts
grep	Search files for a pattern	
open	Open a file or directory in the default application	open search_log.txt
history	Print the history of commands issued to the shell	history

If you are looking to expand your general command line toolkit even further, there is an enormous number of high-quality tutorials online. Now that you have a basic foundation, learning will be faster. However, as mentioned earlier, I recommend against taking a completionist approach. Instead of trying to learn everything at once, get comfortable with this foundation and expand your knowledge in a problem-driven way. That way, you will have time to practise and make interacting with your computer feel more natural, fast, and automatic.

Further Reading

In general, the best way to deepen your knowledge of open source computing, for research or otherwise, is to learn more about Linux and command line computing. You'll find plenty of excellent free resources about Linux and open source computing online, but if you're looking for a more guided and scaffolded tour that doesn't throw you right into the deep end, I would recommend Shott's (2019) *The Linux Command Line* or Ward's (2021) *How Linux Works*.

Now let's learn how to use some more specialized command line tools that enable us to do our work in more transparent, auditable, and reproducible ways.

1.4 Open Source Software

To actually *do* computational research, we need much more than the shell. In what follows, I'll discuss some of the other essential tools you'll need, including a good text editor, Python3, Jupyter Notebooks, and more.

A good text editor

A good text editor is an essential part of your research toolkit. You will primarily use it for writing code, but you can also use it for writing your academic articles, chapters, theses, books, and so on. There are many good text editors available, and these days most have more or less the same capabilities. While editors differ in how they look and feel, you can customize their appearance and behaviour extensively. Picking an editor can be a bit of a struggle, but it needn't be. One need look no further than Wikipedia's article on the Editor War between Emacs and Vi for an example of how disagreements over comparatively minor differences in text editor functionality can spiral into intractable generation-spanning rivalries. To quote Brian Ward (2021) from *How Linux Works*, 'Most UNIX wizards are religious about their choice of editor, but don't listen to them. Just choose yourself' (p. 24). You should try a few out and pick one that works well for you.

If this is your first time using a proper text editor, or the first time you are thinking of a text editor as one of the core tools you use to get your research and writing work done, I suggest you start with VS Code, which is free/open source, runs on any operating system, and has many community packages that simplify writing code and text. It also has extremely good extensions for working in Python and for doing technical writing. Finally, it has out-of-the-box support for working with files on remote machines that is far better than any other editor I have seen, and it has some other neat functionality for collaborative coding.

Further Reading

Kieran Healy's (2018b) 'The plain person's guide to plain text social science' is a good guide to writing scientific papers with plain text tools.

The Anaconda Python 3+ distribution

Python is a general-purpose language with a mature and exciting set of tools for doing data analysis. The Python data science community is a subset of the larger Python community, and the suite of packages and other tools that have been developed for doing research computing are all part of a 'scientific Python' ecosystem which builds upon the 'base' Python language.

While it is possible to install all of these packages and tools on their own, a better solution is to download the Anaconda Python 3 distribution from Continuum Analytics, which bundles many of those research computing tools together and makes them available 'out of the box'. It includes thousands of packages that are very useful in research computing and a number of IDEs that make it easier to write Python code. It also provides a special command line tool for downloading and installing Python packages and a tool for managing 'virtual environments' that enable you to create isolated project environments with the specific version of Python and Python packages used in your project, thus affording a higher level of reproducibility. We will discuss both in this chapter.

Installers for macOS, Windows, and Linux are available at anaconda.com/products/individual. You can use one of the graphical installers, or you can use the command line installer.

Jupyter Notebooks/Jupyter Lab

The Anaconda Python 3 distribution that you downloaded in the previous section comes with a number of IDEs that can improve the process of writing Python code in research contexts considerably. The most widely used IDE for research computing with Python is the Jupyter Notebook, or the more recently developed Jupyter Lab. If you are coming from the world of R, Jupyter Lab and the other Python IDEs function similarly to RStudio. The Jupyter Notebook format is very similar to the R Markdown set of tools, chiefly the R Markdown Notebook.

Jupyter Notebooks enable you to mix narrative text, code, equations, and inline results in an interactive 'notebook' that runs in your browser. They were initially inspired by Galileo's notebooks documenting his discovery of the moons of Jupiter in 1612–13. The ability to seamlessly mix code, narrative text, and inline tables and graphs in well-organized Jupyter Notebooks offers a very powerful way to think, and really shines in the context of exploratory data analysis, when you are learning something new, or when you are developing or prototyping a new idea.

As previously mentioned, Jupyter Notebooks run in your browser. If you are working locally (i.e. on your own laptop or desktop computer rather than a remote server), you need to launch a local server from the command line to start creating notebooks and executing code. Here, we have two options. We can launch either (a) the minimalistic Jupyter Notebook server or (b) the Jupyter Lab IDE, which adds some additional tools to the minimalistic Notebooks and is a bit more RStudio-like.

To start the Jupyter Notebook server, cd to your project directory in your terminal app, type the following on the command line, and then hit 'Return':

```
jupyter notebook
```

Alternatively, to launch the Jupyter Lab IDE, cd to your project directory and type

```
jupyter lab
```

Both commands will automatically open a new tab in your browser showing a Project Jupyter interface. In the traditional Notebook IDE, you will see a list of the files and subdirectories contained in the directory from which you launched your notebook. The Jupyter Lab interface shows the directory contents on the left-hand side. From both interfaces, you can create a new Python 3 Jupyter Notebook. Figures 1.1 to 1.3 are screenshots of the Jupyter Lab interface (version 2.1.5), but you should feel free to use the Jupyter Notebook interface if you prefer it.

Once you have launched your Jupyter server, you can create a new Python 3 notebook or you can open an existing notebook. In this case, we will create a new Python 3 notebook. By default, it will be 'Untitled', but you can change the notebook's filename by right clicking on the new notebook in the file manager on the left side of the screen. In the traditional Jupyter Notebook, you can rename it by clicking on the title of the notebook – 'Untitled' – in the upper left corner. This interface is shown in Figure 1.1.

The right side of the screen in Figure 1.1 displays the actual contents of the Jupyter Notebook itself, which consists of 'cells' that will contain your text or code. The first cell that you see in your new notebook is a code cell. If you click the + button (to the right of the save button and to the left of the cut button), you will see that more code cells are added to the notebook. You can change a cell from a code cell (which contains executable Python code) to a markdown cell by clicking on the drop-down menu that says 'Code' and changing it to markdown. You type narrative text into markdown cells, and executable code into the code cells.

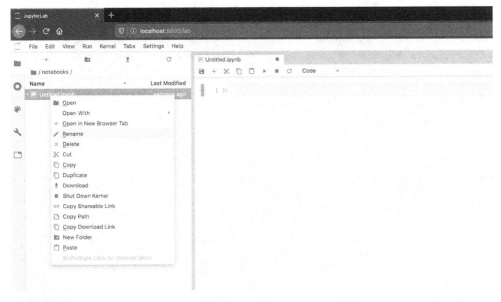

Figure 1.1   Renaming a notebook in Jupyter Lab

The example notebook shown in Figure 1.2 starts with a markdown cell with a header and some text, followed by a series of empty code cells. The # indicates that this is a first-level heading. If we used ##, Jupyter would format the text as a second-level heading. You can 'run' the text cell and the code cell one at a time by pressing 'Shift + Return' on your keyboard, or by clicking the 'Run' button in the Jupyter toolbar (which has a play button icon). The results are shown in Figure 1.3. As you can see, the text is cleanly formatted.

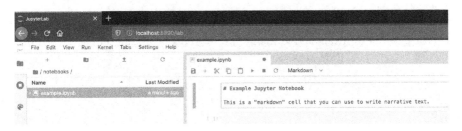

Figure 1.2   A Jupyter Notebook with a markdown cell in edit mode

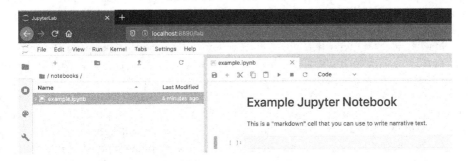

Figure 1.3   A Jupyter Notebook showing the formatted markdown cell when it is not in edit mode

Executing code in Jupyter Notebooks

Now you've seen how the Jupyter Lab interface works, and you've created a notebook with some markdown cells, let's take a moment to see how code cells work by writing our first bit of Python code. In a new code cell, (1) type the following and then (2) press 'Shift + Return' or click the 'Run' button in the Jupyter toolbar:

```
print('Doing Computational Social Science')

Doing Computational Social Science
```

When you execute the code cell – in this case, a `print()` statement – the results are displayed inline, directly below the code cell. This is also true for the results of any mathematical expression or other computation.

```
2050-1986

64
```

You might have noticed that when you used 'Shift + Return', your cursor advanced to the next Jupyter cell. This is a handy behaviour in most cases, as you'll often have several cells of code or text that should be worked through sequentially. There are some instances, however, where it might be handy to have a cursor that remains in place after executing code: in such cases, use 'Ctrl + Return' (for Linux/Windows) or 'Command + Return' (for macOS).

In this book, I'll assume you are executing code in Jupyter Notebooks/Lab, but this is not the only way to write and execute Python code. Once you start to get comfortable with Python, you may wish to write your code in scripts (using your text editor!) that you execute from the command line. The online supplementary learning materials provide some advice on how to get your work done this way.

There are two additional sets of tools that are essential to doing computational social science: version control software and virtualization software. Below, I'll provide a brief overview of each and explain how they work.

1.5 Version Control Tools

Real research projects can become complex messes very quickly. While there are organizational strategies you can adopt to keep the messiness to a minimum, a good version control system is essential. Version control systems watch your full project and record all the changes that happen everywhere, to every file (unless you tell it to ignore a file or subdirectory). It keeps logs of who did what, to what files, when, and if you use it properly, it can even keep log files and other notes associated with each change to the project. It eliminates the 'need' for long descriptive filenames with information about dates, authors' comments, and revision stages, or emailing the 'final version' of a docx file back and forth between collaborators. At any given point, you can roll back in time to a previous state of the project. They also unlock *enormous* potential for collaboration – in fact, the version control system I recommend, git, is used to manage what is arguably the largest and most complex software development project in the world, the Linux kernel, built by more than 5000 individual developers from more than 400 organizations around the world.

The model for `git` and other version control systems is that you store your project in a repository. Once your repository has been 'initialized', you work on your files as you normally would. From time to time – say each time you start and finish working on some piece of your project – you 'add' or 'stage' your changes and then 'commit' them to the repository along with a brief log message about what you did and why. If your repository is linked to a remote server, such as GitHub, you can also 'push' your changes to the remote repository.

As you do this, you build up a complete record of the history of your project, including who (your past self included) did what and why. You can roll back to any place in the history of your project, create experimental branches of the project to explore other lines of enquiry, and so on. Your collaborators can also have access to the remote repositories and can 'clone' (i.e. download) the repository with the full history, make their own changes, add them, commit them, and push them back to the remote repository. You can get those changes yourself by 'pulling' down new changes.

Let's say you are starting a new web scraping project. You've written some code, all stored inside a directory called `scraping_project`. To use `git` to manage your project, you would `cd` into the project directory and initialize `git`. You only have to initialize `git` once for a project.

```
cd scraping_project
git init
```

Once you've made some changes to your project, you can 'stage' the changes using `git add`. You can track individual file changes, but the easiest thing to do is to track any changes that have been made to the whole project directory. You can do this by specifying that you are adding changes for the full directory using the . (Remember: the . indicates the current directory.)

```
git add .
```

Next, you'll want to write a commit message that *briefly* describes the changes we've made. For example, we might write

```
git commit -m "A brief description of what I did..."
```

`git` provides a number of other useful commands that you'll make frequent use of. For example, if you have an account on GitHub, GitLab, or some other service for managing `git` repositories, you can push your changes to the remote version by using `git push`. Similarly, you could also 'pull' down an up-to-date version of the project on another computer, once again making your work more portable. Other useful `git` commands are provided in Table 1.2.

Table 1.2 The subset of `git` commands you need to do 99% of your work with

Command	Action	Example
init	Initialize a new `git` repository	`git init .`
add	Stage changes	`git add .` or `git add article.md`
commit -m	Commit changes with log message	`git commit -m "drafted introduction"`
push	Push changes to remote repository	`git push`

(Continued)

Table 1.2 (Continued)

Command	Action	Example
status	Compare local repository with remote repository	`git status`
pull	Update your local repository with changes from a remote repository	`git pull`
clone	Clone a remote repository	`git clone [URL]`

Using version control software like `git` has many benefits, not the least of which is that when you return to your work after a period of working on something else – say, when a chapter is being reviewed by your committee or a paper is under review – you will know exactly what you did and why later. When it comes to accountability, transparency, and reproducibility, this is perhaps the most important thing: *you must always know what you did.*

Further Reading

Using tools like `git` make transparency, accountability, and reproducibility possible, but only if you use them properly. As you become more comfortable with these tools, you'll want to see out advice on how people use them for different types of projects. I recommend working almost entirely within Patrick Ball's (2016) 'principled data processing' (PDP) framework (see McLevey et al., 2021, for a discussion of Python-based tools). Eric Ma's (2021) *Data Science Bootstrap: A Practical Guide to Getting Organized for Your Best Data Science Work* provides a lot of excellent advice for scientific computing more generally, and for setting up workflows for projects that don't lend themselves well to the PDP framework.

Finally, as a computational social scientist, you'll need to understand and make use of 'virtualization' tools.

1.6 Virtualization Tools

It is important to keep in mind that, like other software, the Python programming language evolves over time, and code written for one version of Python may not execute as expected in other versions. When running old code or code written on another person's computing set-up, these incompatibilities can cause serious issues. The solution to these and other problems is virtualization, which is a type of technology that enables us to create simulated environments with their own isolated resources on our host machines. For example, you might create a virtual machine that runs a Linux operating system (say, Ubuntu 20) on a laptop running macOS, enabling you to work *as if* you were on a machine where the host operating system was Ubuntu 20. In the context of computational social science research, it lets us create isolated project-specific working environments with the specific versions of Python, Python packages, and other software that is needed to execute our project code exactly as we intend. We can share these environments with others, or simply use them on multiple machines, in ways that make our research work completely transparent and reproducible.

Although many types of virtualization are in common usage, we're only going to focus on one type of virtualization: the virtual environment. You can learn about other types of virtualization solutions in the online supplementary learning materials.

Creating and using virtual environments

Virtual environments add very little overhead to a workflow, and once they are in place, they are mostly invisible. The simplest way to use them is the conda env implementation that ships with Anaconda. The Anaconda installation also provides a GUI application called 'Anaconda Navigator' that you can use to manage your conda environments, which can be especially helpful for quickly taking stock of your existing environments. However, the command line is faster and generally easier for actually making changes when used in the context of a larger computing workflow system that is managed from the command line.

From the command line, cd into your project directory and create and activate a new conda environment. To create an environment called test_env, for example, you would execute the following code on the command line:

```
conda create --name test_env
conda activate test_env
```

Notice that once you have activated a conda environment, the command prompt in your terminal application will look a little different. More specifically, you will see that the command line now starts with the name of the virtual environment that is active inside a pair of brackets. In this case, the command line would start with (test_env). This makes it easy to know which environment you are in at any given time.

You can also customize the versions of Python and Python packages that are used in your environment at the same time as you create the environment, if you wish. The software you install into your environment will be 'sandboxed' from other software on your machine. Fortunately for us, conda environments have Python as a dependency and will take care of downloading and installing whatever version of Python you want. For example, if you wanted a specific version of Python (say 3.6), as well as version 0.24 of pandas and the latest version of NumPy (two Python packages that we will make extensive use of in this book), the command would be

```
conda create --name py36_pandas24_numpy python=3.6 pandas=0.24 numpy
conda activate py36_pandas24_numpy
```

From this point forward, you'll always have access to the conda activate command – you don't need to run the conda create line each time you start your computer. Alternatively, you can install a package within the currently active environment using conda install:

```
conda install pandas=1.2
```

When you use conda install to install Python packages, conda checks the Anaconda servers for the most recent source code for the requested package. However, it is also possible to download packages that are not on the Anaconda servers. These different places to look for packages are called 'channels'. One of the most useful 'unofficial' channels in data science and computational social science is called `conda-forge`. We can tell `conda` to search for packages using `conda-forge` if it can't find the package on the official `anaconda` channel by executing the following command:

```
conda config --append channels conda-forge
```

1.7 Putting the Pieces Together: Python, Jupyter, `conda`, and `git`

It might seem like this is a *huge* amount of overhead just to do your research, but it is not nearly as involved as it might seem. While using these tools will slow you down at first, you will soon be using them together in ways that feel very natural and normal. You will find it difficult to imagine going back to doing your computational research any other way. To wrap up this introduction to setting up your scientific computing environment, I'll walk you through using these tools to download the supplementary learning materials for this book.

The supplementary learning materials described in the previous chapter are stored in an online `git` repository, hosted on GitHub.com. In order to use these materials, you'll want to 'clone' the `git` repository, set up the `conda` environment, and launch a Jupyter server. Let's do it!

Getting and using the supplementary learning materials

First, you'll want to `cd` into whatever directory you want to use to store the supplementary materials. For example, if you want to store them in the `Documents` folder on macOS, you would `cd` into that directory:

```
cd ~/Documents
```

You can then use `git` to clone the repository of supplementary materials to your local machine with the `git clone` command. You'll use the link to the hosted repository on GitHub as an argument.

```
git clone https://github.com/UWNETLAB/doing_computational_social_science.git
```

Next, you can `cd` into that directory. If you type `ls`, you'll see all the downloaded materials:

```
cd doing_computational_social_science.git
ls
```

One of the files in the repo you just cloned is `environment.yml`. This file is what you need to install the custom `dcss` conda environment that you can use to access the specific versions of Python and Python packages used in this book. You only need to install the environment once, after which you can simply activate or deactivate it as needed. To install it (from the `doing_computational_social_science` directory):

```
conda env create -f environment.yml
```

Once `conda` has finished installing your environment and all of the required Python packages, you can activate it by typing

```
conda activate dcss
```

You'll see your command prompt change; it will now start with `(dcss)`.

The final thing you need to do to get up and running is launch your Jupyter server. You can do that by typing

```
jupyter notebook
```

or

```
jupyter lab
```

depending on which interface you prefer.

Once your Jupyter server is up and running, you can navigate around the repository of supplementary learning materials using the Jupyter interface. You'll discover plenty of useful things in there, though some won't make much sense to you until you get to the relevant section of the book.

Feel free to make this local copy of the learning materials your own. You can create new directories within it, and create as many scripts and Jupyter Notebooks as you need to follow along with the code in this book. Go ahead and create a new directory called `learning_python` and a new Jupyter Notebook inside it. You can use that notebook to follow along with the Python code introduced in the next two chapters.

1.8 Conclusion

The key points in this chapter are as follows:

- We do scientific computing on the command line using the shell.
- We will use Python, Anaconda, and Jupyter for programming.
- We will use virtual environments (via `conda`) and version control (via `git`) to help enable transparency, accountability, and reproducibility.

Visit the website at https://study.sagepub.com/mclevey for additional resources

2

PYTHON PROGRAMMING: THE BASICS

2.1 Learning Objectives

By the end of this chapter, you should be able to do the following:

- Understand and use basic data types in Python (strings, integers, floats, and Booleans)
- Understand and use assignment for objects
- Understand and use methods for manipulating strings
- Understand and use comparison and control flow to perform conditional execution
- Understand how to read and learn from the `Tracebacks` Python produces when something interrupts the execution of your code, such as an error
- Use `try/except` to handle exceptions and other potential interruptions to the execution of your code.

2.2 Learning Materials

If you followed the set-up instructions in Chapter 1, you can find the online learning materials for this chapter in `doing_computational_social_science/Chapter_02`; then `cd` into the directory and launch your Jupyter server.

2.3 Introduction

It's time to start writing Python code! Make sure to open a Jupyter Notebook or a Python console and follow along as you work through this chapter. If you load up the supplementary learning materials as described in Chapter 1, you'll find a series of chapter-specific Jupyter Notebooks to get you started. You'll want to use `chapter_02_notes.ipynb` as you work through this chapter, or alternatively you can create your own empty notebook. After you've worked through the chapter, you can deepen and test your knowledge by completing the problem sets in `chapter_02_problem_sets.ipynb`. Other chapters will also use this `_notes` and `_problem_sets` naming convention, to keep things simple.

Our primary goal in this chapter is to lay a foundation of general Python knowledge. We'll start with the basics: data types, assignment, using methods and functions, control flow, and handling errors. What you learn here is not specific to scientific computing, but you will find yourself using this knowledge *constantly*. Thus, you don't necessarily need to have 'mastered' this content before moving on. You will have plenty of opportunities to practice your Python programming as you progress through the book. You can always come back to this chapter if you need a refresher.

2.4 Learning Python

Python is designed to maximize human readability, and as a consequence, it's common to *feel* that you have a good understanding of something because the code on the page makes sense and seems obvious, only to find yourself at a loss when you try to write the same code yourself. That's totally normal. You must resist the temptation to copy and paste. You will understand more, identify what you don't understand, and gain mastery faster, if you actually type the code out yourself. Your future self will thank you.

If you are new to Python but have some experience doing scripted data analysis in another language, I suggest that you approach Python as if you were a beginner. It is common to start working in Python by 'translating' your R or Stata scripts into Python, for example. While there are many generic programming concepts that are used in those languages and many others, most efforts to 'translate' your scripts will lead to writing poor Python code and will slow down your learning, causing problems later. While a certain amount of this is unavoidable, you will benefit from minimizing it. When you are working in Python, it is generally better to embrace doing things the 'Pythonic' way.

2.5 Python Foundations

Basic data types and expressions

Every value in Python has a single data type. The key data types to know are *integers* (e.g. 42), *floats* (e.g. 42.0), and *strings* (e.g. 'The Hitchhiker's Guide to the Galaxy' or 'cats are the best'). Strings are sequences of characters that are wrapped in single or double quotes. They both work the same way, but you must be consistent when starting and ending a string, and you can't use quotes of one type inside quotes of the same type. Having the option for both enables us to include quotes and apostrophes within a string.

```
"That's correct."

"That's correct."

'My teacher said, "That is correct."'

'My teacher said, "That is correct."'
```

An *expression* consists of two or more values joined by an operator. The following examples use Python like a calculator:

```
2 + 2 # Addition

4

2 * 9 # Multiplication

18

10 / 2 # Division

5.0

2 ** 6 # Exponential

64

2 + 9 * 7

65
```

Python has mathematical operators for addition, subtraction, multiplication, division, floor division, exponents, and modulus/remainder when working with numbers. Given expressions with multiple operators, Python follows the conventional mathematical order of operations.

Some of these operators can also be used to perform operations on strings, but they represent different things. For example, when used in an expression with two strings, the + operator performs string concatenation by joining the two strings together. We demonstrate this below. The following expression is contained inside a print() function, it appropriately prints the result inline for notebooks or to the screen if you are executing scripts:

```
print('Miyoko is interested in ' + 'a career in data science.')

Miyoko is interested in a career in data science.
```

Python can determine whether + should be addition or string concatenation based on context: whether both items being operated on are strings or numbers. However, Python will throw an error if you try to add, or concatenate, a number and a string. To demonstrate, create a new code cell and type 42 + 'is the answer'. You will see an error message – a 'Traceback' – print below the code cell. We will discuss errors and how to interpret them later. If you wrap the 42 in quotes and execute the cell again, you will see that Python now treats 42 as a string and performs concatenation:

```
42 + 'is the answer'

---------------------------------------------------------------------------
TypeError                                 Traceback (most recent call last)

<ipython-input-9-c30245934d2d> in <module>
----> 1 42 + 'is the answer'

TypeError: unsupported operand type(s) for +: 'int' and 'str'

'42 ' + 'is the answer'

'42 is the answer'
```

We can also convert numbers to strings with the `str()` function. Notice the lost white space we had with '42':

```
str(42 ) + 'is the answer'
```

```
'42 is the answer'
```

We can also use the * operator with strings, where it becomes a string replicator, which requires a string and an integer. For example,

```
print('Sociology ' * 5)
```

```
Sociology Sociology Sociology Sociology Sociology
```

Variables and assignment

We can store data in 'variables' by 'assignment', indicated by the = operator. We can call variables anything we want, provided

1   we only use numbers, letters, and the underscore character (_);
2   we don't start the name with a number; and
3   we do not use any special words that are reserved for Python itself (e.g. `class`).

Use descriptive names for your variables (e.g. call the variable storing your last name as a string `last_name`, not `ln`). It makes your code much more readable and easier for you, or your collaborators, to understand after a bit of time has passed.

You can think of a variable as a labelled container that stores specific information. In the example below, the container has a 'label' called `a_number` and stores the integer value 16:

```
a_number = 16
print(a_number)
```

```
16
```

Once you have created a variable, you can use it in expressions. For example,

```
a_number * a_number
```

```
256
```

```
city = 'Cologne'
country = 'Germany'
```

```
print(city + country)
```

```
CologneGermany
```

```
print(city + ' is the fourth-most populous city in ' + country)
```

```
Cologne is the fourth-most populous city in Germany
```

We are not limited to printing the results of an expression. We can save our results in a new variable:

```
sentence = city + ' is the fourth-most populous city in ' + country
print(sentence)
```

```
Cologne is the fourth-most populous city in Germany
```

Objects and methods, illustrated with strings

Python is an 'object-oriented' language, which means that it performs computations using 'objects'. An in-depth discussion of object-oriented programming is beyond the scope of this book, but you should understand a few simple concepts. To illustrate, let's use a silly but inform-ative analogy. I have two cats, Dorothy and Lando Catrissian, who know how to perform vari-ous actions, like squeezing into small cardboard boxes to take a nap, drinking from a trickling faucet, lying directly on my keyboard while I am using it, and tearing up yoga mats with their claws if you walk away from the mat for more than 2 minutes. Dorothy and Lando are both specific 'instances' of the general 'class' of cats. As cats, they can perform some special actions, including those listed above.

In Python, (almost) *everything* is an object of one kind or another. Like Dorothy and Lando, objects are specific instances of more general classes. Being specific instances, they typically have a name that differs from their class; the `sentence` object is an instance of the `string` class. Objects are capable of a variety of actions – called `methods` – that they share with other objects of the same class. In Python, strings have methods for switching between cases, check-ing for the presence of a value, replacing one substring with another, and many more. As computational social scientists, we frequently work with real-world text data; Python's `string` methods are indispensable for doing so. To learn about a particular class and its methods, you can usually check online documentation, use Jupyter's ? function (e.g. a_number?), or Python's `dir()` function (e.g. `dir(a_number)`).

Changing case

The examples below illustrate some common string manipulation tasks. Any time we use a method, we provide the name of the object followed by a . and the name of the method. For example, to change the case of the characters in a string, we can use the `.upper()`, `.lower()`, and `.title()` methods. Let's try on the `city` variable from earlier:

```
city.upper()
```

```
'COLOGNE'
```

```
city.lower()
```

```
'cologne'
```

```
city.title()
```

```
'Cologne'
```

Technically, the `.upper()` and `.lower()` methods don't actually change the string itself, they create a new string. The code above printed those new strings, but Python did not change the string contained in `city`. To do that, we need to overwrite `city` with the new string:

```
print(city)
city = city.upper()
print(city)

Cologne
COLOGNE
```

We can also check whether a string contains another string. To check whether the variable `sentence` contains the string 'Germany', we can use the `in` operator. Python will return `True` if 'Germany' is in `sentence` or `False` if it is not:

```
'Germany' in sentence

True
```

We can also use the `.index()` method to return the starting index position for where a substring – `city` – appears in a string – `sentence`. If the substring is not in the string, this method will throw an error.

```
sentence.index('Germany')

44
```

To replace one substring with another substring, we can use the `.replace()` method. For example, to replace Cologne with Köln:

```
sentence = sentence.replace('Cologne', 'Köln')
print(sentence)

Köln is the fourth-most populous city in Germany
```

Joining and splitting strings

When working with strings and other text data, you will often find yourself needing to split a string up into multiple pieces, or to join things together into a specific string. If we use the `split()` method on a string with no arguments, it will split the string on white space and return something called a list:

```
sent_split_1 = sentence.split()
print(sent_split_1)

['Köln', 'is', 'the', 'fourth-most', 'populous', 'city', 'in', 'Germany']
```

Alternatively, we can tell the `.split()` to split a string at specific substrings:

```
sent_split_2 = sentence.split('populous')
print(sent_split_2)
```

```
['Köln is the fourth-most ', ' city in Germany']
```

```
sent_split_3 = sentence.split('-')
print(sent_split_3)
```

```
['Köln is the fourth', 'most populous city in Germany']
```

To join these items back into a single string, we use `.join()`. To use this method, we first provide the `separator` we want `.join()` to place between the items, and then pass the items we want to reassemble into a string:

```
joined = " ".join(sent_split_1)
joined
```

```
'Köln is the fourth-most populous city in Germany'
```

```
also_joined = "-".join(sent_split_1)
also_joined
```

```
'Köln-is-the-fourth-most-populous-city-in-Germany'
```

Removing white space

Strings containing text data from the real world – which appear frequently in this book – often have a lot of white space. To remove this white space, we can use the `.strip()`, `.lstrip()`, or `.rstrip()` methods to strip out extra white space from the whole string (not including the spaces between words), or from the beginning or end of the string:

```
with_whitespaces = ' This string has    extra whitespace. '
print(with_whitespaces)
```

```
  This string has  extra whitespace.
```

```
print(with_whitespaces.strip())
```

```
This string has    extra whitespace.
```

```
print(with_whitespaces.lstrip())
```

```
This string has    extra whitespace.
```

```
print(with_whitespaces.rstrip())
```

```
  This string has  extra whitespace.
```

Putting strings inside other strings with the .format() method and f-string

While we can use + for string concatenation, it is often better to use Python's built-in tools for string formatting. One such tool is the appropriately named string formatting method called format(). The easiest way to understand how string formatting works is to see it in action, so let's look at a few examples. In the examples below, we will use the information stored in the variables city and country:

```
a_string = "{} is the fourth-most populous city in {}."
print(a_string.format(city.title(), country))
```

```
Cologne is the fourth-most populous city in Germany.
```

The string on the first line includes two {}s, and the format() method on the next line has two arguments – city.title() (recall that .title() produces a string with characters in title case) and country. When executed, the method replaces the first {} with the value of city.title() and the second {} with the value of country.

We can also do this in a cleaner way. We can put an f before our string to tell Python to use an f-string, which enables us to include the name of the variable containing the relevant value inside each {}:

```
print(f"{city.title()} is the fourth-most populous city in {country}.")
```

```
Cologne is the fourth-most populous city in Germany.
```

In Python, a string can be as short as zero characters ("" contains no characters, but is a valid string), or arbitrarily long (provided it fits in your system's memory). Sometimes, you'll want to create or manipulate longer strings, such as the chapter of a book or the entirety of a congressional report. In such cases, it's possible to preserve a long text's layout using 'newline' characters (\n) everywhere there's a paragraph break in the text. As you can imagine, however, this gets messy very quickly. Luckily, Python has a built-in syntax for representing multiline strings, namely three single (''') or double (""") quotation marks in a row:

```
multiline_string = """
You can work with strings longer than War and Peace, if you want.

The strings can contain line breaks.
"""
```

```
print(multiline_string)
```

```
You can work with strings longer than War and Peace, if you want.

The strings can contain line breaks.
```

Let's set strings aside for now. We will return to them with some more advanced concepts later in the book.

Comparison and control flow

We know how to tell our computer to execute individual instructions (e.g. evaluate 2 + 2). However, we often don't want our computer to simply execute a series of individual instructions top to bottom. Instead, we want to be able to tell our computer to execute code *depending on one or more conditions*. This is called 'control flow'.

Control flow statements include a 'condition' that can be evaluated to either True or False (these are Boolean values, after the mathematician George Boole), followed by a 'clause' which is an indented block of code to execute depending on whether the condition evaluates to True or False. In other words, we will execute the clause code *if the condition returns True* and skip over that code if the expression evaluates to False. Usually, the condition contains one or more of the comparison operators in Table 2.1.

Table 2.1 Python comparison operators

Comparison Operator	Means
==	Equal to
!=	Not equal to
>	Greater than
>=	Greater than or equal to
<	Less than
<=	Less than or equal to

All the comparison operators in Table 2.1 will resolve an expression to a Boolean value.

```
country == country.upper()
```

```
False
```

```
country != country.upper()
```

```
True
```

```
country == country
```

```
True
```

```
23 < 33
```

```
True
```

```
33 >= 33
```

```
True
```

We can use these comparison operators to execute code *conditionally*. Let's make this less abstract with a simple example that uses an if statement.

if, elif, else

An `if` statement starts with `if`, followed by an expression that can be evaluated to `True` or `False` and a colon `:`. The expression is the *condition*, and the colon indicates that what follows will be the *clause*: the indented code to run if the condition is `True`.

The cell below illustrates control flow using a simple `if` statement. It executes the same `if` statement on two variables, checking if a variable has the value 'Cologne' and printing a string if the condition evaluates to `True`:

```python
if city == 'COLOGNE':
    print("city has the value: 'COLOGNE'")
else:
    print("city does not have the value: 'COLOGNE'")
if country == 'Cologne':
    print("country has the value: 'COLOGNE'")
else:
    print("country does not have the value: 'COLOGNE'")
```

```
city has the value: 'COLOGNE'
country does not have the value: 'COLOGNE'
```

Notice that we have included another line of code; an `else` statement indicates that if the previous condition does not evaluate to `True`, Python should execute the indented clause code under `else`. In this case, we use the `else` statement to indicate when a variable did not match the condition.

Let's examine the `==` operator more closely.

```python
if 'doing computational social science' == 'Doing Computational Social Science':
    print("The second two strings are equal to each other!")
if 'doing computational social science ' == 'doing computational social science':
    print("The first two strings are equal to each other!")
if 'doing computational social science' == 'doing computational social science':
    print("The third two strings are equal to each other!")
```

```
The third two strings are equal to each other!
```

There are a few things to note here. First, Python cares about differences in capitalization (the first `if` statement) and white space (the second `if` statement) when comparing strings. The strings `'doing'`, `'Doing'`, and `'Doing '` are all different.

This might seem frustrating at first, but Python's capacity for specificity can pay dividends. We can also anticipate these issues and use some string manipulation methods to exert a bit more control over the comparison. For example, we can enforce title case and strip out white space using the string methods we just learnt.

```python
if 'doing computational social science '.title().strip() == 'Doing Computational
    Social Science':
    print("These two items are equal to one another!")
else:
    print("These two items are NOT equal to one another.")
```

These two items are equal to one another!

In this example, there are only two options: if the strings are equal, do one thing, if not do another. We can use `elif`, or *else–if statements*, to introduce code to execute on different conditions. Note that using an `elif` statement is functionally equivalent to nesting an `if` statement within the clause of an `else` statement. It will only run if a previous condition has evaluated to false.

```python
we_do_sentence = "We're doing learning control flow"
learning_string = "learning control flow"

if we_do_sentence == learning_string:
    print("These two strings are equal to each other!")
elif learning_string in we_do_sentence:
    print("The second string is in the first string, but they are not equal to each
    other.")
else:
    print("The two strings are NOT equal to each other and the second string is NOT
    in the first string.")
```

The second string is in the first string, but they are not equal to each other.

We can read this code as following this logic: if the first condition is `True`, then execute the first print statement. If the first condition is false, check if the second condition is `True`. If it is, execute the second print statement. If the preceding `if` and `elif` statements were all `False`, then execute the final print statement.

Also note that we used strings that contain `'`, such as `We're`. If we used single quotes to open and close those strings, Python would have thrown an error, because it would have interpreted the `'` in `'s` as indicating the end of the string. If your string contains a `'`, then you need to open and close the string with double quotes.

Very importantly, the indentation in our code is meaningful. All indented code following a `condition` is a `clause` and will only be executed when the condition is met. Jupyter, VS Code, and other IDEs and text editors generally do a good job of managing indentation for you as you write your code, but you can still make mistakes. This is a double-edged sword: by making indentation syntax-relevant, Python has eliminated the need for much of the explicit statement formatting required by other languages and is thus far easier to read; in doing so, it demands that we be vigilant about finicky indentation levels, lest our code execute incorrectly.

While loops

`if` statements are probably the most common type of statements used in control flow, but they are not the only ones. We can also use a `while` statement to conditionally execute code. A `while` statement starts with the word `while` and is followed by an expression that can be evaluated down to `True` or `False`. You can read a while loop as if it were saying 'If `condition` is `True`, execute `clause`. Repeat this process until `condition` is `False` or told to stop.'

In the following example, we will use a while loop to print a string until we have reached the end of a course. In plain language, we say 'while the current week is less than or equal to the last week, print "The course is still in progress" and increase the week by 1'.

```
week = 1

while week <= 12:
    print(f"It's Week {week}. The course is still in progress.")
    week += 1 # equivalent to `week = week + 1`
print('\nThe course is "complete". Congratulations!')
```

```
It's Week 1. The course is still in progress.
It's Week 2. The course is still in progress.
It's Week 3. The course is still in progress.
It's Week 4. The course is still in progress.
It's Week 5. The course is still in progress.
It's Week 6. The course is still in progress.
It's Week 7. The course is still in progress.
It's Week 8. The course is still in progress.
It's Week 9. The course is still in progress.
It's Week 10. The course is still in progress.
It's Week 11. The course is still in progress.
It's Week 12. The course is still in progress.

The course is "complete". Congratulations!
```

Remember that the *indentation is meaningful*; because the last line is not indented, Python knows it is not part of the while loop and only runs it when the while loop has completed.

Also, note that the fifth line contains a comment. Comments in Python start with #. Anything on the line after the # is not considered code and will not be executed. Comments can be very useful to include in your code. Initially, you might use comments to remind yourself what certain chunks of code do. As you become more comfortable with Python, you will want to avoid writing comments that translate the code into ordinary language and instead write comments that remind your future self – or inform a collaborator – about what you were trying to do, or what you were thinking at the time. These tend to be much more useful comments than descriptive translations, which become less helpful as your Python skills develop.

A third thing to notice is that, unlike the if clause from above, this example is a loop. If the condition on the third line evaluates to True, the clause (the code block on the fourth and fifth lines) will be executed over and over again until the third line evaluates to False, at which point Python exits the loop.

You may already be anticipating this, but it is possible to write your code in a way that leads Python into an infinite loop, in which it keeps executing the same code over and over again, for ever, or until something unexpected interrupts it, like a power outage. Infinite loops are caused when the condition always evaluates to the same value. For example, if we forgot to include the + in the += on the fifth line above, then Python would not add 1 to the variable week. Instead, it would simply keep reassigning 1 to week, the third line will always evaluate to True, and Python is stuck in an infinite loop. To get out of an infinite loop, press 'Ctrl + C'. If you are in a Jupyter Notebook, press the stop button to interrupt the kernel.

Combining comparisons with connectives

It can be useful to combine comparisons in a condition with connectives such as and or or to exert even more control over the code that is executed under various conditions. For example, to use the and connective in a conditional:

```
book = 'Doing Computational Social Science'
if len(book) > 30 and book == 'Doing Computational Social Science':
    print("Correct! That's the name of this book")
```

Correct! That's the name of this book

The conditional on the first line above uses and to chain together two comparisons. When using and, the line will evaluate to True if *both* comparisons are True. If one of them evaluated to False, then the line evaluates to False.

Alternatively, we could use the or connector. Below, this line evaluates to True if *either* of the two comparisons evaluate to True. Obviously, the code executes without returning an error even though there is a 'mistake' in this code: not every string longer than 30 characters is the name of this book!

```
if len(book) > 30 or book == 'Doing Computational Social Science':
    print("Correct! That's the name of this book")
```

Correct! That's the name of this book

It might sound a bit strange, but we can also use not to make an expression return True (and therefore execute a clause) if it evaluates to False:

```
if not book == 'Doing Computational Social Science':
    print("Sorry, that's not the name of this book")
```

It is possible to combine as many comparisons as you like, though if you go too far you can make your code a little more difficult to read. The convention in Python is to wrap each comparison in (), which makes the code cleaner and easier to read.

```
if (len(book) > 30 and len(book) < 100) or (book == 'Doing Computational Social
    Science'):
    print("Correct! That's the name of this book")
```

Correct! That's the name of this book

Tracebacks

Sometimes, something goes wrong with our code. When errors occur, Python will provide a special report called a Traceback that identifies what the nature of the problem was and where it was encountered. Traceback reports can contain a lot of information and may be a bit overwhelming at first, but if you understand *what* Python is providing and why it is providing it, you can diagnose problems with your code and, over time, become a better Python programmer.

In general, you should read a Traceback from the bottom up. The final line of the Traceback tells you what kind of problem Python encountered, as well as an error message that helps you understand why the exception was raised. Lines that appear earlier in the Traceback show you where in your code the error occurred. Depending on your code, the Traceback may be short and concise, or long and nested.

At this point, the `Tracebacks` that you are most likely to encounter are `NameErrors` (you use a variable that is not yet defined), `TypeErrors` (you perform an operation on an incorrect data type), and `SyntaxError` (you broke Python's grammar rules). We saw an example of a `ValueError` earlier, when we tried to use + on a string and an integer.

try/except

We can distinguish between at least two classes of error. If code has broken one of the grammar rules of Python, like not properly closing brackets, you will get a syntax error. An exception occurs when syntactically correct code still manages to produce an error. While both are errors, syntax errors are detected while the code is being parsed, *before* the code is executed, resulting in its not running at all. Exceptions occur during execution and *may* not cause the execution to fail.

When it encounters an `exception` of any type, Python's default behaviour is to halt execution of your code and provide you with a `Traceback`. While this is often a useful feature, it isn't always what we want. Sometimes, we know that some of the code we've written is likely to encounter a *very particular* type of error, and we would rather Python handle the error in some way and continue executing the rest of our code. In these cases, we can use `try` and `except` statements. In general, you should not use `try`/`except` to handle syntax errors. It's usually impossible because, as mentioned, the syntax error will halt execution before it even attempts to execute the code.

The `try` statement is used before an indented block of code, and it indicates that Python should attempt to execute the code in the indented block. When Python encounters an error whilst executing the code contained within a `try` block, it doesn't immediately halt execution: instead, it first checks all of the following `except` statements to see if the exception it has encountered is listed (e.g. `except KeyError:`). If so, Python then executes the code in the pertinent `except` block before carrying on as normal. Let's consider an example.

Let's expand on the example we used for the `while` block. Rather than assuming that users will always start from the first week, let's pretend the code now allows users to input the week they wish to start from, so long as it's one of the first 3 weeks. We have stored our hypothetical user's input in the `user_input` variable. If its value is an integer equal to or less than 12, you'll see one line of printout for each of the remaining weeks. What happens if the user had typed in 'seven' instead of a number?

```
print("Please enter which week you will start in.")
user_input = "seven"
week = int(user_input)

while week <= 12:
    print(f"It's Week {week}. The course is still in progress.")
    week += 1 # equivalent to week = week + 1

print('\nThe course is "complete". Congratulations!')

Please enter which week you will start in.


---------------------------------------------------------------------------
ValueError                                Traceback (most recent call last)
<ipython-input-53-9d4cb53a15de> in <module>
```

```
    1 print("Please enter which week you will start in.")
    2 user_input = "seven"
---> 3 week = int(user_input)
    4
    5 while week <= 12:
```

ValueError: invalid literal for int() with base 10: 'seven'

You should see a `ValueError` exception. This makes sense. Python isn't inherently aware of how to interpret the string seven as an integer, and even though it *can*, we have not told it to do so. We can use `try` and `except` to catch some of the cases of the value error without sacrificing any of our original functionality. To do this, we'll have to start by figuring out where the error is coming from. We can do this by using the `Traceback` Python printed when it encountered the exception: looks like line 4 is the culprit. Let's try wrapping that line in a `try` block, and then using `except` `ValueError` plus some handwritten string comprehension to handle the error. Let's assume that people can only start the course in the first 3 weeks, and account for those in our `try` block:

```python
print("Please enter which of weeks.")
user_input = "three"
try:
    week = int(user_input)

except ValueError:
    if user_input.lower().strip() == "one":
        week = 1
    elif user_input.lower().strip() == "two":
        week = 2
    elif user_input.lower().strip() == "three":
        week = 3
    else:
        raise ValueError("I don't recognize that as a valid number! Try again!")

while week <= 12:
    print(f"It's Week {week}. The course is still in progress.")
    week += 1 # equivalent to week = week + 1
print('\nThe course is "complete". Congratulations!')
```

```
Please enter which of weeks.
It's Week 3. The course is still in progress.
It's Week 4. The course is still in progress.
It's Week 5. The course is still in progress.
It's Week 6. The course is still in progress.
It's Week 7. The course is still in progress.
It's Week 8. The course is still in progress.
It's Week 9. The course is still in progress.
It's Week 10. The course is still in progress.
It's Week 11. The course is still in progress.
It's Week 12. The course is still in progress.

The course is "complete". Congratulations!
```

Notice that the else statement, if executed, re-raises ValueError (albeit with a different message). Rather than assume your workaround will work in every case, it's good practice to manually raise an exception if all else fails; that way, Python will have a way of letting you know that your fix was a bust, and that it's time to head back to the drawing board.

When used judiciously, try and except are invaluable tools that will serve you well. That said, try and except – like many of the tools we will cover in this book – are prone to abuse. If you don't specify an individual exception after your except statement, your try/except will cover *all* possible exceptions. When a deadline looms, the clock has struck 4.00 am, and you're at your wits' end trying to hunt down the one error-throwing bug preventing your code from executing, the siren song of try and except may be very tempting. Simply wrap all of your code in a try statement, and provide a wildcard except at the end. Poof! No more errors! Problem solved, right?

Sadly no. In Python programming, as in life, errors occur for a reason: *something is wrong.* If you don't know what's causing an error, *you should not trust your code.* Code that cannot be trusted is worthless at best, and potentially harmful. Avoid doing this at all costs.

2.6 Conclusion

The key points in this chapter are as follows:

- Python is a highly readable general-purpose programming language that features an extensive array of community-made open source packages for data science and machine learning.
- We explored a few of Python's built-in methods and functions for string processing/ manipulation.
- We covered some Python fundamentals such as data types, assignment, using methods and functions, comparison and conditional execution, and error handling.
- Our Python journey continues in the next chapter!

Visit the website at https://study.sagepub.com/mclevey for additional resources

3

PYTHON PROGRAMMING: DATA STRUCTURES, FUNCTIONS, AND FILES

3.1 Learning Objectives

By the end of this chapter, you should be able to do the following:

- Perform common operations on Python's built-in data structures, including lists, tuples, and dictionaries
- Use for loops and comprehensions to perform operations on items in lists, tuples, and dictionaries
- Use the operators in, not in, and isinstance in control flow
- Articulate what it means for a Python object to be 'iterable'
- Design, develop, and use your own custom functions
- Read data from, and write data to, external files

3.2 Learning Materials

You can find the online learning materials for this chapter in doing_computational_social_ science/Chapter_03. cd into the directory and launch your Jupyter server.

3.3 Introduction

In this chapter, you will learn about Python's most common built-in data structures: lists, tuples, and dictionaries. We start by learning the basic syntax for each of these data structures, followed by some of the most common methods and operations used to perform operations on the items contained in each. We will place a particularly heavy emphasis on understanding how to iterate over the items in a data structure using for loops and comprehensions. Finally, we will then learn how and why to write our own custom functions and how to work with external files.

3.4 Working With Python's Data Structures

Working with lists and tuples

In Python, lists are ordered collections of *any* object, such as strings, integers, floats, or other data structures – even other lists. The items in a list may be of the same type, *but they do not have to be*. Python lists are very flexible. You can mix information of various kinds in a list, you can add information to the list on-the-fly, and you are able to remove or change any of the information the list contains. This is not always the case in other languages. The most basic list looks like this:

```
my_list = []
```

The above code produces an empty list; it contains no objects. You can also create an empty list by referring directly to the built-in type:

```
my_list = list()
```

All lists begin and end with square brackets [], and elements are separated by a comma. Below, we define two lists containing strings (megacities in one list and their countries in another) and one list containing numbers (city population in 2018). Note that we are using _ as a thousands separator to make our code more readable. As far as Python is concerned, 37_468_000 and 37468000 are identical numbers, but the former is easier to read.

```
megacities = ['Tokyo','Delhi','Shanghai','Sao Paulo','Mexico City','Cairo','Dhaka','
    Mumbai','Beijing','Osaka']
countries = ['Japan','India','China','Brazil','Mexico','Egypt','Bangladesh','India','
    China','Japan']
pop2018 = [37_468_000, 28_514_000, 25_582_000, 21_650_000, 21_581_000, 20_076_000, 19
    _980_000, 19_618_000, 19_578_000, 19_281_000]
```

Every item in a list has an index based on its position in that list. Indices are integers and, like most other programming languages, Python's indexing starts at 0, which means that the first item in any list – or anything else that is indexed in Python – starts at 0. In the megacities list, the index for Tokyo is 0, Delhi is 1, Shanghai is 2, and so on. Figure 3.1 illustrates the idea.

Figure 3.1 Indexing in Python starts at 0, not 1

We can use the index to select a specific item from a list by typing the name of the list and then the index number inside square brackets:

```
megacities[3]
```

```
'Sao Paulo'
```

We can also access individual items by working from the end of the list. To do so, we use a '–' sign in the brackets. Note that unlike counting up from 0, we are not counting down from '–0'. While [2] gives the third element, [-2] gives the second-from-last element. To select 'China' from countries, we could use

```
countries[8]
countries[-2]
```

```
'China'
```

When we access an individual item from a list, Python returns the item in its expected data type. For example, megacities[3] returns 'Sao Paulo' as a string, and pop2018[3] returns the integer 21650000. We can use any methods we want that are associated with that particular data type:

```
pop2018[3]*3
```

```
64950000
```

```
megacities[3].upper()
```

```
'SAO PAULO'
```

Using square brackets to access an element in a list (or tuple, or set, or dictionary) is called *subscripting*, and it is capable of accepting a wider variety of indices than a simple integer. One particularly useful way to subscript an object is to use slice notation, where two index positions are separated by a colon:

```
megacities[0:3]
```

```
['Tokyo', 'Delhi', 'Shanghai']
```

Using a slice to subscript a list returns the item at the first integer's position, plus every item at every position between the first and the second integers. It does *not* return the item indexed by the second integer. To retrieve the last three entries of our list, you would use

```
countries[7:10]
```

```
['India', 'China', 'Japan']
```

You can also use slice notation with one integer missing to return all of the items in a list up to – or starting at – a particular index position. The following gives us the first three megacities,

```
megacities[:3]
```

```
['Tokyo', 'Delhi', 'Shanghai']
```

and this returns the last seven:

```
megacities[-7:]
```

```
['Sao Paulo', 'Mexico City', 'Cairo', 'Dhaka', 'Mumbai', 'Beijing', 'Osaka']
```

Looping over lists

Python's lists are iterable objects, which means that we can iterate (or loop) over the list's elements to execute code for each one. This is commonly done with a for loop. Below, we iterate over the list megacities and print each item:

```
for city in megacities:
    print(city)
```

```
Tokyo
Delhi
Shanghai
Sao Paulo
Mexico City
Cairo
Dhaka
Mumbai
Beijing
Osaka
```

This code creates a *temporary variable* called city that is used to refer to the current element of megacities being iterated over. After a full loop, city will have been used to refer to each element in the list. The name for this variable should be something descriptive that tells you something about the elements of the list.

Modifying lists

Lists can be changed in a number of ways. We can modify the items in the list like we would other values, such as changing the string 'Mexico City' to 'Ciudad de México' using the value's index:

```
megacities[4] = 'Ciudad de México'
print(megacities)
```

```
['Tokyo', 'Delhi', 'Shanghai', 'Sao Paulo', 'Ciudad de México', 'Cairo', 'Dhaka', '
    Mumbai', 'Beijing', 'Osaka']
```

We often want to add or remove items from a list. Let's add Karachi to our three lists using the `.append()` method:

```
megacities.append('Karachi')
countries.append('Pakistan')
pop2018.append(16_000_000)

print(len(megacities), len(countries), len(pop2018))
```

```
11 11 11
```

Our lists now contain 11 items each; our Karachi data was appended to the *end* of each list.

You will use `.append()` frequently. It's a very convenient way to dynamically build and modify a list. This book has many examples of creating an empty list that is populated using `.append()`. Let's create a new list that will contain a formatted string for each city.

```
city_strings = []

for city in megacities:
    city_string = f"What's the population of {city}?"
    city_strings.append(city_string)
for city_string in city_strings:
    print(city_string)
```

```
What's the population of Tokyo?
What's the population of Delhi?
What's the population of Shanghai?
What's the population of Sao Paulo?
What's the population of Ciudad de México?
What's the population of Cairo?
What's the population of Dhaka?
What's the population of Mumbai?
What's the population of Beijing?
What's the population of Osaka?
What's the population of Karachi?
```

Removing items is just as straightforward. There are a few ways to do it, but `.remove()` is one of the more common ones:

```
megacities.remove('Karachi')
countries.remove('Pakistan')
pop2018.remove(16_000_000)
```

Sometimes we want to change the organization of a list. This is usually sorting the list in some way (e.g. alphabetical, descending). Below, we make a copy of `megacities` and sort it alphabetically. We don't want to modify the original object, so we explicitly create a new copy using the `.copy()` method:

```
megacities_copy = megacities.copy()
megacities_copy.sort()
print(megacities_copy)
```

```
['Beijing', 'Cairo', 'Ciudad de México', 'Delhi', 'Dhaka', 'Mumbai', 'Osaka', 'Sao
    Paulo', 'Shanghai', 'Tokyo']
```

Note that we do not use '=' when we call .sort(). This method occurs 'in-place', which means it modifies the object it called on. Assigning megacities_copy.sort() will actually return None, a special value in Python.

Once we change the order of items in a list using the .sort() method, the original order is lost. We cannot 'undo' the sort unless we keep track of the original order. That's why we started by making a copy. To temporarily sort our list without actually changing the order of items in the original list, use the sorted function: sorted(megacities).

When applied to a list of numbers, .sort() will reorder the list from the smallest to the largest:

```
pop_copy = pop2018.copy()
pop_copy.sort()
print(pop_copy)
```

```
[19281000, 19578000, 19618000, 19980000, 20076000, 21581000, 21650000, 25582000,
    28514000, 37468000]
```

To sort a list in reverse alphabetical order, or numbers from the largest to the smallest, use the reverse=True argument for .sort():

```
pop_copy.sort(reverse=True)
print(pop_copy)
```

```
megacities_copy.sort(reverse=True)
print(megacities_copy)
```

```
[37468000, 28514000, 25582000, 21650000, 21581000, 20076000, 19980000, 19618000,
    19578000, 19281000]
['Tokyo', 'Shanghai', 'Sao Paulo', 'Osaka', 'Mumbai', 'Dhaka', 'Delhi', 'Ciudad de
    México', 'Cairo', 'Beijing']
```

The fact that lists are *ordered* makes them very useful. If you change the order of a list, you could easily introduce costly mistakes. Let's say, for example, that we sorted our pop2018 list above. pop2018, megacities, and countries are now misaligned. We have lost the ability to do the following:

```
print(f'The population of {megacities[4]} in 2018 was {pop2018[4]}')
```

```
The population of Ciudad de México in 2018 was 21581000
```

Zipping and unzipping lists

When you have data spread out over multiple lists, it can be useful to zip those lists together so that all the items with an index of 0 are associated with one another, all the items with an index of 1 are associated, and so on. The most straightforward way to do this is to use the `zip()` function, which is illustrated in Figure 3.2 and the code block below. Clever usage of `zip()` can accomplish a great deal using very few lines of code.

```
                         megacities = [  countries = [     pop2018 = [
Index = 0    ⇨              'Tokyo',       'Japan',       37_468_000,
Index = 1    ⇨              'Delhi',       'India',       28_514_000,
Index = 2    ⇨            'Shanghai',      'China',       25_582_000,
Index = 3    ⇨            'Sao Paulo',     'Brazil',      21_650_000,
Index = 4    ⇨          'Mexico City',     'Mexico',      21_581_000,
Index = 5    ⇨              'Cairo',       'Egypt',       20_076_000,
Index = 6    ⇨              'Dhaka',     'Bangladesh',    19_980_000,
Index = 7    ⇨              'Mumbai',      'India',       19_618_000,
Index = 8    ⇨             'Beijing',      'China',       19_578_000,
Index = 9    ⇨              'Osaka'        'Japan'        19_281_000
                              ]              ]               ]

                 list(zip(magacities, countries, pop2018))

         Index = 0    ⇨     [('Tokyo', 'Japan', 37468000),
         Index = 1    ⇨      ('Delhi', India', 28514000),
         Index = 2    ⇨      ('Shanghai', 'China', 25514000),
         Index = 3    ⇨      ('Sao Paulo',a'Brazil', 21650000),
         Index = 4    ⇨      ('Mexico City', 'Mexico', 21581000),
         Index = 5    ⇨      ('Cairo', 'Egypt', 20076000),
         Index = 6    ⇨      ('Dhaka', 'Bangladesh', 1998000),
         Index = 7    ⇨      ('Mumbai', 'India', 19618000),
         Index = 8    ⇨      ('Beijing', 'China', 19578000),
         Index = 9    ⇨      ('Osaka', 'Japan', 19281000)]
```

Figure 3.2 The `zip()` function is useful for joining/unjoining the items of an iterable object

```
for paired in zip(megacities,countries, pop2018):
    print(paired)

('Tokyo', 'Japan', 37468000)
('Delhi', 'India', 28514000)
('Shanghai', 'China', 25582000)
('Sao Paulo', 'Brazil', 21650000)
('Ciudad de México', 'Mexico', 21581000)
('Cairo', 'Egypt', 20076000)
('Dhaka', 'Bangladesh', 19980000)
('Mumbai', 'India', 19618000)
('Beijing', 'China', 19578000)
('Osaka', 'Japan', 19281000)
```

The actual *object* that the `zip()` function returns is a 'zip object', within which our data is stored as a series of tuples (discussed later). We can convert these zipped tuples to a list of tuples using the `list()` function:

```
zipped_list = list(zip(megacities,countries,pop2018))
print(zipped_list)
```

```
[('Tokyo', 'Japan', 37468000), ('Delhi', 'India', 28514000), ('Shanghai', 'China',
    25582000), ('Sao Paulo', 'Brazil', 21650000), ('Ciudad de México', 'Mexico',
    21581000), ('Cairo', 'Egypt', 20076000), ('Dhaka', 'Bangladesh', 19980000), ('
    Mumbai', 'India', 19618000), ('Beijing', 'China', 19578000), ('Osaka', 'Japan',
    19281000)]
```

It is also possible to unzip a zipped list using the * operator and multiple assignment (which is also called 'unpacking'), which allows us to assign multiple values to multiple variables in a single line. For example, the code below returns three objects. We assign each to a variable on the left side of the = sign.

```
city_unzip, country_unzip, pop_unzip = zip(*zipped_list)
print(city_unzip)
print(country_unzip)
print(pop_unzip)
```

```
('Tokyo', 'Delhi', 'Shanghai', 'Sao Paulo', 'Ciudad de México', 'Cairo', 'Dhaka','
    Mumbai', 'Beijing', 'Osaka')
('Japan', 'India', 'China', 'Brazil', 'Mexico', 'Egypt', 'Bangladesh', 'India', 'China
    ', 'Japan')
(37468000, 28514000, 25582000, 21650000, 21581000, 20076000, 19980000, 19618000,
    19578000, 19281000)
```

List comprehensions

Earlier, we created an empty list and populated it using .append() in a for loop. We can also use list comprehension, which can produce the same result in a single line of code. To demonstrate, let's try counting the number of characters in the name of each country in the countries list using a for loop, and then with list comprehension.

```
len_country_name = []
```

```
for country in countries:
    n_chars = len(country)
    len_country_name.append(n_chars)
```

```
print(len_country_name)
```

```
[5, 5, 5, 6, 6, 5, 10, 5, 5, 5]
```

```
len_country_name = [len(country) for country in countries]
print(len_country_name)
```

```
[5, 5, 5, 6, 6, 5, 10, 5, 5, 5]
```

List comprehensions can be a little strange at first, but they become easier with practice. The key things to remember is that they will always include:

1   the expression itself, applied to each item in the original list,
2   the temporary variable name for the iterable, and
3   the original iterable, which in this case is the list.

Above, the expression was `len(country)`, `country` was the temporary variable name, and `countries` was the original iterable.

   We often wish to add conditional logic to our for loops and list comprehensions. Let's create a new list of cities with populations greater than 20,500,000 with the help of the `zip()` function:

```
biggest = [[city, population] for city, population in zip(megacities, pop2018) if
    population > 20_500_000]
print(biggest)
```

```
[['Tokyo', 37468000], ['Delhi', 28514000], ['Shanghai', 25582000], ['Sao Paulo',
    21650000], ['Ciudad de México', 21581000]]
```

The result – `biggest` – is a list of lists. We can work with nested data structures like this using the same tools we use for flat data structures. For example,

```
for city in biggest:
    print(f'The population of {city[0]} in 2018 was {city[1]}')
```

```
The population of Tokyo in 2018 was 37468000
The population of Delhi in 2018 was 28514000
The population of Shanghai in 2018 was 25582000
The population of Sao Paulo in 2018 was 21650000
The population of Ciudad de México in 2018 was 21581000
```

When should you use a for loop and when should you use list comprehension? In many cases, it's largely a matter of personal preference. List comprehensions are more concise while still being readable with some Python experience. However, they become unreadable very quickly if you need to perform a lot of operations on each item, or if you have even slightly complex conditional logic. In those cases, you should definitely avoid list comprehensions. We always want to ensure our code is as readable as possible.

   List comprehension is very popular in Python, so it's important to know how to read it. Since for loops and list comprehension do the same thing in slightly different ways, there is nothing to prevent you from sticking to one or the other, but you should be able to convert one into the other and back again.

Copying lists

Earlier, we copied a list using the `.copy()` method, which is helpful if we want to preserve our original list. Could we accomplish this using the familiar '=' operator?

```
countries_copy = countries
print(countries_copy)
```

```
['Japan', 'India', 'China', 'Brazil', 'Mexico', 'Egypt', 'Bangladesh', 'India', 'China
    ', 'Japan']
```

This approach *appears* to create a copy of `countries`, but it is an illusion. When we copy a list using the '=' operator, we are not creating a new *object*. Instead, we have created a new variable *name* that points to the original object in memory. We have an object with two names, instead of two distinct objects. Any modifications made using `countries_copy` will change the same object in memory described by `countries`. If we append Karachi to `countries_copy` and print `countries`, we would see Karachi, and vice versa. If we want to preserve the original list and make modifications to the second, this will not do.

Instead, we can use the `.copy()` method to create a shallow copy of the original list, or `.deepcopy()` to create a deep copy. To understand the difference, compare a flat list (e.g. `[1, 2, 3]`) with a list of lists (e.g. `[[1, 2, 3], [4, 5, 6]]`). The list of lists is nested; it is *deeper* than the flat list. If we perform a shallow copy (i.e. `.copy()`) of the flat list, Python will create a new object that is independent of the original. But if we create a shallow copy of the nested lists of lists, Python only makes a new object for outer list; it's only one level deep. The contents of the inner lists `[1, 2, 3]` and `[4, 5, 6]` were not copied, they are only references to the original lists. In other words, the outer lists (length 2) are independent of one another, but the inner lists (lengths 3) are references to the same object in memory. When we are working with nested data structures, such as lists of lists, we need to use `.deepcopy()` if we want to create a new object that is fully independent of the original.

not in or in?

Lists used in research contexts are usually far larger than the examples in this chapter. They may have thousands, or even millions, of items. To find out if a list contains, or does not contain, a specific value, rather than manually searching a printed list, we can use the in and not in operators, which will evaluate to True or False:

```
'Mexico' in countries
```

```
True
```

```
'Mexico' not in countries
```

```
False
```

These operators can be very useful when using conditions. For example,

```
to_check = 'Toronto'

if to_check in megacities:
    print(f'{to_check} was one of the 10 largest cities in the world in 2018.')
else:
    print(f'{to_check} was not one of the 10 largest cities in the world in 2018.')

Toronto was not one of the 10 largest cities in the world in 2018.
```

Using enumerate

In some cases, we want to access both the item and its index position from a list at the same time. We can do this with the `enumerate()` function. Recall the three lists from the megacity example. Information about each megacity is spread out in three lists, but the indices are shared across those lists. Below, we enumerate `megacities`, creating a temporary variable for the index position (`i`) and each item (`city`), and iterate over it. We use those values to print the name of the city, and then access information about country and city population using the `index` position. Of course, this only works because the items in the list are ordered and shared across each list.

```
for i, city in enumerate(megacities):
    print(f'{city}, {countries[i]}, has {str(pop2018[i])} residents.')
```

```
Tokyo, Japan, has 37468000 residents.
Delhi, India, has 28514000 residents.
Shanghai, China, has 25582000 residents.
Sao Paulo, Brazil, has 21650000 residents.
Ciudad de México, Mexico, has 21581000 residents.
Cairo, Egypt, has 20076000 residents.
Dhaka, Bangladesh, has 19980000 residents.
Mumbai, India, has 19618000 residents.
Beijing, China, has 19578000 residents.
Osaka, Japan, has 19281000 residents.
```

As previously mentioned, we can include *as many lines as we want* in the indented code block of a for loop, which can help us avoid unnecessary iteration. If you have to perform a lot of operations on items in a list of tuples, it is best to iterate over the data structure *once* and perform all the necessary operations rather than iterate over the list multiple times, performing a small number of operations each time. Depending on what you need to accomplish, you might find yourself wanting to iterate on the temporary objects in your for loop. Python allows this! Inside the indented code block of your for loop, you can put *another* for loop (and another inside that one, and so on). When you need to get a lot out of your lists, keep this in mind!

Tuples, for when your lists won't change

In Python, every object is either *mutable* or *immutable*. We've just shown many ways that lists are *mutable*: adding and removing items, sorting them, and so on. Any data type in Python which allows you to change something about its composition (number of entries, values of entries) is *mutable*. Data types that do *not* permit changes after instantiation are *immutable*.

Generally speaking, computational social scientists prefer to work with *mutable* objects such as lists. The flexibility we gain by working with a *mutable* data type usually outweighs the advantages of working with *immutable* types – but not always. In order to convince you to keep immutable types in mind, we'll start by introducing its most prolific ambassador: the `tuple`.

A `tuple` is an *ordered, immutable* series of objects. You can think of `tuples` as a special kind of list that can't be modified once created. In terms of syntax, values in a tuple are stored inside `()` rather than `[]`. We can instantiate an empty tuple in a similar fashion to lists:

```
my_empty_tuple_1 = ()
my_empty_tuple_2 = tuple()
```

That said, an empty `tuple` isn't generally of much use, because it won't ever be anything but empty: immutability will see to that! Just like with lists, we can instantiate our `tuples` with preloaded values:

```
a_useful_tuple = (2, 7, 4)
```

We can easily convert between tuples and lists using the `tuple()` and `list()` functions, respectively:

```
print(type(countries))
countries_tuple = tuple(countries)
print(type(countries_tuple))

<class 'list'>
<class 'tuple'>
```

There are many uses for tuples: if you *absolutely* must ensure that the order of a series of objects is preserved, use a tuple and you can guarantee it. To illustrate, let's use the list method `.sort()` to change the order of items in our countries list. Note that we will use the `.copy()` method to preserve a record of the original order.

```
countries_sorted = countries.copy()
countries_sorted.sort()
countries_sorted

['Bangladesh',
 'Brazil',
 'China',
 'China',
 'Egypt',
 'India',
 'India',
 'Japan',
 'Japan',
 'Mexico']
```

Great! Now, the countries are in alphabetical order. Nice and tidy – except for the fact that the `countries_sorted` list is out of order with the `megacities` and `pop2018` lists. Sometimes, in a particularly large project, you might accidentally `sort` a list that shouldn't have been sorted; this might create some serious mismatches in your data, and these mismatches might have a deleterious effect further down the line. To prevent something like this from happening, it's worth considering storing your `lists` as `tuples` instead; that way, if you try to use the `.sort()` method on a `tuple`, Python will throw an error and disaster will be averted.

    `tuples` have a few other advantages over `lists`: for one, using tuples can considerably speed up your code and reduce your memory usage; this is true of most *immutable* data types when compared to their *mutable* counterparts. `tuples` can also be used in some places where *mutable* data structures cannot. You cannot use a `list` as a key for a `dictionary` (more on dictionaries below), as all `keys` must be *immutable*. A `tuple` works just fine!

Finally, even though lists are mutable and tuples are immutable, they have another feature in common: they are both iterable. Any of the forms of iteration that can be applied to `lists` can be applied to `tuples` too.

Dictionaries

Another Python data structure that you will frequently see and use is the dictionary. Unlike lists, dictionaries are designed to connect pieces of related information. Dictionaries offer a flexible approach to storing key–value pairs. Each key must be an *immutable* Python object, such as an integer, a float, a string, or a `tuple`, and there can't be duplicated keys. Values can be any type of object. We can access values by specifying the relevant key.

Where lists use square brackets [], and tuples use round brackets (), Python's dictionaries wrap `key:value` pairs in curly brackets {}, where the keys and values are separated by a colon :, and each pair is separated by a ,. For example,

```
tokyo = {
    'country' : 'Japan',
    'pop2018': 37_468_000
}

print(tokyo)

{'country': 'Japan', 'pop2018': 37468000}
```

We can use as many keys as we like when we create a dictionary. To quickly access a list of all the keys in the dictionary, we can use the `.keys()` method:

```
print(tokyo.keys())

dict_keys(['country', 'pop2018'])
```

To access any given value in a dictionary, we provide the name of the dictionary object followed by the name of the key whose value we want to access inside square brackets and quotes. For example, to access the population from our `tokyo` dictionary,

```
tokyo['pop2018']

37468000
```

Like lists, but unlike tuples, dictionaries can be modified as we work. We can add a new key–value pair to `tokyo` – say the population density of the Tokyo Metropolitan Area – using the same syntax we learnt for referencing a key, only we will also assign a value. Because the key we are referencing doesn't exist in the dictionary, Python knows we are creating a new key–value pair, not replacing an old one with a new value. When we print the dictionary, we can see our new pairing has been added.

```
tokyo['density'] = 1_178.4
print(tokyo)

{'country': 'Japan', 'pop2018': 37468000, 'density': 1178.4}
```

In this case, we started with a dictionary that contained some key–value pairs from when we first defined the dictionary. But we could have also started with an empty dictionary and populated it with key–value pairs using the method we just learnt.

```
delhi = {}

delhi['country'] = 'India'
delhi['pop2018'] = 28_514_000
delhi['density'] = 11_312

print(delhi)
```

```
{'country': 'India', 'pop2018': 28514000, 'density': 11312}
```

Nested data structures

Lists, tuples, and dictionaries can all be nested in a variety of ways, including using dictionaries as items in a list, lists as items in lists, and lists as items in dictionaries. Other types of nested data structures are also possible. Working with these nested structures is straightforward. Whatever value you are working with, no matter its position in the nested data structure, you can use the methods appropriate to that type.

If we have a dictionary that has lists as values, we can subscript the values after accessing them with the appropriate key.

```
japan = {}
japan['cities'] = ['Tokyo', 'Yokohama', 'Osaka', 'Nagoya', 'Sapporo', 'Kobe', 'Kyoto',
    'Fukuoka', 'Kawasaki', 'Saitama']
japan['populations'] = [37, 3.7, 8.81, 9.5, 2.7, 1.5, 1.47, 5.6, 1.5, 1.3]

print(japan)
```

```
{'cities': ['Tokyo', 'Yokohama', 'Osaka', 'Nagoya', 'Sapporo', 'Kobe', 'Kyoto', '
    Fukuoka', 'Kawasaki', 'Saitama'], 'populations': [37, 3.7, 8.81, 9.5, 2.7, 1.5,
    1.47, 5.6, 1.5, 1.3]}
```

```
japan['cities'][4]
```

```
'Sapporo'
```

Lists of dictionaries

We can also store dictionaries as elements in a list. Earlier we created dictionaries `tokyo` and `delhi`. Both contain the same keys: `country` and `population`. Adding them, or any other dictionaries, to a list is straightforward. For example,

```
top_two = [tokyo, delhi]

for city in top_two:
    print(city)
```

```
{'country': 'Japan', 'pop2018': 37468000, 'density': 1178.4}
{'country': 'India', 'pop2018': 28514000, 'density': 11312}
```

While any number of arrangements is possible, things can quickly become very complicated the more deeply data structures are nested. If you find yourself building data structures like this, I suggest that you take a moment to really think about what problem you are trying to solve and assess the approach you are taking. There is almost certainly a way you could approach the problem that is cleaner and simpler, which would reduce the likelihood of making a difficult-to-detect mistake while also making your code more readable.

3.5 Custom Functions

So far we have used a few functions that are built into Python, such as `print()` and `len()`. In these and other cases, built-in functions take an input, perform some operations, and then return an output. For example, if we pass the `len()` function a string, it computes the number of characters in that string and returns an integer:

```
seoul = 'Seoul, South Korea'
len(seoul)
```

```
18
```

We could have computed the length of that string without using `len()`, for example

```
length = 0
for character in seoul:
    length += 1
print(length)
```

```
18
```

Both chunks of code compute the length of the string stored in `seoul`, but using `len()` avoids doing unnecessary work. We use functions to take advantage of abstraction: converting repeated tasks and text into condensed and easily summarized tools. Modern software such as Python is built on decades of abstraction. We don't code in binary because we have abstracted that process, moving into higher-level languages and functions that save us time, space, and brain power. This is what you should aim to do when you write your own functions: identify small tasks or problems that you repeat often, and write a well-named function that deals with them the same way every time, enabling you to combine functions to tackle bigger and more complex problems.

Imagine a set of operations that we need to apply multiple times, each time with a different input. You start by picking one of those inputs and writing the code that produces the end result you want. Where do you go from here? One option, *which I do not recommend*, is to copy and paste that code for each of the inputs. Once your code is copied, you change the names of the inputs and outputs so that you get the desired output for each input.

What happens if you discover a problem in the code, or decide to improve it? You have to change the relevant parts of your code in multiple places, and each time you risk missing something or making a mistake. To make matters worse, the script is *far* longer than it needs to be, and the sequence of operations is much harder to follow and evaluate.

Instead, we could write our own functions that let us strategically reuse chunks of code. If we discover a problem or something we want to change, then we only have to make the change in one place. When we execute our updated function, it will reliably produce the newly desired output. We can store our functions in a separate script and import them elsewhere, which makes those scripts and notebooks more concise and easier to understand. And, if we use good descriptive names for our functions – something we will discuss later – then we can abstract away low-level details to focus on the higher-level details of what we are trying to do. This is always a good idea, but it is especially helpful, if not essential, when working on large projects.

Writing our own functions, then, is a very powerful way of compartmentalizing and organizing our code. It offers us many of the same advantages of using built-in functions or functions from other packages, while also introducing a few additional benefits:

- Reusable – don't do work that has already been done
- Abstraction – abstract away low-level details so that you can focus on higher-level concepts and logic
- Reduce potential error – if you find a mistake you only need to fix it in one place
- Shorter and more readable scripts – much easier to read, understand, and evaluate

Writing custom functions

To define a function in Python, you start with the keyword `def` followed by the name of the function, parentheses containing any arguments the function will take, and then a `:`. All code that is executed when the function is called is contained in an indented block. Below, I define a function called `welcome()`, which accepts a name and prints a greeting:

```python
def welcome(name):
    print(f'Hi, {name}! Good to see you.')

welcome('Miyoko')
```

```
Hi, Miyoko! Good to see you.
```

In this case, the function prints a new string to screen. While this can be useful, most of the time we want to actually do something to the input and then return a different output. If a function does not return an output for whatever reason, it will still return `None`, like the `.sort()` method.

```python
def clean_string(some_string):
    cleaned = some_string.strip().lower()
    return cleaned

cleaned_str = clean_string(' Hi my name is John McLevey. ')
print(cleaned_str)
```

```
hi my name is john mclevey.
```

User-defined functions can be as simple or as complex as we like, although you should strive to design functions that are *as simple as possible*. The first and most important step is to know what problem you are trying to solve. If you understand a problem, you can often break it down into smaller sub-problems, some of which might be repeated many times. Rather than write an enormous block of code that handles everything, you can write several subfunctions that individually handle these smaller problems, letting you better organize your approach.

There is plenty more that could be said about writing your own functions; however, we will set any further discussions aside for now. Throughout the rest of this book, we will see many examples of custom functions, and you will have many opportunities to write and improve your own.

3.6 Reading and Writing Files

When working with data, you will routinely find yourself reading and writing files to disk. We will cover specifics around the very common .csv file format later on and, instead, focus on another common file type in computational social science: a text file containing unstructured text. In this case, we will work with a hypothetical text file that contains 'Hello World!'.

When we work with external files in Python, we need to do three things, regardless of whether we are reading in, or writing to, a file: (1) open the file, (2) perform some sort of operation, and (3) close the file.

There are a number of ways to open a file in Python and read its content in memory, but it is best to use an approach that will automatically close a file and free up our computer's resources when we are finished working with it. We will use with open() as x for this purpose:

```
with open('some_text_file.txt', mode='r', encoding='utf-8') as file:
    text_data = file.read()
    print(len(text_data))
```

12

The open() function requires a file to open, which in this case is some_text_file.txt stored in a directory called data. The with at the very start tells Python to automatically close the file when we are finished with it. Finally, the as file part at the end of the line tells Python to create a file object called file, which we use (like other temporary variable names used in this chapter) when we want to actually do something with the file.

We also passed open() two *optional* arguments, mode and encoding. Technically both of these arguments are optional, but it's generally a good idea to use them. mode='r' tells Python to open the file in read mode, which is the default behaviour of the open() function. There are a number of alternatives, however, including:

- w or write mode, which allows Python to write to a new file. If a file with the given name exists, Python will overwrite it with the new one, otherwise Python will create a new file.
- a or append mode, which allows Python to append new text to the end of a file. If a file with the given name doesn't exist, Python will create a new file.
- rb or binary mode, which is helpful when used for file formats with binary data, such as images and videos.

There are other options and combinations of these options that you can learn about if and when you need to.

We also used the optional encoding argument to tell Python to use the utf-8 encoding. While optional, this is a good habit because default encodings vary across operating systems, and few things are as frustrating and unnecessary as being unable to read a file because of encoding issues.

After we create the file object, we need to actually perform some operation, such as reading the contents of the file. When *reading* data, there are several methods that we can use, the main choices being .read() and .readlines(). We use the .read() method, which returns the contents of the file as a single string. When we print the length of the string using the len() function, Python computes the number of individual characters contained in the string. In this case, it's 0 because the file is empty. Alternatively, we could have used the .readlines() method to read the contents of a file one line at a time and add each string to a list:

```
with open('some_text_file.txt', mode='r', encoding='utf-8') as file:
    list_of_lines = file.readlines()
    print(len(list_of_lines))
```

```
1
```

We will see many examples of using with open() as x throughout this book, but we will also introduce some other useful approaches, such as reading and writing multiple files at once, reading and writing structured datasets using csv and other file formats, and reading and writing data in a common data structure called json. When you understand the basic logic of opening, processing, and closing files in Python, and when you have a handle on some more specialized methods for working with common data structures, you will be capable of working with any type of data you like, from single text files to directories containing millions of image and video files. Python enables you to do it all!

3.7 Pace Yourself

There is, of course, far more to Python than what we have learnt here. But as I have mentioned before, there is no value in being a completionist here – you can't, and shouldn't, try to start by learning *everything* before you get on to the real research work. As we move through the book, we will introduce additional Python knowledge as it is useful in specific research contexts. This is the way I suggest you continue to learn – focus on building a solid general foundation that covers the basics, and then adopt more complex approaches and acquire new tools over time, when you need them or when they are useful.

Further Reading

As with Linux and open source computing more generally, there is no shortage of great free online resources for learning Python. However, if you are looking for more than what is included here and you want something more carefully scaffolded than what you will find online, I recommend Severance's (2016) *Python for Everybody*.

3.8 Conclusion

The key points in this chapter are as follows:

- We learnt the fundamentals such as data types, assignment, using methods and functions, comparison and conditional execution, and error handling.
- We discussed Python's most common built-in data structures – lists, tuples, and dictionaries – and how to perform common operations on them, and on the data they store. In doing so, it also introduced the idea of iteration, and showed how to iterate over the items in a list, tuple, or dictionary using for loops and comprehensions. It also introduced indices and subscripting, and some useful functions such as `zip()` and `enumerate()` that allow us to perform some powerful operations using index positions.
- We developed custom functions.
- We learnt how to work with external files in Python.

Visit the website at https://study.sagepub.com/mclevey for additional resources

4

COLLECTING DATA FROM APPLICATION PROGRAMMING INTERFACES

4.1 Learning Objectives

By the end of this chapter, you should be able to do the following:

- Develop a mental model of what application programming interfaces (APIs) are, how they work, and how they can be used for data collection
- Apply your general mental model to understand specific APIs in order to collect the data you want
- Put your knowledge of Python programming to work by developing scripts to query specific APIs and programmatically collect and store data according to best practices
- Work effectively with the *Guardian* REST (representational state transfer) API

4.2 Learning Materials

You can find the online learning materials for this chapter in `doing_computational_social_science/Chapter_04`. `cd` into the directory and launch your Jupyter server.

4.3 Introduction

It's time to use your new Python programming skills to start collecting data from the web! In this chapter, you will learn how to collect data programmatically using web-based application programming interfaces (APIs). You will learn what APIs are, how they work, and how to write code to collect the data you want from specific APIs. In this chapter, we will walk through using APIs to collect data from news stories.

APIs provide a number of benefits when it comes to collecting data from the web. With rare exceptions, rules about what data we can collect and how we can collect it using APIs are explicitly stated, which removes some of the legal uncertainties that can complicate other data collection methods. Widely used APIs are generally well-documented and maintained, and the data returned is usually well-structured and easy to work with.

It's not *all* good, though. There are two main downsides to working with APIs. First, there may be restrictions on what data is provided, and if there are, those restrictions are often grounded in business interests rather than technical requirements and limitations. That said, the data that API providers *choose to include* is almost always complete because it is often generated programmatically as a by-product of their platform, and applications depend on it. Second, APIs change, sometimes unexpectedly (see Freelon, 2018; Hogan, 2018; Jünger, 2021).

In this chapter, the primary learning objective is to understand how web-based APIs work *in general* and to develop a simple mental model to better understand *specific* APIs in order to get the data we need. To that end, we will begin with a conceptual overview of what APIs are and how they work, which will include a pretty high-level discussion of how the internet works. Then, we will deepen our understanding of core API concepts and put that general knowledge to use by collecting data from an API for the *Guardian*.

4.4 What Is an API?

It's usually very easy to find instructions for pulling data from an API. The major barrier is having the knowledge foundation to understand these instructions and their technical terminology. In the first part of the chapter, our goal is to develop a general mental model of APIs and their component parts, which we can use to better understand and work with any specific API.

We start with the notion of an interface – the I in API. You already have a mental model of what an 'interface' is thanks to the many user interfaces you interact with on an everyday basis (e.g. light switches, dials on a laundry machine, or the 'buttons' you 'press' when browsing the web or using an app on your phone). In the context of computers, user interfaces allow a human to interact with a computer to complete specific tasks, such as saving a file or changing the volume on your speakers, without needing to understand *how* that task is actually accomplished.

Well-designed user interfaces make it easier for us to get a computer to do what we want by bundling up many low-level processes into simple intuitive actions. As a result, we tend not to notice or think too much about them when they are well-designed and work as we expect. When you are editing a photo, for example, you might adjust the highlights by moving a slider to the left or right. This feels natural. Users understand the relationship between what they do and what happens on the screen. However, few users actually understand everything that the computer is doing to make those edits and render them on the screen. They don't need to! Similarly, you can respond to a message from your partner or a friend without understanding the networking and security protocols that are involved in that exchange of messages.

Like user interfaces, APIs make difficult things easier by abstracting away a lot of low-level processes. Recalling our discussion of custom functions from the previous chapter, APIs have done much of the hard work of creating custom functions and bundled them up to be especially easy to understand and use.

You may have already realized this, but the functions you use when writing Python code are themselves APIs! One of the reasons why programming languages like Python can be designed around the principle of maximizing human readability is because over time common low-level tasks have been abstracted away into more intuitive high-level functions. Do you know what is actually happening, at the level of 1s and 0s, when you execute a print statement? Probably not; it's APIs all the way down. All you really need to know is how to use the print() function without throwing an error.

RESTful APIs

When it comes to programmatic data collection, we are almost always interested in web-based APIs, and more specifically REST (representational state transfer) APIs. To better understand how REST APIs work, we once again need to build up a bit of general foundational knowledge, this time about how the internet works, and how REST APIs sit on top of this general architecture.

Put simply, the internet is a network of networks that enables many billions of devices to 'talk' to one another using established protocols (i.e. rules and standards). The internet can grow and evolve as long as new devices that connect to it use those established protocols.

Any device that connects to the internet does so using an internet protocol (IP) address that enables it to communicate with other connected devices. When you browse the internet, you type a domain name (or URL [uniform resource locator]) like nytimes.com or theguardian.com into your browser, not the IP address of the server from which you are requesting data. Your computer first contacts a domain name system (DNS) server and asks for the IP address associated with the domain name you typed. The DNS server returns the IP address to your computer, which can then contact the web server with a GET request using the hypertext transfer protocol (which you likely know as HTTP).

When the web server receives a GET request from your computer, it sends the requested content to your computer's IP address (which was shared by your computer when it made the request). It does this by breaking the requested information down into separate packets, each of which includes information about its origin (the server) and destination (your computer). These packets then travel through the network guided by routers, which are like traffic controllers, ensuring that packets travel the network in a relatively efficient fashion. Individual packets generally take different paths along the network before they arrive, out of order, at your computer.

When your computer receives packets from a server, it checks whether it received everything the web server said it would send. This process is managed by the transmission control protocol, which ensures all the necessary packets have arrived. If a packet is missing, your computer tells the web server to send it again. When your computer has all the necessary packets, it assembles them in the correct order and renders the content you requested. This general process applies regardless of whether you are browsing the web, sending an email using a mail application, using an app on your phone, or dimming your bedroom lights using an app on your phone.

REST APIs sit on top of this general architecture to abstract away many of the complexities of *programmatically* transferring data between a client and a server. So far, we have described what happens when your browser makes requests to a server. With REST APIs, a program includes the GET requests in code, and they are sent when your program is executed, rather than executed at the click of a button in your browser or in an app.

Making requests with Python

We have just learnt, at a relatively high level, what happens when your computer (the 'client') makes a request for a web page (the 'resource') from a server. In a similar fashion, you can write programs that make GET requests for resources from a server. These resources can be just about anything, but as researchers, we usually want to retrieve some sort of data or metadata from a web server. To do so, we send our requests to a specific 'endpoint'.

An endpoint is a location on the internet where you send a request for a specific resource. Recall that 'resource' is an abstract term for just about anything that we want to retrieve from a web server. If you are working with a Twitter API, for example, you will see that there are endpoints for requesting data about tweets and an endpoint for requesting data about users. If you are working with the API for the *Guardian* or another news organization, you will see that there is an endpoint for 'content', among other things. To access the resources we want, we have to send our request to the correct endpoint. In nearly all cases, this will be in the form of a URL.

The URLs that we use to send requests to endpoints typically include several important pieces of information that enable us to specify what we want the API to return. For example, the URL may include information about our query, as well as some optional parameters and filters. Usually, this information is combined into a single URL.

If web servers receive too many requests at once – whether intentionally, in the form of a coordinated attack, or unintentionally, in the form of a poorly written or inconsiderate script – they can be overwhelmed. To prevent this from happening, most APIs use rate limiting to restrict the number of requests that a user can make within specific time frames. As of June 2020, the *Guardian* content endpoint limits users to making 12 requests per second and a maximum of 5000 calls per day. Other APIs will have their own restrictions, which you can learn about in the API terms of service. Most of the time, APIs enforce rate limits by detecting overuse and then disconnecting or throttling users, while others use an honour system but heavily penalize users who are found to be violating those limits, such as blacklisting the user.

API keys or tokens

To make requests to an API, you will usually need an API key, or API Token. You can think of these as a username and password that identify you to the API. Unlike usernames and passwords, you don't set them yourself. Instead, the API provides them to you when you sign up for its service and agree to its terms of service. We will see several examples of obtaining and working with different API tokens in the examples that follow.

It is *crucial* that you do not share your API tokens. Do *not* write them directly into your scripts or inadvertently commit them to a public repository (e.g. on GitLab or GitHub). Doing so is comparable to sharing usernames and passwords you use for any other web service and any misuse will be tied to you as the user. If someone obtained your API keys for the *Guardian*, they could access the service as if they were you, and you will suffer the consequences. If you believe your access token has been compromised for some reason, find an appropriate point of contact and inform them. They have an interest in ensuring that *no one* is using compromised tokens. Later in the chapter, we will learn how to use your keys while maintaining a high level of security.

Responses

When we make a GET request to an API, we get a response in return. These responses have numerical codes, such as the familiar 404 (Page Not Found) error you get when you follow a dead link. There are many possible response codes, most of which you don't see when you're just browsing the web. For example, if your request was successful, you will get a 200 (OK) response code. On the other hand, if there was some sort of problem with your request, you will likely get a response code such as 401 (unauthorized), 403 (forbidden), 500 (internal server error), or 503 (the server is unavailable). When you are developing scripts to programmatically collect data from APIs, it is always a good idea to check the status of any given request. Because there are many possible responses for errors, it is better to check for success (i.e. 200) than failure.

Technically, web-based APIs can return anything, but by far the most common way of providing data is json, which stands for JavaScript Object Notation. json is a nested data structure that looks a lot like a Python dictionary in that the data is stored using key–value pairs inside curly brackets. For this reason, working with json is relatively painless in Python. If you import the standard library json, you can easily read and write json files, and when loaded in memory, you can use dictionary methods to work with that data. Additionally, it is possible to use the Pandas package (discussed in later chapters) to read json directly into a dataframe using the .read_json() method. We will see many examples of working with json throughout the rest of this chapter.

4.5 Getting Practical: Working With Apis

Now that we have a conceptual understanding of what APIs are and how they work in general, we can get a bit more practical. In the rest of this chapter, we make these abstract concepts more concrete by comparing several practical examples of collecting data programmatically via web-based APIs. Remember, these examples are not intended to be comprehensive recipes for working with specific APIs. Instead, the idea is that you will deepen your *general* understanding of APIs by comparing multiple examples. When doing your own research, you will likely want to use some feature of an API that I haven't covered, but you will have the foundational knowledge and understanding required to understand the documentation and solve the problem yourself.

The *Guardian*

Many major newspapers provide access to non-trivial amounts of data on their published articles via APIs, and the *Guardian* is no exception. As of January 2021, it offers five endpoints:

1   The content endpoint provides the text and metadata for published articles. It is possible to query and filter the results. This endpoint is likely the most useful for researchers.
2   The tags endpoint provides API tags for greater than 50,000 results, which can be used in other API queries.
3   The sections endpoint provides information on groupings of published articles into sections.
4   The editions endpoint provides content for each of the regional main pages: US, UK, Australia, and International.
5   The single items endpoint returns data for specific items, including content, tags, and sections.

Often, the easiest way to work with an API is to use a 'client'. Python clients for the *Guardian* API or other APIs are no different from any other Python package: they provide functions that abstract away some of the complexities of authenticating with, making requests to, and processing results from the API. You may want to use clients from time to time, such as when working with large and relatively complex APIs. Here, however, we will work directly with the *Guardian* API using a package called requests. This affords a bit more flexibility and freedom in how we interface with the API and will help make some of the previously introduced concepts more concrete.

Accessing the *Guardian* API

As with most other APIs, you need to register for an API key to access the *Guardian* API. This key enables them to monitor your access to their data and ensure you are following their terms of service. Once you have your API key, you can make 12 calls per second and up to 5000 calls per day. You can access the article text (but not images, audio, or video) for millions of articles for free. As with many other APIs, it's possible to unlock more content by paying for a commercial licence.

You can obtain your API keys by registering on the *Guardian*'s website. The process is outlined on its developer page. We won't review all the steps here, as they can easily change and result in confusion. However, the process is straightforward and well-explained.

In this case, your API key will be a single alphanumeric string. To store and use this key securely, open a new text file with the following one liner:

```
GUARDIAN_KEY = 'paste_your_key_here'
```

Save this file with the name `cred.py` and store it in the same directory as whatever notebook or script will contain the code you write to query the API. If you are using `git` for version control, you can add `cred.py` to a `.gitignore` file to ensure that `git` ignores the file. Alternatively, you can store your `cred.py` file outside of the `git` repository. If you do this, I would recommend saving the file somewhere where you can easily access it. You can add API keys for other APIs in this file, which simplifies the process of authenticating with the many APIs you might use frequently.

Once you have saved `cred.py`, you can load your keys into your script and authenticate with the API. To do so, import your `cred` file into a new script or notebook and assign the key to a variable by accessing the attribute with dot notation:

```
import cred
GUARDIAN_KEY = cred.GUARDIAN_KEY
```

We are now ready to make requests to the API.

Making requests

We'll use a package called `requests` to make our API requests. Once the package has been imported, we can do this by providing the `.get()` method with the base API URL for the content endpoint. We will also create a dictionary called PARAMS, which will contain a key–value pair for our API key. Later, we will add more key–value pairs to this dictionary to change what the API returns.

The actual call to the API is made in the seventh line of the code block below, where `requests` authenticates us with the *Guardian*'s servers by sending a GET request to the API with our API key. The API returns a response, including some `json` data that we store in the variable `response_dict`:

```
import requests
import pprint as pp # pretty print!

API_ENDPOINT = 'http://content.guardianapis.com/search'
PARAMS = {'api-key': GUARDIAN_KEY}
```

```
response = requests.get(API_ENDPOINT, params=PARAMS)
response_dict = response.json()['response']
print(len(response_dict))
```

```
9
```

If you print the `response_dict` – `pp.print(response_dict)`, you will see there is quite a lot of information included here, and we haven't even provided any specific search criteria! Why is that?

By default, the *Guardian* is returning a sample of current news stories. Let's start by digging into the fields contained in this response. Remember, since `json` is essentially identical to a Python dictionary, it's natural to store it as a dictionary. We can get a list of the available fields by using the `.keys()` method:

```
print(response_dict.keys())
```

```
dict_keys(['status', 'userTier', 'total', 'startIndex', 'pageSize', 'currentPage', '
    pages', 'orderBy', 'results'])
```

The most useful data is contained in the `results` field, which you can access with `response_dict['results']`. This is where the actual article context is stored.

If you look at the contents of `response_dict['results']`, you will find a list of 10 dictionaries, each corresponding to one of the 10 retrieved stories, which is the default number of stories returned. Each story has several key–value pairs containing useful article metadata such as an ID, a type, section IDs, publication date, the title, the URL for the story and for further API access, and so on. The actual content of the publications is not included, though; we will learn how to retrieve it shortly.

Filtering results

Earlier, I mentioned that we can use queries and filters to retrieve specific types of content from an API. You can use queries to find content just as you would if you were using a search engine, and you can use filters to narrow the returned content on the basis of specific metadata. The API documentation provides information on what kinds of filters are available. For example, in the code block below, we can use filters to specify

- a specific date or range of dates when the articles were last published,
- the language,
- the production office, and
- a term to search for.

```
PARAMS = {
    'api-key': GUARDIAN_KEY,
    'from-date': '2020-04-10',
    'to-date': '2020-04-10',
    'lang': 'en',
    'production-office': 'uk',
    'q': 'coronavirus'
}
```

```
response = requests.get(API_ENDPOINT, params=PARAMS)
response_dict = response.json()['response']
```

Notice that the resulting `response_dict` – which you can print to screen with `pp.pprint(response_dict)` – contains more information than our last set of results:

```
print(response_dict.keys())
```

```
dict_keys(['status', 'userTier', 'total', 'startIndex', 'pageSize', 'currentPage', '
    pages', 'orderBy', 'results'])
```

There are several new fields here, but still no article content or bylines. To retrieve this and other data, we can specify it using the `show-fields` parameter. Let's add it to our search.

```
PARAMS = {
    'api-key': GUARDIAN_KEY,
    'from-date': '2020-04-10',
    'to-date': '2020-04-10',
    'lang': 'en',
    'production-office': 'uk',
    'q': 'coronavirus',
    'show-fields': 'wordcount,body,byline'
}

response = requests.get(API_ENDPOINT, params=PARAMS)
response_dict = response.json()['response']
```

Now, when you print the content of `response_dict`, you will see we have the additional data we were looking for. I won't print all of that here, but you can by executing the following code:

```
for response in response_dict['results']:
    print(response['fields']['body'])
```

Note that the text itself contains HTML (HyperText Markup Language) tags – we will discuss these in the next chapter.

Asking for more data

We've now seen how to get useful data from article publications that meet our search criteria, but we still only have that data for 10 stories. To get more, we need to dig into some additional API concepts. Three of the keys of our `response_dict` describe the volume of data we receive: `total`, `pages`, and `pageSize`. They all work together, in a fashion similar to the results that would be returned by a search engine. `Total` is a count of the total number of stories available. These results can be broken up into multiple `pages`, again, like results returned from a search engine. The number of stories included in any given page is determined by the `pageSize`. If we want the API to return all available stories, we need to change these parameters when we make our request. We can do this by specifying how many stories should be returned in a single page, and then request stories from multiple pages, much as we might click to navigate to the second, third, *n*th page of results in a search.

Below, we update our search parameters with a new parameter specifying `pageSize`. We will increase it from 10 to 50.

```
PARAMS = {
    'api-key': GUARDIAN_KEY,
    'from-date': '2020-04-10',
    'to-date': '2020-04-10',
    'lang': 'en',
    'production-office': 'uk',
    'q': 'coronavirus',
    'show-fields': 'wordcount,body,byline',
    'page-size': 50,
}


response = requests.get(API_ENDPOINT, params=PARAMS)
response_dict = response.json()['response']
```

Increasing the number of stories on any given page is not actually necessary to obtain all of the data we want, since we can simply request more pages. However, we have to make a new API request for each page, which increases the load on the *Guardian* servers. Instead, we reduce the number of calls we need to make by increasing the amount of data returned in each individual call. You could probably get away with increasing this number, but there are a couple of good reasons why you might want to keep it at a modest setting. First, many APIs have rate limits or maximum thresholds above which they'll refuse to return any data; haphazardly increasing the amount of data you ask for in a single request might run you foul of these limits. Second, it's simply more considerate! Other people and organizations are likely trying to use the same API, and the API itself only has so much bandwidth (both literally and figuratively); just because you can push the limits doesn't mean you should.

To iterate through each page of results, we will use yet another parameter: `page`. However, unlike before, we will update this parameter dynamically, enabling us to make new requests for each page of available data until we have collected all results.

The dictionary `PARAMS` has been written and rewritten several times now, but the most recent version contains our fully developed search, including the increased number of stories on each page. We will execute this search multiple times, each time retrieving data for a new page. Because we want to use the `page` parameter and to update it dynamically, we will use a while loop:

```
all_results = []
cur_page = 1
total_pages = 1


while (cur_page <= total_pages) and (cur_page < 10): # with a fail safe
    # Make a API request
    PARAMS['page'] = cur_page
    response = requests.get(API_ENDPOINT, params=PARAMS)
    response_dict = response.json()['response']
```

```
        # Update our master results list
        all_results += (response_dict['results'])

        # Update our loop variables
        total_pages = response_dict['pages']
        cur_page += 1

len(all_results)
```

82

Don't forget, we need to be very careful about rate limiting when we automate our API requests like this, to be mindful of the *Guardian* servers, and to prevent losing access. To ensure that you're not overtaxing the API, consider adding in `time.sleep()` calls, which will have the effect of spacing out your requests. During testing, it's also a good idea to keep your requests to an absolute minimum.

Storing your data

At this point, we have learnt how to use the `requests` package and our API key to make GET requests to the *Guardian*'s API, and how to use parameters to query and filter results returned from the content endpoint. We also learnt that the data we want is split up into multiple 'pages' of results, and to retrieve everything, we have to make individual requests for each page. In doing so, we need to adopt an approach to automating API requests that ensures we stay within the rate limits and don't violate any other terms of service.

Now that we have our data, we need to write it to disk so that it is easily accessed, now or later, without making redundant calls to the API. This will also enable us to decouple the code used to collect this data from any code we develop to clean and analyse it. Remember, that kind of code separation is considered best practice *in general* and is a key component of specific computational research workflows, such as the principled data processing framework.

We can use the `json` module to write this data to disk using the `with open(x) as` approach:

```
import json
FILE_PATH = 'guardian_api_results.json'
with open(FILE_PATH, 'w') as outfile:
    json.dump(all_results, outfile)
```

Now that we have a firm grasp on how to query data from the *Guardian*'s relatively simple REST API, you're ready to move on to a more powerful and complex API. Unfortunately, we don't have the room to cover additional APIs here, but the supplemental learning materials will help you get started with Twitter and other social media APIs.

Further Reading

Russell and Klassen (2019) provide a good introduction to working with social media APIs with Python, including Twitter, Facebook, Instagram, GitHub, and LinkedIn. Sloan and Quan-Haase (2017b) provide a very broad range of chapters related to social science research with social media data.

4.6 Conclusion

The key points in this chapter are as follows:

- This chapter provided an overview of APIs, which offer researchers the ability to programmatically collect data from the web.
- REST APIs are the most common type of APIs; APIs that stream data in real time are also useful to understand.
- We worked through extensive practical examples of how to work with, and store data from, an API using the example of the *Guardian*.

Visit the website at https://study.sagepub.com/mclevey for additional resources

5

COLLECTING DATA FROM THE WEB: SCRAPING

5.1 Learning Objectives

By the end of this chapter, you should be able to do the following:

- Learn how to study the source code for a website to make a plan for collecting the data you need
- Use the Requests package to programmatically make GET requests to web servers
- Use the BeautifulSoup package to parse HTML and CSS (Cascading Style Sheets) code to extract and clean data from web page source code
- Change URLs programmatically to scrape multiple pages of a website
- Explain the ethical and legal issues involved in web scraping projects

5.2 Learning Materials

You can find the online learning materials for this chapter in `doing_computational_social_science/Chapter_05`. cd into the directory and launch your Jupyter server.

5.3 Introduction

This chapter introduces web scraping as a method of programmatically collecting data from the web. While application programming interfaces (APIs) provide direct access to the data behind a website using documented protocols, web scraping requires studying the source code of a website as displayed in a browser, and then writing scripts that take advantage of HyperText Markup Language (HTML) and Cascading Style Sheets (CSS) to extract specific pieces of data.

We will begin by introducing the basics of HTML and CSS, which are essential to understand when developing a web scraper, followed by an explanation of how to use browser-based developer tools to study the source code of a website and isolate the data you want to extract. We will then work through several examples of scraping text data from websites using the packages Requests and BeautifulSoup. These examples cover many common web scraping needs and can easily be extended to cover more.

It is possible to collect virtually any data from the web by writing web scrapers, but that doesn't mean you should. As with APIs, you always need to ensure that you are collecting data in a way that meets high ethical standards, and that you are respecting a website's terms of service. We'll discuss ethics, including for digital data collection, in detail in Chapter 18.

5.4 An HTML and CSS Primer for Web Scrapers

This chapter builds on the previous chapter's foundations; I will begin by describing how the content on web pages is structured using HTML and CSS, and then explain how to write web scrapers that take advantage of these types of markup to programmatically extract data from web pages. As you learn this material, keep in mind that *it takes far less knowledge to scrape a website than it does to develop it in the first place.* A little knowledge goes a long way.

As someone who frequently reads and writes 'documents' (news stories, blog posts, journal articles, Tweets, etc.), you are already familiar with the basics of structuring and organizing documents using headings, subheadings, and so on. This chapter, for example, has all those features and more. As humans, we parse these organizational features of documents *visually*.

If you create a document using a WYSIWYG ('what you see is what you get') word processor like Open Office, Microsoft Word, Apple Pages, or Google Docs, you apply different styles to parts of the text to indicate whether something is a title, a heading, a paragraph, a list, and so on. HTML documents also have these organizational features but use special 'markup' to describe structural features of the document (HTML) as well as how things should appear (CSS).

HTML consists of 'elements' (e.g. paragraphs) with opening and closing tags. You can think of these tags as containers. The tags tell your browser about the text that sits between the opening and closing tags (or 'inside the container'). Here's an example:

```html
<html>
    <head>
        <title>This is a minimal example</title>
    </head>
    <body>
        <h1>This is a first-level heading</h1>
        <p>A paragraph with some <emph>italicized</emph> text.</p>
        <img src="image.pdf" alt="This is an image">
        <p>A paragraph with some <strong>bold</strong> text.</p>
        <h2>This is a second-level heading</h2>
        <ul>
            <li>first list item</li>
            <li>second list item</li>
        </ul>
    </body>
</html>
```

In our example above, the paragraph element opens a paragraph with <p> and closes it with </p>. The actual text – what you see in your browser – lives between those tags. We can see examples of them on the seventh and ninth lines in the HTML code above.

The outermost element in any HTML document is the html element. Your browser knows that anything between <html> and </html> tags should be processed as HTML markup. Most of the time, the next element in an HTML page will be a head element. The text inside the <head> and </head> tags will not actually be rendered by your browser. Instead, it contains metadata about the page itself. This is where the page title is contained, which is displayed on the tab in your browser.

Inside the HTML tags, you'll also find a body element. Anything inside the <body> and </body> tags will be displayed in the main browser window (e.g. the text of a news story). Inside the body tags, you will typically find elements for headings (e.g. <h1> and </h1>, <h2> and </h2>, etc.), paragraphs (<p> and </p>), bold text (<strong> and </strong>), italicized text (<em> and </em>), as well as ordered and unordered lists, tables, images, links, and so on.

Sometimes elements include 'attributes', which provide more information about the content of the text. For example, a paragraph element may specify that the text contained within its tags is American English. This information is contained inside the opening bracket: <p lang="en-us">American English sentence here...</p>. As you will soon learn, attributes can be *extremely* useful when scraping the web.

Before moving on, it's important to understand one final type of HTML element you'll frequently encounter when developing web scrapers: the division tag div. This is simply a generic container that splits a website into smaller sections. Web developers often use it to apply a particular style (e.g. switch to a monospaced font to display code) to some chunk of text in the HTML document, using CSS. Splitting web pages into these smaller pieces using div tags makes websites easier for developers to maintain and modify. They also make it easier for us web scrapers to drill down and grab the information we need. You'll see this in action in the examples to follow.

When scraping the web, you will also encounter CSS, which I previously mentioned is used to *style* websites. To properly understand how CSS works, remember that the vast majority of modern websites are designed to separate content (e.g. actual words that mean things to humans) from *structure* and *style*. HTML markup tells your browser what some piece of text is (e.g. a heading, a list item, a row in a table, a paragraph) and CSS tells your browser what it should look like when rendered in your browser (e.g. what font to use for subheadings, how big to make the text, what colour to make the text, and so on). If there is no CSS, then your browser will use an extremely minimal default style to render the text in your browser. In most cases, developing a good web scraper will require a deeper understanding of HTML than CSS, so we will set aside discussion of CSS for now, but will return later when knowledge of CSS can help us develop a better scraper.

A full inventory of HTML and CSS elements is, of course, beyond the scope of this book. The good news is that you don't need exhaustive knowledge of either to write a good web scraper. You need to have a basic understanding of the key concepts, and you need to know what the most common tags mean, but *more than anything else*, you need to be willing to spend time investigating the source code for websites you want to scrape, attempt to solve problems creatively, and work interactively.

Further Reading

With this foundational knowledge, you'll be able fill gaps in your knowledge of HTML and CSS with web searches as you develop scrapers to collect data for a research project. Still, I recommend setting aside a bit of time to browse some basic tutorials. Better yet, spend some time browsing Jon Duckett's (2011) beautiful resource book *HTML & CSS: Design and Build Websites*, which is an excellent resource for learning the basics.

5.5 Developing Your First Web Scraper

Now that you have a baseline understanding of how your computer retrieves and renders websites, and the role that HTML and CSS play in that process, we can demystify web scraping even further. First, we know that the information we want to retrieve from a website will be sent to our computer from a remote web server following a GET request. Web pages are provided as source code, which is parsed and rendered by our web browser of choice.

Before jumping into coding a scraper, you need to familiarize yourself with the sources you plan to gather data from – this is good advice to apply to any data you plan to use for research purposes. The best way to study the source code of a website is to use the developer tools built into browsers such as Firefox, Chrome, or Brave. Here, and throughout the rest of this book, I will use Firefox, but the developer tools we use here are available in the other browsers as well. We'll start by learning how to study the source code of a web page we want to scrape, and then move into writing the actual code for the scraper.

Studying website source code with developer tools

First, navigate to a website in Firefox. I've selected a story from the front page of the *Guardian* on 2 August 2019, 'Charming But Dishonest and Duplicitous: Europe's Verdict on Boris Johnson'. The specific story you select doesn't really matter, however. If you are writing and executing code along with me as you read this book, and for some reason this story is no longer available, you could select another story from the *Guardian* instead and follow along just fine.

Once the story is loaded in Firefox, you can right click anywhere on the page and select 'Inspect Element' to open a pane of developer tools. (You can also open this pane by selecting 'Toggle Tools' from the 'Web Developer' section of the 'Tools' menu in the toolbar.) We can use these tools to study our target web page interactively, viewing the rendered content and the raw source code of the web page simultaneously.

One especially useful strategy is to highlight some information of interest on the web page and then right click and select 'Inspect Source' (or 'View Selection Source' or 'Inspect Element' or similar). This will jump to that specific highlighted information in the HTML code, making it much easier to quickly find what tags the information you need is stored in. From here, we can strategize how best to retrieve the data we want.

Figure 5.1 is a screenshot of the developer tools pane open in a Firefox tab for the story about Boris Johnson. Since it's a bit difficult to fully read on the printed page, I recommend consulting the high-resolution screenshot available in the online materials. The text 'As the Brexit deadline looms, Europe remains wary of the poker player behind the clown mask' is highlighted and revealed in the inspector tool at the bottom of the page. We can see in the developer tools that the text we've highlighted is enclosed in simple paragraph tags (`<p>As the Brexit deadline looms, Europe remains wary of the poker player behind the clown mask</p>`). That's precisely the kind of information we can exploit when developing a web scraper. Let's see how exactly it's done.

As we develop our web scraper, we progressively narrow down to the information we need, clean it by stripping out unwanted information (e.g. white spaces, new line characters), and then write it to some sort of dataset for later use. Next, we'll cover the steps one might take to develop a functional scraper from the ground up.

One very useful way to extract the data we want is to make use of CSS selectors. Many of the HTML elements on a website have `class` attributes, which allow web developers and designers to style specific chunks of content using styles defined in CSS. In addition to

Figure 5.1 A screenshot of the Firefox developer tools pane open for the story 'Charming But Dishonest: Europe's Verdict on Boris Johnson', published in the *Guardian* on 2 August 2019. A high-resolution colour image is available in the online supplementary learning materials

class attributes, we may encounter an id attribute for some elements. Unlike the class attributes, the id in an element is unique. It refers to that element, and that element only. If you're looking for a way to grab multiple elements that are some subset of all the elements of that type, then you want to use class attributes. But if you want a single element, and that element has an id, then use the id!

One final thing that's very helpful to know here is that almost all web pages use a Document Object Model (DOM) to organize the elements they display. The DOM is a hierarchical structure resembling a tree, the trunk of which is the web page itself. In this model, all the elements can be thought of as branches of the trunk, or branches of those branches, and so on. Many sources use language borrowed from family trees to describe elements' relationships to one another, as most elements in the page will have other elements nested within them. These nested elements are 'children' of the larger 'parent' element they are nested within. If we follow through with the metaphor, the nested elements can be thought of as each other's 'siblings'.

This family tree structure of the DOM is useful to understand, especially in cases when you need to grab data from an element that doesn't have an id and also doesn't have a unique class attribute, such as what you often find for the headlines of news stories. In such cases, we can exploit the nested, hierarchical structure of the DOM to find the information we want: all we need to do is locate the element's parent, at which point we can get information about all of its children and extract the data we need.

If you find that the website design is consistent across the pages you want to scrape, you could determine whether the element you want is always *nested* at the same level. If it is, you could provide a full path to the data you want to scrape, even when given the vaguest of elements. This might mean that you want to always grab the text located at `<body><div><div><article><div><h1>`. If you need to access the second of two `<div>` elements that are at the same depth (and, thus, a sibling of the first), it can be referred to in the same way you would access an element in a Python list, by `<div[1]>`.

Coding a web scraper for a single page

In order to get our scraper operational, we'll need a way to actually get data from the web pages into Python. Normally, the process of requesting and rendering a page is handled by our browser, but as you learnt in the previous chapter this isn't the only way to request HTML documents from a web server. We can also connect to a web server from a Python script using a package such as Requests and load the HTML provided by the web server into our computer's memory. Once we have this HTML in memory (rather than rendered in a browser), we can move onto the next step, which is to start parsing the HTML and extracting the information we want.

When we load an HTML document in Python, we're looking at the raw markup, not the rendered version we see when we load that file in a browser. If we're lucky, the information we want will be consistently stored in elements that are easy to isolate and don't contain a lot of irrelevant information. In order to get that information, we need to parse the HTML file, which can be done using a Python package called BeautifulSoup. Note that BeautifulSoup's naming conventions are a little confusing. The package is called BeautifulSoup, but you have to install it using `beautifulsoup4` and import it into Python using `bs4`. Clear as mud. Let's make all of this a little less abstract by working through a specific example.

To get started, let's grab the title and body text of the article on Boris Johnson mentioned previously. We will (1) request the HTML document from the *Guardian's* web server using the Requests package, (2) feed that HTML data into BeautifulSoup to construct a soup object that we can parse, and then (3) extract the article title and text, and store them in a couple of lists.

In the code block below, we import the three packages we will use, get the HTML, construct the soup object using an `lxml` parser, and then – *just because we can* – print the raw HTML DOM to our screen (though not to this page!):

```
import requests
from bs4 import BeautifulSoup
import pandas as pd

url = 'https://www.theguardian.com/politics/2019/aug/02/europes-view-on-boris-johnson'

r = requests.get(url)
soup = BeautifulSoup(r.content, 'lxml')
```

To save space, I will not actually reproduce the DOM here, but you can do so by running

```
print(soup.prettify())
```

Now we need to get the title. I know from inspecting the source that the article title is stored inside a `<title>` element. I use the `findAll` method from BeautifulSoup to retrieve that part of the text, which BeautifulSoup returns in the form of a list with one item. To get the string,

I simply select the first item in the list using its index (`[0]`) and add `.text` to strip away the markup. Finally, although it is not strictly *necessary* at this point, I strip out any invisible new line characters by ending the line with `.replace('\\n', '')`:

```
article_title = soup.findAll('title')[0].text.replace('\n', '')
print(article_title)
```

```
Charming but dishonest and duplicitous: Europe's verdict on Boris Johnson | Boris
    Johnson | The Guardian
```

Getting the body text is even easier, as all body text is contained inside <p> elements. We can construct a list of paragraphs with the `findAll` method:

```
paragraphs = soup.findAll('p')
```

The ninth paragraph in the list is

```
paragraphs[8].text
```

```
'Another lifelong anglophile, André Gattolin, the vice-president of the French
    senate's European affairs committee, said the new prime minister had carefully
    cultivated a "caricatural image - the hair, the gags, the flags, the zip-wire, the
    provocations".'
```

Sometimes it's useful to combine all the text from an article into one long string (as we will discuss in the chapters on text analysis). We can do this by joining the items in the list, separated by white space:

```
all_text = " ".join(para.text for para in paragraphs)
```

And with that, we have written our first scraper! It was a relatively simple one, in that our goal was simply to pull out a title and body text for an article in a newspaper. We could have collected a bit of other data if we wanted, such as the author of the page and the date it was published. However, one nice thing about our rather minimal scraper is that we can use it to grab text from other stories posted by the *Guardian* as well. In other words, simple web scrapers can be used in a broader variety of contexts, because they are not overly tailored to the content of any one specific page. The main takeaway here is that you should keep your web scrapers *as simple and portable as possible*. Avoid adding complexity unless it's necessary to retrieve the data you need.

Let's wrap these steps up in a simple function, grab some text from a few more news stories, and then construct a Pandas dataframe with article titles in one column and article text in another. We will provide a much deeper explanation of the Pandas package and dataframes in the next chapter.

```
def scrape_guardian_stories(url):
    soup = BeautifulSoup(requests.get(url).content, 'lxml')
    article_title = soup.find('title').text.replace('\n', '')
```

```
paras = " ".join(para.text.replace('\n', '') for para in soup.findAll('p'))
    return [article_title, paras]
```

The function we just defined follows the same process we just used to scrape the text of the first story on Boris Johnson, but this time wraps the code up in a single function that returns a list containing two items: the title of a story and the main body text. To produce the `dataframe`, we will provide a list of URLs and apply our function to each individual story. This will return a `list` of `lists` as a result, which we can then convert into a `dataframe`.

In the code block below, I read in a text file called `guardian_story_links.txt`. This file contains four URLs, each saved on its own line. When I read those lines in, each URL becomes an element in a list. I can then use list comprehension to iterate over the URLs and scrape their content.

```
with open('../data/scraping/guardian_story_links.txt') as f:
    stories = [line.rstrip() for line in f]

scraped = [scrape_guardian_stories(s) for s in stories]
df_scraped = pd.DataFrame(scraped, columns=['Title', 'Article Text'])
print(df_scraped.info())
```

```
<class 'pandas.core.frame.DataFrame'>
RangeIndex: 5 entries, 0 to 4
Data columns (total 2 columns):
 #   Column        Non-Null Count  Dtype
---  ------        --------------  -----
 0   Title         5 non-null      object
 1   Article Text  5 non-null      object
dtypes: object(2)
memory usage: 208.0+ bytes
None
```

We'll use a `dataframe` to summarize the result; `dataframes` are a form of structured data that we will be using frequently throughout the book; in the next chapter, we'll go over them in detail. In this `dataframe`, the titles appear in one column and the article text in another.

Obviously, a simple script like this would not be especially helpful to us if we were only analysing the text of three or four articles. But social scientists are almost *never* concerned with the content of just a few articles. With very little code, we can collect a lot of text very efficiently and store it in a dataset that we can analyse using a variety of methods, from traditional content analysis to the types of computational text analysis introduced later in this book. All you need is a list of URLs, which you can construct manually (although this is not the best approach), by scraping links from some sort of index page (or possibly the front page), or by writing a more complex web crawler. Web crawling is beyond the scope of this book, but you can read about it in Ryan Mitchell's (2018) excellent book *Web Scraping with Python*.

Working with many web pages

In many cases, the data you want to scrape isn't neatly packaged for you on a single web page but is instead spread out across several different pages on a single website. In most cases, there will be some kind of ordering principle that undergirds each of those web pages' URLs; we can take advantage of this to greatly simplify and expedite the scraping process. Just as we studied the source code for a web page to determine how best to scrape it, we have to study how the website handles URLs to determine how best to get the data we want from multiple pages.

Let's talk first about detecting patterns when you browse through pages on a website. This is as simple as navigating through your page from some starting point (say the front page of nytimes.com) and then clicking through to different sections and news stories. As you do this, you'll notice that some parts of the URL change and other parts stay the same. For example, you might see that a new chunk of string is added to the URL when you navigate to parts of the website that cover international news and a different string appears when you're reading op-eds or the lifestyle section.

As you click through pages, make notes on how the URL changes. Then start simply entering new values into parts of the URL (e.g. different numbers for pages) and see what the results are. Does it return a valid page or not? Did it return what you expected? This is just one way of doing the necessary detective work – in terms of both the web page source code and how the website handles URLs – to get the content we want from those pages. Figure 5.2 presents an overview of these two interconnected processes.

Let's make this all a little less abstract by looking at a specific example of programmatically iterating over URLs to scrape a page.

Consider the UN's Sustainable Development Goals Partnerships Platform. This website contains a directory of sustainable development projects that the UN's Department of Economic and Social Affairs is supporting. Here's an example of one such project's page on the website: https://sustainabledevelopment.un.org/partnership/?p=35711. Here, we can see that the 'Future Rangers Program' is an anti-poaching initiative designed to train a new generation of wildlife conservationists.

Let's say you wanted to scrape information about 30 projects approved by this initiative. These project pages are informative, but it will take a fair bit of time to find URLs for each of those 30 projects and then put them into a list (as we did with the *Guardian* in the examples above). Luckily for us, there's an easy way to iterate through the project pages on this website: the key can be found in the ?p=35711 at the trailing end of the URL we examined. Each of the projects listed on the website has a project number and each project's page can be accessed by replacing the number at the end of our example URL with the project number you want to access. Give it a try!

After plugging in a few random numbers, you'll discover that not every five-digit number has a corresponding project (you can use 35553, if you'd like to see one that works), and that continuing to use hand-typed numbers until we reach our desired threshold of 30 projects will take a very long time. Let's write some code to move things along:

```python
def scrape_UNSD_project(url):
    result = requests.get(url)
    if result.ok:
        soup = BeautifulSoup(result.content, 'lxml')
        headline = soup.find(id='headline').getText()
        intro = " ".join(
            [segment for segment in soup.find(id='intro').stripped_strings])
        return [headline, intro]
    else:
        return None
```

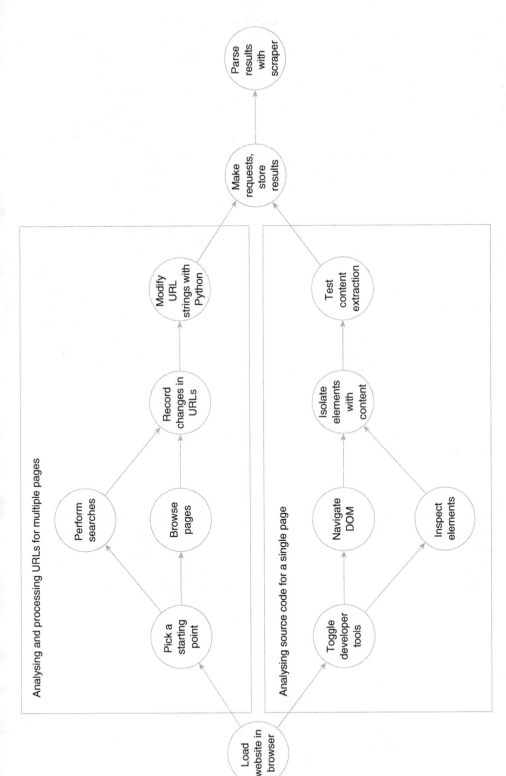

Figure 5.2 An overview of the front end investigatory work that goes into web scraping. You must spend time studying URLs and the source code of the pages you want to scrape. DOM = Document Object Model

In the above code block, we define a function that takes one parameter (a URL) and retrieves textual data about a project from its page on the UN Sustainable Development (UNSD) website (defined by the URL). This function does things a little differently than in previous examples, so it's worth going through it line by line.

The first thing the function does is pass the URL it was supplied to the `requests.get` function, which returns a result. Not all results are useful, though, and as you may have discovered while entering random numbers into the UNSD website, most project IDs don't have a publicly visible project associated with them. Whenever an HTTP GET requests a page that the server can't find, it returns a 404 code, indicating that it couldn't locate what we were asking for. When it *can* find what we're looking for, the server will usually return a 200 code, indicating that everything is okay. There are a variety of HTTP Status Codes that a server can return, and each of them carries a specific meaning (visit https://www.restapitutorial.com/httpstatuscodes. html for a list of what each code means). Generally speaking, codes from 0 to 399 indicate a successful GET request, whereas anything 400 or above indicates that something went wrong.

Luckily for us, the Requests package was designed with ease of use in mind, and provides a convenient way of checking if our GET request was successful: ok. The ok attribute is False if something went wrong, and True in all other cases. As such, we can use `result.ok` to provide a Boolean operator to an if-else statement; we'll cover how this fits into the larger picture a few paragraphs from now. If the result is ok, the function then uses BeautifulSoup to parse it. We'll use find to isolate the text we're interested in, but this time we'll use the named ids 'headline' and 'intro' to retrieve it.

The next block of code simply sets the starting parameters for our scrape – we'll use them later on. In this case, we've used three variables to indicate to our scraper which URL we want it to start at (base_url and starting_number), and how many pages we want to collect (target_records):

```
base_url = "https://sustainabledevelopment.un.org/partnership/?p={}"
starting_number = 30000
target_records = 30
```

We're going to get Python to repeatedly replace those curly brackets ({}) in our URL with different numbers, corresponding to the project IDs we want to gather information about.

The final code block of this section puts the pieces together, starting by defining a list, which we'll populate using our scraper. Then, it uses a while statement with the condition that the number of scraped documents contained in scraped is smaller than target_records; this means that the code inside the while block will repeat until the condition is no longer true.

```
scraped = []

current_number = starting_number

while len(scraped) < target_records:
    url = base_url.format(current_number)
    try:
        output = scrape_UNSD_project(url)
        if output is not None:
            print(f"scraping {current_number}")
            scraped.append(output)
```

```
    except AttributeError:
        pass
    current_number += 1


df_scraped = pd.DataFrame(scraped, columns=['Headline', 'Introduction'])


print(df_scraped.info())
```

```
scraping 30028
scraping 30034
scraping 30076
scraping 30108
scraping 30110
scraping 30116
scraping 30146
scraping 30166
scraping 30200
scraping 30206
scraping 30214
scraping 30248
scraping 30266
scraping 30292
scraping 30312
scraping 30314
scraping 30366
scraping 30372
scraping 30411
scraping 30462
scraping 30477
scraping 30483
scraping 30489
scraping 30492
scraping 30537
scraping 30540
scraping 30564
scraping 30573
scraping 30579
scraping 30633
<class 'pandas.core.frame.DataFrame'>
RangeIndex: 30 entries, 0 to 29
Data columns (total 2 columns):
 #   Column        Non-Null Count  Dtype
---  ------        --------------  -----
 0   Headline      30 non-null     object
 1   Introduction  30 non-null     object
dtypes: object(2)
memory usage: 608.0+ bytes
None
```

When using `while` blocks, exercise caution! If you use a while loop with an end state that isn't guaranteed to be met (or might not be met in a reasonable time frame), your computer will keep executing the same code over and over until the end of time (or Windows forces your computer to update – sorry, I couldn't resist). In our case, we've used a condition that will eventually be broken out of by the code inside the `while` block. Here's how:

- First, it uses `format` to replace the curly brackets inside `base_url` with the current value of `starting_number`, giving us our `url`.
- Second, it attempts to retrieve text data using the `url` and our `scrape_UNSD_project` function, storing the result in `output`.
- After checking to see if `output` contains anything (it can sometimes be empty, which we don't want), our code appends `output` to our `scraped` list.
- Finally, it increments `starting_number` by one and if the number of successful scrapes is fewer than 30, it uses the new `starting_number` to begin another scrape on the next project.

Now we have a `dataframe` containing text describing 30 different projects from the UNSD website, and we've accomplished this without having to navigate the site using links or redirects – we just changed one number! While such an approach is extremely useful, it isn't compatible with all websites. If the approaches we've covered thus far won't work (which can happen when a website is dynamically generated or interactive, for instance), then we'll have to call in the cavalry. In this case, the cavalry is a Python package called `selenium`. Since my editors at Sage feel it would be best if one could carry this book without the assistance of a hydraulic lift, we're not going to have room to cover `selenium` in-text. If you want to read more about how to scrape the interactive web, we've prepared an online supplement that will guide you through the process.

5.6 Ethical and Legal Issues in Web Scraping

While it's theoretically possible to systematically step through every page and element of a website and store it (sometimes called a site-dump), most websites would prefer you didn't, may forbid it in their terms of service, or, in some cases, may seek legal recourse if you were to use that data anywhere. Thankfully, academic researchers are under greater scrutiny over the ethics of their work than your average web hacker trying to harvest content, but you may not have your research plan vetted by people who understand the legal and ethical issues involved in web scraping. Even if you do, you shouldn't rely on them to tell you whether your plan is going to violate the terms of service for a website. You most definitely want to avoid a threat of legal action when web scraping, so be sure you are *always* checking the terms of service for any website you scrape.

A general rule to follow here is that if websites want to provide access to data at scale, they will set up an API to provide it. If they haven't, err on the side of *not* collecting data at scale, and limit your data collection efforts to what you need rather than gathering all of it and filtering later. You may recall that websites will sometimes deny service after receiving too many requests. Sometimes, their infrastructure can struggle to even send out the needed denials of service, and will crash. It's very unlikely that you could cause this type of problem, which is usually performed by many computers at once in a distributed denial of service (DDoS) attack that is either orchestrated or the product of computer viruses. That said, it is likely you will run across denial of service errors, perhaps when doing a more extensive URL iteration like in the example above and may want to think about implementing a modest rate limit in your script.

Finally, there is not yet a widely held standard, in academia or elsewhere, for the boundaries between ethical and unethical web scraping. The most widely held position seems to be that public content online should be treated with the same standards that one would apply when observing people in public settings, as ethnographers do. If this is the position you take, you may sometimes need to think very carefully about what types of online content are 'reasonably public'. If you were scraping some personal blog platform, for example, and found that you could iterate through URLs to access pages that aren't linked to anywhere, this likely would not be considered 'reasonably public' because it's possible the blog owner thought they were no longer accessible. This ongoing debate will inevitably include web scraping practices, so should be an important one to research and keep track of. We'll discuss these issues in more depth in Chapter 18.

Further Reading

To further develop your web scraping skills, I strongly recommend Ryan Mitchell's (2018) *Web Scraping with Python*. It covers a broader range of practical problems than I cover in this chapter, including parsing documents such as PDFs (portable document formats).

5.7 Conclusion

The key points in this chapter are as follows:

- Web scraping is a powerful approach for collecting data from the web, useful when data is not available in an API but could still be obtained ethically and legally.
- BeautifulSoup is a very useful tool for processing HTML from websites, but it cannot obviate the need to understand a web page's DOM.
- The 'iron rule of web scraping' is that you must put in the proper time and energy to investigate the source code of the pages you want to scrape.
- The only true limits on the data you can collect from scraping the web are ethical and legal.

Visit the website at https://study.sagepub.com/mclevey for additional resources

6

PROCESSING STRUCTURED DATA

6.1 Learning Objectives

By the end of this chapter, you should be able to do the following:

- Use Pandas to load, manipulate, and summarize data
- Preview data using head, tail, and sample
- Understand Pandas data structures (Series and DataFrames), indices, and `datetime` objects
- Extract subsets of a dataset by selecting columns and filtering rows
- Group observations in a dataframe and perform operations on groups to enable systematic comparisons
- Combine multiple dataframes by row and by column
- Understand the power (and pitfalls) of record linkage

6.2 Learning Materials

You can find the online learning materials for this chapter in `doing_computational_social_science/Chapter_06`. `cd` into the directory and launch your Jupyter server.

6.3 Introduction

It's time to shift from using Python as a general programming language to using it to process data using specialized data management and analysis packages. We are going to rely primarily on a package called Pandas, which is part of a collection of packages widely referred to as Python's 'scientific stack'. Pandas was created by Wes McKinney for analysing panel data (hence the name). It comes with special data structures, functions, and methods that you can use to take care of the vast majority of data processing operations for structured quantitative data. Pandas is built on top of another packaged called NumPy, which is a lower-level package for efficient computation and maths. We don't have the space to cover NumPy in any significant detail here, but you can learn about it in the supplementary learning materials.

In this chapter, I will start with the basics of getting data in and out of Pandas dataframes and previewing subsets of data. Next, I will dig deeper into Pandas core data structures (Series and

DataFrames), as well as `index` and `datetime` objects. I then discuss more advanced operations, such as grouping data for systematic comparisons, working with `datetime` objects for time-series analysis, and combining dataframes.

Pandas is a very large and complex package with an enormous amount of power, but you don't have to learn it all at once. In fact, you shouldn't even try! Like most other packages you will encounter in this book, you will use a small number of features very heavily, and a large number of features very rarely.

Imports

```
import pandas as pd
pd.set_option("display.notebook_repr_html", False)
```

6.4 Practical Pandas: First Steps

Getting data into Pandas

The Pandas package makes it easy to load data from an external file directly into a `dataframe` object. It uses one of many reader functions that are part of a suite of I/O (input/output, read/write) tools. I've listed some common examples in Table 6.1. Information on these and other reader functions can be found in the Pandas documentation, which also provides useful information about the parameters for each method (e.g. how to specify what sheet you want from an Excel spreadsheet, or whether to write the index to a new CSV file).

Table 6.1 Input/output methods for Pandas

Data Description	Reader	Writer
CSV	read_csv()	to_csv()
JSON	read_json()	to_json()
MS Excel and OpenDocument (ODF)	read_excel()	to_excel()
Stata	read_stata()	to_stata()
SAS	read_sas()	NA
SPSS	read_spss()	NA

I will focus on the `read_csv()` function to demonstrate the general process. The only *required* argument is that we provide the path to the file location, but there are many useful arguments that you can pass, such as the file encoding. By default, Pandas assumes your data is encoded with UTF-8. If you see an encoding error or some strange characters in your data, you can try a different encoding, such as latin1.

This chapter will use data from the Varieties of Democracy (VDEM) dataset. VDEM is an ongoing research project to measure the level of democracy in governments around the world, and updated versions of the dataset are released on an ongoing basis. The research is led by a team of more than 50 social scientists who coordinate the collection and analysis of expert assessments from more than 3200 historians and country experts. From these assessments, the VDEM project has created a remarkably complex array of indicators designed to align with five high-level facets of democracy: electoral, liberal, participatory, deliberative, and egalitarian. The dataset extends back to 1789 and is considered the gold standard of quantitative data about global democratic developments. You can find the full codebook online, and I strongly recommend that you download it and consult it as you work with this data. You can find the full data-set at www.v-dem.net/en/data/data/v-dem-dataset-v11/ and the codebook at www.v-dem.net/media/filer_public/e0/7f/e07f672b-b91e-4e98-b9a3-78f8cd4de696/v-dem_codebook_v8.pdf. Alternatively, a filtered and subsetted version is provided in the data/vdem directory of the online learning materials.

Let's load the CSV file into a Pandas dataframe:

```
df = pd.read_csv('../data/vdem/V-Dem-CY-Full+Others-v10.csv', low_memory=False)
```

Once you have your data loaded, one of the first things you will want to know is how many rows and columns there are. You can do this using the .shape attribute of the dataframe:

```
df.shape
```

```
(27013, 4108)
```

This is a fairly large dataset. It has 27,013 observations and 4108 variables! First, I will construct a new dataframe *from this one* that contains only the columns I want.

What do you need? Selecting columns

I will create a list of the variable names I want to retain, and call the original dataframe followed by the name of the list in square brackets. In this case, I will retain the following variables:

1   The country name
2   The country ID
3   The geographic region
4   The year
5   The polyarchy index
6   The liberal democracy index
7   The participatory democracy index
8   The deliberative democracy index
9   The Egalitarian Democracy Index
10 Whether internet users' privacy and their data are legally protected
11 How polarized the country is on political issues
12 Levels of political violence
13 Whether or not the country is a democracy

I will call the new dataframe sdf, for 'subsetted dataframe'. Of course, you can call it anything you like. If you are going to be working with multiple dataframes in the same script or note-book, then it's a good idea to give them much more descriptive names. For now, I am only working with two, so I will use df for the full dataframe and sdf for the dataframe with a subset of the original variables.

```
subset_vars = ['country_name', 'country_text_id', 'e_regiongeo', 'year', '
    v2x_polyarchy', 'v2x_libdem', 'v2x_partipdem', 'v2x_delibdem', 'v2x_egaldem', '
    v2smprivex', 'v2smpolsoc', 'v2caviol', 'e_boix_regime']
sdf = df[subset_vars]
sdf.shape
```

```
(27013, 13)
```

We've created a new dataframe called sdf. It still has 27,013 rows but only 13 variables. We can print their names using the .columns attribute for the dataframe:

```
list(sdf.columns)
```

```
['country_name',
 'country_text_id',
 'e_regiongeo',
 'year',
 'v2x_polyarchy',
 'v2x_libdem',
 'v2x_partipdem',
 'v2x_delibdem',
 'v2x_egaldem',
 'v2smprivex',
 'v2smpolsoc',
 'v2caviol',
 'e_boix_regime']
```

What's in your dataframe?

We can use the .info() method to see the total number of observations, the total number of columns, the names of the columns, the number of non-missing observations for each, the data type for each variable, the number of variables that contain data of each type (e.g. integers and floats), and the total amount of memory used by the dataframe:

```
sdf.info()
```

```
<class 'pandas.core.frame.DataFrame'>
RangeIndex: 27013 entries, 0 to 27012
Data columns (total 13 columns):
#    Column          Non-Null Count   Dtype
---  ------          --------------   -----
0    country_name    27013 non-null   object
1    country_text_id 27013 non-null   object
2    e_regiongeo     27013 non-null   int64
3    year            27013 non-null   int64
```

```
4    v2x_polyarchy     25342 non-null   float64
5    v2x_libdem        24350 non-null   float64
6    v2x_partipdem     24923 non-null   float64
7    v2x_delibdem      18557 non-null   float64
8    v2x_egaldem       18557 non-null   float64
9    v2smprivex        3562 non-null    float64
10   v2smpolsoc        3562 non-null    float64
11   v2caviol          12745 non-null   float64
12   e_boix_regime     16270 non-null   float64
dtypes: float64(9), int64(2), object(2)
memory usage: 2.7+ MB
```

The data types in this dataframe are float64 (numbers with decimals), int64 (integers), and object. In Pandas, object refers to columns that contain strings, or mixed types, such as strings and integers (object encompasses many more things, too: it's a catch-all category). Pandas can also work with Booleans (True or False), categorical variables, and some specialized datetime objects. Recall how we selected columns to make our dataset. In the code below, I use the same idea to show only a few variables. We will explain this a little more later in the chapter.

We can also use the .describe() method to get summary information about the quantitative variables in our dataset, including the number of non-missing information, the mean and standard deviation, and a five-number summary:

```
sdf[['e_regiongeo', 'year', 'v2x_polyarchy']].describe()
```

	e_regiongeo	year	v2x_polyarchy
count	27013.000000	27013.000000	25342.000000
mean	9.266575	1926.556177	0.262821
std	5.733007	63.754335	0.260966
min	1.000000	1789.000000	0.007000
25%	4.000000	1878.000000	0.057000
50%	8.000000	1937.000000	0.171500
75%	14.000000	1980.000000	0.367000
max	19.000000	2019.000000	0.924000

Heads, tails, and samples

We can also inspect the 'head' or the 'tail' of our dataframe using the .head() and .tail() methods, which default to the first or last five rows in a dataframe unless you provide a different number as an argument, such as .head(10):

```
sdf[['country_name', 'year', 'v2x_libdem']].head()
```

	country_name	year	v2x_libdem
0	Mexico	1789	0.043
1	Mexico	1790	0.040
2	Mexico	1791	0.040
3	Mexico	1792	0.040
4	Mexico	1793	0.040

```
sdf[['country_name', 'year', 'v2x_libdem']].tail(3)
```

```
            country_name  year  v2x_libdem
27010  Piedmont-Sardinia  1859       0.150
27011  Piedmont-Sardinia  1860       0.148
27012  Piedmont-Sardinia  1861       0.149
```

If you would prefer a random sample of rows, you can use the `.sample()` method, which requires you to specify the number of rows you want to sample:

```
sdf[['country_name', 'year', 'v2x_libdem']].sample(15)
```

```
                      country_name  year v2x_libdem
8132                     Indonesia  1814      0.010
15992                        China  1879      0.015
22301                   Luxembourg  1932      0.519
10336     Central African Republic  1948      0.091
8360                    Mozambique  1922      0.025
3176                      Portugal  1869      0.194
26221                      Hanover  1805      0.029
1387                 Burma/Myanmar  1903      0.094
11804                    Guatemala  2004      0.418
24839                    Singapore  2015      0.315
17320                   Kazakhstan  1990        NaN
10901                  Timor-Leste  1980        NaN
23072                  New Zealand  1983      0.757
25514                     Zanzibar  1911      0.075
18392                    Sri Lanka  2014      0.254
```

What do you need? Filtering rows

When we executed the `.describe()` method earlier, you may have noticed that the range for the `year` variable is 1789–2019. Let's say we have a good reason to focus on the years from 1900 to 2019. We will have to filter the data to have only the rows that meet our needs.

There are several ways to filter rows, including slices (e.g. all observations between index *i* and index *j*), or according to some sort of explicit condition, such as 'rows where the year >= 1900'. Note that when we filter or slice a dataframe, the new object is just a *view* of the original and still refers to the same data. Pandas will warn us if we try to modify the filtered object, so a lot of the time, things are smoother if we make a new copy.

```
rowfilter = sdf['year'] >= 1900
fsdf = sdf[rowfilter].copy()
fsdf.info()
```

```
<class 'pandas.core.frame.DataFrame'>
Int64Index: 18787 entries, 111 to 25622
Data columns (total 13 columns):
```

#	Column	Non-Null Count	Dtype
---	------	---------------	-----
0	country_name	18787 non-null	object
1	country_text_id	18787 non-null	object
2	e_regiongeo	18787 non-null	int64
3	year	18787 non-null	int64
4	v2x_polyarchy	18663 non-null	float64
5	v2x_libdem	18424 non-null	float64
6	v2x_partipdem	18587 non-null	float64
7	v2x_delibdem	18557 non-null	float64
8	v2x_egaldem	18557 non-null	float64
9	v2smprivex	3562 non-null	float64
10	v2smpolsoc	3562 non-null	float64
11	v2caviol	12745 non-null	float64
12	e_boix_regime	11841 non-null	float64

```
dtypes: float64(9), int64(2), object(2)
memory usage: 2.0+ MB
```

We could also do this using the `.query()` method, which accepts a Boolean expression as a string:

```
alternate_fsdf = sdf.query('year >= 1900').copy()
alternate_fsdf.info()
```

```
<class 'pandas.core.frame.DataFrame'>
Int64Index: 18787 entries, 111 to 25622
Data columns (total 13 columns):
```

#	Column	Non-Null Count	Dtype
---	------	---------------	-----
0	country_name	18787 non-null	object
1	country_text_id	18787 non-null	object
2	e_regiongeo	18787 non-null	int64
3	year	18787 non-null	int64
4	v2x_polyarchy	18663 non-null	float64
5	v2x_libdem	18424 non-null	float64
6	v2x_partipdem	18587 non-null	float64
7	v2x_delibdem	18557 non-null	float64
8	v2x_egaldem	18557 non-null	float64
9	v2smprivex	3562 non-null	float64
10	v2smpolsoc	3562 non-null	float64
11	v2caviol	12745 non-null	float64
12	e_boix_regime	11841 non-null	float64

```
dtypes: float64(9), int64(2), object(2)
memory usage: 2.0+ MB
```

Our final dataframe – which I have called fsdf for *filtered* and *subsetted dataframe* – now has 13 columns (from 4108) and 18,787 observations (from 27,013).

Writing data to disk

Just as I read our initial CSV file into Pandas using the `read_csv()` function, I can write this new dataframe to disk using the `to_csv()` method:

```
fsdf.to_csv('../data/vdem/filtered_subset.csv', index=False)
```

6.5 Understanding Pandas Data Structures

Now let's discuss Pandas' main data structures, Series and DataFrames, and how they relate to one another.

The series

Each column in a dataframe is an object called a Series. A Series is a one-dimensional object (e.g. a vector of numbers) with an index, which is itself a vector, or array, of labels.

For example, the column `v2x_delibdem` in `fsdf` is a Series containing floats and the index label for each observation. Printing a sample of 15 observations gives me a numerical index for each observation on the left and the actual value on the right. The index values are ordered in the Series itself, but they are out of sequence here because we pulled a random sample. As this is for demonstration purposes, I've included a random_state value to ensure you get the same sample that I do if you rerun this block.

```
fsdf['v2x_delibdem'].sample(15, random_state = 42)
```

```
8437      0.305
25197     0.059
6661      0.079
19266     0.390
7633      0.632
1230      0.727
8829      0.020
10118     0.008
8996      0.047
2360      0.048
18407     0.018
153       0.132
10794     0.805
14375     0.800
24240       NaN
Name: v2x_delibdem, dtype: float64
```

In most cases, the default `index` for a Series or DataFrame is an immutable vector of integers:

```
fsdf.index
```

```
Int64Index([ 111, 112, 113, 114, 115, 116, 117, 118, 119,
             120,
```

```
    . . .
    25613, 25614, 25615, 25616, 25617, 25618, 25619, 25620, 25621,
    25622],
    dtype='int64', length=18787)
```

We can easily modify an index so that it is made up of some other type of vector instead, including a string. Surprisingly, index values do not need to be unique. This enables some powerful techniques, but most of the time you should avoid manually changing indices.

Accessing a specific row by its index

We can use the index to retrieve specific rows from a dataframe or specific values from a Series, much as we would if we were selecting an element from a list, tuple, or array. The easiest way to do this is to pass the index value (e.g. 202) to .loc[]. As you can see below, the result is the observation-specific value for each variable in the dataframe:

```
fsdf.loc[202]
```

```
country_name       Mexico
country_text_id       MEX
e_regiongeo            17
year                 1991
v2x_polyarchy       0.435
v2x_libdem          0.221
v2x_partipdem       0.246
v2x_delibdem         0.31
v2x_egaldem         0.214
v2smprivex            NaN
v2smpolsoc            NaN
v2caviol            -0.71
e_boix_regime         0.0
Name: 202, dtype: object
```

```
fsdf['v2x_delibdem'].loc[202]
```

```
0.31
```

```
fsdf['v2x_delibdem'].loc[20000]
```

```
0.081
```

Note that .loc does *not* refer to the 202nd row of the dataframe. If you were looking closely at the .index command above, you might have noticed the dataframe only contains 18,787 rows but .loc can still return row 20,000 – the index didn't change when you removed a bunch of rows from the dataframe. Think of .loc as accessing a dictionary of the index values – it will even give a KeyError if you ask for an element that doesn't exist.

Instead, if we want to access the *n*th row of a dataframe, we can use `.iloc[n]`. Think of the index as a list and you're referring to an element of that list by its list index. Let's use `.iloc` to select the last element in the dataframe. Note that the index position for the last element will be 18,786 even though the dataframe length is 18,787, because Python data structures are almost always zero-indexed. Here you see the index of the row, which was formerly the row number, as the `Name` at the bottom:

```
fsdf.iloc[18786]
```

```
country_name         Zanzibar
country_text_id           ZZB
e_regiongeo                 8
year                     2019
v2x_polyarchy           0.245
v2x_libdem               0.18
v2x_partipdem           0.083
v2x_delibdem            0.183
v2x_egaldem             0.187
v2smprivex             -1.843
v2smpolsoc             -0.848
v2caviol               -0.181
e_boix_regime             NaN
Name: 25622, dtype: object
```

If there isn't a reason to retain the original indexing of the unfiltered dataframe, it's usually a good idea to reset the index:

```
fsdf.reset_index(inplace = True, drop = True)
fsdf.loc[18786]
```

```
country_name         Zanzibar
country_text_id           ZZB
e_regiongeo                 8
year                     2019
v2x_polyarchy           0.245
v2x_libdem               0.18
v2x_partipdem           0.083
v2x_delibdem            0.183
v2x_egaldem             0.187
v2smprivex             -1.843
v2smpolsoc             -0.848
v2caviol               -0.181
e_boix_regime             NaN
Name: 18786, dtype: object
```

Afterwards, `.loc` and `.iloc` become fairly interchangeable, with a few exceptions: `.loc` has dictionary-like capabilities, whereas `.iloc` is more list-like. Now, let's take a closer look at the dataframe.

Dataframes

Dataframes in Pandas are really just collections of Series that are aligned on the same index values. In other words, the Series we worked with previously have their own indices when we work with them as stand-alone Series, but in the `fsdf` dataframe, they share an index.

As you've already seen, dataframes are organized with variables in the columns and observations in the rows, and you can grab a single Series from a dataframe using square brackets – let's do that now, using the `fsdf` dataframe:

```
deliberative = fsdf['v2x_delibdem']
```

Note that we can also use dot notation to select columns. `fsdf.v2x_delibdem` is functionally equivalent to `fsdf['v2x_delibdem']` and may be used interchangeably.

We are not limited to selecting columns that already exist in our dataset. You can also create and add new ones. For example, you can create a new column called '21 Century' and assign a Boolean value based on whether the observation is in the 2000s:

```
fsdf['21 Century'] = fsdf['year'] >= 2000
fsdf[['21 Century']].value_counts()
```

```
21 Century
False           15225
True             3562
dtype: int64
```

Sometimes, the new columns created are transformations of a Series that already exists in the dataframe. For example, you can create a new `missing_political_violence_data` column which will be `True` when the v2caviol Series (levels of political violence) is empty and `False` otherwise:

```
fsdf['missing_political_violence_data'] = fsdf['v2caviol'].isna()
fsdf['missing_political_violence_data'].value_counts()
```

```
False    12745
True      6042
Name: missing_political_violence_data, dtype: int64
```

As you can see from executing `value_counts()`, there is missing data on levels of political violence for 6042 observations.

Missing data

It's important to understand how missing data is handled. Missing data is common in real-world datasets, and it can be missing for multiple reasons! Generally, Pandas uses the `np.nan` value to represent missing data. NumPy's `np.nan` value is a special case of a floating point number representing an unrepresentable value. These kinds of values are called NaNs (Not a Number).

```
import numpy as np

type(np.nan)

float
```

np.nan cannot be used in equality tests, since any comparison to a np.nan value will evaluate as False. This includes comparing np.nan to itself.

```
n = np.nan
n == n

False
```

np.nan values do not evaluate to False or None. This can make it difficult to distinguish missing values. You can use the np.isnan() function for this purpose, and it is especially useful in control flow.

```
if np.nan is None:
    print('NaN is None')
if np.nan:
    print('NaN evaluates to True in control flow')
if np.isnan(np.nan):
    print('NaN is considered a NaN value in NumPy')

NaN evaluates to True in control flow
NaN is considered a NaN value in NumPy
```

Additionally, np.nan values are generally excluded from Pandas functions that perform calculations over dataframes, rows, or columns. For example, documentation often stipulates that a calculation is done over all values, excluding NaN or NULL values.

```
total = len(fsdf['v2caviol'])
count = fsdf['v2caviol'].count()
print(f'Total: {total}')
print(f'Count: {count}')
print(f'Diff: {total-count}')

Total: 18787
Count: 12745
Diff: 6042
```

The total number of items in the v2caviol column (political violence) is much higher than the counts received from the count() function. If what we learnt above is correct, this difference should be accounted for when we discover how many items in this column are NaNs.

```
nans = fsdf['v2caviol'].isna().sum()
print(' NaNs: {}'.format(nans))
```

```
NaNs: 6042
```

As you can probably tell, the .isna() method, which is similar to np.isnan() but covers additional cases, can be very useful in transforming and filtering data.

6.6 Aggregation and Grouped Operations

Data analysis projects often involve aggregation or grouped operations. For example, we might want to compute and compare summary statistics for observations that take different values on a categorical variable. It can be helpful to be able to carve up the dataset itself, performing operations on different subsets of data. We're going to do that using the .groupby() method, which partitions the dataframe into groups based on the values of a given variable. We can then perform operations on the resulting groups. Let's group our countries into geographic regions using the e_regiongeo variable:

```
grouped = fsdf.groupby('e_regiongeo')
```

The above code returns a grouped object that we can work with. Let's say we want to pull out a specific group, like South-East Asia, which is represented in the data using the numerical ID 13. I know this because the relevant information is provided in the VDEM codebook, which I suggest you keep open whenever you are working with the VDEM data.

We can use the get_group() method to pull a group from the grouped object. (Note that the .get_group() code below is equivalent to fsdf[fsdf['e_regiongeo'] == 13].)

```
south_east_asia = grouped.get_group(13)
south_east_asia[['country_name', 'year', 'e_boix_regime']].head()
```

	country_name	year	e_boix_regime
838	Burma/Myanmar	1900	NaN
839	Burma/Myanmar	1901	NaN
840	Burma/Myanmar	1902	NaN
841	Burma/Myanmar	1903	NaN
842	Burma/Myanmar	1904	NaN

The data stored in south_east_asia is all of the observations of South-East Asian countries in the VDEM data, stored now in their own dataframe. .get_group() is yet another way to extract a subset of a dataframe (by way of a groupby object), and is especially useful when the subset of data you want to work with is only observations with a particular value for a categorical variable in your data.

Generally speaking, when we group a dataset like this, it's because we want to compute something for a group within the dataset or for multiple groups that we want to compare. We can do this by specifying the grouped object, the Series we want to perform an operation on, and finally the operation we want to perform. For example, let's compute the median polyarchy score for countries in each of the regions in the dataset:

```
poly = grouped['v2x_polyarchy'].median()
poly.head()
```

```
e_regiongeo
1    0.7940
2    0.8170
3    0.3890
4    0.2385
5    0.0955
Name: v2x_polyarchy, dtype: float64
```

It would be more useful to see the name of the region rather than its numeric label. We can do this by creating a dictionary that maps the numeric IDs to the region name, and then use the .map() method to tell Pandas where to look up the values it needs to create a new column with the country names. First, the dictionary:

```
regions = {
       1:'Western Europe',
       2:'Northern Europe',
       3:'Southern Europe',
       4:'Eastern Europe',
       5:'Northern Africa',
       6:'Western Africa',
       7:'Middle Africa',
       8:'Eastern Africa',
       9:'Southern Africa',
       10:'Western Asia',
       11:'Central Asia',
       12:'East Asia',
       13:'South-East Asia',
       14:'South Asia',
       15:'Oceania', # (including Australia and the Pacific)
       16:'North America',
       17:'Central America',
       18:'South America',
       19:'Caribbean' # (including Belize Cuba Haiti Dominican Republic)
}
```

And now we can pass this dictionary into the .map() method applied to the fsdf['e_regiongeo'] Series, creating a new Series called fsdf['Region']:

```
fsdf['Region'] = fsdf['e_regiongeo'].map(regions)
```

It is also possible to group by multiple variables, such as geographic region and year, and then perform an operation on *those* slightly more fine-grained groups. This will result in 2211 groups, so we will preview a random sample of 10:

```
grouped = fsdf.groupby(['Region', 'year'])
poly = grouped['v2x_polyarchy'].median()
poly.reset_index()
pd.DataFrame(poly).reset_index().sample(10)
```

```
              Region   year   v2x_polyarchy
1802   Southern Europe   1971          0.1500
1877    Western Africa   1926          0.0370
1073   Northern Europe   1962          0.8090
167    Central America   1947          0.1990
24           Caribbean   1924          0.1415
1394        South Asia   1923          0.0470
1574   South-East Asia   1983          0.1720
830      North America   1959          0.7110
1548   South-East Asia   1957          0.2870
227    Central America   2007          0.5730
```

We can perform other types of operations on the grouped object itself, such as computing the number of observations in each group (equivalent to `value_counts()`):

```
grouped.size().sort_values(ascending=False)
```

```
Region            year
Eastern Africa    2015    20
                  2012    20
                  2019    20
                  2018    20
                  2017    20
                          ..
Central Asia      1904     1
                  1903     1
                  1902     1
                  1901     1
                  1914     1
Length: 2211, dtype: int64
```

Finally, we can perform *multiple* operations on a grouped object by using the `agg()` method. The `agg()` method will apply one or more aggregate functions *to a grouped object*, returning the results of each:

```
with_agg = grouped['v2x_polyarchy'].agg([min, np.median, 'max', 'count'])
with_agg.reset_index().sample(10)
```

```
              Region   year    min   median    max  count
330        East Asia   1939  0.018   0.0935  0.176      6
1770  Southern Europe   1939  0.044   0.1130  0.244      7
1451       South Asia   1980  0.054   0.1560  0.675      9
2106   Western Europe   1915  0.168   0.2970  0.604      7
```

```
1766   Southern Europe   1935   0.060   0.1720   0.562       7
722       Middle Africa   1971   0.009   0.1160   0.204       9
343           East Asia   1952   0.076   0.1560   0.610       7
986     Northern Africa   1995   0.072   0.1915   0.217       6
173     Central America   1953   0.145   0.2600   0.629       7
1095   Northern Europe   1984   0.823   0.8460   0.904       7
```

We can even define our own function for agg() to use! If we're willing to pass a dictionary, .agg() also lets us apply different functions to multiple variables at the same time! Instead of passing one list per function, you can use a dictionary where the column names are the keys and the functions are the values (you can also pass a list of functions) to perform some truly involved aggregation all in one line of code.

6.7 Working With Time-Series Data

Many real-world datasets include a temporal component. This is especially true if you are working with data that comes from the web, which may have precise timestamps for things like the time an email was sent, or a news story was published. Strings are often used to store dates and times, but this is not ideal because strings don't take advantage of the unique properties of time. It is difficult to sort dates if they are stored in strings with strange formats; for example,

```
"Monday Mar 2, 1999" > "Friday Feb 21, 2020"
```

```
True
```

Extracting features like day, month, or time zone from strings can be time-consuming and error-prone. This is why Pandas and Python have implemented special types for date/time objects, called Timestamp and Datetime.

The VDEM data contains an enormous amount of temporal data, but all at the level of the year. Let's switch over to a different dataset that has more fine-grained temporal data and more closely resembles data that you would obtain from the web. In this case, we are going to use some data on Russian information operations targeting the 2016 American Presidential Election. You can read a bit about this data on the FiveThirtyEight blogpost 'Why We're Sharing 3 Million Russian Troll Tweets'.

Unlike the VDEM data, the Russian Troll Tweets come as a collection of CSV files. We will use a clever little trick to load up all the data in a single dataframe. The code block below iterates over each file in the russian-troll-tweets/ subdirectory in the data directory. If the file extension is csv, it reads the csv into memory as a dataframe. All of the dataframes are then concatenated into a single dataframe containing data on approximately 3 million tweets.

```
import os
data_dir = os.listdir("../data/russian-troll-tweets/")

files = [f for f in data_dir if 'csv' in f]

tweets_df = pd.concat((pd.read_csv(
```

```
    f'{"../data/russian-troll-tweets/"}/{f}',
    encoding='utf-8', low_memory=False) for f in files), ignore_index=True)

tweets_df.info()

<class 'pandas.core.frame.DataFrame'>
RangeIndex: 2946207 entries, 0 to 2946206
Data columns (total 21 columns):
 #    Column                 Dtype
---   ------                 -----
 0    external_author_id     object
 1    author                 object
 2    content                object
 3    region                 object
 4    language               object
 5    publish_date           object
 6    harvested_date         object
 7    following              int64
 8    followers              int64
 9    updates                int64
 10   post_type              object
 11   account_type           object
 12   retweet                int64
 13   account_category       object
 14   new_june_2018          int64
 15   alt_external_id        object
 16   tweet_id               int64
 17   article_url            object
 18   tco1_step1             object
 19   tco2_step1             object
 20   tco3_step1             object
dtypes: int64(6), object(15)
memory usage: 472.0+ MB
```

As you can see, we have two data types in our dataframe: object and int64. Remember that Pandas uses object to refer to columns that contain strings, or which contain mixed types, such as strings and integers. In this case, they refer to strings.

One further thing to note about this dataset: each row is a tweet from a specific account, but some of the variables describe attributes of the tweeting accounts, not of the tweet itself. For example, followers describes the number of followers that the account had at the time it sent the tweet. This makes sense, because tweets don't have followers, but accounts do. We need to keep this in mind when working with this dataset.

We can convert date strings from a column or Series into Timestamps using the to_datetime function. We will do that here, assigning the new datetime objects to new variables. Note that this code will take a bit of time to run when executed on all 3 million tweets (if your computer isn't especially powerful, you might want to consider first using the .sample() method to reduce the size of the dataframe by pulling a random sample of observations).

```
tweets_df['dt_publish_date'] = pd.to_datetime(tweets_df['publish_date'])
tweets_df['dt_harvested_date'] = pd.to_datetime(tweets_df['harvested_date'])
```

```
                              author    \
dt_publish_date
2015-08-03 23:39:00          EXQUOTE
2015-09-08 21:51:00        PETRGORELOV
2015-09-19 03:20:00          RIAFANRU
2017-05-19 03:02:00  KANSASDAILYNEWS
2016-02-10 12:32:00        HIIMKHLOE

                                                            content    \
dt_publish_date
2015-08-03 23:39:00  '@bucknall407 Agreed RT Me no like workout lat...
2015-09-08 21:51:00            United Airlines         ...
2015-09-19 03:20:00                  -              ...
2017-05-19 03:02:00  Statewide Silver Alert issued for Republic Cou...
2016-02-10 12:32:00  RT @LatuffCartoons: Rabbi Rabbi Susan Talve: #...

                            publish_date
dt_publish_date
2015-08-03 23:39:00   8/3/2015 23:39
2015-09-08 21:51:00   9/8/2015 21:51
2015-09-19 03:20:00   9/19/2015 3:20
2017-05-19 03:02:00   5/19/2017 3:02
2016-02-10 12:32:00  2/10/2016 12:32
```

```
tweets_df[['author', 'content', 'publish_date']].sample(5)
```

In order, the `datetime` object fields are as follows: `year-month-day hour:minute:second:microsecond`. To retrieve an integer corresponding to the month when the tweet was published:

```
tweets_df['dt_publish_date'].dt.month
```

```
0          1
1          1
2          1
3          1
4          1
          ..
2946202    9
2946203    9
2946204    9
2946205    9
2946206    9
Name: dt_publish_date, Length: 2946207, dtype: int64
```

When our `date` and `time` variables are stored as `datetime` objects, we can access many time-specific attributes using dot notation. The Pandas documentation includes many examples of the kinds of temporal units and other functionality.

We can also sort our dataframe based on publish_date because Pandas knows that it is working with datetime objects:

```
sorted_df = tweets_df.sort_values(['dt_publish_date'])
```

We can also add and subtract datetime columns to create new columns:

```
tweets_df['days_until_harvest'] = tweets_df['dt_harvested_date'] - tweets_df['
    dt_publish_date']
tweets_df['days_until_harvest'].sample(10)
```

```
932727      0 days 00:00:00
1078375     0 days 00:00:00
2167959     0 days 00:00:00
1210330     0 days 00:01:00
2357447     0 days 00:00:00
2108476     0 days 00:00:00
356753      0 days 00:00:00
2413535     4 days 03:22:00
2627310     0 days 00:00:00
2049317     0 days 00:00:00
Name: days_until_harvest, dtype: timedelta64[ns]
```

Let's create new variables for the year, month, and day each tweet was created on. We can do this by using the year, month, and day attributes on the datetime object:

```
tweets_df['Year'] = tweets_df['dt_publish_date'].dt.year
tweets_df['Month'] = tweets_df['dt_publish_date'].dt.month
tweets_df['Day'] = tweets_df['dt_publish_date'].dt.day
```

Pandas offers specialized tools for grouping data into various segments of time. This involves converting a time series at one level into another (e.g. from days to weeks), and is known as resampling. Within resampling broadly, upsampling aggregates dates/times and downsampling disaggregates dates/times. Let's upsample our data to plot the number of tweets per day.

The first thing we will do is use the datetime object dt_publish_date as an index. This will let us easily group observations by resampling dates.

```
tweets_df = tweets_df.set_index('dt_publish_date')
```

We can now use the .resample() method with the argument D to specify that we want to group by day. Table 6.2 provides some other options you can use when resampling dates.

Table 6.2 Units of time in Pandas

Value	Description
B	Business day frequency
C	Custom business day frequency (experimental)
D	Calendar day frequency

Value	Description
W	Weekly frequency
M	Month end frequency
BM	Business month end frequency
CBM	Custom business month end frequency
MS	Month start frequency
BMS	Business month start frequency
CBMS	Custom business month start frequency
Q	Quarter end frequency
BQ	Business quarter end frequency
QS	Quarter start frequency
BQS	Business quarter start frequency
A	Year end frequency
BA	Business year end frequency
AS	Year start frequency
BAS	Business year start frequency
BH	Business hour frequency
H	Hourly frequency
T	Minutely frequency
S	Secondly frequency
L	Milliseconds
U	Microseconds
N	Nanoseconds

Note: You can use any of these units to upsample or downsample temporal data.

We will also use the .size() method to determine the number of tweets that were produced each day:

```
grouped_cal_day = tweets_df.resample('D').size()
grouped_cal_day

dt_publish_date
2012-02-02     4
2012-02-03     0
2012-02-04     1
2012-02-05     1
2012-02-06     3
              ..
2018-05-26    44
2018-05-27    49
2018-05-28    43
2018-05-29    49
2018-05-30    32
Freq: D, Length: 2310, dtype: int64
```

At this point, we are going to visualize the results of our work with a line plot. We are going to do this with the Seaborn and Matplotlib packages, which we will discuss in the next chapter. For now, focus on the visualization and ignore the code. The code blocks below produce Figures 6.1 and 6.2.

```
import seaborn as sns
import matplotlib.pyplot as plt
from dcss.plotting import custom_seaborn
custom_seaborn()

sns.lineplot(data=grouped_cal_day, color='#32363A')
sns.despine()
plt.show()
```

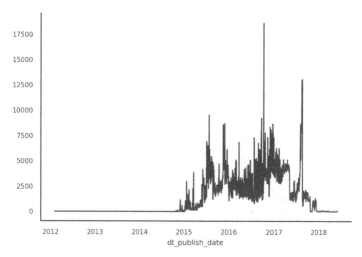

Figure 6.1　A line plot showing the number of tweets published per day. Aggregating by day produces a somewhat hectic plot, which might not be the most useful for our purposes

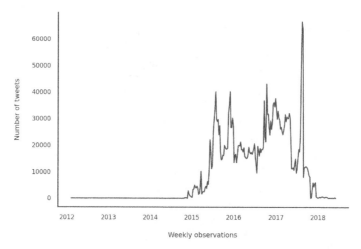

Figure 6.2　A line plot showing the number of tweets published per week. Despite the loss of fidelity, aggregating by day has produced a more intelligible result

Days may not be the best unit of time to work with in this case. We can, of course, upsample from days to weeks instead, and produce the same plot.

```
weekly = tweets_df.resample('W').size()
weekly.head()
```

```
dt_publish_date
2012-02-05        6
2012-02-12       14
2012-02-19        5
2012-02-26       11
2012-03-04        1
Freq: W-SUN, dtype: int64
```

```
ax = sns.lineplot(data=weekly, color='#32363A')
ax.set_xlabel('\nWeekly observations')
ax.set_ylabel('Number of tweets\n')
sns.despine()
plt.show()
```

The plot is much cleaner when we count at the level of weeks rather than days.

6.8 Combining Dataframes

Combining dataframes is a *very* common task. In fact, though it might not seem obvious, combining datasets is one of the most valuable skills you can have when doing computational social science. Here, we will consider some of the most common approaches, namely concatenating and merging, and we will briefly describe a more advanced set of methods commonly referred to as record linkage.

Concatenating a dataframe is conceptually pretty simple – think of it like attaching the rows or columns of one dataframe below or to the right of the last row or column of another dataframe. For this to be useful, the two dataframes should have at least one row or column in common.

```
full_df = pd.read_csv("../data/vdem/filtered_subset.csv")
df_australia = full_df.query("country_name == 'Australia'")
len(df_australia)
```

```
120
```

```
df_sa = full_df.query("country_name == 'South Africa'")
len(df_sa)
```

```
120
```

The default behaviour for `pd.concat()` is to perform a row-wise join, which it refers to as `axis=0`. We can override this default by specifying `axis=1`, which will produce a column-wise join:

```
concatenated = pd.concat([df_australia, df_sa], axis=1)
len(concatenated)
```

```
240
```

When we concatenate the two dataframes, the number of columns stays the same but the number of rows increases, accounting for the rows in both the original dataframes. Normally, this kind of concatenation would result in a different number of columns, but in this case, the two dataframes we joined had the *exact* same columns (which makes sense, given that they were both extracted from the same parent dataframe).

Merging

An alternative way to combine datasets is to merge them. If you want to create a dataframe that contains columns from multiple datasets but is aligned on rows according to some column (or set of columns), you probably want to use the merge() function. To illustrate this, we will work with data from two different sources. The first is the VDEM data we used in the first part of this chapter (fsdf). The second is a dataset from Freedom House on levels of internet freedom in 65 countries. More information is available at https://freedomhouse.org/countries/freedom-net/scores.

```
freedom_df = pd.read_csv( "../data/freedom_house/internet_freedoms_2020.csv")
```

To merge these dataframes, we need to find a column which can be used to match rows from one dataframe to the rows in the other. The columns don't need to have the same name, just values that can be matched with one another. Whatever columns we choose will be called 'keys' in our merge. In our case, this will be the country name columns from each dataset.

```
fsdf.columns
```

```
Index(['country_name', 'country_text_id', 'e_regiongeo', 'year',
       'v2x_polyarchy', 'v2x_libdem', 'v2x_partipdem', 'v2x_delibdem',
       'v2x_egaldem', 'v2smprivex', 'v2smpolsoc', 'v2caviol', 'e_boix_regime',
       '21 Century', 'missing_political_violence_data', 'Region'],
      dtype='object')
```

```
freedom_df.columns
```

```
Index(['Country', 'Total Score', 'Status', 'Obstacles to Access',
       'Limits on Content', 'Violations of User Rights'],
      dtype='object')
```

We will use the merge function to combine these two dataframes using 'country_name' and 'Country'. We're going to do an inner merge, which is the default if the option isn't set, and will keep only the keys (i.e. countries) that appear in both dataframes:

```
merged = pd.merge(fsdf, freedom_df, how='inner', left_on='country_name', right_on='
    Country')
print('merged has {} rows and {} columns'.format(len(merged), len(merged.columns)))
```

```
merged has 6434 rows and 22 columns
```

```
len(fsdf) + len(freedom_df)
```

```
18852
```

You should see five new columns in the merged dataframe compared to the fsdf one. Notice how many rows each of the dataframes have: many fewer rows than the original VDEM dataframe but many more than the Freedom House dataframe. So in our case, if a row's country doesn't appear in the other dataset, that row will not be included in the merged dataframe.

This can be adjusted using the how parameter. There are five ways of merging dataframes in Pandas: left, right, outer, inner, and cross. Check out the documentation to see how the other four methods work.

There are ways to improve the matching, either manual methods or semi-automated methods such as record linkage, described below. Let's see which countries aren't common between the dataframes, using a set operation ^ (XOR), which returns a set of elements from the combination of set 1 and set 2 that are either not in set 1 or not in set 2:

```
fsdf_set = set(fsdf['country_name'].tolist())
freedom_set = set(freedom_df['Country'].tolist())

unmatched = fsdf_set ^ freedom_set

print('Total countries: ' + str(len(fsdf_set) + len(freedom_set)))
print('Unmatched countries: ' + str(len(unmatched)))
```

```
Total countries: 248
Unmatched countries: 122
```

We can then use the & set operator to see which of the missing countries are present in each of the country sets. If the data is small enough, we can print the two sets as sorted lists in a dataframe. The most obvious manual change we could do here is make 'United States' and 'United States of America' consistent but we would also expect Myanmar to be in the VDEM data. We could also make this change manually by knowing that Myanmar was referred to as Burma until 1989. However, it just so happens that at the top of the south_east_asia aggregated group dataframe from earlier, 'Burma/Myanmar' was the name used, rather than Burma alone. For a more complex but automated solution to disambiguating different versions of country names, we would have to use some form of record linkage, discussed briefly below.

```
fsdf_missing = list(fsdf_set & unmatched)
fsdf_missing.sort()
freedom_missing = list(freedom_set & unmatched)
freedom_missing.sort()
pd.DataFrame({'VDEM': pd.Series(fsdf_missing), 'Freedom': pd.Series(freedom_missing)})
```

	VDEM	Freedom
0	Afghanistan	Myanmar
1	Albania	United States
2	Algeria	NaN
3	Austria	NaN

4	Barbados	NaN
..	...	...
115	United States of America	NaN
116	Uruguay	NaN
117	Vanuatu	NaN
118	Yemen	NaN
119	Zanzibar	NaN

[120 rows x 2 columns]

Record linkage

The `merge` function works great when you can make *exact* matches between columns. It also works really well because checking for exact matches has been optimized in Pandas. However, it's often the case that we need to combine datasets which cannot be merged based on exact matches.

Instead, we often have to use inexact matching (aka 'fuzzy matching' or 'approximate matching') to combine datasets. Typically, this involves using some similarity metric to measure how close two keys are to one another. Then a match is made based on thresholds, rules, or a nearest-neighbour approach. However, naively calculating similarity between all possible key combinations results in incredibly lengthy compute times. Instead, there are ways to exclude some key pairs from the beginning. This allows you to drastically reduce the number of comparisons you need to make. Additionally, inexact matching can leverage machine learning techniques which uses human-curated examples to learn to predict whether two rows should be matched with one another.

If this 'more advanced' approach to combining datasets is of interest, I highly suggest looking into the `recordlinkage` Python package.

Further Reading

Much of what I introduce in this chapter is foundational; you'll build on that foundation in later chapters. But if you are looking for a slower and more comprehensive introduction to Pandas and NumPy, then I would recommend VanderPlas's (2016) *Python Data Science Handbook*.

6.9 Conclusion

The key points in this chapter are as follows:

- In this chapter, we expanded into the world of processing structured data using Pandas; these are *critical* skills for computational social scientists.
- We covered the basic Pandas data structures, Series and DataFrames, and the `index` and `datetime` objects.
- We discussed how to subset dataframes by selecting columns and filtering rows, followed by a discussion of how to do systematic comparisons by performing operations on grouped dataframes.
- We then discussed how to combine multiple dataframes using `merge` and `concatenate` and introduced the general idea of record linkage.

Visit the website at https://study.sagepub.com/mclevey for additional resources

7

VISUALIZATION AND EXPLORATORY DATA ANALYSIS

7.1 Learning Objectives

By the end of this chapter, you should be able to do the following:

- Understand the iterative logic of research workflows, specifically 'Box's loop'
- Build an intuitive understanding of what makes for good data visualization
- Explore techniques for visualizing univariate data and distributions
- Explore techniques for exploratory data analysis for multivariate data and distributions

7.2 Learning Materials

You can find the online learning materials for this chapter in `doing_computational_social_science/Chapter_07`. `cd` into the directory and launch your Jupyter server.

7.3 Introduction

In this chapter, we'll continue to build foundational data processing skills by introducing the basics of data visualization and exploratory data analysis (EDA). EDA encompasses a broad range of data processing activities that enable you to get to know your data and to *iteratively* develop, critique, and redevelop formal, statistical, and machine learning models. In other words, EDA and model development are intimately linked in *iterative* workflows. In this chapter and throughout the book, I will emphasize a generic iterative workflow for data analysis and modelling known as 'Box's loop'.

In what follows, we will make extensive use of the Seaborn package (V0.11+), a high-level statistical visualization package built on top of the older and more complex Matplotlib package. Because it's built on top of Matplotlib, you can usually combine Matplotlib code and Seaborn code, which we will occasionally do to take advantage of the low-level capabilities of Matplotlib while working in more user-friendly Seaborn.

7.4 Iterative Research Workflows: EDA and Box's Loop

Traditionally, the term *exploratory data analysis* typically refers to the work you do to explore, examine, clean, and make sense of a dataset prior to any formal, statistical, or machine learning modelling. The idea is that we should get to know our data (i.e. exploration) before getting into any serious modelling (i.e. confirmation). However, it is important to understand that the relationship between 'exploratory' and 'confirmatory' analysis is rarely clear-cut in practice. In fact, many prominent statisticians and social scientists have proposed approaches that explicitly link exploratory and confirmatory approaches. Andrew Gelman (2004), for example, points out that we can think of both approaches as sharing the same underlying logic: learning by comparing what we observe empirically to a set of expectations that come from an *implicit* or *explicit* model. While there are different ways of thinking about EDA, all share the idea that EDA is a crucial component of iteratively developing almost any model, simple or complex, implicit or explicit. Let's briefly consider this framework for thinking about the role of EDA in quantitative and computational research. We will do so using an idealized framework known as Box's loop, first proposed by the statistician George Box.

Let's say we want to better understand the effect of education on attitudes towards vaccination. The first step in Box's loop, before we even load a dataset, is to imagine an initial model. At this point, we are simply (1) clarifying what we want or need to know and (2) thinking through a few ways that we might go about analysing our data to gain some preliminary insights into our research questions. This could be as simple as selecting a few simple statistical visualizations and computing a correlation or two, or it might involve thinking deeply about the processes/mechanisms that might shape attitudes towards vaccination, and the potential relationships between some set of variables that we expect to be important. It can be useful to do this work the old-fashioned way – with pen and paper, or marker and whiteboard – before you write any code. I suggest you do this graphically, writing down the names of variables and drawing arrows between those you think are likely to be associated (perhaps causally) with one another. This visual representation is known as a 'graphical model'; we will discuss them later in the book. Keep your model simple and resist the urge to try to account for *everything* that could be relevant. If you are doing this work prior to data collection, then your initial model should give you some insight into the kind of data you will need to collect, and how you should collect it.

We use this first model to analyse our data in Step 2 with the goal of producing an initial answer to our research question. We critically assess the analysis in Step 3. Does our model make sense? Does it fit the data well? Is there anything surprising? If there is, does it suggest an unforeseen issue with the data? Is it the best answer to our question that we can get? Are there additional factors that should be accounted for? Like the rest of us, you'll typically find your first analysis lacking; that critique is the starting point for the next round of analysis and modelling. It's a 'loop' because this cycle of developing, critiquing, and then redeveloping continues, bit by bit, until we have a model we are satisfied with. At that point, we break the loop.

Remember that your initial model might be as simple as visualizing distributions. Imagine, for example, that we have a continuous measure of support for policies that mandate COVID-19 vaccinations on university campuses that ranges from –1 (strongly against) to 1 (strongly in support). Our initial model in Step 1 may be a simple histogram to visualize the distribution of our support measure. We create that histogram in Step 2 and critique it in Step 3. Perhaps we notice that our support measure has a multi-modal distribution, suggesting that there could be subgroups in our data, each of which has their own central tendency. We use this new information to help develop a new model in Step 4. This new model may also be fairly simple; perhaps we create another histogram, but this time conditioned on some other variable, such as sex, gender identity, race, ethnicity, type or level of education, or whether the participant lives in a rural or urban setting. Or perhaps we decide to fit a more complex model, such as a mixture model (dicussed later in the book). We repeat this process again and again until we are satisfied that we can produce a good answer to our research question, at which point (Step 5) we stop development and apply our final model.

Box's loop is summarized in Figure 7.1. You'll see this loop, or variations of it, repeatedly throughout the rest of the book.

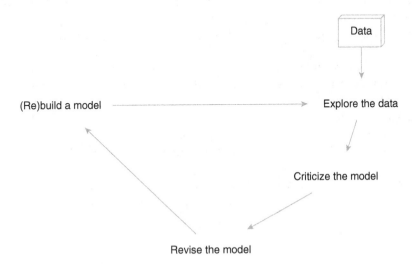

Figure 7.1 Box's loop, showing how to use an iterative approach to modelling and inference

In this chapter, we will work on developing your EDA skills in the more classical sense – the first steps you take with a new dataset – and with a heavy emphasis on visualization. However, as your skills develop chapter by chapter, we will start to use Box's loop to more tightly integrate exploratory analysis and model development. With a bit of experience, you may find yourself further appreciating Gelman's argument that even the most basic EDA work is a kind of implicit modelling, which further tightens the links between the kind of work we will consider here and the more complex statistical and machine learning models we will focus on in later chapters.

EDA is often broken down into graphical and non-graphical methods for analysing single variables (i.e. univariate graphical and univariate non-graphical) and graphical and non-graphical methods for analysing two or more variables (i.e. multivariate graphical and multivariate non-graphical). We will discuss methods within these four categories that can be used for categorical and quantitative data. First, let's discuss visualization *in general* – specifically what differentiates good plots from bad plots and ways to make creating good plots a bit easier.

7.5 Effective Visualization

Guidelines for effective visualization

I'll admit, I'm fastidious when it comes to the aesthetics of data visualization. But when I talk about good visualizations versus bad ones, I'm *not* talking about the fine distinctions between colours or typefaces. You can create good visualizations while being clueless about those things.

No, I'm talking about more fundamental things like knowing what you want to learn or communicate.

Creating graphs to visualize distributions, relationships, and so on, is relatively straight-forward in Python. Creating *good* graphs has little to do with Python and everything to do with the decisions you make about what to show and how to show it. Some of these decisions are high level, like the *kind* of graph and how it should be structured. Other decisions are low level, like selecting colours and shapes. What differentiates a really good visualization from a really bad one is rarely taste. It's almost always the amount of thought behind those fundamental decisions.

As Kieran Healy (2018a) points out, 'bad graphs' tend to be bad for one of three reasons:

1   Aesthetics: there are unnecessary details or modifications (e.g. unnecessary 3D effects, shadows, rotated axes). These 'infographic' visualizations may be memorable but are difficult to interpret correctly. Avoid creating these at all costs. If a collaborator asks you to make one, politely decline.
2   Substantive data problems: the graph looks good and follows best practices, but the data themselves are bad or have been incorrectly processed, sending a misleading message. Avoid this by doing extensive EDA.
3   Being inattentive to the realities of human perception, and therefore making poor visualization choices that may mislead you or your readers.

As I have stressed, effective data visualization requires adopting an *iterative approach*. Start by thinking carefully about what you want to learn (if you're doing EDA) or what you want to com-municate (if you're producing a graph for publication). Try sketching the plot with pen and paper. It refines your thinking before you start coding and helps clarify what *kind* of plot you need.

Once you know what you want and need, *then* you start coding. Again: iterate. Start with the default settings for the kind of plot you want, such as a scatter plot. Then gradually modify the defaults, and add and remove elements, until you have a plot that clearly shows what you want it to show. Work slowly: change one thing at a time.

If you think of visualization as a communication problem, you need to consider the reali-ties of perception and the human vision system. Perception is more complicated than simply creating a 1:1 mental representation of what we are looking at. Think of the many examples of visual effects and optical illusions.

There is a sizeable empirical literature on perception and statistical visualization, largely built on Bill Cleveland's work in the 1980s and 1990s. Psychologists, statisticians, and applied data analysts have documented many specific factors that affect the probability of drawing an incorrect conclusion from a graph. These include the following:

•   Selecting the wrong type of colour palette increases the chance of misperception (e.g. it's diverging when it should be qualitative, it's not colour-blind friendly).
•   Using area or angles to represent important properties increases the chance of misperception because humans are inherently bad at comparing similar angles and areas.
•   Using length and position increase the chance of correct perceptions because humans are good at comparing differences in length and position.

These lead to some useful guidelines. One of the most important, and very easy to implement, comes from knowing we have an easier time perceiving some colours, shapes, and relationships than others. Visualizations that require comparing angles and areas – such as pie charts, bubble charts, and stacked bar charts – are non-starters. Follow this basic rule and you'll avoid plenty of bad and misleading visualizations.

Pie charts are easy to criticize, but are stacked bar charts and bubble charts really all that bad? Yes. With stacked bar charts, each block has a different baseline/starting point in each bar. Given how bad we are at comparing areas, your reader will be more likely to interpret your graph incorrectly. Don't make them. Bubble charts are slightly more complex. Sometimes, it can be effective to change the size of points in a scatter plot, but be careful; you shouldn't expect a reader to perceive small differences between points.

Distances are very important and meaningful in almost all data visualizations. Most of the time, bar graphs and dot plots should have a y-axis that starts at 0, but contrary to common wisdom there are some *rare* cases when this is not the best choice. Generally, default to axes that start at 0 but don't be dogmatic. Again, know exactly what you want to show and why. If you want to be instantly discredited by a quantitatively literate reader, exaggerate differences by manipulating the range of the y-axis. Otherwise, don't do this!

Humans tend to see patterns in data even when these patterns are meaningless. As such, it's usually a mistake to use visualizations without doing some statistical modelling, just as it is a mistake to model your data without visualizing it. Recall Gelman's argument: all EDA is done in reference to an implicit or explicit model. While we won't get into statistical modelling until later in the book, I want to emphasize that you should pursue these two types of analysis simultaneously. In this chapter, we pair visualization with summary statistics that are commonly used in EDA.

In addition, here are some straightforward rules to reduce the chances of creating bad visualizations:

- If you can show what you need to using a type of graph that is widely used and well-understood, do so. Don't invent new graphics for the sake of it. Make it easy for you and your readers to interpret your graphs.
- Less ink is usually better than more ink. Simplify as much as possible, but no more. Find the balance of information density and visual minimalism by working on your visualizations iteratively.
- Avoid 3D (three-dimensional) visualizations of any kind. If you have to add a third dimension, consider using either colour or shape, but not both.
- The dimensions of a line plot have a *huge* effect on our perception of slope/rate of change. Exercise extreme care when selecting the dimensions. *Do not intentionally mislead your readers.*
- Do not vary colour or shape unless you are encoding important information in colours and shapes. A multicoloured bar plot might look nicer than a solid grey, but if the colours aren't meaningful, it dramatically increases the chances of misperception. Readers will always assume differences in colour are meaningful, so don't use different colours unless that is the case.

Finally, ask others to critique your visualizations and practise! Learning any new skill takes time and effort.

Now, let's get into the code!

━━━━━━━━ **Further Reading** ━━━━━━━━

In addition to what's provided here, I suggest reading Healy and Moody (2014) on the state of data visualization in sociology and other social sciences. And though it uses R rather than Python, Healy (2018a) is an outstanding introduction to good data visualization practice.

7.6 Univariate EDA: Describing and Visualizing Distributions

We're going to make use of the VDEM data once again. You should refresh yourself on the data and variables description before proceeding. We will start by reading in the filtered and subsetted dataframe `fsdf` that we produced earlier and saved as a CSV file and get the mean, median, and standard deviation from some of its variables.

Imports

```
import os
import pandas as pd
pd.set_option("display.notebook_repr_html", False)
import numpy as np

import matplotlib as mpl
import matplotlib.pyplot as plt
import seaborn as sns

from dcss.plotting import format_axes_commas, custom_seaborn
custom_seaborn()

fsdf = pd.read_csv('../data/vdem/filtered_subset.csv')
fsdf.shape

(18787, 13)

egal = fsdf['v2x_egaldem']
print(f'Median Egalitarian Democracy Score: {egal.median()}')
print(f'Mean Egalitarian Democracy Score: {egal.mean()}')
print(f'Standard Deviation: {egal.std()}')

Median Egalitarian Democracy Score: 0.142
Mean Egalitarian Democracy Score: 0.2368012609796842
Standard Deviation: 0.23019217079493423
```

Since the values returned from operations on Series are essentially equivalent to a NumPy array, we can use NumPy methods on quantitative Series. For example, here you can use the `round()` method to round these descriptives to a few decimal points:

```
print(f'Median Egalitarian Democracy Score: {round(egal.median(),3)}')
print(f'Mean Egalitarian Democracy Score: {round(egal.mean(), 3)}')
print(f'Standard Deviation: {round(egal.std(), 3)}')
```

```
Median Egalitarian Democracy Score: 0.142
Mean Egalitarian Democracy Score: 0.237
Standard Deviation: 0.23
```

If the Series is categorical, we can also easily compute useful information such as the number of unique categories, the size of each category, and so on. For example, you can use the .unique() method to get a list of the unique countries from the country_name Series. Here these values are cast as a list and sliced to display the first 10 elements.

```
list(fsdf['country_name'].unique())[0:10]
```

```
['Mexico',
 'Suriname',
 'Sweden',
 'Switzerland',
 'Ghana',
 'South Africa',
 'Japan',
 'Burma/Myanmar',
 'Russia',
 'Albania']
```

With a categorical variable like this, you can also use the value_counts() method to see how many observations you have for country_name in the dataset. Since there are 73, you might not want to print everything to screen. Instead, you can just peek at the top 10 and bottom 10 rows.

```
fsdf['country_name'].value_counts().head(10)
```

```
Cuba            120
Cyprus          120
Norway          120
Paraguay        120
South Africa    120
Zanzibar        120
Benin           120
Italy           120
Nepal           120
Mali            120
Name: country_name, dtype: int64
```

```
fsdf['country_name'].value_counts().tail(10)
```

```
Turkmenistan        30
Kyrgyzstan          30
```

```
Tajikistan                    30
Azerbaijan                    30
Kazakhstan                    30
Ukraine                       30
North Macedonia               29
Bosnia and Herzegovina        28
Kosovo                        21
South Sudan                    9
Name: country_name, dtype: int64
```

Visualizing marginal distributions

It's a good idea to visualize distributions for individual variables (i.e. ' marginal distributions') before getting into more complex analyses. As with numerical summaries, graphical approaches to examining distributions will typically answer questions about the range of values, their central tendency, whether they are highly skewed, whether there are potentially influential outliers, and so on.

Count plots and frequency tables for categorical variables

For a single categorical variable, we are limited to examining frequencies, percentages, and proportions. For example, you can visualize the number of countries in each geographical region defined by the United Nations (the e_regiongeo categorical variable) using the .countplot() function. You want the bars in the count plot to be horizontal rather than vertical, so use the argument y='e_regiongeo' instead of x='e_regiongeo'. The code below produces Figure 7.2:

```
ax = sns.countplot(data=fsdf, y='e_regiongeo', color='darkgray')
sns.despine()
plt.show()
```

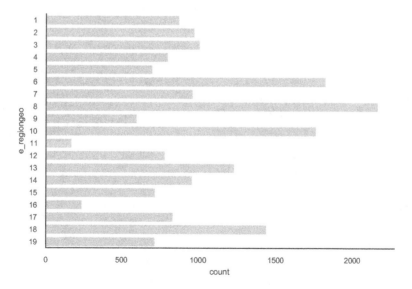

Figure 7.2 A count plot of e_regiongeo

This graph could use some improvements. Let's iterate! First, it would be better if the data were in descending order by counts. Second, it would be better if it had region names rather than number IDs. Third, a few small aesthetic adjustments would improve the overall look of the graph, like removing the black line on the left side of the graph.

It is best to address these issues one at a time. First, let's deal with the order issue, which can be solved by using the `order` argument for `.countplot()`. The code below orders the bars by sorting the `fsdf['e_regiongeo']` Series, and produces Figure 7.3:

```
ax = sns.countplot(data=fsdf, y='e_regiongeo', color='darkgray',
                   order = fsdf['e_regiongeo'].value_counts().index)
sns.despine()
ax.set(xlabel='Number of Observations', ylabel='Geographic Region')
plt.show()
```

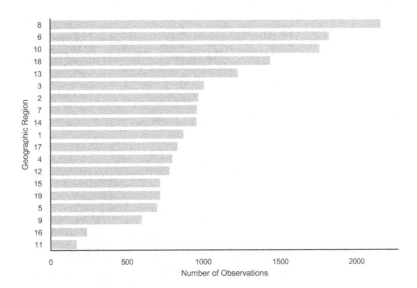

Figure 7.3 A count plot of `e_regiongeo`, ordered by frequency

Let's replace the numerical region IDs with a string ID. The dictionary below is the mapping between IDs (keys) and the region strings (values) provided in the VDEM codebook:

```
region_strings = {
    1: "Western Europe",
    2: "Northern Europe",
    3: "Southern Europe",
    4: "Eastern Europe",
    5: "Northern Africa",
    6: "Western Africa",
    7: "Middle Africa",
    8: "Eastern Africa",
    9: "Southern Africa",
```

```
    10: "Western Asia",
    11: "Central Asia",
    12: "East Asia",
    13: "South-East Asia",
    14: "South Asia",
    15: "Oceania", # (including Australia and the Pacific)
    16: "North America",
    17: "Central America",
    18: "South America",
    19: "Caribbean" # (including Belize, Cuba, Haiti, Dominican Republic and Guyana)
}
```

You can now use a Pandas method called .replace() to replace each numerical ID with the string representation:

```
fsdf.replace({'e_regiongeo': region_strings}, inplace=True)
```

inplace=True changes the values in the original dataframe. If you create the same count plot again, the region names will be used as the labels on the *y*-axis. The code below produces Figure 7.4:

```
ax = sns.countplot(data=fsdf, y='e_regiongeo', color='darkgray',
                   order = fsdf['e_regiongeo'].value_counts().index) # orders the bars
sns.despine(left=True)
ax.set(xlabel='Number of Observations', ylabel='')
ax.xaxis.set_major_formatter(mpl.ticker.StrMethodFormatter('{x:,.0f}')) # comma
    formats x-axis
plt.show()
```

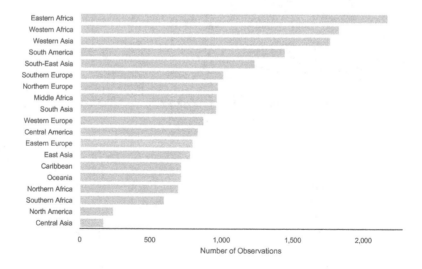

Figure 7.4 A count plot of e_regiongeo, ordered by frequency, with value labels

We can easily produce frequency tables with Pandas; in fact, we have already done this using .value_counts() at the country level. The code below creates a frequency table for the same data you just plotted:

```
fsdf['e_regiongeo'].value_counts()
```

```
Eastern Africa      2166
Western Africa      1824
Western Asia        1762
South America       1440
South-East Asia     1231
Southern Europe     1011
Northern Europe      975
Middle Africa        966
South Asia           962
Western Europe       876
Central America      837
Eastern Europe       802
East Asia            784
Caribbean            720
Oceania              720
Northern Africa      700
Southern Africa      600
North America        240
Central Asia         171
Name: e_regiongeo, dtype: int64
```

Univariate histograms and density estimation

When working with continuous variables, it is common to use histograms to visualize how the data is distributed and where it clusters. As a reminder, histograms are a kind of bar chart, where the x-axis contains the range of all values for a particular variable and the y-axis indicates a count of the number of observations. In other words, the height of each bar represents the number of observations of x values between the left and right boundaries of each bar. Histograms are generally a more easily digestible summary of a variable than the .describe() method used earlier.

Let's use Seaborn's histplot() to create a histogram of the Egalitarian Democracy Index variable from the fsdf dataframe. The code below produces Figure 7.5:

```
ax = sns.histplot(data=fsdf, x='v2x_egaldem')
sns.despine(left=True, right=True, top=True)
ax.set(xlabel='Egalitarian Democracy Index', ylabel='Count')
ax.yaxis.set_major_formatter(mpl.ticker.StrMethodFormatter('{x:,.0f}'))
plt.show()
```

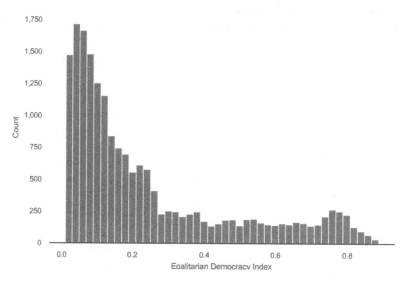

Figure 7.5 A histogram of `v2x_egaldem`

The histogram clearly shows that most of the `v2x_egaldem` values in the dataset can be found at the lower end of the range, quickly sloping down and then evening out with a few gentle peaks. Note that the function has made an important decision implicitly – we didn't specify the number of bins, so it used a built-in method that provides generally good defaults. However, you should always double-check the default parameters. Overly wide bins can 'hide' peaks or troughs in the distribution if they fit entirely inside a bin. Overly narrow bins can produce visualizations that are especially sensitive to 'noise'. Narrower bins will tend to result in graphs with sharper spikes as small clusters and gaps get magnified.

You can manually check for these cases by providing explicit values to the `bins` or `binwidth` parameters. Below, I provide extreme examples of overly wide and narrow bins to highlight the issues with both. The code below produces Figure 7.6:

```
ax = sns.histplot(data=fsdf, x='v2x_egaldem', bins=3)
sns.despine(left=True, right=True, top=True)
ax.set(xlabel='Egalitarian Democracy Index', ylabel='Count')
ax.yaxis.set_major_formatter(mpl.ticker.StrMethodFormatter('{x:,.0f}'))
plt.show()
```

The code below produces Figure 7.7:

```
ax = sns.histplot(data=fsdf, x='v2x_egaldem', binwidth = 0.001)
sns.despine(left=True, right=True, top=True)
ax.set(xlabel='Egalitarian Democracy Index', ylabel='Count')
ax.yaxis.set_major_formatter(mpl.ticker.StrMethodFormatter('{x:,.0f}'))
plt.show()
```

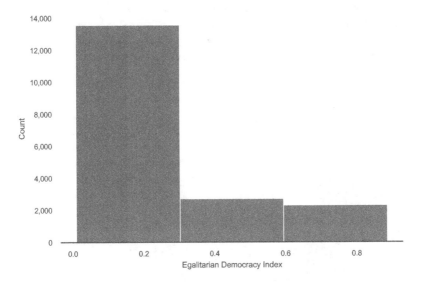

Figure 7.6 A histogram of `v2x_egaldem` with extremely wide bins

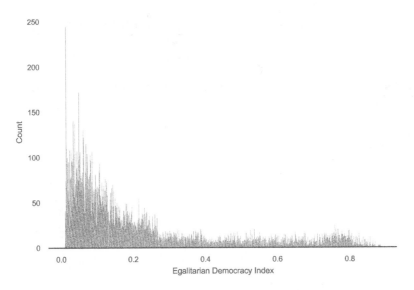

Figure 7.7 A histogram of `v2x_egaldem` with extremely narrow bins

We can also use kernel density estimation (KDE) to visualize a distribution. KDE is a classical technique for estimating the probability density function of a random variable. Rather than visualizing the raw counts in combined bins, it estimates the probability of every possible value using a smooth function. KDE attempts to reduce the random noise in the data, smoothing out the spikes.

You can add a KDE line to histograms by providing the parameter `kde = True`. The code below produces Figure 7.8:

```
ax = sns.histplot(data=fsdf, x='v2x_egaldem', kde=True)
sns.despine(left=True, right=True, top=True)
ax.set(xlabel='Egalitarian Democracy Index', ylabel='Count')
ax.yaxis.set_major_formatter(mpl.ticker.StrMethodFormatter('{x:,.0f}'))
plt.show()
```

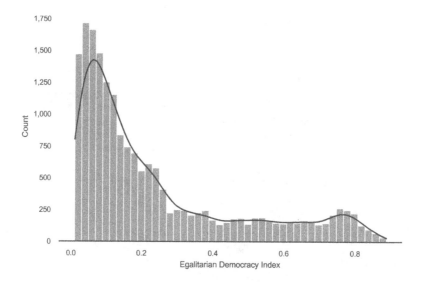

Figure 7.8 A histogram of `v2x_egaldem` with kernel density estimation overlaid

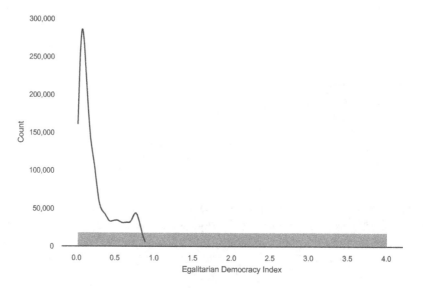

Figure 7.9 A histogram of `v2x_egaldem` with a preposterously wide bin which covers the entire dataset; the kernel density estimation from Figure 7.8 remains

Seaborn provides a large number of ways to customize and refine your visualizations. However, with great power comes great responsibility. In this case, you are responsible for creating visualizations that make sense; the package will not stop you from making mistakes. Consider the previous histogram with `binwidth=4`. The entire range of `v2x_egaldem` is less than 1. The visualization is technically possible, but obviously useless. I left the KDE line to help keep track of where the data actually is. The code below produces Figure 7.9:

```
ax = sns.histplot(fsdf['v2x_egaldem'], kde=True, binwidth=4)
sns.despine(left=True, right=True, top=True)
ax.set(xlabel='Egalitarian Democracy Index', ylabel='Count')
ax.yaxis.set_major_formatter(mpl.ticker.StrMethodFormatter('{x:,.0f}'))
plt.show()
```

Marginal empirical cumulative distributions

Empirical cumulative distributions (ECDs) combine several of the advantages of the previously described visualizations. Unlike histograms, you do not need to bin your data because every data point is represented. This makes it easy to assess the shape of the distribution. For example, one can easily visually identify the five-number summary. Finally, they make it much easier to compare multiple distributions.

Plotting empirical cumulative distributions

To visualize an ECD, set one axis to be the variable of interest. The second axis represents the proportion of observations that have a value equal to or lower than a given cut-off point. Consider a five-number summary: the minimum value; the first, second, and third quartiles; and the maximum value. If a point on an ECD represents a value of our variable and the proportion of observations with equal or lower value, the minimum value must be given by the very first point: the lowest, and leftmost point on the plot. The first quartile is necessarily found at the point where proportion equals 0.25. The second quartile is where proportion equals 0.50, and so on for the third quartile and the maximum value. Since the proportion axis captures each observation and all lower-valued ones, proportion can never decrease as the variable increases.

Unfortunately, ECDs are less common than point or box-based visualization techniques, so we have less experience reading them. Like all skills, though, it can be developed with time and practice. Most importantly, you can think of the slope of the line as telling you where data is clustered. A steep slope indicates a large portion of the data is clustered around those values. Consider the ECD of `v2x_egaldem`. The code below produces Figure 7.10:

```
ax = sns.displot(fsdf, x="v2x_egaldem", kind="ecdf", color='darkgray')
sns.despine()
ax.set(xlabel='Egalitarian Democracy Index')
plt.xlim(0, 1)
plt.show()
```

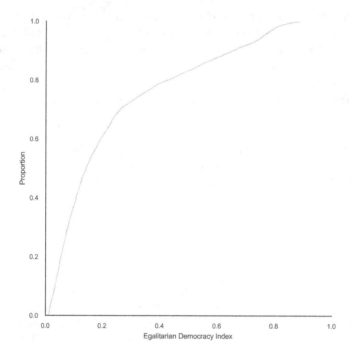

Figure 7.10 A plot of the empirical cumulative distribution for `v2x_egaldem`

The slope shows us that proportion rises very rapidly between `v2x_egaldem` values of 0.0 and 0.2. Much of the data is clustered in that area, and the slope slowly tapers off afterwards, telling us the same thing we saw in the histogram: the number of observations decreases as `v2x_egaldem` increases, with a slight blip around 0.75.

Histograms, KDE, and ECDs have different strengths and weaknesses; each makes some things easier to see and others harder. I advise you to use all three types when exploring your data.

7.7 Multivariate Eda

Visualizing conditional distributions

Sometimes we might want to visualize a variable of interest conditioned on another variable. Perhaps we want to visualize only those instances of a variable X that are associated with a particular value of Y.

Conditional histograms

Let's visualize the egalitarian index of countries, conditioned on whether the country is a democracy or not. A conditional distribution will exclude any observations that do not meet the condition, so for completeness we can visualize both cases separately, side by side.

The `displot` function allows us to visualize univariate (a single variable) or bivariate (two variables) data distributions across multiple subplots. Below, we will create a visualization that displays a `v2x_egaldem` histogram for each value of `e_boix_regime`, a binary variable. Thus, when we give the column parameter `col` the values for `e_boix_regime`, we should get two columns, one for each value it can take. The code below produces Figure 7.11:

```
ax = sns.displot(fsdf, x="v2x_egaldem", col="e_boix_regime", multiple="dodge")
ax.set(xlabel='Egalitarian Democracy Index')
plt.show()
```

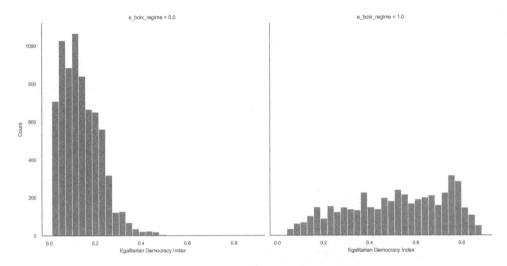

Figure 7.11 Two conditional histograms of `v2x_egaldem`; the left is for `e_boix_regime` = 0, the other for `e_boix_regime` = 1

The results are the two conditional distribution histograms in Figure 7.11. If you were to add the two together, you would get the original `v2x_egaldem` marginal distribution histogram we produced earlier. While this method makes very clean graphs, it can be hard to compare the graphs, especially if you want to graph many different conditions. One way around this would be to plot both conditional distributions on the same plot, but colour them differently and make them slightly transparent. We can do this by passing `e_boix_regime` to the hue parameter, rather than `col`. The code below produces Figure 7.12:

```
grayscale_cmap = sns.cubehelix_palette(50, hue=0.05, rot=0, light=0.9, dark=0, as_cmap
    =True)
```

```
ax = sns.displot(fsdf, x="v2x_egaldem", hue="e_boix_regime", palette=grayscale_cmap)
ax.set(xlabel='Egalitarian Democracy Index')
plt.show()
```

This plot makes it much easier to compare the two distributions, and we can clearly see where they overlap and where they don't. However, it adds visual clutter and can quickly become hard to read as more conditions are added. This is one reason why it is good to develop your visualizations iteratvely.

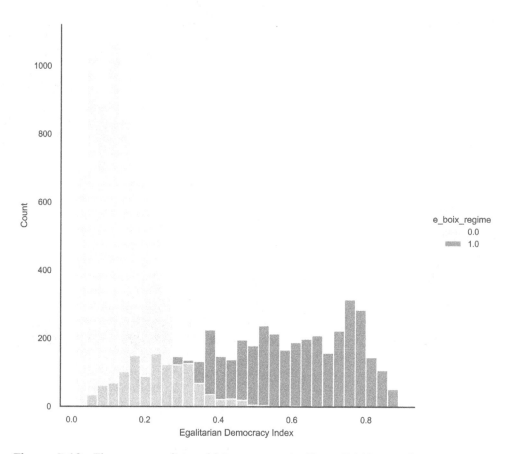

Figure 7.12 The same conditional histograms as in Figure 7.11 but with some different aesthetics

Conditional KDE

As before, we can add KDEs to existing histograms by passing kde = True, or we may visualize just the KDE to reduce visual clutter by passing kind = "kde". The code below produces Figure 7.13:

```
ax = sns.displot(fsdf, x="v2x_egaldem", hue="e_boix_regime", kde = True, palette=
    grayscale_cmap)
ax.set(xlabel='Egalitarian Democracy Index')
plt.show()
```

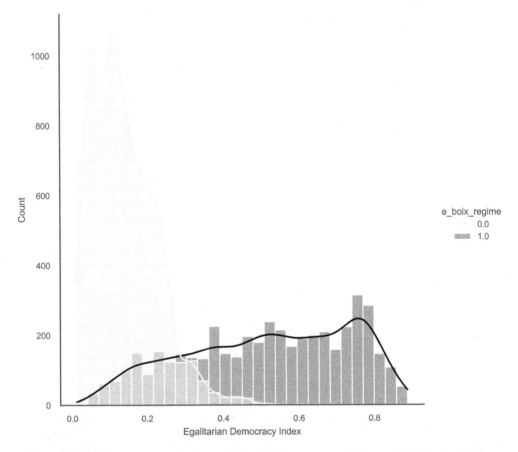

Figure 7.13 The same overlaid conditional histograms as in Figure 7.12, but with the addition of the conditional kernel density estimations for both

The code below produces Figure 7.14:

```
ax = sns.displot(fsdf, x="v2x_egaldem", hue="e_boix_regime", kind = "kde", palette=
    cmap)
ax.set(xlabel='Egalitarian Democracy Index')
plt.show()
```

In all of these plots, countries with a value of 1.0 for e_boix_regime are electoral democracies. Those with 0.0 are not. The comparative plots we have been creating show, unsurprisingly, that non-democratic countries tend to have lower scores on the Egalitarian Democracy Index.

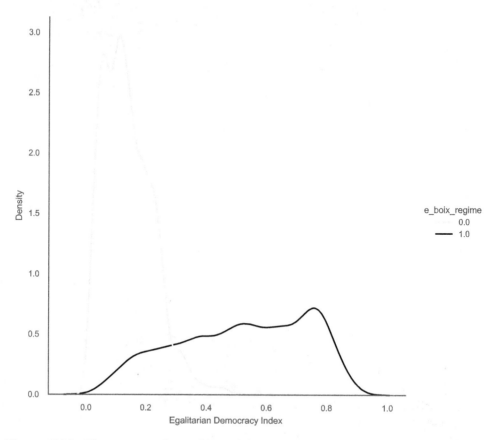

Figure 7.14 The same conditional kernel density estimations as in Figure 7.13, but with underlying histograms removed

Conditional ECDs

Extending an ECD to conditional distributions is as easy as passing e_boix_regime to the hue parameter. Consider the previous example of plotting the histograms of v2x_egaldem conditioned on e_boix_regime. Histograms involve a lot of 'ink', resulting in a lot of visual clutter compared to ECDs, and get hard to read very quickly as the number of conditions increases. The code below produces Figure 7.15:

```
ax = sns.displot(fsdf, x="v2x_egaldem", kind = "ecdf",
                 hue="e_boix_regime", palette=grayscale_cmap)
sns.despine()
ax.set(xlabel='Egalitarian Democracy Index')
plt.xlim(0, 1)
plt.show()
```

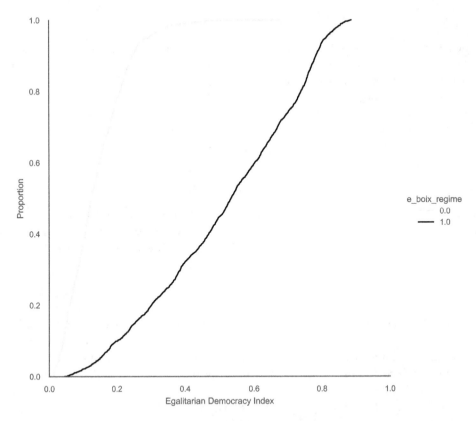

Figure 7.15 Two conditional empirical cumulative distribution plots of `v2x_egaldem`; the left is for `e_boix_regime = 0`, the other for `e_boix_regime = 1`

We can see from the slope for `e_boix_regime = 0.0` (non-democratic countries) that observations are clustered towards the lower values of `v2x_egaldem`, and they very rapidly taper off. The maximum value can be found around `v2x_egaldem = 0.5`. Conversely, the slope for `e_boix_regime = 1.0` (democratic countries) is more gradual, telling us that the distribution is much more evenly distributed across all values, with a few spikes where the slope increases around 0.55 and 0.75. If we look back at the histograms, we can confirm that the visualizations agree with one another.

Visualizing joint distributions

While the marginal and conditional distributions of the earlier section are useful for understanding the shape of our data, we often want to examine the relationships between variables. We can visually represent these relationships by visualizing *joint* distributions. Let's first look at two of the most common ways of visualizing joint distributions: cross tables for categorical variables and scatter plots for continuous variables.

Cross tables

When we want to visualize the joint distribution of two categorical variables we can produce a cross table: an extension of a frequency table. A cross table, sometimes shortened to crosstab, shows a grid, with the possible values of one categorical variable along one axis and the same for the other variable along the other axis. Each cell in the grid shows the number of observations that have *both* (hence joint) categorical variable values corresponding to its row and column.

Let's create a cross table using the `.crosstab()` function for the categorical variables `e_regiongeo` and `e_boix_regime`. The resulting table will tell us how many observations (country–year combinations) there are of each regime type for each geographic region.

```
ct = pd.crosstab(fsdf.e_regiongeo, fsdf.e_boix_regime)
```

If we want to know how many non-democratic countries there were in Western Europe across all years in the VDEM dataset, we would look at the corresponding row and inspect the 0 columns (non-democratic), which shows 110. The number of democratic observations, 703, is shown in the 1 column.

Scatter plots

A scatter plot shows the relationship between two variables by plotting each observation on a graph, where the *x*-axis represents the value of one variable and the *y*-axis represents the value of the other. Let's use the `scatterplot` function to plot the relationship between the egalitarian democracy and polyarchy indices. The code below produces Figure 7.16:

```
ax = sns.scatterplot(data = fsdf, x="v2x_egaldem", y="v2x_polyarchy")
sns.despine()
ax.set(xlabel='Egalitarian Democracy Index', ylabel='Polyarchy Index')
plt.xlim(0, 1)
plt.ylim(0, 1)
plt.show()
```

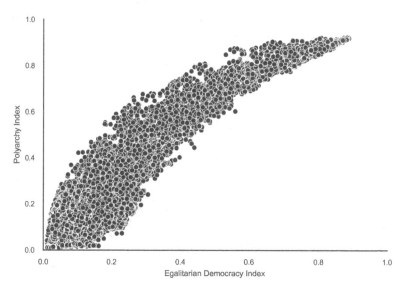

Figure 7.16 A scatter plot of `v2x_egaldem` and `v2x_polyarchy`

At first glance, this seems to suggest a non-linear, but definitely positive relationship between the two variables. If an observation has a high value for one of the two variables, the other is also high. At lower values, the relationship is a bit less tight where we can see the points are less densely clustered, but the overall pattern remains visible. We can use different alpha (transparency) values to see where overlapping points are obscuring underlying points. The code below produces Figure 7.17:

```
ax = sns.scatterplot(data = fsdf, x="v2x_egaldem", y="v2x_polyarchy", alpha = 0.1)
sns.despine()
ax.set(xlabel='Egalitarian Democracy Index', ylabel='Polyarchy Index')
plt.xlim(0, 1)
plt.ylim(0, 1)
plt.show()
```

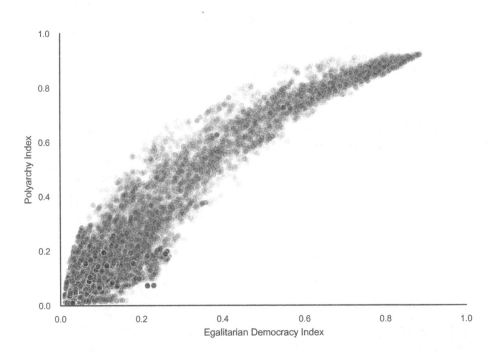

Figure 7.17 A scatter plot of `v2x_egaldem` and `v2x_polyarchy`, but with a modest transparency setting, which provides a better sense of the data's distribution

The code below produces Figure 7.18:

```
ax = sns.scatterplot(data = fsdf, x="v2x_egaldem", y="v2x_polyarchy", alpha = 0.01)
sns.despine()
ax.set(xlabel='Egalitarian Democracy Index', ylabel='Polyarchy Index')
plt.xlim(0, 1)
plt.ylim(0, 1)
plt.show()
```

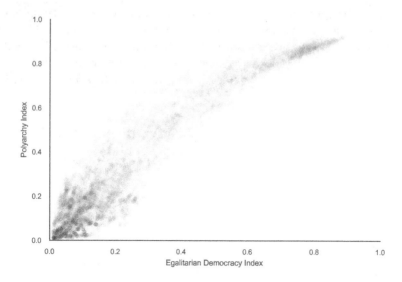

Figure 7.18 The same scatter plot as in Figure 7.17, but with a suspiciously low `alpha` argument, which renders most of the data points nearly invisible

Bivariate histograms

We can extend the idea of histograms to bivariate visualizations. To do so, we divide both the *x*- and *y*-axes into bins, producing square bins. The square bins are coloured based on the number of observations within each box. Since our *y*-axis is now being used to define another dimension of the box, we use colour instead of bar height to indicate how densely observations are clustered within a bin. The code below produces Figure 7.19:

```
ax = sns.displot(fsdf, x="v2x_egaldem", y="v2x_polyarchy")
sns.despine()
ax.set(xlabel='Egalitarian Democracy Index', ylabel='Polyarchy Index')
plt.xlim(0, 1)
plt.ylim(0, 1)
plt.show()
```

Upon inspection, the majority of observations can be found clustering around low values of `v2x_polyarchy` and `v2x_egaldem`. There appears to be another, less dense cluster at the top right portion of the distribution as well.

Like univariate histograms, we can refine our visualization by explicitly setting parameter values, like `binwidth`. We can even provide a further layer of information by including a rug plot, which acts like a one-dimensional scatter plot for each axis. For visualizations with lots of data, use alpha values to avoid solid black bars as shown in Figure 7.20. The code below produces Figure 7.20:

```
ax = sns.displot(fsdf, x="v2x_egaldem", y="v2x_polyarchy", binwidth = 0.01,
rug=True)
sns.despine()
ax.set(xlabel='Egalitarian Democracy Index', ylabel='Polyarchy Index')
plt.xlim(0, 1)
plt.ylim(0, 1)
plt.show()
```

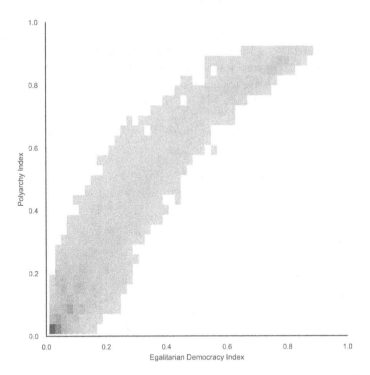

Figure 7.19 A bivariate histogram of `v2x_egaldem` and `v2x_polyarchy`; this plot uses the default bin width

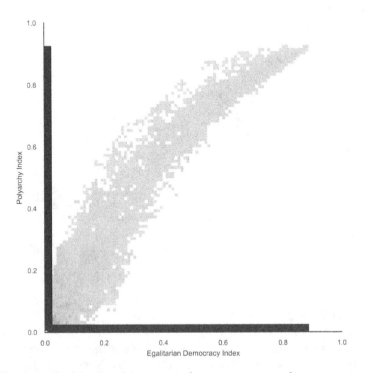

Figure 7.20 A similar bivariate histogram of `v2x_egaldem` and `v2x_polyarchy` with the addition of an unreadable rug plot; this plot uses a much smaller bin width than that in Figure 7.19

Bivariate kernel density estimation

Like histograms, we can also use KDE to smooth the bins to give an idea of the underlying probability distribution. In this case, it takes the form of a 2D contour plot. Let's also improve the appearance of the rug plot by providing rug_kws with a dictionary describing values for its parameters: in this case setting an alpha of 0.01. The code below produces Figure 7.21:

```
ax = sns.displot(fsdf, x="v2x_egaldem", y="v2x_polyarchy", kind="kde", rug = True,
    rug_kws = {"alpha": 0.01})
sns.despine()
ax.set(xlabel='Egalitarian Democracy Index', ylabel='Polyarchy Index')
plt.show()
```

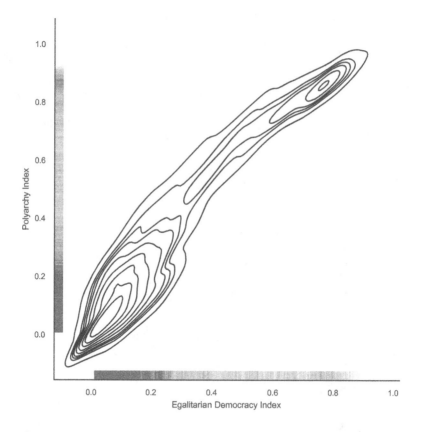

Figure 7.21 A bivariate kernel density estimation plot of v2x_egaldem and v2x_polyarchy

If you are familiar with reading contour maps, many closely spaced lines indicate areas of rapid change in elevation, or in this case, density. The slopes of our ECD plots are analogous to the slopes described by contour plots. Looking at the above visualization, we can see two major clusters: one at the lower left and a smaller, but still significant, one in the upper right.

The line of best fit

The visualizations in this section try to strike a balance between showing as much of the data as possible while conveying the relationship between the two variables as simply as possible. These two goals are in tension with each other, as plots become more complex the more data we attempt to visualize. One way of displaying the relationship between two variables as simply as possible is to fit a regression line to a scatter plot. We could draw a wide variety of different lines, of course; the 'line of best fit' is the line that minimizes the distance between itself and each observation.

The 'line of best fit' is very closely tied to Frequentist regression analysis, which differs from the Bayesian approach to regression models that I will emphasize later in the book. For now, we can think of the line of best fit as a simple way of describing a linear relationship between two variables using the formula for a straight line:

$$y = mx + b$$

Scatter plots display the data in great detail, while the line of best fit portrays a potential linear relationship between our two variables very concisely. Together, they can tell us quite a lot about our data. Let's reproduce the earlier scatter plot with a line of best fit. To do this, we will use the `regplot` function. The code below produces Figure 7.22:

```
ax = sns.regplot(data = fsdf, x = "v2x_egaldem", y = "v2x_polyarchy", color='darkgray'
    , scatter_kws = {"alpha": 0.05}, line_kws={"color": "black"})
sns.despine()
ax.set(xlabel='Egalitarian Democracy Index', ylabel='Polyarchy Index')
plt.show()
```

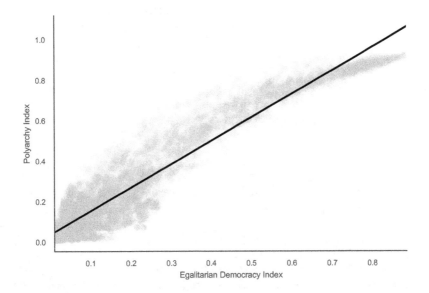

Figure 7.22 A regression plot (or line of best fit plot) of `v2x_egaldem` and `v2x_polyarchy`

Correlation

As with the line of best fit and many of the graphs introduced in this chapter, I assume you already have some baseline knowledge of correlation; still, let's briefly cover the basics. Correlation is a measure of the linear relationship, or dependency, between two variables. If two variables have a strong linear relationship – in other words if there is a high degree of dependence among them – then we can use the values of one variable to predict the values of the other. Correlation describes the standardized direction of a linear relationship between variables as well as the strength of that relationship. Correlation coefficients range between –1 and +1, with a coefficient of 1 representing a perfectly linear dependent relationship for any two variables. A coefficient of –1 also represents a perfectly linearly dependent relationship, but in the opposite direction.

Let's calculate some correlations. To do so, we call .corr() on a variable and pass another of equal length as an argument:

```
corr_libdem_partipdem = fsdf.v2x_libdem.corr(fsdf.v2x_partipdem)
corr_libdem_year = fsdf.v2x_libdem.corr(fsdf.year)

print(f'Correlation of v2x_libdem and v2x_partipdem: {corr_libdem_partipdem}')
print(f'Correlation of v2x_libdem and year: {corr_libdem_year}')

Correlation of v2x_libdem and v2x_partipdem: 0.9699497043536189
Correlation of v2x_libdem and year: 0.3827966897553837
```

Note that here we access dataframe columns by name using 'dot notation' rather than the square brackets we used earlier. I'm not trying to confuse you here! Both methods see frequent use, so it's a good idea to get used to seeing them as largely interchangeable.

While the maths behind correlation coefficients is beyond the scope of this chapter, it's useful to have an idea of what I mean when I say that it is *standardized* and what a *linear relationship* actually means. To demonstrate, let's create a new variable that is just year multiplied by 100 and correlate that with v2x_libdem like we did in the previous cell:

```
df_new = fsdf.copy()
df_new['year_x100'] = fsdf['year'].apply(lambda x: x*100)

new_corr_libdem_partipdem = df_new.v2x_libdem.corr(df_new.v2x_partipdem)
new_corr_libdem_year = df_new.v2x_libdem.corr(df_new.year_x100)

print(f'Correlation of v2x_libdem and v2x_partipdem: {new_corr_libdem_partipdem}')
print(f'Correlation of v2x_libdem and year*100: {new_corr_libdem_year}')

Correlation of v2x_libdem and v2x_partipdem: 0.9699497043536189
Correlation of v2x_libdem and year*100: 0.3827966897553833
```

The correlation remains the same, despite multiplying one of the variables by 100. This is because the correlation coefficient is defined so that its value will always be between –1 and 1. As for linear relationships, recall the line of best fit in a scatter plot. If we plot observations of two variables, the strength of the linear relationship between the two is how closely those points lie on a straight line. If you can draw a straight line through every single point, the two variables have a perfect linear relationship. When we multiplied year by 100, all we did was change the angle of the line; we did not change the direction of the relationship, or the strength of it, so the correlation coefficient remains the same.

Just as there are different kinds of data, there are different ways of calculating correlation coefficients. We have been using Pearson's correlation coefficient so far; it's the default in Pandas .corr() method. This is not the only option. One of the most common alternatives to Pearson's correlation, Spearman's correlation, is intended for use with rank data, where a variable has some order, but the distance between values is not necessarily consistent. Consider a sprint; we know the first-place runner finished before the second-place runner, but we might not know by how much. The distance between first and second could be very different from the distance between second and third place. To calculate the Spearman rank-order correlation coefficient in Pandas, we simply provide the .corr() function with the appropriate method parameter.

Correlation matrices and heat maps

Sometimes we want to look at all the pairwise relationships between variables in a dataset. We could calculate a correlation coefficient for each pair of variables but it's more efficient to create a correlation matrix and visualize the results. A correlation matrix provides the correlation coefficient for every pair of variables in an $n \times n$ table, where n is the number of variables.

To create a correlation matrix, we need to select only the appropriate columns. In this case, we will use Pearson's correlation coefficient to look at the relationships between each pair of continuous variables in our data. Previously, we used the .corr() method to calculate the correlation between two columns. If we use it on a dataframe without specifying any columns, it will produce a correlation matrix for all possible pairings of our variables.

```
fsdf_corr = fsdf[['v2x_polyarchy', 'v2x_libdem', 'v2x_partipdem', 'v2x_delibdem', '
    v2x_egaldem']].corr()
```

Note the diagonal line of 1s arranged from top left to bottom right. Any variable correlated with itself should provide a coefficient of 1: a variable will always be perfectly associated with itself. Secondly, the coefficients are mirrored across the diagonal. The coefficient for the v2x_pol-yarchy row and the v2x_libdem column is the same as the one for the v2x_libdem row and the v2x_polyarchy column. Pearson's correlation is commutative, so $corr(X,Y) = corr(Y,X)$.

We can also create a heat map to help us scan the data quickly for correlations that especially stand out. The code below produces Figure 7.23. Unlike me, you have more colour options. I would recommend using a colour palette other than greyscale.

```
ax = sns.heatmap(data = fsdf_corr, vmin = 0.9, vmax = 1, cmap=grayscale_cmap)
plt.show()
```

First, note the scale. While scales should typically start at 0, the values are highly clustered at top of the range, and *what I want to learn* is which correlations stand out from the others. If I included the whole scale, each box would be a nearly identical colour. Guidelines can help you make decisions about visualizations, but they can't replace thinking about what you're doing and why.

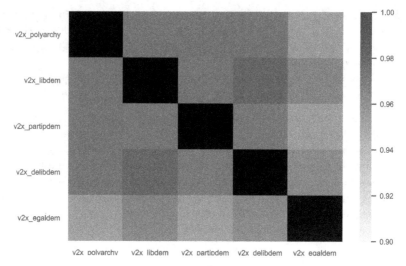

Figure 7.23 A heat map showing the covariance between each pairwise combination of the five high-level indices from the VDEM dataset

To create a heat map that doesn't duplicate data and is less cluttered, we can use a 'mask' to cover up the upper triangle. The code below produces Figure 7.24:

```
mask = np.triu(np.ones_like(fsdf_corr, dtype = bool))
ax = sns.heatmap(fsdf_corr, mask = mask, vmin = 0.9,
                 vmax = 1, cmap=grayscale_cmap)
plt.show()
```

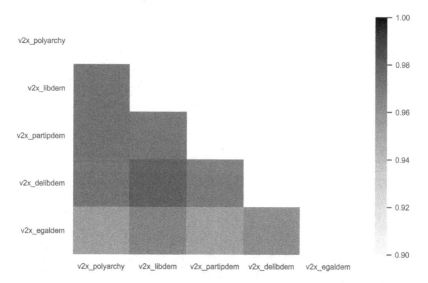

Figure 7.24 A heat map showing the covariance between each pairwise combination of the five high-level indices from the VDEM dataset, omitting diagonal and upper triangular cells

Visualization with more informational density

I've mentioned that good visualization practice involves thinking about what to display. That requires exercising restraint regarding what you add to a graph. Less is *usually*, but not always, more. Sometimes we find ourselves in situations where the best option is to layer several simple visualizations together in ways that substantially increase the overall information density of a visualization while still keeping things as simple as possible. This is often preferable to, for example, generating a large number of separate graphs that you, or a reader, would have to consult simultaneously to learn from. Again, think about what *exactly* you are trying to learn or show, and construct a visualization for that purpose and no other.

The two primary examples of more informationally dense visualizations we will consider here are (1) graphs that combine marginal and joint distributions, and (2) small multiples and pair plots. We will only briefly introduce these visualizations here.

Layering marginal and joint distributions

Previously, we have occasionally combined different distributions or visualizations in the same plot. We plotted conditional histograms together, histograms with KDEs, scatter plots with lines of best fit and rug plots, and so on. This time, let's focus on supplementing a scatter plot with histograms and KDE to visualize the marginal distributions of each variable in the joint distribution. The code below produces Figure 7.25:

```
ax = sns.jointplot(data=fsdf, x="v2x_polyarchy", y="v2x_egaldem", kind="reg", color='
    darkgray',
               joint_kws={'line_kws':{'color':'black'},
                      'scatter_kws':{'alpha':0.03}})
```

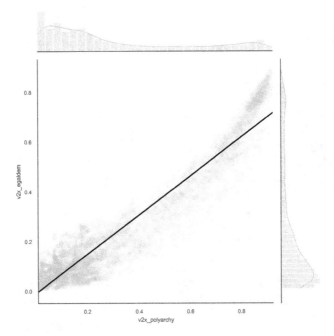

Figure 7.25 A joint plot of `v2x_egaldem` and `v2x_polyarchy` including kernel density estimations, histograms, scatter plot, and line of best fit

The above visualization provides us with a wealth of information, letting us see individual points as well as the relationship between the two variables with the joint distribution. The marginal distributions show us the observed distributions and an estimate of the underlying probability distribution.

Quick comparisons with pair plots

Rather than choosing which variables to plot against each other, we can use the `pairplot` function to produce a grid of scatter plots, pairing every variable against every other variable. Where a variable would be paired with itself (the diagonal of the grid), we instead get a histogram of the marginal distribution of that variable. A `pairplot` is a great way to get a sense of your data before letting theory and research questions guide more focused analysis and visualization. The code opposite produces Figure 7.26:

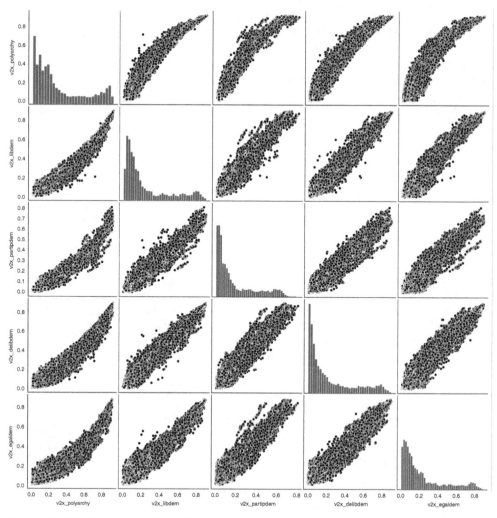

Figure 7.26   A pair plot of the five high-level indices from the VDEM dataset

```
high_level_indexes = ['v2x_polyarchy', 'v2x_libdem', 'v2x_partipdem', 'v2x_delibdem',
    'v2x_egaldem']
ax = sns.pairplot(fsdf[high_level_indexes])
plt.show()
```

In later chapters, we will often produce 'small multiples' that have a structured subplot design like the pair plots. We will set that aside until later, however.

Further Reading

In addition to being a good introduction to Pandas and NumPy, VanderPlas's (2016) Python Data Science Handbook contains a good introduction to Matplotlib, which Seaborn is built on top of. Regrettably, I don't have space to get into Matplotlib in this book, but it's a *very* powerful package. We use little bits of Matplotlib code to supplement Seaborn in this book. If you want to take more control over the aesthetics of your plots, it's well worth learning more about Matplotlib.

7.8 Conclusion

The key points in this chapter are as follows:

- This chapter introduced the concept of EDA and iterative research workflows in general, and introduced Box's loop as a specific approach to EDA that is commonly used in computational social science.
- We explored some basic guidelines for creating effective visualizations.
- We applied those guidelines to univariate and multivariate data drawn from a large and complex real-world dataset.

Visit the website at https://study.sagepub.com/mclevey for additional resources

8

LATENT FACTORS AND COMPONENTS

8.1 Learning Objectives

By the end of this chapter, you should be able to do the following:

- Explain what latent variables, components, dimensions, and clusters are
- Explain what the 'curse of dimensionality' is and why it matters in computational social science
- Explain what dimensionality reduction methods are and describe the basic logic of linear dimensionality reduction using theory-driven approaches (exploratory factor analysis) and data-driven approaches (principal component analysis)
- Perform linear dimensionality reduction using principal component analysis

8.2 Learning Materials

You can find the online learning materials for this chapter in `doing_computational_social_science/Chapter_08`. `cd` into the directory and launch your Jupyter server.

8.3 Introduction

This chapter introduces additional methods for exploratory data analysis and inductive discovery. You may have encountered them previously when learning multivariate statistics. In machine learning, these methods are typically referred to as 'unsupervised' because we discover and interpret latent patterns in the data *inductively*, but for now, you can think of them as a form of multivariate exploratory data analysis.

We will begin with an introduction to the idea of latent variables: abstract constructs that we cannot actually observe. In this chapter, we will distinguish between two main ways of dealing with this problem: factor analysis (FA) for theory-driven efforts to measure latent variables, and principal component analysis (PCA) for data-driven efforts to mitigate the 'curse of dimensionality', facilitate more inductive and interpretive work, and improve the quality of downstream analyses. Latent variables is a major theme in this book; you'll learn other ways of thinking about, and working with, latent variables in later chapters.

Imports and data preparation

We will make extensive use of the Sklearn package in this chapter. Sklearn is very important and widely used in machine learning, and it features heavily in the rest of this book. Some of the methods we introduce here are also implemented in other Python packages, including Statsmodels, which implements a wide variety of statistical models within the Frequentist paradigm. If it suits your needs better, you should feel free to use Statsmodels instead.

```python
import pandas as pd
pd.set_option("display.notebook_repr_html", False)
import numpy as np
from scipy.stats import zscore
import random

from sklearn.preprocessing import StandardScaler
from sklearn.decomposition import PCA
from sklearn.cluster import KMeans
from sklearn.metrics import silhouette_score, silhouette_samples

import matplotlib as mpl
import matplotlib.pyplot as plt
import seaborn as sns

from dcss.plotting import format_axes_commas, custom_seaborn
custom_seaborn()
```

We will continue working with the VDEM data in this chapter, filtered to contain observations from 2019 only.

```python
df = pd.read_csv('../data/vdem/V-Dem-CY-Full+Others-v10.csv', low_memory=False)
df = df.query('year == 2019').reset_index()
df.shape
```

```
(179, 4109)
```

Now that we have the VDEM data from 2019 loaded up, we can select the columns we will use in our analyses. In this case, we want the country name as well as a series of variables related to political deliberation, civil society, media and internet, private and political liberties, and the executive. The specific variables we will use in each of these categories are given in Table 8.1. Given that I don't have space to discuss each variable (there are 35 of them in total), I recommend that you consult the VDEM codebook to ensure you know what each represents.

Table 8.1 VDEM variables used in this chapter

Deliberation	Civil Society	Media and Internet	Private and Political Liberties	The Executive
v2dlreason	v2cseeorgs	v2mecenefm	v2cldiscm	v2exrescon
v2dlcommon	v2csreprss	v2mecenefi	v2cldiscw	v2exbribe
v2dlcountr	v2cscnsult	v2mecenefibin	v2clacfree	v2exembez
v2dlconslt	v2csprtcpt	v2mecrit	v2clrelig	v2excrptps
v2dlengage	v2csgender	v2merange	v2clfmove	v2exthftps
v2dlencmps	v2csantimv	v2mefemjrn		
v2dlunivl	v2csrlgrep	v2meharjrn		
	v2csrlgcon	v2meslfcen		
		v2mebias		
		v2mecorrpt		

Note: VDEM = Varieties of Democracy.

We will create a list of these indicator variables' names that we can use to subset the larger dataframe:

```
indicators = [
    'v2dlreason', 'v2dlcommon', 'v2dlcountr', 'v2dlconslt', 'v2dlengage',
    'v2dlencmps', 'v2dlunivl', 'v2cseeorgs', 'v2csreprss', 'v2cscnsult',
    'v2csprtcpt', 'v2csgender', 'v2csantimv', 'v2csrlgrep', 'v2csrlgcon',
    'v2mecenefm', 'v2mecenefi', 'v2mecenefibin', 'v2mecrit', 'v2merange',
    'v2mefemjrn', 'v2meharjrn', 'v2meslfcen', 'v2mebias', 'v2mecorrpt',
    'v2exrescon', 'v2exbribe', 'v2exembez', 'v2excrptps', 'v2exthftps',
    'v2cldiscm', 'v2cldiscw', 'v2clacfree', 'v2clrelig', 'v2clfmove'
]
```

We can now subset the original dataframe so that it includes only these variables, and then use the country names as the dataframe index:

```
countries = df['country_name'].tolist()
df = df.set_index('country_name')[indicators]
df.shape
```

```
(179, 35)
```

The resulting dataframe has 179 observations (each one a country in 2019) and our 35 variables. Before moving on, we can do a quick check to see whether we have any problems with missing data. The code below counts the number of variables with missing (1) and non-missing (0) data. None of our variables have missing data.

```
df.isna().sum().value_counts()
```

```
0    35
dtype: int64
```

All we need to finish preparing our data is to get our indicator variables into a NumPy array. We will do some additional cleaning a bit later in the chapter.

```
X = df.to_numpy()
```

8.4 Latent Variables and the Curse of Dimensionality

Before getting into 'latent variables', let's clear up a bit of terminology. In this chapter, and many that follow, we'll talk about the 'dimensions' and 'dimensionality' of dataframes and matrices. All of this talk of 'dimensions' is really just about the number of variables we are using. If we have 10 variables, we have 10 dimensions; 147,002 variables, 147,002 dimensions. When we have a *lot* of variables, we often describe our dataset as 'high-dimensional'.

High-dimensional datasets pose all sorts of problems for statistical and machine learning models that low-dimensional datasets do not. That's why we refer to this situation as the 'curse of dimensionality' even if it might seem at first to be an embarrassment of riches. Typically, we reduce the number of variables we are working with by manually selecting the variables of interest and/or by performing some sort of 'dimensionality reduction' on the dataset that mitigates the problems associated with the curse of dimensionality. Below, you will learn about two different but related approaches to dimensionality reduction; one is deductive and driven by theory and measurement, the other inductive and driven by patterns in the data.

Theory first: measuring latent variables with factor analysis

We social scientists spend a huge amount of time trying to measure things that we can't directly observe. If you take a moment, you can probably list dozens of such things: political ideology, religiosity, well-being, job satisfaction, social capital, opportunity costs, social anxiety, confirmation bias, populism, introversion, personality types, emotional labour, resource mobilization, and so on. In earlier chapters of this book, we spent a fair amount of time working with five variables that measure things we can't directly observe:

1   A country-level measure of the principle of electoral democracy (polyarchy)
2   A country-level measure of the principle of liberal democracy
3   A country-level measure of the principle of participatory democracy
4   A country-level measure of the principle of egalitarian democracy
5   A country-level measure of the principle of deliberative democracy

When I say that none of these five 'principles' of democracy can be directly observed, I mean that literally: you can't look at a country and eyeball the amount of deliberative democracy as if it had material form. That's because deliberative democracy is not a material thing in the world, it's an abstract concept developed by social scientists and political philosophers in the context of theoretical debate and applied research. Because these are unobservable abstract concepts, we call the random variables that represent them 'latent', 'hidden', or 'unobserved'.

When we develop theoretical concepts, we can't assume other researchers share our meanings, or that our meaning is somehow self-evident. Instead, we put in quite a lot of work to ensure conceptual clarity, as that is the only way to advance the state of our collective knowledge. These abstract concepts are *essential* in the quest to advance collective knowledge, but to treat them as if they were 'real' material things, and not theoretical constructs, is a mistake called reification.

Abstract concepts, like the principles of democracy above, are meaningful both in our everyday lives and in relation to broader theories and paradigms, but because they can't be directly observed, they are difficult to measure empirically. This requires us to adopt measurement strategies that combine careful reasoning and logic with measurement models that we carefully and transparently validate. The first step in this process is specification, which involves developing conceptual and operational definitions of concepts. Specification is essential because it helps ensure we are talking about the same thing; in social science, as in everyday life, you can't get very far just making up your own definitions of things, however good those definitions might be.

A conceptual definition involves defining an abstract concept in relation to other concepts whose meaning is more widely shared, usually by breaking it down into more concrete aspects or dimensions. For example, my friend and colleague Igor Grossmann conducts fascinating psychological research on wisdom. What exactly is 'wisdom' and how does one study it scientifically? Even something as grand and abstract as 'wisdom' can be specified in terms of concrete dimensions that, together, speak to the more general concept. For example, as Brienza et al. (2018) propose, wisdom can be represented by the extent to which people demonstrate intellectual humility, recognition of uncertainty and change, consideration of the broader context at hand and perspectives of others, and the integration of these perspectives/compromise in specific situations.

The various dimensions that are specified in the conceptual definition of wisdom are, of course, *other concepts*. The difference between an operational definition and a conceptual one is that an operational definition describes the specific operations that one would have to perform to generate empirical observations (i.e. data) for each of the various dimensions. The variables that contain data on these specific dimensions are typically called indicator variables. Operational definitions involve specifying things like the level at which to measure something, the type of variables to use (e.g. ordinal, interval, ratio, categorical), the range of variation those variables should have, and so on. A good operational definition of a concept enables one to measure the concept by measuring its dimensions with a high degree of reliability and validity, and then aggregating the measures of specific dimensions into a measure of the abstract concept that *also* has high reliability and validity. In the case of measuring wisdom, for example, Brienza et al. (2018) outline an explicit measurement strategy that attempts to mitigate social desirability biases (which inevitably come into play when you ask people about the wisdom of their reasoning) by assessing how people respond to specific scenarios. They provide an online supplement that includes the specific survey instruments used to collect the data according to the operational definitions laid out in their article.

Let's return to our abstract 'principles of democracy'. The principle of electoral democracy, for example, is represented by the five dimensions listed below. The set of accompanying questions come straight from the VDEM codebook (Coppedge et al., 2021).

1 *Freedom of expression:* 'To what extent does government respect press and media freedom, the freedom of ordinary people to discuss political matters at home and in the public sphere, as well as the freedom of academic and cultural expression?' (variable: `v2x_freexp_altinf`)
2 *Freedom of association:* 'To what extent are parties, including opposition parties, allowed to form and to participate in elections, and to what extent are civil society organizations able to form and to operate freely?' (variable: `v2x_frassoc_thick`)

3 *Share of adult citizens with suffrage:* 'What share of adult citizens (as defined by statute) has the legal right to vote in national elections?' (variable: `v2x_suffr`)

4 *Free and fair elections:* 'To what extent are elections free and fair?' (variable: `v2xel_frefair`)

5 *Officials are elected:* 'Is the chief executive and legislature appointed through popular elections?' (variable: `v2x_elecoff`)

Each dimension is a bit more concrete than 'electoral democracy', but for the most part, we still can't directly observe these dimensions. Perhaps you noticed that some contain multiple questions! The first dimension, for example, contains several questions about freedom of the press and media, freedom of ordinary people, and freedom of academic and cultural expression. In this case, each of the five dimensions that make up the higher-level measure of electoral democracy are called *indices*, which is a type of measure that is constructed by combining the values of lower-level indicator variables.

For example, the *freedom of expression* dimension represented by the index variable `v2x_freexp_altinf` is constructed from the values of the variables government censorship effort (`v2mecenefm`), harassment of journalists (`v2meharjrn`), media self-censorship (`v2meslfcen`), freedom of discussion (`v2xcl_disc`), freedom of academic and cultural expression (`v2clacfree`), levels of media bias (`v2mebias`), how critical the media is (`v2mecrit`), and the diversity of perspectives promoted by the media (`v2merange`). These lower-level indicators are easier to observe than the higher-level index variables above them, or the even higher still indices representing types of democracies. If you want to learn more about the conceptual and operational definitions of these principles of democracy, as well as the specific measurement models used, you can consult Coppedge et al. (2020).

The difference between these indices and indicator variables maps directly back to the process of specification; the variables we use to record observations about the specific dimensions of concepts are indicator variables because they *indicate* part of the concept, and the overall concept is measured by combining the values for those indicators into an index. Indices are composite measures because they are created by systematically and transparently combining multiple indicators.

When we want (or need) to measure something really big and abstract like a concept that is part of a larger theory (e.g. the amount of deliberative democracy that we see in a given country at some point in time), we break the big abstract concept down into various different dimensions, and sometimes we break *those* dimensions down into even smaller ones. The measures for the higher-level concepts are indices constructed by combining the values of lower-level indicator variables.

This general idea is sketched out in Figure 8.1, with example indicator variables on the top feeding into mid-level index measures for latent concepts (in grey), which in turn feed into the high-level index measures of the latent concept of the principle of electoral democracy, or 'polyarchy' (also in grey). The . . .s are meant to emphasize that there are other indicators that feed into the mid-level indices in addition to those shown here.

When trying to measure latent variables, such as the state of electoral democracy or freedom of association in a country, we typically perform some sort of factor analysis that tells us whether the indicators we observed and measured (e.g. the share of adult citizens with voting rights and the power of the head of state relative to the head of government) are indeed likely to reflect some underlying 'factor'.

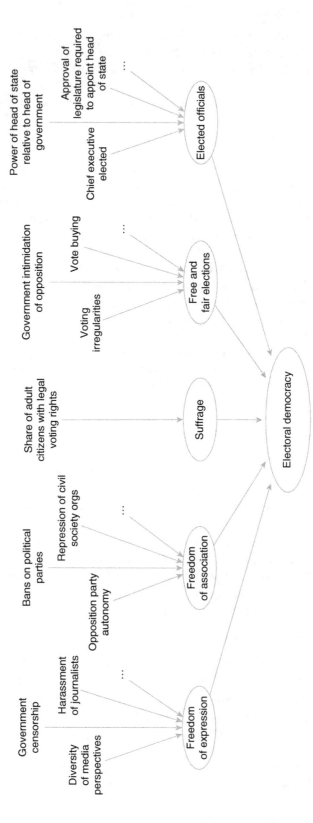

Figure 8.1 Latent variables – at the top are observable features; the red bubbles in the middle and bottom layers are latent variables which are amalgamations of one or more other variables (latent or otherwise). orgs = organizations

A 'factor' is simply a subset of highly correlated variables that have been combined into a single composite variable. If v2x_freexp_altinf, v2x_frassoc_thick, v2x_suffr, v2xel_frefair, and v2x_elecoff are all highly correlated with one another (and not strongly correlated with other variables), it might be because they are all indicating different dimensions of the same underlying latent construct: *electoral democracy*. The factor analysis lets us take a larger set of variables, of which some are highly correlated with one another, and reduce them to a smaller subset of explanatory factors. Depending on the type of factor analysis you conduct, these factors may or may not be correlated with one another.

When we conduct a factor analysis, we also compute factor loadings that clarify the relationship between each of the original variables in our analysis and the underlying factors extracted in the analysis. Variables that are strongly associated with the latent factor contribute more to that factor, and hence have higher loading. The specific factor loadings we can compute vary a bit depending on how we are approaching things. If we assume that the latent variables might be at least somewhat correlated with one another (which is a very reasonable assumption!), then we compute two sets of factor loadings, one being the Pearson correlation coefficients between the variables and the latent factors (a 'structure matrix') and one being coefficients from a linear regression (a 'pattern matrix').

If we assume that the latent variables are not correlated with one another (rarely a reasonable assumption, but it has its place), then there is only one set of factor loadings (either the correlation coefficients or the regression coefficients, which in this scenario would be the same). These loading scores are often 'rotated' to help make them more substantively interpretable. Though we won't discuss them here, the type of rotation you perform depends on whether you think the factors are correlated with one another. If you suspect they are at least somewhat correlated with one another, then you would use an oblique rotation, and if you suspect they aren't, you would choose an orthogonal rotation.

Factor loadings describe how specific *variables* (e.g. government intimidation of the opposition) contribute to a latent factor. Factor scores, on the other hand, tell us how specific *observations* (e.g. the USA in 2020) score on a given latent factor (e.g. electoral democracy). You can probably see where I'm going with this: if the latent factors represent meaningful variables that we want to measure but can't directly observe, then the factor scores that describe how an observation is related to that latent factor *is* the measurement of that observation for that latent factor. For example, on the egalitarian democracy measurement variable in 2019, Namibia scored 0.453, Egypt scored 0.118, France scored 0.773, North Korea scored 0.096, Vanuatu scored 0.566, Senegal scored 0.517, Canada scored 0.776, and Ukraine scored 0.316. Where did these numbers come from? The egalitarian democracy variable is a latent index variable constructed from several other indices, which are in turn constructed from more concrete low-level indicators. The latent variables and the individual country scores are mathematically constructed using factor analysis.

In the interest of space, we will not actually conduct a theory-oriented factor analysis in this chapter. Instead, we will focus on a different approach that is more inductive and data driven: PCA.

Further Reading

Chapter 13 from Barbara Tabachnick and Linda Fidell's (2007) *Using Multivariate Statistics* and Chapter 17 of Field et al. (2012) *Discovering Statistics Using R* both provide a good introduction to EFA and PCA as widely used practices in the social and cognitive sciences. Both are written from a

(Continued)

Frequentist perspective. Chapter 8 of Géron's (2019) *Hands-On Machine Learning with Scikit-Learn, Keras, and TensorFlow* and Chapter 3 of Müller and Guido's (2016) *Introduction to Machine Learning with Python* provide a good introduction to 'dimensionality reduction' in machine learning.

8.5 Conducting a Principal Component Analysis in Sklearn

Standardization

We did most of the necessary preprocessing at the start of the chapter when we imported our data, filtered the rows, selected the relevant columns, and then converted the data to a NumPy ndarray, which is a nice way of storing matrix data. There is, however, one very important piece of preprocessing that we need to do before we conduct a PCA: scaling our variables via z-score normalization, or 'standardization'.

Remember, PCA reduces the dimensionality of a dataset by constructing 'principal components' from highly correlated features. If the variance contained in any one component differs from the variance contained in another because of the scales for the features that contribute to it, then PCA will make consequential mistakes. In short, PCA is *heavily* impacted by feature scaling. To prevent any such issues, we can use Sklearn's StandardScaler(), which performs z-score normalization on each feature. The z-score normalization ensures we are comparing things on the same scales.

```
X = StandardScaler().fit_transform(X)
```

Many statistical and machine learning models require standardization. If you need a refresher, you can consult the subsection below. Otherwise, you are free to skip over it.

A brief refresher on variance, standard deviation, and z-score normalization

First, let's *very* briefly revisit the concepts of variance and standard deviation. *Variance* is a statistical measure of how spread out or clustered the values in a dataset are. More specifically, it's a measure of how far each value is from the mean. Variance is usually represented with the symbol σ^2. A larger variance means that the values are more spread out, while a smaller variance means that they are more clustered around the mean. Let's use some very simple examples to see how this works:

```
ABCD = {
    'A': [1, 1, 1, 1, 1], # no variance...
    'B': [1, 2, 3, 4, 5], # some variance...
    'C': [-1, 1, 3, 5, 7], # a bit more variance...
    'D': [-10, -9, 3, 4, 4] # still more variance...
}
for k, v in ABCD.items():
    print(f'{k} has a variance of {np.round(np.var(v), 3)}.')

A has a variance of 0.0.
B has a variance of 2.0.
C has a variance of 8.0.
D has a variance of 41.84.
```

The *standard deviation* of a dataset is the square root of the variance (σ^2), and is therefore represented with the symbol σ.

```
for k, v in ABCD.items():
    print(f'{k} has a standard deviation of {np.round(np.std(v), 3)}.')
```

```
A has a standard deviation of 0.0.
B has a standard deviation of 1.414.
C has a standard deviation of 2.828.
D has a standard deviation of 6.468.
```

A z-score is a measure of how far an observation's value (x) is from the mean (μ), standardized by dividing by the standard deviation (σ). Thus, an observation x has a z-score

$$z = \frac{x - \mu}{\sigma}$$

There are other ways of standardizing data, but converting each observed value into a z-score is the most common approach. Below, we use the zscore() function from the stats module of a package called SciPy. Note that the values in A all return nan because they have a standard deviation of 0, which means there is no variance.

```
for k, v in ABCD.items():
    print(f'The values in {k} have the following Z-scores: {np.round(zscore(v), 3)}.')
```

```
The values in A have the following Z-scores: [nan nan nan nan nan].
The values in B have the following Z-scores: [-1.414 -0.707 0.    0.707 1.414].
The values in C have the following Z-scores: [-1.414 -0.707 0.    0.707 1.414].
The values in D have the following Z-scores: [-1.299 -1.144 0.711 0.866 0.866].
```

Back to PCA!

Now that our data has been standardized, we can conduct the PCA. When we initialize the model object with PCA(), we have the option of telling Sklearn to compute a specific number of components (e.g. pass the number 15 to get back the 15 principal components that account for the most variance) or a float specifying the amount of variance we want to be accounted for by the PCA (e.g. pass the number 0.9 to produce a solution that accounts for 90% of the variance). In this example, we will not specify either.

Once we initialize the model object, we can use the .fit_transform() method on our standardized array X:

```
pca = PCA()
pca_results = pca.fit_transform(X)
```

Let's take a look at the results!

Below, we create a dataframe representation of the NumPy matrix returned by pca.fit_transform(X) because it's a bit easier to read. As you can see, each country is represented as a row and each principal component as a column. The cells indicate the association between each country and component pairing. These scores don't have any meaning to us just yet, but they will become more clear shortly.

```
res = pd.DataFrame(pca_results, index=countries)
res.columns=[f'PC {i}' for i in res.columns]

res['PC 0'].head()
```

```
Mexico          -1.202027
Suriname        -2.341024
Sweden          -6.869927
Switzerland     -7.507582
Ghana           -2.319518
Name: PC 0, dtype: float64
```

Each of the 35 principal components we have constructed accounts for some amount of variance in the dataset. The components are ordered such that the first component accounts for the most variance, followed by the second, third, fourth, and so on. The amount of variance that each individual component accounts for is stored in the pca model object as an attribute (explained_variance_ratio_), which means we can access it using dot notation. Because we used the default parameters, rather than specifying the n_components parameter, the explained variance ratio scores will sum to 1, which means that *together* the principal components account for 100% of the variance in the data.

```
evr = pca.explained_variance_ratio_
evr
```

```
array([0.59924733, 0.0891026,  0.04201601, 0.03184165, 0.02871048,
       0.0247993,  0.01937897, 0.01704044, 0.0161068,  0.01216557,
       0.01137465, 0.010775,   0.0093373,  0.00825962, 0.00759738,
       0.00674564, 0.00614955, 0.00572312, 0.00529913, 0.00488844,
       0.00461487, 0.00445199, 0.00423259, 0.00407862, 0.00380965,
       0.00361415, 0.00304708, 0.00285819, 0.00265381, 0.00240895,
       0.00215666, 0.00177851, 0.00154364, 0.00134978, 0.00084251])
```

The first value in the evr array above is roughly 0.6, which means that the first principal component contains roughly 60% of the variance in the dataset. You can interpret the rest of the numbers the same way: the second component contains roughly 9% of the variance, the third roughly 4% of the variance, and so on. In this particular example, a quick glance at this array alone suggests that the first component accounts for substantially more variance than any of the others.

```
print(f'The sum of the array is: {np.round(np.sum(evr), 2)}')
```

```
The sum of the array is: 1.0
```

Usually, we want to see how much *cumulative* variance is accounted for by some subset of principal components, starting with the first component. In other words, how much variance is accounted for by each component *and those before it.* The cumulative variance of the first three components, for example, is

```
np.sum(evr[:3])
```

```
0.7303659455066264
```

Knowing how the explained cumulative variance changes with each additional principal component is useful because we typically want to work with some subset of the components rather than the entire set of variables or even principal components. That is, after all, generally the point of using a data-driven dimensionality reduction method like PCA. If you are going to work with a subset, you should know how much information you kept and how much you threw away.

Let's create a Series containing information on the cumulative explained variance for the components in our PCA. We can do this by passing the array of explained variance ratios (evr) to NumPy's cumsum() function, which is short for cumulative sum. The Series tells us how much variance is accounted for by each component and those preceding it (remember, the index starts with 0, so the zeroth element of the series represents the first component).

```
cve = pd.Series(np.cumsum(evr))
cve[:12]
```

```
0     0.599247
1     0.688350
2     0.730366
3     0.762208
4     0.790918
5     0.815717
6     0.835096
7     0.852137
8     0.868244
9     0.880409
10    0.891784
11    0.902559
dtype: float64
```

In this case, a simple preview of the cumulative explained variance tells us that the first two components alone account for 68% of the variance in the dataset, which is a *very* substantial amount. Similarly, we can see that the first 12 components still account for 90% of the variance – pretty good considering we started with 35 indicator variables!

This is only part of the picture, though. Let's plot the proportion of cumulative explained variance for each successive principal component. Notice that, by default, PCA will construct a number of components equal to the number of original variables in the dataset. You should be able to see the diminishing returns, here, even if they set in rather smoothly. The code below produces Figure 8.2:

```
fig, ax = plt.subplots()
sns.lineplot(x=cve.index, y=cve)
```

```
plt.scatter(x=cve.index, y=cve)
ax.set(xlabel='Principal component ID',
       ylabel='Proportion of explained variance (cumulative)')
ax.set(ylim=(0, 1.1))
sns.despine()
plt.show()
```

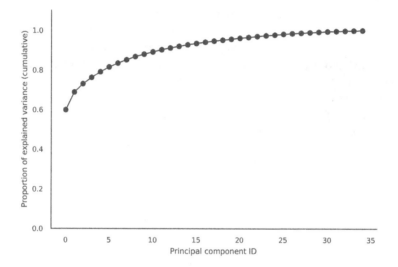

Figure 8.2 A plot of the proportion of variance explained, cumulatively, by each of the components in the principal components analysis

Matrix decomposition: eigenvalues, eigenvectors, and extracting components

When you conduct a PCA, you only want to keep some components. You're trying to *reduce dimensionality* while preserving as much information (in the form of variance) possible. So, which components do you extract?

The above plot of cumulative variance accounted for can be helpful if you want to preserve a certain amount of variance in the data. An alternative approach is to construct a scree plot to determine which components are substantively important enough to use. To understand how to construct and interpret a scree plot, you need to know a little bit more about how PCA works, and more specifically what role eigenvalues and eigenvectors play in a PCA, and how those roles differ from loadings in factor analysis.

As discussed earlier, PCA creates a covariance matrix of standardized variables (or sometimes a correlation matrix). We can understand the structure and other properties of these matrices mathematically using eigen-decomposition. We won't get into the linear algebra here, but here's the basic idea: We can decompose the matrix into two parts. The first are the principal components themselves, which are *directions* of axes where there is the most variance (eigenvectors). The second part is the *amount* of variance that is accounted for by the principal components (eigenvalues). Every eigenvector has an eigenvalue, and there is an eigenvector (principal component) for every variable in the original data. A very important feature of PCA is that the first principal component accounts for the greatest possible variance in the dataset. The second principal component is calculated in the same way as the first, except that it cannot be correlated with the first. This continues for each principal component until you have as many as you do variables. It is important to remember that all the information about scale (the amount of variance explained) is contained in the eigenvalues. The eigenvectors in a PCA do not tell us anything about the magnitude of explained variance.

Scree plots graph the eigenvalues for each component in the PCA, which you now know represents the amount of variance that each component accounts for. *The higher the eigenvalue, the more important the component.* Because eigenvalues represent the amount of explained variance, Sklearn helpfully stores them in the `explained_variance_` attribute of the PCA model object. This also makes it very straightforward to create a scree plot. The code below produces Figure 8.3:

```
eigenvalues = pd.Series(pca.explained_variance_)

fig, ax = plt.subplots()
sns.lineplot(x=eigenvalues.index, y=eigenvalues, data=eigenvalues)
plt.scatter(x=eigenvalues.index, y=eigenvalues)
ax.set(xlabel='Principal component ID', ylabel='Eigenvalue')
sns.despine()
plt.show()
```

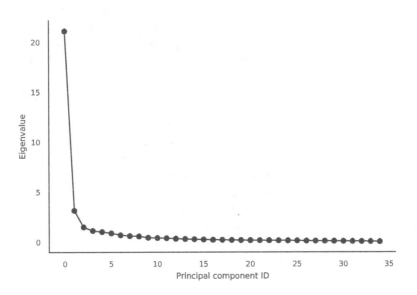

Figure 8.3 A scree plot, showing an inflection point at the second principal component

This plot should be straightforward to understand. The first few components are more important than the others. In a scree plot, you are usually looking for an inflection point where the

---

If you are looking for the eigenvectors, Sklearn stores them in the .`components_` attribute.

slope of the line changes rather abruptly. Usually, that point is clear, but we can also inspect the eigenvalues themselves if we want a bit more precision; just remember that the eigenvalues are zero-indexed, so 0 represents the first component, 1 represents the second component, and so on.

```
eigenvalues.head(10)
```

```
0     21.091486
1      3.136111
2      1.478822
3      1.120719
4      1.010512
5      0.872852
6      0.682074
7      0.599766
8      0.566905
9      0.428187
dtype: float64
```

We might use the fact that dropping from 3.14 to 1.48 (a decrease of more than 50%) is significantly greater than the drop from 1.48 to 1.12, and from 1.12 to 1.01, to identify an inflection point at 1.48. The general rule is that you extract the components to the left of the inflection point, excluding the component at the inflection point itself. However, there are debates about whether it is best to keep all components with eigenvalues higher than some threshold, such as 1, the idea being that this is still quite a lot of variation *even if less than the other components*. In this example, cutting at the inflection point would be the third component, which means we would extract the first two. On the other hand, if we go with a threshold of 1, then we would take the first five.

When different rules suggest different courses of action, the best solution is the one most aligned with your research objectives. One reason why researchers perform PCA is because they want to do some sort of regression analysis but have a *bad* multicollinearity problem. In that case, keep lots of components! It is better to keep information than throw it away unless you *really* need to throw some away. If, conversely, you are trying to visualize a high-dimensional dataset by collapsing it down to two significant dimensions, then you should only extract those two components *provided they contain a lot of variance* (which you should always report).

Here, we will extract the first two because they preserve a *lot* of variance, and because the next thing I want to do is create a simple visualization of where the countries in our analysis are positioned in terms of these latent dimensions, and creating informative visualizations in three or more dimensions is a fool's errand.

```
component_1 = pca_results[:, 0]
component_2 = pca_results[:, 1]

PC12 = pd.DataFrame(zip(component_1, component_2), columns=['PC1', 'PC2'])
```

We can now easily visualize how the countries in our dataset are positioned in relation to these two principal components. Let's grab the country names from our metadata variables to use in the visualization, which will be a simple density plot with country names indicating where each country is given these two components.

```
PC12['Country'] = countries

ax = sns.kdeplot(data=PC12, x='PC1', y='PC2', alpha=.8, fill=True)
for i, country in enumerate(PC12['Country']):
    ax.text(PC12['PC1'][i],
            PC12['PC2'][i],
            country,
            horizontalalignment='left',
            size=3,
            color='black',
            weight='normal')
ax.set(xticklabels=[], yticklabels=[])
ax.set(
    xlabel=
    f'$\longleftarrow$ PC1 (eigenvalue: {np.round(eigenvalues.loc[0], 2)}) $\
    longrightarrow$',
    ylabel=
    f'$\longleftarrow$ PC2 (eigenvalue: {np.round(eigenvalues.loc[1], 2)}) $\
    longrightarrow$'
)
plt.show()
```

While the text is dense in Figure 8.4 (a high-resolution version is available in the online supplement), careful inspection should lead to noticing several patterns. The first principal component is defined by the opposition between countries like Norway, Denmark, Switzerland,

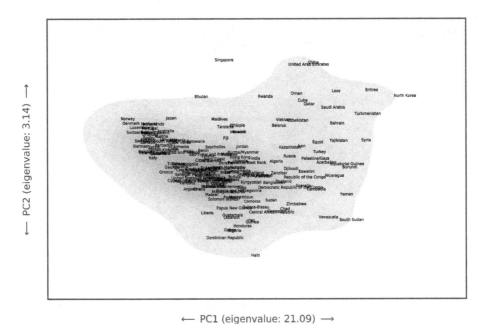

← PC1 (eigenvalue: 21.09) →

Figure 8.4 Each of the countries in the dataset plotted according to their position on the two most powerful principal components (PC1 and PC2)

Luxembourg, and Germany on the one hand, and by Burundi, Turkmenistan, Syria, Eritrea, and North Korea on the other. The second principal component is defined by the opposition of countries like Haiti, Dominican Republic, Nigeria, Gabon, and Honduras on the one hand, and by Laos, Eritrea, United Arab Emirates, China, and Singapore on the other. The eigenvalue is *much* higher for the first principal component, suggesting that the interpretation of the differences between countries on the left and the right of the graph is most important.

This is not a factor analysis. We have not guided the PCA towards this solution. Instead, we have obtained these two latent dimensions *mathematically*, through matrix decomposition, and projected the countries onto that latent space. These two dimensions only represent 68% of the variance in the dataset, but when you think about it, that's a lot of information for just two variables! The challenge, given that this is computationally *inductive*, is to do the qualitative and historical work necessary to interpret this representation of the latent structure in the data. However, don't forget that the only information the PCA has to work with comes from our original variables, so those variables are a great place to start.

8.6 Conclusion

The key points in this chapter are as follows:

- We learnt about latent variables and the differences between theory-driven and data-driven dimensionality reduction.
- We discussed the distinctions between factor analysis and PCA.
- We also conducted a PCA.

Visit the website at https://study.sagepub.com/mclevey for additional resources

PART II
FUNDAMENTALS OF
TEXT ANALYSIS

9

PROCESSING NATURAL LANGUAGE DATA

9.1 Learning Objectives

By the end of this chapter, you should be able to do the following:

- Describe the main components of spaCy's natural language processing pipeline
- Effectively use spaCy's `doc`, `token`, and `span` data structures for working with text data
- Describe why normalizing text data can improve the quality of downstream analyses
- Describe the difference between stemming and lemmatization
- Use part-of-speech labels to select and filter tokens from documents
- Examine noun chunks (i.e. phrases) that are detected by spaCy's pipeline
- Examine subject, verb, and object triplets

9.2 Learning Materials

You can find the online learning materials for this chapter in `doing_computational_social_science/Chapter_09`. `cd` into the directory and launch your Jupyter server.

9.3 Introduction

In this chapter, we will shift our focus from working with structured quantitative data to natural language data stored in the form of unstructured text. We will begin by learning how to use the package spaCy for common natural language processing (NLP) tasks, such as cleaning and normalizing text data, followed by a discussion of labelling words by their part of speech, manipulating syntactic dependencies between words, and using all of this to create a rough three-word summary of the content in a sentence. Later, we will put this knowledge to use for custom text preprocessing functions to use for downstream tasks in other chapters of the book.

Package imports

```
import pandas as pd
pd.set_option("display.notebook_repr_html", False)
```

```
import seaborn as sns
import matplotlib.pyplot as plt

from dcss.plotting import format_axes_commas, custom_seaborn
from dcss.text import bigram_process, preprocess

import spacy
from spacy import displacy
from sklearn.feature_extraction.text import CountVectorizer, TfidfVectorizer
from sklearn.decomposition import TruncatedSVD

custom_seaborn()
```

9.4 Text Processing

With the exception of some recent neural network and embedding-based text methods that we will consider later in this book, the quality of most text analyses can be dramatically improved with careful text processing prior to any modelling. For data cleaning, common text processing tasks include removing punctuation, converting to lower case, normalizing words using techniques such as stemming or lemmatization, and selecting some subset of terms to use in the analysis. When selecting the subset of terms, it is possible to use a vocabulary that you curate yourself (in which case it is referred to as a dictionary) or to select terms based on some sort of criteria, such as their frequency or part of speech (e.g. noun, adjectives).

You can process your text data any number of ways in Python, but my advice is that you use a package called spaCy. spaCy is, to put it plainly, head and shoulders above the rest when it comes to processing natural language data in Python, or in any other language for that matter. If you are interested in NLP, spaCy alone is reason to do your work entirely in Python. In the first part of the chapter, we will introduce spaCy with an emphasis on its built-in data processing pipelines and data structures, and then we will practise using it to process a dataset consisting of political speeches.

Getting to know spaCy

One of the major benefits of using spaCy is that it is tightly integrated with state-of-the-art statistical language models and trained using deep learning methods that you will start learning about in later chapters. We are not yet ready to get into the details of these pretrained statistical language models, but we will briefly touch on them here since knowing a *bit* about them is an important part of learning how to use spaCy to process natural language data.

In recent years, NLP (and computer vision research) has been revolutionized by 'transfer learning', in which the output of a machine learning model that was trained in one context is reused in another context. Typically these are deep learning models that take an enormous amount of time and energy to train. In NLP, the basic idea is to train such a model on massive datasets (e.g. crawls of the entire open web) so that the model learns a lot about language *in general*, but perhaps not much about any specific domain. The output from the pretrained model can then be made available to researchers, who can update it using annotated data from the specific domain they are interested in, such as news stories reporting on the Black Lives Matter movement. For most tasks, this transfer learning approach outperforms models that have been trained on a massive dataset but have not been updated with domain-specific data, or models trained the other way around.

While we haven't actually gotten into machine learning yet (let alone deep neural networks and transfer learning), it is useful to keep this general idea of reusing models in a transfer learning framework in mind. In this chapter, for example, most of the methods you will learn make use of a statistical language model that has been pretrained on a massive general text corpus, including web data from commoncrawl.org and the OntoNotes 5 corpus, which contains data from telephone conversations, newswire, newsgroups, broadcast news, broadcast conversation, and weblogs. The pretrained language models that spaCy provides can be used as is, or they can be updated with domain-specific annotated data. In the rest of this chapter, we will not update the pretrained models.

spaCy's pretrained models come in three sizes – small, medium, and large. Each is available in multiple languages[1] and follows a simple naming convention: language + model name (which is the type of model + genre of text it was trained on + the model size). The medium core English model trained on news data is en_core_news_md, and the large English core model trained on web data (blogs, comments, and online news) is en_core_web_lg.

These models vary in what they do, how they do it, how fast they work, how much memory they require, and how accurate they are for various types of tasks. As we now know, it is important to pick the model that is best suited to the specific research application. The smaller models are, of course, faster and less memory-intensive, but they tend to be a bit less accurate. For most general-purpose tasks, they work fine, but your case is probably not 'general purpose' – it is probably fairly domain specific, in which case you may want to work with a larger model, or a model that you can train and update yourself.

Models are not installed with spaCy, so you will need to download them to your machine. You can do this on the command line with the following command:

```
python -m spacy download en_core_web_sm
python -m spacy download en_core_web_md
python -m spacy download en_core_web_lg
```

Once they have been downloaded, we can use spaCy's pretrained models by loading them into memory using the .load() method and assigning the model to a language object, which is spaCy's NLP 'pipeline'. As we will see below, this object contains everything needed to process our raw text. You can call it whatever you want, but the convention is to call it nlp. Once we have imported spaCy and loaded one of the 'core' models, we are ready to start processing text. We don't need the named entity recognition or syntactic dependency parser for this part, so we'll disable those components of the pipeline.

```
nlp = spacy.load("en_core_web_sm", disable=['ner', 'parser'])
```

We've now created an instance of spaCy's text processing pipeline. Let's put it to use!

---

[1] At the time of writing, spaCy provides these models for English, German, Spanish, Portuguese, French, Italian, Dutch, Norwegian, and Lithuanian. It is also capable of processing multilingual documents and tokenization for more than 50 languages to allow model training. In the rest of this chapter and those that follow, we will use English-language models.

The spaCy NLP pipeline

Once the language model has been loaded (nlp), we can start processing our raw text by passing it through spaCy's default text processing pipeline, which is illustrated in Figure 9.1. This is often the slowest part of an NLP workflow because spaCy does a *lot* of heavy lifting right at the start. The result of this process will be something called a Doc object, which we will discuss momentarily; for now, let's focus on the big picture and then circle back and fill in the details on each pipeline component and data structure later.

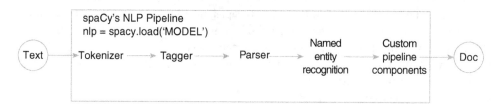

Figure 9.1 A flowchart depicting the steps in spaCy's generic natural language processing (NLP) pipeline

As shown in Figure 9.1, as soon as our original text enters spaCy's pipeline, it encounters the *tokenizer*, which identifies the boundaries of words and sentences. Most of the time, punctuation makes it relatively simple for computers to detect sentence boundaries but periods in abbreviations (Dr., Inc.), for example, can complicate this simple approach. Even tokenizing individual words can be tricky, as this process involves making decisions like whether to convert contractions to one token or two (e.g. it's vs. it is), or whether to tokenize special characters like emoji or sequences of characters that together form an emoticon: ¯_(ツ)_/¯ spaCy tokenizes text using language-specific rules, differentiating between punctuation marking the end of a sentence and punctuation used in acronyms and abbreviations. It will also use predefined language-specific rules to split tokens like don't into do and n't. Although these rules are language specific, if spaCy doesn't already have a tokenizer for a language you need, it is possible to add new languages. Instructions on how to do this are available in the spaCy documentation.

In the second step of the pipeline, spaCy assigns each a tag based on its *part of speech* using its pretrained statistical models. In doing so, spaCy combines rules-based expertise from linguistics with supervised machine learning models. The third step maps syntactic dependencies between words (e.g. which words in a sentence depend on or modify other words in a sentence) using its neural network model. This dependency *parsing* is the basis for accurate sentence segmentation in spaCy and enables more complex linguistic analysis. The fourth step in the processing pipeline is to recognize *named entities*. This is a very useful and important task for computational social scientists but is relatively complex and tends to be highly dependent on the data used to train the model. Therefore, we will set named entity recognition aside until later, where we can explore it in more depth and learn how to train models that are customized to work best for our specific research applications (see Chapter 32). Note that when we loaded the pretrained language model and initialized the nlp pipeline, we disabled the ner component. Since we are not going to use it here, disabling it in the pipeline speeds up text processing a noticeable amount, because it means spaCy won't spend time executing that part of the pipeline.

The general processing pipeline I have just described is summarized in Figure 9.1, which is reproduced from the spaCy documentation. Note the 'Custom pipeline components' on the right side of the processing pipeline. This indicates the option of adding additional steps to the pipeline, such as categorizing texts based on some predefined set of labels; assigning customized attributes to the Doc, Token, and Span objects; merging noun chunks or named entities into single tokens; and so on. Technically, you can add your own custom steps to any part of the spaCy pipeline, not just at the end. These custom steps are beyond the scope of this chapter, but now you know it's possible to add them.

Now that we understand how to download, load, and use pretrained statistical models as part of spaCy's default text processing pipeline, it's time to learn about spaCy's containers: Docs, Tokens, and Spans.

The spaCy containers

We'll use a simple example to illustrate spaCy's containers. We start by passing some raw input text into the processing pipeline and then demonstrate how to work with the containers that store the output of that pipeline.

As an example, let's consider the abstract for Bart Bonikowski's (2017) journal article 'Ethno-Nationalist Populism and the Mobilization of Collective Resentment' published in *The British Journal of Sociology*. Here is the raw text of the abstract:

Scholarly and journalistic accounts of the recent successes of radical-right politics in Europe and the United States, including the Brexit referendum and the Trump campaign, tend to conflate three phenomena: populism, ethno-nationalism and authoritarianism. While all three are important elements of the radical right, they are neither coterminous nor limited to the right. The resulting lack of analytical clarity has hindered accounts of the causes and consequences of ethno-nationalist populism. To address this problem, I bring together existing research on nationalism, populism and authoritarianism in contemporary democracies to precisely define these concepts and examine temporal patterns in their supply and demand, that is, politicians' discursive strategies and the corresponding public attitudes. Based on the available evidence, I conclude that both the supply and demand sides of radical politics have been relatively stable over time, which suggests that in order to understand public support for radical politics, scholars should instead focus on the increased resonance between pre-existing attitudes and discursive frames. Drawing on recent research in cultural sociology, I argue that resonance is not only a function of the congruence between a frame and the beliefs of its audience, but also of shifting context. In the case of radical-right politics, a variety of social changes have engendered a sense of collective status threat among national ethnocultural majorities. Political and media discourse has channelled such threats into resentments toward elites, immigrants, and ethnic, racial and religious minorities, thereby activating previously latent attitudes and lending legitimacy to radical political campaigns that promise to return power and status to their aggrieved supporters. Not only does this form of politics threaten democratic institutions and inter-group relations, but it also has the potential to alter the contours of mainstream public discourse, thereby creating the conditions of possibility for future successes of populist, nationalist, and authoritarian politics.

I have the abstract saved in a text file called 'bonikowski_2017.txt'. To feed this abstract into the spaCy pipeline, we'll read it into memory, assign it to a variable, and then call our `nlp()` object on it.

```
with open('../data/txt_files/bonikowski_2017.txt', 'r') as f:
    abstract = f.read()
```

Doc

In spaCy, the first data structure to understand is the `Doc` object returned from the default processing pipeline indicated in Figure 9.1. The `Doc` object contains the linguistic annotations that we will use in our analyses, such as information about parts of speech. As indicated in Figure 9.1, we create the `Doc` object by running our data through the NLP pipeline. We'll call the `Doc` object doc, but of course we could call it pretty much anything we want.

```
doc = nlp(abstract)
print(f'There are {len(doc)} tokens in this document.')
```

```
There are 346 tokens in this document.
```

spaCy's Doc object is designed to facilitate *non-destructive* workflows. It's built around the principle of always being able to access the original input text. In spaCy, no information is ever lost, and the original text can always be reconstructed by accessing the `.text` attribute of a Doc, Sentence, or Token object. For example, `doc.text` recreates the exact text from the abstract object that we fed into the pipeline. Note that although we access `.text` as we would an attribute of an object, as though the text is stored plainly as a variable attached to it, `.text` is actually a class method that retrieves the original text from spaCy's underlying C storage structure.

Each `Doc` object includes information about all of the individual sentences and tokens that are used in the raw text. For example, we can print each individual sentence in the Doc. In the code block below, we print each sentence from the abstract. I won't print the full text here, but you will see it on your screen if you follow along with the code.

```
for sent in doc.sents:
    print(sent, '\n')
```

Similarly, we can iterate over the Doc object and print out each token. Iterating tokens is the default behaviour of a Doc object, so we don't need to use `.tokens` to access them.

```
for token in doc:
    print(token)
```

The ability to iterate over tokens greatly simplifies the process of cleaning and extracting relevant information from our text data. In the sections below, we'll iterate over tokens for a variety of important text processing tasks, including normalizing text and extracting words based on their part of speech, two tasks we turn to shortly.

The Doc object itself can be stored on disk and reloaded later, which can be very useful when working with large collections of text that take non-trivial amounts of time to pass through the default processing pipeline. This can be done in a few different ways, including the new DocBin class for serializing and holding the contents of multiple Doc objects, which can then be saved as a .spacy file using DocBin.to_disk(). The to_array() method exports an individual Doc object to an ndarray (from numpy), where each token occupies a row and each token attribute is a column. These arrays can also be saved to disk using numpy, but the DocBin method is the most convenient.

```
from spacy.tokens import DocBin

doc_export = DocBin()
doc_export.add(doc)
doc_export.to_disk('../data/misc/bart_bonikowski_doc.spacy')
```

Of course, it is possible to read these Docs back into memory using methods like DocBin. from_disk(), or loading the saved ndarray and using Doc.from_array(). Loading from DocBin is the most convenient, but you will need a vocabulary from the nlp() object to recreate the Doc objects themselves.

```
doc_import = DocBin().from_disk('../data/misc/bart_bonikowski_doc.spacy')
docs = list(doc_import.get_docs(nlp.vocab))
doc = docs[0]
print(f'There are {len(doc)} tokens in this document.')
```

```
There are 346 tokens in this document.
```

Token

The second type of object to know about is the Token. A token is each individual element of the raw text, such as words and punctuation. The Token object stores information about lexical types, adjacent white space, the parent Doc that a token belongs to, and 'offsets' that index precisely where the token occurs within the parent Doc. As we will see in subsequent chapters, all of this Token metadata can be used to accomplish specific NLP tasks with a high degree of accuracy, such as the information extraction tasks covered in later chapters.

Tokens are stored as hash values to save memory, but just as we can access the raw input text of a Doc object using .text, we can see the textual representation of a given token using .text. We can also access each token by specifying its index position in the Doc or by iterating over the Doc.

```
for token in doc:
    print(token.text)
```

An enormous amount of information is stored about each Token, most of which can be retrieved using methods discussed extensively in the documentation. We'll cover examples of some fairly important ones, including methods for accessing the normalized forms of the token such as a lemma, its part of speech, the dependency relations it's embedded in, and in some cases, even an estimate of the token's sentiment.

Span

The final data structure to understand before moving on is the Span, which is a slice of a Doc object that consists of multiple tokens but is smaller than the full Doc. When you iterate sentences in a document, each of those is actually a Span. Knowing how spans work can be very useful for data exploration, as well as programmatically gathering contextual words that are adjacent to a target type of token, such as a type of named entity. We can specify a span by using slice notation. For example, we could define a Span by providing the range of token indices from 5 to 15. Note that this span will include token 5 but not token 15!

```
a_span = doc[5:15]
```

Given a span, we can use many of the same methods available for Docs and Tokens, as well as merging and splitting Spans, or copying them into their own Doc objects.

Now that we have a solid foundational understanding of spaCy's statistical models, processing pipeline, and containers, we can take a closer look at two important components of the text processing pipeline that are *very* useful when preprocessing text data for the type of analyses we will perform in this chapter: (a) normalizing text via lemmatization and (b) part-of-speech tagging.

9.5 Normalizing Text via Lemmatization

When we work with natural language data, we have to decide how to handle words that are very similar but have different surface forms (e.g. consequence, consequences, consequential, consequentially). On the one hand, leaving words as they appear preserves potetntially important nuances in language. As a result, those words are tokenized and counted separately, as if they had no semantic similarity. An alternative approach is to normalize the text by grouping together highly similar words and reducing them to the same token. The idea, in short, is to define classes of equivalent words and treat them as a single token. Doing so loses some of the nuance but can dramatically improve the results of most text analysis algorithms. The two most widely used approaches to text normalization are stemming and lemmatization.

Stemming is a rule-based approach to normalizing words that ignores the roles words play in a sentence (e.g. noun or verb), or the surrounding context. For example, the Snowball stemmer takes in each individual word and follows rules about what parts of the word (e.g. 'ing') should be cut off. As you might imagine, the results you get back are usually not themselves valid words.

Rather than chopping off parts of a word to reduce it to the stem, *lemmatization* normalizes words by reducing them to their base dictionary form. As a result, it always returns valid words, which makes it considerably easier to interpret the results of almost any text analysis. In addition, lemmatization can be done either with a simple language-specific lookup table or in a rule-based way that considers a token's part of speech (discussed below), which enables it to differentiate between ways of using the same word (e.g. 'meeting' as a noun, 'meeting' as a verb) and identical words that have different normalization rules in different contexts. Lemmatization is extremely accurate and is almost always a better choice than stemming. It is also more widely used.

Keeping in mind that our most common goal with computational text analysis is to see the shape and structure of the forest, not any individual tree, you can probably see why this is useful in the context of analysing natural language data. Although we lose some nuance by normalizing the text, we improve our analysis of the corpus (i.e. the 'forest') itself.

As mentioned earlier, spaCy's `nlp()` does most of the heavy computing upfront. As a result, our `Doc` object already includes information about the lemmas of each token in our abstract. By default, the latest (3.0+) version of spaCy uses the simpler lookup lemmatizer. To use the newer rule-based lemmatizer that incorporates part-of-speech information, we'll install the additional data and modify the pipeline component to use the rule-based one.

You can install the `spacy-lookups-data` package in a virtual environment with

```
pip install spacy-lookups-data
```

Alternatively, if you are not using a virtual environment for some reason, you can run

```
pip install --user spacy-lookups-data
```

This new lemmatizer needs to replace the existing one, but it *also* needs to come after the other default pipeline components that assign part-of-speech tags. Unfortunately, simply using `nlp.replace()` puts the new lemmatizer after the parser but before the tags are mapped by the `AttributeRuler` part of the pipeline. (It's unclear whether this is intentional or a minor bug due to the fact that spaCy is in the middle of a major transition to version 3.) The easiest approach currently is to exclude the default lemmatizer during loading, then add the new one back in at the end. The lemmatizer also needs to be initialized in order to load the data from `spacy-lookups-data`.

```
nlp = spacy.load('en_core_web_sm', disable=['ner'], exclude = ['lemmatizer'])
lemmatizer = nlp.add_pipe('lemmatizer', config = {'mode': 'rule'})
lemmatizer.initialize()
```

We can iterate over each token in the `Doc` and add its lemma to a list. It's worth noting that using `.lemma_` on a token returns only the lemmatized text, not the original token, so the `lemmas` object we create here is a standard Python list of strings. To do additional spaCy-specific operations, we have to return to the original `Doc` object.

```
doc = nlp(abstract)
lemmatized = [(token.text, token.lemma_) for token in doc]
```

The list we just created contains all the tokens in our original document as well as their lemmas *where appropriate*. If not appropriate, the same token is added twice. To get a sense of the difference between the original tokens and their lemmas, and how minimal (and yet helpful) this normalization can be, let's take a peek at the lemmas from the first 100 words of the abstract:

```
for each in lemmatized[:100]:
    if each[0].lower() != each[1].lower():
        print(f'{each[0]} ({each[1]})')
```

```
accounts (account)
successes (success)
```

```
politics (politic)
including (include)
phenomena (phenomenon)
are (be)
elements (element)
are (be)
resulting (result)
has (have)
hindered (hinder)
accounts (account)
causes (cause)
consequences (consequence)
existing (exist)
```

This simple process of iterating over tokens and selecting some, but not all, is something we will do again and again in this chapter. There are more efficient ways to do this kind of preprocessing work – specifically by writing a custom function – but we will put that task on hold until we've covered each of the individual pieces.

9.6 Part-of-Speech Tagging

In some research applications, you may want to restrict the subset of words that you include in your text analysis. For example, if you are primarily interested in understanding *what* people are writing or talking about (as opposed to *how* they are talking about something), then you may decide to include only nouns and proper nouns, or noun chunks (discussed below) in your analysis. In our example abstract, nouns and noun chunks like 'Europe', 'radical-right politics', 'Brexit referendum', 'Trump campaign', 'causes and consequences', 'ethno-nationalist populism', and so on tell us far more about the *content* of this abstract than words such as 'and', 'has', 'recent', or 'available'. We can do this by filtering words based on their part of speech.

If you're a little lost at this point, that's a good thing; it means you're paying attention, and are justifiably struggling to acquire a new way of thinking about language in general, and text data specifically. At this point, an example might help show how these processes play out in action. Returning to our example abstract, we'll start by examining each word and its part of speech.

```
for item in doc[:20]:
    print(f'{item.text} ({item.pos_})')
```

```
Scholarly (ADJ)
and (CCONJ)
journalistic (ADJ)
accounts (NOUN)
of (ADP)
the (DET)
recent (ADJ)
successes (NOUN)
of (ADP)
```

```
radical (ADJ)
- (PUNCT)
right (NOUN)
politics (NOUN)
in (ADP)
Europe (PROPN)
and (CCONJ)
the (DET)
United (PROPN)
States (PROPN)
, (PUNCT)
```

spaCy classifies each word into one of 19 different parts of speech, each of which is defined in the documentation. However, if you are uncertain about what a part-of-speech tag is, you can also ask spaCy to explain() it to you. For example, spacy.explain('ADJ') will return adjective, and spacy.explain('ADP') will return adposition. Because the part of speech a word plays can vary depending on the sentence – 'meeting' can be a noun or a verb, depending on the context – spaCy's approach to part-of-speech tagging combines language-based rules and statistical knowledge from its trained models that can be used to estimate the best part of speech for a word given the words that appear before and after it.

If these 19 parts of speech are not sufficient for your purposes, it is possible to access fine-grained parts of speech that include additional information, including verb tenses and specific types of pronouns. These fine-grained parts of speech can be accessed using the .tag attribute rather than .pos_. As you likely expect, there are far more fine-grained parts of speech than coarse-grained ones. Their meanings can all be found online in the spaCy documentation.

Because spaCy assigns a part of speech to each token when we initially call nlp(), we can iterate over the tokens in our abstract and extract those that match the part of speech we are most interested in. For example, the following code will identify the nouns in our abstract:

```
nouns = [item.text for item in doc if item.pos_ == 'NOUN']
print(nouns[:20])
```

```
['accounts', 'successes', 'right', 'politics', 'referendum', 'campaign', 'phenomena',
    'populism', 'ethno', 'nationalism', 'authoritarianism', 'elements', 'right', '
    right', 'lack', 'clarity', 'accounts', 'causes', 'consequences', 'ethno']
```

We can do the same for other parts of speech, such as adjectives, or for multiple parts of speech:

```
adjectives = [item.text for item in doc if item.pos_ == 'ADJ']
adjectives[:20]
```

```
['Scholarly',
 'journalistic',
 'recent',
 'radical',
 'important',
 'radical',
 'coterminous',
```

```
'limited',
'analytical',
'nationalist',
'contemporary',
'temporal',
'discursive',
'public',
'available',
'radical',
'stable',
'public',
'radical',
'pre']
```

```
parts = ['NOUN', 'ADJ']
words = [item.text for item in doc if item.pos_ in parts]
words[:20]
```

```
['Scholarly',
 'journalistic',
 'accounts',
 'recent',
 'successes',
 'radical',
 'right',
 'politics',
 'referendum',
 'campaign',
 'phenomena',
 'populism',
 'ethno',
 'nationalism',
 'authoritarianism',
 'important',
 'elements',
 'radical',
 'right',
 'coterminous']
```

The accuracy of the part-of-speech tagger in version 3 of spaCy is 97% for the small English core model and 97.4% for the large English core models, both of which are trained using convolutional neural networks. As mentioned earlier, you will only see modest gains in accuracy by switching to a larger statistical model. Ultimately, as you will soon learn, the accuracy of these kinds of models depends in large part on the data they're trained on. The good news is that the accuracy rates for part-of-speech tagging are consistently high regardless of the corpus used for training, and for researchers like us who are more interested in applying these algorithms than developing them have nothing to gain from trying to beat the 97% accuracy.

9.7 Syntactic Dependency Parsing

The third component of the spaCy processing pipeline (see Figure 9.1) is the syntactic dependency parser. This rule-based parser rests on a solid foundation of linguistic research and, when combined with machine learning models, greatly increases the accuracy of a variety of important text processing tasks. It also makes it possible to extract meaningful sequences of words from texts, such as short phrases, or components of larger narratives and frames. We will consider the power of this approach by looking at how spaCy extracts noun chunks from text, setting aside more complex manipulations of the dependency tree until later.

When we communicate in natural languages such as English, we follow sets of commonly held rules that govern how we arrange words, clauses, and phrases in sentences. For the most part, we learn these rules – grammar – implicitly via socialization as children, and then more explicitly later in life. For non-linguists, some explicit forms of instruction about the 'correct' and 'incorrect' way of doing things in a language are what probably come to mind when we think about grammar, but from a linguistic point of view grammatical rules should *not* be seen as proscriptive but rather as cultural and evolving in populations over time. Grammatical 'rules' are about dominant patterns in usage in a population (linguists use the word 'rule' in the way sociologists and political scientists do, not the way physicists do). They are one of the best examples of shared culture and implicit cultural rules we have! Rather than proscription, linguists are focused on *description* and *explanation* of grammatical rules, and there is an enormous amount of formal linguistic theory and research on modelling grammar. Pānini's study of the grammatical structure of Sanskrit was written in the fourth century and is still discussed today (Jurafsky and Hand, 2009)!

One of the most enduring ways of modelling grammar is dependency parsing, which has its origins in ancient Greek and Indian linguistics (Jurafsky and Hand, 2009). Dependency parsing is a rules-based approach that models the relationships between words in a sentence as a directed network. The edges in the network represent various kinds of grammatical relationships between the pairs of words. You may already be able to think of some important grammatical relations, such as clausal argument relations (e.g. a word can be a *nominal subject* of another word, a *direct* or *indirect object*, or a *clausal complement*), modifier relations (e.g. *adjectives* that modify a noun, *adverbs* that modify a verb), or others such as coordinating conjunctions that connect phrases and clauses in sentences. Linguists have documented many important grammatical relations and have systematically compared how they operate across different languages (e.g. Nivre and Fang, 2017). spaCy combines this rules-based dependency parsing with machine learning models, which results in extremely high levels of accuracy for a broad range of NLP tasks, such as part-of-speech tagging, discussed earlier.

There are some rules around how these dependency relation networks are constructed that are helpful to understand. First, every sentence has one root word (i.e. node) that is not dependent on any other words. It's the starting point for our sentence from which *all* other words 'grow'. Second, with the single exception of the root word, every word has one and only one dependency relationship with another word. Finally, there is a path that starts at the root word and connects to every other word in the tree. This directed acyclic network is usually represented with the text written horizontally left to right, with arcs connecting and labelling specific dependency relationships between words.

The syntactic dependency parser built into spaCy is powerful, accurate, and relatively fast. spaCy also simplifies the process of understanding these syntactic dependencies by using a visualization tool called displaCy, which is especially useful for researchers with little background knowledge of formal linguistic theory. For example, let's use displacy to visualize the syntactic dependencies in a short sentence. Below, we do this for a short and simple sentence. If you're executing code from a script, you should use the `.serve()` method. If you're in a Jupyter Notebook, you should use `.render()` instead.

```
sentence = nlp("This book is a practical guide to computational social science")
```

The dependency relations that spaCy identified in this simple sentence are shown in Table 9.1 and in Figure 9.2 (produced using displacy). As you can see, spaCy has mapped each word in our document to another word, based on a specific type of dependency relationship. These dependency types are actually labelled on the arcs in the visualization. In Figure 9.2 and Table 9.1, each word has a 'head' (which sends a directed link to the word as a 'child') but only some have 'children' (which receive an incoming link from a word if they depend on it).

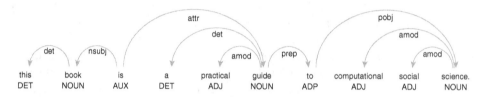

Figure 9.2 A visualization of syntactic dependency relationships between words

Table 9.1 A table view of the syntactic dependencies shown in Figure 9.2

Text	Dependency	Head Text	Head Part of Speech	Children
this	det	book	NOUN	[]
book	nsubj	is	AUX	[this]
is	ROOT	is	AUX	[book, guide, .]
a	det	guide	NOUN	[]
practical	amod	guide	NOUN	[]
guide	attr	is	AUX	[a, practical, to]
to	prep	guide	NOUN	[science]
computational	amod	science	NOUN	[]
social	amod	science	NOUN	[]
science	pobj	to	ADP	[computational, social]
.	punct	is	AUX	[]

For now, what's important to understand is that spaCy does this dependency parsing as part of the default processing pipeline (and like other parts of the pipeline, it is possible to disable it if you don't need it). However, we can extract information about these dependency relations directly from the syntactic tree, which in turn enables us to extract a variety of useful information from text with a very high degree of precision and makes it possible to partially automate methods such as quantitative narrative analysis, briefly discussed below, which are otherwise very laborious and time-consuming.

Noun chunks

One substantial benefit of dependency parsing is the ability to extract coherent phrases and other sub-sentence chunks of meaning from text. We will learn a bit about how to navigate the dependency tree shortly, but for now we can get a sense of the power of dependency parsing by looking at the example of noun phrases, which spaCy calls 'noun chunks'.

Noun chunks consist of a single word (the noun) or a string of words including a noun and the words that modify that noun. These are usually 'premodifiers', meaning words (e.g. adjectives) that appear *before* the focal noun, not after. A base noun phrase is a phrase that has a noun as its head, and which does not itself contain another noun phrase.

Below, we iterate over the doc containing the text of Bonikowski's (2017) article and print each noun chunk:

```
for item in list(doc.noun_chunks)[:10]:
    print(item.text)
```

```
Scholarly and journalistic accounts
the recent successes
radical-right politics
Europe
the United States
the Brexit referendum
the Trump campaign
three phenomena
populism
ethno-nationalism
```

Remember, the computer doesn't actually know the meaning of any of these words or phrases. Given that the results are surprisingly accurate, it should be clear how useful this kind of simplification could be for working with large volumes of text! In a later chapter, we will take a closer look at detecting noun chunks, using a machine learning approach designed specifically for this task.

Extracting words by dependency labels: subject, verb, and object triplets

Earlier, you learnt how to process a large collection of Docs and extract Tokens from each based on several criteria, including their part of speech. We can also extract tokens from documents based on other criteria, such as their dependency relationships with other words. For example, if we wanted to extract a very small representation of an action–object narrative from a sentence (e.g. 'Kat (subject) plays (verb) bass (object).'), we could extract the transitive verb (i.e. a verb that takes an object, 'plays') and the direct object of that transitive verb (i.e. 'bass'). To do this, we simply check the .dep_ tags for each token rather than the .pos_ tags. For example, the loops below create a list of tuples containing the transitive verbs and direct objects for each sentence in doc:

```
for sent in doc.sents:
    tvdo = [(token.head.text, token.text) for token in sent if token.dep_ == 'dobj']
    print(tvdo)
```

```
[('conflate', 'phenomena')]
[]
[('hindered', 'accounts')]
[('address', 'problem'), ('bring', 'research'), ('define', 'concepts'), ('examine', '
    patterns')]
[('understand', 'support')]
[('shifting', 'context')]
[('engendered', 'sense')]
[('channelled', 'threats'), ('activating', 'attitudes'), ('return', 'power')]
[('threaten', 'institutions'), ('has', 'potential'), ('alter', 'contours'), ('creating
    ', 'conditions')]
```

When analysing text in terms of these semantic dependencies, we are often looking to extract information in the form of a semantic triplet of subject–verb–object, also known as an SVO. In social science text analysis, these triplets are most closely associated with the quantitative narrative analysis framework developed by Roberto Fransozi (2004). The idea, in short, is that these SVOs contain crucial information about *who* did *what* to *whom*. We will see examples of working with this kind of data in later chapters, but let's take a preliminary look at the kind of thing we can expect when extracting SVOs.

Walking through the linguistic technicalities of a fully functional SVO workflow is outside the scope of this chapter, but we can use the subject_verb_object_triples() function included in the dcss package to see the results of a reasonably complex implementation of the basic idea, as outlined by researchers such as Fransozi:

```
from dcss.svo import subject_verb_object_triples
```

```
list(subject_verb_object_triples(doc))
```

```
[(accounts, tend, to conflate),
 (three, are, elements),
 (lack, has hindered, accounts),
 (I, bring, research),
 (I, bring, define),
 (I, bring, examine),
 (variety, have engendered, sense),
 (discourse, has channelled, threats),
 (that, promise, to return),
 (form, threaten, institutions),
 (form, threaten, relations),
 (it, has, potential)]
```

Some of these look pretty good, but others leave a little to be desired. As you can probably imagine, there are an enormous number of challenges involved in automating this kind of language processing. To get things *just right,* you have to consider how people write and speak in different contexts, how sentence construction varies (active, passive; formal, informal), how statements differ from questions, and so on. It is possible to get very high-quality results by building complex logic into the way you walk through the dependency trees, but in general you can expect to find that the signal-to-noise ratio in automated SVO analyses typically means you have to do a good amount of manual work to clean up the results.

Further Reading

Vasiliev (2020) provides a fairly deep dive into spaCy for a variety of natural language processing tasks. The spaCy documentation is itself also *very good*, although some parts of it might be a bit challenging to fully understand until you know a bit more about neural networks and large-scale pretrained language models. Those topics are covered later in the book.

9.8 Conclusion

The key points in this chapter are as follows:

- We discussed a variety of common text processing tasks and demonstrated how to use them on a small text dataset and a very large one.
- We learnt about how spaCy's text processing pipeline is organized and how to use its data structures.
- We used spaCy's pipeline and data structures to normalize text via lemmatization.
- We filtered and selected words based on the part of speech and their syntactic dependencies.
- We learnt how to approximately extract noun chunks, and how to identify the subject, verb, and object in a sentence.

Visit the website at https://study.sagepub.com/mclevey for additional resources

10
ITERATIVE TEXT ANALYSIS

10.1 Learning Objectives

By the end of this chapter, you should be able to do the following:

- Describe how text preprocessing, exploratory text analysis, close reading, and computational modelling all connect in larger text processing pipelines and workflows
- Explain the difference between manifest and latent content in text data
- Explain why there is disagreement about whether coding (also known as annotating or labelling) or count-based feature extraction methods are the best tools for constructing quantitative representations of text data
- Describe the 'bag-of-words' approach to representing text
- Explain what a document-term matrix is, and compare matrices with term counts and term weights (e.g. term frequency–inverse document frequency [TF-IDF])
- Explain how TF-IDF word weights are computed
- Explain the role of close reading in computational text analysis
- Describe the computational grounded theory framework

10.2 Learning Materials

You can find the online learning materials for this chapter in `doing_computational_social_science/Chapter_10`. `cd` into the directory and launch your Jupyter server.

10.3 Introduction

The previous chapter introduced some basic methods for processing natural language data stored as unstructured text. Typically, these methods are part of a much larger project; we are preparing text data for some other downstream analysis. Before we get there, this chapter offers a bigger picture view of generic text processing pipelines and workflows. The goal is to understand how the various text-analytic methods that are introduced in this book fit together and to highlight a few core challenges in text analysis.

Before we get started, I want to clarify exactly what I mean by 'pipelines' in this chapter. As a reminder, we briefly discussed spaCy's text processing pipeline in the previous chapter. In this chapter, I am using 'pipelines' to refer to the same general idea; it's the sequence of operations in which we are pushing our data through a series of steps, transforming the data and fitting various kinds of models along the way. However, we are focusing on an idealized text analysis pipeline for an entire project.

10.4 Exploration in Context: Text Analysis Pipelines

The methods introduced in the previous chapter are rarely used on their own. Instead, they are paired with other methods and models in larger text analysis pipelines. Let's start by discussing these larger pipelines to provide context for what you've already learnt and what is still to come. This chapter will focus on summarizing and describing the *content* of many different documents. We will consider other possible goals later in the book.

Figure 10.1 is a high-level overview of a typical computational text analysis pipeline focused on describing the content of many documents in a corpus. Keep in mind that this is a *typical* project pipeline and the details may differ in any specific project. At the top left of the figure is the 'original data'. At this stage, we don't want to be sitting around waiting for our code to execute, which is often the case when working with large text datasets. To enable quick, iterative, and multi-method analyses, we can start by drawing a smaller random sample.

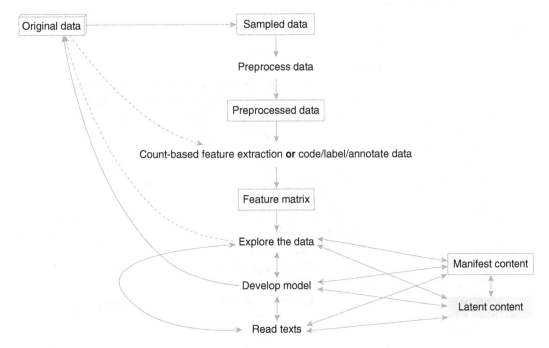

Figure 10.1 A flowchart depicting the steps involved in performing iterative exploratory data analysis

Once we have our sample, we perform some initial processing, or preprocessing, which usually involves a combination of cleaning and prescreening text using methods introduced in the previous chapter. The cleaning tasks vary by project, but may include converting characters to lower case, removing punctuation, and normalization via lemmatization. I think of prescreening as the selection of relevant text, rather than filtering of unwanted text, because we are not modifying the original data; our research workflows are always non-destructive.

The methods introduced conceptually in this chapter and concretely in the next are represented in the next stage of the pipeline, which is the construction of a feature matrix. There are two main ways to do this: (1) by extracting features from the text itself and (2) by 'coding' the data (also known as labelling and annotation). This is a somewhat controversial stage in the process, as researchers and methodologists disagree about the 'best' way to accomplish this task. Both approaches have their merits and demerits, and you should select the approach that will best enable you to answer your research questions.

The next step in the pipeline is exploratory analysis, the focus of the next chapter. The main purpose of these exploratory methods is to develop a deeper understanding of both the manifest and latent content in a corpus. Manifest content is plainly communicated, whereas latent content is 'below the surface' of the text and therefore requires more interpretation from the researcher. I want to emphasize that this interpretive work is done *iteratively*, by going back and forth between data-driven exploration of the kind introduced here, formal modelling (discussed in later chapters), and careful close readings of individual documents. Recall the discussion of Box's loop from Chapter 7. Exploratory text analysis serves the same purpose as the techniques from Chapter 7: better understanding our data and analysis so we can iteratively critique, revise, and improve our text analysis and modelling.

Counting, coding, reading

Social scientists have been answering questions about our social, political, psychological, and economic lives by systematically collecting, interpreting, and drawing inferences from text data for more than 100 years, long before anyone had the kind of computational power at their fingertips that we do now. (Humanists have been doing it even longer, of course.) Formal content analysis techniques have been a core part of the social sciences' methodological toolkits since shortly after the First World War, when researchers such as Lasswell (1927) started developing methods for analysing propaganda and political discourse in newspapers (Krippendorff, 2019). It should hardly come as a surprise that the explosion of possibilities afforded by *computation* and large-scale textual data is viewed in part through the lens of this long history, much of which has revolved around competing ideas about the best way to analyse latent content.

For many years, these differences divided text analysts, with some being more oriented towards scientific approaches and others towards the humanities. These divisions are not so clear-cut in practice, and they involve far more rigour and depth than their oversimplified names suggest. The methods used by these groups are sometimes summarized as 'counting' (identifying patterns in the manifest content of text), 'coding' (identifying latent content through careful specification of concepts), and 'reading' (of the painstaking variety practised by our friends in the humanities).

Rather than rehashing comparisons of specific approaches (see Ignatow and Mihalcea, 2016), we will focus on understanding why manual coding and the role of interpretation have been so divisive, and how these debates have informed multiple scientific approaches to content analysis, be they quantitative, qualitative, computational, or hybrid (Krippendorff, 2019; see also Neuendorf, 2016).

The distinction between manifest and latent content played an important role in the early development of mainstream quantitative approaches to content analysis (Berelson, 1952; Krippendorff, 2019; Neuendorf, 2016). Focusing on manifest content is often considered more *objective* because it involves relatively little interpretation. With manifest content, meanings are unambiguous and sit at the surface level of text. Analysing latent content, however, is a little too close to *subjective* judgement for some. The distance from words on the page to the latent meanings and messages behind them requires a greater leap of interpretation. Any analysis of latent content necessarily requires us to use our human brains – wired as they are with preconceived notions, theories, and cultural schemas, and prone to cognitive biases like conformation bias and motivated reasoning – to interpret ambiguous meanings. This is unfortunate, as latent content tends to be much more interesting than manifest content.

To be clear, counting techniques are in no way free of subjectivity; the main goal of 'counting' is feature extraction under different constraints (e.g. occurrences, co-occurrences) *which can then be modelled*. No serious social scientist should be satisfied with a table of word co-occurrences and no further interpretation. The major difference is where the interpretations take place and how accessible and transparent they are.

Further Reading

Evans and Aceves (2016) provide a great review of the intersection of natural language processing and social science content analysis. If you want to learn more about the general methodological foundations of quantitative content analysis in the social sciences, Krippendorff (2019) and Neuendorf (2016) are widely used sources. Ignatow and Mihalcea (2016) provide a broader methodological discussion that includes high-level discussions of text analysis methods from the social sciences and humanities as well as computer science.

Differences in interpretations of latent content are bound to arise. For a very long time, the mainstream solution for dealing with this problem has been careful specification, which we've already discussed in the context of working with latent factors (Chapter 29), and manual coding. Researchers specify precise operational definitions that indicate what concepts mean, and what types of things would constitute an observation of that concept in a document. Once defined, researchers *manually* construct the quantitative representation of their text data by coding each document.

In this context, 'coding' is the process of transforming unstructured documents into structured datasets by manually labelling data according to some set of variables that are coupled to theoretical concepts via the specification process. While there are different coding styles, they tend to follow a similar pattern. First, you have a research question you want to answer. Usually you also have some idea of what you expect, grounded in some larger theory. For example, if you wanted to compare the tone and argumentative style of letters to the editor addressing local or non-local issues (e.g. Perrin and Vaisey, 2008), you would first decide what types of tones and argumentative styles are relevant, and then you would carefully operationalize those tones and styles based, at least in part, on theory. Then you would read each text and assign codes based on the presence or absence of specific tones and argumentative styles. If resources allow, you would have multiple trained researchers (including yourself) code the documents. This makes it possible to compare the codes assigned to documents by different researchers and compute an inter-coder reliability rate (Krippendorff, 2019). Codes with a reliability rate above a given threshold (e.g. 90% agreement between coders) are retained, shifting the coding process from one based on *subjective interpretation* to *intersubjective agreement*. In short, the coding approach is one that hinges on good specification, careful interpretation, and ideally high levels of intersubjective agreement.

Though widely practised, and despite plenty to love, there are some valid concerns about manual coding that go beyond the time (and money) it requires. The difference between approaches that 'code' and those that count and map was the subject of an animated debate in the *American Journal of Cultural Sociology* following the publication of Monica Lee and John Levi Martin's (2015a) 'Coding, Counting, and Cultural Cartography'. (I've provided the references for this debate in the 'Where to Go Next' section at the end of the chapter.) Lee and Martin start by engaging with an argument made by Richard Biernacki (2009, 2012) that, in short, manual coding just makes things worse. Biernacki thinks that any good content analysis requires the kind of careful interpretation that our colleagues in the humanities practise. From his perspective, manual coding both lowers the quality of the interpretation (by virtue of being coupled to theoretical concepts and hypotheses) and obscures it.

Consider an example. If I were to code the presence or absence of different types of political arguments in a collection of news stories about immigration reform, I would start specifying the types of political arguments I think are relevant and likely to be found. I would have to be explicit about what constitutes an observation of one type of political argument versus another (i.e. operationalization). Researchers who question the validity of the coding approach would likely point out that my (or any) choice of coding scheme would invariably misrepresent the texts themselves. As a result, my codes could be contested by researchers who see the same text differently, and any results I obtained from analysing the final dataset would likely not be replicated by another researcher. Their second objection would be that this potential interpretive chaos is hidden away behind the codes, where other researchers and readers can't see it.

Biernacki's (2015) solution is to reject coding altogether and to replace it with humanistic approaches to interpretation. Somewhat surprisingly, he argues that this approach is actually more scientific because it 'better engages standards for validity, transparency, producing competing hypotheses, generalizing and hypothesis testing by recalcitrant detail' (p. 313). Lee and Martin (2015a, 2015b) accept Biernacki's (2015) critique that manual coding *hides* the essential but messy work of interpretation rather than eliminates it, but they disagree that turning to humanistic approaches is the only, or the best, response to the problem. Instead, they propose a refinement of the 'counting' methods that begins by representing original texts in a simplified form, like a map represents terrain in simplified form. To be a good 'map', these simplified representations need to remove a lot of information from the texts while still faithfully representing the core features of the original texts. Lee and Martin (2015a, 2015b) offer semantic networks (discussed in later chapters) as an approach, which work by exploiting the low-level relationships between words within semantic units like sentences and paragraphs.

Lee and Martin's (2015a, 2015b) goal is not to eliminate interpretation, but rather to move it out into the open where it can be seen, evaluated, and potentially contested. The idea is that this becomes possible if we have formal procedures for producing map representations from text. This leaves the researcher to openly and transparently interpret the map rather than hiding interpretive judgements behind codes and then analysing relationships among the codes as if no really challenging interpretation had taken place at all.

This debate boils down to whether, and how, to make complex interpretive research, which is absolutely unavoidable, more open and transparent. The debate between coding and count-based approaches is largely a debate about where the inevitable interpretation should happen and who should be able to see and assess it. Those who code and those who count both break with Biernacki (2015), and personally I think that's a good thing because the approach he recommends – close reading – is *not an alternative* to counting or coding. Coding and counting both have many strengths, but should *always* be paired with close reading of a subset of documents. In other words, Biernacki (2015) is right that close reading and interpretation are essential, but it doesn't follow that manual coding has no place in text analysis, or in social science more broadly. For the same reason, Lee and Martin (2015a, 2015b) are right to shift interpretation out into the open, but their critique of manual coding is also overly dismissive and 'maps' don't just magically reveal their unambiguous meanings to us. We should not abandon manual coding in favour of an exclusive commitment to humanistic interpretation or formalism; we should combine close reading, manual coding, formal approaches, and other methods.

In the rest of this chapter, and in subsequent chapters focused on text data, I will assume the following:

1   Close reading is not an alternative to any other method, it must be paired with other methods.
2   'Coding' and 'counting' approaches need not be pitted against each other either, as they can be used together to mitigate the limitations of employing either approach in a vacuum.
3   Any computational approach to text analysis benefits from combining all of these approaches in some way.

In the rest of this chapter, we will introduce some important count-based feature extraction methods for constructing quantitative representations of text, and we will see how to use these representations to compare high-level differences in manifest language use and to explore the *latent* dimensions of text data. Like the methods you learnt in the previous chapter, the methods you learn here are useful regardless of whether you want to interpret a 'map' or model your data a bit further downstream. In later chapters, we will discuss several ways of doing this using different types of machine learning. We will also return to the idea of close reading and how to integrate it into larger text analysis workflows.

10.5 Count-Based Feature Extraction: From Strings to a Bag of Words

Any quantitative or computational text analysis requires some sort of quantitative representation of the text to operate on. Once you've constructed that representation, the analysis typically involves going back and forth between algorithmic manipulations and modelling of the quantitative representation on the one hand and careful interpretation of the textual representation on the other hand. For this reason, it is very useful to have the following four things accessible to you at any point in the analysis process:

1   The original texts
2   Any relevant metadata about the texts, such as who produced them
3   The preprocessed versions of the texts
4   A quantitative representation of the texts

There are two main types of quantitative representations of text that you will learn in this book: (1) long sparse vectors and (2) short dense vectors. The long and sparse vector representation is usually referred to as a bag of words, and the most widely used data structure is the document-term matrix (DTM). The short dense vector representations have come to be known as embeddings. Alternative ways of representing texts quantitatively, such as networks, can easily be interpreted as variations on these two types of representation. We will set embeddings aside for now and focus on DTMs.

Long and sparse representations with DTMs

The first step in constructing a quantitative representation of text is to learn the 'vocabulary', which is the set of unique terms (i.e. words and short phrases) that are used across the entire corpus. In our dataset of political speeches by UK MPs, for example, the corpus would consist of the full text across all speeches by all political parties in our *sampled* dataset. Note that the vocabulary depends on how we define the corpus. If we define it as the original speech data, then the vocabulary will consist of every unique token used across all speeches. If we define it as our *preprocessed* speech data, then the vocabulary will consist of all the unique words that make it through our preprocessing step in the text analysis pipeline. This process of defining the corpus, learning the vocabulary, and constructing the DTM is an example of automated count-based feature extraction.

When we create a DTM representation of our text data, each unique term in the corpus vocabulary will become an individual feature (i.e. column) unless we specifically set some sort of condition that filters terms out (e.g. must appear in a minimum of five documents).

The cells in a DTM typically represent one of three things:

1   The presence or absence of a token in the relevant document (0 or 1)
2   A count of the number of times a token appears in the relevant document (integers)
3   Some measure of word importance or relevance, such as TF-IDF (floats), which we will discuss below.

The DTM shape will always be equal to the number of unique tokens in the vocabulary (minus any that we screen out in the process of constructing the DTM) and the number of documents (i.e. rows). Table 10.1 is a hypothetical example of a DTM with term counts in each cell.

Table 10.1   A hypothetical document-term matrix

Documents	Token 1	Token 2	Token 3	Token 4	Token ...	Token n
Document 1	0	0	3	0	2	8
Document 2	2	0	1	1	0	0
Document 3	1	0	0	0	1	4
Document 4	0	2	1	0	1	3
Document ...	0	0	0	1	2	1
Document n	1	0	0	1	5	1

In this case, each row of the matrix is a vector representation for a document and each column is a vector representation for a token in the vocabulary. The long sparse vector representation for document 1, then, would be all of the numbers in the first row of the table

(Document 1: [0,0,3,0,2,8]) and the long sparse vector representation for token 1 would be all of the numbers in the column (Token 1: [0,2,1,0,0,1]).

When we describe vectors as 'long and sparse', we are typically referring to the document vectors, which are long because each element in the vector (i.e. feature in the matrix) represents a unique term in the vocabulary used across the entire corpus. Vocabularies are almost always large, and most words in the vocabulary do not appear in most documents. As a result, these vector representations are mostly full of 0s; hence sparse.

Weighting words with TF-IDF

In many approaches to computational text analysis, working with simple count data is rarely ideal because the words that occur the most frequently are function words (e.g., 'the', 'and', 'of') that carry very little information about the actual *content* of a document. Extremely rare words are also generally uninformative. The most informative words tend to be somewhere in between these two extreme ends of the frequency distribution. We typically identify these words using some sort of word weight, the most common of which is a measure called TF-IDF.

TF-IDF stands for 'term frequency–inverse document frequency', and it is intended to measure the usefulness of any given token for helping reveal what a document is about relative to other documents in a corpus. It *weights* words rather than counts them, where the weights are lower for words that are either too common or too rare. To understand how it works, let's break it down and look at term frequency and inverse document frequency separately, and then the full measure. To do so, we will use a hypothetical example of a dataset of 150 journal article abstracts.

As you might expect, term frequency is a measure of how common a word is in some document. Rather than using a straight count (which would be biased towards longer documents), we multiply the number of times the word appears in a document by the inverse ratio of the number of documents that have the term compared to the total number of documents in the corpus. Let's say, for example, that the word 'environment' appears four times in a 200-word abstract for a journal article about environmental activism. The term frequency $TF_{i,j}$ for 'environment' *in this specific document* would be 0.02:

$$TF_{environment} = \frac{4}{200} = 0.02$$

Now let's say there are a total of 150 abstracts in our dataset and the word 'environment' appears 42 times in the full dataset. We want to know how important the word 'environment' is across the whole collection, so we calculate the inverse document frequency, IDF, using the following equation:

$$IDF = \log\left(\frac{N}{DF_i}\right)$$

where N is the total number of documents in the dataset, and DF_i is the number of documents that the word i appears in. The IDF score for 'environment' is the log of this value, which is 0.55:

$$IDF_{environment} = \log\left(\frac{150}{42}\right) = 0.55$$

To compute the TF-IDF weight for any word in any document in a corpus, we multiply *TF* with *IDF*:

$$W_{i,j} = TF_{i,j} \times \log\left(\frac{N}{DF_i}\right)$$

Putting it all together, TF-IDF is as its name suggests: Term frequency × Inverse document frequency. The TF-IDF weight of a word in a document increases the more frequently it appears in that document but decreases if it also appears across many other documents. Rare, but not *too* rare, words are weighted more than words that show up across many documents. The result is a set of words that, while not the most common, tell us a lot about the content of any one document relative to other documents in the collection. This measure is far more useful than raw counts when we are attempting to find meaningful words. In the next chapter, we will further clarify TF-IDF by comparing word weights with their frequencies in our political speech dataset.

10.6 Close Reading

So far, I've sketched out a pretty high-level and idealized pipeline that explains how different types of text processing, analysis, and modelling fit together. I've also explained the challenges involved in one crucial step: the approach used to represent text *quantitatively*. These challenges have led to disagreements over whether and how to represent text quantitatively, with some arguing in favour of coding over counting, others counting over coding, and others for throwing the baby out with the bathwater. Now let's turn our attention to another issue, which is the role of close reading in a computational text analysis. The idea, illustrated in the pipeline, is that you engage in deep reading *as you iteratively explore your data and develop models*.

In computational text analysis, methodologists are beginning to think through ways of *systematically* combining various inductive and deductive approaches to computational text analysis with good old-fashioned reading. Why? Because:

1   mixed-methods research (Small, 2011) is especially valuable when one of the methodologies is less familiar to the scientific community (as computational text analysis often is), and/or when it pulls the researcher further away from the original data than more familiar methods (validation and triangulation);
2   there is a lot to be gained by thoughtfully combining induction and deduction; and
3   machines and humans are good at different types of things, and we want to use both our brains and our computers for the things they are best at.

Most computational text analyses involve machine learning of one kind or another, and the impressive results that these models produce, combined with the use of metaphors like 'reading' and 'learning', can make it easy to forget, at least temporarily, that computers are not *actually* reading; they don't understand words, sentences, or meaning (manifest or latent) in the same way that humans do. When computers 'read', they are applying mathematical operations to internal representations of data. More inductive computational models, such as probabilistic topic models (introduced in Chapter 29), identify patterns in documents that, hopefully, correspond to what we humans recognize as reasonably coherent themes and 'topics'. Despite finding the pattern, the computer doesn't know what a topic is, or what a word is for that matter. To really know, understand, and assess the validity of the computational analysis, we humans need to read things carefully. Systematic comparisons of manual and computational text analysis support this combination (Nelson et al., 2018). There is no way around it; whatever our specific interests or text analysis methodology, we have to read carefully. That's a good thing.

Humans with domain knowledge should do the things that humans are good at and computers are bad at (e.g. interpretation, critical thinking), and computers should do the things that computers are good at but humans are comparably bad at (e.g. computing the similarity of two massive vectors of numbers). In the next section, we explore one practical implementation of human–computer division of labour: computational grounded theory.

Computational grounded theory

One of the most exciting and promising examples of a mixed-approach framework is Laura Nelson's (2017) 'computational grounded theory'. It is, to date, the most systematic and sophisticated approach to combining machine learning and computation more generally with deep reading and interpretation by humans. As the name of the framework suggests, Nelson's (2017) approach builds on the qualitative foundations of grounded theory (Charmaz, 2006; Glaser and Strauss, 1999), which is (somewhat confusingly) both a process and a product. To risk oversimplifying things, the process involves *inductively* identifying, integrating, and refining categories of meaning in text. This is accomplished through a variety of specific procedures, the most common of which is the method of 'constant comparison' of cases. The product is a set of relatively abstract concepts and statements (i.e. theory) that are 'grounded' in the data.

Nelson (2017) builds on this methodological foundation because it is well-established, unapologetically inductive, and emphasizes the interpretive work that is unavoidable in text analysis. But, as she points out, grounded theory does not scale well to large datasets, and the results can be difficult to validate and replicate. Her computational framework is designed to address these problems while retaining the good parts of the original approach.

Computational grounded theory involves three basic steps. The first is pattern detection using exploratory and computationally inductive methods – such as those introduced in the next chapter, as well as in Chapters 29 and 32 – to discover latent themes and topics in a corpus. This is a shift in the logic of the grounded theory method. In classic grounded theory, the researcher is doing interpretive work to develop and refine categories of meaning. In computational grounded theory, the computer identifies potential categories of meaning (i.e. topics) using unsupervised methods that can be replicated; the researcher interprets and evaluates those categories.

This is the starting point for the second step – 'guided deep reading' – in which the researcher makes informed decisions about specific texts to read and interpret. The *guided* part is key here, because it allows the researcher to select texts that are representative of some larger theme or topic, not an unusual outlier. This helps mitigate the effects of confirmation bias and other cognitive biases that can affect the judgements of even the most well-intentioned researcher. It also makes the interpretive part of the analysis easier to validate and replicate. Think of it as the difference between exploring an unfamiliar city with and without a map. Without a map, you may end up seeing the same amount of the city, but if you have a map, you can make more informed decisions about where to go and you will have a better sense of what you did and did not see. You can also trace your route on the map, making it easier for someone else to understand where you went and potentially to go there themselves.

To summarize, we use computationally inductive methods to discover some potential themes and estimate how they are distributed within and across texts in our corpus. We then use the results of that analysis to select a sample of texts that are representative of specific themes and, through a process of 'deep reading', use our human brains to develop a better and more sophisticated understanding of what those themes are. This enables us to come to an understanding of the text that is better than any one method could have produced on its own.

The third and final step of the computational grounded theory framework is pattern confirmation. For Nelson (2017), this step forces the researcher to operationalize concepts and ideas discovered in the first two steps, and then check to see how common they are across the corpus. One way to do this is to go through the supervised learning process covered in Chapters 20 and 21, but we will set further discussion of supervised learning methods aside for now.

The full process is summarized in Figure 10.2, which is based on a figure from Nelson's (2017) article. I encourage you to read her article carefully, in part because she thoroughly illustrates each step with examples from her work on the political logics underlying the women's movement in New York and Chicago from 1865 to 1975 (Nelson, 2015). It's an excellent article with fascinating examples.

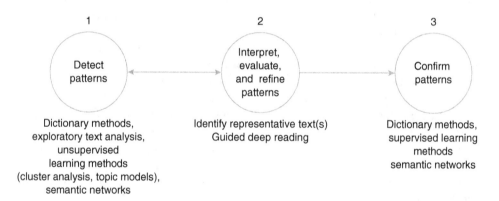

Figure 10.2   A flowchart depicting the steps involved in performing computational grounded theory

Further Reading

If you are interested in the debate over coding and counting that was discussed in this chapter, I would recommend reading the original articles by Lee and Martin (2015a, 2015b), Biernacki (2015), Reed (2015), and Spillman (2015).

In addition, I recommend reading Laura Nelson's (2017) original article on computational grounded theory, and her 2021 article 'Cycles of conflict, a century of continuity: The impact of persistent place-based political logics in social movement strategy' in the *American Journal of Sociology* for an exemplary application of the method. You can also learn more about the original grounded theory method by consulting Glaser and Strauss (1999) or Charmaz (2006). Finally, Small (2011) offers a great overview of various different ways of doing mixed-methods research.

10.7 Conclusion

The key points in this chapter are as follows:

- We outlined a generic text analysis pipeline that starts with sampling and preprocessing text, as well as constructing quantitative representations of unstructured text data using manual coding and/or automated count-based feature extraction.
- We discussed the challenge of transparently interpreting latent content and the tensions between the coding, counting, and close reading approaches.
- We highlighted Laura Nelson's (2017) computational grounded theory framework as an exemplar pipeline for iterative multi-method text analysis.

Visit the website at https://study.sagepub.com/mclevey for additional resources

11

EXPLORATORY TEXT ANALYSIS – WORKING WITH WORD FREQUENCIES AND PROPORTIONS

11.1 Learning Objectives

By the end of this chapter, you should be able to do the following:

- Build a 'bag-of-words' representation of unstructured text
- Use feature extraction tools from Sklearn
- Build familiarity with chunks, triplets, and *n*-grams
- Explain 'document-term matrices' and how they can be used
- Describe high-level patterns of language use in a corpus, and across subsets of documents in a corpus, using counts, frequencies, and term weights

11.2 Learning Materials

You can find the online learning materials for this chapter in doing_computational_social_science/Chapter_11. cd into the directory and launch your Jupyter server.

11.3 Introduction

The generic text analysis pipeline introduced in the previous chapter stresses the interconnectedness of data exploration and iterative model development. In Chapter 7, I stressed the importance of exploratory data analysis to this kind of iterative development. In the case of exploratory text analysis, we requires some additional tools. I'll start by showing you how to scale up preprocessing methods to a large text dataset, and will discuss using Gensim's Phraser module in order to detect *n*-grams. We will then consider how to use Sklearn to construct feature matrices. This enables a broad range of exploratory analyses and sets the stage for starting to explore the latent thematic dimensions of text datasets, which we will turn to in the next chapter.

Package imports

```
import pickle
from pprint import pprint
import pandas as pd
pd.set_option("display.notebook_repr_html", False)
import numpy as np
import seaborn as sns
import matplotlib.pyplot as plt

from dcss.text import bigram_process, preprocess, bow_to_df
from dcss.plotting import format_axes_commas, custom_seaborn
from dcss.utils import sparse_groupby
custom_seaborn()

import spacy
nlp = spacy.load('en_core_web_sm')

from sklearn.feature_extraction.text import CountVectorizer, TfidfVectorizer
from sklearn.decomposition import TruncatedSVD
from sklearn.preprocessing import Normalizer
import scipy
```

11.4 Scaling Up: Processing Political Speeches

In this chapter, we're going to work with text data from speeches made by British members of parliament (MPs) between 2016 and 2019, available in full from the British Hansards dataset. We will drop any observations that are missing values from the `party`, `speakername`, or `speech` columns.

```
columns = ['speech', 'speakername', 'party', 'constituency', 'year']
uk_df = pd.read_csv("../data/british_hansards/hansard-speeches-v301.csv", usecols=
    columns)
uk_df.dropna(subset=['party', 'speakername', 'speech'], inplace=True)
uk_df = uk_df.query('year > 2016')
uk_df['party'].value_counts()
```

```
Conservative                      139197
Labour                             49068
Scottish National Party            15658
Labour (Co-op)                      9911
Speaker                             9685
```

```
Liberal Democrat                        4896
Democratic Unionist Party               3802
Independent                             1858
Plaid Cymru                             1030
Green Party                              454
The Independent Group for Change         155
Social Democratic & Labour Party         138
Change UK - The Independent Group         90
Ulster Unionist Party                     75
Alliance                                  45
UK Independence Party                     12
Name: party, dtype: int64
```

The Conservative Party has made far more speeches than other parties within this time frame due to the fact that they have been the governing party for that entire window, first under Theresa May (2016–19), later under Boris Johnson (2019+).

We will also ignore speeches made by the Speaker of the House and Independents. We will focus only on parties whose MPs collectively made more than 400 speeches within our 4-year window.

```
parties_keep = [
    'Conservative',
    'Labour',
    'Scottish National Party',
    'Labour (Co-op)',
    'Liberal Democrat',
    'Democratic Unionist Party',
    'Plaid Cymru',
    'Green Party'
]

party_subset = uk_df[uk_df['party'].isin(parties_keep)].copy()
party_subset.reset_index(drop=True, inplace=True)

total_speech_counts = party_subset['party'].value_counts()
total_speech_counts
```

```
Conservative                139197
Labour                       49068
Scottish National Party      15658
Labour (Co-op)                9911
Liberal Democrat              4896
Democratic Unionist Party     3802
Plaid Cymru                   1030
Green Party                    454
Name: party, dtype: int64
```

This leaves us with 224,016 speeches.

So far, all of the text processing we have done has been on a very small amount of text. When scaled up to data of this size, things inevitably take a lot longer. Powerful computers help a lot, of course, but even then you can spend a lot of time just waiting around for code to finish running, and that's not ideal when you are rapidly iterating over many different analyses. Instead, it can be helpful to work with a smaller representative sample of the full dataset – you can always execute your code against the full dataset when it is fully developed. The best way to do this is by drawing a random sample, of course.

We will draw a stratified random sample where the strata are political parties. In the code block below, we do this by grouping the dataframe by political party and then drawing a random sample of 30% from each strata. This is done without replacement; once a speech has been sampled, it can't be sampled again. We set the random_state to ensure that your sample matches mine.

```
sampled_speeches = party_subset.groupby('party').sample(replace=False,
                                                         frac=.3,
                                                         random_state=23)

len(sampled_speeches)
```

```
67204
```

```
with open('../data/pickles/sampled_british_hansard_speeches.pkl', 'wb') as fp:
    pickle.dump(sampled_speeches, fp)
```

```
sampled_speech_counts = sampled_speeches['party'].value_counts()
```

```
sample_sizes = pd.DataFrame(zip(total_speech_counts, sampled_speech_counts),
                            columns=['Total', 'Sample'],
                            index=parties_keep)
```

There are now 67,204 speeches in our dataset, sampled from eight political parties (if we treat Labour Co-op as if it were a separate party, which it *sort of* is) proportional to the number of speeches each made within our 4-year window.

Let's start by quickly taking a look at the length of speeches by politicians from each party. We will do so by computing the length of each string (i.e. the number of tokens in each speech):

```
sampled_speeches['speech_len'] = sampled_speeches['speech'].apply(lambda x: len(x.
    split(" ")))
```

Now we can group by political party, extract each group from the grouped object, and plot the kernel density estimate for our new speech length variable. We will put each plot side by side, as small multiples, to facilitate comparisons. Note that in Figure 11.1, the kernel density estimate shows the density for speeches *within each party*, not across parties.

We will define a function called party_subplot() to avoid needlessly repeating code. The result is shown in Figure 11.1.

```
parties = sampled_speeches.groupby('party')
```

```
def party_subplot(subgroup, title, position):
    sns.kdeplot(ax = position, data=subgroup, x='speech_len',
                log_scale=True, fill=True, alpha=.5, linewidth=0, color='black')
    position.set(xlabel='Number of tokens (log scale)', title=title)
```

```
fig, ax = plt.subplots(2, 4, sharex=True, sharey=True, figsize=(10, 4))
party_subplot(parties.get_group('Conservative'), 'Conservative', ax[0,0])
party_subplot(parties.get_group('Labour'), 'Labour', ax[0,1])
party_subplot(parties.get_group('Scottish National Party'), 'Scottish National Party',
        ax[0,2])
party_subplot(parties.get_group('Labour (Co-op)'), 'Labour (Co-op)', ax[0,3])
party_subplot(parties.get_group('Liberal Democrat'), 'Liberal Democrat', ax[1,0])
party_subplot(parties.get_group('Democratic Unionist Party'), 'Democratic Unionist
        Party', ax[1,1])
party_subplot(parties.get_group('Plaid Cymru'), 'Plaid Cymru', ax[1,2])
party_subplot(parties.get_group('Green Party'), 'Green Party', ax[1,3])

plt.tight_layout()
plt.show()
```

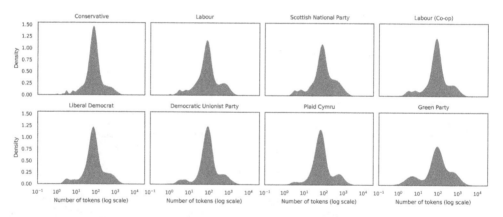

Figure 11.1 A plot of the kernel density estimate for the speech length variable, separated by UK political party

```
parties['speech_len'].median()
```

```
party
Conservative                  72.0
Democratic Unionist Party     84.0
Green Party                   89.5
Labour                        75.0
Labour (Co-op)                81.0
Liberal Democrat              73.0
Plaid Cymru                   66.0
Scottish National Party       80.0
Name: speech_len, dtype: float64
```

We can see that the distributions for each party follow roughly the same pattern of proportions. The distribution of speech lengths is strongly skewed, with the median length generally being in the ballpark of 70 to 90 terms for all parties.

From rule-based chunks and triplets to statistically dependent *n*-grams

Previously, you learnt how to extract phrases contained in spaCy docs by accessing the noun chunks attribute (`.noun_chunks`), and you saw how to leverage the syntactic dependency labels assigned to each token to extract information such as verb–object pairs, and subject–verb–object triplets (SVOs). Although the results of an automated SVO extraction often involve a lot of noise, there is a fair amount we can do to improve the results by customizing them to our research contexts (e.g. changing how we walk through the dependency trees when working with social media data).

Each of these methods is especially helpful when we are exploring text data or trying to extract specific pieces of information. Often, however, we want to identify *n*-grams, which are phrases that denote some sort of concept that we want to treat *as if they were a single token*. The *n* in *n*-gram refers to the number of tokens in the phrase. For example, bigrams are two tokens that make up a phrase that ostensibly has a different meaning than the two constituent tokens. For example, `climate` and `change` tokens could be transformed into a single `climate_change` token. Don't forget, your computer has *no idea* what the tokens 'climate', 'change', or 'climate change' mean, so it can only estimate when two tokens co-occur frequently enough to be considered a phrase, rather than simply being adjacent tokens from time to time. It's important to keep this in mind at all times when working with advanced computational techniques.

The `Phrases` model class in Gensim is widely used for this task, in part because it's a well-optimized way to detect bigrams in a corpus without a lot of effort or processing time. It's a statistical model that calculates maximum likelihood estimates for token co-occurrences (pairs of tokens that co-occur too frequently to be random). In other words, it scores tokens that appear next to each other based on their *statistical* dependencies rather than their *syntactic* dependencies (i.e. not based on linguistic rules and domain expertise).

Gensim's `Phrases` includes two scoring functions for the likelihood estimation, pointwise mutual information (PMI) and normalized pointwise mutual information (NPMI). Neither scoring method is inherently better or worse, and the choice between them depends on your objective. NPMI is generally better at prioritizing frequent co-occurrences, while the PMI scorer tends to favour less frequent cases. As you may have guessed from the name, NPMI scores modify PMI ones by normalizing them to a scale from –1 to 1, where a score of 1 would mean that the two tokens only ever appear together and negative scores indicate that they appear together less than expected by chance. The normalized values are also easier to interpret comparatively, and as you will see, the trained `Phraser` model class (which is a leaner form of the `Phrases` class when you no longer need to update the model) can return a dictionary of all bigrams and their associated scores. This can be helpful to get a better sense of the parameters that result in higher scores for the bigrams that you expect.

In this example, I'll use the `npmi` scorer because we will be training the model on a very specific domain (political speeches), so we can reasonably expect that meaningful bigrams in that context will be repeated frequently. With that said, it's always worth comparing the results of the various options and configuration parameters. There are ways to quantitatively evaluate the model, but often it's enough to look at the text itself with the merged tokens because the poor results tend to be noticeable right away if the parameters weren't set to capture the results you want, or if the input data wasn't preprocessed correctly.

As of 2021, Gensim is transitioning to a major new version, and some of the planned changes impact the `Phraser` class implementation. Rather than publish Gensim code that will soon be out of date, I've included the relevant code in the dcss package (enabling it to be updated as appropriate) in the form of two functions, bigram_process() and preprocess(). We won't actually call the bigram_process() function directly. Instead, we will call the preprocess() function from the dcss package that *includes* the bigramming process as an option alongside other preprocessing steps. The bigram_process() function is simply a few lines of code that passes our text into Phrases in the form Gensim expects and returns the exact same text but with pairs of words detected as bigrams joined (i.e. word1_word2). I've set the default scoring threshold pretty high: 0.75 out of a maximum of 1.0. Sometimes it's preferable to process the text with a strict threshold like this and miss some bigrams rather than worry about handling too many nonsense results from a relaxed score minimum.

By default, the preprocess() function also selects nouns, proper nouns, and adjectives; and removes stop words. Stop words (e.g. function words such as 'and' or 'the') are important in communication but do not convey content. They can be a bit tricky to deal with because of sociolinguistic variation within and across groups of people. The idea here is that different cultural groups, large or small, tend to have their own culture-specific stop words that we generally want to disregard in text analyses that are focused on *content*. 'Social' might be a stop word in a dataset of documents produced by sociologists, but not for chemists, classicists, or East Anglian dwile flonkers. In a specialized domain or culture-specific application, we want to be able to identify words like this and exclude them along with more language-specific stop words (e.g. English, Spanish, Korean).

Below, we call the function using the speeches from all the selected parties, rather than a random sample. Fair warning, *this is gonna take a while*. We've got a lot of text to process.

```
bigram_model, preprocessed = preprocess(sampled_speeches['speech'], nlp=nlp, bigrams=
    True, detokenize = True, n_process=4)
len(preprocessed)
```

```
67204
```

Sometime later, you'll be left with a list of ~67,000 speeches that have been thoroughly prepared for downstream analysis. spaCy is ridiculously fast relative to comparable packages, but this much text will still take a good amount of time to analyse. That's why we worked with a stratified random sample earlier!

When your code finishes running, you'll want to save the results to disk so they can be easily reloaded later. Below, we do this with pickle, which stores Python data structures in binary format, which is OK for data generated within a larger pipeline as that data can be regenerated if necessary. The pickle package is remarkably adaptable and can safely interact with *most* Python objects, but it's important not to rely on it unless you've tested whether or not what you want to save can be converted to and from binary without ill effect. In this case, we know it's going to work out just fine. We can save and load our preprocessed and bigram_model objects to and from memory, respectively, using the dump() and load() functions from the pickle package:

```
with open('../data/pickles/processed_sample_british_party_subset_hansards.pkl', 'wb')
    as fp:
    pickle.dump(preprocessed, fp)
```

```
with open('../data/pickles/sample_british_party_subset_hansard_bigram_model.pkl', 'wb'
    ) as fp:
    pickle.dump(bigram_model, fp)


with open ('../data/pickles/processed_sample_british_party_subset_hansards.pkl', 'rb')
    as fp:
    preprocessed = pickle.load(fp)
```

To briefly recap, we've just used a function called `preprocess()` that applied a series of operations to a sample of political speeches. Specifically, it:

1   detected bigrams using Gensim's `Phraser` class and merged them into single tokens;
2   filtered out English-language stop words and tokens containing fewer than two characters from the remaining tokens;
3   selected nouns, proper nouns, and adjectives; and
4   replaced each selected token with its lemma.

In the rest of this chapter, we will primarily work with the data that resulted from that process. We can reaccess that data *anytime* by loading the pickle we created, which is very handy because you don't want to be sitting around needlessly re-preprocessing your data all the time.

It's a good idea to do your text analysis in a non-destructive way, and to always have on hand the following:

1   The original text data, in full
2   Any relevant metadata, such as who created the text data
3   The preprocessed text data, pretransformation into a feature matrix or other quantitative representation
4   The feature matrix itself (created later in this chapter).

Let's add the preprocessed speech data to our `sampled_speeches` dataframe to help keep everything together. As you can see, it will contain two series with text data, one with the original full speech text, such as this remark from Theresa May:

```
sampled_speeches.iloc[700]['speech']
```

```
'My right hon. Friend is absolutely right on that last point. The question of the
    withdrawal agreement and the fact that it could not be reopened was reiterated
    again by the European Council in its decision yesterday. It is the case that it
    was some weeks ago that I first offered the Leader of the Opposition the
    opportunity to talk. We had an initial meeting. There was then not the same level
    of follow-up meetings and the same level of interest. What I am pleased about is
    that there is, I think, a change in the approach that is being taken: we are
    both sitting down seriously, looking at these issues in detail and looking at
    them constructively.'
```

And another with the version that was produced by our preprocessing function:

```
sampled_speeches['preprocessed'] = preprocessed
sampled_speeches.iloc[700]['preprocessed']
```

```
'right hon friend right point question withdrawal_agreement fact european council
    decision yesterday case week leader opposition opportunity initial meeting level
    meeting level interest pleased change approach issue detail'
```

As you can see, our preprocessing has removed a *lot* of information. When working with small datasets or individual documents, this would make little sense. But when you are trying to understand the content of a large *collection* of documents, it's enormously helpful. It helps us understand the forest for the trees.

Now that our data is ready, let's move to the next step in our pipeline. If you recall from the previous chapter, our next task is to construct a quantitative representation of our text data. We're going to use feature extraction methods in Sklearn. We'll start with simple term counts.

11.5 Creating DTMs with Sklearn

In Sklearn, we can construct document-term matrices (DTMs) with Boolean or count data using CountVectorizer() and with TF-IDF weights using TfidfVectorizer(). The process of learning the vocabulary is a method of the vectorizer itself, so the first thing we will do is make a decision about which vectorizer to use and how to tune it. Let's start with the CountVectorizer.

Once we initialize a vectorizer object, Sklearn learns the vocabulary in our corpus using the fit() method. It can then transform our raw unstructured text data into a DTM using the transform() method. In the resulting DTM, each document is a row and each token (i.e. word) in our corpus vocabulary is a column.

As always, the quality of any text analysis depends in large part on the quality of the data we provide, and what we've done to clean and prepare that data for downstream tasks. In the context of feature extraction methods, such as the construction of a DTM from text data, we can influence the quality of the final matrix by (1) preprocessing our data and/or (2) customizing the feature extraction process by changing specific parameters in our vectorizer. You've already learnt how to do the first part. We can use our preprocessed list from earlier in the vectorization process below.

Count vectorization

Sklearn's CountVectorizer has a number of parameters that we can tune. For a simple example: we often want to avoid words that are too generic to the corpus, so we can use the max_df parameter to specify that we don't want to keep tokens that appear more than *n* times, or in more than *n*% of the documents in our collection. This can be especially helpful when working with text datasets that include a lot of specialist language. Similarly, we can use the min_df parameter to specify that we do not want to keep tokens that appear in fewer than three documents in our collection. While some parameters might be useful, others will be irrelevant to your task. I encourage you to read the documentation to get a better idea of what you can do with Sklearn.

Which parameters should you use? These decisions are part of a large and complex literature on 'feature selection', and there is no one rule you can follow that will get the best results every time. The best advice I can give you is to keep things as simple as you can and align your decisions with your research needs. If it makes sense to do something given the question you are trying to answer, then do it and describe and justify the decision when you report on the rest of your methodological decisions. If it doesn't, don't do it just because you can. In this case, our spaCy preprocessing and bigram detection with Gensim took care of most of what we would want to do. However, given the volume of data we are working with, we will also

- ignore tokens that appear very frequently and very infrequently and
- strip accents from characters.

Make note of the parameters we are using here; consider the effects they will have, given the data.

```
count_vectorizer = CountVectorizer(max_df=.1,
                                   min_df=3,
                                   strip_accents='ascii',
                                   )
```

Once we have instantiated our CountVectorizer with the relevant arguments, we want to learn the vocabulary and construct the DTM. We can use the fit_transform() method to do this, which simply combines the fit() and transform() methods. Below, we do this for preprocessed texts:

```
count_matrix = count_vectorizer.fit_transform(preprocessed)
vocabulary = count_vectorizer.get_feature_names()

count_matrix.shape

(67204, 16428)
```

Let's pickle both of these objects for future use:

```
with open('../data/pickles/brit_hansards_sample_party_subset_count_matrix.pkl', 'wb')
    as fp:
    pickle.dump(count_matrix, fp)

with open('../data/pickles/brit_hansards_sample_party_subset_vocabulary.pkl', 'wb') as
    fp:
    pickle.dump(vocabulary, fp)
```

Our vectorizer has produced a DTM with 16,428 unique tokens (all of which met the criteria specified in the arguments passed to CountVectorizer()) from 67,204 documents (i.e. speeches). We could also have used the ngram_range argument to return *n*-grams up to three tokens long if we're using the default word analyser (although this is not a replacement for Gensim's statistical bigrammer), or a chosen number of letters if we're using the character analyser. There are two versions of the character *n*-gram analyser: `char_wb` will respect token boundaries, while `char` could result in a trigram with the last letter of one token, a space, and the first letter of the next token.

Comparing token frequencies and proportions

We can start discovering some very high-level patterns in our text data just by working with these simple frequencies, akin to doing exploratory data analysis prior to modelling. For example, we can convert the `count_matrix` to a dataframe and add a column indicating the party of the speaker, group the dataframe by party, and then compare some simple aggregate patterns in word usage across each political party. We'll start by creating the dataframe, which with data this size will require staying within the sparse matrix framework (unless you're working with a system that has a great deal of memory resources); 67,000 speeches is not a particularly huge text dataset by modern standards, but keeping track of 26,000 features for *each* of those speeches becomes a huge memory burden when most of the values for those features are zeroes. To illustrate, let's compare the size of our data when stored as sparse and dense matrices:

```
count_data = pd.DataFrame.sparse.from_spmatrix(count_matrix)
count_data.columns = vocabulary

count_data.index = sampled_speeches['party']
count_data.shape

(67204, 16428)
```

The sparse form of the count vectorizer data uses only about 21 MB of memory, because the density is around 0.001 – only 0.1% of the values are non-zero and sparse matrices don't actually store the zero or `np.nan` values. In fact, you are able to select whatever value you like to 'fill' the empty areas of the matrix.

```
print('sparse size: ' + str(count_data.memory_usage().sum()/1048576) + "MB")
print('sparse density : ' + str(count_data.sparse.density))

sparse size: 21.371265411376953MB
sparse density :  0.0016509075275485574
```

The code block below will turn a sparse matrix into a dense one then calculate the size. You probably won't want to run it yourself!

```
count_data_d = count_data.sparse.to_dense()
print('dense size: ' + str(count_data_d.memory_usage().sum()/1048576) + "MB")
```

The dense version occupies a straight-up remarkable 8400 MB of memory! Clearly, it is better to stick with sparse matrices when working with a lot of text data.

The next step is to group the dataframe by the subset of parties, aggregate the token frequencies, and calculate their proportions within each party. We will use some full matrix manipulations for this, storing the percentages in the `results` dataframe and then transposing it so that each row is a token (indexed by the token string itself) and each column contains the token proportions for each party. With sparse matrix handling in the current version of Pandas, aggregation with a groupby operation is unfortunately extremely slow. The function sparse_groupby from dcss.utils is a handy trick that makes sum aggregation very fast.

Now we can create the dataframe, transpose it, and look at a random sample of word proportions:

```
party_counts = sparse_groupby(sampled_speeches['party'], count_matrix, vocabulary)
results = party_counts.div(party_counts.sum(axis=1), axis=0)
results_t = results.T
results_t.sample(20, random_state=10061986)
```

	Conservative	Democratic Unionist Party	Green Party \
grammar	3.487351e-05	0.000021	0.000000
complimentary	2.179594e-06	0.000000	0.000000
tracking	5.085720e-06	0.000000	0.000142
restorative	6.538783e-06	0.000000	0.000000
architectural	2.906126e-06	0.000000	0.000000
newbury_richard	1.598369e-05	0.000000	0.000142
natasha	7.265314e-07	0.000000	0.000000
intercommunal	2.179594e-06	0.000000	0.000000
mayhem	5.812251e-06	0.000021	0.000000
guideline	1.075266e-04	0.000106	0.000000
misnomer	1.453063e-06	0.000000	0.000000
hobby	5.812251e-06	0.000021	0.000000
continuous	6.030211e-05	0.000042	0.000000
zonal_attachment	3.632657e-06	0.000000	0.000000
decarbonising	7.265314e-07	0.000000	0.000000
extractive	0.000000e+00	0.000000	0.000000
chaotic_cluelessness	0.000000e+00	0.000000	0.000000
august	9.735521e-05	0.000255	0.000000
gymnastic	2.906126e-06	0.000000	0.000000
occupant	1.525716e-05	0.000042	0.000000

	Labour	Labour (Co-op)	Liberal Democrat	Plaid Cymru \
grammar	0.000045	0.000031	0.000054	0.000000
complimentary	0.000000	0.000000	0.000000	0.000000
tracking	0.000014	0.000015	0.000000	0.000000
restorative	0.000002	0.000000	0.000000	0.000000
architectural	0.000009	0.000008	0.000000	0.000000
newbury_richard	0.000008	0.000000	0.000000	0.000000
natasha	0.000002	0.000000	0.000018	0.000000
intercommunal	0.000000	0.000000	0.000000	0.000000
mayhem	0.000008	0.000008	0.000000	0.000000
guideline	0.000112	0.000101	0.000161	0.000074
misnomer	0.000003	0.000000	0.000000	0.000000
hobby	0.000000	0.000000	0.000018	0.000000
continuous	0.000053	0.000031	0.000036	0.000074

zonal_attachment	0.000000	0.000000	0.000000	0.000000
decarbonising	0.000000	0.000000	0.000018	0.000000
extractive	0.000002	0.000000	0.000072	0.000000
chaotic_cluelessness	0.000000	0.000000	0.000000	0.000000
august	0.000112	0.000201	0.000161	0.000074
gymnastic	0.000002	0.000008	0.000036	0.000000
occupant	0.000011	0.000008	0.000018	0.000000

	Scottish National Party
grammar	0.000019
complimentary	0.000005
tracking	0.000005
restorative	0.000000
architectural	0.000000
newbury_richard	0.000000
natasha	0.000000
intercommunal	0.000000
mayhem	0.000005
guideline	0.000082
misnomer	0.000000
hobby	0.000010
continuous	0.000029
zonal_attachment	0.000000
decarbonising	0.000005
extractive	0.000005
chaotic_cluelessness	0.000019
august	0.000116
gymnastic	0.000014
occupant	0.000010

With this dataframe, we can easily retrieve (and compare) the proportions for any given token across each of our parties. For example, if we search for scotland, we find that the Scottish National Party (SNP) comes out on top. Note how small the differences in scores are across Plaid Cymru, Labour (Co-op), Labour, Conservative, and SNP:

```
search_term = 'scotland'
results_t.loc[search_term].sort_values(ascending=False)
```

```
Scottish National Party      0.013615
Plaid Cymru                  0.002512
Liberal Democrat             0.001757
Conservative                 0.001387
Labour (Co-op)               0.000983
Democratic Unionist Party    0.000658
Labour                       0.000559
Green Party                  0.000000
Name: scotland, dtype: Sparse[float64, nan]
```

While it is useful to compare the proportion of *specific tokens* of interest across each group, we can also compare parties by inspecting the top *n* tokens for each:

```python
n_top_words = 5
top_words_per_party = {}

for party in results_t.columns:
    top = results_t[party].nlargest(n_top_words)
    top_words_per_party[party] = list(zip(top.index, top))

for k, v in top_words_per_party.items():
    print(k.upper())
    for each in v:
        print(each)
    print('\n')
```

```
CONSERVATIVE
('bill', 0.006218382261590537)
('service', 0.0050770014305403285)
('business', 0.004968748251783816)
('deal', 0.004288714860400624)
('lady', 0.004075841159892851)

DEMOCRATIC UNIONIST PARTY
('northern_ireland', 0.024837738090187928)
('party', 0.007169219021762186)
('united_kingdom', 0.0058117337632036655)
('constituency', 0.0051754125482543585)
('decision', 0.005111780426759428)

GREEN PARTY
('environmental', 0.010475651189127973)
('bill', 0.010050962627406568)
('eu', 0.009484711211778029)
('standard', 0.008210645526613816)
('deal', 0.007219705549263873)

LABOUR
('bill', 0.005798510334341296)
('service', 0.0055913094008465634)
('child', 0.005147307400500709)
('prime_minister', 0.005064738607453937)
('deal', 0.00441665147712455)

LABOUR (CO-OP)
('service', 0.006464849798699288)
('bill', 0.006426138123257975)
('public', 0.0050634871477237536)
```

```
('child', 0.004908640445958501)
('deal', 0.004831217095075875)

LIBERAL DEMOCRAT
('brexit', 0.005289392526715915)
('deal', 0.005235602094240838)
('business', 0.004894929355232016)
('prime_minister', 0.004876999211073657)
('bill', 0.0048232087785985795)

PLAID CYMRU
('wale', 0.02312352245862884)
('welsh', 0.015218676122931441)
('british', 0.011894208037825059)
('brexit', 0.0076832151300236405)
('uk', 0.007166075650118203)

SCOTTISH NATIONAL PARTY
('scotland', 0.013614973572070461)
('scottish', 0.011039820657267923)
('uk', 0.009860951405463383)
('bill', 0.006522432335803806)
('prime_minister', 0.006189063571973833)
```

Finally, we can compute the difference of proportions between any given pair of document groups. This will result in a single vector of positive and negative numbers, where tokens with the largest positive values are associated with the first group and not the second, and tokens with the largest negative values are associated with the second group but not the first.

```
diff_con_snp = results_t['Conservative'] - results_t['Scottish National Party']
diff_con_snp.sort_values(ascending=False, inplace=True)

con_not_snp = diff_con_snp.head(20)  # Conservatives but not SNP
con_not_snp
```

```
lady        0.003259
local       0.002403
school      0.002009
course      0.001568
area        0.001491
council     0.001423
sure        0.001383
business    0.001360
clear       0.001265
police      0.001261
great       0.001230
service     0.001081
number      0.001061
funding     0.001009
```

```
opportunity    0.000992
nhs            0.000955
able           0.000932
prison         0.000921
hospital       0.000910
department     0.000880
dtype: Sparse[float64, nan]
```

```
lab_not_snp = diff_con_snp.tail(20) # SNP but not Conservatives
lab_not_snp
```

```
power            -0.000971
office           -0.000986
week             -0.001019
pension          -0.001083
poverty          -0.001137
family           -0.001164
conservative     -0.001184
eu               -0.001205
woman            -0.001214
leader           -0.001250
glasgow          -0.001608
snp              -0.001793
party            -0.001872
tory             -0.002508
parliament       -0.003324
prime_minister   -0.003792
brexit           -0.004404
uk               -0.006066
scottish         -0.009727
scotland         -0.012228
dtype: Sparse[float64, nan]
```

We can concatenate these two series to more easily visualize their differences. The results are shown in Figure 11.2.

```
dop = pd.concat([con_not_snp, lab_not_snp])

fig, ax = plt.subplots(figsize=(6, 6))
sns.swarmplot(x=dop, y=dop.index, color='black', size=4)
ax.axvline(0) # add a vertical line at 0
plt.grid() # add a grid to the plot to make it easier to interpret
ax.set(xlabel=r'($\longleftarrow$ Scottish National Party) (Conservative Party
    $\longrightarrow$)',
        ylabel='',
        title='Difference of Proportions')
plt.tight_layout()
plt.show()
```

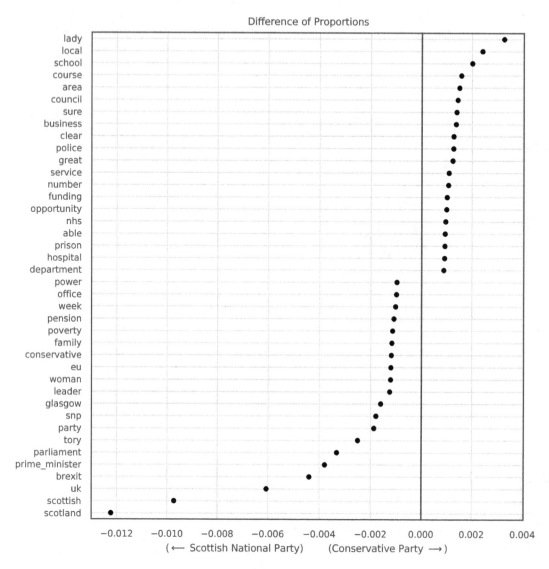

Figure 11.2 A dot plot comparing to what degree words are more strongly associated with the Scottish National Party (left) or the Conservative Party (right)

As you can see, simple token frequencies and proportions can be very useful when we are starting to explore our text data. Before moving on to the larger problem of exploring latent topics, let's discuss an alternative way of scoring tokens in a DTM. In the next chapter, we will take a look at term frequency–inverse document frequency (TF-IDF) weights.

Further Reading

The count-based methods we discussed in this chapter are the foundation of 'dictionary-based' approaches that are widely used in the literature. For example, Bonikowski and Gidron (2016) use count-based dictionary methods to study populist claims-making in the 2016 US general election. Nelson et al. (2018) discuss dictionary-based methods alongside machine learning methods that we will cover later in the book.

11.6 Conclusion

The key points in this chapter are as follows:

- We learnt about chunks, triplets, bigrams, and *n*-grams.
- We used Gensim's `Phraser` with spaCy to detect *n*-grams.
- We used Sklearn to create a DTM.
- We discussed differences between using token counts and proportions.

Visit the website at https://study.sagepub.com/mclevey for additional resources

12

EXPLORATORY TEXT ANALYSIS – WORD WEIGHTS, TEXT SIMILARITY, AND LATENT SEMANTIC ANALYSIS

12.1 Learning Objectives

By the end of this chapter, you should be able to do the following:

- Compute and interpret term frequency–inverse document frequency (TF-IDF) weights for terms in a corpus
- Compute the similarity between pairs of documents using cosine similarity
- Represent documents in latent semantic space using matrix decomposition methods, more specifically latent semantic analysis (LSA) via truncated singular value decomposition (SVD)

12.2 Learning Materials

You can find the online learning materials for this chapter in `doing_computational_social_science/Chapter_12`. `cd` into the directory and launch your Jupyter server.

12.3 Introduction

The previous chapters (1) focused on using spaCy and Gensim to process natural language data stored in the form of unstructured text; (2) considered how various different types of text processing and modelling fit together into larger pipelines; (3) discussed the differences between two ways of creating quantitative representations of text data, coding (or 'labelling'/'annotation') and count-based feature extraction; (4) constructed DTMs using count-based approaches; and (5) identified some high-level patterns using simple frequencies and proportions.

In this chapter, I will show how to use Sklearn to construct feature matrices with TF-IDF weights, followed by a discussion of some useful descriptive and exploratory methods of text analysis. In particular, I'll emphasize the difference between high-level patterns of language use that we can observe directly (e.g. words used, not used) and latent patterns that we can't observe directly. You will learn how to explore 'latent semantic space' using a method called singular value decomposition (SVD), which is closely related to the latent variable and dimensionality reduction methods introduced in Chapter 8.

Package imports

```
import pickle
from pprint import pprint
import pandas as pd
pd.set_option("display.notebook_repr_html", False)
import numpy as np
import seaborn as sns
import matplotlib.pyplot as plt

from dcss.text import bigram_process, preprocess, bow_to_df, get_topic_word_scores
from dcss.plotting import format_axes_commas, custom_seaborn
from dcss.utils import sparse_groupby
custom_seaborn()

import spacy
nlp = spacy.load('en_core_web_sm', disable=['ner'])

from sklearn.feature_extraction.text import CountVectorizer, TfidfVectorizer
from sklearn.decomposition import TruncatedSVD
from sklearn.preprocessing import Normalizer
```

TF-IDF vectorization

When analysing *content*, we are rarely interested in the most and the least frequent words, as the former tend to be domain- or group-specific stop words and the latter are too rare. As discussed in Chapter 10, the main benefit of using TF-IDF is that it preserves *all* tokens (words) in the corpus but decreases the weights of tokens that are at the extremes of the frequency distribution.

When we call TfidfVectorizer instead of CountVectorizer, the values assigned to each token (i.e. features) are TF-IDF scores rather than binary (presence/absence) or frequencies. Similar to the example in Chapter 11, we can use this vectorizer to produce a document-term matrix (DTM).

Alternatively, we could use Sklearn's TfidfTransformer() to convert the count-based DTM from Chapter 11 to TF-IDF.

```
with open ('pickles/processed_sample_british_party_subset_hansards.pkl', 'rb') as fp:
    preprocessed = pickle.load(fp)

tfidf_vectorizer = TfidfVectorizer(max_df=.1,
                                   min_df=3,
                                   strip_accents='ascii')

tfidf_matrix = tfidf_vectorizer.fit_transform(preprocessed)
tfidf_matrix.shape
```

```
(67204, 16428)
```

To help clarify the differences between the count data and the TF-IDF scores, let's construct a dataframe with the counts from the previous chapter and the above TF-IDF scores for each token across all documents. In this case, the shape of the resulting matrix will be identical to the frequency matrix we constructed in the previous chapter, but only because we are passing identical arguments to the vectorizer, which is deterministic, and fitting it to the exact same preprocessed data. If our data or parameters were different, we would, of course, obtain different results. The vocabulary is also identical, so we can use the same one for both matrices.

```
with open ('pickles/brit_hansards_sample_party_subset_count_matrix.pkl', 'rb') as fp:
    count_matrix = pickle.load(fp)

tfidf_scores = np.ravel(tfidf_matrix.sum(0))
tfidf_scores = tfidf_scores/np.linalg.norm(tfidf_scores)
term_counts = np.ravel(count_matrix.sum(0))
term_counts = term_counts/np.linalg.norm(term_counts)
vocabulary = tfidf_vectorizer.get_feature_names()

df = pd.DataFrame({'Term': vocabulary, 'TFIDF': tfidf_scores, 'Count': term_counts})
df.sort_values(by='TFIDF', ascending=False, inplace=True)
```

The code below creates a scatter plot showing each token in the corpus by count and TF-IDF. The result is Figure 12.1.

```
sns.jointplot(data=df.head(5000), x='Count', y='TFIDF', kind='hist')
plt.show()
```

When you inspect this plot, you should notice that:

1   most tokens in the vocabulary are used very rarely, and so the marginal distribution of counts is skewed towards low values;
2   most tokens in the vocabulary have relatively low TF-IDF scores;
3   the tokens with high count values almost always have low TF-IDF values; and
4   the tokens with high TF-IDF scores tend to have lower counts.

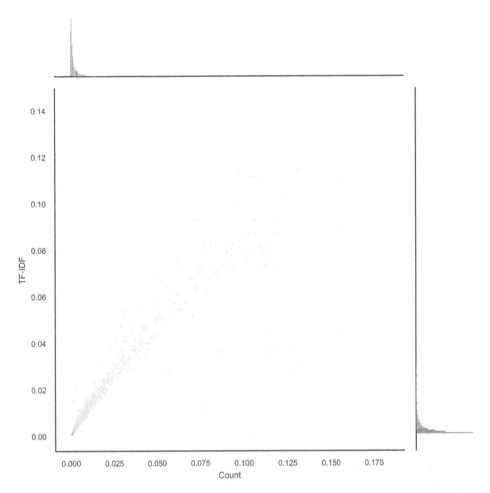

Figure 12.1 A scatter plot showing each token in the corpus by count and TF-IDF (term frequency–inverse document frequency); includes histograms of both axes in the margins

If you understand the TF-IDF formula, this should make intuitive sense. If it doesn't, I recommend reviewing the formula, as you don't want to proceed with a text analysis that relies on a token scoring method that you don't understand.

To visualize the relationship between counts and TF-IDF weights, we used two matrices (`count_matrix` and `tfidf_matrix`) with the same shape. Recall that one of the reasons why those two matrices have the same shape is because we passed the same arguments to both vectorizers. While this helps develop some intuition about the differences between word frequencies and TF-IDF weights, *we should not use the* `min_df` *and* `max_df` *arguments with* `TfidfVectorizer`. The reason is because TF-IDF assigns very low scores to the tokens at the top and bottom of the frequency distribution, so removing them is unhelpful and can change the actual scores that are computed. Before continuing to analyse our dataset with tokens weighted by TF-IDF, let's construct a final TF-IDF DTM without the `min_df` and `max_df` arguments:

```
tfidf_vectorizer = TfidfVectorizer(strip_accents='ascii', sublinear_tf=True)

tfidf_matrix = tfidf_vectorizer.fit_transform(preprocessed)
tfidf_matrix.shape
```

```
(67204, 34625)
```

Computing semantic similarity and clustering documents

In the previous chapter, I mentioned that each feature and each document has an associated vector of numbers. The documents, or row vectors, assign a specific value to the document for each feature in the DTM. The features, or column vectors, tell you how a specific feature is distributed across documents. Because each document is represented by a vector, this approach is also known as a vector space model, or VSM; the documents are represented by 'long and sparse' vectors that position them *in relation to one another in a high-dimensional vector space*. This makes it relatively simple to assess the semantic similarity between documents using measures of the distance or similarity between their vectors' representations.

Perhaps the most basic of these measures is Euclidean distance, which is a flat measure of the distance between two points in a Euclidean space like you find in classical geometry. This measure works fine when you just want to compare the literal text contained in documents, as in plagiarism detection software. For that purpose, the importance of individual tokens in a document matters less than the degree to which two documents have similar tokens that appear with similar frequency. This is a pretty reliable measure of how similar the text strings are between documents.

Euclidean distance has some limitations when it comes to measuring semantic similarity, however, and especially when we are working with term counts rather than TF-IDF weights. This is because Euclidean distance tends to overestimate the importance of tokens that appear frequently, as they increase the magnitude of the vectors in space. For example, imagine two documents about natural language processing in some larger corpus. If the term 'language_processing' appears 100 times in the first document about that topic but only once in the other, then there's a good chance that the Euclidean distance between these two documents will be large, suggesting (incorrectly) that they are about totally different topics! This overestimation is most pronounced when comparing texts of different lengths, as longer documents will of course have higher token counts. These problems can be mitigated to some extent by using TF-IDF scores rather than frequencies, since TF-IDF takes differences in document length into account.

Unlike Euclidean distance, cosine similarity compares the angle between two vectors; whereas Euclidean distance measures how far the vector has extended into space in a given direction, cosine distance considers only the direction the vector is headed in. The result is a document similarity score that better compares the two documents in terms of their conceptual/abstract similarity rather than their physical make-up. Let's see what this looks like by comparing the cosine similarity between speeches by MPs from different parties using the `tfidf_matrix` produced above.

We'll use the same `sparse_groupby` function we used in the previous chapter to aggregate the TF-IDF scores into a dataframe where each row is a vector for the entire party:

```
with open ('../data/pickles/sampled_british_hansard_speeches.pkl', 'rb') as fp:
    speech_df = pickle.load(fp)
```

```
party_names = speech_df['party']
tfidf_vocabulary = tfidf_vectorizer.get_feature_names()
party_scores = sparse_groupby(party_names, tfidf_matrix, tfidf_vocabulary)


len(party_names)
```

```
67204
```

Because we've aggregated the TF-IDF scores by summing them, we should normalize them again to unit norm. We can use the `Normalizer()` preprocessing utility from Sklearn to handle the maths for us here. The main benefit of doing it this way is that the Sklearn code is highly optimized (it's actually running C code in the background, which is super-efficient) and operates on the whole matrix at once.

```
normalize = Normalizer()
party_scores_n = normalize.fit_transform(party_scores)
```

Now that we've normalized the matrix, we'll compute the cosine similarity between each pair of vectors. The maths are beyond the scope of this chapter, but what you need to do to compute the cosine similarity between political parties here is to compute the product of our rectangular party-by-feature and a transpose of that same matrix. The result will be a square 'self-to-self' cosine similarity matrix. In the code below, the @ symbol is used to compute the product of two matrices:

```
sim_matrix = party_scores_n @ party_scores_n.T
sim_df = pd.DataFrame.sparse.from_spmatrix(sim_matrix).sparse.to_dense()
```

The top left to bottom right diagonal will always be 1 in a self-to-self cosine similarity matrix because the diagonal reports how similar each entity (in this case, political party) is to itself. Perfect similarity every time! You might also notice that the data below the diagonal is mirrored above the diagonal. We can use NumPy to clean it up a bit for us by filling the diagonal and one of the triangles (above or below the diagonal, it doesn't matter which) with `np.nan`. If we use the `.values` attribute for Pandas dataframes, we can use NumPy array functions directly without doing any conversions from Pandas to NumPy.

```
np.fill_diagonal(sim_df.values, np.nan)
sim_df.values[np.tril_indices(sim_df.shape[0], -1)] = np.nan
```

Now let's add in the party names as the index and column names for our fresh, shiny, new cosine similarity matrix:

```
sim_df.index = party_scores.index
sim_df.columns = party_scores.index
```

With a matrix this size, it's possible to eyeball what's going on, but when you have a lot of comparisons to make, it can be handy to write a bit of code to show you the highlights. For example, we might want to print the three most similar and the three least similar party pairings for each party. We can do this by using Pandas' `.stack()` method to flatten the dataframe dimensions so that .nlargest() and .nsmallest() return results for the entire matrix rather than row by row:

```
print(sim_df.stack().nlargest(3))
```

```
Labour          Labour (Co-op)      0.975790
                Liberal Democrat    0.950330
Labour (Co-op)  Liberal Democrat    0.946272
dtype: float64
```

```
print(sim_df.stack().nsmallest(3))
```

```
Green Party                      Plaid Cymru   0.562094
Democratic Unionist Party        Plaid Cymru   0.586745
                                 Green Party   0.636776
dtype: float64
```

We can see that Labour and Labour (Co-op) have very high similarity, and that both have similarities with the Liberal Democrats (who from time to time have had pacts with Labour). All three of these parties are considered left-of-centre. On the other hand, the Green Party and Plaid Cymru are also considered left-leaning, but Plaid Cymru is a Welsh nationalist party seeking independence from the UK, so we should expect to see that they differ from the other parties despite being social democratic. The Democratic Unionist Party is a right-leaning socially conservative party in Northern Ireland, so their lower similarity to the other two parties also makes some sense.

We know that there are similarities between the *content* of what Labour and Lib Dem MPs have focused on in their speeches, and that Plaid Cymru and the Democratic Unionist Party differ from the others. One way to gain a bit of insight into these comparisons is to look at the tokens that are most strongly associated with each party. Below, we'll print the 10 most associated tokens for each of the four parties. Note that these will differ a bit from the scores we previously computed because we are working with TF-IDF scores, not counts.

```
party_scores_df = pd.DataFrame.sparse.from_spmatrix(party_scores_n)
party_scores_df.index = party_scores.index
party_scores_df.columns = tfidf_vectorizer.get_feature_names()


for party in ['Labour','Liberal Democrat','Democratic Unionist Party','Plaid Cymru']:
    print(party + '\n')
    print(party_scores_df.loc[party].nlargest(10))
    print('\n')
```

```
Labour


government    0.241095
minister     0.216044
secretary    0.182925
hon          0.171087
```

```
people        0.170363
state         0.162468
way           0.158298
house         0.149029
member        0.144188
year          0.129809
Name: Labour, dtype: Sparse[float64, 0]
```

Liberal Democrat

```
government    0.226466
minister      0.213624
way           0.202180
hon           0.193127
people        0.183703
gentleman     0.175649
secretary     0.167834
member        0.147524
state         0.145406
house         0.136900
Name: Liberal Democrat, dtype: Sparse[float64, 0]
```

Democratic Unionist Party

```
northern_ireland    0.429030
minister            0.216100
hon                 0.195505
way                 0.182133
secretary           0.160904
people              0.158602
state               0.158254
issue               0.145663
gentleman           0.138184
house               0.135264
Name: Democratic Unionist Party, dtype: Sparse[float64, 0]
```

Plaid Cymru

```
wale          0.459598
welsh         0.342678
government    0.227643
state         0.146535
british       0.143649
hon           0.129486
secretary     0.127324
brexit        0.125425
minister      0.124787
way           0.119684
Name: Plaid Cymru, dtype: Sparse[float64, 0]
```

The highest-scoring tokens for Labour and the Liberal Democrats are not particularly noteworthy in this case. The Northern Irish and Welsh parties, on the other hand, have very high scores for the terms that refer to their respective countries. Remember that TF-IDF scores terms highly if they appear frequently in a given document but don't appear in many documents in the corpus. The high scores in this case indicate that these parties more often refer to their home countries in parliament and/or that other parties don't talk about them much.

While cosine similarity performed on token count (e.g. `count_matrix` from the `CountVectorizer()`) and TF-IDF weights (e.g. `tfidf_matrix` from the `TfidfVectorizer()`) does a better job of measuring meaningful similarity between documents, it still relies on exact term matches to calculate the spatial distances. This is a significant limitation of using long sparse vector representations. In later chapters, we will discuss short dense vector representations called word embeddings that allow us to go beyond identical token matches to compare the semantic similarity of tokens and documents that are *conceptually* close. Using these short and dense word embeddings in similarity analysis means that seemingly identical words with different meanings can be differentiated based on their usage contexts, while other words that are not identical can be considered *conceptually* close. For now, we'll move on to another set of exploratory text analysis methods: latent semantic analysis, or LSA.

12.4 Exploring Latent Semantic Space With Matrix Decomposition

So far, we've discussed how to represent unstructured text data as long and sparse vectors. These vectors are stored as structured matrices, where the rows are documents, the columns are tokens, and the cells are either Boolean (a token is present or absent), frequencies, or TF-IDF weights. You saw how we can use token frequencies and proportions to do some preliminary comparisons of language use across document collections, and how to perform some simple semantic similarity comparisons. While useful, there are some limitations in using these methods to learn about the actual topical content of the documents in our corpus.

Remember, our DTMs are made up of *long and sparse vectors*. One of the first substantial breakthroughs in contemporary 'topic modelling' was the realization that one could use matrix decomposition methods to construct a latent 'semantic space.' The dimensionality reduction process enables us to draw inferences about the unobservable features of text (e.g. their latent topics) from observable features (e.g. words). The dimensions of the latent semantic space are typically interpreted as topics, and documents that are close to one another tend to be about the same topics.

In Chapter 8, you learnt about dimensionality reduction methods with an emphasis on principal component analysis (PCA). As a brief reminder, PCA and other dimensionality reduction methods reduce the number of features in a dataset by combining highly correlated, or covarying, features into principal components. These principal components represent *latent* dimensions of a dataset, always at a higher level of abstraction than the original features. When we are performing dimensionality reduction on text data, we often used a method called truncated SVD rather than PCA. SVD and PCA are very similar, but SVD is an extension that can be used for non-square matrices (recall that PCA starts by converting data to a square matrix, e.g. correlation) and it handles sparse matrices efficiently. When SVD is used in the context of text analysis and the vector space model, it is called LSA.

Latent semantic analysis with truncated singular value decomposition

As previously mentioned, SVD is a dimensionality reduction method comparable to PCA. Other than relatively small differences in how PCA and SVD decompose matrices, the salient difference between the latent variable analyses here and those in Chapter 8 is *interpretation*. When the original features are individual tokens from the vocabulary, the latent components that are produced via the linear combination of highly correlated features are *interpreted as topics*. This is just another latent variable problem where we attempt to learn about the latent variables (topics) by decomposing matrices of observed features (tokens) using linear algebra.

We won't get deep into the mathematics here, but it is important that you have at least a conceptual understanding of how SVD works. It all starts with a feature matrix, which in a text analysis like this will typically be a DTM. In this example, we will use our tfidf_matrix DTM.

SVD decomposes the DTM into three smaller matrices, each of which contains essential information that can be used to accurately reconstruct the original matrix:

1   **U** is a matrix with documents in the rows and latent topics in the columns. The columns are orthogonal to one another.
2   **S** is a diagonal matrix of singular values indicating the importance of each topic.
3   **V** is a matrix with latent topics in the rows and tokens from the vocabulary in the columns. The rows are orthogonal to one another.

When you multiply these three matrices, you get a matrix that is extremely close, or approximately equivalent, to the original matrix (i.e. our DTM). This is represented in the following equation:

$$\text{DTM} \approx \mathbf{U} \cdot \mathbf{S} \cdot \mathbf{V}$$

Figure 12.2 further clarifies the relationships between these three matrices.

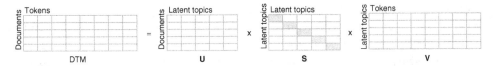

Figure 12.2   Decomposition of a document-term matrix into **U**, **S**, and **V** matrices

We can use these three matrices to interpret the latent topics in our dataset. We can use **V** to learn about the tokens most strongly associated with each latent topic, enabling us to interpret what that latent topic represents. We can use **S** to learn roughly how important the topic is relative to the other topics. Finally, we can use **U** to better understand how the discovered topics are distributed across the documents in our corpus.

As with PCA, when we perform an SVD we will get back a number of latent components equal to the number of features in the original matrix, and those components will be sorted such that the ones explaining the most variance come first, and those explaining the least amount of variance come last. We are almost never interested in using all of the topics, so we usually select some subset of the latent components to interpret. This is called truncated SVD and is the approach implemented in Sklearn. This means we have to tell Sklearn in advance how many components we want.

LSA via SVD in Sklearn

To conduct an LSA analysis with Sklearn, we first initialize a `TruncatedSVD()` object and indicate the number of latent topics we want by using the `n_components` argument. In this case, we will set the number of components to work with to 100:

```
lsa = TruncatedSVD(n_components=100, n_iter=6, random_state=12)
```

Now we can fit it to our `tfidf_matrix` (or `count_matrix`, for that matter) to actually execute the LSA:

```
lsa = lsa.fit(tfidf_matrix)
```

As previously mentioned, the singular values (the diagonal matrix **S**) summarize the relative importance of each of the latent dimensions. We can access these values from the `.singular_values_` attribute of the fitted `lsa` model object. Plotting them gives us a quick view of how important each latent dimension is. Let's look at the top 20 singular values:

```
svs = lsa.singular_values_[:20]
svs
```

```
array([31.98920783, 20.38742083, 18.84947969, 17.43700962, 16.33938111,
       15.7103002,  15.38935603, 14.83683502, 14.67931961, 14.17851146,
       14.00815732, 13.83193669, 13.53645288, 13.25627776, 13.03047778,
       12.98201512, 12.70899053, 12.64315814, 12.62438539, 12.44770159])
```

Each dimension contains a *little bit* of pretty much every term in the vocabulary.

When you are interpreting the meaning of the dimensions, you want to look for terms that have the highest values. To make this a bit easier, we can transpose the `lsa.components_` matrix **V** (see Figure 12.2) to create a dataframe where the rows are terms in the vocabulary and each column represents one of the latent dimensions. The score in each cell tells you how strongly associated that word is for the given topic.

```
word_topics = pd.DataFrame(lsa.components_).T # transpose  the dataframe
column_names = [f'Topic {c}' for c in np.arange(1,101,1)]
word_topics.columns = column_names
```

```
word_topics.shape
```

```
(16428, 100)
```

Let's get a list of the tokens in the vocabulary and use them as an index for our dataframe:

```
terms = tfidf_vectorizer.get_feature_names()
word_topics.index = terms

word_topics.sort_values(by='Topic 2', ascending = False)['Topic 2'].head(20)
```

```
deal                     0.543486
eu                       0.260769
trade                    0.212182
prime_minister           0.172854
european_union           0.165233
brexit                   0.148985
agreement                0.125763
vote                     0.101002
referendum               0.086761
negotiation              0.086367
custom                   0.082417
uk                       0.079995
parliament               0.079693
union                    0.074415
european                 0.064705
united_kingdom           0.062308
withdrawal_agreement     0.054508
scotland                 0.050980
future                   0.049220
amendment                0.048934
Name: Topic 2, dtype: float64
```

Now we can easily use .loc[] on our dataframe to get the scores for any specific word across all latent topics. To get the topic scores for England, we would pull the row vector for the row indexed with england. Since the result is simply a Pandas Series, we can sort it to print the topics in order of most to least strongly associated. Note that we have to make do with wale rather than wales because the word has been lemmatized during preprocessing. Using named entity recognition, which you will learn about in later chapters, you can ensure that this doesn't happen during preprocessing.

```
compare_df = pd.DataFrame()

compare_terms = ['england', 'scotland', 'wale', 'ireland']

for i, term in enumerate(compare_terms):
    scores = word_topics.loc[term].sort_values(ascending=False)
    compare_df[i] = scores.index
    compare_df[term] = scores.values

compare_df.head()
```

```
           0     england        1   scotland      2      wale        3    \
0    Topic 76   0.079782  Topic 32  0.251529 Topic 84  0.209919  Topic 27
```

1	Topic 22	0.078304	Topic 26	0.221033	Topic 81	0.206131	Topic 33
2	Topic 54	0.072457	Topic 11	0.166615	Topic 79	0.194224	Topic 25
3	Topic 63	0.062456	Topic 14	0.155068	Topic 78	0.166255	Topic 48
4	Topic 72	0.061198	Topic 89	0.142264	Topic 65	0.153478	Topic 77

```
        ireland
0       0.048944
1       0.033966
2       0.028820
3       0.025367
4       0.023717
```

Note that for many terms (including england and ireland), the requested terms are not strongly loaded for any particular theme. This is different for scotland and wale, however. This suggests that there may be a topic here that is focused on issues related to Ireland, but perhaps not for Scotland and Wales. Now, it turns out this is a bit tricky, so let's think things through for a moment. Perhaps most importantly, we need to understand what these loadings (weights) tell us. When looking at a given topic, the loading of a word between –1 and 1 is the contribution it makes to the composition of that latent topic. A score closer to 1 means the *presence* of that word contributes to the definition of the topic, while a score closer to –1 means the *absence* of that word contributes to the definition of the topic. Scores around 0 have very little impact. In LSA, words are considered in relation to the words they appear with, so a focal word might only indicate a certain topic if some other word isn't in the document.

An example of an ideal outcome can be helpful here: if your focal word was escape and it appeared in the same document as backslash, you could assume the topic of the document was related to computers or programming. If instead the word prison appeared in the document, it would suggest the topic of the document was a prison escape. So for the latent topic of 'computing', the word prison could end up fairly negatively loaded, as it distinguishes between the two different uses of escape. LSA is capable of distinguishing between different uses of the same word, but it's important to put some thought into what the negative loadings mean in relation to the positive ones.

In both of these cases, we can find out what topics a given word is most associated with, but since there is no guarantee that the word we are interested in is actually important (or even really relevant) to the topic, this is not an especially helpful way to discover what the topic is about. Instead, if we want to know what words are most strongly associated with each topic, we can pull the top (and bottom!) scoring words for each.

To do so, we can use the utility function get_topic_word_scores() from the DCSS package. One of the arguments is all_topics. By default, this argument is set to False, which means the function will return data on the top *n* words and their scores for the specified topic. If changed to True, the function returns a full dataframe with all the other topics alongside the topic of interest. The word scores for these other topics tell you the relationship that the top words for the topic of interest have across the other topics, so it is important to interpret this properly. Let's explore the topic that's most relevant to 'scotland':

```
word_topics.loc['scotland'].sort_values(ascending=False)
```

```
Topic  9    0.421203
Topic  8    0.278695
```

```
Topic   16    0.221600
Topic   11    0.212515
Topic   43    0.174956

                ...

Topic   46   -0.106769
Topic   93   -0.108168
Topic   76   -0.155765
Topic   19   -0.169195
Topic   50   -0.197856
Name: scotland, Length: 100, dtype: float64
```

```
get_topic_word_scores(word_topics, 10, 'Topic 8')
```

```
[('business', 0.4459),
 ('scotland', 0.2787),
 ('scottish', 0.2544),
 ('school', 0.1669),
 ('tax', 0.1221),
 ('party', 0.1196),
 ('small', 0.1041),
 ('labour', 0.0953),
 ('economy', 0.0908),
 ('parliament', 0.0895),
 ('home', -0.1055),
 ('prison', -0.1183),
 ('service', -0.1222),
 ('officer', -0.1231),
 ('trade', -0.1315),
 ('eu', -0.1417),
 ('crime', -0.1436),
 ('department', -0.1646),
 ('step', -0.188),
 ('police', -0.2884)]
```

A key topic related to Scotland seems to be about business and school, but is also distinguished by *not* being about crime and police. To learn more, we could examine other topics comparatively as well as return to the original source documents to better understand why Scotland, school, business, and the absence of talk about crime and police would be a topic of British parliamentary debate.

Before moving on, let's briefly take stock of what we've done in this illustrative LSA. First, we constructed a DTM using Sklearn's `TfidfVectorizer()`, fit to our preprocessed data. Then we decomposed the DTM with truncated SVD, which produced a matrix with the component coefficients for each of the 67,204 sampled political speeches on 100 latent dimensions, which we can interpret as representing *latent topics*. The final step is to interpret the results by inspecting the terms that contribute the most to each latent dimension. Computational text analysis should always be mixed-method and iterative. The next step would be to examine the latent topics comparatively, and to closely read the original text from documents that load heavily on each latent topic.

Further Reading

If you want to deepen your understanding of LSA, and what it was originally developed to do, I would suggest reading papers by some of the major contributors to the methodology. I recommend Dumais (2004) and Deerwester et al. (1990). These works are an important foundation for some of the machine learning models used for text analysis that we discuss later in the book.

12.5 Conclusion

The key points in this chapter are as follows:

- We used spaCy's `TfidfVectorizer` to compute TF-IDF scores for weighting tokens.
- Vector space models represent documents using vectors that are long (many features) and sparse (few non-zero values).
- We learnt about semantic similarity measures including Euclidean distance and cosine similarity.
- We conducted an LSA using truncated SVD.

Visit the website at https://study.sagepub.com/mclevey for additional resources

PART III

FUNDAMENTALS OF NETWORK ANALYSIS

13

SOCIAL NETWORKS AND RELATIONAL THINKING

13.1 Learning Objectives

By the end of this chapter, you should be able to do the following:

- Explain how social network analysis and relational thinking differs from approaches to quantitative social science that examine associations between attributes of statistically independent individuals
- Differentiate between four common ways of conceptualizing social networks:
  - affective ties/patterns of sentiments
  - access and opportunity structures
  - structures of durable role relations
  - behavioural interactions
- Compare different ways of representing relationships in network data (e.g. directed or undirected, signed or unsigned)
- Work with relational data in the form of edge lists and NetworkX graph objects
- Explain what walks, trails, paths, and cycles are

13.2 Learning Materials

You can find the online learning materials for this chapter in `doing_computational_social_science/Chapter_13`. cd into the directory and launch your Jupyter server.

13.3 Introduction

In this chapter and the four that follow, we shift our focus from text analysis to network analysis. We will start with a three-chapter sequence on descriptive and exploratory methods and a two-chapter sequence on modelling diffusion processes. We will set aside more complex statistical and computational models for network data until later chapters.

This chapter is organized into three main sections. The first section clarifies what social networks are and why they matter. We'll start by discussing how structural and relational thinking differentiates network analysis from the predominant focus on attributes of statistically independent individuals in much of traditional quantitative social science, and we will briefly discuss some prominent perspectives about what networks are and why they matter. This sets the stage for comparing common ways of conceptualizing social networks, including as patterns of (1) sentiments, (2) access and opportunity structures, (3) socially constructed role relations, and (4) behavioural interactions (Kitts, 2014; Kitts and Quintane, 2020). These ways of thinking about networks have important implications for the questions, data, theory, methods, and models we will use.

The second section focuses on storing and working with network data. I describe some common ways researchers represent the complexity of real-world network structures and processes using relational data structures, including edge lists, matrices, and attribute files. These data structures are capable of encoding a wide variety of relational information and can be adapted to the specifics of your research projects. You will learn how to construct graph objects from these data structures using the NetworkX package. The third section introduces the ideas of a network 'walk structure' (the chains of direct and indirect connections that link pairs of nodes in a network) and 'contagions' flowing through network structure.

The concepts introduced in this chapter are foundational to many methods and models in network analysis and will be referenced frequently in future chapters, so it is important to be familiar with them before tackling more complex methods and models.

Finally, before we dive in, I want to briefly acknowledge that network analysis is a massive interdisciplinary field with a history that is more than 100 years old in the social sciences and several decades old in other sciences. While many of the foundational ideas endure, the theories, methods, measures, and models that define the field have transformed many times (e.g. see Freeman, 2004) and are changing again with the adoption of new kinds of datasets and the creation and improvement of computationally intensive models. It's impossible to offer a comprehensive introduction to network analysis in the chapters dedicated to networks in this book, so I've had to make some very difficult decisions about what to emphasize. I've elected to focus on some of the most enduring ideas in these initial three chapters and to emphasize computational approaches to inferential network analysis in Chapter 30. I set aside many topics that are fascinating and worthy to keep this a general introduction to computational social science. Where appropriate, I have tried to include directions to other resources that can better cover topics beyond the scope of this book.

13.4 What Are Social Networks?

From independent individuals to networks

Linton Freeman's (2004) history of social network analysis starts with a colourful (and slightly unsettling) quote from an American sociologist in the late 1960s that gets straight to the core of the difference between network analysis and the traditional quantitative social science of his day:

> For the last thirty years, empirical social research has been dominated by the sample survey. But as usually practiced, using random sampling of individuals, the survey is a sociological meatgrinder, tearing the individual from his [sic] social context and guaranteeing that nobody

in the study interacts with anyone else in it. It is a little like a biologist putting his [*sic*] experimental animals through a hamburger machine and looking at every hundredth cell through a microscope; anatomy and physiology get lost, structure and function disappear, and one is left with cell biology . . . If our aim to is to understand people's behaviour rather than simply to record it, we want to know about primary groups, neighbourhoods, organizations, social circles, and communities; about interaction, communication, role expectations, and social control. Allen Barton (1968, p. 1)

While many people still practise this kind of 'meat grinder' research, Barton's (1968) distinction is much less salient now than it used to be. Mainstream quantitative social science has changed a *lot* since he wrote that in 1968, and again since he was quoted by Freeman in 2004. For one thing, network analysis is no longer just an obscure undertaking of mathematically inclined sociologists, social psychologists, and other social scientists; it's well within the mainstream of applied quantitative science across dozens of disciplines and is an important research area in contemporary statistics.

Network analysis is one of several major developments in quantitative data analysis that attempts to model interdependent relationships and institutional contexts. Another, multilevel analysis (or hierarchical modelling), will be covered in Chapter 28. Both seek to explicitly model the complex interdependencies between entities (e.g. people) by emphasizing their shared *contexts*, *relationships*, and *interactions*. However, in network analysis, an entity's context is typically their connections to other entities and their structural position in a network (a concept we will discuss briefly here and again in later chapters). In multilevel analysis, an entity's context is typically some sort of institutional environment that is shared with other entities, such as classrooms in a school, teams in a league, provinces or states in a country, or countries in the world polity (on world polity theory and Stanford school institutionalism see Buhari-Gulmez, 2010; Meyer et al., 2009). In a multilevel network analysis (see Lazega and Snijders, 2015), the context would be the entities' concrete connections with one another nested in one of many possible shared institutional contexts, such as networks of informal relations between employees nested in the specific firms they work for (e.g. Brailly et al., 2016).

We care about these network connections and shared institutional contexts for many reasons. Perhaps the most obvious is that we think complex interdependencies have important effects on specific outcomes that we care about. For example, we might hypothesize that whether someone believes misinformation that vaccines cause autism depends in part on the beliefs of the people they interact with frequently or whom they trust the most. Or we might hypothesize that a person's overall health and well-being depend in part on the health and well-being of the people with whom they spend the most time. The logic is similar for multilevel analysis, but what follows 'depends in part on' would refer to some sort of shared institutional context or environment rather than a complex network of concrete relationships and interactions.

Not all hypotheses about how networks influence individual outcomes are based on *direct* connections, however. My friends influence me, but their friends (including those whom I am not friends with) influence them, and my friends' friends' friends influence them, and so on. Each step out in such a friendship network usually brings new, but diminished, influences. Networks are *complex systems*; what happens in one region of the network can affect disparate regions, and seemingly small differences in micro-level interaction processes (e.g. norms around who you interact with, how you interact with them, and what they mean to you) can have dramatic macro-level outcomes. For example, we might design a network study to better understand how micro-level social norms generate macro-level structures that shape disease transmission dynamics (Bearman et al., 2004), or how network structures differently impact the spread of an infectious disease through a population and the adoption of health behaviours necessary to mitigate the spread of that disease (Centola, 2018).

We also care about networks and institutional contexts because, as social scientists, we want to understand networks and institutions for their own sakes, inclusive of the social and political processes that generate different kinds of structural configurations. This might be because we are interested in advancing scientific knowledge by doing rigorous theory-driven research, or because we want to leverage that knowledge for some applied reason, such as intervening in a network to mitigate the effects of misinformation and disinformation, to disrupt the diffusion of a violent political ideology, or to improve health and well-being.

This is what makes networks so interesting and beautiful: we are all linked together in a vast and dense web of intersecting, meaningful, and mutually influential relationships. But this complexity can quickly get out of hand. There's a reason why old-fashioned quantitative social science worked like a meat grinder: it was extremely difficult to do much of anything else. Consequently, the history of network analysis is full of fascinating stories of intrepid sociologists, social psychologists, anthropologists, and other social scientists coming up with clever new mathematical models to describe and analyse interdependent relationships and developing research software to use those models in applied research. Now that network analysis is being practised across so many scientific fields, methods and models are improving at breakneck speed.

Just about anything that a social scientist might be interested in can be usefully described in network terms, and just about any research question you might ask could be cast as a question about networks, where the network or some network-based variable might be:

- part of an explanation for something else, such as why some people practise safe sex, while others do not; or
- the thing we are trying to explain, such as why some schools have racially segregated friendship networks, while others do not.

Does this mean you *should* model everything as a network and pose every question as a question about networks? No (though as a network scientist and sociologist I'm tempted to say yes). Recall Box's loop: your model should be whatever will best answer your question.

Freeman didn't include it in his excerpt of Barton's 1968 article, but just a bit further down the page, Barton (1968) poses an important question: *what do we want?* Different things, of course. Network analysis is diverse and interdisciplinary, and you can find meaningful divisions between different groups of network analysts who use different tools to answer different questions. But what unites network scientists of virtually every social science, now and in the past, is a paradigmatic preference for holistic research strategies that focus on people and groups embedded in complex interdependent relationships. Let's turn towards some of the various ways network analysts have conceptualized those relationships.

What is a network?

Network analysis has grown rapidly within and across many scientific and technical fields. One downside of this otherwise welcome development is that the same phenomena can be known by several different terms. These interchangeable terms can be confusing when you first run into them. For clarity, we will say that networks consist of a set of entities, which we will usually call nodes (also called vertices or actors), and the relationships between those entities, edges (also called ties or in some cases arcs). In theory, a node can be any kind of entity and an edge can be any kind of relationship or interaction between such entities. In the social sciences, we typically work with *social* networks where the nodes have some sort of agency, such as individual people or groups of people (e.g. an organization), and the edges represent some sort of meaningful relationship between them, although this is starting to change (Tindall et al. 2022). Following Kitts (2014) and Kitts and Quintane (2020), we can categorize these common types of edges as defined by:

1   *patterns of sentiment*, such as who likes or dislikes whom;
2   *socially constructed role relations*, such as friendships, research collaborations, romantic partnerships, doctoral student and supervisor relationships, family;
3   *behavioural interactions and contact over time*, such as who messages whom; and
4   *providing access to resources, support, information, and opportunities*, such as who contacts whom for advice in a personal crisis, to discuss a problem at work, or to pick up your groceries while quarantining in a global pandemic.

These four types of edges provide us with a high-level framework for talking about *types* of networks based on the relational information they encode and, importantly, the questions we want to answer and the theories we are using. In many respects, the type of relation that defines the edges in a network is the most important thing in determining what *type* of network you have and what you can reasonably do with it. One of the most common mistakes that novices make is trying to answer a research question, or apply a theory, that is a poor match for the type of network, like trying to answer a question about power and inequality with data on a network recording whether people attended the same events. It *can* work with the right data and a bit of mental gymnastics, but it shouldn't have to. *As with any other type of research*, this is a match that you want to ensure you get right. This is, once again, a matter of good research design.

Graphically, we can represent nodes as points and edges as lines that connect those nodes. Figure 13.1 is a hypothetical network with five nodes (Chen, Nate, Anika, Anvita, and Patrick) and the relationships between them. When two nodes are connected, such as Chen and Anvita, we say they are *adjacent*. If we choose to focus on a specific node, we refer to it as the *ego*, and the nodes ego is directly connected to can be referred to as *alters*. Together, an ego's alters represent a *neighbourhood*. For example, if we are focused on Patrick, Patrick is 'ego', and their neighbourhood would consist of the alters Anvita, Chen, and Anika.

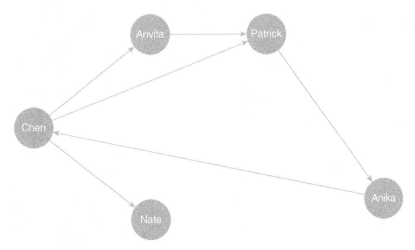

Figure 13.1   A simple directed network showing how the three nodes – Anika, Chen, and Patrick – are connected

We'll come up with a fictitious story about information sharing in this network later in the chapter. For now, let's just focus on learning some technical vocabulary and understanding how we can represent social networks with relational data structures.

The edges have arrows because the network is directed as opposed to undirected. For example, there is an arrow pointing from Anika to Chen because Anika *sends* something to Chen, or initiates something with Chen, that Chen may not reciprocate. Many interactions and relationships can be represented this way. Email and SMS communication can be modelled as directed interactions: 'Anika *emails* Chen' becomes an edge *from* Anika *to* Chen. Requests for support or advice can be modelled as coming from one person ('Help, please!') and the support or advice being sent back in return ('Here you go!'). In a network defined by patterns of sentiment, one person may like another who may or may not like them back. Other types of relationship don't make sense to represent as directed. While one node might nominate another node as a 'friend' and not be nominated in return (tragic!), this really shouldn't be the case in co-authorship. If Anika wrote a book with Chen, Chen must also have written a book with Anika.

Networks are simply relational mathematical objects and have no inherent visual form. Figure 13.1 is just a common and convenient way of *representing* relational data for small networks. However, just as a scatter plot is a representation of data, rather than the data itself, so too is Figure 13.1. With networks, as with text, it's matrices all the way down. In this case, it's a square adjacency matrix. Consider Figure 13.2, which shows how the graphical network representations of the network (directed on the left, undirected on the right) align with two different adjacency matrices.

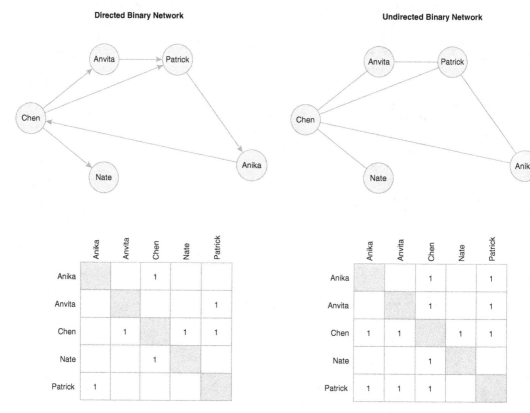

Figure 13.2 A slightly larger and more complex directed network between five nodes

First, for both the directed network (left) and the undirected network (right), many cells are empty, which represents 0, or the absence of an edge. The diagonals are highlighted in grey, but this is just to emphasize them. The diagonals are 0 because the nodes in these networks are not permitted to connect to themselves, which means that there are no self-loops. In other types of networks, such as email communication networks, self-loops might be possible, and a self-loop could be created by an action such as a node emailing themselves.

If you look closely at the undirected network's adjacency matrix, you will notice that the data above and the data below the diagonal are mirror images of one another, but not in the directed network. That's because you can have relational asymmetry in a directed network (Anika can send a tie to Chen that Chen does not reciprocate) but not in an undirected network.

Both of these networks are binary; the adjacency matrices contain 0s (not shown) to represent the absence of an edge and 1s to represent their presence. However, we can populate these cells with plenty of other information, often interpreted as some sort of edge weight. For example, in an interaction network, we might populate cells with count data representing frequency of interaction within a given time frame. In a sentiment network, we might populate the cells with numbers that indicate different types or levels of sentiment, such as a Likert-type scale from 1 to 5 or a set of distinctions such as 'strong' and 'weak'. There is a lot of flexibility in how this data is collected, and it is largely up to you to make decisions that make sense in the context of your research project.

Traditionally, researchers have focused on *positive* ties like friendship, support and sharing, or collaboration and collective action. But as Harrigan et al. (2020) and others have pointed out, 'some relationships harm. Others are characterised by avoidance, dislike, or conflict' (p. 1). These negative ties are (hopefully) less common, but are disproportionately impactful in our lives. They also operate in ways that are fundamentally different from positive ties. Networks that incorporate data on the positive and negative ties are called signed graphs, and are a major area of theoretical and methodological development in contemporary network analysis.

Let's make two final distinctions. First, the network we are working with here is *unipartite*, which means there is only one type of node (people) and the matrix storing the data is square, with the same set of nodes in the rows and the columns. However, it is also possible to consider networks with two types of nodes, such as between people and organizational affiliations, or between people and events. This kind of network is *bipartite*, because there are two types of nodes, and the underlying matrix is a rectangular *incidence matrix* (or *affiliation matrix*) with one node type represented on the rows and the other in the columns. There are fascinating theoretical and methodological literatures on bipartite networks (for some foundational ideas, see Breiger, 1974; Mützel and Breiger, 2020), but regrettably we don't have the space to discuss bipartite networks here.

Finally, the example we are working with is a whole network, in contrast to an ego network. As I mentioned, we can think of each node in a network as 'ego' with a neighbourhood composed of their direct connections (alters). If the network data is collected to capture all the relevant relationships within some network boundary (e.g. all students in a classroom), then we are working with a whole network, and the main data collection tasks include specifying the boundaries of the network (e.g. the classroom) within which we want to record relationships. If, however, we collect some sample of people and then collect data on their individual relationships, then we are working with a collection of ego networks, one for each node in the study. Ego networks, fascinating though they are, are also out of scope for this book. If you are interested in learning more about ego network analysis, I recommend Crossley et al. (2015) and Small et al. (2021), as well as the 2020 special issue of *Network Science* on ego network analysis edited by Perry et al. (2020).

Further Reading

There is no shortage of outstanding conceptual introductions to network analysis. Crossley et al. (2015) provide a great introduction to ego network analysis, which regrettably is not covered in this book. Christina Prell's (2012) *Social Network Analysis*, John Scott's (2017) *Social Network Analysis*, Garry Robins' (2015) *Doing Social Network Research*, and Borgatti et al.'s (2018) *Analyzing Social Networks* are all great general introductions to network analysis. If you want to know more about data collection in network analysis, I recommend jimi adams' (2020) *Gathering Social Network Data*.

13.5 Working With Relational Data

With these generalities out of the way, let's start getting into the details of working with relational data.

Edge lists and node lists

As I mentioned earlier, matrices are the heart of network analysis, but they are not ideal ways to enter, store, or manage network data for anything other than small networks. In contemporary practice, most network data is stored in the form of edge lists and node lists. In Figure 13.3, the same relational data that is represented in the graph, and encoded in the adjacency matrix in Figure 13.2, is encoded as an edge list. The first two columns of the edge list are where the relational data itself is stored. The columns are labelled source and target because the network is directed; the node in the `source` column sends an edge to the node in the `target` column.

Figure 13.3 The structure of a node list and edge list for the five-node graph from Figure 13.2

While an edge list only requires pairs of nodes, we can also include additional columns that provide data *about the relationship*. There is nothing special or unique about data that describes these edges except for the fact that they describe characteristics of the *relationship* between two entities rather than characteristics of the entities themselves. Just as we carefully specify variables for describing the attributes of entities, we can carefully specify variables for describing the attributes of relationships between entities. For example, we might have a variable that categorizes edges by the *type* of relationship (e.g. family, friend, foe, professional, romantic, people who dance together, people who do intravenous drugs with one another) or by its sentiment (positive, neural, negative) to suggest just a couple of possibilities. Just as we can with an adjacency matrix, we can record edge weight (e.g. interaction frequency) as a variable in the edge list. In longitudinal or dynamic networks (discussed in later chapters), we might also record the wave that a relationship was observed in, or perhaps a timestamp of when the interaction occurred (e.g. when Chen sent an email to Anvita). It may be a simple point, but it's very important to understand: we can record any empirical observations of the attributes of relationships. The same considerations about what to observe and record apply for edges as with nodes. There is nothing special about edge data except that it describes edges.

NetworkX graph objects from edge lists (and matrices and more)

Let's examine some actual data. In the code block below, we will import a couple of packages and load up some relational data collected from a group of French high school students in 2013. This dataset is one of several collected by the SocioPatterns research team (with collaborators the ISI Foundation in Turin, the Centre de Physique Théorique in Marseilles, and Bitmanufactory in Cambridge). The particular dataset we will use describes a network of face-to-face contacts between high school students in Marseilles over a 5-day period in December 2013. This data was collected via contact diaries, in which students recorded who they came into contact with (restricted to other students in the study) and for how long. Similar data was also collected with wearable sensors, but we will just focus on the contact diaries for now.

The edge data is provided in a CSV file with three columns: i, j, and weight. Physical co-presence is, of course, naturally undirected. It is not possible to be physically co-present with someone who is not also physically co-present with you. Therefore, the edge list names the columns with i and j instead of source and target. This also means that a tie from i to j is the same as a tie from j to i. Finally, edge weight data is stored in the weight column and is coded as follows:

- weight = 1 if i and j were co-present for at most 5 minutes
- weight = 2 if i and j were co-present for 5 to 15 minutes
- weight = 3 if i and j were co-present for 15 to 60 minutes
- weight = 4 if i and j were co-present for more than 60 minutes

We can load this edge data in a Pandas dataframe and perform any necessary cleaning before reading the edge data into the NetworkX package to create a graph object that we can analyse using network methods:

```
import pandas as pd
pd.set_option("display.notebook_repr_html", False)
import networkx as nx
import matplotlib.pyplot as plt
from dcss.plotting import custom_seaborn
import seaborn as sns
custom_seaborn()

contact_diaries = pd.read_csv("../data/SocioPatterns/Contact-diaries-network_data_2013
    .csv", sep=' ')
contact_diaries.head()

contact_diaries.info()
```

```
<class 'pandas.core.frame.DataFrame'>
RangeIndex: 502 entries, 0 to 501
Data columns (total 3 columns):
 #    Column   Non-Null Count   Dtype
---   ------   --------------   -----
 0    i          502 non-null   int64
 1    j          502 non-null   int64
 2    weight     502 non-null   int64
dtypes: int64(3)
memory usage: 11.9 KB
```

All three columns in this data are numeric: the nodes in columns i and j are represented by numerical IDs rather than the names of the participants in the study. There are 502 rows in this edge list, which means there are 502 observed edges.

We can import this weighted edge list into the Python package NetworkX, which will transform our edge data into a graph object that we can analyse using methods and models from network analysis. NetworkX provides a number of useful functions for doing this. We'll use from_pandas_edgelist() because our data is stored in an edge list format in a Pandas dataframe. When we construct the network G, we'll provide NetworkX with the names of the columns that contain the IDs for each node in an edge. Any other columns in the dataframe will be treated as edge attribute data. Finally, we will also tell NetworkX that this is an *undirected* graph by passing the argument create_using=nx.Graph(). This tells NetworkX that, when it is creating the network, an edge from i to j is the same as an edge from j to i. If we were working with a *directed* network, we could pass the argument create_using=nx.DiGraph() instead.

```
G = nx.from_pandas_edgelist(contact_diaries, 'i', 'j', create_using=nx.Graph())
G.name = 'Reported Contacts (Diary Data)'
print(nx.info(G))
```

```
Name: Reported Contacts (Diary Data)
Type: Graph
Number of nodes: 120
Number of edges: 348
Average degree: 5.8000
```

Like the .info() method for Pandas dataframes, the info() function from NetworkX provides some simple descriptive information about a network object. In this case, info() tells us that the network type is Graph (undirected) and that there are 120 nodes (students) and 348 edges (contact/interactions) between them. Of course, there are many descriptive statistics for network data that we might be interested in that are not reported here. We won't discuss them yet, though. We need to build up some more knowledge of network structures and processes first.

```
print(nx.info(G))
```

```
Name: Reported Contacts (Diary Data)
Type: Graph
```

```
Number of nodes: 120
Number of edges: 348
Average degree:   5.8000
```

You might be wondering why the number of rows in the edge list differs from the number of edges in the network object G. The reason is because different students report the same relation. i might say they spent between 15 and 30 minutes with j, and j might later report the same contact with i. However, it seems that not all students reported all interactions (if they had, we would expect there to be 502 reports of 251 edges). Because we believe that students are more likely to forget to record an interaction than they are to fabricate one in their contact diary, we symmetrize the relationship, making it undirected (if i spent time with j, then the reverse must necessarily be true). We have informed NetworkX that this network should use undirected edges by specifying a Graph object rather than a DiGraph (directed graph).

Finally, before moving on, let's create a quick visualization of this network (Figure 13.4). This is an inherently challenging task as networks are high-dimensional objects, and we are limited to two dimensions. It's best not to rely on visualizations such as these for any serious analytic work, but for relatively small networks they can still be informative.

```
layout = nx.nx_pydot.graphviz_layout(G)

fig, ax = plt.subplots(figsize=(12, 12))
nx.draw(G,
        pos=layout,
        node_color='gray',
        edge_color='lightgray',
        node_size=10,
        width=.5)
plt.show()
```

You'll see similar visualizations in the coming chapters. Each time you'll develop a deeper understanding of what to look for, such as clusters of densely connected nodes, or pendants hanging off a dense cluster of nodes at the core of a network. For now, let's keep moving.

NetworkX has a variety of functions for reading network data stored in other formats as well, and you can find the one that works with your data's format by checking the documentation, which you can find at https://networkx.org/documentation/latest/. Some of the formats supported at the time of writing include edge lists and matrices stored in Python's built-in data structures (e.g. dictionaries) as well as NumPy arrays and matrices, SciPy matrices, and Pandas dataframes. In addition to these edge list and matrix data structures, NetworkX can also read and write network objects using file formats commonly used by other network analysis software, including GraphML, GEXF, JSON, and Pajek files. Unless you have a specific need for them, my recommendation is that you store your network data in the form of an edge list and a node list in separate plain text CSV files.

Now it's time to turn our attention to the 'walk structure' of a network, and the notion of network flow. This is intended to get you to start thinking about networks in a particular way in preparation for content that appears in later chapters.

Figure 13.4 The structure of the SocioPatterns face-to-face contacts network

13.6 Walk Structure and Network Flow

One of the most foundational ideas in social network analysis is that your position in a network affects your ability to access or shape the flow of things – such as resources, information, or knowledge – through that network. These things are often called *contagions*, or *social contagions*, even when they are not literally contagious in the way an infectious disease is (and most contagions that social scientists are interested in do *not* spread like infectious diseases, as you will learn in Chapter 17). Depending on where a node is positioned in the network, they can control or otherwise manipulate how a contagion is flowing through a network. For example, they may prevent someone from learning about some important information by feeding them incorrect information or by betraying their trust and spilling their secrets to the rest of the office.

This notion of contagions *flowing* along the structure of a network enables disparate regions of that network to influence one another. In a friendship network, for example, we are influenced by our friends, by our friends' friends, by our friends' friends' friends, and so on. But exactly *how* does that happen, and to what degree? Which of the many possible paths do contagions flow on? All of them at once? Some subset of paths? If so, which ones? Perhaps a single *most optimal* one?

Walks, trails, paths, and cycles

Earlier, I mentioned that we would spin up a fictitious story about our five-person network (Chen, Patrick, Anika, Anvita, and Nate). We'll do that now to help clarify some of the essential terminology, but we'll start with a slightly smaller version – just Anika, Chen, and Patrick – and then add the others in.

Imagine a research lab with an upcoming team meeting with an ominous sounding item on the agenda. One member of the team, Chen, knows something about the context for this item and shares it with another member of the team, Patrick. In this scenario, Chen sends the information to Patrick (remember, this makes them *adjacent*).

As we've discussed, nodes are also linked to other nodes *indirectly*. Let's say Chen's information came from another team member, Anika. Anika and Patrick are not adjacent, but they are indirectly connected via Chen. How can we describe this relationship? And why does it matter whether we describe it at all?

In network analysis, we are often interested in whether something (e.g. information about the ominous-sounding agenda item) can travel from node *i* (e.g. Anika) to node *j* (e.g. Patrick). If it is indeed possible for that to happen, how many people would it have to go through to get there? And is there more than one way it might get there? If so, are some ways more efficient than others? If so, which ones? We can answer questions such as these about any nodes in a network by invoking the concept of a walk, which also provides both general and specific terminology for describing a wide variety of indirect relationships (Borgatti and Everett, 2020). Consider the hypothetical network in Figure 13.5, which we just described with words.

Figure 13.5 A simple directed network showing how the three nodes – Anika, Chen, and Patrick – are connected

A *walk* is simply any sequence of adjacent nodes and edges that start with some node and end with a node. They can even start and end with the same node. In fact, the same node can appear in a walk more than once, and so can the same edges! In short, a walk is a very general way of describing *any* way that you can go from one node to another by 'walking' along the edges, even if what you want to do is get back to where you started. There are no restrictions provided the edges to walk on actually exist (or rather, are observed). This opens up all kinds of useful ways of thinking about the *distances* between nodes, operationalized in terms of lengths of walks, which are defined in terms of the number of edges contained in the walk. In the above network, the walk from Anika to Patrick passes through one node, Chen, but has a length of 2 because it consists of the relationship between Anika and Chen, and between Chen and Patrick (two edges).

Let's complicate this just a wee bit by introducing a few additional team members, our fictitious friends Anvita and Nate. Chen, especially anxious about the ominous agenda item, shares the information with Anvita and Nate. Anvita doesn't know Patrick already knows, so shares the information with Patrick. Patrick doesn't know the information ultimately came from Anika, so sends the information back to Anika. Nate prefers not to pass the information along because he isn't sure how credible it really is. Figure 13.6 shows the structure of this network with the new information-sharing relations. Note that you can't read this representation left to right! The information flow process started with Anika in this hypothetical example.

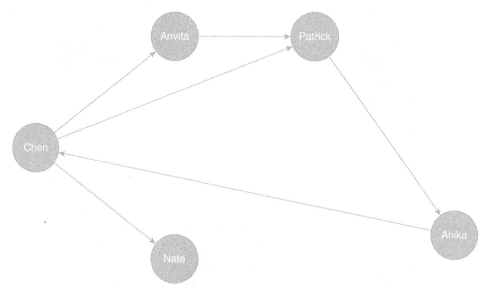

Figure 13.6   A slightly larger and more complex directed network between five nodes

Our initial walk from Anika to Patrick still exists, of course, but now we also have the possibility of many other walks. Anika to Chen to Nate is a walk. Anika to Chen to Anvita to Patrick and back to Anika is a walk. More specifically, it is a closed walk because it starts and ends with the same node: Anika.

In empirical networks, the number of possible walks between any pair of nodes can be vast, but we can impose some order by grouping them into different *kinds* of walks, such as trails, paths, and cycles. A trail is a type of walk where *edges* are not allowed to repeat themselves. For example, Anika to Chen to Anvita to Patrick to Anika is a trail but the exact same walk would *not* be a trail if we included another step to Chen (as that would be repeating an edge). The length of a trail is equal to the number of edges contained in the trail, which in the example above would be 4. A path is a type of walk where *nodes* are not allowed to be repeated. This means that the trail from Anika to Chen to Anvita to Patrick to Anika is *not* a path, because Anika is repeated twice, but Anika to Chen to Anvita to Patrick is. As with trails, the length of a path is equal to the number of edges it contains. Finally, cycles are types of closed walks that (1) involve a minimum of three nodes where the only node that is repeated is the node that starts and ends the walk and (2) no edges are repeated.

All of these examples are walks. Some of these walks are trails, and some of these trails are paths and others are cycles. *If there is a path between two nodes*, say between Anika and Nate, then we say that these two are reachable.

In connected networks, there are typically *many* possible paths that connect any given pair of nodes in a network, but they are not all equally efficient. While information and other resources can certainly travel through a network via inefficient routes, the likelihood of actually going the distance is much greater when travelling on efficient paths. For this reason, we are commonly interested in focusing on the shortest paths between nodes. We will spend a good amount of time in the next chapter discussing shortest paths, followed by a discussion of some alternative assumptions about how contagions flow in a network.

We will leave our discussion of walk structures for now. The key thing to emphasize right now is the general logic of traversing a social network this way and to understand that the structure of the network affects the flow of contagions through it, meaning people in the network will be differentially exposed to those contagions, good or bad. We will return to this issue in the next chapter.

13.7 Conclusion

The key points discussed in this chapter are as follows:

- Relational thinking provides new, different, and valuable ways of approaching social science.
- Different types of ties change how we should think about a network.
- We learnt how to work with network files and data types in NetworkX.
- We discussed walks, paths, cycles, and trails: ways of describing how things can move or traverse through a network.

Visit the website at https://study.sagepub.com/mclevey for additional resources

14

CONNECTION AND CLUSTERING IN SOCIAL NETWORKS

14.1 Learning Objectives

By the end of this chapter, you should be able to do the following:

- Compare different micro-structural configurations at the level of dyads and triads
- Learn how to conduct a triad census
- Detect subgroups in social networks using the following:
  - k-clique communities
  - Louvain community detection
  - Leiden community detection
  - k-components and structural cohesion analysis
  - k-core decomposition

14.2 Learning Materials

You can find the online learning materials for this chapter in `doing_computational_social_science/Chapter_14`. `cd` into the directory and launch your Jupyter server.

14.3 Introduction

This chapter expands on the general introduction to social networks in the previous chapter by widening our discussion to micro- and meso-level structures in social networks. We begin with the building blocks of network structure: dyads. Dyads provide the basis for discussing triads, which are in turn the basis for the more complex meso-level structures we discuss afterwards: cohesive subgroups and communities. There are many ways of detecting cohesive subgroups in networks, some of which start with micro-level structural configurations that overlap to form larger and more complex structures, and others that start at the level of the network itself and work their way down to smaller structures. We will start with two common 'bottom-up' approaches, (1) k-clique communities and (2) Louvain and Leiden community detection, followed by two 'top-down' approaches to describing network structure, (3) k-component structural cohesion analysis and (4) k-core decomposition. While these ideas are not unique to 'computational' approaches to network analysis, much computational network analysis rests on top of these more general foundations, so they are essential to understand first.

Imports

```
import pandas as pd
pd.set_option("display.notebook_repr_html", False)
import numpy as np

from sklearn.metrics.pairwise import euclidean_distances
from scipy.cluster import hierarchy

import networkx as nx
from networkx.algorithms.community import k_clique_communities
from networkx.algorithms.triads import triadic_census
import community

import matplotlib
import matplotlib.pyplot as plt
import seaborn as sns

import random

from dcss.plotting import format_axes_commas, custom_seaborn
custom_seaborn()
```

Data

In this chapter, we'll use both randomly generated networks and the 2013 data on reported contacts collected from the high school students in Marseilles. Technically, this is a directed network, but some of the methods we will cover in this chapter are not implemented for directed networks. Instead, we will treat it as an *undirected* network.

```
contact_diaries = pd.read_csv("../data/SocioPatterns/Contact-diaries-network_data_2013
    .csv", sep=' ')

G = nx.from_pandas_edgelist(contact_diaries, 'i', 'j', create_using=nx.Graph())
G.name = 'Reported Contacts (Diary Data)'
print(nx.info(G))

Name: Reported Contacts (Diary Data)
Type: Graph
Number of nodes: 120
Number of edges: 348
Average degree:   5.8000

contact_diaries.j.unique()[:5]

array([ 28, 106, 147, 177, 295])
```

14.4 Micro-Level Network Structure and Processes

The smallest *relational* units in a network are dyads (two nodes) and triads (three nodes). Much of network analysis rests on aggregations of these simple structures into more complex configurations, so it is important to understand the vocabulary that network analysts use to describe the different forms that dyads and triads take. Let's start with dyads.

Dyads and reciprocity

A dyad consists of the presence or absence of an edge between two nodes, the minimum number of nodes and edges that can define a relation. I say 'presence or absence' because *absence matters*. Edges that do not exist are as informative as edges that do exist (the case of missing data leads to a very interesting literature including covert and illicit networks that is beyond our present scope). Whole networks are built up from the presence and absence of edges between every pair of nodes in the network.

   If our network is directed, it is possible to observe dyads that differ from those in undirected networks. In Figure 14.1, for example, we have two nodes i and j. There are three possible configurations of nodes and the relationships between them: mutual (i and j both send edges to one another, $i \leftrightarrow j$, which is an indication of reciprocity), asymmetric (one sends an unreciprocated edge to the other, either $i \to j$ or $j \leftarrow i$), and null (the absence of an edge between i and j). The possibilities are summarized in Figure 14.1. For obvious reasons, we refer to this as the MAN framework: *m*utual, *a*symmetric, and *n*ull.

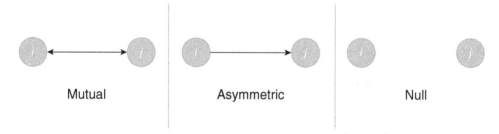

Figure 14.1   The three different types of pairwise relationship between two nodes

   In directed social networks, we may or may not expect to see reciprocity. This is one of many structural forms that we hypothesize about, *look for*, and model. For example, in communication networks among friends, we should expect to see that when one person sends another person a message, *they respond*. However, in an advice-giving network, we might expect to see more asymmetry; graduate students turn to their supervisors for career advice more often than supervisors turn to their graduate students for career advice. The key takeaway here is that there is a social process, *reciprocity*, that is reflected in the edges of directed networks. The social process *generates* the structural form. Other types of social processes manifest in other types of structural forms, and this is one reason why network analysis is a powerful tool for thinking systemically about our interdependencies with one another.

   Dyads are foundational to social network analysis, though they tend to get less attention because they cannot by themselves speak to higher-order concepts such as community structure or network positions. In order to get at those ideas, we need to introduce another level of complexity.

Triads and triadic closure

The next micro-level structure is the triad, just one level up from the dyad. As the name would suggest, triads are the extension of dyads to three ordered nodes. Triads have an especially important place in network analysis, and theoretical work on their importance can be traced back to the classic works of the German sociologist Georg Simmel in 1901. Simmel observed that the addition of a third person to a triad has *far* more dramatic effects than adding a fourth person to a triad, or any other additions that increase the size of the group. The transition from two people to three people is a substantial qualitative change in the relationship and entirely changes what is possible (see excerpts in Wolff, 1950). One of Simmel's examples, that is by no means the most insightful but which drives the point home, is the difference between couples with and without a child. The difference between couples who have a child and those who are child-free is much bigger than the difference between a couple with one child and a couple with two. More generally, the introduction of a third person means that two people can ally themselves to pressure the third, and so on.

Because triads allow relations between two nodes to be understood within the context of a third person, and because of all the qualitative relational differences that the introduction of a third person poses, we can think of triads as the smallest structural elements of larger groups, communities, and societies. For example, when a dyad disagrees, there is no recourse to outside influence, be it mediators, tie-breaking votes, or the like. When a dyad disagrees within a triad, the third node has the opportunity to influence or be influenced by it.

MAN for triads

Earlier, we introduced the MAN framework for differentiating between different types of dyads in a directed network: *m*utual, *a*symmetric, and *n*ull. The possibilities are fewer for an undirected network: present or absent. With an undirected network, the possibilities for triads are also fairly straightforward. We can observe triads with no edges between the nodes, with one edge, with two edges, or with three edges.

Things become considerably more complex for directed networks. Whereas a dyad in a directed network has 3 possible configurations, a triad in a directed network has 16 possible configurations, and differentiating between them requires some specialized vocabulary. We'll use a framework proposed by Davis and Leinhardt (1967) to describe every possible configuration of a triad with directed edges. This framework rests on the MAN framework for dyads, also introduced by Davis and Leinhardt (1967).

The description of a triad under the MAN framework takes the form of a three-digit number, where each digit represents the number of mutual, asymmetric, and null relations within the triad. Thus, the triad described by 003 would be a triad with zero mutual relations, zero asymmetric relations, and three null relations. In short, it's a graph of three nodes with no edges. The triad described by 300 is a triad where each node has a mutual relation with the others. In other words, there are three dyads embedded in this triad. If we name the nodes A, B, and C, we have $A \leftrightarrow B$, $A \leftrightarrow C$, and $B \leftrightarrow C$.

Since the MAN relations describe all possible edge configurations within a dyad, the sum of the three digits in a MAN triad will always be 3. That gives us the following possible configurations: 300, 210, 201, 120, 102, 111, 030, 021, 012, and 003.

That might seem like a lot, but it describes only 10 of the 16 possible configurations for triads in a directed network. Consider the case of 030, the triad where each dyad has a single directed edge between them. This configuration might be cyclical or it might be transitive. A cyclical triad is simply a cycle (discussed in the previous chapter) made with three nodes. A transitive triad takes the form $A \rightarrow B$, $B \rightarrow C$, and $A \rightarrow C$. One node sends two edges. One node sends an edge and receives an edge. The last node receives two edges.

These two sub-configurations are given a capital letter to differentiate them, giving us 030C and 030T, respectively. The full set of 16 configurations is shown in Figure 14.2.

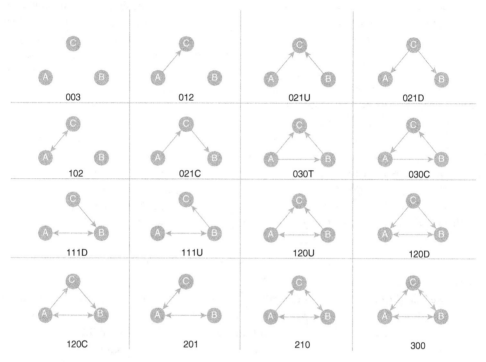

Figure 14.2 All 16 possible triadic configurations possible within the MAN (*mutual, asymmetric, null*) framework

We can count the number of every one of these 16 configurations in a directed network by conducting a triad census. This gives us some insight into the kinds of micro-level structures that are more or less prevalent in the network we are analysing. This requires examining *every combination of three nodes* in the network to identify which MAN triad they belong to. The number of such combinations in a network of any moderate size quickly becomes infeasible to conduct by hand, so we turn to computer algorithms.

To build a bit of intuition about the complexities involved here, and their implications for other network methods, we'll simulate a network, execute a triad census, modify it a bit, and then conduct another census. Let's simulate a random network with 50 nodes using the gn_graph() function, which creates a growing network with directed edges:

```
from networkx.algorithms.triads import triadic_census

gn_50 = nx.gn_graph(50, seed = 42)
sim_50 = pd.Series(triadic_census(gn_50))
sim_50
```

```
003       17464
012        1920
102           0
021D          0
021U        184
021C         32
111D          0
111U          0
030T          0
030C          0
201           0
120D          0
120U          0
120C          0
210           0
300           0
dtype: int64
```

While we might notice certain configurations are more prevalent than others, it's important to remember that interpreting and comparing these counts is not so straightforward. Two triads may overlap. The mutual relationship between the dyad of *A* and *B* will show up in the *ABC* triad, but also the *ABD* triad, and the *ABE* triad, and so on. A triad census will *necessarily* count every dyad multiple times, and every triad will have multiple overlaps with others. Consider another issue. Network density is the proportion of *potential* connections in a network that are realized. As network density decreases, we would certainly expect to see a greater number of triads with more null relationships.

Let's generate a new network with only 20 nodes. We will also define a function that prints the number of nodes, edges, and network density. Finally, we will create a simple visualization of this network (Figure 14.3).

```
gn = nx.gn_graph(20, seed = 42)
gn.name = "Simulated DiGraph with 20 Nodes"

def describe_simulated_network(network):
    print(f'Network: {network.name}')
    print(f'Number of nodes: {network.number_of_nodes()}')
    print(f'Number of edges: {network.number_of_edges()}')
    print(f'Density: {nx.density(network)}')

describe_simulated_network(gn)

Network: Simulated DiGraph with 20 Nodes
Number of nodes: 20
Number of edges: 19
Density: 0.05
layout = nx.fruchterman_reingold_layout(gn, seed=12)

nx.draw(gn, layout, node_color='darkgray',
        edge_color='gray', node_size=100, width=1)

plt.show()
```

Figure 14.3 The structure of our simulated directed network

Now let's conduct a triad census on the network.

```
sim_20_a = pd.Series(triadic_census(gn))
sim_20_a
```

```
003       858
012       222
102         0
021D        0
021U       51
021C        9
111D        0
111U        0
030T        0
030C        0
201         0
120D        0
120U        0
120C        0
210         0
300         0
dtype: int64
```

Now, let's add a single node *with no edges* and see how it affects our triad census.

```
gn.add_node("an isolate")
describe_simulated_network(gn)
```

```
Network: Simulated DiGraph with 20 Nodes
Number of nodes: 21
Number of edges: 19
Density: 0.04523809523809524
```

We've added just a single new node with no edges, an 'isolate'. The number of edges in the network is the same, and the difference in the density is minor. But what happens when we run the triad census again?

```
sim_20_b = pd.Series(triadic_census(gn))
sim_20_b
```

```
003      1029
012       241
102         0
021D        0
021U       51
021C        9
111D        0
111U        0
030T        0
030C        0
201         0
120D        0
120U        0
120C        0
210         0
300         0
dtype: int64
```

We can simplify the comparison by making it visual. Below we'll plot the counts for each of the triadic configurations for both networks. The values for the original network are shown in Figure 14.4 with grey points. The values for same simulation with a single isolate added are shown with crimson plus marks.

```
fig, ax = plt.subplots()
sns.scatterplot(x=sim_20_a,
                y=sim_20_a.index,
                s=50,
                alpha=.8,
                label="Simulated network")
sns.scatterplot(x=sim_20_b,
                y=sim_20_b.index,
                color='crimson',
```

```
                marker="+",
                s=80,
                label="Simulated network + one isolate")
ax.set(xlabel='Count', ylabel='Triad configurations')
sns.despine()
plt.legend()
plt.show()
```

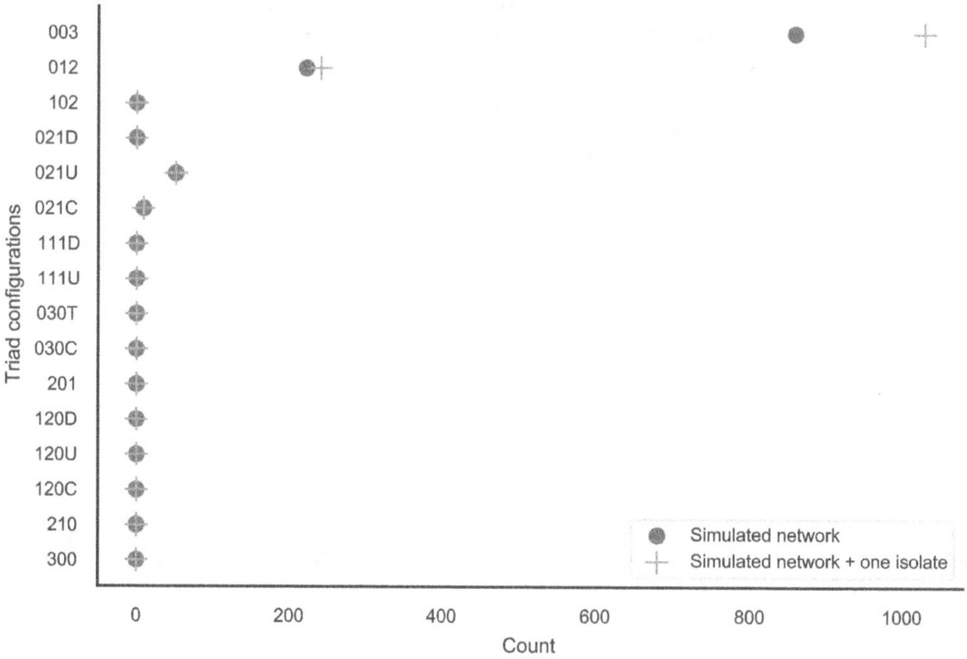

Figure 14.4 The results of the triad census for the original simulated network (grey points) and the simulated network plus one isolate (red plus signs)

We've added quite a few new 003 triads (171 to be precise) and a non-trivial number of 012 triads (19) – all this despite the fact that there has been no appreciable change in the structure of the network.

Finally, let's consider two networks with the same number of nodes and edges. One network will contain a very dense group, while the other will not.

```
clustered_g = nx.null_graph(create_using=nx.DiGraph())
nodes = range(0,20)

for node in nodes:
    clustered_g.add_node(str(node))

for i in range(0,9):
    for j in range(0,9):
```

```
        if i != j:
            clustered_g.add_edge(str(i), str(j))

clustered_g.name = 'Simulated DiGraph, Clustered'
describe_simulated_network(clustered_g)

Network: Simulated DiGraph, Clustered
Number of nodes: 20
Number of edges: 72
Density: 0.18947368421052632

import random

not_clustered_g = nx.null_graph(create_using=nx.DiGraph())

for node in nodes:
    not_clustered_g.add_node(str(node))

for i in range(0,72):
    random_from = str(random.randint(0,19))
    random_to = str(random.randint(0,19))
    while not_clustered_g.has_edge(random_from, random_to):
        random_from = str(random.randint(0,19))
        random_to = str(random.randint(0,19))
    not_clustered_g.add_edge(random_from, random_to)

not_clustered_g.name = 'Simulated DiGraph, Not Clustered'
describe_simulated_network(not_clustered_g)

Network: Simulated DiGraph, Not Clustered
Number of nodes: 20
Number of edges: 72
Density: 0.18947368421052632
```

Now let's compute a census for both simulated networks and then compare the results visually (Figure 14.5).

```
tc_clustered = pd.Series(triadic_census(clustered_g))
tc_not_clustered = pd.Series(triadic_census(not_clustered_g))

fig, ax = plt.subplots()
sns.scatterplot(x=tc_clustered,
                y=tc_clustered.index,
                s=50,
                alpha=.8,
                label="Simulated network, clustered")
sns.scatterplot(x=tc_not_clustered,
                y=tc_not_clustered.index,
```

```
                    color='crimson',
                    marker="+",
                    s=80,
                    label="Simulated network, not clustered")
ax.set(xlabel='Count', ylabel='Triad configurations')
sns.despine()


plt.legend()
plt.show()
```

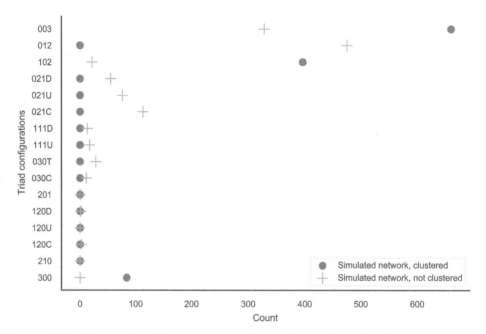

Figure 14.5 The results of the triad census for the clustered simulated network (grey points) and the unclustered simulated network (red plus signs)

Remember, these two networks have the same number of nodes and edges, but one has a dense cluster and the other does not. What has happened is that the dense cluster has a monopoly on the edges, there is a large number of heavily overlapping 300 triads, a much greater number of 003 null triads created by there being more isolates, and there are many more 102 triads representing two isolates and a member of the dense cluster.

The key point to take away from these simple simulations is that raw counts of microstructural configurations in a network, for example via a triad census, can be deceiving. They are nested and highly complex. However, a triad census can be part of an initial exploratory analysis if you are being careful *and intentional*. Among other things, they may help you think through what types of processes and mechanisms might be contributing to the specific structural forms a network takes.

Consider a network of journal articles that cite other journal articles. If we perform a triad census on a citation network, we should absolutely expect to see many more 030T triads than

030C triads. In fact, *we might see no 030C triads at all*, as such a triad suggests that a paper *A* cited a paper *B*, that cited a paper *C*, that cited the original paper *A*. Given that most articles cite papers that have already been published, rather than papers that are yet to be published, such triads should be exceedingly rare, though technically not impossible.

14.5 Detecting Cohesive Subgroups and Assortative Structure

There are many ways of detecting cohesive subgroups, often called communities, in social networks. Some methods start with micro-level structural configurations that overlap to form larger and more complex structures, while others start at the level of the network itself and work their way down to smaller structures. In the subsections that follow, we will explore a variety of methods for such techniques.

We will start with the *k*-clique communities approach, which starts by identifying small groups of densely connected nodes (*k*-cliques) and builds up to larger communities by combining adjacent groups of densely connected nodes. This approach is designed to allow nodes to belong to more than one community, as is the case in real life. We will then discuss Louvain and Leiden community detection, both of which partition networks into mutually exclusive communities where nodes have more connections internally to one another than they do externally to other regions of the network.

The final approach we will cover – *k*-core analysis – identifies the most connected nodes in a component, revealing a component's 'core'. Other methods, like structural cohesion analysis, reveal the core of a component by progressively disconnecting components at their weakest points. Like *k*-clique communities, the *k*-core approach allows nodes to be part of multiple cohesive subgroups, but this means something a little different from what is meant by the *k*-clique communities approach. Here, cohesive subgroups are hierarchically nested, so one can be part of multiple cohesive subgroups in the sense that some subgroups are nested inside other, larger, subgroups.

Let's work our way through each of these approaches.

Cliques and *k*-clique communities

You are probably familiar with the idea of a clique from your everyday life. In network analysis, we use the term a little differently: a 'clique' is a set of nodes that is *completely* connected, meaning that every node is connected to every other node in the clique. As this is the only requirement, cliques can vary in sizes. However, they tend not to be especially large, since most real social networks are fairly sparse, and *complete* connection is an extremely high bar.

The *k*-clique is a variation on this idea, where *k* is the number of nodes in the clique. For example, if *k* = 5, we want to find all groups of five nodes where each node in the set of five is connected to all other nodes. If four of the five nodes are completely connected but the fifth node is missing a connection to one of the other nodes, it is *not* a five-clique, it's a four-clique.

The *k*-clique communities approach to detecting cohesive subgroups is based on the idea that larger 'community' structures in a network are built up from overlapping lower-level structures, such as triads and cliques. This basic idea – large overlapping communities composed of smaller overlapping structures – is an extremely appealing one because it better fits how we view social relations (e.g. as overlapping groups, or intersecting social circles) than alternative approaches that require nodes to be members of only one community (e.g. Louvain, which we will discuss shortly).

How do we know whether two cliques sufficiently overlap to be considered a 'community'? Following Palla et al. (2005), we can say that two k-cliques overlap when they share at least $k - 1$ nodes. In other words, if $k = 4$, then two cliques that have three nodes in common (again, $k - 1$) are overlapping, or 'adjacent'. Those two cliques are then merged into one community. This process continues until there are no more overlapping cliques.

Detecting cliques can be very computationally intensive, especially for large networks. Fortunately, there are variations on the basic idea that make it possible to do this type of analysis on larger and more complex graphs. The most common approach is the clique percolation method. In short, clique percolation works by;

1   finding all the maximal cliques in a network,
2   creating a clique adjacency matrix where the cells represent the number of nodes shared by two cliques,
3   thresholding the matrix using the value $K - 1$ so as to prevent merging cliques that overlap but below the $K - 1$ threshold, and
4   forming communities from the connected components that remain after thresholding.

This clique percolation method is implemented in NetworkX and is used when we run the `k_clique_communities()` function. We can select any value for K, but remember that larger values will identify fewer cliques and fewer communities because large cliques are relatively rare in real-world social networks, and larger overlaps will also be rare. Inversely, small values of K will result in more cliques detected. The number of nodes required for communities to form from overlapping k-cliques is also smaller, so communities will be more diffuse.

```
k = 5
ccs = list(k_clique_communities(G, k))
print(f'Identified {len(ccs)} {k}-clique communities.')
```

```
Identified 6 5-clique communities.
```

If we set $K = 5$, as we do above, we find n clique communities in the graph. We can print the node IDs for each of the communities by iterating over the lists produced by the code in the previous cell:

```
communities = [list(c) for c in ccs]
for c in communities:
    print(c)
```

```
[480, 771, 21, 791, 15]
[771, 21, 200, 826, 15]
[1828, 1412, 1295, 1201, 1594, 1214]
[232, 488, 210, 120, 89, 285]
[471, 681, 970, 475, 124]
[400, 145, 945, 489, 428]
```

Remember, the central idea here is that communities are *overlapping*, so we should see some nodes that appear in multiple communities. Let's create a new dictionary where the keys are node IDs and the values are a list of the k-clique communities that the node is embedded in.

If a node is not part of any *k*-clique communities, we will leave their list empty. We will just use numerical IDs (derived from the index in the outer list) for the community IDs.

```
kccs = {}
for node in G.nodes():
    kcliques = [communities.index(c) for c in communities if node in list(c)]
    kccs[node] = kcliques
```

We can print the list of overlapping nodes by simply checking for keys in the dictionary that have more than 1 *k*-clique community. We will also create another list that includes the node IDs for all nodes that are embedded in *any* *k*-clique component. This list can be used to determine the percentage of nodes in the network that are part of a community. We will also use it in a network visualization below.

```
overlapping_nodes = []
in_any_kclique = []


for k, v in kccs.items():
    if len(v) > 1:
        overlapping_nodes.append(k)
    if len(v) >= 1:
        in_any_kclique.append(k)

print(
    f'{len(overlapping_nodes)} nodes belong to multiple $k$-clique communities: {
    overlapping_nodes}.'
)
print(
    f'{len(in_any_kclique)} nodes ({np.round(len(in_any_kclique)/len(G), 2)*100}% of
    the network) are embedded in at least one $k$-clique community.'
)
3 nodes belong to multiple $k$-clique communities: [15, 21, 771].
29 nodes (24.0% of the network) are embedded in at least one $k$-clique community.
```

Again, we can use some simple network visualizations to help interpret the results of our *k*-clique analysis. This time, let's construct a visualization where all nodes and edges are initially grey. Then we will overlay a visualization of the nodes that are embedded in at least one *k*-clique component in crimson. Finally, we will print labels for nodes indicating the numerical ID of the community they are embedded in. The result is the network shown in Figure 14.6.

To do all this, we need to do a little bit of prep work. Specifically, we need to get a list of tuples for the edges embedded in a *k*-clique community and we need to create a dictionary of node labels: in this case, the numerical IDs for each detected community.

```
layout = nx.nx_pydot.graphviz_layout(G)

edges_in_kcliques = [
    e for e in G.edges() if e[0] in in_any_kclique and e[1] in in_any_kclique
]
```

```
labs = {}
for k, v in kccs.items():
    if len(v) == 1:
        labs[k] = v[0]


nx.draw(G,
        layout,
        node_color='darkgray',
        edge_color='lightgray',
        node_size=50,
        width=.5)
nx.draw_networkx_nodes(G,
                       layout,
                       node_color='crimson',
                       node_size=50,
                       nodelist=in_any_kclique)
nx.draw_networkx_edges(G,
                       layout,
                       edge_color='crimson',
                       edgelist=edges_in_kcliques)
labs = nx.draw_networkx_labels(G,
                               layout,
                               labels=labs,
                               font_size=6,
                               font_color='white')
```

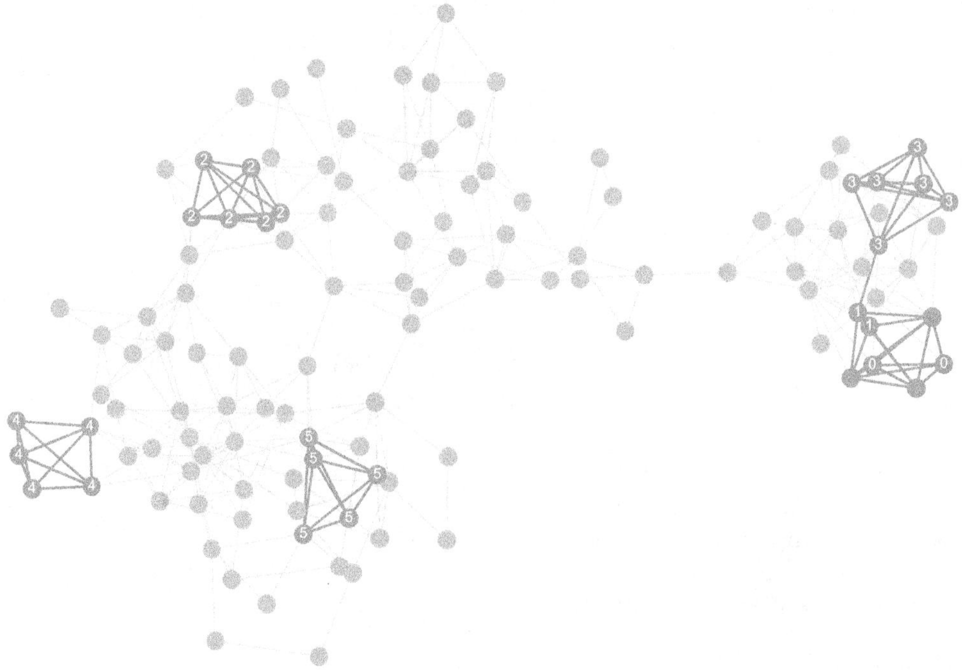

Figure 14.6 The SocioPatterns network with the *k*-cliques overlaid in red; note the overlapping *k*-clique on the right-hand side of the figure

In this particular network, the *k*-clique community approach has identified a few communities that do indeed seem to be very cohesive and cliquish relative to other nodes in the network. It also seems like our aggregation rules for going from small cliques to larger communities is preventing the algorithm from identifying some small clusters of nodes in the network that probably should be considered 'cohesive'.

Let's flip the script a little and turn our attention to techniques that sort *everyone* in the network into one community or another. This solution may be a bit better, but the downside is that these approaches don't allow overlap; everyone is a member of one and only one community.

Community detection using Louvain and Leiden

Identifying cliques in a network is useful, but there are times when we want to know more about how group membership is spread across all of the nodes in a network. In these cases, we typically turn to a community detection algorithm. One of the most widely used in recent years is the 'Louvain' community detection algorithm.

The Louvain community detection algorithm relies on a measure called modularity (Q), which is a quantitative summary of how modular the structure of a given network is, and which is produced by analysing the density of edges within a group relative to edges outside the group. The value of Q ranges between a minimum of $-\frac{1}{2}$ and a maximum of 1. The more modular a network is (closer to 1), the more distinct 'communities' it is composed of. In other words, networks with higher Q are made up of communities that have many internal ties and relatively few external ties. To gloss over many details, the Louvain algorithm tries to optimize Q by checking how much moving a node into a community will increase Q, and moving it into the community that increases Q the most (if any move is positive). Once Q can't be improved by moving nodes between communities, it creates a new representation of the graph where each community is a node. It then repeats the process of trying to improve Q until there is only a single node.

In the modularity algorithm world, each algorithm varyingly provides some kind of modularity 'guarantee'. For example, Louvain guarantees that when it is finished, no merging of communities can increase Q further. If one iterates the algorithm, one can eventually guarantee that no nodes can be moved that would increase Q. However, it makes no guarantee that this unimprovable partition is the *best* partition. It also doesn't guarantee that moving a node to a different community will not disconnect an existing community. In short, this introduces a weakness, identified by Traag et al. (2019), where a bridging node that holds two parts of a community together can be moved to another community. The result would be that the first community is now disconnected, in the sense that the only way to move from one part of it to the other is through a node that is now in an outside community. Traag et al. (2019) also point out that relatively common problem of 'detecting' poorly connected communities. Despite these and other problems, Louvain is very popular because it still tends to produce better results than many competing algorithms, and it tends to be fairly fast.

The Louvain algorithm is implemented in the `best_partition()` method from the `community` package we imported earlier. Although the Louvain algorithm has been developed over time and is said to be adaptable to directed and weighted networks, the original implementation is for undirected binary networks and the Python package doesn't have the extensions implemented. We will talk about an alternative shortly that can make full use of the contact diary data.

```
part = community.best_partition(G)
q = community.modularity(part, G)
print(f"The modularity of the network is {np.round(q, 3)}.")
```

```
The modularity of the network is 0.71.
```

We can use this community membership data in a variety of ways. The code below, for example, shows community membership differentiated by colour. Figure 14.7 is printed in greyscale, but you can find the full-colour version in the online supplementary learning materials.

```
colors = [part[n] for n in G.nodes()]
my_colors = plt.cm.Set2
```

```
fig, ax = plt.subplots(figsize=(12, 8))
nx.draw_networkx_nodes(G,
                       pos=layout,
                       node_size=100,
                       node_color=colors,
                       cmap=my_colors)
nx.draw_networkx_edges(G, pos=layout, edge_color='lightgray', width=1)
plt.axis('off')
```

```
plt.show()
```

Figure 14.7 The SocioPatterns network with the results from Louvain community detection overlaid

Louvain seems to have done a better job of identifying distinct clusters of densely connected nodes in this network than our *k*-clique community approach. There are, however, limitations. While some of the communities seem well-defined (the one on the right is clear-cut), others get a little messy and appear to be overlapping; these may not be good partitions, but in this case it's hard to tell because we have very limited information about the nodes, as this is an anonymized public dataset.

Sometimes it is useful to bump things up a level of analysis, such as by looking at networks of cohesive subgroups rather than networks of individuals who cluster into groups. Once you have detected communities with the Louvain algorithm, you can aggregate the communities into single nodes and assign edges between them when a node from one community has a tie to a node in another community. This can be done by simply passing the Louvain partitions and the network object to the `induced_graph()` function from the `community` package. Note that we will also collect data on edge weights to size the thickness of the edges in this induced network, similar to how we sized nodes based on their centrality in the previous chapter. The result is Figure 14.8.

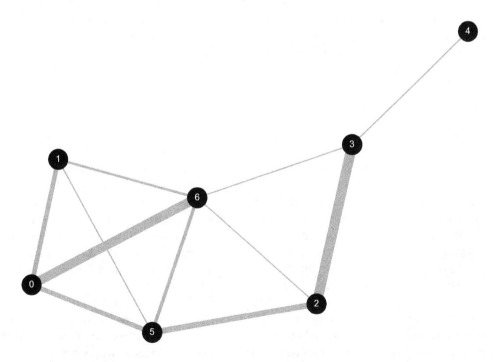

Figure 14.8 The connections between the communities identified in the previous figure

```
inet = community.induced_graph(part, G)
inet.name = "Induced Ego Network"

weights = [inet[u][v]['weight'] for u,v in inet.edges()]
ipos = nx.nx_pydot.graphviz_layout(inet)

nx.draw(inet,
        node_color = 'black',
        pos = ipos,
        with_labels = True,
        font_color = 'white',
        font_size = 8,
        width=weights,
        edge_color = "gray")
```

To help interpret this induced graph, we can look up the names of the nodes in each community. For example, if we wanted to know which nodes make up the community 2 node:

```
community = 14
for k,v in part.items():
    if v == community:
        print(k)
```

The Louvain algorithm does a reasonably good job of identifying cohesive subgroups in networks, but there are some non-trivial limitations in the algorithm. The most obvious of these limitations are that (1) nodes must belong to one and only one community because communities can't overlap and (2) small communities may not be accurately identified and may end up being merged into larger communities. Earlier, I discussed some issues with the algorithm, raised by Traag et al. (2019).

From Louvain to Leiden

To address the issues they identified with Louvain, Traag et al. (2019) propose the Leiden algorithm; it includes some additional processes that give it more flexibility about how it treats communities and the nodes within them. While Louvain optimizes modularity by moving individual nodes to other communities and then kicks off the aggregation step to choose community merges, Leiden adds a step in the middle where each community is considered in isolation and its modularity is maximized. In this way, a poorly connected community that should be split into multiple, smaller communities doesn't get swallowed up as a single unhappy unit in the aggregation stage that follows. Aside from guaranteeing that all of the communities identified will actually be connected, this optimal subcommunity assignment also allows Leiden to find smaller, distinct communities. Leiden also implements a number of clever performance refinements that have been proposed to improve Louvain's often lengthy convergence time. These are less important to understanding how and when to use Leiden for community detection, so we don't need to get to the bottom of them here. Instead, let's see some example results from applying Leiden to the same data we used with the Louvain algorithm above.

If you are curious, I suggest consulting this blog post, which does a great job of explaining what Leiden is doing. https://timoast.github.io/blog/community-detection/

Leiden is available for Python via pip, but it requires the package Python-igraph as a dependency. igraph is substantially more performant than NetworkX due to the C++ back end that it's built around, but the documentation (for the Python implementation) is not nearly as extensive as NetworkX, which is one of the reasons why we have used NetworkX so far.

Let's start by building an igraph undirected graph object, basically identical to the one above. Thankfully, our Pandas dataframe is in exactly the format that igraph expects, where the first two columns are the `from` and `to` nodes from NetworkX terminology.

```
import igraph as ig
import leidenalg as la
```

We create the network object, then use `leidenalg` to calculate the partition memberships for each node:

```
H = ig.Graph.DataFrame(contact_diaries, directed = False)
part_leiden = la.find_partition(H, la.ModularityVertexPartition)
```

For consistency, it's nice to be able to use the same layout for a graph to compare the community detection results. Drawing graphs in NetworkX is more straightforward, and the `graphviz_layout` algorithm produces nice layouts. We can access attributes of the `leidenalg` partition class object to modify a copy of the NetworkX `partition` object, which is just a dictionary of `{node_name:community_id}`. The attribute `_graph` of the `partition` class is itself an igraph `graph` class, from which we can access the `.vs['name']` attribute that is populated from the dataframe and will match the NetworkX node names:

```
partition = part.copy()
for membership, node in zip(part_leiden._membership, part_leiden._graph.vs['name']):
    partition[node] = membership
```

Now we can draw the graph just as we did with the networks above. You will notice from Figure 14.9 (once again, printed in greyscale but with a full-colour version available in the online supplementary learning materials) that we end up with more communities here than we did with Louvain community detection, and some are considerably smaller. Also note that although the communities in the bottom left of the graph seem pretty intermingled, this is because the layout was calculated only by the connections between nodes, rather than by any sophisticated community detection. Importantly, none of these communities have disconnected nodes despite being split into twice the communities detected by Louvain, which is a promise of the Leiden algorithm.

```
colors = [partition[n] for n in G.nodes()]
my_colors = plt.cm.Set2

fig, ax = plt.subplots(figsize=(12, 8))
nx.draw_networkx_nodes(G,
                       pos=layout,
                       node_size=100,
                       node_color=colors,
                       cmap=my_colors)
```

```
nx.draw_networkx_edges(G, pos=layout, edge_color='lightgray', width=1)
plt.axis('off')

plt.show()
```

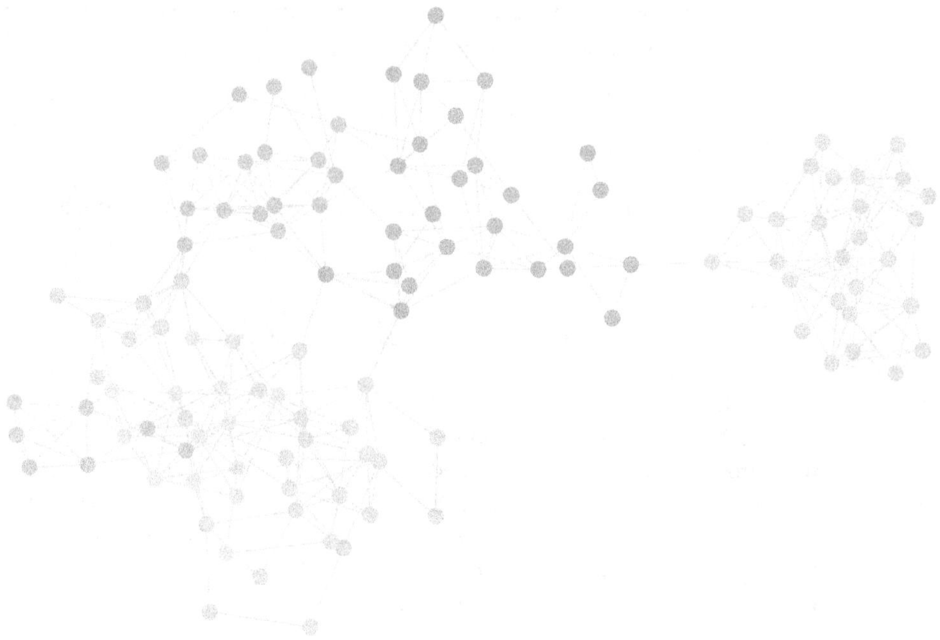

Figure 14.9 The SocioPatterns network with the results from Leiden community detection overlaid

The `leidenalg` package also accepts directed networks with edge weights – we will provide those to the partition detection function and then see how much it changes the communities that are detected.

```
dH = ig.Graph.DataFrame(contact_diaries, directed = True)
part_leiden = la.find_partition(dH, la.ModularityVertexPartition, weights = dH.es['
    weight'])

for membership, node in zip(part_leiden._membership, part_leiden._graph.vs['name']):
    partition[node] = membership
```

In the resulting image (Figure 14.10), it's possible to simply observe the changes because there's actually only one! The middle community at the top of the graph is split into two individual communities.

```
colors = [partition[n] for n in G.nodes()]
my_colors = plt.cm.Set2

fig, ax = plt.subplots(figsize=(12, 8))
nx.draw_networkx_nodes(G,
```

```
                    pos=layout,
                    node_size=100,
                    node_color=colors,
                    cmap=my_colors)
nx.draw_networkx_edges(G, pos=layout, edge_color='lightgray', width=1)
plt.axis('off')

plt.show()
```

Figure 14.10 The SocioPatterns network – now including edge weights and directionality – with the results from Leiden community detection overlaid

Components and *k*-cores

Components

The *k*-clique, Louvain, and Leiden approaches to subgroup detection that we have covered so far detect higher-level structures (communities) by working their way *up* from lower-level structures. Now we are going to switch our focus to another set of approaches that work the opposite way: from the top down. The first thing we need to do is discuss components. A component is simply a connected graph. Most of the networks we have seen so far have been single components, but we have seen a few examples where a few nodes exist off on their own, detached from the rest of the networks. In these cases, each connected group of nodes is a component. Components are generally not considered 'communities' in and of themselves, but they are the starting point for community detection algorithms that start at the top level of a network and work their way down to the lower levels of a network, revealing increasingly cohesive subgroups of nodes along the way.

NetworkX makes it easy to figure out how many components a network has. In this case, we already know the answer from the network visualizations above (3), but let's execute the code anyway:

```
nx.number_connected_components(G)
```

```
1
```

We can use a bit of list comprehension to get the number of nodes in each component:

```
comps_sizes = [len(c) for c in sorted(nx.connected_components(G), key=len, reverse=
    True)]
print(comps_sizes)
```

```
[120]
```

This network consists of a single component with 120 nodes. If there were multiple components, we would refer to the largest as the giant component.

Many network methods require operating on a connected graph (i.e. a single component). If we need to use a method or a model that requires a fully connected network but the network we are analysing has more than one component, there are a number of possible actions we could take. One would be to decompose the network into a series of networks (one for each component) and analyse them separately. Alternatively, we could extract the giant component by identifying all the components in the network ('connected component subgraphs') and then selecting the largest one. In most cases, it is best not to limit your analysis to the giant component unless the other components are all very small (e.g. isolates).

```
components = sorted(nx.connected_components(G), key=len, reverse=True)
giant = G.subgraph(components[0])
giant.name = "Communication Network, Giant Component"
print(nx.info(giant))
```

```
Name: Communication Network, Giant Component
Type: Graph
Number of nodes: 120
Number of edges: 348
Average degree:   5.8000
```

k-cores

From a top-down perspective on community structure, components are a bit like Russian nesting dolls; the component itself is 'cohesive' insofar as it is, and stays, connected, but much *more* cohesive subgroups, such as cliques, are nested inside them. Just as we worked our way *up* to communities earlier, we can work out *down* from components to reveal more cohesive groups inside of components.

With social networks, it is common to find a set of nodes that are densely connected with one another at the 'core' of a component. As you move further away from that densely connected core towards the edges of the network, you find nodes that are less densely connected. This is typically referred to as a core–periphery structure.

K-Cores are one of the most common ways of identifying the cohesive group(s) of nodes at the core of a component. In this approach, *k* represents a minimum degree value. For example, if *k* = 5, then the *k*-core will consist of the largest connected subgraph where all nodes have *at least* a degree of 5. A *k*-core with *k* = 2 would be made up of nodes with a degree of at least 2, and so on. As the value of *k* increases, denser and more cohesive regions of the component are revealed. Note that the definition of *k*-core accounts for a node's degree before identifying the core, so such an analysis could reveal pockets of dense connections which are themselves only weakly connected. For example, imagine a long chain of nodes with a degree of 4: each node in the chain is connected to the next and has an additional 2 pendants hanging off. The backbone of this chain would be identified by a 4-core, while the pendants would not.

Let's extract a series of *k*-cores from the SocioPatterns contact diaries network (G) and compare the number of nodes and edges that are part of the *k*-core at different values for *k*.

```
ks = [1,2,3,4,5,6,7,8]
nnodes = []
nedges = []


for k in ks:
    kcore = nx.k_core(G, k)
    nnodes.append(kcore.number_of_nodes())
    nedges.append(kcore.number_of_edges())


kdf = pd.DataFrame([ks,nnodes,nedges]).T
kdf.columns = ['Value of K', 'Number of Nodes', 'Number of Edges']
kdf
```

	Value of K	Number of Nodes	Number of Edges
0	1	120	348
1	2	117	345
2	3	105	324
3	4	83	262
4	5	18	60
5	6	0	0
6	7	0	0
7	8	0	0

We can see here that *if there were isolates in this network*, they would have been dropped by *k* = 1. The number of nodes and edges in the network drops slightly with *k* = 2. There are fairly large drops in size for *k* = 3 and 4. No nodes or edges are retained for *k* = 8 in this particular network.

Let's see what the *k*-cores look like for *k* = 4 and 5. To do so, we will extract and then visualize the *k*-core subgraphs overlaid on the full network.

```
kcore_4 = nx.k_core(G, 4)
kcore_5 = nx.k_core(G, 5)
```

To emphasize the *nestedness* of these *k*-cores, let's layer visualizations of each. In Figure 14.11, we first draw our base graph, with all nodes and edges in the giant component in light grey. Then we overlay a visualization of the four-core using the same layout coordinates, but colouring the nodes and edges dark grey (the colour palette I can use for this book is highly constrained!).

Finally, we overlay a visualization (Figure 14.11) of the 5-core, again using the same layout coordinates, but colouring the nodes and edges crimson. The resulting visualization shows how the most locally dense regions of the network are embedded in larger and less cohesive regions of the network, *much like the Russian nesting dolls previously mentioned.*

```
## BASE NETWORK
nx.draw(G, layout, node_color = 'lightgray', edge_color = 'lightgray', node_size = 30)

## DRAW THE NODES IN THE 4-CORE GRAY
nx.draw_networkx_nodes(kcore_4, layout, node_size = 30, node_color = 'gray')
nx.draw_networkx_edges(kcore_4, layout, node_size = 30, edge_color = 'gray')

## DRAW THE NODES IN THE 5-CORE IN CRIMSON
nx.draw_networkx_nodes(kcore_5, layout, node_size = 30, node_color = 'crimson')
nx.draw_networkx_edges(kcore_5, layout, node_size = 30, edge_color = 'crimson')
plt.show()
```

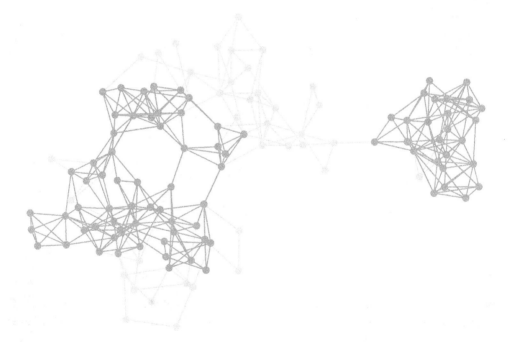

Figure 14.11 The SocioPatterns network with various *k*-cores overlaid; dark grey represents *k* = 4, and red represents *k* = 5

These visualizations should help build some intuition for how *k*-cores work, and how they can help you uncover a particular type of network structure with a cohesive subgroup, or several groups, at the core of a component, and more peripheral nodes loosely connected to the core.

=========== **Further Reading** ===========

If you are looking to learn more on cohesive subgroups and community structure, Chapter 11 of Borgatti et al.'s (2018) *Analyzing Social Networks* provides a good overview.

14.6 Conclusion

The key points in this chapter are as follows:

- Dyads (two nodes) and triads (three nodes) are the primary micro structures that are used to describe networks.
- We conducted a triad census.
- We learnt how micro structures combine to create larger macro structures such as cliques and communities (bottom-up).
- We learnt how network structure can be broken down to find smaller subgroups (top-down).
- We conducted a community analysis using k-clique communities, Louvain community detection algorithm, k-components, and k-core decomposition.

Visit the website at https://study.sagepub.com/mclevey for additional resources

15

INFLUENCE, INEQUALITY, AND POWER IN SOCIAL NETWORKS

15.1 Learning Objectives

By the end of this chapter, you should be able to do the following:

- Explain what centrality analysis is and how it relates to theoretical ideas
- Explain what a shortest path is
- Compare shortest path and current flow betweenness
- Compare degree, eigenvector, and Bonacich power centrality
- Explain the conceptual and graph-theoretic underpinnings of:
  - Shortest path and current flow betweenness centrality
  - Degree centrality, eigenvector centrality, and Bonacich power centrality
- Explain why it is *essential* to think carefully about what specific centrality measures mean given the nature of the edges in an observed network

15.2 Learning Materials

You can find the online learning materials for this chapter in `doing_computational_social_science/Chapter_15`. `cd` into the directory and launch your Jupyter server.

15.3 Introduction

This chapter focuses on 'centrality analysis', which is widely used for analysing social networks with an emphasis on influence, inequality, status, dependence, and power (among many other things). The literature on social networks contains a huge number of centrality measures, each designed to operationalize and measure some specific theoretical idea. It's not possible to cover all of them here, nor especially desirable. I will cover two important frameworks for thinking about centrality. For each framework, I will describe some of the most foundational centrality measures and clarify the connections between these empirical measures and their conceptual and theoretical underpinnings. This should help you develop a good understanding of centrality *in general* so you can make sense of other centralities.

This chapter is organized into three main sections. The first section begins with a brief high-level discussion of centrality. I then introduce the first centrality framework: a 'central' node describes a network position that has more influence over the flow of things through the network. This perspective is anchored in ideas of 'walks' on a network and 'contagions' that 'flow' through those walks, two ideas that were briefly introduced in the previous chapter. The second section of this chapter builds up an intuitive understanding of these concepts and culminates in a discussion of 'shortest path betweenness centrality' and 'current flow betweenness centrality'.

The third section addresses the second centrality framework, which ultimately boils down to counting connections, the sum of which is known as a node's 'degree'. At the most basic level, nodes that are connected to many other nodes (high degree) are more popular than nodes with few relationships (low degree). This simple idea is the foundation of more complex ideas. For example, the popularity of the nodes that one is connected to also matters, and because of the structure of social networks, this idea expands out to include all reachable nodes in a network. In other words, being connected to a small to moderate number of very well-connected nodes can unlock more advantages in a network than being connected to a very large number of nodes who are not themselves well connected (e.g. it's probably better to have 20 friends who each have 5 friends than to have 100 friends who are only connected to you). This is will lead us to eigenvector centrality and its close relation Bonacich power centrality.

These different ways of thinking about – and operationalizing – influence, inequality, status, dependence, and power came from researchers studying different networks in a wide array of contexts. A centrality measure developed to measure the influence in a friendship network may not translate well to measuring influence in an information brokerage network. As Kitts (2014) has argued, a common problem with centrality analysis is that researchers implicitly assume there is some inherent meaning behind specific centrality measures that holds up regardless of the type of relationships that are operationalized as the edges of a network. In fact, the interpretation of a measure depends as much on the nature of the relations measured as it does on the mathematics of the measure itself (see also Kitts and Quintane, 2020).

As always, we're just scratching the surface of what is possible here, but if you really understand the conceptual basis of these measures and how they are computed from network data, you'll have a solid foundation for learning about other centrality measures.

Package Imports

```
import networkx as nx
import pandas as pd
pd.set_option("display.notebook_repr_html", False)
import numpy as np

import matplotlib
import matplotlib.pyplot as plt
import seaborn as sns

from dcss.plotting import format_axes_commas, custom_seaborn
from dcss.networks import *
custom_seaborn()

import collections
import random
```

Data

We will continue to work with data from the SocioPatterns project – specifically, the relational data reported by students in their contact diaries:

```
contact_diaries = pd.read_csv("../data/SocioPatterns/Contact-diaries-network_data_2013
    .csv", sep=' ')
```

```
G = nx.from_pandas_edgelist(contact_diaries, 'i', 'j', create_using=nx.Graph())
G.name = 'Reported Contacts (Diary Data)'
print(nx.info(G))
```

```
Name: Reported Contacts (Diary Data)
Type: Graph
Number of nodes: 120
Number of edges: 348
Average degree:   5.8000
```

Recall from the previous chapter that `create_using=nx.Graph()` means we are creating an undirected network. The output of the `info()` function confirms this by telling us we have a `Graph` object, not a `DiGraph` object (directed).

15.4 Centrality Measures: The Big Picture

A node's location in a social network matters. It determines what they are exposed to; the support, opportunities, and resources they have access to; their social status and prestige; and their ability to exercise power and influence over others. In network science, centrality measures are one of the main ways in which abstract concepts such as these are mapped onto concrete measurable variables that can be computed from relational data.

Consider power. Like many other social science approaches to conceptualizing power, the network perspective is relational. It emphasizes relationships and situations where one person is dependent upon another, with the assumption that these dependency relations determine consequential things in our lives, both good and bad. We are embedded in a complex intersection of many such relationships, regardless of how aware we are of the dependency dynamics. To name just a few examples:

- A child or young adult who depends upon a parent for *everything*
- A graduate student who depends upon a supervisor's expertise, support, and connections
- An academic department chair whose approval or disapproval partially determines a faculty member's performance evaluations and salary increases (in a non-unionized context)
- A friend who depends upon another friend for support in a crisis

These dependency relations can, of course, be exploited. Parents can be unloving, and physically or emotionally abusive. Supervisors can take credit for their students' work. Department chairs can be jealous, or petty, and favour others. Friends can take advantage of us.

In these cases, one person has asymmetric control and power in the relationship. The person can impose their will and make life better or worse for the dependent individual. The point is *outcomes for ego, such as health and well-being, are at least partially in the hands of alter.* But it's not just about one-to-one relationships, and this is one of the critical reasons for thinking about these dependency relations in the context of larger networks of relations, not just dyads.

If a student can jump ship and find a better supervisor, if a friend can turn to another friend, if a faculty member can be evaluated by a committee rather than by a department chair, then the dependency is lessened and power is less concentrated. Children and adults in toxic and abusive relationships are more obviously constrained in their ability to reduce their dependencies. Children don't get to choose their parents, and there are most certainly specific reasons why people are prevented from leaving toxic and abusive relationships. The structure of social networks can constrain people in comparable ways, making it difficult to break free from the control of others. This is further complicated by the fact that most of us don't *really* know all that much about the structure of the networks that we live our lives in. As Hanneman and Riddle (2005) put it so pithily, 'Ego's power is alter's dependence.'

This insight has profound implications. The structural properties of a social network determine the amount of power available in general, its distribution among nodes, and therefore the extent to which some nodes can influence others. In some networks, power may be relatively evenly distributed and opportunities for control and domination are rare. In others, it may be centralized around a small subset of nodes. In other words, the structure of our social networks determines the extent to which we are *able* to influence and control one another, with some network structures enabling more influence and control and others enabling less. We can change lives *dramatically*, for better or for worse, by changing the structure of dependency relations.

Centrality analysis provides tools we can use to examine power empirically via dependency relations, but this is only one possibility. Centrality analysis can be used to assess the opportunities and constraints for any node, given the specific ways they connect to other nodes in a network, which we can refer to as a node's 'position'.[1] Some positions may be more or less likely to result in exposure to novel information and ideas, or they may afford easy access to elites or resources that are more difficult for others in less advantageous positions to access.

There are various centrality measures designed to capture these differences and others. At this point, it's important to note the following:

1   Being central is not inherently good or desirable. The same types of central positions that give one early access to useful information can also mean early exposure to infectious diseases.
2   Being central is not a guarantee that a node will experience the hypothesized effects of their position, good or bad. Having the opportunity to access elites is not the same thing as seizing that opportunity.

There are usually specific types of structural positions that you expect to be important given your research question. As always, *theory is really important here*. Rather than computing every centrality score, you should select those that correspond to your research question or operationalize a relevant concept. You may want to identify information brokers in a collaboration network. This could help you study whether people who are in a position to influence the flow of information over walks (a concept we will turn to momentarily) in the collaboration

---

[1] In later chapters, we will expand the idea of positions in a network, but for the time being, we can think of position primarily in terms of centrality.

network have different career outcomes than those who are not in such positions, or perhaps find key individuals in a needle-sharing network for a public health intervention. In that case, you could use betweenness centrality, which we discuss shortly. While you certainly should analyse multiple centralities, you need to think deeply about the question you are trying to answer, what these specific centralities mean and how they work, and how well those align.

15.5 Shortest Paths and Network Flow

Shortest paths/geodesics

The first framework for thinking about centrality is interested in the access that a node has to the rest of the network. It's probably intuitive that the most efficient way to exchange something (information, resources, power) between two points is to find the shortest distance between them (i.e. the path between two nodes that involves the smallest number of nodes and edges). These 'shortest paths' are also called geodesics.

We can identify the *shortest* path between any two nodes using the shortest_path() function in NetworkX. If we use the function without specifying a specific pair of nodes, it will compute all the shortest paths between every possible start and end points between every pair of nodes in a network. Even for small networks, that's a *lot* of paths.

To help build some intuition about paths, we will define a couple of functions that will let us quickly query the paths between any pair of nodes, and then highlight those paths in simple network visualizations. Note that we are constructing our visualizations a little differently than we did in Chapter 14.

Our plot_path() function requires a layout for the network visualization. We will use the kamada_kawai_layout() function to compute the layout for a visualization of the contact diary network data from SocioPatterns, which we used to construct the network object G at the start of this chapter:

```
layout = nx.kamada_kawai_layout(G)
```

The nodes in the SocioPatterns data are, of course, anonymized. The research team assigned each node an integer ID. You can see those IDs with G.nodes().

Now that we have our functions defined, and we know what the IDs are for the nodes in our network, let's look at a few examples. We will provide our get_shortest_paths() function with the integer IDs for our source and target nodes. For example, let's find the shortest path between nodes 173 and 48:

```
path_a, es_a = get_shortest_paths(G, 173, 48)
print(path_a)
```

```
[173, 295, 954, 691, 642, 605, 687, 496, 134, 45, 48]
```

In order for some information that 173 has to reach 48 along the shortest path, it would have to first go through nodes 295, 954, and so on. What does this path look like? Let's visualize it. In Figure 15.1, the shortest path between 173 and 48 will be highlighted.

```
plot_path(G, layout, path_a, es_a)
```

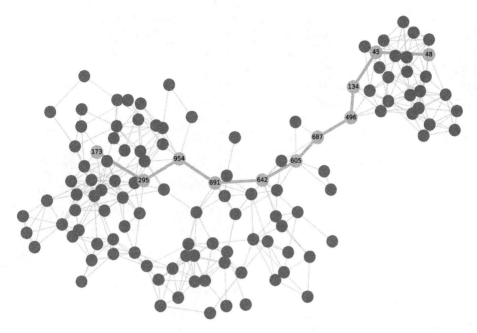

Figure 15.1 The SocioPatterns contact diary network, with one of the shortest paths between nodes 173 and 48 overlaid in red

Multiple shortest paths

If there are more than one shortest paths between nodes, then get_shortest_paths() picks one at random to return. We can get the full list of shortest paths using the all_shortest_paths() function. Let's see the other paths between 173 and 48:

```
sps = [path for path in nx.all_shortest_paths(G, source=173, target=48)]
path_nodes = set([item for sublist in sps for item in sublist])
```

```
for path in sps:
    print(path)
```

```
[173, 295, 954, 691, 502, 582, 687, 496, 87, 488, 48]
[173, 295, 954, 691, 642, 582, 687, 496, 87, 488, 48]
[173, 295, 954, 691, 642, 605, 687, 496, 87, 488, 48]
[173, 295, 954, 691, 502, 582, 687, 496, 134, 45, 48]
[173, 295, 954, 691, 642, 582, 687, 496, 134, 45, 48]
[173, 295, 954, 691, 642, 605, 687, 496, 134, 45, 48]
[173, 295, 954, 691, 502, 582, 687, 496, 388, 45, 48]
[173, 295, 954, 691, 642, 582, 687, 496, 388, 45, 48]
[173, 295, 954, 691, 642, 605, 687, 496, 388, 45, 48]
[173, 295, 954, 691, 502, 582, 687, 496, 388, 79, 48]
[173, 295, 954, 691, 642, 582, 687, 496, 388, 79, 48]
[173, 295, 954, 691, 642, 605, 687, 496, 388, 79, 48]
[173, 295, 954, 691, 502, 582, 687, 496, 448, 845, 48]
[173, 295, 954, 691, 642, 582, 687, 496, 448, 845, 48]
[173, 295, 954, 691, 642, 605, 687, 496, 448, 845, 48]
```

Notice that in these shortest paths that *start* with 173 and *end* with 48, there are some nodes that appear on *all* the shortest paths, such as 295 and 954. This enables us to count the number of shortest paths that involve any given node. Nodes that are involved in a larger number of shortest paths may be considered more central, as being involved in more shortest paths offers some distinct advantages for power and influence.

Let's plot all of these paths (Figure 15.2):

```
fig, ax = plt.subplots(figsize=(12, 8))

nx.draw_networkx_nodes(G, pos=layout, node_size=200, node_color='#32363A')

nx.draw_networkx_edges(G,
                       pos=layout,
                       edge_color='darkgray',
                       width=1)

## THE PATHS!

nx.draw_networkx_nodes(G,
                       pos=layout,
                       node_size=200,
                       node_color='crimson',
                       nodelist=path_nodes)

for p in sps:
    edges = set(zip(p, p[1:]))
    nx.draw_networkx_edges(G,
                           pos=layout,
                           edgelist=edges,
                           edge_color='crimson',
                           width=4)

plt.axis('off')
plt.show()
```

Shortest path lengths can also be computed, which can be useful when the distance between two nodes matters more than the specific paths connecting them. We can do this with the shortest_path_length() function. Recall from earlier that we are counting *edges* on a path between a source and target node, so the length will always be equal to 1 – the number of nodes in the path itself. This can be useful to know because information and influence usually degrade over longer distances. That's why shorter paths are likely to be more important than longer ones. The shortest_path_length() function tells us that, regardless of the specific path, the closest that 173 and 48 can be is 10 steps:

```
nx.shortest_path_length(G, source=173, target=48)
```

```
10
```

Finally, we can also compute the average length shortest paths in a connected network using the average_shortest_paths() function. This is an average across *all pairs* of *i, j* nodes in the full network.

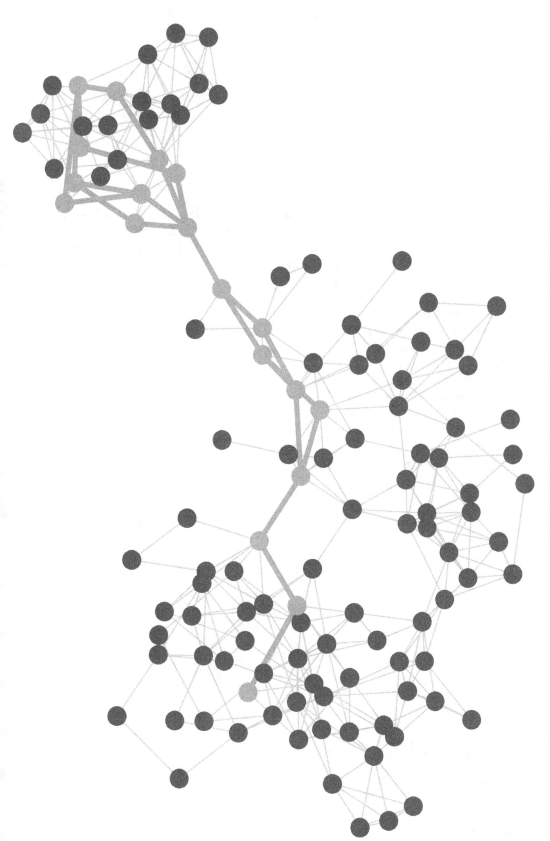

Figure 15.2 The SocioPatterns contact diary network, with all of the shortest paths between nodes 173 and 48 overlaid in red

```
np.round(nx.average_shortest_path_length(G), 2)
```

```
5.36
```

Note that the path lengths between 173 and 48 are higher than the average path lengths in the network.

15.6 Betweenness Centrality, Two Ways

This discussion of paths and network walk structure has been building a foundation for our discussion of betweenness centrality. In brief, the idea is that nodes that lie between nodes or, better yet, between groups of densely connected nodes (such as 'communities') often have advantages and opportunities that other nodes do not have. For example, information tends to be more homogeneous within clusters of densely connected nodes and more diverse across such clusters. As a result, nodes that are embedded *within* a cluster tend not to have information that is unknown to their adjacent peers, but nodes that lie *between* clusters get access to diverse sources of information. In some cases, these nodes may be able to influence and perhaps even control the flow of information through the network. For example, they may filter and frame information in ways that increase their own power over others who depend on them for access to that information. In other words, they are in potential brokerage positions. Consider the hypothetical network in Figure 15.3. Which node is the in-between broker? If we consider the shortest paths in this network, which nodes will be on more shortest paths than others?

```
nx.draw(nx.barbell_graph(5,1), node_size=300, node_color='#32363A')
```

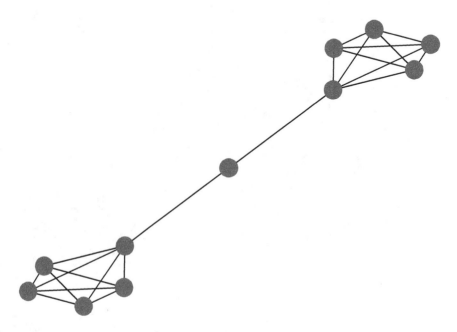

Figure 15.3   A barbell graph

Further Reading

If you want to deepen your understanding of brokerage dynamics in social networks, I recommend Katherine Stovel and Lynette Shaw's (2012) review article 'Brokerage', which touches on many interesting theoretical ideas related to centrality.

There are two main ways of computing betweenness centrality: shortest path and current flow. As you might expect, shortest path betweenness is computed based on shortest paths, which are central to any process where a contagion (e.g. information) spreads through a network.

To compute shortest path betweenness for any given node, we first determine the shortest paths between every pair of nodes in the network. We then compute the proportion of shortest paths that include the node in question for each i, j pair of nodes in the network. Those proportions are then summed to obtain a single number. If a node does not lie on *any* shortest paths, then its betweenness score will be 0 (e.g. if it is an isolate). It will have the maximum value if it lies on *all* shortest paths between *all* pairs of nodes in the network. Note that this is a systematic implementation of the general idea we considered earlier when noting that some nodes lie on more shortest paths than others.

Let's quickly visualize the distribution of betweenness scores with a histogram (Figure 15.4).

```
sp_bet = pd.Series(nx.betweenness_centrality(G))

ax = sns.histplot(sp_bet, kde=True)
ax.set(xlabel='Shortest path betweenness centrality',
       ylabel='Number of nodes')
sns.despine()
plt.show()
```

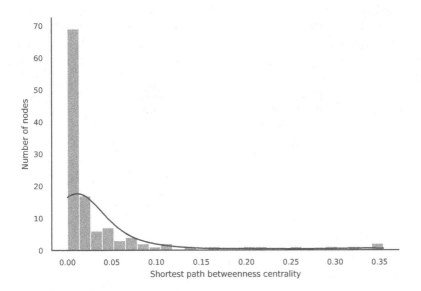

Figure 15.4 A histogram and kernel density estimate of the shortest path betweenness centralities of each node in the SocioPatterns contact diary network

Most nodes in the network have low shortest path betweenness; only a few have higher scores.

Unlike shortest path betweenness, current flow betweenness takes into account the strength of relationships when it conceptualizes how a contagion flows through a network. Current flow betweenness draws on the analogy of electric current flowing through a *resistance network*, where edges are resistors. A detailed discussion of electromagnetism is, unsurprisingly, beyond the scope of this book, so we will gloss over the details and focus on some quick takeaways.

A circuit where resistors are arranged in a single line between the source and the target is a series circuit. The current can only flow through one path, so the current is the same between each node on the path between the source and the target. The *effective resistance* of the circuit is the sum of the resistances of all the resistors. Thus, for a given path, adding another edge at the end can only increase the effective resistance: information flows less well through longer chains. Consider the flow of people leaving a crowded stadium. This stadium is poorly designed and everyone has to leave via a single path consisting of a series of rooms. Each time you add a room, you add a door that has to be opened, you give people more chances to stumble, and generally the whole flow of people from the stadium (source) to the exit (target) will slow down.

A circuit where resistors are arranged such that multiple paths lie between the source and the target is a parallel circuit. The current will split where paths branch and flow down each of the possible paths, with more current flowing through more efficient paths. As you add parallel resistors, the effective resistance of the whole circuit decreases. Consider the stadium example: if we have multiple exits, people will be leaving through all of them. Some exits will be more efficient because they have fewer rooms and/or larger doors, and people will flow through those faster. If you add another exit, even if it's a small side door, people will necessarily be able to leave faster. In current flow betweenness, the strength of a relationship corresponds to how efficient the flow of current is between nodes. In our example, rooms with larger doorways between them could be represented with greater edge weights.

This example sounds like a directed network, but the network we are working with is undirected. To calculate the circuit flow betweenness of a node, we consider that each node in the network could be a source or a target, and calculate the current flow for that node averaged across every possible pairing of source and target nodes. Bringing it back to the stadium example, this is like shuffling the stadium seats and the stadium exit through all the rooms so that we consider every possible pairing and take the average flow through a room across all those pairings.

The code below computes current flow betweenness and then constructs a scatter plot (Figure 15.5) to compare the scores against the shortest path version.

```
cf_bet = pd.Series(nx.current_flow_betweenness_centrality(G))
betweenness = pd.concat([sp_bet, cf_bet], axis=1)
betweenness.columns = ['Shortest Path Betweenness', 'Current Flow Betweenness']

sns.jointplot(data=betweenness,
              x='Shortest Path Betweenness',
              y='Current Flow Betweenness',
              alpha=.7)
plt.show()
```

```
<seaborn.axisgrid.JointGrid at 0x7f9d648f2d60>
```

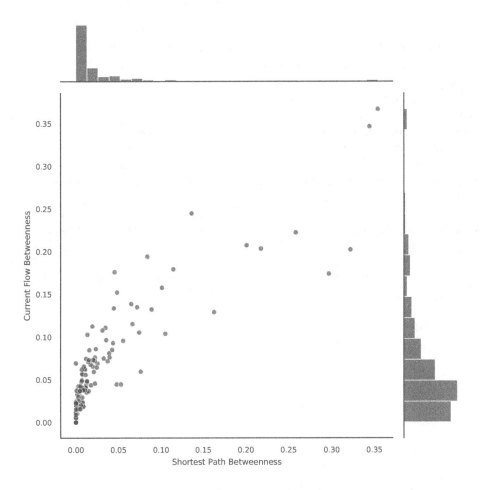

Figure 15.5 A scatter plot with marginal histograms of the shortest path and current flow betweenness centralities of each node in the SocioPatterns contact diary network

While similar, the two measures are not equivalent to one another. At very low values, shortest path betweenness and current flow betweenness are quite densely clustered and the relationship between the two seems stronger, but as we look at the larger (and rarer) values, the relationship becomes much weaker. Consider why this might be. Being on a single shortest path will necessarily have a low shortest path and low current flow betweenness score because the flow of contagion/current can only be a small amount of the larger network. However, as we increase the number of shortest paths that a node is on, we are also increasing the chances of a node being part of a parallel circuit (metaphorically speaking). Current flow betweenness conceptualizes that flow between nodes takes the routes other than the shortest path, albeit at a reduced rate. Thus, we would likely expect a wider distribution of current flow betweenness values.

Let's move on from the idea of things flowing through a network and consider another way of thinking about centrality.

15.7 Popularity, Power, and Influence

The second centrality framework is focused less on the ideas of paths and flow, and more on popularity, status, and prestige. The idea is that more – and 'better' – relationships are associated with greater popularity, status, and prestige.

To demonstrate this, let's work with another network dataset collected from the same French high school students by the SocioPatterns team. The previous network represented reported *contacts* that we coerced into an undirected network. The network we will use in this example is a directed friendship network produced by students identifying other students as their friends. Unfortunately, some friendships are asymmetrical; one may feel the relationship is strong enough to nominate the other, but it may not be reciprocated. For this, we will use a DiGraph (directed graph).

```
reported_friendships = pd.read_csv("../data/SocioPatterns/Friendship-network_data_2013.
csv", sep=' ')

G_friendships = nx.from_pandas_edgelist(reported_friendships,
                                        'i', 'j', create_using=nx.DiGraph())

G_friendships.name = 'Reported Friendships'
print(nx.info(G_friendships))

Name: Reported Friendships
Type: DiGraph
Number of nodes: 134
Number of edges: 668
Average in degree: 4.9851
Average out degree: 4.9851

layout = nx.nx_pydot.graphviz_layout(G_friendships)
```

Degree, degree centrality, and connection inequality

One of the most critical pieces of information in this approach to centrality is the number of connections a node has. For an undirected network, that count is called degree. If I have 50 connections, my degree is 50. Nodes with higher degree are, by definition, more connected. For a directed network, we distinguish between edges leaving a node, *out-degree*, and edges arriving at a node, *in-degree*. In a hypothetical advice network at a business where a directed edge represents 'gave advice to', we would expect the most senior and experienced employees to have higher out-degree (they are giving advice to more people) and the most junior would have higher in-degree (they are receiving advice from more people). While an individual node can have different in-degree and out-degree, the network *as a whole* will have a balanced in-degree and out-degree because each directed edge is necessarily an outgoing *and* an incoming edge for two different nodes. We can still use the concept of degree for directed networks, simply by adding a node's in-degree and out-degree to count all edges connected to a node.

Let's compute the out- and in-degrees for the nodes in the SocioPatterns contact network. Then we'll visualize the network a couple of times, once with the node sizes as a function of in-degree and once as a function of out-degree. Since we intend to execute the visualization code a couple of times, let's define a custom function:

```
def visualize_digraph(network, layout, node_size=50, title=''):
    fig, ax = plt.subplots(figsize=(12, 8))
    ax.set_title(title, fontsize=16)
    nx.draw_networkx_nodes(network,
                           pos=layout,
                           node_size=node_size,
                           node_color='#32363A')
    nx.draw_networkx_edges(network,
                           pos=layout,
                           edge_color='#98989C',
                           arrowsize=5,
                           width=1)
plt.axis('off')
plt.show()

in_degree = dict(G_friendships.in_degree())
out_degree = dict(G_friendships.out_degree())
```

If we supply NetworkX with the original in- and out-degree scores as node sizes, even the most popular and active nodes will be extremely tiny. Instead, we will multiply every score by 20 to get them into a range of values that are large enough to use as node sizes in the visualization (Figure 15.6):

```
sized_by_indegree = [v * 20 for v in in_degree.values()]
sized_by_outdegree = [v * 20 for v in out_degree.values()]

visualize_digraph(G_friendships, layout, sized_by_indegree)
```

Figure 15.6 The SocioPatterns friendship network, with node size scaled by in-degree

And now we'll do the same for out-degree (Figure 15.7):

```
visualize_digraph(G_friendships, layout, sized_by_outdegree)
```

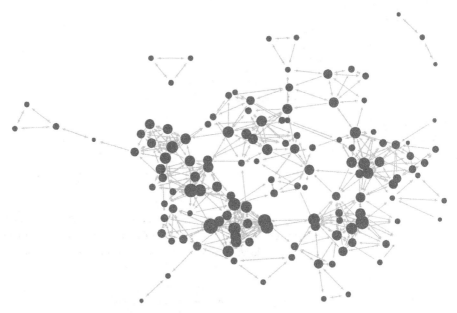

Figure 15.7 The SocioPatterns friendship network, with node size scaled by out-degree

If you squint, you might notice some apparent differences in the popularity (in-degree) and activity (out-degree) across nodes in the network, but for the most part, it seems as if the nodes that have higher in-degree also have higher out-degree. We can confirm our hunch by plotting the two degree scores (Figure 15.8):

```
fig, ax = plt.subplots()
sns.scatterplot(x=in_degree, y=out_degree, alpha = 0.2)
sns.despine()
ax.set(xlabel='Indegree',
       ylabel='Outdegree')
plt.show()
```

Recall that we are working with reported friendships, where out-degree means that one node, *i*, has nominated another node, *j*, as a friend. If *i* and *j* are indeed friends, then they should both nominate each other. (*Reciprocity!*) It follows that in a network such as this one, nodes that have a high score on one of the two degree measures will likely also have a high score on the other. The network visualizations and the scatter plot clearly suggests that there are some high-activity students who both nominated and were nominated by more people, and while closely related, it is also clear that in-degree and out-degree are not equal for all students. Not every friendship in this network was reciprocated.

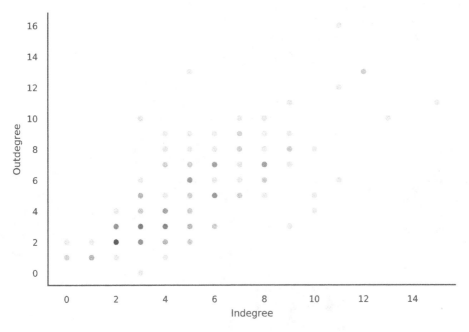

Figure 15.8 A scatter plot of the out-degree and in-degree of each node in the SocioPatterns friendship network

Connection inequality

Inequalities in connectedness, visible as inequalities in node in-/out-degree, can have many consequences. We are often concerned with extreme levels of inequality, which in network science are often analysed in terms of cumulative advantage processes – the rich get richer, the more well connected become more connected (Barabási and Albert, 1999; DiPrete and Eirich, 2006; Merton, 1968; Price, 1965, 1986).

Even moderate levels of inequality can have surprising effects, however. Consider what Scott Feld (1991) has called 'the friendship paradox', which states that on average, people's friends have more friends than they do (on average, people have fewer friends than their friends do). To demonstrate, consider the following: a person (ego) has 20 friends (alters) who each have 10 friends. As a consequence of this inequality, every alter has a below-average number of friends. This connection inequality in personal networks can impact how we perceive the world around us and what we judge to be 'normal'. Although they are a minority overall, the most well-connected people are over-represented in most people's personal networks, and everyone else, though quantitatively more common, are under-represented in other people's networks (Feld, 1991). In other words, the preferences and behaviours of the most popular people are disproportionately represented and are therefore more visible in our lives than those of their under-represented peers. As a result, our personal connections are rarely a good indication of the types of preferences and behaviours that are more common in the general population.

Let's use degree as a measure of popularity for now. We can visualize connection inequalities by plotting the degree distribution. In Figure 15.9, we see the number of nodes (*y*-axis) with each possible degree value (*x*-axis).

```
degree_sequence = sorted([d for n, d in G_friendships.degree()], reverse=True) #
    degree sequence
degreeCount = collections.Counter(degree_sequence)
deg, cnt = zip(*degreeCount.items())

fig, ax = plt.subplots(figsize=(6,4))
plt.bar(deg, cnt, width=0.80, color="#32363A")
ax.spines['right'].set_visible(False)
ax.spines['top'].set_visible(False)
ax.set_xlabel('Degree')
ax.set_ylabel('Number of nodes')
plt.show()
```

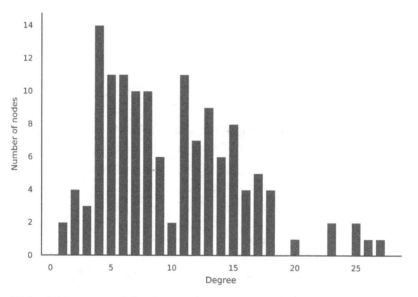

Figure 15.9 A histogram of the degree of each node in the SocioPatterns friendship network

Because there is often a lot of inequality in connectedness, especially in larger networks, it is often more informative to plot the degree distribution with both axes on a log scale. If the result is a relatively straight negative line from the upper right to the bottom left, you might want to formally check for a power law distribution, which would indicate extreme inequality and potentially some sort of cumulative advantage process.

Another way of inspecting the degree distribution is to produce a plot that ranks nodes based on their degree and plots their rank and degree on a log–log scale (Figure 15.10). The top-*ranked* node in the graph is shown in the upper left of the graph (at 10^0, which is 1). As you would expect, nodes in this upper left corner have higher degree centrality than any other nodes in the network (27). We see the decreasing degree of each successive node in the ranked list as we move along the x-axis. As we get towards the end of the list, we start to see nodes with very low degree. As there are no isolates in this network, the lowest degree score is 1 (or 10^0).

```
fig, ax = plt.subplots(figsize=(6,4))

ax.loglog(degree_sequence,
          'black',
          marker='o',
          markersize=3)

plt.title("Degree Rank Plot")
plt.ylabel("Degree")
plt.xlabel("Rank")

ax.spines['right'].set_visible(False)
ax.spines['top'].set_visible(False)
```

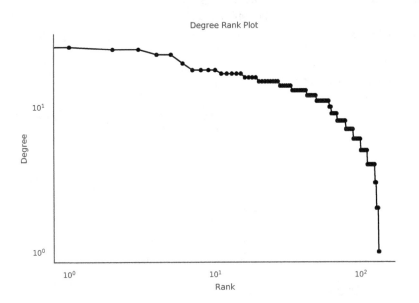

Figure 15.10 A degree–rank plot for each node in the SocioPatterns friendship network

Degree is commonly treated as a proxy for 'popularity', but that's not the only option. Our interpretation of any centrality measure *must be based on the type of ties in the network*. In the earlier example of the contact diary network, the edges in the network simply indicate whether two nodes came into contact with each other within a given time frame. One could make an argument for 'popularity' there, but it would make more sense to think of degree in the contact network as something like mobility: moving more may produce more opportunities for contact. Returning to the idea of contagions flowing through a network, degree could be a measure for exposure, with more connections indicating more exposure. The specific details of the relations encoded in the network matter as much, or more than, the formal mathematics of the measure when it comes to interpreting centrality.

Eigenvector centrality

Degree centrality is an intuitive way of thinking about how connected people are, but analytically it doesn't get us very far on its own. However, many other centrality measures are built on degree and can be used to operationalize more complex and interesting ideas. Eigenvector centrality is based on the simple idea that being connected to well-connected people matters: even if your degree doesn't change, if your neighbour's degree increases, your connection to the network also increases.

Consider our friendship network again. This time we are going to look at the 'neighbourhoods' (immediate alters) of two specific nodes and their extended neighbourhoods (alters' alters). I will pick two focal nodes, 1519 and 196, and assign them the colour crimson. Their immediate alters will be plotted in black, their extended neighbourhood in dark grey, and the rest of the nodes in light grey. I have chosen these two nodes to compare because they have the same degree (the size of their immediate neighbourhoods are identical).

We'll use the plot_nodes() function defined below to simplify some of the visualization code. The resulting plots are shown in Figures 15.11 and 15.12.

```python
def plot_nodes(which_network, which_nodes, what_color, where):
    if type(which_nodes) is list:
        nx.draw_networkx_nodes(which_network,
                               pos=where,
                               node_size=100,
                               node_color=what_color,
                               nodelist=which_nodes)
    else:
        nx.draw_networkx_nodes(which_network,
                               pos=where,
                               node_size=100,
                               node_color=what_color,
                               nodelist=[which_nodes])


alters = nx.ego_graph(G_friendships, 1519, radius=1, undirected=True)
alters_2 = nx.ego_graph(G_friendships, 1519, radius=2, undirected=True)

fig, ax = plt.subplots(figsize=(12, 8))
plot_nodes(G_friendships, list(G_friendships.nodes()), 'lightgray', layout)
plot_nodes(G_friendships, list(alters_2.nodes()), 'gray', layout)
plot_nodes(G_friendships, list(alters.nodes()), 'black', layout)
plot_nodes(G_friendships, 1519, 'crimson', layout)

nx.draw_networkx_edges(G_friendships, pos=layout, edge_color='lightgray',
                       arrowsize=3,
                       width=1)

plt.axis('off')
plt.show()

alters = nx.ego_graph(G_friendships, 196, radius = 1, undirected = True)
alters_2 = nx.ego_graph(G_friendships, 196, radius = 2, undirected = True)
```

Figure 15.11 The SocioPatterns friendship network with the focal node – 1519 – in red, alters in black, second-order alters in dark grey, and the rest of the network in light grey

```
fig, ax = plt.subplots(figsize=(12,8))
plot_nodes(G_friendships, list(G_friendships.nodes()), 'lightgray', layout)
plot_nodes(G_friendships, list(alters_2.nodes()), 'gray', layout)
plot_nodes(G_friendships, list(alters.nodes()), 'black', layout)
plot_nodes(G_friendships, 196, 'crimson', layout)

nx.draw_networkx_edges(G_friendships, pos=layout, edge_color='lightgray',
                       arrowsize=3,
                       width=1)

plt.axis('off')
plt.show()
```

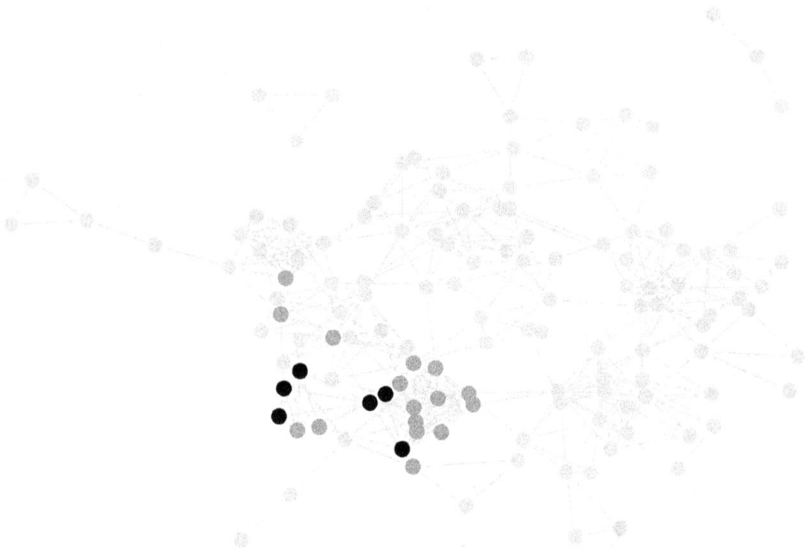

Figure 15.12 The SocioPatterns friendship network with the focal node – 196 – in red, alters in black, second-order alters in dark grey, and the rest of the network in light grey

Despite their immediate neighbourhoods (black) being the same size, 196 has much greater reach with their extended neighbourhood because their immediate neighbours are better connected.

Think about *influence* in this context: 196 influences and is influenced by their direct alters, who in turn influence and are influenced by *their* direct alters. Influence on 196 is most strong from their immediate alters, followed by their alters' alters, followed by their alters' alters' alters, and so on.

Let's consider how this is reflected in eigenvector centrality. Technically, a node's eigenvector centrality is proportional to the sum of the centralities of their alters (Borgatti et al., 2018). In this sense, eigenvector centrality can also be interpreted as a measure of popularity, but it differs from degree centrality because a node can have high eigenvector centrality but low degree centrality (i.e. they are connected to only a few people, but those people are well connected).

Both 1519 and 196 have degrees of 11 (five reciprocated nominations and one unrecipro-cated), but when we look at the network, we can probably intuit that they occupy different types of positions given *who* they are connected to, and how those people are connected. Just by eyeballing the network, we can see that 196's connections are more connected than 1519's are. When it comes to *influence* and *power* in a network, being connected to well-connected people is more useful than being connected to less well-connected people.

Eigenvector centrality is based on this fundamental idea that when it comes to influence, the connections of the people we are connected to matter. We have to think, and 'see' beyond our immediate social neighbourhoods.

Computing eigenvector centrality

Let's take a look at the distribution of eigenvector centrality scores to degree (Figure 15.13):

```
dn = pd.Series(dict(nx.degree(G_friendships)))
ec = pd.Series(nx.eigenvector_centrality(G_friendships))

fig, ax = plt.subplots()
sns.scatterplot(x=dn, y=ec, alpha=.6)
ax.set(xlabel='Degree', ylabel='Eigenvector centrality')
sns.despine()
plt.show()
```

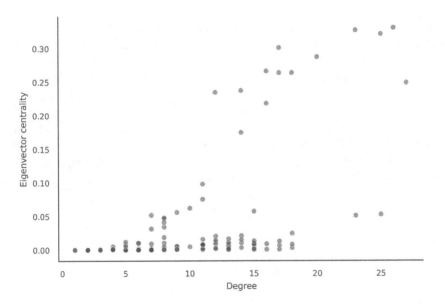

Figure 15.13 A scatter plot of the eigenvector centrality and degree of each node in the SocioPatterns friendship network

We can see that degree and eigenvector centrality are somewhat positively correlated. As degree increases, eigenvector tends to increase as well, though some individuals with high degree centrality are especially well-positioned and take a lion's share of the eigenvector centrality.

Bonacich power centrality

Eigenvector centrality is often used, among other things, as a proxy for power. However, as Phillip Bonacich (1987) pointed out, being more 'central' is not necessarily the same thing as being more powerful. Being connected to well-connected others makes you more reachable, *but less powerful* because the people you are connected to are connected to a lot of other people; they do not *depend* on you because they are connected to a lot of others. On the other hand, if the people you are more connected to are *not* themselves well connected, then their connection to you matters more; they are more dependent on you, and therefore, you are more powerful. For Bonacich, then, ego is more central when their alters are densely connected with one another, but this makes ego *less* powerful; instead, ego gains power when their alters have few connections to one another.

We might expect to see this in access and exchange networks, where being connected to people who have a lot of other exchange partners reduces your 'bargaining power'. Being connected to people who have few exchange partners, on the other hand, increases your bargaining power. Bonacich (1987) power centrality conceptualizes power in terms of an ego's access to alters who are dependent on them.

Bonacich (1987) power centrality makes this distinction with a β parameter that represents how a node's degree centrality is influenced, positively or negatively, by the degrees of its alters. A positive β parameter indicates that being connected to alters who are well connected is 'better' and is, therefore, closer to the original idea of eigenvector centrality. In fact, larger values of β will approach eigenvector centrality. On the other hand, a negative β parameter indicates that power comes from being connected to alters who are poorly connected to one another.

A β parameter of 0 indicates that the degree of a node's alters has no bearing on its centrality, thus duplicating degree centrality. In this way, Bonacich power centrality is the most flexible centrality measure that we have examined in this chapter, technically containing several others under its rather large umbrella. However, this flexibility comes at a cost. How does one choose a specific β parameter? This is a tricky question that is beyond the scope of this chapter. Instead, we'll build a bit of intuition of the effects of different β parameters.

At the time of writing, NetworkX does not have an implementation of Bonacich power centrality, so I computed the scores in R using the implementation in igraph. The code block below executes the R script using the os Python package. The `.system()` method is executing a command as it could be executed directly on your command line.

```
G = nx.from_pandas_edgelist(contact_diaries, 'i', 'j', create_using=nx.Graph())
G.name = 'Reported Contacts (Diary Data)'

import os
nx.write_edgelist(G, "intermediary.csv", delimiter=',', data=False)
os.system('Rscript power_centrality.R')
```

The output of the `power_centrality.R` R script is a CSV file called `boncent.csv`. We can read it back into Python below, add the scores for different β values to our NetworkX object as node attributes, and then create a series of visualizations to get a sense of what the scores are indicating. The custom function `size_by_beta_centrality()` pulls the relevant centrality score from the power dataframe, multiplies them by 10,000 to get them into a range of values large enough to see, and then passes the value to our previously defined function `visualize_digraph()`. The plot is shown in Figure 15.14.

```
power = pd.read_csv('boncent.csv', index_col=0)
power = power.round(4)


layout = nx.nx_pydot.graphviz_layout(G)


def size_by_beta_centrality(network, beta_value, title):
    size = power[beta_value].tolist()
    scale = abs(min(size))+0.0001
    size = [(s+scale)*1000 for s in size]
    visualize_digraph(G, layout, size, title)


size_by_beta_centrality(G, 'b0', title=r'$\beta$ = 0 (i.e., Degree Centrality)')
```

β = 0 (i.e., Degree Centrality)

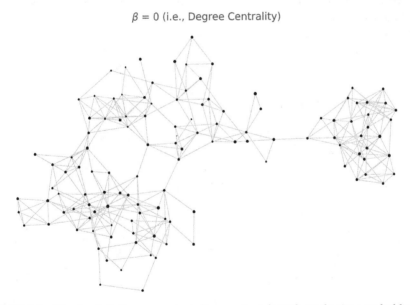

Figure 15.14 The SocioPatterns contact diary network with node sizes scaled by Bonacich, $\beta = 0$

The case of $\beta = 0$ should be relatively straightforward. Feel free to check this yourself, but the Bonacich power centrality scores for this network are linearly dependent on the degree centrality scores: they are perfectly correlated. See Figure 15.15.

```
size_by_beta_centrality(G, 'b_neg.4', title=r'$\beta$ = -0.4')
```

Here we can see $\beta = -0.4$. Notice how some previously large nodes have become much smaller relative to their neighbours. In particular, the largest node in the left cluster is now one of the smallest, while its neighbours have increased in size relative to it. Similarly, several moderate-sized

$\beta = -0.4$

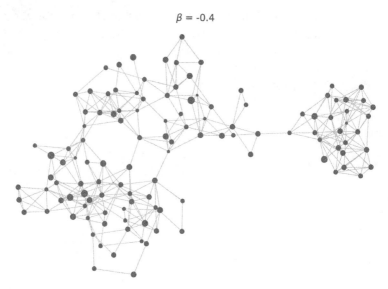

Figure 15.15 The SocioPatterns contact diary network with node sizes scaled by Bonacich, $\beta = -0.4$

nodes have become much larger despite having relatively low degree centralities because they are connected to nodes that have very few connections.

Now let's go in the other direction, more 'centrality' less 'power'. See Figure 15.16.

```
size_by_beta_centrality(G, 'b.4', title=r'$\beta$ = 0.4')
```

$\beta = 0.4$

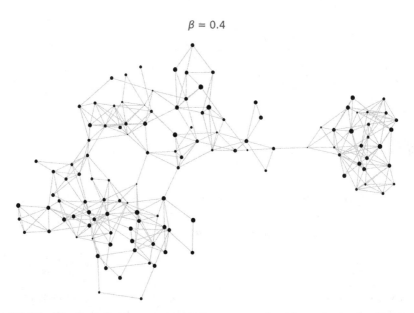

Figure 15.16 The SocioPatterns contact diary network with node sizes scaled by Bonacich, $\beta = 0.4$

Finally, we have $\beta = 0.4$, which shows eigenvector centrality seeming to 'cluster' in the especially dense parts of the network, as those are areas where nodes are connected to nodes that are also well connected.

Rather than worry about the specific calculation of Bonacich power centrality scores, let me once again stress that you must ensure that the centrality measures you use are *appropriate* to the network and the kinds of relations present within it. This is a contact network, so *what would degree centrality actually capture?* It may be a decent measure of mobility, or activity. Someone who is constantly moving around is more likely to make contact with different people, increasing their degree. What would eigenvector centrality capture? If $\beta = 0$ is capturing mobility/activity, $\beta = 0.4$ would describe highly active people who are connected to highly active people. Perhaps this might describe individuals who are in a good position to mobilize cohesive groups en masse? Conversely, $\beta = -0.4$ would describe highly active people who are connected to less active people. These people might be the best individuals to contact in order to reach the fringes of the network. Note that in this interpretation, we are not using Bonacich's measure for what he intended. That's because we understand how it works and what it does. In that situation, we can reason about the meaning of the resulting scores when applied in contexts that differ from the ones they were originally intended for. There is no way to get away from thinking carefully about what the measures mean *given what the edges mean*.

Further Reading

If you are looking to learn more on centrality analysis, Chapter 10 of Borgatti et al.'s (2018) *Analyzing Social Networks* provides a good overview. Borgatti and Everett (2020) contrast three different perspectives on network centrality. Kitts (2014) and Kitts and Quintane (2020) offer a useful perspective on social networks in 'the era of computational social science', with implications of how we interpret centrality measures with networks constructed using behavioural and interactional data.

15.8 Conclusion

The key points in this chapter are as follows:

- We learnt two major ways of thinking about what centrality means: shortest paths through the network and counting edges.
- We learnt some of the most common centrality measures.
- We connected centrality measures to the theories and concepts they operationalize.
- We visualized the distribution of different centrality measures within the same network.

15.9 Chapter Appendix

Optional: formulae for centrality measures covered in this chapter

If you're interested in the formulae for these centrality measures, you can find them below. However, as promised, equations don't carry any explanatory burden in this book, so you should feel free to skip over the formulae if you don't find them enlightening.

Shortest path betweenness

The shortest path betweenness centrality of a node, i, is given by the following:

$$B(i) = \sum_{i \neq j \neq k} \frac{\sigma_{j,k}(i)}{\sigma_{j,k}}$$

where:

- $B(i)$ is the betweenness centrality of i
- $\sigma_{j,k}(i)$ is the number of shortest paths between node j and node k that pass through node i
- $\sigma_{j,k}$ is the number of shortest paths between node j and node k

Current flow betweenness

The current flow betweenness centrality of a node, i, is given by the following:

$$CFB(i) = \frac{\sum_{s,t} tF_i^{s,t}}{\frac{1}{2}n(n-1)}$$

where:

- $F_i^{s,t}$ is the current flow through a node, i, for a source node and target node, s and t, respectively
- s, t are all possible source and target pairs
- n is the number of nodes in the network

Thus, $CFB(i)$ is the average current flow through a node i averaged across all possible source–target pairings.

Current flow betweenness is mathematically very complex, and a full explanation is beyond the scope of this book. For further details, see Brandes and Fleischer (2005).

Eigenvector centrality

The eigenvector centrality of a node, i, is given by

$$\lambda e_i = \sum_j A_{ij} e_j$$

where:

- λ is a constant that gives equations a non-zero solution
- e_i is the centrality of node i
- A is the adjacency matrix
- e_j is the centrality of node j

Note that e_j will also be defined in terms of e_i, so calculating eigenvector centrality involves multiple iterations to refine the values.

Using matrix notation, eigenvector centrality is given by

$$\lambda e = Ae$$

where e is an eigenvector of the adjacency matrix A, and λ is its associated (preferably largest) eigenvalue. This is where the term *eigenvector* centrality comes from.

Visit the website at https://study.sagepub.com/mclevey for additional resources

16

GOING VIRAL: MODELLING THE EPIDEMIC SPREAD OF SIMPLE CONTAGIONS

16.1 Learning Objectives

By the end of this chapter, you should be able to do the following:

- Explain what simple contagions are
- Describe processes/mechanisms that enable simple contagions to spread rapidly via network connections
- Configure an agent-based simulation of the spread of simple contagions through social networks using the Python package NDlib
- Interpret aggregate results produced by many different executions of a simulation model
- Explain the basic idea of an SIR (*susceptible*, *infected*, *recovered/removed*) model, and describe how network-based SIR models deviate from SIR models based on differential equations
- Execute a simulation model on empirical network data, both cross-sectional and dynamic

16.2 Learning Materials

You can find the online learning materials for this chapter in `doing_computational_social_science/Chapter_16`. `cd` into the directory and launch your Jupyter server.

16.3 Introduction

In the previous chapters on networks, I emphasized the idea that network structures govern the spread of various kinds of things, such as infectious diseases, information, beliefs, and behaviours. In this chapter, we will dig deeper into theory, methods, and models that can help us understand how such contagions spread through networks. We will start by discussing the basics of a network-based approach to diffusion, and we will introduce the idea of 'simple contagions' like information or infectious diseases. Then I'll compare traditional models of epidemic spread with some simple network models and finish by extending our discussion of simple contagions to dynamic networks.

16.4 Epidemic Spread and Diffusion

Scientific approaches to studying the spread of contagions through populations have been developing for well over a century. Epidemiologists have been using mathematical models of disease spread like the SIR model since at least the 1920s (Kermack and McKendrick, 1927). Some of the fundamental ideas behind this particular type of model, which partitions populations into different 'compartments' (Susceptible, Infected, Recovered/Removed, etc.) and models transitions between them, can even be traced back to models developed by the famous Dutch mathematician Daniel Bernoulli in 1766, which sought to understand the effect that eliminating smallpox would have on life expectancy (Dietz and Heesterbeek, 2002).

Traditional epidemiological models make some strong simplifying assumptions. The advent of network analysis has led epidemiologists to incorporate network structure and dynamics into their work to address some of those assumptions. Since it can be *incredibly* challenging, not to mention costly and time-consuming, to collect the relevant data, these models typically combine observational data with carefully specified simulation models that we can run thousands of times. We can then step back and look at the most common outcomes from these many simulations.

The value of a network approach to questions of diffusion is not limited to epidemiology. Network analysts are interested in the spread of many different kinds of contagions, infectious diseases being only one (important) example. In network analysis, we use the term *contagion* to mean some 'thing' that spreads through a network; it may be a disease, or perhaps news, a new fashion trend, safe-sex behaviours, or some other quality. Usually, contagions are things that are not consumed as they spread, but propagate and increase in total. A sum of money being shared through a network, for example, is not usually called a contagion, nor is it subject to epidemic spread and diffusion.

To better understand the spread of a contagion through a network, there are some key terms that are important to know. A node is *activated* when they've adopted, caught, or been 'infected' by whatever contagion is flowing over the network. For example, they might catch a cold or adopt a belief. A node is *exposed* to the contagion when an adjacent node is activated.

Consider the hypothetical network shown in Figure 16.1, through which an information-based contagion spreads over time. At first (Time 0), Yevgen has some interesting gossip he is eager to share. Since Yevgen and Eric are directly connected, Eric is 'exposed'. Once Yevgen shares the information with Eric at Time 1, Eric becomes activated and his alters become exposed. Eric's switch from exposed to activated is a *state change*. All state changes in the figure are represented by changes in node colour from white (not activated, not exposed) to grey (exposed) to crimson (activated).

This is some *really* interesting gossip, and Eric can hardly contain it. He doesn't. He shares it with his contacts, triggering another set of state changes at Time 2. Finally, at Time 3, all of Eric's neighbourhood has been activated, and the process continues to spread beyond the boundaries of the figure.

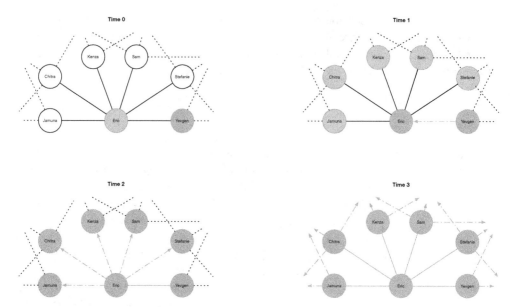

Figure 16.1 A four-part figure depicting how a simple contagion might spread through a simple hypothetical network

This is an illustration of a *simple contagion* process. It's 'simple' in several respects, the most salient of which is that transmission between any two people is *practically effortless*. A single interaction between two people is all that is needed to enable a simple contagion like information to spread. This is not just true for informational contagions, of course. Other simple contagions, such as COVID-19 (coronavirus disease 2019) or a sexually transmitted infection, spread with the same sort of ease. And yet, we don't learn new information from every conversation, contract COVID-19 from every face-to-face interaction, or develop an STI (sexually *transmitted infection*) following every sexual encounter. And despite having much in common, there are substantial differences in the specific diffusion patterns for these and other simple contagions.

There are two things that are especially important to keep in mind here. First, most contagions are not *automatically* transmitted after a single exposure. Therefore, we think about these transmission events in a probabilistic way rather than a deterministic way: each exposure increases the *likelihood* of activation. The second thing to understand is specifically related to social networks, and it's another simple idea that turns out to have profound scientific and practical consequences. All contagions are ultimately spread by specific transmission *mechanisms* like conversation (e.g. informational contagions), being co-present in the same spaces (e.g. COVID-19), and so on. These are social mechanisms. There are culturally specific rules, norms, and conventions that govern how we interact with one another. Of course, we often violate these conventions. Yet, despite individual variation and deviations, the highly patterned micro-level behaviours are strong enough to generate large-scale social networks that take on different shapes and structural configurations. Once formed, these emergent networks take on something of a life of their own and work in a top-down fashion to structure and constrain what happens at the micro level, further shaping diffusion dynamics.

Our day-to-day information-sharing networks have *very* different structures than our sexual contact networks; consider the norms and attitudes associated with each. We are all embedded in these and countless other evolving networks at the same time, each defined by a host of factors, sociological and otherwise. So while simple contagions spread through networks in the same way (exposed nodes activate and expose other nodes), there are still a variety of factors that might lead them to spread differently from one another, and understanding these differences is vital. For network structure and processes, this is both a bottom-up and a top-down process.

These are the two things that matter most for the spread of simple contagions: increased *likelihood* of transmission based on repeated exposures and the effects of emergent and evolving network structure on the spread of a contagion as to spreads through ties, activating some but not others. *Complex contagions* behave differently, which we'll address in the next chapter.

16.5 Modelling Spreading Processes with NDlib

Understanding network diffusion is not always intuitive, especially when we discuss complex contagions. To lay the foundation for the next chapter, we will begin by modelling simple contagions. The models we execute in this chapter are agent-based simulations (see Bruch and Atwell, 2015; Epstein, 2006; Macy and Flache, 2009; Macy and Willer, 2002; Shaw, 2015, 2019) that unfold over time in a series of discrete steps. This means each node is equipped with some set of simple rules that govern what they can do and how they respond to their local neighbours. In the case of simple contagions, this is generally just a matter of probability of infection when two nodes come into 'contact' in the simulation. As the model steps through time, it repeatedly executes these rules, changing each node's state accordingly. This process continues for a fixed number of iterations that we determine ourselves, or until no further changes are possible. When the runs are finished, we can step back and look at overall patterns across the many different iterations.

We will use the NDlib package to develop our models of epidemic spread and diffusion (see Rossetti et al., 2017, 2018). NDlib is built on top of NetworkX and, as of 2021, supports 27 different diffusion models for both simple and complex contagions out of the box. NDlib also contains utilities for specifying custom models from scratch, which gives us a good deal of freedom.

The basic workflow for developing simulation models with NDlib involves the following:

1   Creating or loading network data in the form of a NetworkX graph object
2   Selecting and configuring a diffusion model, or creating one from scratch
3   Executing the simulations
4   Visualizing the results, interpreting macro-level patterns, and drawing inferences about spreading processes

We will execute several diffusion models, starting with epidemiological SIR models. To develop some intuition of how the modelling process works, we'll start with a simple model that is based *entirely* on simulated data. Then, we'll see how to go from executing a single simulation to executing hundreds, and finally how to execute these models using empirically observed network data.

━━━━━━━━━━ **Further Reading** ━━━━━━━━━━

Rossetti et al. (2018) provide an overview of the design of NDlib. If you want to learn more about network theories of diffusion, I would recommend the first two chapters of Damon Centola's (2018) *How Behavior Spreads* and the first few chapters of Centola's (2021) *Change: How to Make Big Things Happen*.

Simple contagions, beyond your neighbourhood

Since simple contagions can spread with only a single source of exposure, they can 'go viral' fairly easily, even if most ultimately do not. Think, for a moment, about the kinds of networks that enable the spread of COVID-19, mass email chains, or internet memes. What are the features of these networks that you would expect to be most relevant? There is, of course, the trivial example of a completely connected network, where every node is connected to every other node, in which case simple contagions can spread with astonishing speed and efficiency. If someone sends a hilarious cat video to everyone on a listserv, then anyone who opens the email will have been activated by the action of a single node. Social networks are *very rarely* completely connected, however.

We can also think of network effects that are related to differences in how central people are. In Chapter 15, we discussed two betweenness centrality measures: shortest path and current flow. Nodes with high betweenness centrality are especially important in the transmission of simple contagions because they are disproportionately likely to be the conduit between densely connected clusters of nodes (e.g. the cohesive subgroups we considered in Chapter 14). Once a simple contagion enters a cohesive subgroup, the members of that group generally become activated *very* quickly. The more paths that lead into the cluster, the more quickly the process happens, but if the paths are few in number, or if they are rarely used (i.e. i and j talk, but infrequently), then the contagion may never make the leap from one to the other. We'll see this dynamic in action when we turn to the simulations a bit later in the chapter.

This way of thinking about network effects on information diffusion owes much to Mark Granovetter's (1973) classic article 'The Strength of Weak Ties'. Granovetter, a grad student at the time, was interested in understanding how blue-collar workers in the Boston area got information about job opportunities. He found that the most efficient sources of information were contacts with whom the jobseeker had relatively infrequent contact, and that this was primarily due to the fact that these contacts were not part of the seeker's usual cluster of friends and family, who tended to have access to the same information. The 'strength of weak ties' idea, then, is that ties that are affectively weaker (i.e. we don't know them as well, we interact with them less frequently, we don't *feel* close) can be structurally stronger because they are a conduit of novel information into our tight clusters of personal ties, within which quite a lot of redundant information circulates. This was an important finding that not only laid the foundation for much of the research into diffusion that followed, but also serves as a reminder that we should not expect all contagions to act the same.

Several network measures can give us imperfect insights into diffusion processes. One of the simplest is network diameter, which is equal to the length of the longest shortest path in the network. If a contagion is spreading along shortest paths, network diameter will tell us the maximum number of exposures needed to reach the whole network from a given starting node. A network with smaller diameter will likely be more conducive than a similar network with larger diameter. Unfortunately, however, network diameter tells us little to nothing about the network's overall structure, since it only gives us information about a single path (or multiple equal paths).

Ideally, a network-level measure that could offer insight into how diffusion processes might unfold over time would include more information about the structure and dynamics of the network *in general*. Think back to shortest path betweenness centrality for a moment. As we discussed above, nodes with high betweenness centrality are likely to play a very important role in the diffusion of *simple* contagions through a network, because they are efficient routes between distant parts of a network. However, a single node's betweenness centrality does not give us a good idea of the network's structural effects on the spread of a simple contagion. Instead, we could calculate the average length of *all* the shortest paths in the network, which would give us a better idea of how easy it is for any one node to reach any other. And since simple contagions spread easily within clusters, a single activated node will expose most or all of a cluster. Given this theoretical knowledge, we could calculate a network's clustering coefficient, which summarizes the tendency for nodes to cluster together. Higher clustering coefficients indicate that nodes are more likely to be found in closed triplets (triangles), which at a larger scale tends to produce very dense clusters.

Putting these two things together, we could hypothesize that networks that have low average shortest paths and high clustering coefficients are very likely to facilitate the spread of a simple contagion. In fact, this is *exactly* the case, and what we've described is known as a small-world network, the properties of which were famously exposed by Watts and Strogatz (1998).

Simulating a small world

To get started with modelling diffusion processes, we'll simulate a simple network with 300 nodes. The particular type of network we are simulating here is a 'small-world' network (i.e. low average shortest paths and high clustering coefficients). Each node in this simulated network, shown in Figure 16.2, will be connected to four other nodes. Obviously, this network differs substantially from just about any existing social network that we might observe empirically, but it's a useful starting point. Once we've developed some intuition of how these types of models work, we'll switch over to using empirical data on interaction networks.

Imports

```
import pandas as pd
pd.set_option("display.notebook_repr_html", False)
import networkx as nx
import matplotlib as mpl
import matplotlib.pyplot as plt
import seaborn as sns
import pickle

import ndlib.models.ModelConfig as mc
import ndlib.models.epidemics as ep
from ndlib.utils import multi_runs

from dcss.plotting import custom_seaborn
from dcss.networks import *
custom_seaborn()
```

```
population_size = 300
G = nx.watts_strogatz_graph(population_size, 4, 0.15)
G.name = "A Simulated Small World"

print(nx.info(G))

Name: A Simulated Small World
Type: Graph
Number of nodes: 300
Number of edges: 600
Average degree:   4.0000

layout = nx.nx_pydot.graphviz_layout(G)

fig, ax = plt.subplots(figsize=(12, 12))
nx.draw(G,
        pos=layout,
        node_color='gray',
        edge_color='gray',
        node_size=100,
        width=.5)
plt.show()
```

Figure 16.2 The structure of a simulated small-world network

16.6 Simple Contagions and Epidemic Spread

Let's start by simulating the spread of a simple contagion through our simulated small-world network. Since we've already constructed our NetworkX object (G), we can jump straight to the second step of the workflow, which is to configure the parameters for our first model.

The SIR model

We'll be developing several SIR models to better understand the spread of simple contagions. SIR is a compartmental model of disease spread that partitions a population into three compartments:

1   susceptible people, who may become infected in the future
2   infected people, who may spread the disease
3   recovered/removed people, who, depending on the model, have either died or recovered and developed immunity

Traditional SIR models describe transitions between these compartments using a set of differential equations. Note that the equation for each population takes into account other population compartments; as one changes, the others also change. The susceptible population will become infected at a rate proportional to the number of infected and susceptible (the more there are of one or the other, the faster a disease will spread), but slowed down by the total population size, a kind of proxy for population density. The infected population will increase at the same rate that the susceptible population decreases, as people move from one compartment to the other, but it will also decrease at a rate relative to its size and how quickly people recover from the disease. Similarly, the recovered compartment will increase at the same rate that the infected compartment is losing population. We'll see this happen in the simulations that follow:

$$\frac{dS}{dt} = -\left(\frac{a}{N}\right)IS$$

$$\frac{dI}{dt} = -\left(\frac{a}{N}\right)IS - bI$$

$$\frac{dR}{dt} = bI$$

subject to $R_0 = \frac{a}{b}$, where

- $\frac{dS}{dt}$, $\frac{dI}{dt}$, and $\frac{dR}{dt}$ represent the *rates of change* in the relevant population compartment;
- N is the total population;
- R_0 represents the ability of a single infected individual to infect others, the basic reproduction rate; and
- a and b are parameters that can be related to the typical time between contacts and the typical time until an 'infected' becomes 'recovered'.

While powerful in its simplicity, the differential equation SIR model pays for that simplicity by assuming that there is homogeneous mixing between populations. Human agency and behaviour are abstracted away until people act like atoms bouncing into each other.

Initializing and configuring the SIR model

As we are interested in the epidemic spread of contagions *through networks*, we won't be using differential equations. Instead, we will be conducting many *simulations* using NDlib. There are a few differences in how NDlib handles SIR models compared with the above differential equations. The above equations are continuous, while NDlib uses strict integer counts of nodes for each status/compartment and time steps. The differential equation SIR model is deterministic, but NDlib uses probabilistic infection and recovery. For the sake of clarity, NDlib uses status instead of compartment, and 'removed' instead of 'recovered'. These last two differences are purely semantic, and you can use whichever is most appropriate for your particular model.

The parameters governing how the simulation will unfold are stored in a special model configuration object. As just described, the SIR model takes two parameters. For the sake of clarity, I have used a and b in the differential equation model and the more traditional β and γ for the probabilistic NDlib parameters:

- β is the probability of infection and
- γ is the probability of recovery.

In addition to these two parameters, we have to specify the percentage of nodes that are activated/infected at the start of our simulation – the dawn of time for our simulated society. We'll start by setting the probability of infection at 5% and the probability of recovery at 1%, and by randomly infecting 10% of the network.

Since we'll be executing multiple simulations, we'll define a custom function that lets us simplify the process of configuring new SIR models:

```
def sir_model(network, beta, gamma, fraction_infected):
    model = ep.SIRModel(network)

    config = mc.Configuration()
    config.add_model_parameter('beta', beta)
    config.add_model_parameter('gamma', gamma)
    config.add_model_parameter("fraction_infected", fraction_infected)

    model.set_initial_status(config)
    return model

sir_model_1 = sir_model(G, beta=0.05, gamma=0.01, fraction_infected=0.1)
sir_model_1
```

```
<ndlib.models.epidemics.SIRModel.SIRModel at 0x7f96629f5820>
```

Executing the simulations

NDlib offers two different methods for executing the simulations. The .iteration() method executes a single iteration (one step through time) and .iteration_bunch() executes *n* iterations. Below, we'll execute 200 iterations, which means we will step through 200 moments in time, executing the probabilistic model's rules, and assessing node states at each step. We'll set the argument node_status to True so that the method returns information about the status of each node in each iteration, rather than just summary statistics for the overall population. We will use %%capture to suppress the overly verbose output that NDlib produces to report on the progress of each iteration:

```
%%capture

sir_1_iterations = sir_model_1.iteration_bunch(200, node_status=True)
```

.iteration_bunch() returns a list containing data on each of the 200 iterations in our simulation. The data pertaining to each individual iteration is provided in the form of a dictionary with the following key–value pairings:

- *iteration* tells us which iteration of the simulation the data pertain to.
- *status* is another dictionary. Each key in this dictionary is a node ID, and the corresponding value indicates their status at that particular iteration. The length of this dictionary is therefore equal to the number of nodes in the population.
- *node_count* is another dictionary where the keys represent node states and the values indicate the cumulative sum of nodes with that state, up to and including the present iteration.
- *status_delta* is yet another dictionary, this time providing information about how the number of nodes in each of the status categories has changed since the previous iteration. For example, a delta of 2 for the 'infected' status would indicate that two additional people were infected in this iteration. A value of –3 for the 'susceptible' status would indicate that three nodes switched from susceptible in the previous iteration to a different state in the present iteration.

In other words, most of the data returned by .iteration_bunch() is in the form of dictionaries nested inside other dictionaries, organized as a list. The innermost dictionaries are what tell us what has happened in any particular point in time during the simulation process. For example, to get data that can be used to plot the trend line for each status, we could iterate over the list and extract the 'node_count' data for each iteration. Below we preview the first 10:

```
[iteration['node_count'] for iteration in sir_1_iterations][:10]

[{0: 270, 1: 30, 2: 0},
 {0: 270, 1: 30, 2: 0},
 {0: 265, 1: 35, 2: 0},
 {0: 255, 1: 44, 2: 1},
 {0: 248, 1: 50, 2: 2},
 {0: 242, 1: 55, 2: 3},
 {0: 240, 1: 56, 2: 4},
```

```
{0: 233, 1: 62, 2: 5},
{0: 230, 1: 65, 2: 5},
{0: 219, 1: 76, 2: 5}]
```

Iterating over the models results is straightforward, but since we're going to be performing a fair number of simulations and we'll be looking for the same nested information each time, we'll define a few custom functions that allow us to easily extract the information we want.

The `simulation_overview()` function, defined below, iterates over the results of the simulations and extracts:

1   The number of nodes in each state at each iteration, converted to a proportion of the overall population.
2   The status deltas for each iteration, which tell us how the numbers of nodes in each status category change between simulation runs, such as +3 infected, −3 susceptible.

Both are returned as dataframes.

```
def simulation_overview(iteration_results, network, prop=True):
    population_size = network.number_of_nodes()

    trends = []
    deltas = []

    for iteration in iteration_results:
        trends.append(iteration['node_count'])
        deltas.append(iteration['status_delta'])

    columns = ['Susceptible', 'Infected', 'Removed']

    # trends DF
    trends = pd.DataFrame(trends)
    trends.columns = columns
    if prop is True:
        trends = trends.div(population_size)

    # deltas DF
    deltas = pd.DataFrame(deltas)
    deltas.columns = columns

    return trends, deltas
```

We'll use our custom function `simulation_overview()` to parse the output from the simulation model we just executed and create our two dataframes:

```
sir_1_trends, sir_1_deltas = simulation_overview(sir_1_iterations, G)
sir_1_trends.head()
```

	Susceptible	Infected	Removed
0	0.900000	0.100000	0.000000
1	0.900000	0.100000	0.000000
2	0.883333	0.116667	0.000000
3	0.850000	0.146667	0.003333
4	0.826667	0.166667	0.006667

From here, we can plot (1) trends in the number of susceptible, infected, and removed nodes and (2) the compartment deltas. The results are shown in Figure 16.3.

```
fig, ax = plt.subplots()
sns.lineplot(data=sir_1_trends)

ax.set(xlabel='Iteration / step in time', ylabel='Proportion of nodes')
sns.despine()
plt.legend()
plt.show()
```

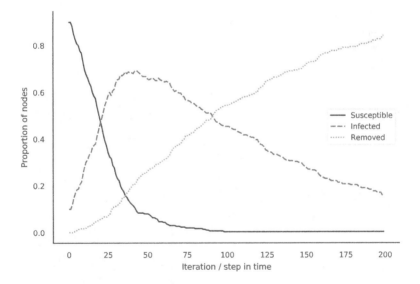

Figure 16.3 A plot featuring three lines tracing the proportion of nodes susceptible, infected, and removed as a function of time. The infection spikes rapidly and then tapers off

This plot offers a high-level summary of what has happened to our simulated society over time. In this particular case, we can see the proportion of infected nodes increases dramatically, infecting more than 70% of the population in fewer than 50 iterations (when you factor in those who had already recovered by iteration 50, about 90% of the population had been infected, but some had already recovered). At the same time, the number of susceptible nodes decreases (which we should expect, given the zero-sum and unidirectional nature of the SIR model). Over time, there is a fairly steady increase in the number of nodes who are removed from the simulation due to immunity or death.

Let's also take a quick look at the deltas for each state (Figure 16.4):

```
fig, (ax1, ax2, ax3) = plt.subplots(3,1, figsize=(8,8), sharex=True)
sns.lineplot(ax = ax1, data=sir_1_deltas['Susceptible'], color='gray')
sns.lineplot(ax = ax2, data=sir_1_deltas['Infected'], color='gray')
sns.lineplot(ax = ax3, data=sir_1_deltas['Removed'], color='gray')

## EMPHASIZE DEVIATIONS FROM 0
ax1.axhline(0, color='crimson')
ax2.axhline(0, color='crimson')
ax3.axhline(0, color='crimson')

ax3.set(xlabel='Iteration')
plt.show()
```

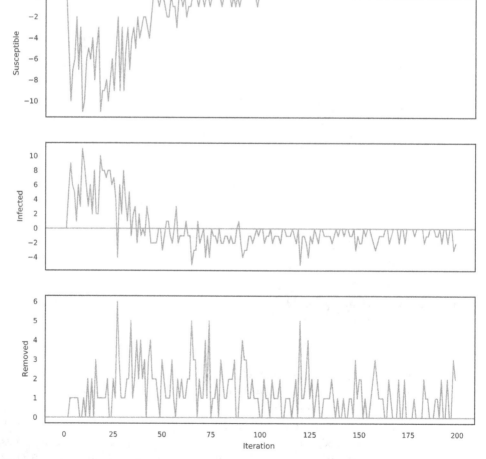

Figure 16.4 A three-part graph showing the number of nodes entering or leaving a category (delta) over time

Figure 16.5 The same simulated small-world network as before, displayed 20 times – once for each of the first 20 time steps in the simulation of epidemic spread through the network

This plot shows how the number of nodes in each of the three possible node states changes from one iteration to the next and is not cumulative. It should make some intuitive sense: in the SIR model, a susceptible node can either stay susceptible or become infected, an infected node can either stay infected or become removed, and a removed node cannot change state. Therefore, the susceptible population should always decrease, the infected population can increase or decrease, and the recovered population should always increase.

Wait, who did we just infect?

Recall that NDlib is performing simulations on a network rather than solving differential equations. Figure 16.5 provides a bit of additional insight into what has happened to our simulated society throughout this process. We took 200 steps through time, but a lot of action happened in just the first 20 steps. Each of the subplots in Figure 16.5 represents one of the first 20 iterations. At each iteration, the nodes are crimson if they are newly infected, or were infected in a previous iteration. Grey nodes are susceptible. Some of these nodes, of course, transitioned to the 'removed' state, but for pedagogical reasons, my interest here is in highlighting the specific paths the contagion moves along. Though there are, of course, some clusters that form around the initial seed infections, there is no indication that the contagion gets 'stuck' in those clusters. It spreads easily to infect surrounding nodes.

There is another (more important) pedagogical reason for this figure: to emphasize that it's just *one* of many possible outcomes. We've performed a *single simulation* over 200 time steps. Showing this sequence of snapshots of the network over time is a useful reminder that at any point in this process, including Time 0 where we see the nodes that were randomly infected at the start of our model, *things could have gone differently* (unlike with deterministic SIR models using differential equations, which always give the same results). We might have selected a different random subset to initially infect, for example. Since the transmission process is probabilistic, minor differences in which nodes get infected at any given point in the process could have an impact on what happens later, such as opening up or closing off certain regions of the network to the contagion. All of this and more is possible with the *exact* same model we used, with the same probabilities of infection and removal.

What should we do? Simulate a *whole lot more* and look at aggregate patterns across all of those simulations. Let's do that now.

Let's do that 500 more times

NDlib's multi_runs() function enables us to easily execute many simulations from the same model, and because each simulation is independent of the others, they can be executed efficiently in parallel. This time, let's use multi_runs() to execute 500 simulations, each with 200 iterations:

```
%%capture
trends = multi_runs(sir_model_1, execution_number=500, iteration_number=200,
    infection_sets=None, nprocesses=4)
```

The results returned by multi_runs() are very similar to that returned by iteration_bunch(), only more deeply nested. The custom function visualize_trends() from the utilities package parses the output and produces a trend plot (Figure 16.6).

```
visualize_trends(trends, network=G, proportion=True, return_data=False)
```

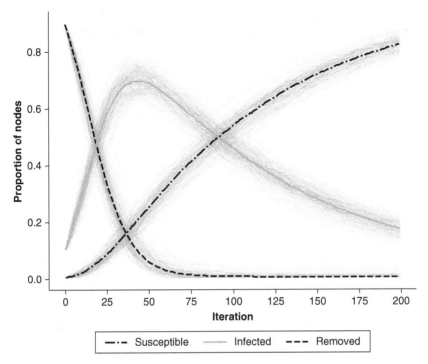

Figure 16.6 A plot featuring many simulated lines tracing the proportion of nodes susceptible, infected, and 'removed' as a function of time; the thicker, more pronounced lines represent the mean values across each iteration of the simulation. The infection spikes rapidly and then tapers off

Figure 16.6 conveys the same type of information as the first trend plot we produced, only this time it does so for 500 simulations with 200 iterations rather than one simulation with 200 iterations. Each thin grey line represents the trend for one of the three possible states across the iterations of a single simulation, and the three more prominent lines represent the median trend across all 500. As you can see, there are a few simulations that deviate from the pack, but for the most part the patterns are very clear, and things don't fluctuate wildly across runs.

Now that we've seen the logic of how to develop diffusion models in NDlib, and we've seen how to parse the results of the simulations and visualize their results, we're ready to start using actual empirical network data.

From simulated societies to Denmark

For the rest of this chapter, we will make use of network data collected as part of the Copenhagen Networks Study (see Sapiezynski et al., 2019; Stopczynski et al., 2014). This dataset is a multi-layer temporal network made up of more than 700 university students in Copenhagen. It was collected using smartphones, third-party APIs, and online questionnaires. The layers consist of a physical proximity network using Bluetooth signal strength, phone calls, text messages, and Facebook friendships. Each of these network types has additional information regarding the relations, including timestamps, phone call duration, and so on. I recommend reading Sapiezynski et al. (2019) to learn more about this dataset in general.

The data we'll use here is a subset of the Bluetooth physical co-location network data that I've filtered to include interactions that occurred over a roughly 24-hour period:

```
bluetooth_contact = pd.read_csv("../data/copenhagen_networks_study/
    cns_bluetooth_filtered.csv", sep=',')
bluetooth_contact.head()
```

```
  # timestamp   user_a   user_b   rssi
0     1217400       55       52    -57
1     1217400       58       37    -58
2     1217400      111       58    -48
3     1217400      578      176    -36
4     1217700       55       52    -55
```

As we've done in the previous chapters, we can use the `from_pandas_edgelist()` function to create a NetworkX graph object from the `bluetooth_contact` dataframe. In this case, the researchers have used `user_a` and `user_b` instead of i and j, but as long as NetworkX knows which two columns represent an edge, it's perfectly content:

```
g_bluetooth_contact = nx.from_pandas_edgelist(bluetooth_contact, 'user_a', 'user_b',
    create_using=nx.Graph())
g_bluetooth_contact.name = 'CNS Bluetooth Contact'
print(nx.info(g_bluetooth_contact))
```

```
Name: CNS Bluetooth Contact
Type: Graph
Number of nodes: 621
Number of edges: 2942
Average degree:   9.4750
```

```
layout = nx.nx_pydot.graphviz_layout(g_bluetooth_contact)
```

This network is quite dense, so visualizing it is a bit tough. In Figure 16.7, I overlay a contour plot to give an idea of where the density lies, and what kind of gradient it follows.

```
for_contour = pd.DataFrame([v for k,v in layout.items()])
```

```
fig, ax = plt.subplots(figsize=(12, 12))
sns.kdeplot(x=for_contour[0],y=for_contour[1])
```

```
nx.draw(g_bluetooth_contact,
        pos=layout,
        node_color='gray',
        edge_color='gray',
        node_size=100,
        width=.5,
        alpha=.3)
```

```
plt.show()
```

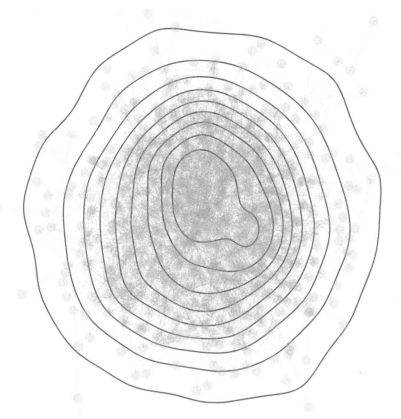

Figure 16.7 A co-presence network from the Copenhagen Networks Study

Let's also inspect the degree distribution (Figure 16.8):

```
fig, ax = plt.subplots()
sns.ecdfplot(pd.Series(dict(g_bluetooth_contact.degree())))
sns.despine()
ax.set(xlabel='Node degree')
plt.show()
```

Now we're ready to develop our second SIR model. We'll keep the same beta (*β*) and gamma (*γ*) parameters, and the same proportion of initially infected nodes. Unlike last time, we'll let our simulations run for 300 iterations, and we'll execute a batch of 500. In order to compare our results against future models, we're going to set the initially infected nodes so we can isolate the effects of changing parameters. While we are choosing the nodes randomly, we'll set a seed for the random number generator to keep results consistent for the book. You would not normally do this for research purposes. Since we're running 500 simulations, we will produce 500 initial infection sets.

The results are shown in Figure 16.9.

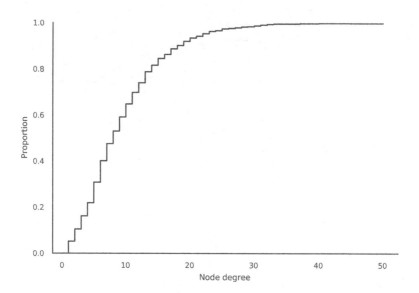

Figure 16.8 An empirical cumulative distribution plot of the degree distribution for the co-presence network from the Copenhagen Networks Study

```
import random
import copy

random.seed(42)

def rand_infection_set(network, frac):
    node_list = list(network.nodes())
    return random.sample(node_list, int(round(len(node_list)*frac, 0))) # randomly
    select nodes from node_list without replacement

infect_sets = [rand_infection_set(g_bluetooth_contact, 0.1) for x in range(500)]

%%capture
sir_model_2 = sir_model(g_bluetooth_contact,
                        beta=0.05,
                        gamma=0.01,
                        fraction_infected=0.1)

sir_model_2_trends = multi_runs(sir_model_2,
                                execution_number=500,
                                iteration_number=300,
                                infection_sets=infect_sets,
                                nprocesses=4)

visualize_trends(sir_model_2_trends, network=g_bluetooth_contact, proportion=True,
    return_data=False)
```

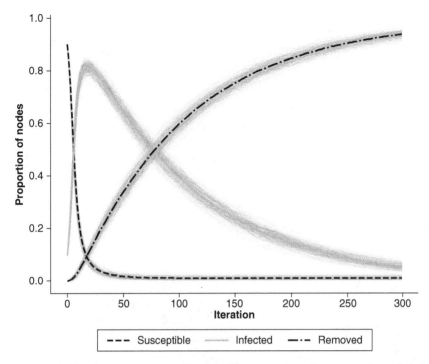

Figure 16.9 A plot featuring many simulated lines tracing the proportion of nodes susceptible, infected, and 'removed' in the co-presence network from the Copenhagen Networks Study as a function of time, with a beta of 0.05 and a gamma of 0.01; the thicker, more pronounced lines represent the mean values across each iteration of the simulation

We see the same general pattern we saw before, with an early spike of infections that spreads rapidly through the population, accompanied by a decline in the proportion of susceptible nodes. And as before, we see a fairly steady increase over time in the number of nodes that are removed by immunity or death. By the 100th iteration, nearly every susceptible individual has been infected, and all that remains is the recovery process. Note, however, that if we had more isolated components in the network, rather than one large one, some simulations might have had very different results. Since contagions cannot spread without an interaction, each component would need to have at least one infected node at Time 0 to make infection possible. In general, the higher the number of components in a network, the more important the number and distribution of initial infections will be.

Another thing to note from these visualizations is that the trends across all simulations are usually more tightly clustered together right at the dawn of simulated time than they are as the simulation progress. Since each simulation starts with the same conditions, they have little room to diverge from each other, but as the infection spreads over time, different parts of the network may open up at different rates.

Now let's model a simple contagion with $\beta = 0.01$, dramatically dropping the probability of transmitting an infection. The results are shown in Figure 16.10.

```
%%capture
sir_model_3 = sir_model(g_bluetooth_contact,
                        beta=0.01,
                        gamma=0.01,
                        fraction_infected=0.1)

sir_model_3_trends = multi_runs(sir_model_3,
                        execution_number=500,
                        iteration_number=300,
                        infection_sets=infect_sets,
                        nprocesses=4)

visualize_trends(sir_model_3_trends, network=g_bluetooth_contact, proportion=True,
    return_data=False)
```

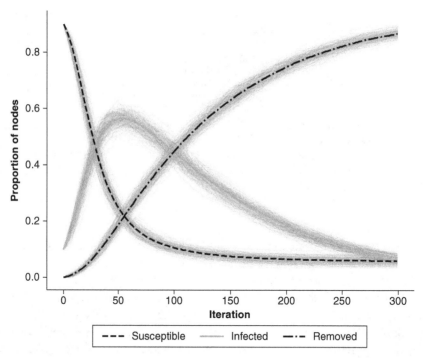

Figure 16.10 A plot featuring many simulated lines tracing the proportion of nodes susceptible, infected, and 'removed' in the Copenhagen Networks graph as a function of time, with a beta value of 0.01; the thicker, more pronounced lines represent the mean values across each iteration of the simulation

Lowering the probability that an infected person transmits the contagion to a neighbour results in several noticeable differences. First, the initial spike of infections is much less sharp, and its effects are more spread out over time. Public health interventions during a pandemic will often focus on reducing the disease's β because it helps 'flatten the curve'. A region's health-care facilities usually operate close to their maximum capacity during non-pandemic times for the sake of efficiency, but that means that sudden spikes can overwhelm the available resources.

Reducing the rate of infection, by mandating wearing masks, for example, can help buffer the system against rapid shocks.

You may also notice that susceptible populations in the simulations tend to settle at a higher point than in the previous model, roughly in the 5% to 10% range. This is because individuals are spreading the contagion less before recovering, resulting in the recovered/removed individuals forming a barrier around small portions of the network and preventing further spread into those areas.

Simple contagions on dynamic networks

So far, we have only examined static networks; the network's structure does not change over the course of the contagion's spread. A discussion of dynamic networks is unfortunately beyond the scope of this book, but if you are interested, the process is a generalization of what we have just done. The key difference is that we pass NDlib a series of snapshots of the network as observed at different time points. A brief example is provided in the online supplementary learning materials.

16.7 Conclusion

The key points in this chapter are as follows:

- We learnt key social contagion terminology.
- We discussed the differential equation SIR model and contrasted it against the network simple contagion model.
- We used NDlib to run network contagion simulations.
- We laid the groundwork for discussing complex contagions.

Visit the website at https://study.sagepub.com/mclevey for additional resources

17

NOT SO FAST: MODELLING THE DIFFUSION OF COMPLEX CONTAGIONS

17.1 Learning Objectives

By the end of this chapter, you should be able to do the following:

- Differentiate between simple and complex contagions
- Compare the typical diffusion processes for simple and complex contagions
- Explain the role that contagion, network structure, and individual thresholds play in threshold models of diffusion and social influence
- Develop simulations and computational experiments of complex diffusion processes with NDlib

17.2 Learning Materials

You can find the online learning materials for this chapter in `doing_computational_social_ science/Chapter_17`. `cd` into the directory and launch your Jupyter server.

17.3 Introduction

In the previous chapter, we discussed the epidemic spread of simple contagions through networks, focusing on simple epidemiological models of disease spread. Many people use analogies to infectious diseases to describe how other types of things spread through networks, such as beliefs and behaviours, but this is a highly consequential mistake. To understand why, I'll introduce the idea of complex contagions and compare them with simple contagions. We'll also break down some of the most important differences in the mechanisms and network structures that govern their spread. Then I'll introduce threshold models for complex contagions and show you how to configure, execute, and interpret them using NDlib.

17.4 From Simple to Complex Contagions

Complexity is an important concept that takes the idea of multiple exposures a step further than mere counts. Just like the network perspective on simple contagions, it does so by taking the relationship between micro-level contexts and macro-level network structures very seriously. The difference is in the details.

Whereas simple contagions can spread easily with exposure from even a single contact with a single alter, complex contagions require multiple exposures from multiple *sources* to spread, and require one to *choose* whether to become activated, or to 'adopt' the contagion. For example, you don't 'choose' to catch a cold from your cousin's kid; exposure is sufficient. But you can choose whether to sign up for the latest social media platform, to wear the same style of clothes in 2022 that my parents wore in 1991 (which, inexplicably, is a thing), or to join a violent far-right mob and storm the US Capitol Building. In all these cases *and many others*, there is some sort of cost or risk involved in activation, which may range from small ('My millennial friends will tease me for dressing like their parents did in 1991') to large ('Things might end poorly for me if I join a violent far-right mob and storm the US Capitol Building').

In his groundbreaking work on complex contagion, Damon Centola (2018) pointed out that social confirmation, or social proof, is much more important when there is a lot at stake, or when there is a lot of risk and uncertainty involved. More specifically, he proposes four social mechanisms that shape the spread of complex contagions in ways that differ profoundly from simple contagions:

1. *Strategic complementarity* comes into play when a contagion becomes more useful as the number of other adopters increases. Using an open source end-to-end encrypted messaging app like Signal is a great idea, but it's not very useful if you're the only one using it. It becomes much more valuable if the people you want to communicate with are also using it.
2. *Credibility* comes into play when a contagion is unknown, untested, or considered risky, and therefore, nodes are unlikely to activate until they have seen several neighbours do so without negative consequences or prove the value of activating (again, 'social proof').
3. *Legitimacy* comes into play when the perception of social risk or value of a behaviour depends on the number of activated neighbours. If a dramatic new fashion trend puts you at the edge of your comfort zone, seeing multiple neighbours wearing that style may make you more comfortable adopting it.
4. *Emotional contagion* comes into play when the excitement of adopting the contagion is influenced by, or influences, the excitement of neighbours.

Credibility and legitimacy may seem closely related, or even the same, as they both relate to perceptions of risk. The distinction arises out of where the risk is perceived. Credibility relates to the risk of the contagion: 'this new technique is potentially dangerous'. Legitimacy relates to the *social* risks of being activated. The risk (or the perception of risk) comes from one's neighbours, not from the contagion itself. Ensuring a contagion is credible may require only a few positive examples. Ensuring a contagion is legitimate may require a certain portion of one's neighbours be activated. This will come up in our discussion of *thresholds* later. A complex contagion may be driven by any combination of the above mechanisms.

Consider, then, what complex contagions need to spread. The basic idea is illustrated in Figure 17.1. In this scenario, let's say Eric is considering signing up for a new fitness app that he heard about on a podcast. The app is free to use as long as you complete the workouts you say you're going to complete, but if you skip a workout without a good reason, the app charges your card and donates £10 to a cause you find morally and politically objectionable. Ouch. What a gut punch that would be.

Exposure from one source does not lead Eric to activate.

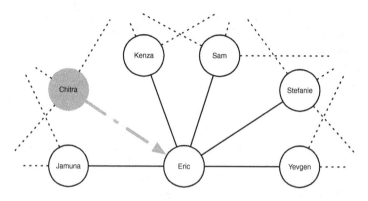

Exposure from two sources does not lead Eric to activate.

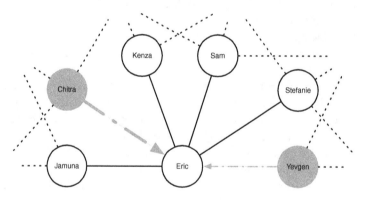

Exposure from a third source leads Eric to activate.

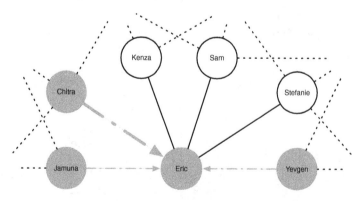

Figure 17.1   A three-part figure depicting how a complex contagion might spread through a simple hypothetical network

Eric's friend Chitra is already using the app. She loves the idea and enthusiastically promotes it to everyone she knows, including Eric. (The size of the arrow reflects her energetic promotion of the app.) But most of Eric's good friends don't use the app and Chitra's enthusiasm alone is just not enough to tip Eric into adopting. Then Eric learns that Yevgen has also been using the app and, having recently lost £10 to the campaign of a politician he finds morally objectionable, has never been so fired up about glute bridges and Romanian split squats. Still, Eric doesn't budge. The idea of losing £10 to a politician with a penchant for spreading bullshit is just too high a risk. But then Jamuna adopts the app. Maybe it's not so bad?

Eric adopts.

In these cases, we've focused on differences in what simple and complex contagions need to spread through a network. The main difference boils down to whether exposure from a single source is sufficient to activate a node ('Karen told me she's storming the US Capitol Building on Wednesday. I am most definitely not doing that'.) or whether more social confirmation is required to make a decision to activate (*'Everyone I know is storming the Capitol Building on Wednesday* . . . I guess that's a thing that happens now? And Karen graciously offered to give me a ride to the riot, so maybe I should go?').

I realize that in the example above, I'm making light of an extremely serious situation. I'm using an extreme case to drive home an important point: there are some things that most of us are highly unlikely to do just because we know someone who is doing it, and this is most certainly the case for decisions that involve a non-trivial amount of risk and uncertainty. But it also raises another interesting dimension of the problem: our own individual thresholds for social confirmation might vary. Some people might be willing to storm the Capitol Building when their favoured candidate loses an election because 1/2 of their closest friends are storming the capital. For others, it might take 3/4 or 7/8 of their friends. Or perhaps all they need is to know a total of 10 people. Or perhaps they would *never* storm the Capitol Building no matter who else was.

How can we take these variations into account? And how does the nature of the contagion, variability in individual thresholds, the social and interaction rules governing the formation of ties in a network, and the emergent structure of the network interact? How do we deal with the probabilistic nature of all of this? *How do we manage all this complexity?*

We'll be in a position to dig into these questions with some models very soon. But first, let's take a closer look at some of the ways in which network structure matters in a more *global* sense, and how it relates to the notion of variability in individual-level thresholds.

Further Reading

Damon Centola's (2018) *How Behavior Spreads* is the best place to learn about complex contagion theory. Centola and Macy's (2007) 'Complex contagions and the weakness of long ties' is one of the classic articles on complex contagion theory, and Guilbeault et al.'s (2018) 'Complex contagions' is a more recent review.

17.5 Beyond Local Neighbourhoods: Network Effects and Thresholds

We know that micro-level social mechanisms shape specific exposure events in somewhat predictably ways and govern the transmission of a contagion from one individual to another. We discussed several examples in the previous chapter. These micro-level processes give rise to specific macro-level structures that act in a top-down fashion to constrain our actions and determine the shape and scale of spread through a population. Importantly, these processes differ for simple and complex contagions. If we incorrectly assume that every contagion spreads like a simple contagion, then our efforts to promote specific beliefs (e.g. this vaccine is safe, the election was not rigged) and behaviours (e.g. wearing a mask reduces the likelihood of spreading COVID-19 [coronavirus disease 2019], using condoms helps reduce the spread of STIs [sexually transmitted infections]) are in vain and may even backfire. Centola (2018), for example, has shown through ingenious experimental design and carefully designed simulations that the same network structures that accelerate the spread of a disease ('simple' contagion) can *inhibit* the spread of behaviours ('complex' contagion) needed to combat those same diseases. These differences are therefore vital to understand if we want to successfully conduct interventions, broadly conceived, and are highly relevant to efforts to promote social and political change (Centola, 2021).

In this section, we'll discuss some meso- and macro-level network properties that have a strong influence on diffusion. Our starting point is that some network structures are more conducive to spreading processes than are others. The most obvious and straightforward example of this is that it's hard for a contagion to spread through a network composed of many isolated components (which is why lockdowns during COVID-19 have been an effective public health intervention despite causing other problems, such as worsening mental health). Following this discussion, we'll see how it all plays out when we conduct hundreds or thousands of simulations conditioned on empirical network data.

Complex contagions, narrow bridges, wide bridges, and thresholds

Understanding complex contagions tends to be, appropriately, more complex than understanding simple contagions. The requirement that a node be exposed to a contagion through multiple sources immediately suggests a diminished role for weak ties and high betweenness peers. The same things that make those 'weak ties' ideally suited for spreading simple contagions make them poor conduits of complex contagions. They are, almost by definition, *narrow bridges* between clusters of densely connected nodes. The more they fit that idealized profile of a weak tie, the less likely they are to contribute to the kind of collective pressure that propels the spread of complex contagions.

Centola's work has shown us that complex contagions require *wide bridges* that involve multiple different sources repeatedly exposing us to the contagion. The question is *how wide do those bridges need to be?* Or, to put it another way, how many different sources of exposure would it take to flip our state from exposed to activated?

This question of 'how many people does it take?' is a question of individual thresholds, and once again, some of the key insights into how to model the role of individual thresholds in diffusion processes are inspired by the work of Mark Granovetter (1978). There are two main things to consider:

1 Should we use a threshold that is uniform for all nodes in the network or one that varies for each node?
2 Regardless of whether they are uniform or variable, should thresholds be count-based (e.g. activate if at least three alters are activated) or fractional (e.g. activate if 1/3 of alters are activated)?

The first consideration is largely about whether you want a model that is as simple as possible or one that is more realistic. The second is a bit more difficult because it has significant consequences for how easily different types of nodes in a network can be activated. If the network has a uniform degree distribution (every node has the same degree), a fractional threshold would be effectively identical to a count threshold. If every node has a degree of 3 and a threshold of 2/3, it's the same as saying they have a count threshold of 2. If, however, there is an uneven degree distribution (as there almost always is), the fractional threshold of 2/3 for a node with degree 3 would be very different from a node with degree 300: 2 versus 200!

How should we decide whether a threshold should be a count or fractional? Theory and domain knowledge! *Think about the mechanisms of complexity mentioned earlier, and ask yourself which are likely at play.* Where diffusion is a matter of credibility, for example, we might expect a count threshold. If scientists are deciding whether to incorporate a new technique into their work, they might only need a few concrete examples of it working to consider adopting it. The efficacy of the technique does not especially rely on how much of their network has adopted the technique. Where diffusion is a matter of legitimacy, on the other hand, we might expect a fractional threshold. If your friend tells you that the 70s are back in fashion, you might wait until some proportion of your personal network has adopted the look before you yourself seriously consider adopting it. If at least half of your friends are bringing back the 70s, you might be a lot more comfortable joining in, or even feel pressured into joining in. This kind of peer pressure/acceptance is very different depending on the size of your personal network, of course.

There could, of course, also be countervailing forces at play here. You may recall that in a previous chapter I mentioned the notion of negative ties (dislike, distrust, disesteem, etc.) that can be observed on their own, or alongside positive ties in a signed graph. It is, of course, possible that adoption decisions are also driven by observing what our *negative* ties do. Consider once again the example of scientists who are considering adopting some new technique. Seeing their peers adopt the technique only signals credibility *if they trusts the judgement of their peers*. Normally networks researchers collect data on positive ties, which might include asking questions about who you admire or respect. If we were to collect data on negative ties, we might very well find that increases in adoption among those we are negatively tied to decreases the likelihood of our own adoption. However, we should expect that there is individual variability here too, and, hopefully, few people are embedded in such a mess of negative ties that the weight of those negative ties overwhelms that of the positive. But they might. Despite being rarer than positive ties, we know that negative ties are disproportionately influential.

There are many benefits to really thinking this through carefully for any given research problem, but as with anything pertaining to complex systems, our intuitions will inevitably fail us, and we will be quickly humbled by what we can learn from even simple models. Let's turn to them now.

17.6 Threshold Models for Complex Contagions

Let's start by importing the same Bluetooth contact data from the previous chapter. This will help us see the differences between modelling simple and complex contagions without having to worry about differences in the networks.

Imports

```
import pandas as pd
pd.set_option("display.notebook_repr_html", False)
import networkx as nx
import matplotlib as mpl
import matplotlib.pyplot as plt
import seaborn as sns
import pickle

import ndlib.models.ModelConfig as mc
import ndlib.models.epidemics as ep
from ndlib.utils import multi_runs
from dcss.plotting import custom_seaborn
custom_seaborn()

from dcss.networks import *

bluetooth_contact = pd.read_csv("../data/copenhagen_networks_study/
    cns_bluetooth_filtered.csv", sep=',')
g_bluetooth_contact = nx.from_pandas_edgelist(bluetooth_contact, 'user_a', 'user_b',
    create_using=nx.Graph())
g_bluetooth_contact.name = 'CNS Bluetooth Contact'
print(nx.info(g_bluetooth_contact))

Name: CNS Bluetooth Contact
Type: Graph
Number of nodes: 621
Number of edges: 2942
Average degree: 9.4750
```

Now let's create some *threshold models* for complex contagions. I'll start with a simple example, using a fractional threshold of 0.1, and infecting 0.1, or 10%, of the population at Time 0. I will then contrast this against a model with a fractional threshold of 0.35 and the same initially infected nodes. Then I will compare this second model with a third that has a fractional threshold of 0.35 and an initial infection of 0.15, or 15%, of the population.

Note that we have changed only one variable between models 1 and 2, increasing the fractional threshold from 0.1 to 0.35 while keeping the same initially infected nodes. With model 3, we are increasing the number of initially infected nodes. To keep the comparison as close as possible between models 2 and 3, we will define new sets of initially infected nodes that contain the same nodes as before and simply add new ones until the appropriate fraction has been reached.

The results are shown in Figures 17.2, 17.3, and 17.4.

```
infect_sets = [rand_infection_set(g_bluetooth_contact, 0.1) for x in range(500)]
infect_sets_2 = add_to_infection_set(infect_sets, 0.05, g_bluetooth_contact)

%%capture
thresh_model = ep.ThresholdModel(g_bluetooth_contact)
thresh_config = mc.Configuration()
```

```
threshold = 0.1
fraction_infected = .1

thresh_config.add_model_parameter("fraction_infected", fraction_infected)

for n in g_bluetooth_contact.nodes():
    thresh_config.add_node_configuration("threshold", n, threshold)

thresh_model.set_initial_status(thresh_config)

threshold_trends = multi_runs(thresh_model,
                        execution_number=500,
                        iteration_number=40,
                        infection_sets=infect_sets,
                        nprocesses=4)

visualize_trends(threshold_trends,
                network=g_bluetooth_contact,
                states=[0, 1],
                labels=['Not Activated', 'Activated'],
                proportion=True,
                return_data=False)
```

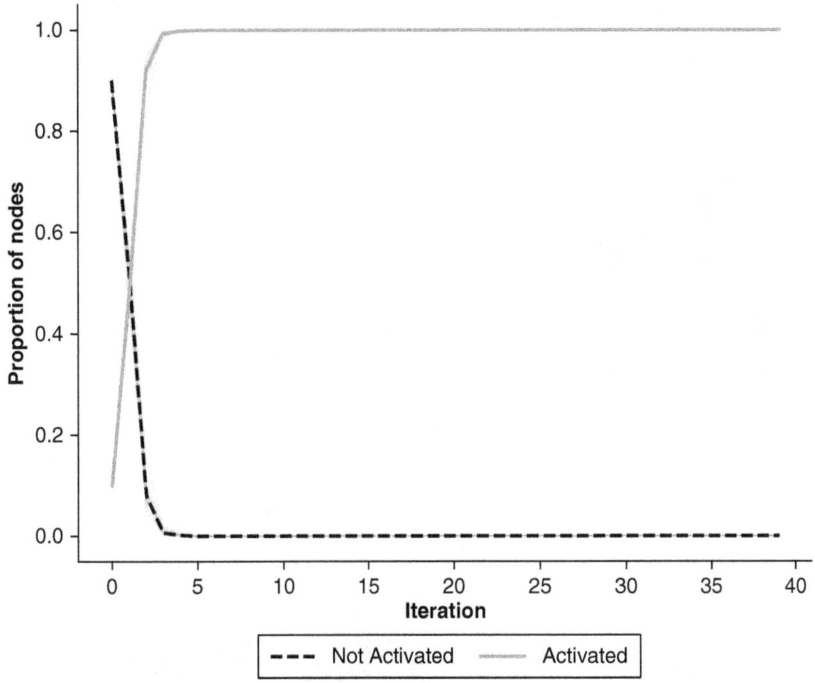

Figure 17.2 A plot showing the proportion of nodes in a network who have been 'activated' over time (iterations); each of the small translucent lines represent the results of one of the 500 simulations run, the red line represents the average 'activated' proportion, and the black dashed line represents the average 'not activated' proportion. This model started with 10% of the population activated and a fractional threshold of 0.1

```
%%capture
thresh_model_2 = ep.ThresholdModel(g_bluetooth_contact)
thresh_config_2 = mc.Configuration()

threshold_2 = 0.35
fraction_infected_2 = .1

thresh_config_2.add_model_parameter("fraction_infected", fraction_infected_2)

for n in g_bluetooth_contact.nodes():
    thresh_config_2.add_node_configuration("threshold", n, threshold_2)

thresh_model_2.set_initial_status(thresh_config_2)

threshold_trends_2 = multi_runs(thresh_model_2,
                                execution_number=500,
                                iteration_number=40,
                                infection_sets=infect_sets,
                                nprocesses=4)

visualize_trends(threshold_trends_2,
                 network=g_bluetooth_contact,
                 states=[0, 1],
                 labels=['Not Activated', 'Activated'],
                 proportion=True,
                 return_data=False)
```

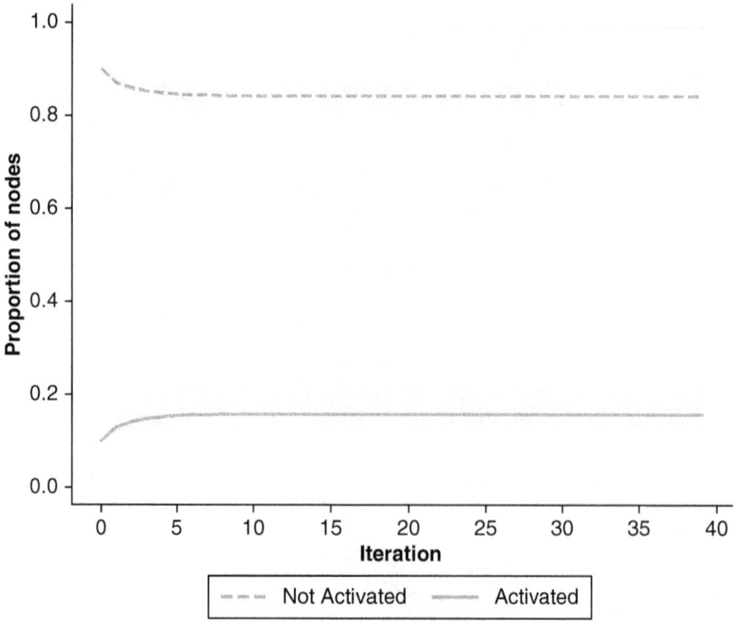

Figure 17.3 A plot showing the proportion of nodes in a network who have been 'activated' over time (iterations); each of the small translucent lines represent the results of one of the 500 simulations run, the red line represents the average 'activated' proportion, and the black dashed line represents the average 'not activated' proportion. This model started with 10% of the population activated and a fractional threshold of 0.35

```
%%capture
thresh_model_3 = ep.ThresholdModel(g_bluetooth_contact)
thresh_config_3 = mc.Configuration()

threshold_3 = 0.35
fraction_infected_2 = .15

thresh_config_3.add_model_parameter("fraction_infected", fraction_infected_2)

for n in g_bluetooth_contact.nodes():
    thresh_config_3.add_node_configuration("threshold", n, threshold_3)

thresh_model_3.set_initial_status(thresh_config_3)

threshold_trends_3 = multi_runs(thresh_model_3,
                        execution_number=500,
                        iteration_number=40,
                        infection_sets=infect_sets_2,
                        nprocesses=4)

visualize_trends(threshold_trends_3,
                network=g_bluetooth_contact,
                states=[0, 1],
                labels=['Not Activated', 'Activated'],
                proportion=True,
                return_data=False)
```

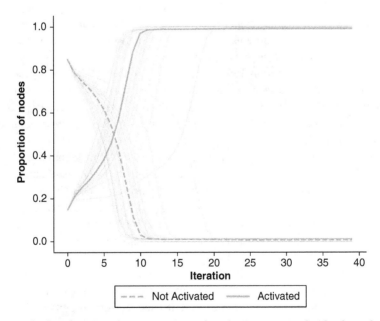

Figure 17.4 A plot showing the proportion of nodes in a network who have been 'activated' over time (iterations); each of the small translucent lines represent the results of one of the 500 simulations run, the red line represents the average 'activated' proportion, and the black dashed line represents the average 'not activated' proportion. This model started with 15% of the population activated and a fractional threshold of 0.35

Let's take a look at model 1. Despite starting with only 10% of the population infected, this contagion spreads to the whole population in less than five iterations in every simulation. This complex contagion spreads faster than the simple contagions I modelled earlier! After a moment's reflection, this should make sense. Model 1 has a fractional threshold of 0.1, which means that a node only needs 10% of its neighbours to be activated for the contagion to spread. Given that the average degree is less than 10, this will usually translate to needing a single activated neighbour. While I have technically defined a threshold model for a complex contagion, this contagion will effectively act like a simple contagion with perfect transmissibility for most of the population!

Now let's compare the results against model 2, where I have set the fractional threshold to 0.35. This is a much stricter threshold. Nodes will now need a little over a third of their neighbours to be activated for a contagion to spread to them. Where model 1 usually required the narrowest of bridges possible, model 2 will require much thicker bridges. As a result, we see that the contagion takes a bit longer to reach its steady state, but perhaps only a few iterations more. The really dramatic difference, though, is how incredibly variable the outcomes are! In most simulations, the contagion doesn't even infect 20% of the network, while in others, it infects the entire network. In most cases, the initial infections are not situated in the right places to infect the thick bridges key to reaching the whole network, which is one reason why we run so many simulations. The positions of the initial infected nodes can *dramatically* influence the results of a particular simulation, as they may be the difference between a key node, cluster, or bridge activating or not. Based on only these plots, it seems that there may be some key choke points or important feature(s) in the network that are difficult for the contagion to infect without the right initial conditions. Recall our earlier visualization of the network in conjunction with the decisions we made about the model, and consider what might be going on. A consequence of the fractional threshold condition is that non-adopters apply pressure on their neighbours. Having lots of non-adopter neighbours makes it harder to activate. As a result, hubs are harder to activate than dense portions of the network. Keeping in mind the strong core–periphery structure of the network that we visualized, it would be reasonable to hypothesize that, in most cases, the initially infected nodes were too dispersed across the network and unable to activate enough nodes in the core to spread further. Conversely, in the cases where the contagion did manage to spread, the initial infection was likely clustered in key areas, enabling it to build up enough momentum to break into the hub, resulting in rapid infection rates and eventual domination of the network.

In model 3, we increase the proportion of initially infected nodes from 10% to 15% of the population. While this is a relatively small increase, we once again see dramatic differences. The simulations now take more than 10 iterations to reach their steady state, and the median proportion of the population infected has risen to almost 100%. In some cases, portions of the network resist infection. The sensitivity to initial conditions and parameter values that these three models and their variability display is one of the major reasons that complex contagions require very careful consideration and thorough investigation.

Let's take a moment to compare these results to the simple contagions we modelled in the previous chapter. The earlier SIR models allowed a node to have one of three states, namely susceptible, infected, and recovered/removed, but these threshold models allow only inactivated and activated states. Once a node has been activated, there is no mechanism to deactivate it (in this model, you cannot forget that juicy gossip or let go of the 70s), so the number of activated nodes can only ever stay the same or increase. This is why we don't see the peak and drop that occurred in the SIR model. This version of the threshold model is also deterministic once the initially infected nodes have been chosen. Once a node has reached its threshold, it *immediately* activates. This immediate activation is the main reason we see such a small number of iterations needed to get to the final steady state. The probabilistic SIR model with low probabilities of infection and recovery can have many steps where nothing changes, or very little changes, even though the *potential* for change is great. It's just unlikely, so it takes longer. Of course, just as more advanced SIR models exist, so do more advanced threshold models exist that might have probabilistic activation once a threshold has been met or allow nodes to deactivate based on some condition. Well consider such models a bit later in the chapter.

Complex contagions with variable thresholds

So far, what we've seen should make some intuitive sense. When the contagion is simple and the thresholds for activation are low, the contagion spreads quickly and activates most of the nodes in the network with little trouble. When the contagion is complex, and the individual thresholds are higher for all the reasons we discussed previously, then the contagion travels much more slowly over wide bridges, and eventually hits a plateau where some cohesive subgroups in the network are activated and others are not. Hopefully this also helps deepen your understanding of how and why beliefs, behaviours, and norms can be relatively homogeneous within cohesive subgroups and heterogeneous across them.

All of the earlier threshold models had uniform thresholds for activation. However, as we have mentioned, that is a rather dramatic simplifying assumption. In the real world, not everyone has identical thresholds! Some people have very low thresholds, changing their beliefs and behaviours quickly and easily; others have a high threshold and are unwilling to change no matter what anyone around them thinks or does. Most, probably, sit somewhere in between. If we expect real people to have some variability in their activation thresholds, perhaps we should account for that in our simulations.

There are a variety of ways we could go about assigning variable thresholds. Here, we will assign each node a threshold by randomly sampling values between 0 (*always adopts*) and 1 (*never adopts*) from a probability distribution. There are a number of distributions we could choose from here (we will get into some of the details of sampling from different probability distributions in Chapter 25), but as Centola (2018) suggests, the best choice is probably a Gaussian (i.e. normal) distribution. With variable threshold models, there are even more parameters we can tweak to try to model the spread of a complex contagion. For the sake of brevity, we will compare two models using the same network as before, and the same 10% initially infected nodes. One model will use a Gaussian distribution of threshold scores from 0 to 1 with a mean of 0.35 and a standard deviation of 0.001. The other will be the same, but with a standard deviation of 0.1. Intuitively, we might expect the first model to resemble our earlier uniform threshold model with a threshold of 0.35, and the second model might have a higher variance.

```
from scipy.stats import truncnorm
def get_truncated_normal(mean, sd, low, upp):
    return truncnorm((low - mean) / sd, (upp - mean) / sd, loc=mean, scale=sd)


model_cc_vt = ep.ThresholdModel(g_bluetooth_contact)
config_cc_vt = mc.Configuration()
```

```
fraction_infected = .1

random_thresholds = []
threshold_dist = get_truncated_normal(mean=.35, sd=.001, low=0, upp=1)

for n in g_bluetooth_contact.nodes():
    threshold = threshold_dist.rvs()
    config_cc_vt.add_node_configuration("threshold", n, threshold)
    random_thresholds.append(threshold)

## WITH THAT DONE, WE CAN ADD THE OTHER MODEL INFORMATION TO THE CONFIG.
config_cc_vt.add_model_parameter("fraction_infected", fraction_infected)

model_cc_vt.set_initial_status(config_cc_vt)
```

As a quick check, let's quickly visualize the distribution of randomly sampled individual thresholds using an ecdf, which should be centred on 0.35 (see Figure 17.5):

```
sns.ecdfplot(random_thresholds)
sns.despine()
plt.show()
```

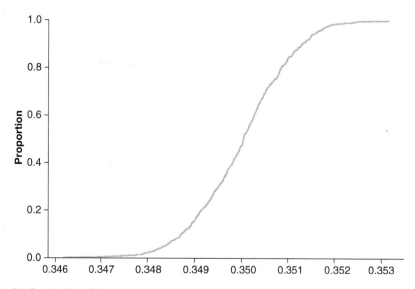

Figure 17.5 A plot of the empirical cumulative distribution of the thresholds in the simulated network with variable threshold scores

And now let's run the final models, shown in Figures 17.6 and 17.7.

```
%%capture
threshold_trends_vt = multi_runs(model_cc_vt,
                                 execution_number=500,
                                 iteration_number=40,
                                 infection_sets=infect_sets,
                                 nprocesses=4)
```

```
visualize_trends(threshold_trends_vt,
                 network=g_bluetooth_contact,
                 states=[0, 1],
                 labels=['Not Activated', 'Activated'],
                 proportion=True,
                 return_data=False)
```

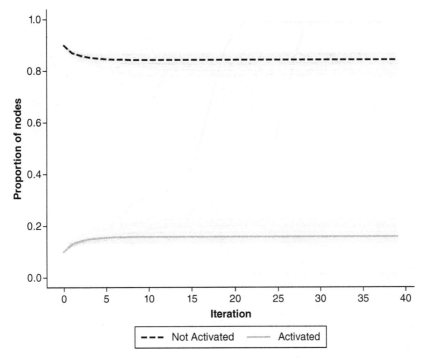

Figure 17.6 A plot showing the proportion of nodes in a network with variable thresholds who have been 'activated' over time (iterations); each of the small translucent lines represent the results of one of the 500 simulations run, the red line represents the average 'activated' proportion, and the black dashed line represents the average 'not activated' proportion. This model started with 10% of the population activated and a fractional threshold of 0.1. The thresholds scores were drawn from a Gaussian distribution with mean of 0.35 and a standard deviation of 0.001

```
%%capture
model_cc_vt_2 = ep.ThresholdModel(g_bluetooth_contact)
config_cc_vt_2 = mc.Configuration()

fraction_infected = .1

random_thresholds_2 = []
threshold_dist_2 = get_truncated_normal(mean=.35, sd=.1, low=0, upp=1)

for n in g_bluetooth_contact.nodes():
    threshold_2 = threshold_dist_2.rvs()
    config_cc_vt_2.add_node_configuration("threshold", n, threshold_2)
    random_thresholds_2.append(threshold_2)
```

```
config_cc_vt_2.add_model_parameter("fraction_infected", fraction_infected)

model_cc_vt_2.set_initial_status(config_cc_vt_2)

threshold_trends_vt_2 = multi_runs(model_cc_vt_2,
                               execution_number=500,
                               iteration_number=40,
                               infection_sets=infect_sets,
                               nprocesses=4)

visualize_trends(threshold_trends_vt_2,
               network=g_bluetooth_contact,
               states=[0, 1],
               labels=['Not Activated', 'Activated'],
               proportion=True,
               return_data=False)
```

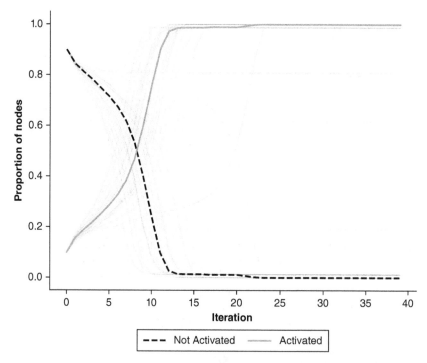

Figure 17.7 A plot showing the proportion of nodes in a network with variable thresholds who have been 'activated' over time (iterations); each of the small translucent lines represent the results of one of the 500 simulations run, the red line represents the average 'activated' proportion, and the black dashed line represents the average 'not activated' proportion. This model started with 10% of the population activated and a fractional threshold of 0.1. The thresholds scores were drawn from a Gaussian distribution with mean of 0.35 and a standard deviation of 0.1

Wow – these two models appear incredibly distinct! Recall that these models are being run on the same network, with the same initially infected nodes, with the same mean threshold of 0.35. The only difference is the size of the standard deviation of their thresholds. For a far deeper and more thorough exploration of variable threshold models, I will once again draw your attention to Centola's (2018, 2021) work. Let this example serve to emphasize a major theme of this chapter: intuitions can be very unreliable when dealing with complex contagions. Explore every facet of your model and the network because due diligence is especially important when models can be sensitive to initial conditions.

Finally, just as NDlib allows us to extend our models of simple contagions to dynamic networks, so too can we extend complex contagions. I urge you to look into the documentation and experiment with these models!

Towards greater realism: stochastic thresholds and network diffusion experiments

In these last two chapters, we've scratched the surface of modelling the spread of simple and complex contagions, and we've only focused on two common types of models! There are a great many others, each of which makes a slightly different set of assumptions about the processes involved in epidemic spread and diffusion. To bring this discussion of diffusion to a close, I want to briefly point to two additional things you might consider. First, it is possible to configure some of these models so that thresholds don't just vary across people in a population but also vary *within a person over time*. This is another step towards greater realism. You know, one day you are feeling pretty open and into new things, another day you aren't. If we introduce this additional bit of realism, does anything change? To find out, we could use stochastic thresholds instead of deterministic ones, drawing a new threshold for each node at each iteration.

The second consideration is bigger picture. While we have done a lot of modelling in these two chapters to better understand the spread of simple and complex contagions, *models are not the real world*. However, as the saying goes: all models are wrong, but some models are useful. In order to know which models are useful, we need to validate them against the real world. In the social sciences, natural experiments are usually our bread and butter because controlled experiments (1) are difficult to design, (2) are expensive, (3) need a lot more work, and (4) may involve ethical challenges that cannot be overcome. However, when a controlled experiment is possible, you should take the opportunity! A full discussion of experimental design in computational diffusion research is beyond the scope of this book, but I highly recommend reading Centola's (2018) *How Behaviour Spreads* for an ingenious series of social experiments that he used to validate many ideas and theories we have considered in this chapter.

17.7 Conclusion

The key points in this chapter are as follows:

- We learnt how complex contagions act differently than simple contagions because they require multiple *sources* of exposure to spread.
- We used NDlib to develop simulations for complex contagions.
- We used the simulations to better understand some of the relations between network structure and complex contagion spread.

Visit the website at https://study.sagepub.com/mclevey for additional resources

PART IV
RESEARCH ETHICS AND MACHINE LEARNING

18

RESEARCH ETHICS, POLITICS, AND PRACTICES

18.1 Learning Objectives

By the end of this chapter, you should be able to do the following:

- Explain the challenges with informed consent in computational social science
- Describe the tensions between the ethical principles of privacy and transparency
- Explain how algorithmic biases and biased training datasets can amplify and exacerbate inequalities
- Explicitly articulate the normative and political values that underlie your research
- Identify the types of computational social science that you will and *will not* do

18.2 Learning Materials

You can find the online learning materials for this chapter in `doing_computational_social_science/Chapter_18`. cd into the directory and launch your Jupyter server.

18.3 Introduction

The chapters following this one will introduce a variety of machine learning methods and models. Before we get there, we're going to consider some of the ethical and political challenges that arise in the context of computational social science. One of the many themes in this chapter is that we are working in unsettled times when it comes to research ethics in computational social science and data science. Many of the methods and models in this book provide access to power that we are not accustomed to dealing with, and for which there are few guidelines and standards. The recent advances in computational approaches to research have far outstripped what we, as social scientists, have been historically capable of, and our ethical standards and practices have not yet caught up. As professional researchers, we need to hold ourselves and one another to high ethical standards. That means doing *more* than making sure we don't *violate currently established* ethical principles, which are not adequate for much of what is introduced in this book (e.g. machine learning).

Rather than being *reactive* (e.g. changing practices and establishing standards after people have already been harmed), we should be *proactive* (e.g. anticipating and mitigating potential harms). We must adopt practices that help ensure we are doing our work in ways that *enable* us to be transparent and accountable to the right people at the right times. It means asking ourselves hard questions about the types of things we will and won't do and making a serious effort to anticipate the potential unintended negative consequences of our work. There is no avoiding constant reflexive practice or the politics of research. We must confront difficult political issues head on and make our normative values explicit and visible in our work. We do this not only to protect ourselves, our participants, and anyone who might be affected by our work once it leaves our hands, but also because it produces better science: science that is transparent, accountable, and reproducible.

We'll start by considering ethics in the context of social network analysis, which we covered in the preceding chapters, followed by matching issues we have to negotiate as we work with machine learning in the following chapters.

18.4 Research Ethics and Social Network Analysis

As researchers, we are not detached from the social and political world we study, and we need to remember that our position as researchers puts us in unique positions of power. In network analysis, knowledge of a network imparts power over it in concrete and tangible ways. Most of us have limited understanding of the structure of the networks we live our daily lives in, and whatever understanding we do have diminishes rapidly as we move beyond our immediate connections. As researchers, we have privileged access to intimate details of the lives of real people and the unique relational contexts that shape their lives, for better and for worse. This information is often sensitive and has the potential to cause harm if not handled properly.

At some point in your research career, you will gain information that is very important, valuable, or compromising to the people participating in your study, and in network analysis that can happen *without any one individual realizing it*. Part of the value of studying networks comes from the ways that micro-level interactions (e.g. friendships, advice, communication) combine to produce highly consequential network structures that are not immediately obvious. When we collect relational data, we gain access to information about an emergent network structure that, though lacking in details, can reveal a picture that's very difficult to see from the inside.

The decisions we make when we collect relational data, construct and analyse networks, and present our findings *all* have important ethical dimensions. For example, in a commentary from a 2021 special issue of *Social Networks* on ethical challenges in network analysis, Bernie Hogan (2021) recounts several experiences where presentations of simple network visualizations caused unintentional harm. In one case, a student gave a presentation that included a visualization of a network of their classmates, revealing that everyone was connected in one large group except a single isolated student. Similarly, after presenting visualizations of an academic network, Hogan describes being contacted by disconcerted academics who were located on the periphery of the network (implying they were marginal), but who felt this unfairly painted them in a poor light as they were primarily active in *other* networks that didn't fall within the presented network's boundaries. These were not necessarily 'marginal' academics, but the definition of network boundaries *portrayed* them as marginal. We don't just *reveal* networks as they really exist, we *construct* them, and in ways that feed back into the world.

═══════════ **Further Reading** ═══════════

To learn more about some salient ethical issues in contemporary network analysis, I recommend reading the 2021 special issue of *Social Networks* edited by Tubaro et al. (2021).

Cases such as these are a reminder that unavoidable and seemingly benign measurement decisions play a significant role in determining who is portrayed as central or marginal within the boundaries of a network *as we define it*; we have a certain amount of control over influential representations of the world that cast some people as more central (and therefore more powerful, influential, and high status) than others. This is what I meant when I said we *construct* networks, we don't just reveal them. Since it is possible to cause harm with our constructions, we should consider the important ethical dimensions of the decisions involved, such as which ties we measure among which people. And since many harms can come from portraying *specific* people as central or marginal, we should also consider the ethical implications of how we share information about networks, whether we are sharing data or presenting results in some other form. All of this is especially problematic for people who are already marginalized. Cases like these are likely more common than we realize.

There are concrete things we can do to help mitigate the negative effects of situations such as those described above, but many problems persist. For example, properly anonymizing network data *can* go a pretty long way. However, this is not just a matter of 'give everyone numeric IDs' because people are often able to make pretty good inferences about who's who in a network they are involved in even if they don't have all the information needed to construct the network in the first place. If someone showed you a visualization of a friendship network that you're part of, I'd wager that with some time and thought you could make very good guesses as to who was where in the network. The ability to use extremely surface-level data to know, with relative certainty, information about individuals is *powerful*.

So how can we present data while protecting anonymity? There are a variety of options. Consider the Faux Magnolia High network data available in the statnet R library (Handcock et al., 2003), for example. It describes a fake high school with 1461 students with attribute data for grade, sex, and race. While it was based on real data, and those variables could potentially have been used to identify individual students, an exponential random graph model (ERGM) was used to infer the broad patterns between these variables and the network structure. Those patterns were then used to create a *randomly generated network* that became the dataset provided to the public. (Unfortunately, I couldn't make space for ERGMs in the networks chapters, but for a good starting point if you are interested in delving further into ERGMs, see Lusher et al., 2013.) Unfortunately, this won't work for all network data, nor for all data in general; the Faux Magnolia High data is primarily used for learning and testing network models. It poses little value for further network research because it is so far divorced from the original data. It makes no claims to represent any relationship between the original data and network structure beyond that captured in the model used to generate it.

This raises difficult questions about the tension between privacy and transparency. We'll turn to these issues directly in a moment, but for now, I want to emphasize that network data collection can sometimes result in information about people who have not provided consent, or specifically *informed consent*. For example, if you collect data on an organization's management team and ask employees to name the people they give advice to and receive advice from, you will likely end up with information about someone who simply wasn't in the office that day, and all the little bits of relational information from many different people add up to paint a picture of that person's position in the advice-sharing network.

As with other ethical challenges we will discuss below, do not assume that you are in the clear because your research passes an ethics review. As I've mentioned, current ethical standards are lagging behind advancing methods, and they are not well-suited to judging how cutting-edge work might be used by others. One of the driving forces for the recent explosion of network analysis derives from the generalizability of methods, measures, and models. At their heart, networks are mathematical constructs. Anything that can be reasonably conceptualized as a collection of things that are meaningfully connected to other things is within its purview. A measure that can be used to describe 'popularity' or 'influence' in sociology can be used for 'risk of exposure' in an epidemiological model or 'importance' in a criminal or terrorist network. Knowledge about networks *in general* is powerful because network analysis itself is so generalizable. You shouldn't assume that your work will only be used in the way you intended it to be used.

While I have focused on how researchers need to consider the ethics of working with networks, we aren't the only ones working on them. Google built one of the most valuable tech companies in the world on the foundation of PageRank (a centrality-like algorithm that uses network analysis to estimate the relative 'quality' of a website based on the links leading to and from it). Similarly police forces and intelligence agencies profit from information about the structure and dynamics of our social networks, and it doesn't especially matter if they have any information about the explicit *content* of those ties. You can make powerful inferences using only your knowledge of the structure of the network as Kieran Healy (2013) cleverly showed in a blog post following revelations in 2012 about the extent of National Security Agency metadata-based surveillance (e.g. Upsahl, 2013). These non-academic groups do not have the same standards we hold ourselves to, but they have access to everything we publish, more data, and far more money and computing power. When we develop new network tools or data, we need to consider what others with more resources might be able to do with it.

In the following section, I move from network data to discussing data more generally, and I will focus more closely on issues of informed consent and balancing the principles of privacy and transparency.

18.5 Informed Consent, Privacy, and Transparency

Digital data collection (including the collection methods we discussed in Chapters 4 and 5) poses greater ethical challenges than more traditional data collection methods, and issues with voluntary informed consent are especially salient. This is largely because we can observe (and interfere) from a great distance, and without the knowledge of the people and groups we are observing (and potentially interfering with, e.g. in online experiments). The massive availability of data online also poses new challenges for privacy, as information that is anonymous in one dataset can quickly become uniquely identifiable when combined with other data. This necessitates a considerable amount of careful ethical thinking and decision-making for individual researchers and teams (Beninger, 2017; Salganik, 2019), as there are no pre-established rules or ethical checklists to rely on in these and many other situations we might find ourselves in when collecting digital data. In research with social media data, where issues around informed consent are ubiquitous (Sloan and Quan-Haase,

2017a), some have argued for increased ethical standards (Goel, 2014), while others have argued that this is unnecessary for minimal risk research on data in the public domain (e.g. Grimmelmann, 2015).

One of the reasons why these debates rage on is because the boundaries between public and private are much more porous with data collected from social media platforms and the open web (see Sloan and Quan-Haase, 2017a). And while people may realize that much of what they do and say online can be read by anyone, they are not necessarily thinking about the fact their words and actions are being recorded, stored, and used for something other than their own intended purpose. And even if they are thinking about that, people may not anticipate how the data collected about them from social media platforms and the open web may be linked up with other data, just like they may not anticipate the richness of the network knowledge that can be gleaned from lots of seemingly trivial details, like the name of the person you call when you need to vent about your insufferable co-worker.

For example, from 2006 to 2009, Lewis et al. (2008) collected a huge volume of Facebook data from a cohort of students over 4 years. With this, they created network datasets with information about the students' home states, cultural tastes such as preferred books and musical genres, political affiliations, the structure of their friendship networks, photos, and so on. All of the Facebook data they collected was from public profiles, but it was *not* collected with informed consent. The researchers linked the Facebook data with data from the college (e.g. on academic major). That's quite the collection of intimate portraits of some 1700 unaware people.

As part of the terms of funds they received from the National Science Foundation, Lewis et al. (2008) made an anonymized version of their data publicly available via Dataverse; they did not identify the institution by name, used identification numbers instead of names, and they delayed releasing personal information like interests in movies, books, and so on. Within days of the first wave of release, Zimmer (2010) and others were able to identify Harvard as the source of the data and show that enough unique information was available to identify individual students.

There is nothing inherently wrong with linking datasets. Researchers do it all the time, and for good reason. But where there is a lack of consent, the data is *extensive and sensitive*, and there is a lack of agreed-upon ethical standards, the risks should be readily apparent. While people know their actions are public, they can't reasonably be expected to anticipate all the things that researchers (or government or industry) will do with that data, what they will link it to, and what the resulting picture of them will look like. So, while they may have consented to publicly releasing certain data on certain platforms, they have not consented to the various ways that we might combine that data in ways they never considered, and which they may not fully realize is even possible. Common privacy protection methods are little defence against dedicated research methods, and we may easily de-anonymize individuals without realizing it in our pursuit of more robust data.

As with network data, anonymized names are not enough to protect people. In the 1990s, a government agency called the Group Insurance Commission collected state employees' health records for the purposes of purchasing health insurance and released an anonymized dataset to researchers (Salganik, 2019). This data included things like medical records, but also information like zip code, birth date, and sex. By combining this data with voting records (that also had zip code, birth date, and sex) purchased for $20, Latanya Sweeney, a grad student, was able to attach the name of the governor of Massachusetts to specific medical records, and then mailed him a copy. By linking records, data that is *internally* anonymous can be used to identify personal information that no one source intended to allow. Whenever you release anonymized data, you need to think very carefully about not just your own data, but what other kinds of data might exist that could be used in harmful ways.

Medical records are an obvious example of informational risk (the potential for harm from the disclosure of information), but this is far from the only example. Latanya Sweeney (2002) has shown, for example, that 87% of the US population could be reasonably identified with just their five-digit zip code, gender, and date of birth. The risk posed by record linkage means that even seemingly innocuous data can be used to unlock much riskier data elsewhere. Even attempts to perturb the data, by switching some values around, may not be enough if enough unchanged data is still available. Given the power of machine learning to make inferences about unseen data, which we will cover later in this book, I will echo Salganik (2019) and stress that you should *start* with the assumption that any data you make available is potentially identifiable and potentially serious.

As researchers, we tend to hyper-focus on the aspects of our data that pertain to our specific research projects, as if we were only responsible for what we ourselves do with the data we collect. After all, we collected the data for a particular purpose, and that purpose can define how we perceive its uses. We should also consider what *other* questions might be answerable with our data, both as a matter of good research and as a matter of protecting the data we have direct responsibility over, and the indirect data that it might unlock.

One response to this type of problem is to simply share nothing; *lock down all the data*. But this collides with another very important ethical principle and scientific norm: transparency, which is a necessary but insufficient condition for accountability. We don't want black box science that nobody can question, challenge, or critique. We will later discuss how datasets can contain racist and sexist data that are learnt by models, put into production, and further propagated, for example. Privacy and transparency are in direct contradiction with one another. So where on the scale should the needle to be? There is no perfect solution for completely transparent research and completely protected privacy, so we consider the importance of both according to the situation. There is no avoiding difficult decision-making and constant ethical reflection and reflexive practice.

'According to the situation' is key here. As Diakopoulos (2020) sums up the key idea about the ethical importance of transparency:

> Transparency can be defined as 'the availability of information about an actor allowing other actors to monitor the workings of performance of this actor.' In other words, transparency is about *information*, related both to outcomes and procedures used by an actor, and it is *relational*, involving the exchange of information between actors. Transparency therefore provides the informational substrate for ethical deliberation of a system's behavior by external actors. It is hard to imagine a robust debate around an algorithmic system without providing the relevant stakeholders the information detailing what that system does and how it operates. Yet it's important to emphasize that transparency is not sufficient to ensure algorithmic accountability. (p. 198)

But as Diakopoulos (2020) points out, we can't understand algorithmic transparency in a binary – transparent or not – as there are many different *types* of transparency, including what types of information and how much is provided, to whom, and for what purposes. The nature of disclosure can also matter, as self-disclosures are self-interested and present things in a certain light. Not all transparency is good transparency, and not all types of transparency lend themselves to accountability. He identifies a number of things we need to consider when trying to strike this delicate balance between privacy and transparency:

- *Human involvement*: Some machine learning algorithms require human input. Supervised machine learning may require data that has been annotated by humans, while others require humans to provide feedback on results, or during operation. Wherever humans have non-trivial input into the process, their decisions should be made open and available.
- *The data*: Machine learning often involves 'training' an algorithm on some set of data. If photo data has been used to train a facial recognition algorithm, biases in the original data, like a disproportionate number of white men on some social media sites, can taint any subsequent work that doesn't match the training data. If we don't know the training data and how it was produced, we can't examine it for biases.
- *The model and code*: While algorithms are executed by computers, humans wrote them. They were written to solve specific problems, sometimes with specific data and goals in mind. Decisions were made about what variables to optimize, and much more. Researchers decide the values of parameters, or decide not to decide and use default values. These decisions should be open and available for review.

In an ideal world, no important *decisions* about our data or models would need to be hidden to protect privacy or confidentiality. In practice, that is often not the case, and we must navigate as best we can our obligations to safeguard our data while making our work as open and transparent as possible. Both are essential; we cannot completely abandon one for the other while still meeting a high standard for ethical research. The answer is not to make all information available; there are too many factors to balance, risks to assess, privacy to protect, and so on. Nor is the answer full transparency, which is not good for anyone. It's *contextually appropriate transparency*, where decisions are made close to the specific cases with the relevant stakeholders. These are the kinds of transparency that are most important to ensuring algorithmic accountability.

In addition to contextual ethical considerations, we can look for ways to build fairness into our practices more deeply (Nielse, 2021) and adopt new privacy-oriented practices such as Sweeney's (2002) proposed *k*-anonymity. This notation should be familiar based on our discussion of *k*-cliques in the networks chapters. The idea behind *k*-anonymity is that no one individual in a dataset can be distinguished from *at least k* other individuals in the same data using a combination of unique 'quasi-identifiers' (e.g. five-digit zip code, gender, and date of birth). The goal here, like in Faux Magnolia High, is to protect privacy by hiding needles in identical needle stacks, but we manage how transparent/anonymous our data is with the value of *k*. With especially sensitive data, we may choose higher values, while lower values may be more appropriate for low-risk stakes. This may mean generalizing some data to make it less specific: if only one person is from Glasgow in your dataset, that might mean replacing their location data with Scotland, or you could remove their location data, or remove them from the data altogether. In every case, we make our data *less transparent*, but we try to preserve the contextually appropriate transparency of the data *while also protecting individual privacy and anonymity*.

As computational scientists, we *must* wield our power responsibly. That means doing our work in ways that are transparent and facilitate accountability while also ensuring privacy and respecting the people represented in our datasets. It also means doing our work in ways that are auditable and which enable us to be accountable for the work we do and the impacts it has. That may manifest in any number of ways, the most obvious of which are to use tools that record every decision, and every step that takes an input and produces an output is recorded and can be understood. There are systems that enable this, and using them is the cost of entry.

However, being aware of the political power we wield and adopting tools and workflows that attempt to make our work as transparent and accountable as possible are, as I mentioned earlier, necessary *but insufficient*. To wield power responsibly, it is necessary to go beyond abstract ethical principles to think more deeply about how and why we do science, and what kinds of science we want to contribute to and advance, and which we want no part of. In the next section, we'll discuss bias and algorithmic decision-making (ADM) as examples of why it is so important to ask ourselves these kinds of questions.

In addition to Diakopoulos (2020), I suggest looking into other articles on transparency and accountability by Diakopoulos (2017) and Ananny and Crawford (2018).

18.6 Bias and Algorithmic Decision-Making

In a widely viewed talk 'How to stop artificial intelligence from marginalizing communities', Timnit Gebru (2018) raises two very important questions about the many machine learning algorithms that are invisibly woven into virtually every aspect of our lives. For any given algorithm:

1   Should it exist at all?
2   If it is to exist, is it robust enough to use in high-stakes contexts (e.g. in the criminal justice system, healthcare, education, etc.)?

Gebru's (2018) questions take aim directly at high-stakes ADM; rightfully so, as ADM is one of the most insidious mechanisms through which systemic inequality is perpetuated. But more importantly, these questions are especially relevant to us as researchers; you will likely have opportunities to contribute to technologies such as these, or others that are similar in one way or another. Given that you could easily find yourself in a situation where that's a possible outcome, it's important for us to ask ourselves these questions early and often, so we can better understand what kinds of technologies we are uncomfortable contributing to, whether because we think they are inherently dangerous or simply too prone to abuse to be worth the risk.

If you don't spend a lot of time thinking about, critiquing, or developing algorithms, it might *seem* like incorporating algorithms into decision-making is reasonable and perhaps even more impartial than the alternative. After all, algorithms are just a series of steps consistently carried out by computers, following mathematical rules and precision. And a computer is incapable of thought, let alone bigotry.

This is a complete fantasy; algorithms don't spring into existence fully formed out of nowhere. They're written by humans to enforce human rules, and I doubt anyone would say that the rules we make are always fair. When our biases are encoded into algorithms, those biases are perpetuated and amplified, often with very serious consequences. These biases disproportionately affect people who are already marginalized. There is a rapidly growing literature (e.g. Angwin et al., 2016; Benjamin, 2019; Buolamwini and Gebru, 2018; Eubanks, 2018; Gebru, 2020; Hamidi et al., 2018; Nelson, 2021; Noble, 2018; O'Neil, 2016; Vries et al., 2019; West et al., 2019), and there is no excuse for ignorance.

Who can we turn to when an algorithm discriminates? Rarely ever one person. ADM technologies are thought up, planned, developed, and implemented by *many* people, diffusing any direct responsibility and allowing any one person or group to somewhat reasonably claim that they cannot be held personally responsible for specific negative outcomes. If you think something is wrong, you can always try to get the organization to change the rules, right?

This is one small part of Virginia Eubanks' (2018) description of the evolution of what she calls the 'Digital Poorhouse': technological systems born from conservative hysteria over welfare costs, fraud, and inefficiency as the 1973 recession hit. With recent legal protections put in place to protect people needing welfare from discriminatory eligibility rules, politicians and state bureaucrats were caught between a desire to cut public assistance spending and the law. So, they found a way to cut spending, and gave it a spin that was hard to dispute at face value. They commissioned new technologies to save money by 'distributing aid more efficiently'. After all, computers could ensure that every rule was being followed, welfare fraudsters couldn't sneak through the cracks in the algorithms, and everyone would be getting equal treatment. Welfare assistance had rules, and computers would simply enforce the rules that were already there. By the 1980s, computers were collecting, analysing, and storing incredibly detailed data on families receiving public assistance. And they were sharing this data with agencies across the US government, including the Department of Defense, state governments, federal employers, civil and criminal courts, local welfare agencies, and the Department of Justice.

Algorithms trawled this data for indications of fraud, criminal activity, or other inconsistencies. Through a combination of new rules and technologies, Republican legislators in New York state set about solving the problem of 'cheats, frauds, and abusers' of the welfare system (Eubanks, 2018). In 1972, almost 50% of citizens living under the poverty line were on public assistance; as of 2018, it was less than 10%. Every new set of rules could be justified if they found a few examples of misuse, which could then be amplified and used to justify the next round of rules. When failure to be on time for an appointment or otherwise missing any case-worker-prescribed therapeutic or job-training activity can be met with sanctions that result in temporary or permanent loss of benefits, this feeds into a cycle of poverty. People in need of assistance are then punished for illness, taking care of dependants, or occupational obligations, which in turn produces greater pressures on health, family, and finances. In protecting against people becoming 'dependent' on the government, algorithms become the walls of the Digital Poorhouse, actively perpetuating the cycle of poverty.

Think back to Gebru's questions. Should these algorithms exist? Are they robust enough for high-stakes contexts? The first question is always difficult, in part because the same algorithms can be used in so many different contexts and to so many different ends. The second question is easier to answer: no, they are not good enough to rely on in these high-stakes contexts. These are questions that we should *always* be thinking about when we produce algorithms that make decisions where humans would otherwise. We need to ask these questions because we are working in areas with important unsettled ethical dimensions where the decisions we make have material consequences on people's lives. These questions should help us determine what kinds of work we will do, and what kinds we will *not*.

In addition to consent, informational risk, the tensions between competing principles such as privacy and transparency, and the highly consequential risks of algorithmic bias and decision paired with ADM, we have to be deeply concerned with the *data* we train our models with, and whether that data contains biases that would be perpetuated if used in an applied context. We'll discuss the details in the next chapter and many that follow, but for now, what you need to know is that machines only 'learn' what we teach them via *many* examples. Certain kinds of machine learning make it very hard to understand what exactly the machine has learnt, which contributes to a lack of accountability in a context where what the model learnt has *very* significant consequences for the lives of real people. Since this data is collected from the real world, it necessarily reflects the biases that exist in the world as well as those of the people who collected it. The latter is an especially challenging problem given the extent to which marginalized people are under-represented in fields like machine learning and artificial intelligence research (e.g. Gebru, 2020; West et al., 2019). Many of these models learn, *or are explicitly trained to learn* (e.g. classification models for social categories such as race, gender, and sexuality), those biases, which are then amplified and further propagated. Sometimes these biases are blatantly obvious once you know to look for them (Buolamwini and Gebru, 2018). Other times they can be much more illusive, even though there are plenty of good reasons to suspect they are there in some form (Bolukbasi et al., 2016; Gonen and Goldberg, 2019; Nissim et al., 2020).

Further Reading

There is a lot of excellent work on ethics and politics of machine learning and artificial intelligence that is important to know. I strongly recommend O'Neil (2016), Eubanks (2018), and Angwin et al. (2016) for general introductions to issues related to systemic social inequality and ADM. Timnit Gebru (2020) provides a good overview of questions related to race and gender in machine learning and ethics. West et al. (2019) provide a close look at issues related to diversity and representation issues in machine learning and artificial intelligence that includes a critique of 'pipeline' research on diversity in STEM (science, technology, engineering, and mathematics) fields.

Abeba Birhane and Fred Cummins' (2019) 'Algorithmic injustices' offers a perspective grounded in philosophical work on relational ethics, and Hanna et al. (2020) offer guidelines for work on algorithmic fairness that is grounded in critical race theory and sociological and historical work on the social construction of race and systemic social inequality. Denton et al. (2020) tackle issues of algorithmic unfairness in benchmark machine learning datasets, which are biased towards white, cisgender, male, and Western people.

18.7 Ditching the Value-Free Ideal for Ethics, Politics, and Science

We've discussed a lot of major challenges in this chapter so far, but we've barely scratched the surface. One thing I hope has been clear so far is that data is not and inherently objective description of reality that *reveals* the truth to us, like some sort of mythical view from nowhere; they are things that we *construct*. It's not a matter of collecting and drawing insights from 'raw data'; *it's models all the way down.* Deciding to collect data in *any* way is in effect a modelling decision that is propagated forward into other models (e.g. univariate distributions), which in turn is propagated forward into more complex models (e.g. machine learning models). At the end of all this, we design digital infrastructure that further entrenches our models in the world, whether it's in the algorithms that recommend friends and news articles, or predictive models that we come to understand and game over time, further restructuring and reimagining our societies. This is sometimes referred to as 'performativity'.

While we should reflect on whether the data we collect and encode represents the world in some statistical sense, this is only the most obvious dimension of the problem of fair representation. It is also crucial to think about how the data we collect, and how we encode it, works *back* on the world. In other words, we need to think about how the ways we collect and encode data represent people and whether the potential impacts from our work are *fair* and *just*. If the idea of doing computational social science with justice in mind is a bit too much for you, then I recommend, at the very least, starting with a commitment not to do computational social science in ways that contribute to *injustices*, which, as the algorithmic injustice literature makes patently clear, is *very easy to do*. In the end, the decision about the kinds of work you will or will not do is up to you and any ethics board/stakeholders you must answer to, but this decision should be *intentional*. Refusing to make a decision *is a decision*, so it's better to know what you're comfortable contributing to so you don't get a nasty surprise later on.

I hope this resonates, but even if it does, it may not sit very well with everyone's understanding of how science is supposed to be done. Shouldn't we strive for impartiality? Shouldn't we be pursuing the 'value-free ideal'? This debate has raged on in some form or another in the sciences and humanities for centuries, and a full discussion is beyond the scope of this chapter. But the point I want to emphasize here is an obvious one whose full implications are rarely appreciated: science is fundamentally a human and cultural activity. For better or for worse, *there is no getting rid of values in science* (Douglas, 2009).

Further Reading

There is plenty of work in science and technology studies as well as the sociology, history, and philosophy of science that is relevant to this discussion. I recommend reading Heather Douglas's (2009) *Science, Policy, and the Value-Free Ideal* and Collins et al.'s (2020) *Experts and the Will of the People*. Both books articulate realistic normative models for science in social and political context. Finally, Green (2021), discussed later is worth reading for a more explicitly political take on the practice of data science.

Not only is it impossible and pointless to try to get rid of values in science, *neutrality itself is an illusion*. Every decision that we make in the context of collecting data, applying models, interpreting outputs, and making decisions is part of imagining and structuring the world in particular ways, and to the extent that those decisions impact who gets what, *these decisions are political*. Neutrality is not an answer here. As Green (2021) points out, efforts to *resist* reform are just as political as any effort *for* reform, and the only people who get to claim 'neutrality' are the ones whose perspective and interests are already widely entrenched. Everyone else is denied that stance. There really is no getting out of politics, whether we want it or not.

Green (2021) uses the case of predictive policing and systemic racism to make an argument we will return to when considering what and how we will and will not do computational social science:

> The very act of choosing to develop predictive policing algorithms is not at all neutral. Accepting common definitions of crime and how to address it does not allow data scientists to remove themselves from politics – it merely allows them to *seem* removed from

> politics, when in fact they are upholding the politics that have led to our current social conditions. (p. 16)

And:

> Whether or not the data scientists . . . recognize it, their decisions about what problems to work on, what data to use, and what solutions to propose involve normative stances that affect the distribution of power, status, and rights across society. They are, in other words, engaging in political activity. (p. 20)

There are three core related insights here: (1) it is not possible to be 'neutral'; (2) striving for neutrality is fundamentally conservative in that it maintains the status quo, whatever that may be; and (3) while you are entitled to conservatism if that's what you want, you should be honest and call it what it is: conservativism, not neutrality. You don't need to adopt a specific political stance to do good science, but doing good science, doing *ethical* and professionally *responsible* science, means articulating those values and making them explicit. You can see this as an extension of transparency if you like: you have values that shape your science, whether you know it or not. It is incumbent upon you to identify those values, understand their role, make them explicit, and use that reflexive knowledge to do better science in service of your articulated and carefully considered values.

Green (2021) argues that abstract ethical principles are not enough, we also need explicit normative values. *But doesn't that run against the value-free ideal?* Yes? Doesn't that make for bad science? *No. Quite the opposite, actually.* Nothing good can come from pretending that science is not fundamentally a human and cultural endeavour (Collins et al., 2020; Douglas, 2009). There is no being free from social standpoints or political and cultural contexts. And that does *not* devalue or diminish science in any way. The problem is *not* that we find values in places (i.e. sciences) where they don't belong, it's that those values are usually hidden, intentionally or unintentionally; they are not *recognized* as values, they are implicit, smuggled in. And they affect people's lives.

Critical questions to ask yourself

We do not just make neutral tools that reveal some value-free truth about the world. How will your tools be used? Are you developing or improving tools that could be used to violate people's rights? That could infringe on their privacy or manipulate their informational environments and emotional/affective states? Could it undermine their autonomy, identities, or self-presentation? Could it out their secrets, or expose intimate details of their lives? Does it assign them membership in groups they don't identify themselves with, such as methods that automatically estimate membership in some sort of social category?

If you consider these questions, you will quite possibly find yourself with the start of your very own 'what I won't build' list, articulated so clearly by Rachael Tatmam (2020; www.rctatman.com/files/Tatman_2020_WiNLP_Keynote.pdf) in her Widening NLP keynote. What will *you* not build? How will you *not do* computational social science or data science?

I am framing this as a question of professional *responsibility* in part because much of the mess that data scientists and computational social scientists can find themselves in, wittingly or unwittingly, stems directly from defining our scientific work and roles in society as *lacking* agency, power, and responsibility for the way our work is used, and how it acts back on the world, and for avoiding politics as if it tainted our science rather than making it better. By framing it as a *professional* responsibility, I'm casting it as the cost of entry: ignoring these issues or defining them as not our/your responsibility is professionally irresponsible at best.

It is not enough to think about these things, they have to have an impact on our professional practice. Some of that, most in fact, is not a matter of technical skill. As we've already discussed, much is a matter of explicating your own values, whatever they might be, and making them more explicit. It's about making decisions about what you *will* and *won't* do for explicitly articulated ethical and political reasons. Doing so does not mean injecting values into 'science' that would otherwise be 'value-free', nor does it mean compromising the integrity of our research work. Doing so results in *better* science, but more importantly, it contributes to a world that is better for everyone, including us.

In addition to decisions about what you will and won't do in data science and computational social science, you will need to make specific decisions about *how* to do the things you've decided you will do. At a minimum, the cost of entry here should be to do your work in ways that are as transparent, accountable, and reproducible as possible.

Further Reading

There is a growing movement in the machine learning community, and more recently computational research in general, towards embedding fairness, transparency, and accountability (see e.g. the FAccT conference) into concrete research practices. It has also motivated discussions of prioritizing interpretable and causal models (e.g. Kusner and Loftus, 2020; Rudin, 2019) and better standards and documentation for data and models (e.g. Gebru et al., 2018; Holland et al., 2020; McLevey et al., 2022; Mitchell et al., 2019; Nielse, 2021), and research with secondary data (e.g. Weston et al., 2019).

In the kinds of cases that Cathy O'Neil (2016) and others discuss, the central idea is that to be *accountable* one has to be able to explain to those whose lives we affect how decisions were made not just in general, but *in their case*. If a bank uses a model that denies you a loan, you have a right to know why. Yet many widely used cutting-edge models in the field, like most contemporary neural network models, can include thousands or millions of parameters that are learnt from data and are extraordinarily difficult to understand. Some of the really large-scale language models that make the news headlines have billions. And the variables these models use – generally known as features – are often low-level, like individual words or pixels. This has prompted two movements towards: (1) using less complex models that produce directly interpretable results, from humble logistic regressions to hierarchical Bayesian models instead of more complex models; and (2) developing new 'explainability' models that attempt to inject a bit of interpretability into more complex models.

Part of doing ethical, fair, and just computational and data science is about using models in ways that are appropriate for the problem at hand. Often this will mean putting down your neural network and picking up your logistic regression. But that doesn't mean that the more complex models don't have a place, they do! In fact, as Nelson (2021) and others have argued, they can even enable approaches to computational research that are informed by intersectionality theory.

As always, part of what makes this a challenge is that there is no checklist here. That said, here's a non-exhaustive checklist to get you *started* thinking through some of these ethical and political considerations in computational social science and data science:

- Have the people represented by my data provided informed consent? If not, have I fully justified its use?
- How important is privacy? Are any participants particularly at risk? Is any data particularly sensitive?
- How important is transparency? How much of my data and process can I reveal to increase accountability and reproducibility?
- What kind of data might my data be linked with? Does this pose any risks?
- What could other people who have more resources do with my work?
- Should this work exist? Is it robust enough to be used in high-stakes contexts? Might others use my work in ethically problematic ways that I did not originally intend?
- What values have I used to guide this research? Have I made those explicitly clear?
- What kind of work will I do? What kind of work will I not do? How does this research fit into that?

If you can provide answers to these questions (and any more that apply) that would satisfy you coming from others, as well as yourself, you will be taking a much more proactive approach to conducting ethical and principled computational social science. But once again, this is just the starting point.

18.8 Conclusion

The key points in this chapter are as follows:

- Knowledge of network structure can provide information that can be used to influence, for good or ill, that network.
- Anonymizing data is not a matter of removing names. The vast wealth of data in the digital age provides many ways to de-anonymize data, so more advanced techniques are needed to protect privacy.
- Transparency in research is important for producing better science that is reproducible, accountable, and more open to critique.
- Privacy and transparency are in direct opposition to each other; we must balance the two principles according to the contextual importance of both.
- Algorithms are not impartial. They reproduce human biases and goals, and they hide individual accountability.
- Science is a human and cultural endeavour. It has never been value-free. We can make science even better by making our values explicit, rather than hiding them.
- While ethical standards lag behind new technologies, doing ethical and principled computational social science requires holding ourselves to higher standards than are the current norm.

Visit the website at https://study.sagepub.com/mclevey for additional resources

19

MACHINE LEARNING: SYMBOLIC AND CONNECTIONIST

19.1 Learning Objectives

By the end of this chapter, you should be able to do the following:

- Describe the difference between supervised and unsupervised learning
- Describe how supervised classification and regression differ
- Explain what unsupervised clustering and dimensionality reduction are useful for, and how they differ from supervised learning
- Describe the differences between the symbolic and connectionist paradigms in artificial intelligence (AI) research

19.2 Learning Materials

You can find the online learning materials for this chapter in `doing_computational_social_science/Chapter_19`. `cd` into the directory and launch your Jupyter server.

19.3 Introduction

Most of what you have learnt about using Python for data analysis has focused on description and exploration, both of which are integral to doing good computational social science. In the rest of the book, we will focus more heavily on developing maching learning and statistical models. The four chapters that follow are devoted to 'supervised' machine learning models and neural networks (both defined below). This chapter sets the stage by explaining some of the salient differences between supervised and unsupervised learning and by describing the types of problems that are typically associated with each type of learning.

Understanding the differences between supervised and unsupervised learning is an important first step. But, once you start *doing* machine learning, you will encounter a host of methods and models that will need more of an organizing framework than these foundational distinctions. You can save yourself a lot of misplaced effort if you understand the paradigms that guided the development of specific families of machine learning models. The second part of this chapter provides some of the intellectual context necessary to develop that organizing framework. It is equally important to understand the relationship between machine learning and statistics, including the similarities and differences between machine learning models and more conventional statistical models. We will set that relationship aside until Chapter 25, where we will shift our attention to generative models, probabilistic programming, and Bayesian data analysis.

I've written this chapter assuming you have no prior knowledge of machine learning. We will take a top-down view from 10,000 feet, glossing over many important details in service of understanding the big picture. I'll fill in many of the missing details in the remaining chapters of this book.

19.4 Types of Machine Learning

Much of machine learning can be divided into supervised learning, where machines are taught via example, and unsupervised learning, where machines use algorithms to uncover patterns on their own, which we then interpret or make use of in downstream analyses. (There are other general types of machine learning too, but we will not cover them in this book.) What we call 'learning' is not actually learning at all, it's just very sophisticated pattern recognition accomplished by running data through sequences of mathematical functions. Let's build some intuition here with a few examples, starting with supervised learning.

Supervised learning

Let's imagine a hypothetical project using the political speeches data we've used in previous chapters. For the sake of simplicity, rather than groundbreaking discovery, our goal is to compare how supportive politicians are of renewable energy. For this example, imagine that the data is organized into two types of files:

- A collection of plain text files containing the actual content of the speeches, one file per speech
- A CSV file containing metadata about each speech, including:
    - the date, time, and location of the speech;
    - the name of the politician who made it; and
    - their party affiliation

Unfortunately, there is nothing in the data that tells us whether any given speech contains a discussion of transitions to renewable energy, let alone whether the speaker is supportive of such transitions. This is a fairly common scenario in machine learning: we have plenty of data, but it doesn't necessarily contain the specific information we need to do our job well. *There is no free lunch.*

In situations such as these, machine learning won't do our work for us. We need to find a way to label speeches as one of the following:

- Containing no references to renewable energy transitions
- Containing negative references to renewable energy transitions
- Containing positive references to renewable energy transitions

It's unreasonable to label thousands of speeches, so we label a sample instead. (There are great tools for this. I prefer Prodigy, which is an efficient and beautiful annotation tool developed by the same people that make spaCy, and tortus, which is an annotation tool that runs in a Jupyter Notebook.) Then, if we plan to use a fairly simple model, we would do quite a lot of data preprocessing and cleaning using methods we learnt in previous chapters.

Having labelled our sample, we use it to train a supervised learning algorithm to model the relationship between features of the speeches, such as the specific words used, and the relevant label we assigned to the speech: no references, negative references, or positive references. If the model performs well, we can then use it to classify the out-of-sample speeches (i.e. all of the speeches that we did not label) according to our three-part schema.

I described 'labelling' a sample of speeches because it is a widely used term in supervised learning. I could have also said 'coding' or 'annotating'. Labelled datasets include information about whatever we want our machines to learn. It's common to refer to these labels as 'ground truth', which simply means that we've observed what we know rather than inferred it; *you read the speech and it contained negative references to energy transitions*. During learning, whatever algorithm you use will constantly compare its estimates (inferences) to the 'ground truth' label (observations) until there are no examples left to learn from.

We want our machine to learn whether a given speech should be *classified* as containing no references, negative references, or positive references to renewable energy transitions (a categorical outcome), which makes this a classification problem. If we were predicting the intensity of positive or negative support on a 10-point scale (a quantitative outcome), then we might model this as a kind of regression problem instead. This is true even if we don't make our quantitative predictions using a regression model, or if we make a categorical prediction using a regression model (e.g. multinomial logistic). In a situation such as this, where you are labelling the data yourself, you are free to treat this as either type of problem. The specific decision here is informed by good research design, not machine learning.

Figure 19.1 shows a simple framework for thinking about types of machine learning. It separates supervised learning into two general types of problems: regression problems and classification problems. Immediately under that distinction are two simplified representations of datasets organized for supervised machine learning. Let's start with the one on the top left, under supervised learning.

Features in machine learning, and variables (or covariates) in applied statistics, are essentially the same thing: they are columns in a matrix that represent characteristics of observations, represented by rows. One important difference, however, is that a matrix contains the same type of data in every cell. You can still combine continuous and categorical data in your matrices, but you have to perform extra steps to ensure that all of your data is numerical and properly configured.

In machine learning, features are commonly low-level characteristics automatically extracted from the data, such as the presence or absence of specific words in a text or the intensity of a pixel in an image. This process is called feature extraction, and you've already conducted it with Sklearn's `CountVectorizer()` and `TfidfVectorizer`. Like variables in statistical models, the features might need to be preprocessed and transformed before they can be used in a machine learning model. This process is called feature engineering.

Returning to our example, we need to perform some feature extraction on the text of the political speeches. We can use Sklearn's vectorizers to create a document-term matrix. In this matrix, the features would be individual tokens (primarily words), the total number of which

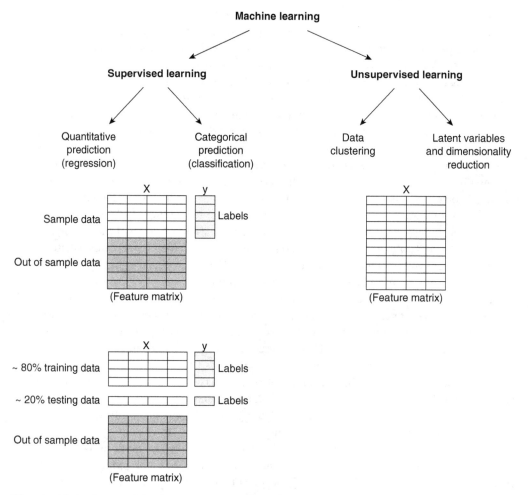

Figure 19.1 Some of the high-level processual distinctions between supervised learning and unsupervised learning

will equal the number of unique tokens used in the entire corpus of speeches. Each speech will have a row in the matrix, and each cell of that row will simply record the number of times that word appeared in that document. This 'vectorization' process of converting words to numbers is an essential step because we can only do machine learning with numbers. In Figure 19.1, we call this feature matrix with many thousands of low-level features X, and the labels, which we manually assigned to each sampled speech, are stored in the vector y. These are simply naming conventions, but you should use them because they make it easier for you to understand other people's machine learning code, and for them to understand yours.

Note that the data in our sample have labels in the y vector, but the data that is out of sample does not. We don't know the ground truth labels for the out-of-sample data, so we are going to use the model to estimate these labels.

In supervised machine learning, we slice our labelled samples many different ways, but the most important split is between the training data and the testing data, typically with roughly

80% of the data being used for training and the remaining data being used for testing. The iron rule of supervised machine learning is *never touch your testing data until you have finished developing all of your models.*

After all this, we have our final feature matrix. We train one of many supervised learning algorithms to learn the underlying patterns that differentiate speeches into three classifications, and we evaluate how well these models learnt by computing various evaluation metrics, calculated using a further held-out portion of the data called the validation data. When we have a model that performs well on both the training and the validation data, we can use that model to classify all of the out-of-sample data. Pretty cool, right?

Now, one thing I hope that you picked up in this very high-level introduction is that the vast majority of the human work involved in all of this *is not actually the machine learning*; it's the often huge amounts of data processing that *precede* the learning (which is one reason why I have devoted so much space in this book to developing these skills). The actual code that kicks off the learning process is often no more than a few lines! *That doesn't necessarily mean those few lines of code will be quick or easy to write, though.* They may include all kinds of complex hyperparameters to tune and configure, which is something we will return to later. The main point is that coding is, generally, not the challenging part. You need to think, interpret, and iterate.

To wrap up this introduction to supervised learning, let me say that this process will vary a bit in different circumstances (some learning algorithms perform best with careful feature engineering, others perform best without it), but the *general* process of supervised learning is the same whether you are dealing with a regression problem or a classification problem. You'll see this demonstrated multiple times throughout the rest of the book.

Unsupervised learning

Now let's jump over to the other side of Figure 19.1: unsupervised learning. Unsupervised learning is also just pattern recognition, but the conditions are radically different because there are no 'ground truth' labels we can use to teach the machine. That means there is no way for the machine to improve prediction by learning from mistaken predictions. Consequently, unsupervised learning is designed to make predictions about different kinds of things, and we analysts interpret the predictions with those differences in mind. The most common prediction tasks associated with unsupervised learning are (1) data clustering and (2) dimensionality reduction and analysis of latent variables. You've already seen how to do some of these things in earlier chapters. Still, let's briefly discuss these methods in relation to machine learning.

Just as in supervised learning, unsupervised learning is performed on a feature matrix X, where observations are in the rows, and the *features* of those observations are recorded in the columns. Note that in the schematic representation of a dataset for unsupervised learning, there is no vector of labels y, and there is no segmenting the data into sample and out-of-sample data, or training and test sets; there is only the feature matrix X. In our example, we classified speeches into one of three categories. This is not possible in the context of unsupervised learning. The closest thing to supervised classification is unsupervised clustering, but it would be a big mistake to conflate the two. Clusters are not classifications, but they can help shed light on latent structure and similarities in our data.

While there is less set-up in unsupervised learning than supervised learning, you pay for it with careful and sometimes painstaking interpretive work. In cluster analysis, as in all unsupervised learning, there is no avoiding interpretation and informed judgements about validity. Face validity is especially important, as good cluster analysis must always 'make sense'. Bad ones usually don't make sense. Never blindly trust the results of a cluster analysis as some sort of ground truth classification. While there are quantitative ways of assessing the quality of a data-driven cluster analysis, these assessments are not the same as the evaluation metrics used in supervised learning. They are tools you can use to strategically inform your decisions as you practise the dark arts of data clustering. Above all else, *use theory and your substantive knowledge and expertise!*

An alternative option to this bottom-up data-driven clustering approach is to use a top-down model-based approach, where we assume there is some latent structure in our data, and rather than attempting to reveal, assess, and interpret that structure using similarity measures, we leverage our substantive and theoretical knowledge to model that latent structure and make principled inferences about which group each observation belongs to. Because these are statistical models, we can assess their goodness of fit. We will discuss a variety of different types of latent variable models for structured, network, and text data in later chapters of this book.

Another common use of unsupervised learning is dimensionality reduction and analysis of latent factors and components. Dimensionality is just another way of referring to the number of features in a dataset, with each feature representing an additional dimension. Datasets with very large numbers of features are high-dimensional, which can cause a lot of trouble for statistical and machine learning models – the curse of dimensionality. Dimensionality reduction is the process of reducing the number of features in a dataset while preserving as much variance as possible by combining highly covarying features into new composite variables.

As you learnt in Chapter 8, there are theory-driven (e.g. exploratory factor analysis) and data-driven (e.g. principal component analysis) approaches to dimensionality reduction. In a theory-driven context, the idea is that some features are highly covarying with each other because they share a common underlying latent factor, and the goal is to measure that underlying unobservable factor. In a data-driven context, we assume that there are latent variables, but we don't purport to measure them with factor analysis. Instead, we try to decompose our feature matrix into 'principal components'. The resulting components can then be used to improve the quality of some downstream analysis task, such as a cluster analysis, or can be analysed inductively as part of a larger effort to understand latent structure in your data.

Clustering, dimensionality reduction, and latent variable models are not new, nor are they unique to machine learning. In fact, principal component analysis was invented in 1901 by Karl Pearson (1901), whose influence on the history and development of statistics can hardly be overstated. The fact that these methods have such long histories in multivariate statistics and scientific research is one of several reasons why I introduced them prior to this discussion of machine learning.

Unsupervised learning has predominantly been used as a way to cluster or reduce the dimensions of data, to identify latent groups or segments in a dataset, or to measure latent variables. All of these methods can be very helpful in exploratory data analysis (EDA) by making it easier to understand what's generally going on in very large datasets that are otherwise impossible to manage with the typical EDA tools. And what's good for EDA is also good for modelling.

Further Reading

James Evans and Pedro Aceves (2016) and Laura Nelson et al. (2018) provide overviews of how supervised and unsupervised learning relate to computational text analysis. Molina and Garip (2019) provide a helpful overview of applications of machine learning in sociology more generally, including for understanding population heterogeneity and causal inference.

Looking for supervision?

The choice between using supervised and unsupervised learning, or between specific approaches within one or the other, depends first and foremost on the problem you are facing. Classification and clustering both assign labels to data, for example, but they are not interchangeable. If what you need is classification, clustering is a very poor substitute. It's highly valuable and useful, but not for the same reasons. If you need clustering, classification is likewise a poor choice. Using machine learning does not mean you are magically free from the challenges of designing good research projects, working hard to understand and clean your data, matching your methods to the problem at hand, and iteratively developing and improving models.

While research design considerations should always come first, your choices will of course be constrained by the resources available to you, the timeline you're working on, and the nature of the data you're working with. While it's typically possible to introduce some amount of supervision into an unsupervised learning process, and thereby exert more control, there are many tasks that can only be accomplished with supervised learning. However, advances in machine learning have begun to blur this distinction in some areas, as you will see in later chapters.

Finally, it's a mistake to view unsupervised learning as simply a less rigorous and trustworthy form of machine learning. Data clustering, dimensionality reduction, and latent variable modelling have long histories in statistics and quantitative science, and recent advances in probabilistic modelling and Bayesian statistics have revolutionized what is possible with these types of methods.

By now, the main differences between supervised and unsupervised learning, and the most common problems associated with each, should be clear. In the next section, we will discuss how the families of machine learning models that are most widely used have been influenced by two paradigms in AI research. *These are not the only two paradigms in machine learning*, but like the distinction between supervised and unsupervised learning, they are foundational. We will introduce a third paradigm, statistical/probabilistic machine learning (more specifically an approach that is often referred to as generative modelling, probabilistic programming, and/or Bayesian data analysis), in Chapter 25.

19.5 Symbolic and Connectionist Machine Learning

So far I've spilled little to no ink on the algorithms that do the actual 'learning'. I want to keep your focus on the big picture here; most of the chapters that follow this one are dedicated to filling in the details. I want to help you develop some understanding about different families of machine learning models, which I hope will help you understand the thinking behind how many of specific algorithms were designed, and what their strengths and limitations might be in different contexts. Most importantly, I hope to bring a bit of order to an area that can otherwise feel like it is simply bursting at the seams with innumerable models and algorithms. Let's now focus on two of the three machine learning paradigms we are concerned with in this book: symbolic and connectionist.

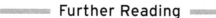

Further Reading

If you want to learn more about the paradigms that have shaped the development of AI and machine learning, I recommend reading Melanie Mitchell's (2019) *Artificial Intelligence for Thinking Humans*.

Machine learning in AI research

How do you teach a machine to ride an elevator? In the early days of AI, researchers thought that they could explicitly provide machines with the necessary rules to perform everyday tasks like these. 'When you get in the elevator, turn around and face the door rather than the back wall or other riders.' Eventually they realized that there are an astounding number of rules, mostly tacit, that would have to be programmed to have a machine perform even the most mundane everyday tasks as a human would. This was not the first time the importance of these implicit rules was discovered. Mid-twentieth-century micro sociologists like Erving Goffman demonstrated their existence and importance exhaustively, using, among other things, extensive ethnographic research. Both AI researchers and micro sociologists, in different intellectual contexts and for different reasons, discovered what has come to be known as the frame problem: it is practically impossible to consciously know and explicate all of the rules that are relevant (i.e. in the frame) in any given situation, even as you use them effectively.

Early AI researchers abandoned the goal of explicating every symbol and rule for every situation and developed machine learning models instead. This shift was a huge benefit to AI. You could celebrate several birthdays hardcoding a set of rules to differentiate spam from regular messages and still do a pretty poor job of things, or you could teach a machine to learn how to correctly and reliably classify messages using the supervised learning approach described earlier. The switch to empirical data-driven machine learning afforded AI researchers other advantages as well, as the programs that make it possible are much shorter and less complex and, thus, easier for humans to write, read, and understand; they are also easier to maintain, and the results are more accurate. If spammers start using new strategies, machine learning algorithms can pick up on those differences even if expert humans have not noticed them.

Under the broad umbrella of machine learning, AI researchers have imported or invented a variety of algorithms to teach machines. Most of these models are associated with one of two major paradigms in AI, the major proponents of which have historically been at odds with one another. A few notable exceptions aside, however, the general trend is for people to move across these paradigmatic boundaries often, *especially outside of AI itself*. The two paradigms are symbolic and connectionist machine learning. We will set aside discussion of a third paradigm, statistical/probabilistic, until Chapter 24.

Each has a collection of models or model variants that are most closely associated with their paradigm. The symbolic and probabilistic paradigms tend to rely on more interpretable models, while connectionist models (neural networks) are more 'black boxed' (meaning opaque and difficult to interpret directly). As a computational social scientist who prioritizes transparency, you should lean towards simple and interpretable models and avoid using black box models in most research contexts, but neural network models certainly have an important role to play in computational social science. I'll provide some guidelines to help you make those decisions later.

The development of machine learning algorithms has been strongly influenced by analogies to human reasoning and critical thinking on the one hand, and biological cognition and perception on the other. These two inspirations are the intellectual foundations upon which the big machine learning paradigms are based. Symbolic (and most statistical/probabilistic) machine learning works at the level of concepts and symbols, which includes just about anything that we can think and reason about, or theorize and measure. Class, gender, race, sexualities, age, financial markets, the global economy, political parties, social movements, emotions, pay gaps, and basically anything else you can think of in the social sciences are examples of symbols and concepts. If the features a machine learning model is using are symbols or concepts such as these, then you can consider it symbolic learning, and depending on the methods and models you are using, possibly statistical or probabilistic machine learning.

Connectionism, on the other hand, is loosely inspired by perception and biological cognition. Like the biological brain, connectionist machine learning models are designed to work with data *below the level of explicit symbols and concepts*. Neural networks are the workhorse model of connectionist learning, and they have unlocked an enormous range of new possibilities when working with unstructured data, especially text and natural language data (to say nothing of the progress they have made in interpreting images and sound data).

Statistical/probabilistic machine learning is the other major paradigm. It's generally closer to symbolic learning than connectionist learning (though there are exceptions, many fairly recent) and is generally considered the most interpretable of the three paradigms. It's also the least 'home grown', as many important probabilists have been statisticians as much as they are computer scientists and AI researchers. We will discuss this further in Chapter 24.

Figure 19.2 is an overview of the some of the types of models that are widely used within the symbolic, probabilistic, and connectionist paradigms. Below, we will consider the 'learning' analogies that inform these various different models to build an intuition of how they work and how they relate to one another.

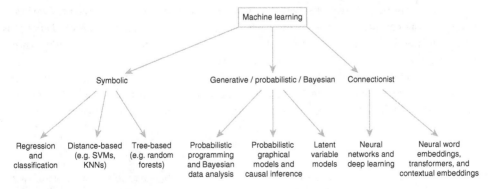

Figure 19.2 The three major machine learning paradigms, along with some of their associated techniques

Symbolic learning, inspired by rules-based reasoning, abstraction, and analogy

Some of the most widely used models in symbolic machine learning were not developed within machine learning and have long histories in many scientific fields. The best examples of such imported (and usually improved) models are linear and logistic regression, cluster analysis, and dimensionality reduction methods. Other models have a closer connection to AI research and cognitive science.

Many early symbolic machine learning models were inspired by reasoning of two types: rules-based reasoning; and abstraction, analogy, and conceptualization. Rules are simply *if–then* statements such as '*if* I mindlessly scroll through social media while watching a movie, *then* I will miss what happened'. As humans, we acquire if–then rules both consciously and unconsciously from experience, and we use and modify them constantly. From a symbolic learning perspective, learning is the outcome of *critical thinking* and *reasoning* such as the evaluation, modification, and application of acquired if–then rules. Do not fall into the trap of romanticizing rationality; these cognitive operations are rarely, if ever, as clean and elegant as formal logic.

When you find yourself in a novel situation, you need to acquire basic *if–then* rules to solve whatever problem you are facing, or simply to make sense of the situation at hand. Acquiring new *if–then* rules directly from experience like this is called 'inductive generalization'. Once you discover rules that seem to work reliably, then you can keep applying them. But across different situations, you encounter some scenarios where the rules you've acquired don't work as expected, so you modify and adapt them. Over time, *if–then* rules can also be synthesized with other rules (which is called chunking), enabling higher-order reasoning. The rules we learn can also become organized into scripts that we follow more or less automatically. When all goes well, we tend not to notice or realize that we are following scripts and acting on learnt rules, but when things go wrong, *we notice!*

Another stylized model within the symbolic paradigm focuses instead on abstract concepts, associations, and analogical thought processes. Abstraction is the ability to recognize something as a specific instance of a more general concept, and it is the basis of all conceptualization (Mitchell, 2019). Analogical reasoning involves accessing knowledge acquired from previous situations; when we encounter a problem or a novel situation, we construct an analogical mapping between the present situations and some abstracted form of prior knowledge. If the mapping is based on relevant similarities, the analogy is good, but *irrelevant* similarities will be misleading.

Many symbolic machine learning models were initially inspired by these stylized models of thinking and reasoning. If two observations are very similar on the relevant features we know about, the more confident we can be that they will be similar in terms of what we *don't* know about them (i.e. whatever we are trying to predict). Similarly, rules-based models of thinking and reasoning have led others to develop models based on decision trees to automatically extract and modify rules from different empirical examples. A number of variations on the decision tree, such as random forests and gradient-boosted machines, have been developed to address problems with overfitting. We will learn more about these models in Chapter 21.

Connectionist learning, inspired by perception and biological cognition

Connectionist machine learning differs paradigmatically from symbolic learning, drawing inspiration from perception and biological cognition. In the early days of connectionist AI, researchers developed models of neurons and neural networks – artificial neural networks

(ANNs) – that sought to replicate biological learning processes. While most contemporary ANN modelling no longer strives to be biologically realistic, the influence endures.

If you were to peek into a brain, you obviously wouldn't see any 'concepts'. Instead, you would see a *massively* dense and complex network consisting of roughly 100 billion brain cells called neurons. More complex mental representations are *distributed a*cross many neurons, each of which contributes to many different mental representations. These clusters of neurons form and become stronger through repeated association. In the late 1940s, Canadian psychologist Donald Hebb first proposed a mechanism we often summarize as 'neurons that fire together wire together'. The connections between neurons that repeatedly fire together becomes stronger the more they are co-activated, forming clusters of neurons that enable higher-level and more complex mental representations. From a connectionist perspective, learning is largely a process of adjusting the weights of the relationships between neurons, or the strength of the signals that one neuron sends another, and the threshold at which the second neuron fires.

Contemporary ANNs are not designed to learn like brains any more than aircraft are designed to fly like birds, but these early inspirations are still relevant to understanding what makes the connectionist's neural network models so different from the families of models used in symbolic machine learning. We will get into the details in Chapters 22 and 23, but the key things to know are the following:

- ANNs are designed to work with low-level features extracted from the objects of interest without feature engineering; the idea is that information should enter into the model like information sent to your brain from your senses, at a very low level (e.g. pixels, not whole images; words in a sequence, not an entire document).
- Higher-level learning (correctly classifying cats and dogs, autocracies and democracies) is the result of an astounding number of really simple computations at lower levels.
- Just as you can't point to a concept in a biological neural network, you can't point to a concept in an ANN. Concepts are represented as many neurons firing together in different configurations.
- The complexity comes from the network itself, not from the individual neurons.

19.6 Conclusion

The key points in this chapter are as follows:

- Supervised learning involves splitting data into training, testing, and validation sets. Its goal is generally to make good predictions on data it has never seen before.
- Unsupervised learning is done with full datasets; there are no splits. Its goal is generally to identify clusters of observations, reduce dimensionality, or measure latent variables.
- Symbolic machine learning is inspired by critical thinking and reasoning, more specifically rules-based cognition, analogies, and abstraction.
- Connectionist machine learning is inspired by our knowledge of perception and the functioning of biological neural networks. Complex networks of 'neurons' are arranged in layers.

Visit the website at https://study.sagepub.com/mclevey for additional resources

20

SUPERVISED LEARNING WITH REGRESSION AND CROSS-VALIDATION

20.1 Learning Objectives

By the end of this chapter, you should be able to do the following:

- Develop, evaluate, and improve machine learning models using Sklearn
- Develop and interpret linear and logistic regression models for supervised learning
- Explain the logic of cross-validation

20.2 Learning Materials

You can find the online learning materials for this chapter in `doing_computational_social_science/Chapter_20`. cd into the directory and launch your Jupyter server.

20.3 Introduction

This chapter is focused on the use of linear and logistic regression for supervised learning, and introduces the logic of cross-validation. We will begin by quickly reviewing the basics of regression. With the basics out of the way, we'll set up a minimal supervised learning environment by preprocessing our data, creating arrays for our response and explanatory variables, and splitting the data into a training set and a test set. Then we will build, fit, and draw conclusions from a variety of models using Python's Sklearn package. In this chapter, we will cover ordinary least squares, ridge, and lasso linear regression models, and logistic regression. Throughout, we will employ cross-validation, taking pains to explain its role in model evaluation and selection.

Imports

```
import pandas as pd
import numpy as np
import matplotlib.pyplot as plt
import matplotlib as mpl
import seaborn as sns
from dcss.plotting import plot_knn_decision_boundaries
from dcss.plotting import custom_seaborn
custom_seaborn()
```

A very brief refresher on linear and logistic regression models

In this chapter, we discuss machine learning models that are based on linear and logistic regression models common to traditional statistics. As this book covers computational social science, I assume that you have at least a passing familiarity with these tools. However, if your memory could do with some jogging, I will *very briefly* outline a few key things here. If you don't need a refresher of the basics, feel free to jump ahead.

In classical statistics, linear regression models attempt to produce a line, a plane, or a hyperplane that minimizes the distance between itself and each individual data point. For a visual example, recall the 'line of best fit' from Chapter 7, where we visualized a scatter plot and the line that best describes the relationship between the variables. When we use a linear regression model with n variables to predict an outcome variable y, we use the following model:

$$y = a1_{x1} + a2_{x2} + \ldots + an_{xn} + b$$

where x_1 represents one of our model's variables, x_2 represents the next, and so on, for each variable in the model, and b is the y-intercept. We don't actually know the values of a_1 through a_n, nor the intercept, b. A linear regression model estimates these 'coefficients', or values. To estimate y, we plug in the values for each variable in the model, multiply each by the relevant coefficient, and add them together. A logistic regression, on the other hand, predicts a binary outcome (0 or 1), rather than a continuous outcome. In this case, the prediction takes the form of log-odds; the outcome reflects the probability that an event will occur.

Again, this is meant to be the barest refresher of what these models look like, *not* as a replacement for learning to develop, assess, and improve them for the first time. If these models are completely unfamiliar to you, I recommend reading an introduction to linear and logistic regression to better acquaint yourself with these models. No need to go too deep; we'll cover (Bayesian) regression models extensively later in the book.

Now, let's develop some simple regression models for supervised learning!

Preparing the data

In this chapter, we're going to create a series of regression models using data on a country's political and electoral freedoms to predict their internet freedoms. We will use data from the VDEM project and from Freedom House's 'Freedom on the Net' dataset, which is an annual report on the online freedoms, or lack thereof, present in countries around the world.

As always, we start by reading in and preprocessing our data. For the VDEM data, we're going to work with a subset of the full dataset that contains variables for the following:

- Country name (`country_name`)
- A four-part regime classification (0 = closed autocracy, 3 = liberal democracy; `v2x_regime`)
- Year (`year`),
- The five high-level democracy indices:
  - Polyarchy (`v2x_polyarchy`)
  - Liberal democracy (`v2x_libdem`)
  - Participatory democracy (`v2x_partipdem`)
  - Deliberative democracy (`v2x_delibdem`)
  - Egalitarian democracy (`v2x_egaldem`)
- The five measures of internet freedom in the VDEM data that we will use in addition to the variables from Freedom House:
  - Government dissemination of false information domestic (`v2smgovdom_osp`)
  - Government internet filtering in practice (`v2smgovfilprc_osp`)
  - Government social media censorship in practice (`v2smgovsmcenprc_osp`)
  - Diversity of online media perspectives (0 = government only, 4 = any perspective; `v2smonper_osp`)
  - Arrests for political content disseminated online (`v2smarrest_osp`)

I encourage you to read about these variables in the VDEM codebook, which is available online. The Freedom House data contains two variables of interest for us:

- `Status`, a categorical variable which indicates the status of a nation's internet freedoms. It has three levels: 'Free', 'Partly Free', and 'Not Free'
- `Total Score`, a continuous numerical measure of a nation's internet freedoms

Fortunately for us, most of the variables we're loading from the VDEM and Freedom House datasets are already in the form of a floating point number (`float` for short), and can be fed into our models without any further preparation or alteration. There are a few categorical variables which must be preprocessed before.

We'll start by loading the data:

```
vdem_fh_df = pd.read_csv("../data/vdem_internet_freedom_combined/vdem_fh_combined.csv")
vdem_df = pd.read_csv("../data/vdem_internet_freedom_combined/vdem_only.csv")
vdem_df.head()
```

The train-test split

Developing supervised machine learning models requires splitting our data: some for training the model and others for testing and validating the model. *This is extremely important*: without splitting our data, our model will simply learn to retrodict data that it has already seen rather than accurately predict data that it has not. To make sure that our machine learning models aren't memorizing the data, we allow our model to train on the training set, tweak hyperparameters, check for overfitting using the validation set, and then assess overall performance using the test set.

Every time you split your data, you remove some of the information your model has available to it; if you remove too much of the data (or don't have much data to begin with), a full train/validation/test split might negatively impact your model's performance. Fortunately, we can sidestep this issue without sacrificing any principles. The process is as follows:

1   Split your data into train and test sets. All of the training data will be fully available to train on. The test set will not be used in any way until a final model has been selected.
2   Use cross-validation (explained below) to produce an optimal set of training hyperparameters.
3   Select the best cross-validated model and evaluate using test data.

We can easily complete this first step in Sklearn using the train_test_split() function. Below, we separate our data into two objects: X and y. Doing so brings us in line with a long-standing convention that the predictor data is stored in an upper-case X, indicating a matrix of covariates, or 'design matrix'. The lower-case y, or the 'target', indicates a vector of outcome values. The machine learning models we employ will learn how to predict the y values using the X values.

In our case, we're going to use the five high-level VDEM indices as our independent variables (which will collectively comprise our design matrix, X), and we'll use the continuous Total Score as our y target:

```
from sklearn.model_selection import import train_test_split

X = vdem_fh_df[['v2x_polyarchy', 'v2x_libdem', 'v2x_partipdem', 'v2x_delibdem', '
    v2x_egaldem',]]
y = vdem_fh_df[['Total Score']]

X_train, X_test, y_train, y_test = train_test_split(X, y, shuffle=True, random_state
    =23)
```

20.4 Supervised Learning with Linear Regression

The linear regression model is about as transparent and interpretable as machine learning gets. Linear regression models are algorithmically simple, and because they have been widely used in the social sciences, your peers who don't know much about machine learning can follow along.

Ordinary least squares regression

In an ordinary least squares (OLS) regression, we model an outcome of interest (*y*) as a function of a weighted sum of input features (*X*) and random error. The 'weights' in a linear model are the coefficients, which are 'learnt' during training. For example, we might predict the degree of internet freedom in a country as a linear function of other regime characteristics, such as whether it holds open elections, the amount of the population with suffrage, and so on.

In the context of machine learning, the goal with a regression model such as this is to find a line (if you have one feature), a plane (if you have two features), or a hyperplane (if you have three or more features) that best fits the data. When we fit our model to the training data, it 'learns' the best value for the intercept and slope by minimizing the *mean-squared error (MSE)*, which is the sum of the squared differences between each observed value in the data and the predicted value from the model.

We now need to create an instance of the machine learning model class we plan to use. In this case, it is LinearRegression. Since we are developing an OLS model, we will call the instance ols:

```
from sklearn.linear_model import LinearRegression
ols = LinearRegression()
```

Once we have initialized our model, we can learn the model parameters by fitting the model to our training data. In Sklearn, we do this using the .fit() method:

```
ols.fit(X_train, y_train)

LinearRegression()
```

The intercept and coefficient (slope) are now accessible as attributes of the ols object and can be accessed using dot notation. Because these are learnt parameters, Sklearn uses _ at the end of the attribute:

```
print("Intercept", list(X_train.columns))
print(ols.intercept_, ols.coef_)
Intercept ['v2x_polyarchy', 'v2x_libdem', 'v2x_partipdem', 'v2x_delibdem', 'v2x_egaldem']
[20.63811519] [[ 50.39585893 39.56204743 -8.08759862 13.15629676 -23.17231143]]
```

While the coefficients might be useful later, we first need to assess how well the model managed to fit our data. For that, we can use the .score() method to get the R^2. Very briefly, the R^2 score measures how much of the variance in the dependent variable can be explained by the model. A score of 1 indicates a perfect fit: the model is capable of making exact predictions of the outcome variable. Let's see what our R^2 score from training was:

```
ols.score(X_train, y_train)

0.8001472299432686
```

Wow – that's an *extremely* high R^2 score! This means that our trained OLS model is capable of accounting for roughly 80% of the variance in the training data with just six parameters (including the intercept). While it's *possible* that our model has teased out the nuance behind our data, it's more likely to have learnt to reproduce the training data, like firing an arrow into a wall, painting a target around the arrow, and calling it a bullseye. Is that what happened here? To get a better picture of how our model is performing, we're going to use cross-validation.

Cross-validation

Throughout the remainder of this chapter, we'll use cross-validation for model evaluation and selection. Doing so enables us to compute accuracy measures that give us some sense of how well our model can generalize to unseen data.

Cross-validation builds on the intuition behind training and testing sets, but does so repeatedly, training and assessing models each time. The most common type of cross-validation in machine learning is *k*-fold cross-validation, which splits our data into a number of equally sized *folds*. The number of folds (*k*) varies but is generally 5 or 10 (Müller and Guido, 2016: 254). We then use these folds as a sliding window of training–validation splits. If we are doing fivefold cross-validation, we segment our dataset into five folds and fit and assess five models. The first model is trained using the data contained in folds 2 to 5 and then validated on the data on in fold 1. The second model is trained on the data in fold 1 and folds 3 to 5 and validated on the data in fold 2, and so on. The model evaluation scores are computed for all five and then examined together, or summarized as an average. If we are using accuracy as our evaluation score, ideally we would see that all five accuracy measures are high and reliable; if there is a lot of variation in our accuracy scores, then the model is likely over-relying on characteristics of data in some of the folds.

Sklearn simplifies cross-validation with the `model_selection` module, and in particular the `cross_val_score()` function, which computes accuracy rates appropriately. To use it, we need to provide it with the model to evaluate as well as the training data for that model. It will perform fivefold cross-validation by default, though we can increase the value of *k* using an additional parameter, `cv`.

Putting the two together: OLS and cross-validation

The code below is going to produce five scores from the five training–validations splits it produces internally. We're primarily interested in the stability of the score (how much it fluctuates between the folds).

If our model is consistent in its performance but not as accurate as we would like, then we have to improve our analysis. We might improve the quality of the input data or make improvements to the model itself. If we see a lot of variation in the model accuracy on different folds, then we have a different problem and we need to change how we segment our data into folds.

Here's a fairly standard cross-validation set-up:

```
from sklearn.model_selection import cross_val_score

cross_val_score(ols, X_train, y_train, cv=5)

array([0.83058131, 0.78927647, 0.49840463, 0.79752537, 0.43638926])
```

Three of the scores are excellent, falling somewhere in the high 0.7 to low 0.8 range. The remaining two are far worse. Our model's performance seems to depend on which data it trains on (and, equivalently, the data upon which it must validate itself).

The gap between our high and low cross-validation scores might indicate that our data is ordered or clustered in some way. It could be that our observations appear in alphabetical order by country name, or something similar. In such cases, it can be useful to *shuffle* the data before we split it to ensure that we are not simply rolling over one group at a time. Doing this is as simple as using Sklearn's `ShuffleSplit()`, which takes two arguments: the number (supplied as an integer) or percentage (supplied as a float) of instances to sample for the training and test sets, and the number of iterations, or splits, to perform. You can then pass the resulting object into `cross_val_score`'s `cv` argument, and Sklearn smoothly handles the rest:

```
from sklearn.model_selection import ShuffleSplit

shuffsplit = ShuffleSplit(n_splits=5, test_size=0.2, random_state=42)

olscv_score = cross_val_score(ols, X_train, y_train, cv=shuffsplit)

olscv_score
```

```
array([0.69717758, 0.75979355, 0.85291181, 0.75438354, 0.82520158])
```

Much, much better. Simply by randomizing the order in which our observations appear, we were able to smooth out our R^2 scores. There's still room for improvement, but the results are stable enough that we can proceed.

Shuffling won't always solve the issue; in such cases, stratified k-fold cross-validation is an excellent choice. Conceptually, this is like the k-fold approach we just learnt, but when it splits the data, it retains the proportions of data belonging to different classes in both the test and training sets for each fold (to the best of its ability). For example, if 35% of the cases in our dataset are autocratic and 65% are democratic, and we are trying to predict regime type, then each fold will preserve that 35%–65% split. This ensures some balance in the distributions of observations across class labels in both the training and the test sets, which eliminates the possibility of limited class diversity in any given fold.

Cheating on the test

Now let's take the mean value across all folds and use that as a point of comparison:

```
olscv_score.mean()
```

```
0.7778936127600505
```

The score from our cross-validation (~0.78) is a little lower than the one we initially received by training on the entire dataset (~0.80), but that's to be expected. We can think of the cross-validation score as a 'validation score' in the sense that it measures our model's performance on data it wasn't able to train on (averaged across five different configurations of that set-up). Our original OLS model, by comparison, was able to train on the entire dataset at once; its score represents how well it fit the data it trained on.

There's one last piece of the puzzle here, and that's how well our model fits the test data. Normally, assessing your validated model's performance on test data should only be done *once you are completely finished developing your models*. The impetus here is that the test data is there to assess how generalizable a model is by mimicking real-world conditions: by the time your model has been used 'in production' or to inform policy decisions, it will be working off completely novel data that it hasn't seen before, and you won't be able to tweak or change its hyperparameters anymore. If you use your test data to help you improve your model, you're causing 'data leakage', wherein knowledge your model shouldn't have access to is being used to improve it. At best, the model is suspect. At worst, the model will be prone to overfitting and could produce hopelessly inept predictions in real-world settings.

I cannot stress enough that in the real world, it is vitally important that you do not view your test score until after you are finished training and validating all of your candidate models. So now, we're going to cheat by doing exactly what I just told you never to do:

```
ols.score(X_test, y_test)
```

```
0.7138660952137659
```

Oof! While that R^2 is relatively good by OLS standards, the score from our fivefold cross-validation model is substantially higher than the test score, which is an indication that our model is overfitting the training data. Overfitting occurs when your model is capable of learning to identify features from your training data and use them to improve prediction; of course, this strategy only works for data the model is capable of learning from, and falls apart when applied to data it hasn't seen before. This typically happens when your model is given too much leeway and/or statistical power (in the form of tunable parameters).

Counter-intuitively, the remedy to this issue is often to make your model *less* powerful or to use some kind of regularization technique. Remember, though, that under normal circumstances, we wouldn't be able to see our model's test score. In an attempt to wean ourselves off of test scores, we're going to spend the next few sections creating regularized models *without* examining the test scores (we'll save that for the very end). Let's begin.

Regularization via ridge regression

We recognize an overfitting problem when the quality of a model drops when making predictions on the test set. To address this, we could provide some additional constraints to prevent our model from learning too much from the training data. One method is ridge regression, which uses L2 regularization to make the coefficients as close to 0 as possible while still making good predictions. In effect, L2 regularization applies a penalty to model parameters that scales with their magnitude. This means that your model is incentivized to keep each parameter value as small as possible. This tension is useful for preventing overfitting.

To fit a ridge regression model, we follow the same process as before, only unlike our OLS model, ridge regression accepts one important hyperparameter: 'alpha' (α). The alpha hyperparameter determines the strength of the regularizing penalty the ridge regression applies to each of our parameters; the higher it is, the stronger it is. It defaults to a value of 1, which is generally a good starting point. We'll start by creating a fresh set of training and test data (with a new random seed):

```
from sklearn.linear_model import Ridge

X = vdem_fh_df[['v2x_polyarchy', 'v2x_libdem', 'v2x_partipdem', 'v2x_delibdem','
    v2x_egaldem',]]
y = vdem_fh_df[['Total Score']]

X_train, X_test, y_train, y_test = train_test_split(X, y, shuffle=True, random_state
    =2)
shuffsplit = ShuffleSplit(n_splits=15, test_size=0.2, random_state=2)

ridgereg = Ridge(1)
ridgecv_score = cross_val_score(ridgereg, X_train, y_train, cv=shuffsplit)
print(ridgecv_score)
print(f"Mean: {ridgecv_score.mean()}")
```

```
[0.76925883 0.6824065  0.55949992 0.8241338 0.68662485 0.70895771
 0.75976052 0.81467692 0.45224363 0.70896388 0.8031883 0.79628239
 0.80544664 0.59523827 0.75607114]
Mean: 0.714850220864512
```

We can see that the use of ridge regression has left us very slightly better off than our original OLS regression, but not by much. It might be possible to improve the cross-validation scores by modifying the alpha parameter, but let's try another regularization.

Regularization via lasso regression

We could use L1 regularization, which penalizes coefficient values that are close to 0 much more harshly than the comparatively light treatment that L2 regularization offers. The result is that the model is forced to use only a subset of the available features, which it selects automatically. All other coefficients are set to 0. This approach is called lasso regression. As with ridge, lasso takes an 'alpha' (α) parameter that determines how aggressive the regularization is. If we have an underfitting problem, then we want to decrease α to soften the constraints and let the model learn more from the training data. Conversely, if we have an overfitting problem, we want to increase 'alpha' to more aggressively push the coefficients towards 0 and learn less from the training data.

Creating a lasso regression model is the same process as before:

```
from sklearn.linear_model import Lasso

lassoreg = Lasso(1)
lassocv_score = cross_val_score(lassoreg, X_train, y_train, cv=shuffsplit)
print(lassocv_score)
print(f"Mean: {lassocv_score.mean()}")
```

```
[0.66584977 0.57869829 0.56643005 0.80293505 0.63309778 0.67545323
 0.68783192 0.76130175 0.40440872 0.6672346  0.70078081 0.75350907
 0.78697977 0.56112952 0.7518551 ]
Mean: 0.6664996955827663
```

Our cross-validation R^2 score is a good deal lower than our score from ridge regression.

We might be able to squeeze a bit more life out of our regularized models by tweaking the 'alpha' hyperparameter. If not specified, 'alpha' defaults to 1. As α increases, the model becomes more simple, more constrained, and more regularized. As it decreases, the model becomes more complex, less constrained, less regularized.

Let's compare the results of a series of ridge and lasso regressions on this data using different 'alpha' parameters. We will define a set of 'alpha' values, estimate a series of ridge and lasso regressions, and then plot their R^2 scores for comparison (Figure 20.1):

```
alphas = np.linspace(0.01, 2, 50)

ridge_r2s = []
lasso_r2s = []

olscv_score = cross_val_score(LinearRegression(), X_train, y_train, cv=shuffsplit)

for alpha in alphas:
    new_ridge = Ridge(alpha)
    ridge_r2s.append(cross_val_score(new_ridge, X_train, y_train, cv=shuffsplit).mean
    ())
```

```
new_lasso = Lasso(alpha)
new_lasso.fit(X_train, y_train)
lasso_r2s.append(cross_val_score(new_lasso, X_train, y_train, cv=shuffsplit).mean
    ())

r2s = pd.DataFrame(
    zip(alphas, ridge_r2s, lasso_r2s),
    columns = ["alpha", "Ridge Regression", "Lasso Regression"])

fig, ax = plt.subplots()
sns.lineplot(x="alpha", y="Ridge Regression", data = r2s, label="Ridge", linestyle='
    solid')
sns.lineplot(x="alpha", y="Lasso Regression", data = r2s, label = "Lasso",
linestyle='
    dashed')
ax.axhline(olscv_score.mean(), label="OLS", linestyle='dotted', color="darkgray")
ax.set(xlabel='alpha values for Ridge and Lasso Regressions', ylabel='R2')
sns.despine()
ax.legend()
plt.show()
```

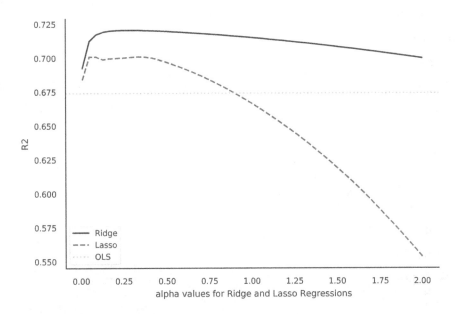

Figure 20.1 A plot depicting lines plotting the R^2 for ridge regression, lasso regression, and ordinary least squares regression over a range of alpha values; this represents the various models' performances on the combined VDEM Freedom House data

Here, we can see that all three of the model types we're testing – ridge, lasso, and OLS – converge as 'alpha' approaches 0 (we didn't actually fit any of the models with an alpha of zero, since the models only accept non-negative, non-zero values for alpha), but rapidly diverge thereafter. As alpha increases, lasso regression's performance increases, falters, and begins a nosedive as 'alpha' approaches 0.5. Ridge regression rises and falls like lasso regression, but over a much larger scale of alpha.

Although the peaks of ridge and lasso are close, it would appear that ridge regression with a haphazardly optimized 'alpha' parameter is our best fit for this model. We'll retrieve that value of 'alpha', fit a new model, and interpret the results:

```
best_alpha = alphas[ridge_r2s.index(max(ridge_r2s))]
best_alpha
```

```
0.2942857142857143
```

Let's use this to fit a ridge regression and get the coefficients:

```
best_ridgereg = Ridge(best_alpha)
best_ridgereg.fit(X_train, y_train)

pd.DataFrame(
    [
        *best_ridgereg.intercept_,
        *np.ravel(best_ridgereg.coef_)],
    index=['Intercept', *X_test.columns]
)
```

	0
Intercept	22.769359
v2x_polyarchy	21.976134
v2x_libdem	20.601121
v2x_partipdem	22.536885
v2x_delibdem	5.303777
v2x_egaldem	7.585864

Now that we've developed a candidate model, validated it, and fit it to the available data, we can assess its performance on the test data:

```
best_ridgereg.score(X_test, y_test)
```

```
0.747274009328536
```

Not bad! Using weak regularization, we've created a ridge regression model that outperforms our OLS model on the test data. The gains are modest, but measurable.

Model interpretation

Let's set aside more rigorous assessment for now and use our model to make predictions on new data, or out-of-sample data. We do this using the .predict() method of the trained model. Below, we use our model to make predictions on the test data, which we split away from the training data earlier.

```
predictions = np.round(best_ridgereg.predict(X_test))

np.ravel(predictions)

array([41., 40., 37., 34., 52., 82., 49., 33., 63., 49., 50., 73., 77.,
       51., 29., 34., 33.])

preds = pd.DataFrame({"Total Score": y_test['Total Score'], "Predicted Score": np.
    ravel(predictions), "Country": vdem_fh_df.loc[y_test.index]['Country']})
preds
```

Not bad! Each of the predictions is off by a modest amount, but there's only one truly off-base prediction (Angola, with a difference of 23). Many predictions are very close! Like most aspects of machine learning, linear regression isn't a one-size-fits-all solution. It's a family of models with a variety of tweakable hyperparameters that deserve your attention. If you put in the effort, you'll likely be rewarded with a model that fits the data well and is highly interpretable. That said, linear regression is not suitable for all tasks; let's look at a model better suited to classification tasks: logistic regression.

20.5 Classification with Logistic Regression

When the goal is classification, logistic regression provides better results than the models in the previous section. It's also highly interpretable and can be used for binary or multi-class classification problems. It's a very flexible model, in part because it doesn't assume a linear relationship between the response variable and our explanatory feature matrix. While similar to linear regression in many ways, rather than predict a numerical outcome for a variable, logistic regression describes the probability that an observation would have a particular value in a categorical variable. Logistic regression is typically conducted using two classes, but it can be extended to multiple classes.

Given that logistic regression is designed to answer different kinds of questions than linear regression, we're going to have to create a new set of training and test data. Let's say we want to predict whether a given country is governed democratically, as opposed to autocratically. We have a variable from the VDEM dataset that will serve for this purpose: it is a 4-point scale, with

- 0 representing closed autocracies,
- 1 representing electoral autocracies,
- 2 representing electoral democracies, and
- 3 representing liberal democracies.

We're going to simplify this down to a 2-point scale, with 0 indicating autocracies, and 1 indicating democracies. Using this recoding, we can use binary logistic regression to predict the probability that any given country in our dataset belongs to one of the two categories. Our predictions will be based on the five measures of internet freedom drawn from the VDEM dataset, briefly discussed when importing our data. I recommend refreshing yourself with them. Let's create our new X and y:

```
y = np.where(vdem_df["v2x_regime"] <= 1, 0, 1).copy()

X = vdem_df[[
                'v2smgovdom_osp',
                "v2smgovfilprc_osp",
                "v2smgovsmcenprc_osp",
                "v2smonper_osp",
                "v2smarrest_osp",
]]
```

Now we perform a new train–test split and estimate our binary logistic regression:

```
from sklearn.linear_model import LogisticRegression

X_train, X_test, y_train, y_test = train_test_split(X, y, random_state=23)
shuffsplit = ShuffleSplit(n_splits=5, test_size=0.2, random_state=42)

log_reg = cross_val_score(
    LogisticRegression(),
    X_train,
    y_train,
    cv=shuffsplit)
print(log_reg)
print(f"Mean: {log_reg.mean()}")

[0.96296296 0.85185185 0.88888889 0.85185185 0.7037037 ]
Mean: 0.8518518518518519
```

As before, we could use regularization to deal with underfitting and overfitting problems. In this case, the parameter that controls regularization is called C. The logic is similar to when we used alpha, but unfortunately goes in the opposite direction. Increasing the value of C reduces regularization and results in more complex models that can learn more from the training data. Decreasing C results in more regularization that constrains how much the model can learn from the training data. So when we set a low value for C, the logistic regression model will force the coefficients to be closer to 0, but not exactly 0. The code for accomplishing this is below:

```
log_reg_regularized = cross_val_score(
    LogisticRegression(C=0.5),
    X_train,
    y_train,
    cv=shuffsplit)
```

```
print(log_reg_regularized)
print(f"Mean: {log_reg_regularized.mean()}")
```

```
[0.96296296 0.85185185 0.88888889 0.85185185 0.7037037 ]
Mean: 0.8518518518518519
```

In this case, altering our regularization parameter didn't help at all. Rather than bury this result or massage it to produce a desirable outcome, we're going to preserve this as a reminder that using reasonable techniques in machine learning can often produce uninteresting, uninformative, or confusing results.

Despite the roadblock we encountered here, it should be clear that it is relatively straightforward to use linear and logistic regression models, with and without regularization to prevent overfitting, within a supervised machine learning framework. You might also have noticed that we did not need to write a lot of code to do the actual learning.

The next chapter will discuss some supervised machine learning algorithms that are probably less familiar and finish with a discussion of evaluation metrics for machine learning.

Further Reading

If you want to learn more about doing supervised machine learning with regression models, I recommend consulting the relevant chapters from Andreas Müller and Sarah Guido's (2016) *Introduction to Machine Learning with Python: A Guide for Data Scientists* or Aurélien Géron's (2019) *Hands-On Machine Learning with Scikit-Learn, Keras, and TensorFlow*.

20.6 Conclusion

The key points in this chapter are as follows:

- We used Sklearn to set up, build, fit, and interpret supervised machine learning models.
- We learnt how to prepare data by splitting our features into two different arrays, one containing the labels we want to predict (quantitative or categorical) and the other containing the values we want to use in our predictions.
- We learnt how to use cross-validation to remove the need for a separate validation split and to harness the entire training set when tuning hyperparameters.

Visit the website at https://study.sagepub.com/mclevey for additional resources

21

SUPERVISED LEARNING WITH TREE-BASED MODELS

21.1 Learning Objectives

By the end of this chapter, you should be able to do the following:

- Explain how decision trees classify data
- Describe how to regularize (or trim) decision trees
- Compare individual decision trees to ensemble classification methods
- Explore how leveraging different metrics can help provide a better sense of how your classification models are performing

21.2 Learning Materials

You can find the online learning materials for this chapter in `doing_computational_social_science/Chapter_21`. cd into the directory and launch your Jupyter server.

21.3 Introduction

In the previous chapter, we did a bit of supervised machine learning with simple and hopefully somewhat familiar models that lend themselves well to the symbolic learning paradigm: OLS, lasso, and ridge linear regression models, and logistic regression models. This chapter will continue that discussion but with a focus on other types of models: decision trees, ensemble learning, random forests, and gradient-boosted machines. We will finish with a description of model evaluation metrics, comparing accuracy, precision, recall, and some ways we can make better use of these metrics.

Imports

```
import pandas as pd
import numpy as np
```

```
import matplotlib.pyplot as plt
import matplotlib as mpl
import seaborn as sns

import graphviz

from dcss.plotting import plot_knn_decision_boundaries
from dcss.plotting import custom_seaborn

custom_seaborn()
```

Preparing the data

As in earlier chapters, we will be using the VDEM data on a country's political and electoral freedoms to predict internet freedoms drawn from the Freedom House dataset.

```
forml = pd.read_csv("../data/vdem_internet_freedom_combined/vdem_fh_combined.csv")
```

The train-test split and cross-validation

As discussed in Chapter 20, developing supervised machine learning models requires splitting our data into different sets: some for training the model and others for testing and validating the model. The most practical way to perform this split involves using cross-validation (introduced in the previous chapter).

```
from sklearn.model_selection import train_test_split

X = forml[['v2x_polyarchy', 'v2x_libdem', 'v2x_partipdem', 'v2x_delibdem', '
    v2x_egaldem',]]
y = forml[['Total Score']]

X_train, X_test, y_train, y_test = train_test_split(X, y, random_state=23)
```

21.4 Rules-Based Learning with Trees

Decision trees

Decision trees, and some more sophisticated models based on decision trees that we will discuss shortly, are the workhorse models of rules-based symbolic learning (as discussed in Chapter 19). They can be used for both classification and regression tasks. We will focus on classification in the example here, but the process is more or less the same for regression problems.

In machine learning, a decision tree is a directed network that starts with a single node 'containing' every instance in your dataset. From there on, it's like playing a *highly* skilled game of 20 questions (Domingos, 2015). In this game, the model is going to 'ask' a series of 'questions' to figure out the correct label if it's a classification problem, or the correct value if it's a regression problem. In a moment, we will learn how the model decides which question to ask, but for now, just know that the model will *always* ask the most informative question possible. The questions will always concern the value for some specific feature for each instance, such as 'Does Canada hold free and fair elections?' or 'Is Canada's score for freedom of the press higher than the median score?'

Every time the model asks a question, a node containing some subset of instances in our dataset splits off into two new nodes. Depending on the answer to the question, each observation moves from the parent node into one of the two child nodes. This process continues until (1) all of the observations contained in a node share the same value for the outcome you want the model to be able to predict, or (2) your tree model runs out of room to ask more questions. When one of these two conditions is met, the branch of the tree terminates in a node called a 'leaf'. The path from the root node (every instance in the dataset) to each leaf in the tree consti-tutes a rule. We can collect all of these rules into a single hierarchical rule base that is relatively easy for humans to interpret and understand.

Now that we understand the basics, it's time to answer a critical question: *how does the model decide which question to ask next?* How does it know what the 'most informative' question is? The most common method is to use the concept of entropy from information theory. In infor-mation theory, entropy is a measure of how much information something contains, expressed in terms of uncertainty.

To use a simplified example, let's say we want to figure out which of the nations in the VDEM dataset are democracies. If you think elections are all you need to be considered a democracy, then you could just ask one question for each case – do they hold elections? *However*, not all elections are the same, and democracies are about much more than elections. So you keep asking questions until you are confident you can make a good judgement. The more questions you need to ask to arrive at a confident judgement, the more accurate your classification of the observations into 'democracies' and 'autocracies' will be. The more purely separated those two classes become, the lower the 'entropy' in your model. In the context of a decision tree analysis, the model will *always* ask the question that will result in the biggest decrease in entropy, usually expressed in terms of 'information gain', which quantifies the decrease in entropy that resulted from asking the question.

At this point, there shouldn't be much doubt about how easily the VDEM dataset we've been using throughout the book can be classified; nevertheless, we're going to use it here again. We're not going to do so because it will provide us with a better classification (we already achieved very good scores using a logistic regression) but rather because the resultant decision tree model will allow us to easily see what information the model finds most useful when decid-ing whether a nation is an autocracy or a democracy.

We'll start, as usual, by splitting our dataset into a matrix, *X*, and an outcome vector, *y*:

```
from sklearn.tree import DecisionTreeClassifier, export_graphviz
from graphviz import Source
from sklearn.preprocessing import LabelEncoder

dem_indices = pd.read_csv("../data/vdem_internet_freedom_combined/dem_indices.csv")

X = dem_indices[[
```

```
                'v2smgovdom_osp',
                "v2smgovfilprc_osp",
                "v2smgovsmcenprc_osp",
                "v2smonper_osp",
                "v2smarrest_osp",
]]


interpretable_names = [
    'Domestic Misinformation',
    'Internet Filtering',
    'Social Media Censorship',
    'Online Media Diversity',
    'Arrests for Political Content'
]


regime_types = [
    'Autocracy',
    'Democracy',
]


le = LabelEncoder()
labels = le.fit_transform(regime_types)


y = np.where(dem_indices["v2x_regime"] <= 1, 0, 1).copy()
```

The technique we're using to convert the 4-point `v2x_regime` scale into a binary variable is identical to the one we employed in Chapter 20.

With *X* and *y* created, we can create our training and test sets, and then create and fit our decision tree classifier using cross-validation (in much the same way as we did in the previous chapter; consult Chapter 20 for more detail on cross-validation).

```
from sklearn.model_selection import cross_val_score
from sklearn.model_selection import ShuffleSplit


X_train, X_test, y_train, y_test = train_test_split(X, y, random_state=23)


shuffsplit = ShuffleSplit(n_splits=5, test_size=0.3, random_state=42)


dtclass = DecisionTreeClassifier(random_state=0)
dt_scores = cross_val_score(dtclass, X_train, y_train, cv=shuffsplit)
print(dt_scores)
print(f"Mean: {dt_scores.mean()}")


[0.68292683 0.73170732 0.7804878 0.75609756 0.82926829]
Mean: 0.7560975609756098


## DEM_INDICES.V2X_REGIME
```

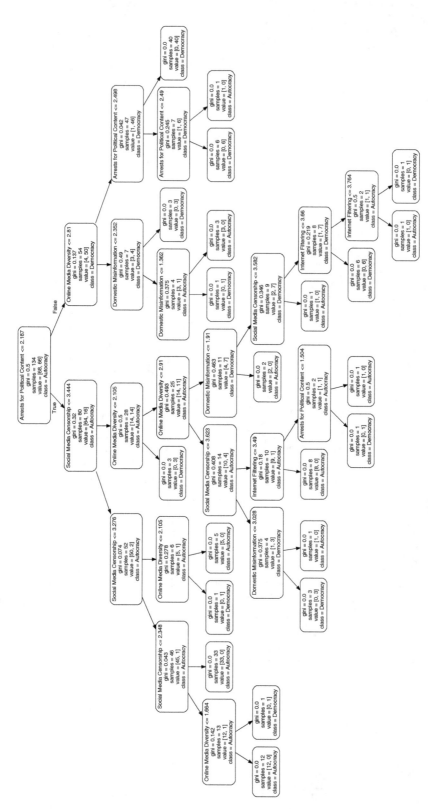

Figure 21.1 The many branches and leaves of the decision tree fitted to the VDEM data; the objective was to sort nations in the dataset into autocracies and democracies

Not bad! In order to get a sense of what our tree is doing under the hood, Figure 21.1 represents our decision tree. You start at the top node, which contains all of the observations (countries in this case). The top line in that node (and every non-leaf node in the remainder of the tree) indicates the rule it will use to split the data. All of the countries for which that statement is true will travel along the 'True' path for further subdivision. All of the nations for whom this condition does not apply travel along the 'False' path.

Figure 21.1 shows the resulting image without colour because it keeps the cost of the print book down. If you change the argument `filled = False` below to `True`, you can get a colour version. In the colour versions, the 'strength' of the colour represents how 'pure' each node is. If there's an equal mix of both classes, the colour should desaturate entirely. The code below also writes the figure to disk. To display it in a notebook, wrap the entire function in `graphviz.Source()`. The same is true for the other decision trees later in the chapter.

```
from sklearn import preprocessing

dt_fitted = dtclass.fit(X_train, y_train)

export_graphviz(
    dtclass,
    out_file='../graphical_models/classified_1.gv',
    filled=False,
    rounded=True,
    feature_names=interpretable_names,
    class_names=le.classes_,
)
```

What about overfitting?

As you may be starting to suspect, decision trees are prone to overfitting. The tree grows bigger with every question, and by the time we've reached the leaves, we know everything we need to know to make predictions that are 100% right 100% of the time . . . *for the data we trained the model on*. This extreme overfitting is sometimes called 'memorizing' the training data. We don't want to do that.

One way to address the overfitting problem with decision trees is to 'prune' them. Remember that the model *always* asks the most informative question first. This means that as the trees get deeper and deeper – as we ask more questions – each feature is weaker or less predictive than those that came before it. As we move further and further out, we risk making decisions based on noise and overfitting the model to the data we have. The full tree, then, is typically *worse* than a pruned tree because it includes weak features that could be specific to our dataset and which do not generalize.

We constrain the depth of the tree by restricting the number of questions or decisions that the model is allowed to ask, and in doing so, we improve the ability of our model to generalize to data it hasn't seen before. If we set the maximum depth of our tree to 6, for example, the models can only ask the six most informative questions, at which point it must make its prediction. Obviously, this reduces the accuracy on the training data, but not as much as you might think. It's the unseen data we care most about, and the pruned model will make much better predictions when it is not overfitted.

In Sklearn, we specify the maximum depth of the tree in advance. This can be done using the `max_depth` argument for the `DecisionTreeClassifier()`. Let's set it to 3. This will produce a very shallow tree, but that's desirable; we want it to have to make the best decisions it can in broad strokes. This way, the model will be less likely to overfit the training data.

```
dtclass_pruned = DecisionTreeClassifier(max_depth=3, random_state=0)
dt_scores = cross_val_score(dtclass_pruned, X_train, y_train, cv=shuffsplit)
print(dt_scores)
print(f"Mean: {dt_scores.mean()}")

[0.75609756 0.73170732 0.7804878 0.73170732 0.85365854]
Mean: 0.7707317073170732


dtclass_pruned.fit(X_train, y_train)

export_graphviz(
    dtclass_pruned,
    out_file='../graphical_models/pruned.gv',
    filled=False,
    rounded=True,
    feature_names=interpretable_names,
    class_names=le.classes_,
)

dtclass_pruned.score(X_test, y_test)

0.8444444444444444
```

Looking good! We've already seen a modest improvement, which probably represents a slight reduction in overfitting (something that cross-validation automatically assesses). Let's examine the tree again (Figure 21.2).

You can see the influence of setting the `max_depth` parameter to 3 in the tree: rather than a sprawling monstrosity, we now have a tree that neatly terminates each branch at the same level. Decision trees have other parameters you can tweak, such as `min_samples_leaf`; it's worth looking at the documentation to see the options available to you! Using only `max_depth`, we managed to get a good result, but we're unlikely to be able to do much better using regularization alone. As we saw with ridge and lasso regression, regularization usually reaches a 'sweet spot' at some modest value, but as the strength of the regularization increases, the model's performance nosedives. Decision trees have, by their nature, low granularity. You can't perform fine-grained regularization on a single decision tree the same way you could for an 'alpha' parameter on a ridge or lasso regression (what would a `max_depth` of 3.5 even look like?). It's likely that no regularization of a single-tree model will eliminate overfitting entirely. Instead, we'll have to turn to a method which will allow us to combine many, many trees.

21.5 Ensemble Learning

One very effective way to get around the overfitting problem is to take an ensemble approach, which combines predictions from multiple models into a single prediction that

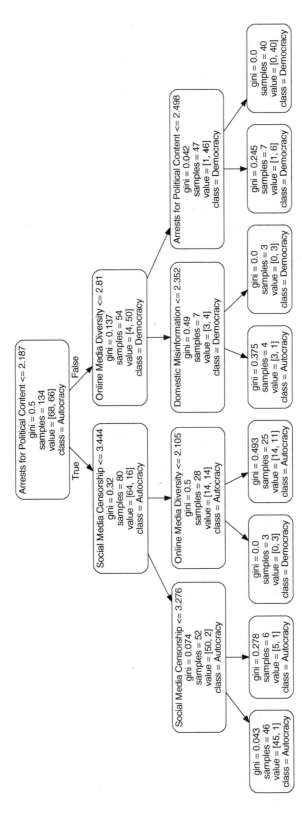

Figure 21.2 A pruned decision tree fit to the same VDEM data; setting the `max_depth` parameter dramatically reduced the size of the tree

is better than that of any individual model. As you will soon learn, this approach tends to produce excellent results and does not require any pruning. Ensembles of decision trees produce better results than any one decision tree, including any of the individual decision trees in the ensemble.

To work with an ensemble of decision trees, we first draw many bootstrapped samples of instances from our overall dataset. In a bootstrapped sample, replacement is allowed, which means that the same instance can be sampled more than once. For each sample, we fit a decision tree and record the model's predictions. The final predictions are made by an 'election' of sorts, where each tree 'votes' on the class they think each observation belongs to. If we take 200 samples, we would fit 200 decision trees. These modes are used collectively – as an ensemble – to make predictions on new instances by taking averages of the predictions made by the models that make up the ensemble. This process is called 'bagging' or 'bootstrapped aggregation', and it can be applied not only to decision trees but also to a wide variety of the classification models implemented in scikit-learn! For now, we'll stick to applying it to decision trees.

Bagging or bootstrapped aggregation goes a very long way in addressing the overfitting problem. One major advantage is that we don't have to prune our decision trees. In fact, it's better if we don't! If we let each tree grow to be as deep and complex as it likes, we will end up with an ensemble that has high variance but low bias. That's exactly what we want when we go to make our final aggregated predictions. The important choice you must make is how many bags to use, or rather, how many bootstrapped samples of instances to draw, and the number of total trees we want to end up with. Let's see what the combination of 100 trees can bring us:

```
from sklearn.ensemble import BaggingClassifier

bag_of_trees = BaggingClassifier(DecisionTreeClassifier(),
                                 n_estimators=100,
                                 bootstrap=True,
                                 random_state=0)

bt_scores = cross_val_score(bag_of_trees, X_train, y_train, cv=shuffsplit)
print(bt_scores)
print(f"Mean: {bt_scores.mean()}")

[0.80487805 0.90243902 0.85365854 0.85365854 0.80487805]
Mean: 0.8439024390243903
```

The unregularized bagging classifier has produced an even better score than the regularized decision tree did! There may yet be more room for improvement if we alter how each of the trees functions using a random forest model.

Random forests

One issue with the bagging approach is that the resulting trees tend to be correlated with one another, mainly due to the fact that they are all trying to maximize the same thing when they ask questions – information gain. If there are some very powerful attributes in our dataset, as there almost always are, the tree we fit for each bag will lean heavily on those features, which makes the whole ensemble approach a lot less useful and degrades the quality of the final prediction. It would be much better for us if the trees are not correlated, or are at best weakly correlated.

Random forests accomplish this with one simple, but highly effective, modification: *they constrain the features that any given node is allowed to ask questions about.* The result is a collection of decision trees that are uncorrelated, or weakly correlated, with one another, which leads to more accurate predictions when they are aggregated.

Random forests are straightforward to train, and because of their clever design, they do a good job of dealing with noise and preventing overfitting, so it is not necessary to trim or prune the trees. They also take only two hyperparameters: the number of trees in the forest (i.e. the number of samples of instances to draw) and the size of the random sample to draw when sampling the features that any given decision tree will select from. You can and should experiment with cross-validation to select values for these hyperparameters that result in the most accurate predictions (we're not doing so here because space is limited).

```
from sklearn.ensemble import RandomForestClassifier

rforest = RandomForestClassifier(n_estimators=100,
                                 max_features=2,
                                 random_state=0)

rforest_scores = cross_val_score(rforest, X_train, y_train, cv=shuffsplit)
print(rforest_scores)
print(f"Mean: {rforest_scores.mean()}")

[0.85365854 0.85365854 0.85365854 0.85365854 0.80487805]
Mean: 0.8439024390243903
```

It would appear that our random forest model, with modest parameters, is producing the *exact same result* as we got with our bagging classifier.

The downside of random forests is that – unlike garden-variety decision trees – the results are not so easy to interpret. For this reason, random forests and other ensemble models are generally considered to be less 'interpretable' than simple decision trees, linear and logistic regressions, or *k*-nearest neighbours. While you can inspect any of the trees in your random forest classifier, this process is complicated somewhat by the fact that our model contains 100 distinct trees, and we can't easily determine how significant any one tree was to the overall decision-making process. Nevertheless, it's a good idea to select a a tree at random and take a look at what it did with the data. Of course, you can do this many different times, if you like. Just select different trees each time. One such tree is shown in Figure 21.3.

```
rforest.fit(X_train, y_train)

export_graphviz(
    rforest.estimators_[6],
    out_file='../graphical_models/rf_classified.gv',
    filled=False,
    rounded=True,
    feature_names=interpretable_names,
    class_names=le.classes_,
)
```

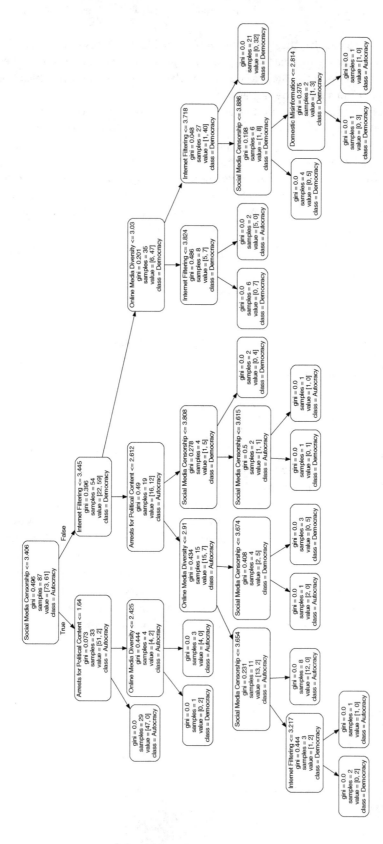

Figure 21.3 A single randomly selected decision tree from the random forest thereof fitted to the VDEM data

There are other ways that can help you interpret your random forest models, such as using `rforest.feature_importances` to get a sense of which features in your dataset had the greatest impact on predictive power.

While our random forest classifier has outperformed decision trees, regularized decision trees, and tied the bagging classifier, there's one last technique we might use to squeeze out a bit more performance: gradient-boosted machines.

Gradient-boosted machines

While random forests remain one of the best and most widely used approaches to supervised machine learning, a slightly newer approach to ensembling decision trees has recently started outperforming random forests and is widely considered to be one of the best algorithms for doing machine learning on anything other than image or perception data (Chollet, 2018). This technique is called 'gradient boosting', and it differs from the random forest approach in that rather than allowing all of the decision trees to randomly pursue the best answer possible in isolation (as random forest does), it attempts to fit trees that better account for the misclassified observations from previous trees. In this way, each tree tackles the 'room for improvement' left behind by the tree that immediately preceded it. The effect here is that the gradient-boosted trees can reach a remarkably high degree of accuracy using only a small handful of estimators (but are accordingly prone to overfitting). Let's try creating one now:

```
from sklearn.ensemble import GradientBoostingClassifier

gboost = GradientBoostingClassifier(n_estimators=100,
                           random_state=0)

gboost_scores = cross_val_score(gboost, X_train, y_train, cv=shuffsplit)
print(gboost_scores)
print(f"Mean: {gboost_scores.mean()}")

[0.80487805 0.85365854 0.85365854 0.7804878 0.7804878 ]
Mean: 0.8146341463414635
```

The gradient-boosted trees achieved worse performance than our previous two models. Usually, we would expect a gradient-boosted trees model to outperform all of our other decision tree models (ensemble or otherwise), but that shouldn't be interpreted as a good reason to skip straight to gradient boost without bothering to specify and fit any other models. What we've seen here is evidence to that point; there's value in fitting 'intermediate' models to see how their performance and idiosyncrasies compare to the cutting-edge techniques. There are a few reasons why this is a vital practice.

Advanced, complicated methods are not intrinsically better than simple methods: not only is this true in our example – given that one of the most demonstrably powerful and widely applicable algorithms, gradient boosting, failed to outperform random forests – but it is often true in general. Cutting-edge methods are indispensable for their ability to tackle cutting-edge issues, but they're often overkill for the kinds of problems they get applied to.

Don't sacrifice interpretability without good cause: explicable, interpretable, transparent models that slightly underperform are often more valuable than top-performing 'black box' models that appear to be more accurate, but for reasons that are hard to establish. Gradient-boosted models are more difficult to interpret than decision tree models, so the advantages of the former over the latter should be considered in light of the interpretability trade-off.

Any problem in machine learning should be tackled using multiple approaches: even if you feel like you can't improve on your model, there may be undiscovered issues lurking beneath the surface. Applying a multitude of modelling strategies to a problem – even in cases where your first model is performing well – may help confirm the defensibility of your primary approach, give you more inferential insight, or uncover contingencies that need to be addressed.

One problem common to all tree-based models (ensemble or otherwise) is that they require an abundance of data and are especially prone to overfitting in cases where such data is not forthcoming. That said, there are many ways to make up for a lack of data; in future chapters, we'll explore methods you can use to get even more out of a limited dataset.

Before we move on, let's take a moment to compare how each of our tree-based models perform on the test set which we split off from the training data right at the beginning of this section and haven't touched since:

```
model_list = [dtclass,
dtclass_pruned,
bag_of_trees.fit(X_train, y_train),
rforest,
gboost.fit(X_train, y_train)]

for model in model_list:
    print(model.score(X_test, y_test))
```

```
0.7555555555555555
0.8444444444444444
0.9111111111111111
0.9111111111111111
0.8888888888888888
```

Looks like the training results match up nicely with the test results.

21.6 Evaluation Beyond Accuracy

So far, we have been using accuracy to evaluate the quality of our machine learning models. While accuracy is important, *it isn't everything*. Consider two issues.

First, bad models can have high accuracy rates. This can happen when the events we want to predict are rare, or the categories we want to classify instances into are very imbalanced. In such scenarios, we can achieve very high accuracy rates by making the same guess every time. We haven't actually learnt anything useful, we just learnt that if something is rare, predicting that the rare thing didn't happen is often correct. Similarly, bad models can achieve high accuracy rates by learning from the wrong things. For example, a deep learning model differentiating pictures of huskies from pictures of wolves – with a high level of accuracy, of course – was shown to be relying on whether or not the image contained snow. That's a *bad* model. We will return to this example later in the chapter.

Second, depending on the purpose of your machine learning, there may be aspects of your model's performance that are more important to optimize than accuracy. Imagine you were tasked with designing a machine learning algorithm capable of detecting when a patient in a hospital requires a dose of analgesic medication; although false negatives in such a setting would be bad, false positives could be deadly and should be avoided at all costs. In that case, we could set a hard constraint on the ratio of false positives to false negatives and ignore any marginal increases that break that constraint.

There are a number of useful measures we can use when accuracy is not ideal. Selecting the best from among them depends on factors such as the data you have, the types of question you are trying to answer, the consequences of false positives or false negatives, and so on. In other words, once again, you need to know what you are trying to do, why you are doing it, and where the risks are. Your evaluation measures should be aligned with those larger goals.

Let's work through some examples of other evaluation measures. In the examples below, we will focus primarily on evaluation measures for classification models, but we will also discuss evaluation for regression models.

Balancing false positives and false negatives in classification models

We can evaluate the quality of a machine learning model in terms of the balance between false positives and false negatives, or Type I and Type II errors, respectively. In the context of binary classification, false positives are when we predict that a negative instance is positive, and false negatives are when we predict that a positive instance is negative. Imagine you have a binary classification model to predict whether any given country is an autocracy. In this model, 'autocracy' is the 'positive' class and 'not autocracy' (i.e. democracy) is the 'negative class'. If your model predicted that New Zealand was an autocracy in 2020, that's a false positive or Type I error. If it predicted that North Korea was a not an autocracy in 2020, that's a false negative or Type II error.

In some cases, we may prefer a model with slightly lower accuracy if it minimizes false positives or false negatives while still having good overall accuracy. This is especially important in models that might have some kind of real-world impact. Again, think about whether there are any potentially negative consequences that could result from one type of error versus the other, and if so, how much overall accuracy would you be willing to accept to reduce the risk of false positives or false negatives?

Generally, it's easier to work with single score summaries for evaluation metrics, like accuracy. The most common alternative single score evaluation metrics are precision and recall. *Precision* is a measure of the number of predicted positive cases that are *actually* positive. Specifically, precision is the number of true positives the model identified divided by the number of total positives (true and false) the model identified. Precision gives us the proportion of correct predictions (true positives). *Recall* is a measure of the number of true positives that the model identified divided by the total number of true positive cases (regardless of whether or not the model identified them as such). Recall is the number of true positives divided by the number of actual positives in the data. In other words, the proportion of positive cases that we were able to identify.

$$Precision = \frac{True\ Positives}{True\ Positives + False\ Positives}$$

$$Recall = \frac{True\ Positives}{True\ Positives + False\ Negatives}$$

Precision should be used when you are trying to reduce false positives, and recall should be used when you are trying to limit false negatives. However, it is generally a bad idea to focus on one of these measures without considering the other. If you *only* care about avoiding false positives, the solution is trivial: you will never produce a false positive if you never predict the positive case! So while one type of error may be more serious than the other, you should consider them *together*. The goal is to strike an acceptable balance between the two types of errors.

One way of considering precision and recall together is to use a measure such as *F-score*, which combines precision and recall into a single measure by computing their harmonic mean as shown below:

$$F = \frac{2}{\text{Recall}^{-1} + \text{Precision}^{-1}}$$

Recalling that precision and recall are proportions, and therefore range between 0 and 1, as precision and recall improve (get closer to 1), the *F*-score will approach 1. As precision and recall get closer to 0, the sum of their inverses grows towards infinity and the *F*-score will approach 0. In short, *F*-scores that are close to 0 are bad and scores that are close to 1 are good.

Sklearn's implementation can be imported from the `metrics` module. Conveniently for us, Sklearn will report the precision, recall, and *F*-score together in a `classification report`. The final column in the report – 'support' – is the number of true instances in that class, or the 'ground truth'. Each class category in the report has its own line, as this is an example of binary classification.

Improving binary classification with curves

Predictions about class labels – Was New Zealand an autocracy in 2020? – depend on some underlying probability threshold. When our model classifies New Zealand as *not* an autocracy, it predicted the negative class because New Zealand is above some probability threshold that separates the boundaries between classes. In other words, the probability of its being a 'not autocracy' is greater than the probability of its being an autocracy. For example, if the probability of a country being an autocracy is greater than 0.5, classify it as an autocracy, otherwise classify it as not an autocracy.

What if there was a different probability threshold? What if, instead, our model would only classify countries as autocracies if the probability of their being in the autocratic class was above 0.8 instead of above 0.5? Shifting the threshold in this way reduces the false positive rate because it would make it harder for any given case to be classified as positive (i.e. autocratic). But what would that do to our rate of false negatives? Does it really matter if we inaccurately classify some autocracies as not autocracies if we prevent our models from incorrectly classifying some non-autocracies as autocracies?

As always, it depends on your case, the questions you are trying to answer, the problems you are solving, and – more than anything else – the consequences of both types of errors. You need to think carefully about these questions every time you begin a machine learning project. Once you have a sense of what an ideal model might look like (e.g. one with very few false positives), you can use precision–recall curves to understand how different probability thresholds separating the positive and negative cases change the balance between false positives and false negatives. We will briefly discuss these, but a full exploration is beyond the scope of this chapter.

Precision-recall curves

How good would your model be if you needed to ensure a minimum of 90% recall – that is, if you needed to correctly identify at least 90% of the true positives in the data? Again, depending on the specifics of your project, maximizing your model's performance on one dimension, *while still being good enough on other dimensions*, is better than relentlessly pursuing small improvements in overall accuracy.

Precision–recall curves let us visualize the trade-offs between these two metrics and understand their impact on the quality of our classifiers at various probability thresholds. Models with high precision and high recall are better, so what we are looking for is a model where the curve is as close as possible to 1 on both axes. Note, however, that we will never *actually* get to 1, because of the inherent trade-off between these two measures.

Alternatively, we can compute the area under the curve, or AUC, to get a one-number summary of the quality of this model. The AUC is not necessarily a better approach when we are assessing one model, but since it is a single-number summary, it does make it easier to compare the performance of multiple models. Very simply, consider a randomly chosen pair of a true positive p and a true negative q: the AUC is a measure of how likely the model is to rank p higher than q, ranging between 0 and 1. A perfect classifier would always rank true positives higher than true negatives, so scores closer to 1 are better. Precision–recall curves are very helpful and informative when the number of cases in each class label is imbalanced.

If you want further information and examples on precision–recall curves, and receiver operating characteristic (ROC) curves, I suggest looking into Géron (2019) and Müller and Guido (2016).

Beyond binary classifiers

So far we have only considered measures for evaluating binary classifiers, but the evaluation metrics for multi-class predictions build on those of the binary tasks, so we can extend what we have just learnt to these more complex models. We don't have the room to cover them here, but if you're interested in exploring multi-class evaluation metrics, feel free to check out our section on them which can be found in the *online supplemental material* for this book.

Further Reading

As with the previous chapter, if you want to learn more about doing supervised machine learning with the models covered in this chapter, and many others, I recommend consulting the relevant chapters from Andreas Müller and Sarah Guido's (2016) *Introduction to Machine Learning with Python* or Aurélien Géron's (2019) *Hands-On Machine Learning with Scikit-Learn, Keras, and TensorFlow*.

21.7 Conclusion

The key points in this chapter are as follows:

* We learnt how to set up, build, fit, and interpret supervised learning with tree-based classifiers, including decision trees and ensemble classifiers.
* We explored how pipelines help prevent data leakage while also facilitating cross-validation.
* We demonstrated the use of parallel processing to expedite model fitting.
* We learnt how to use a variety of performance metrics to balance between false positives and false negatives.
* We created and interpreted graphical measures of threshold trade-offs, including precision–recall and ROC curves.

Visit the website at https://study.sagepub.com/mclevey for additional resources

22

NEURAL NETWORKS AND DEEP LEARNING

22.1 Learning Objectives

By the end of this chapter, you should be able to do the following:

- Describe the basic operation of early neural network models, specifically the perceptron
- Explain the basic components of a neural network and how they work together to learn from data and make predictions
- Explain how 'forward propagation', 'backward propagation', 'gradient descent', and 'autoencoders' improve the performance of neural networks

22.2 Learning Materials

You can find the online learning materials for this chapter in `doing_computational_social_science/Chapter_22`. `cd` into the directory and launch your Jupyter server.

22.3 Introduction

This chapter introduces artificial neural network (ANN) models and deep learning. We will build on the distinctions we drew between the symbolic and connectionist paradigms in Chapter 19. We'll start by introducing the perceptron, which was one of the first artificial simulations of a biological neuron. We will use the perceptron as a relatively simple entry point into the more complex world of contemporary neural network modelling.

Once we have discussed how neural network models work at the level of individual artificial neurons, we will shift our focus to the basic components and algorithms involved in contemporary neural network modelling. We will emphasize the basic components of a multilayer perceptron (MLP) model, as well as the algorithms involved in training these models. More specifically, we will learn how neural network models are organized into layers, with information about our data feeding *forwards* through those layers and information about errors flowing *backwards*. We will learn about activation functions, backpropagation, gradient descent, and learning curves. We will conclude with a high-level discussion of more advanced 'deep learning' neural network architectures and some ethical and political challenges that we need to consider when using them, or when evaluating other research that uses them.

By the end of this chapter, you will have a solid conceptual foundation in neural network modelling and a sense of what makes deep learning so challenging.

22.4 The Perceptron

To really understand how neural networks work, it's necessary to understand what happens at the level of individual artificial neurons. For this reason, we'll start our introduction to neural networks by discussing the first successful attempt to simulate a biological neuron. Recall from Chapter 19 that neural networks are the model family of choice within the connectionist paradigm, which is loosely inspired by biological neural networks and neuroscientific research on perception and cognition more broadly.

The perceptron was a highly simplified model of a biological neuron, proposed by psychologist Frank Rosenblatt (1958). The simulated neuron would receive numerical inputs from multiple sources (i.e. other neurons), each of which would be multiplied by a weight to simulate differences in the strength of each of those incoming signals. Then it would sum all of the weighted inputs and, if the sum exceeded a specific threshold, the perceptron would output 1 (it 'fires'); if not, 0 (it does not fire). Recall the threshold model of complex contagion from Chapter 17 as an analogy. If enough neighbours are activated and sending strong enough signals, ego is likely to activate as well.

For a relatively simple model like this, then, the main questions are as follows:

1   How do you come up with the weights that each simulated neuron uses to multiply incoming signals?
2   What thresholds should you place on the simulated neurons to determine whether the sum of the weighted inputs is enough to cause it to 'fire' (output 1) or not (output 0)?

Rosenblatt's (1958) solution to these problems was influenced by behaviouralist notions of operant conditioning that were dominant in psychology at the time. In brief, he proposed teaching the perceptron to learn the connection weights itself using a process that we would now call supervised learning.

To illustrate the process, imagine you are training a perceptron to differentiate between black and white photos of cats and dogs (which is a pretty tall order for the perceptron, but we'll proceed anyway). In this scenario, your input features are individual pixel values. The number of initial inputs would be equal to however many pixels are in the original image. If each image was 28 pixels by 28 pixels (*much less* than the images we make these days), it would be represented by a total of 784 numerical input features.

To keep things really simple, in this example we will work with just four input features. Figure 22.1 illustrates the basic model. First, we start by assigning weights using a random number generator. It doesn't matter what our initial weights are *as long as they are not all the same*. Positive weights are 'excitatory' and negative weights are 'inhibitory'. The perceptron makes an initial prediction by multiplying each input value with its randomly assigned weight and then summing all of these weighted inputs. For example, in this case, it would perform the following calculation:

$$(0.2 \cdot 0.9) + (0.1 \cdot 0.1) + (0.08 \cdot 0.7) + (0.92 \cdot 0.2) = 0.43$$

If 0.43 is greater than the simulated neuron's fixed threshold, it fires (outputs 1, predicts cat). If not, it does not fire (outputs 0, predicts dog).

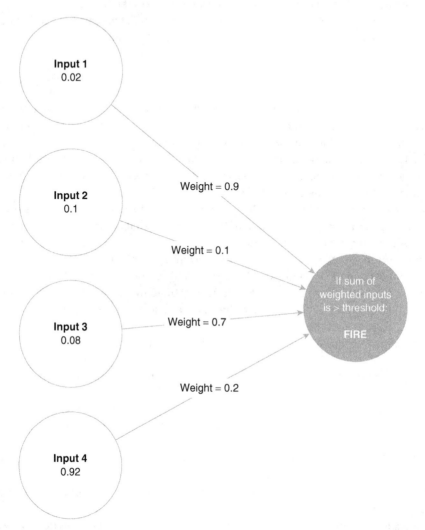

Figure 22.1 The perceptron received numerical inputs, multiplied them by weights to simulate differences in signal strength, and then 'fired' if the sum of weighted inputs was greater than a fixed threshold

Drawing on operant conditioning, if the perceptron makes an incorrect prediction – the image was a dog (output = 0) but the perceptron guessed cat (output = 1) – then it makes a *minor* adjustment to the weights, raising some and lowering others (giving us an early version of supervised learning). Then it makes another prediction on another image using these adjusted weights. It makes further minor adjustments to the weights whenever it makes an incorrect prediction and leaves them as they are when it makes correct predictions.

This is, of course, a dramatically simplified model of neuron. Although contemporary ANNs are considerably more complex, even the more complex models are simple relative to the biological neural networks that inspire them.

It should already be clear from this discussion that symbolic AI (artificial intelligence) and connectionist AI have very different ways of modelling cognition and 'learning' from data. In symbolic AI, declarative knowledge is represented as symbols and rules, and 'cognition' is about performing operations like logical inference on those symbols, as we might when engaging in slow and controlled cognition. Conversely, the connectionist paradigm starts below the level of symbols, with perception itself. Cognition is modelled in the form of massive and dense networks of relatively simple neurons, with 'learning' being a process of adjusting the weights between neurons that are passing information back and forth. Higher-level concepts – or other types of mental representations in a biological neural network – are the products of many neurons firing together.

Brains are 'black boxes' because, as I mentioned in the context of comparing symbolic AI and connectionist AI in Chapter 19, you can't peek inside them and 'see' concepts like cats, Russian Banyas, hardwood flooring, or toxic masculinity. You won't see them if you look inside a perceptron (which is far too simple for anything like this) or a contemporary ANN either (you would just see a massive densely connected network of simulated neurons sending numbers back and forth to one another). These processes are considered *sub-symbolic* because they *underlie* or *give rise* to the higher-level symbols that we *can* communicate about, for example with natural language. That said, in simpler ANN models, it is possible to see individual neurons influencing one another. You can find an excellent interactive example of this at playground.tensorflow.org.

The early perceptron was a very simple machine, but it generated an enormous amount of intellectual hype when Rosenblatt first demonstrated it in the 1950s. Despite the obvious limitations of the model, Rosenblatt and others envisioned networks of these perceptrons processing low-level input signals to perform increasingly difficult high-level tasks, including the kind of computer vision task in our hypothetical example of differentiating between images of cats and dogs. Let's now consider some of the ways that this initial example developed and became more complex, eventually leading to the development of the kinds of neural network models that are dominant today.

22.5 Multilayer Perceptrons

The perceptron provided an important foundation for contemporary ANN models. Let's take a closer look at a powerful extension that is currently in wide use – the multilayer perceptron.

Making sense of layers

As you might expect, MLPs organize networks of simulated neurons into multiple layers: an input layer, one or more hidden layers, and an output layer. This layered organization is illustrated in Figure 22.2.

Our data enters the MLP via the neurons in the input layer. Just like in the perceptron, the input values are numerical. Every neuron in the input layer is connected to every neuron in the hidden layer, and every neuron in the hidden layer is connected to every neuron in the output layer. Therefore, the hidden layer in this MLP is *dense*. Later we will learn that there are other ways of organizing the connections between neurons. This model architecture is also sequential because information has to pass through each layer one at a time to go from one end of the network to another. Non-sequential model architectures are also possible, but we will not discuss them here.

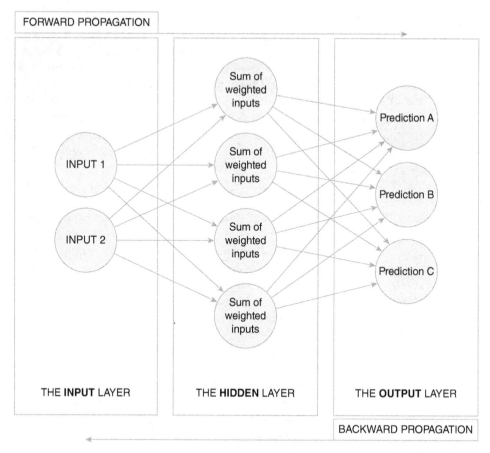

Figure 22.2 Simulated neurons in a multilayer perceptron are assigned to specific layers: an *input* layer, one or more *hidden* layers, and an *output* layer. Information propagates *forwards* (left to right) through the network from the raw data in the input layer to the predictions made in the output later. In training, information about errors are propagated *backwards* (right to left) from the output later to the input layer

Analogous to a biological neural network, the neurons in the input layer send their output values to the nodes in the hidden layers. The neurons in the hidden layer multiply each incoming input value by their weight, which simulates differences in the connection weights between neurons in a biological network. The simulated neuron in the hidden layer then sums all of these weighted inputs to determine what it will output.

Activation functions

At this point, we encounter another important difference between MLPs and their predecessor, the perceptron. Whereas the perceptron had a fixed threshold and would make deterministic binary decisions about whether to fire (1 for yes, 0 for no), the MLP applies an activation function to the sum of weighted inputs and outputs a continuous number. The continuous number is then passed along to all connected neurons in the next layer, which in this case are the neurons in the output layer. There are many possible activation functions one might use, but the three most common are sigmoid, hyperbolic tangent (tanh), and rectified linear unit

(ReLU). We will learn about each in a moment, but first let's clarify what activation functions are simulating *in general*.

Recall from Chapter 19, during our brief discussion of biological neural networks, we learnt that action potentials are triggered in postsynaptic neurons when they receive a level of stimulation that exceeds some threshold. The perceptron simulated this with an actual fixed threshold, and then the neuron would deterministically 'fire' if the weighted sum of inputs exceeds the neuron's threshold. In other words, this is a binary step function that outputs 0s for every number before a threshold and 1s for every number above the threshold. But what if the sum of weighted inputs is just a *wee bit above* or below the threshold?

In a biological neural network, relatively low levels of stimulation are insufficient to trigger an action potential, but once the level of stimulation reaches a certain point, the probability of an action potential jumps way up. Once that point has been reached, additional stimulation has little additional effect. In the 1980s, researchers realized the many benefits of making this simulated process a bit more like the biological process using activation functions. Figure 22.3 illustrates the differences between four different types of activation functions. For each, the x-axis represents the total input from other neurons, and the y-axis represents the neuron's output.

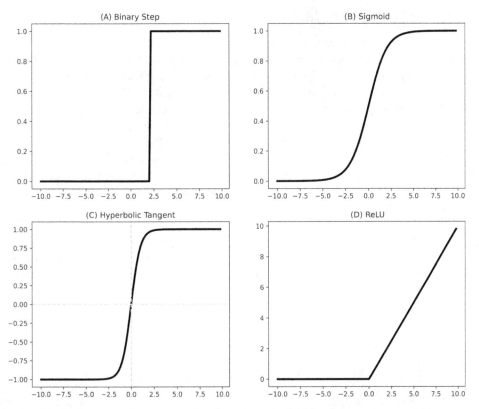

Figure 22.3 Four common activation functions for hidden layer neurons: a binary step function with a hard threshold (A), the sigmoid function (B), the hyperbolic tangent (tanh) function (C), and the rectified linear unit function (ReLU) (D)

The first activation function (Figure 22.3, subplot A) is the original binary step function used in the perceptron: if the sum of weighted inputs exceeds some threshold (in this hypothetical example, the threshold is set to 2), then the neuron outputs 1 (i.e. it fires), else it outputs 0 (i.e. does not fire). In a famous article from 1986, Rumelhart et al. replaced the binary step function with a sigmoid activation function. (You may recognize the sigmoid function, Figure 22.3, subplot B, from the context of logistic regression.) One of the many advantages of their revised approach is that it eliminates entirely the need to use hard thresholds and binary outputs. Instead, the sigmoid function returns a real number between 0 and 1, which can be interpreted as a probability. Similarly, the hyperbolic tangent activation function (Figure 22.3, subplot C) is continuous and S-shaped, but outputs values between −1 and 1.

The fourth activation function shown in Figure 22.3 is the rectified linear unit function, or ReLU, shown in subplot D. ReLU simply accepts the sum of weight inputs, and if the sum is equal to or less than 0, it outputs a 0. If the sum of weighted inputs is greater than 0, it outputs whatever that positive value is. In other words, it also outputs continuous values that have a lower bound of 0 but no upper bound.

The sigmoid, hyperbolic tangent, and ReLU activation functions are all vastly superior to the binary step/hard threshold activation function. Apart from making ANNs slightly closer to their biological counterparts, these functions all output continuous values, which turns out to be *very* useful when training ANNs.

What about the output layer?

Once we've added as many layers consisting of as many neurons as we care to include, we're ready to create an output layer. Neural networks provide you with a remarkable degree of latitude when constructing them; the output layer is no exception. It's up to you to decide what the best output layer for your ANN will be; that decision will rest, in large part, on whether you're interested in performing, for example, a regression task (numerical approximation of a continuous variable) or a classification task (probabilistically sorting observations/cases into two or more different classes). If you're performing a regression task, you can get away with using a simple single-neuron output layer with a fully linear activation function; this will effectively end up producing a (scaled) numerical output representing the summed-up weighted signals from each of the neurons in the preceding layer. If you're performing a classification task with two labels/classes, you can use an output layer that replicates the functionality of a logistic regression. For classification tasks with more than two labels/classes, you can use a 'softmax' activation function, which is a generalization of logistic regression into larger numbers of categories. An intuitive interpretation of a softmax-powered output layer might view it as allowing each part of the preceding layer to 'vote' on which of the categories that part thinks the item belongs to. The softmax function then normalizes each of the 'scores' for each category into a series of probabilities that sum to 1; the item is classified as belonging to the class with the highest probability.

22.6 Training ANNs with Backpropagation and Gradient Descent

One of the major challenges that held back advancing this model for quite some time was that training a multilayered ANN is far more complex than a single neuron (e.g. a perceptron). When ANNs make incorrect predictions, how do we know which weights in the hidden layer of the network to adjust? The possible paths from input through the hidden layer to the output are very complex, and every mistaken prediction could be the result of any number of thousands or millions of weights and thresholds. Which ones should change, in what direction, and by how much? Backpropagation is an algorithm that enables us to answer these questions and better train our ANNs.

Backpropagation

When neurons in the hidden layers of an ANN output continuous values, rather than a binary decision, we can quantify the extent to which each individual weighted connection contributed to an overall prediction error. Just as information flows forwards from an input to a final prediction, it is possible to send information about errors *backwards* from the final prediction to the input layers. This is called backpropagation. The algorithm itself was developed in the 1970s, but Rumelhart et al. (1986) famously showed its usefulness in the context of neural network modelling, and it has greatly improved the ANN training process. In fact, backpropagation may be the most important algorithm in ANN modelling.

Working backwards from a prediction, the backpropagation algorithm starts by using a loss function to compute an overall measure of prediction error. The specific loss function used depends on the context. If you are training a neural network on a regression problem, then mean-squared error (MSE) is a good choice. If you are training a neural network for a multi-class classification problem, categorical cross entropy is a better choice. In short, the loss function you use depends on the type of model you are developing. Once the overall error has been computed, the next step is to calculate how much each individual weight in the ANN contributed to that error. Each weight can then be adjusted in the direction that would best minimize the overall prediction error. These adjustments are *minor* and *local*. Very small adjustments are made to weights based on the impact those changes would have only on connected neurons.

Training an ANN with backpropagation involves two processes for each example provided in training: a forward pass and a backward pass. During the forward pass, information is sent through the network from the input layer, through the hidden layer, and out the output layer. As in Figure 22.3, you can picture this as information moving from left to right. The neurons in the hidden layer output continuous values that result from applying an activation function to the inputs they receive from the neurons in the layer below them. The neurons in the output layer apply a different activation function, but we will discuss that later.

The backward pass starts after a prediction has been made. First, an overall prediction error is computed using a loss function such as MSE or categorical cross entropy. Then the contribution that each connection weight makes to that overall error is computed, and then small adjustments are made to the weights such that the overall error is minimized. Once the adjustments are made, training can proceed with the next example.

Gradient descent

The changes made to connection weights are governed by an optimization algorithm called gradient descent. *In general*, gradient descent is used to find parameter values for some function that minimizes the loss, or cost, as much as possible. In the case of ANN modelling, our goal is to find the optimal values for all of the connection weights across all layers in our ANN. With gradient descent, we do that by making small modifications to the connection weights over *many* iterations. We start with our randomized weights and adjust them iteratively during training, example after example, until we have values that minimize the overall loss measured by our loss function.

In Figure 22.4, loss is represented on the *y*-axis, and the range of possible weight values is represented on the *x*-axis. The connection weights range from –1 to 1, as they might if we were using the hyperbolic tangent activation function (tanh). Let's say that our randomly selected starting point is the point S1 (for 'Step 1'). If this was the value used for the connection weight, the loss for that weight would be the corresponding *y*-value (which in this hypothetical example is not actually shown). If the connection weight was a little higher (e.g. shifted to the right a bit), the loss would decrease. Therefore, we increase our connection weight a bit in the next step, from –0.79 to –0.59, and reduce our loss a little bit.

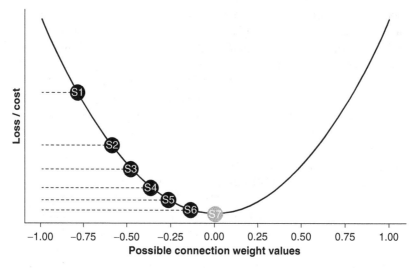

Figure 22.4 An illustration of gradient descent to iteratively find connection weight values that minimize loss. In this example, the optimal weight is 0, but it could have been any value between –1 and 1

At each step, the algorithm calculates how much the loss would change if the weight value was slightly different. Each potential new weight value has a gradient, or slope. Since we want to minimize loss, gradient descent will select a weight value that lets it *descend* (the opposite would be gradient ascent).

We continue these relatively small steps for S3, S4, S5, and S6, gradually increasing the connection weight and reducing the loss. By S7, we reach a connection weight that minimizes the loss. We have *converged* to the minimum loss. From this position, any further adjustments to the connection weight *regardless of the direction* would increase the loss (and would be gradient *ascent*). We can't minimize the loss any further.

Each step in Figure 22.4 is a learning step. The size of these steps is determined by a learning rate parameter in our ANN. In general, small steps are better because they reduce the chance of accidentally stepping over the optimal weight value. In our example, it might mean stepping over the optimal value at the bottom of the curve (0), climbing back up the curve on the other side, and then bouncing back and forth without ever stopping on the optimal value. The downside of using small learning rates is that it takes longer, and more iterations, to find the value that minimizes loss.

There is no reason to assume that the loss function has a nice single-valley shape like the one in Figure 22.4. It could have a wide variety of shapes, such as the one shown in Figure 22.5. This illustrates another issue that we might encounter when using gradient descent to find the optimal value for the connection weights in our ANN. First, imagine you have a random starting point: in this case, the grey S1 point. From here, gradient descent makes adjustments, each time reducing the loss by gradually increasing the weights with Steps 2 to 6 (all represented with the grey points). After the sixth step, any further increases in the connection weight start *increasing* the loss. Gradient descent *thinks* it has found an optimal weight, but it hasn't. It's stuck on a local minimum and doesn't know about the global minimum that it might have found if the random starting point had been the black S1 point further to the right of the figure.

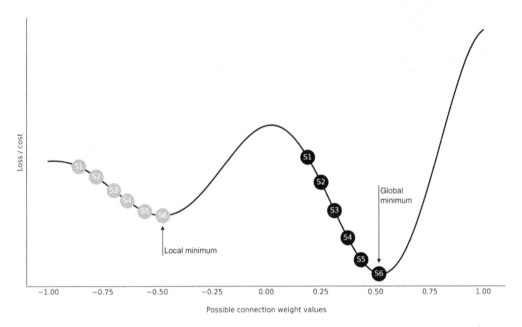

Figure 22.5 An illustration of gradient descent to iteratively find connection weight values that minimize loss

Clearly, the black S6 point in Figure 22.5 is better than the grey S6 point because it has a lower loss value. The more complex the terrain produced by the loss function, the more challenging it is to converge on the *global* minimum. There are variations on the basic gradient descent algorithm that can help with this problem. Stochastic gradient descent (SGD), for example, computes the gradients based on a randomly selected subset of the training data. This causes the loss values to jump around a lot more at each step, but over many iterations, it greatly reduces the risk of getting stuck in local minima and increases the chance we will get at least very close to the global minimum.

Learning curves

As an ANN trains, it uses backpropagation and gradient descent to iteratively tune the weights until it converges on a locally optimal solution (which isn't always the globally optimal solution). It goes through data *repeatedly* to do this. Each pass through the data is a single epoch of training.

As we will see in the next chapter, we can calculate various performance measures during each epoch of training; it is often helpful to plot these measures. Figure 22.6 illustrates this for a hypothetical ANN. In this example, we can see that the accuracy rates for both the training and validation data increases with each epoch and that the two rates are very close together (which suggests the model is not overfitting).

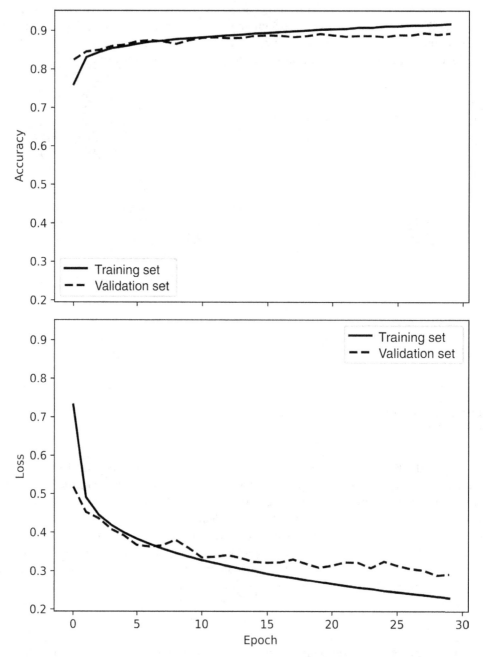

Figure 22.6 Accuracy and loss metrics for the test and validation data at each epoch of training

22.7 More Complex ANN Architectures

Now that we've discussed some fairly simple neural network models and I've explained how some key algorithms (e.g. gradient descent) work, let's turn our attention to some more complex ANN architectures. Focus on the big picture here. The goal here is still conceptual; we want to understand, at a high level, what these types of models do and how they work. I will refer back to these models in later chapters (at which point you might want to flip back to these pages to remind yourself of the big picture).

Stacked autoencoders

Autoencoders are a type of ANN that attempt to produce an output identical to whatever input was received, which is not as pointless as it might sound. Autoencoders have hidden layers that are smaller than their input and output layers. By trying to produce an output that is identical to their inputs, they learn how to create a high-quality representation with a smaller number of bits. (You can think of this as analogous to file compression; when you zip a file, the same file contents are represented using fewer bits.) In practice, this introduces a lot of computational problems, so instead we can use a clever trick. We make the hidden layer *bigger* than the input and output layers, but at any given moment only a small portion of those neurons are allowed to be active, meaning the autoencoder is still forced to learn a more compact representation, but the maths is easier.

Increasingly sophisticated representations can be learnt when autoencoders are stacked together, with the outputs of one becoming the inputs for another. With each autoencoder, the representations are less like low-level perceptual patterns and more like higher-level mental representations analogous to the types of symbols that feature in cognitive science and symbolic AI, such as rules, frames, schemas, scripts, and concepts. In this way, we can use autoencoders as a form of neural-network based-dimensionality reduction; their low-dimensional representations of high-dimensional objects can be very useful! We will see some examples of this later in the book.

Convolutional neural networks

Convolutional neural networks (CNNs, or ConvNets) are ubiquitous in computer vision – working with image data – and are increasingly also used in natural language processing. They were first introduced in the 1980s by Yann LeCun, who was inspired by the work of Kunihiko Fukushima on some of the first deep neural networks developed for computer vision tasks, in this case recognizing handwritten digits. Two of the most common computer vision tasks that CNNs are currently used for are as follows:

1 Image classification
2 Object detection/recognition

Like neural networks, more generally, CNNs are biologically *inspired*. In particular, they are inspired primarily by our brain's vision system. Let's take a moment to understand some basics of the biology to better understand how the artificial version works. It is important to remember that the artificial versions depart from their biological inspirations in important ways; CNNs don't need to work like their biological counterparts any more than an aircraft should fly the same way birds do, but the biology helps provide a framework for making sense of CNNs.

From biological vision to artificial vision

How do we see? The eyes play a very important role, of course, but the brain doesn't simply receive images provided by the eyes. It actively *constructs* those representations. Our retinas convert patterns of light into neural signals using photoreceptors (consisting of rod and cone cells). Special neurons in the retina (bipolar cells) detect light areas on dark background and dark areas on bright backgrounds. Then, at a higher level of neural processing, retinal ganglion cells respond to differences in light within their own receptive field. These cells may activate depending on whether there is light in the centre or the edges of their receptive field, or in some particular orientation (e.g. horizontal), to which they are especially sensitive. Together they enable the detection of edges and other low-level building blocks of vision (Ward, 2020).

After this fairly minimal amount of processing, a neural signal is sent from the eyes to the brain via the optic nerve, where it splits into several different pathways. The most important, for our purposes, is the pathway to the primary visual cortex, located in the back of our brain. Starting in the late 1950s, David Hubel and Torsten Wiesel made a series of discoveries that revealed the *hierarchical* organization our visual system, in which complex abstract representations are built from the bottom up by combining simple low-level representations (e.g. edges). In addition, there is a *top-down* process where our brains are actively involved in the construction of those representations, for example by filling in missing bits of information and creating a three-dimensional model of our environment from two-dimensional inputs (Ward, 2020). These *backward* connections are important – they outnumber the *forward* connections – but are not currently well-understood (Mitchell, 2019).

In the primary visual cortex, then, neurons are organized into hierarchical layers, with those on the bottom detecting low-level features, like edges. The layers above it detect more complex features, from relatively simple shapes to more complex ones, eventually resulting in our conscious perception of faces, objects, and the rest of our environments (Ward, 2020).

How CNNs process data: from pixels to predictions

CNNs, like other ANNs, are inspired by this biology, but they don't mirror it exactly. Drawing on the hierarchical organization of the visual system, CNNs are made up of a sequence of *layers* of neurons, with each layer in the sequence sending its output to the layers of neurons that come next, where they are processed as inputs. As with the MLP and other neural networks, each of these artificial neurons has an activation value that is computed from an input value and a weight.

Let's say we have an image of a cat. We can represent that image as a matrix that encodes information about the brightness and colour of each individual pixel in the image. Each neuron in the first layer corresponds to one of those pixels in the image, so they must be the same size. In other words, if there are 12 million pixels (as there are in an image from an iPhone in 2021, for example), then there must be 12 million neurons in the CNN's first layer.

Each hidden layer in the CNN is itself made up of multiple activation maps (also called feature maps), directly inspired by the hierarchical nature of the vision system. The neurons in each of these activation maps are organized like a grid, with each neuron responding to specific features within specific regions of the image like retinal ganglion cells responding to specific patterns of light within their individual receptive fields. Each activation map is focused on different types of visual features. As in the brain, some activation maps are focused on very low-level features such as edges, detected by variations in the distribution and intensity of reflected light. In layers focused on edge detection, the simulated neurons activate when they detect an edge *within their narrow receptive field* that matches some specific orientation: horizontal, vertical, or any other angle. Their receptive field is a specific pixel location in the input image and a small surrounding area that overlaps with the receptive fields of other simulated neurons in the same activation map.

This is the most important way in which CNNs differ from other types of neural networks that have *dense* layers. The *convolutional* layers in a CNN are designed to learn patterns that are local, in other words within a narrow receptive field. In contrast, the type of neural networks we have learnt about before now had *dense* layers, where every neuron in one layer feeds into every neuron in the next layer, learning more *global* patterns from the entire image. As Chollet (2018) notes, this means that CNNs only have to learn a pattern once; if they learn it in one part of an image, they will recognize it in other parts of the image without having to relearn it, as a densely connected layer would. As a result, CNNs are more efficient with image training data than are networks with densely connected layers.

Each neuron has an activation value that represents the extent to which the input numbers in its receptive field match its expectation, such as for a horizontal edge. Let's say that the receptive field of a given neuron is a grid of 3 by 3 pixels. The numbers for each of the 9 pixels represent how bright the pixel is, from 0 to 255. As with more basic neural network models, these pixel values are multiplied by a given weight. All of these weighted inputs are summed, and the resulting activation value can be passed on.

Within any given activation map inside any given layer, the simulated neurons all use the same weights. In other words, they all multiply the inputs from the pixels within their receptive fields by the same weights before summing them to produce their activation value. Each of these processes of multiplying the inputs in a receptive field by the weights shared by neurons in the same activation map is called a convolution.

Each layer of the CNN has its own set of activation maps, each of which is a grid of neurons looking for a particular pattern within its narrow receptive field. These layers are called convolutional layers. The activation values that result from summing each weighted input are passed from that layer into the next as a new set of input values. Inspired by our biological vision system, the initial layers are focused on very low-level features such as edges, and subsequent layers combine these low-level patterns into more complex shapes and objects. The number of activation maps in each layer and the number of layers in any given CNN vary and are controlled by the researcher.

If we are training our CNN to perform a classification task – like classifying whether images contain a patch of trees or not – then the activation values from the penultimate layer of the CNN are passed to a classification module. This module is itself a neural network that will predict the likelihood of a patch of trees given the input values from the final layer in the CNN, which encodes information about the most high-level features in the image (e.g. grass, leaves, tree branches). The classification model outputs the probability of the image containing a patch of trees. If it were an object detection model, it would output probabilities that the image contains any of the types of objects it knows about.

Other than the organization of layers into activation maps and the process of performing convolutions on the inputs of each neuron's receptive field, CNNs operate like other ANNs. The weights, for example, are learnt using backpropagation during a supervised learning training process. Each pass through the data is a training epoch, and typically many of these are required to train a CNN. When the network 'converges' on a good set of learnt weights, the error is diffused as much as possible via backpropagation, training is complete, and if the model is a good one, you can start using it to make predictions on unseen data.

Biased training data for computer vision: ethical and political concerns

Earlier, I mentioned that CNNs were initially developed by Yann LeCun in the 1980s, but they became ubiquitous in computer vision only recently, and the models have changed little since they were first introduced. Rather, the massive explosion of data and the rapid increases in computing power brought CNNs into the spotlight. A number of widely used training datasets, such as ImageNet, have played an important role in this development, and more recently, social media platforms like Flickr and Facebook that serve up massive collections of labelled datasets harvested from users, such as people tagged in photos posted to Facebook.

There are some *major* ethical and political issues to consider here. First, there is the market for your data; it is entirely possible that your images (as in photos you upload to sites like Facebook or Flickr), uploaded and tagged, are in a training dataset somewhere, perhaps even a public one like ImageNet. But a less obvious, and even more consequential, set of issues concern biases embedded in these massive training datasets, and more importantly appalling misogyny and racism (Buolamwini and Gebru, 2018; Crawford and Paglen, 2019; Gebru, 2020; Steed and Caliskan, 2021; Vries et al., 2019). Crawford and Paglen (2019) state the problem plainly at the start of 'Excavating AI: The politics of images in machine learning training sets':

> you open up a database of pictures used to train AI systems. At first, things seem straightforward. You're met with thousands of images: apples and oranges, birds, dogs, horses, mountains, clouds, houses, and street signs. But as you probe further into the dataset, people begin to appear: cheerleaders, scuba divers, welders, Boy Scouts, fire walkers, and flower girls. Things get strange: A photograph of a woman smiling in a bikini is labeled a 'slattern, slut, slovenly woman, trollop.' A young man drinking beer is categorized as an 'alcoholic, alky, dipsomaniac, boozer, lush, soaker, souse.' A child wearing sunglasses is classified as a 'failure, loser, non-starter, unsuccessful person.' You're looking at the 'person' category in a dataset called ImageNet, one of the most widely used training sets for machine learning. Something is obviously very wrong here. (https://excavating.ai/?fbclid=IwAR0nw_F_f6CMMaJuYem45ODpWPZtomtkJ_-704-zMJVML_fza0_tO45Ye2Q

Sometimes the biases are in the relationship between the image and its label, as with the examples that Crawford and Paglen (2019) cite. In other situations, it is due to asymmetries in who is represented in images and how they are represented (e.g. Buolamwini and Gebru, 2018; Gebru, 2020). White men, for example, are generally far more represented in these training datasets than other people, and as a result, CNNs trained on these datasets tend to perform far better for white men than they do for women or racialized people. For example, a CNN could classify a person as a woman because the person is standing in a kitchen, and the training data contains many more images of women in kitchens than men in kitchens.

A good example of these issues is the 80 Million Tiny Images dataset that was created by and formerly hosted by researchers at MIT (Massachusetts Institute of Technology; see Prabhu and Birhane, 2020). The dataset consisted of images scraped from the web and was annotated using crowdsourcing. However, after being in wide use for 14 years, it was discovered that the training data contained thousands of images annotated with racial slurs, not to mention labels such as 'rape suspect'. The dataset was also found to include many deeply problematic images that were clearly taken (and of course circulated) without consent, such as pictures taken up skirts.

One especially high-profile illustration of the implications of racially biased training data happened in 2015 when Google released a new feature in its photo app that would tag images with captions derived from a CNN trained to classify the primary contents of an image. Because of training data biased towards white people, the CNN tagged a selfie of two black people with 'Gorillas' (Mitchell, 2019). Obviously, this is unacceptable, and any applications of CNNs on image data – including for research in computational social science, not just commercial applications – need to directly address the issues of training data with racial and other biases.

As you know from Chapter 18, there is an ongoing debate about what we should do, given that biases in training data – not just image training data – reflect real biases and inequalities in the real world. On the one hand, we can learn more about these biases and inequalities from the problems that arise from models trained on these biased data. While there may be some merit to this idea within a purely scientific context, datasets used to train these models are very difficult and expensive to collect and build. It's not like we could easily separate out train-ing datasets for commercial applications, in which we work hard to reduce biases, from those intended for scientific research on bias, where we let those biases remain. The same training data is used in both contexts. So at best, using biased training data to study bias is making the best of a bad situation. These biases are amplified by the models and feed back into society, and as we saw in Chapter 18, these negative feedback loops create and solidify inequalities, especially when they are part of facial recognition systems or are part of opaque automated decision-making processes.

While CNNs have many positive benefits in the world, including healthcare applications assisting in diagnoses using medical imaging data, others are obviously deeply problematic and rightfully controversial. None more so than facial recognition (or really anything that involves classifying people), which is used not just to help you find pictures of your friends and adorable cats in your personal digital photo library, but also by police departments and many others. Privacy concerns, as well as the negative consequences of mistakes resulting from hidden biases, disproportionately affect racialized people. Regulation is clearly needed, but we are in the early days of this political debate. Most of the discussion in Europe at the time of writing is focused on transparency and the 'right to explanation' in the context of automated decision-making, such as whether you get a loan or probation. As Melanie Mitchell (2019), Timnet Gebru (2018), and many others have pointed out, debates about the ethics, politics, and risks of deep learning have been far too concerned with the potential threats of intelligent machines and far too unconcerned with the very real and immediate threats of opaque errors rooted in deeply embedded racial and gender biases.

Data isn't the only culprit here. Nor is it the only solution. As computational social scien-tists, it is incumbent upon us to actively interrogate the fairness of the models that we build. If we find them lacking, it is not enough to simply blame the data and move on; we must confront the problem head on. It is up to us to fix our data – to proactively build fairness into what we do.

━━━━━━━━ **Further Reading** ━━━━━━━━━━━━━━━━

Chapter 10 from Géron's (2019) *Hands-On Machine Learning* and the first several chapters of Chollet's (2018) *Deep Learning with Python* offer a deeper dive into neural network modelling than the introduction in this book. Chollet is the original developer of Keras, the Python package we'll use to develop a simple neural network model in the next chapter.

22.8 Conclusion

The key points in this chapter are as follows:

- This chapter introduced neural network models, shallow and deep.
- We examined some early neural network models – the perceptron and Boltzmann machine – and the multilayer perceptron.
- We learnt how the 'backward propagation' and 'gradient descent' addressed critical limitations in their modelling frameworks.
- We explored the difference between 'shallow' and 'deep' neural networks.
- We learnt about an approach to deep learning that involves stacking together 'autoencoders'.
- We learnt about the basics of convolutional neural networks.
- We learnt about ethical and political challenges in deep learning, especially in regards to working with image data.

Visit the website at https://study.sagepub.com/mclevey for additional resources

23

DEVELOPING NEURAL NETWORK MODELS WITH KERAS AND TENSORFLOW

23.1 Learning Objectives

By the end of this chapter, you should be able to do the following:

- Explain how TensorFlow and Keras are related
- Describe how to build a neural network using the Keras sequential API
- Recognize when a model is overfitting and take steps to regularize the model
- Use diagnostic tools, such as the confusion matrix, to assess model fit

23.2 Learning Materials

You can find the online learning materials for this chapter in `doing_computational_social_science/Chapter_23`. cd into the directory and launch your Jupyter server.

23.3 Introduction

Now that you've had a high-level conceptual introduction to artificial neural networks (ANNs), we can start building and training models from the ground up. In this chapter, we will develop ANNs to predict the political affiliation of a politician based on the content of their parliamentary speeches. We'll tackle this problem by developing and training a very simple ANN on the UK Hansard data; in so doing, we'll explore a number of issues related to model construction and overfitting.

Imports

As always, let's begin by importing packages and our dataset. The data we are using is a little large, so be aware that it might take a few minutes for Pandas to load the entire dataframe into memory. To help cut down on the amount of data we're loading, we'll only use a subset of the columns present in the raw dataset and pre-filter the data by dropping any columns that have a null value in the `party`, `speakername`, or `speech` columns.

```
import pandas as pd
pd.set_option("display.notebook_repr_html", False)

import seaborn as sns
import matplotlib.pyplot as plt
from dcss.plotting import custom_seaborn
custom_seaborn()

from numpy.random import seed
from tensorflow.random import set_seed
set_seed(42)
seed(42)

columns = ['speech', 'speakername', 'party', 'constituency', 'year']
uk_df = pd.read_csv("../data/british_hansards/hansard-speeches-v301.csv", usecols=
    columns).dropna(subset=['party', 'speakername', 'speech'])

uk_df.info()

<class 'pandas.core.frame.DataFrame'>
Int64Index: 2392186 entries, 6 to 2651218
Data columns (total 5 columns):
 #   Column       Dtype
---  ------       -----
 0   speech       object
 1   party        object
 2   constituency object
 3   year         int64
 4   speakername  object
dtypes: int64(1), object(4)
memory usage: 109.5+ MB
```

We now have a dataframe of more than 2,000,000 rows representing individual speeches given in the British House of Commons, and each of the five columns beyond the first provides meta-data about that speech (who was speaking, what party they belong to, etc.).

There's a *lot* of data to work with, and as useful as such an abundance could be, working with such a large dataset might pose a bit of a challenge to older or less-powerful computing set-ups. As such, we'll filter our dataframe so that it only includes speeches delivered from 2015 to 2019, inclusive:

```
uk_df = uk_df[uk_df['year'].isin([2015, 2016, 2017, 2018, 2019])]
```

Filtering the data

From the general view of the dataframe alone, we can already see some places where it may be prudent to trim the data down. Since we're interested in predicting party affiliation, we should ensure that each of the rows in our dataset – and, hence, every speech we consider – was spoken by someone who we can identify as a person belonging to a political party (or, more restrictively, was speaking in an overtly partisan capacity). Let's summarize the 'party' column:

```
uk_df['party'].value_counts()
```

```
Conservative                           188154
Labour                                  71317
Scottish National Party                 22664
Speaker                                 12704
Labour (Co-op)                          12655
Liberal Democrat                         7168
Democratic Unionist Party                4885
Independent                              2046
Plaid Cymru                              1482
Social Democratic & Labour Party          722
Green Party                               675
Ulster Unionist Party                     324
The Independent Group for Change          155
UK Independence Party                     141
Change UK - The Independent Group          90
Alliance                                   28
Respect                                    18
Name: party, dtype: int64
```

A significant portion of the speeches in our dataset was delivered by a party known as the 'Speaker' party. There is no 'Speaker' party in the UK. This is what our dataset uses to indicate that a speech was delivered by the Speaker of the House. The Speaker is ostensibly a non-partisan position, and so we would do well to exclude all of the speaker's speeches from consideration:

```
uk_df = uk_df.drop(uk_df[uk_df['party'] == 'Speaker'].index)
uk_df['party'].value_counts()
```

```
Conservative                           188154
Labour                                  71317
Scottish National Party                 22664
Labour (Co-op)                          12655
Liberal Democrat                         7168
Democratic Unionist Party                4885
Independent                              2046
Plaid Cymru                              1482
Social Democratic & Labour Party          722
Green Party                               675
Ulster Unionist Party                     324
The Independent Group for Change          155
UK Independence Party                     141
Change UK - The Independent Group          90
Alliance                                   28
Respect                                    18
Name: party, dtype: int64
```

We also want to limit our analysis to those speeches which impart some kind of substantive information; there are many 'speeches' that consist of only one or two words. We can see some of them by sorting the list of speeches by the number of characters they contain and returning 20 of the smallest:

```
sorted(list(uk_df['speech']), key=lambda x: len(x))[10:20]
```

```
['No.', 'No.', 'No.', 'Oh!', 'No.', 'No.', 'No.', 'No.', 'Me?', 'No.']
```

A significant portion of our corpus is composed of vanishingly brief utterances. Rather than spend hours sleuthing through the data to find the perfect cut-off point, let's assume that any 'speech' which contains fewer than 200 characters is unlikely to be of much value in determining the political leaning of the person who delivered it.

```
uk_df.drop(uk_df[uk_df['speech'].apply(lambda x: len(x)) < 200].axes[0], inplace=True)
```

Categorizing affiliation

Now, we're ready to categorize our data. We'll do this by adding a new column to our dataframe indicating the political affiliation of the politician giving the speech. There are a few parties, such as 'Labour (Co-op)' and 'Liberal', which we will combine with their 'parent' party. The 'Liberal' Party was the senior partner in the 1988 merger which created the Liberal Democratic Party, and 'Labour (Co-op)' is a special appellation applied to MPs elected under the auspices of a co-operation agreement between the Labour and the (aptly named) Co-Operation Party.

We also create an 'other' category containing the names of all the parties that aren't included in one of the other lists (right, centre, left, national):

```
right = ['Conservative']
centre = ['Liberal Democrat']
left = ['Labour', 'Labour (Co-op)']
national = ['Scottish National Party']
other = list(uk_df['party'].value_counts().axes[0].drop([*right, *left, *centre, *
    national]))

uk_df.loc[uk_df['party'].isin(right), 'affiliation'] = "centre-right"
uk_df.loc[uk_df['party'].isin(centre), 'affiliation'] = "centre"
uk_df.loc[uk_df['party'].isin(left), 'affiliation'] = "centre-left"
uk_df.loc[uk_df['party'].isin(national), 'affiliation'] = "national"
uk_df.loc[uk_df['party'].isin(other), 'affiliation'] = "other"

uk_df['affiliation'].value_counts()
```

```
centre-right    158835
centre-left      66887
national         18195
other             8975
centre            6007
Name: affiliation, dtype: int64
```

Taking a stratified sample

There are a couple of other issues we should tackle before going any further. The first is that we have a large imbalance between the various categories; the centre-right dominates the data to the extent that all of the other speeches combined only amount to about two-thirds of the Conservative Party's tally. The second issue is that we simply have too many speeches! We can solve both problems simultaneously by taking a stratified random sample, where we ensure we draw an equal number of speeches from each of the five categories. In order to keep run times modest, let's draw 3000 speeches from each category:

```
uk_df_strat = uk_df.groupby("affiliation", group_keys=False).apply(lambda x: x.sample
    (3000))
uk_df_strat.affiliation.value_counts()
```

```
centre-right    3000
centre-left     3000
other           3000
national        3000
centre          3000
Name: affiliation, dtype: int64
```

Lemmatizing speech

Finally, machine learning algorithms and statistical models alike can get tripped up on trivial differences between semantically similar words. You've already used spaCy to lemmatize a series of documents, intelligently reducing each word (or token) to a basic form that's identical across all tenses, conjugations, and contexts. We'll do the same here (depending on the computing power available to you, this cell might take a while to run):

```
import spacy
from tqdm import tqdm
nlp = spacy.load('en_core_web_sm', disable=['ner', 'textcat', 'parser'])
lem_speeches = []
for doc in tqdm(nlp.pipe(uk_df_strat['speech']), total=15000):
    lem_speeches.append([tok.lemma_ for tok in doc if not tok.is_punct])
lem_speeches_joined = []
for speech in lem_speeches:
    lem_speeches_joined.append(" ".join(speech))
```

```
100%|| 15000/15000 [03:10<00:00, 78.81it/s]
```

With our categories in place, our sample stratified, and our speeches lemmatized, we're ready to get started with ANNs!

23.4 Getting Started With Keras

We're going to be using a combination of TensorFlow and Keras. TensorFlow is a tensor-processing library developed and maintained by Google; it has a wide variety of uses, but it is best known for its neural network applications. TensorFlow is powerful and widely applicable, but it can also be prohibitively difficult to pick up, learn, and use. This is where Keras comes in: formerly, Keras served as a dedicated network API capable of using its comparatively simple ANN syntax to power model training using a wide variety of computational back ends (Theano, MXNet, R, etc.). As of Keras's June 2020 release (version 2.4.0), it is a dedicated interface for TensorFlow exclusively.

For the purposes of this chapter, we'll mostly be working with Keras. When using Keras to build a typical ANN from scratch, you'll generally work your way through the following stages of development:

1. Load, clean, and preprocess data.
2. Define a Keras model and add layers to it.
3. Select a loss function, optimizer, and output metrics for our model.
4. Train and evaluate our model.
5. Select a model.
6. Use the final selected model to make predictions.

Progress through the six steps described above is usually non-linear (save for the final two); when training and evaluating a model, for example, we might find that the model is underperforming or behaving erratically – this might prompt us to return to the third step (e.g. using a different loss function) or the second step (e.g. reconfiguring our model's layers) multiple times. Remember: Box's loop!

Preprocessing/prep work

Even though we preprocessed our data when we first imported, there are a few additional hurdles before we proceed. First, we need to explicitly think through what our inputs and our outputs are going to look like. Conceptually, this should be simple: we want our ANN to take in the full text of a speech delivered in the British House of Commons (our input), and spit out the political leaning of the person who wrote and/or delivered the speech (our output). Thus, we have a classification task.

Now we can start thinking of building a model for our data. ANNs are mathematical constructs and don't generally handle non-numerical input or output values smoothly. We're going to have to use some techniques to transform our data into something our ANN can use. We'll start with the outputs.

Encoding the 'affiliation' column

Currently, the 'affiliation' column in our dataframe is human-readable:

```
uk_df_strat[['affiliation']].sample(5, random_state=1)

        affiliation
2484517 centre-right
2526073     national
2593758  centre-left
2439383  centre-left
2480384       centre
```

This is convenient for us, but we need to create a numerical representation for the ANN. We can do this using scikit-learn's LabelBinarizer. The LabelBinarizer will take in the entire 'affiliation' column and return a series of vectors, each of which will contain five integers – one for each of the categories we defined above. In each of these vectors, one of the integers will be a 1, and the rest will be 0. You might be wondering why we don't just convert the column into a series of numbers ranging from 0 to 4. Doing so would not be in our model's interests; the party classifications are categorical, and even though we've decided to describe them using a left–right continuum, using a numerical scale in our model would implicitly cast the Liberal Democrats as being 'one point' more right-leaning than the Labour Party. We don't want that.

```
from sklearn.preprocessing import LabelBinarizer
affiliation_encoder = LabelBinarizer()
affiliation_encoder.fit(uk_df_strat['affiliation'])
aff_transformed = affiliation_encoder.transform(uk_df_strat['affiliation'])
pd.DataFrame(aff_transformed).sample(5, random_state=1)
```

```
        0 1 2 3 4
7576    0 0 1 0 0
10509   0 0 0 1 0
4253    0 1 0 0 0
5150    0 1 0 0 0
506     1 0 0 0 0
```

Compare the first five rows of the 'affiliation' column with the first five rows of our transformed affiliation data. You'll see the entries in each row of our aff_transformed variable correspond with one of the five 'affiliation' categories. When there's a 1 in the leftmost position and 0 in every other position, that corresponds to the 'centre' affiliation.

We're going to use term frequency–inverse document frequency (TF-IDF; which you've also encountered elsewhere in the book) on the entire corpus of speeches. Here again, we can use scikit-learn to help us:

```
from sklearn.feature_extraction.text import TfidfVectorizer
speech_vectorizer = TfidfVectorizer(strip_accents='unicode', stop_words='english',
    min_df=0.01)
speech_transformed = speech_vectorizer.fit_transform(lem_speeches_joined)


speech_vectorizer.get_feature_names()[40:50]
```

```
['abuse',
'accept',
'access',
'accord',
'account',
'achieve',
'acknowledge',
'act',
'action',
'activity']
```

We now have access to two NumPy arrays – `aff_transformed` and `speech_transformed` – which contain numerical representations of political affiliation and word counts for each speech in our filtered dataset. There should be one entry (row) in `aff_transformed` for each entry (row) in `speech_transformed`. We can confirm this by comparing their 'shape' attributes:

```
aff_transformed.shape
```

```
(15000, 5)
```

```
speech_transformed.shape
```

```
(15000, 1170)
```

In both cases, the first number contained in the `shape` attribute is the number of rows in the array. Both should be the same. They should also have two entries in their `shape` attribute – this means that they are two-dimensional arrays. We can think of the first value as the number of rows contained in the array and the second value as the number of columns. Even though `aff_transformed` and `speech_transformed` must have the same number of rows, they don't need to have the same number of columns.

The 'columns' correspond to the features we extracted. `aff_transform` has five columns because we defined five different categories of political affiliation. `speech_transform` has many, many more columns, because each column corresponds with a unique word which appears in at least one of the speeches in our dataset.

It's time to move onto the last step before we dig into modelling: training, test, and validation splitting!

Training and validation sets

In order to validate your results, you must split your data into training and test sets, and then split your training set into a training set (for real this time) and a validation set. We've covered this process before, but we used 'cross-validation' to achieve the training–validation split (dynamically, at runtime). Cross-validation isn't as common with neural network modelling, so we'll create these splits by hand:

```
from sklearn.model_selection import train_test_split
import numpy as np
import tensorflow as tf
from tensorflow import keras

X_t, X_test, y_t, y_test = train_test_split(
    speech_transformed,
    aff_transformed,
    test_size = 0.1,
    shuffle = True,
    stratify=aff_transformed
)

X_train, X_valid, y_train, y_valid = train_test_split(
    X_t,
```

```
    y_t,
    test_size = 0.2,
    shuffle = True,
    stratify=y_t
)
```

```
### You don't need to pay much attention to the following of code - it's just something
we have to do to make sparse numpy arrays compatible with Keras
```

```
def convert_sparse_matrix_to_sparse_tensor(X):
    coo = X.tocoo()
    indices = np.mat([coo.row, coo.col]).transpose()
    return tf.sparse.reorder(tf.SparseTensor(indices, coo.data, coo.shape))
```

```
X_train = convert_sparse_matrix_to_sparse_tensor(X_train)
X_valid = convert_sparse_matrix_to_sparse_tensor(X_valid)
```

Here again, we can take some time to check that everything is the correct shape. If our splits worked correctly, then X_train and y_train should have the same first dimension:

```
X_train.shape
```

```
TensorShape([10800, 1170])
```

```
y_train.shape
```

```
(10800, 5)
```

We'll also take a moment to store the number of columns in our X data, as we'll need to provide Keras with that number shortly:

```
words = X_train.shape[1]
```

Our data is now ready. I stress that this is a *very* basic approach to preparing the data. It is optimized for speed and ease of understanding rather than for scientific rigour. In the next section, we'll use Keras to build a neural network for classification, train it on the data, and evaluate its performance.

23.5 End-to-End Neural Network Modelling

Building the sequential model

It's common to use pre-built neural network architectures that require little to no assembly, but in this case we're going to build one from the ground up to help deepen your understanding of how neural networks work. There are many ways to build an ANN using Keras; we're going to use the 'Sequential' API, which is one of the simpler methods. You start by instantiating keras.models.Sequential() and assigning it a variable name. We'll call this one the uk_model:

```
uk_model = keras.models.Sequential()
```

Now that we've defined this model, we can start to add layers to it sequentially (hence its name). In ANNs, a 'layer' is simply a group of artificial neurons that share some attributes in common. In the previous chapter, we described various types of layers one might find in a network, so we won't cover them in much detail here.

We can add a layer to our sequential model by using the model's add method. This first layer is going to be a special layer called the input layer. It won't act on the data in any significant way, but it does play an important role in configuring the network overall, as we'll give it information about the shape of the data we plan to feed into it; we've already found and stored that number, which makes this process simple:

```
uk_model.add(keras.layers.InputLayer(words))
```

Next come the 'dense' layers. They're called 'dense' because they're fully connected to the previous layer; every neuron in the input layer can potentially have some impact on any neuron in our first dense layer. Some more advanced forms of neural network architecture intentionally restrict which neurons can affect which other neurons, but that's a topic for another time. Let's start by adding a dense layer with 400 neurons and a relu activation function (introduced in the previous chapter):

```
uk_model.add(keras.layers.Dense(400, activation = "relu"))
```

We can use the summary() method on our model to keep tabs to quickly see what we've built so far. It's a good idea to do this often, as you iteratively develop a model.

```
uk_model.summary()

Model: "sequential"
_____
Layer (type)                Output Shape              Param #
===============================================================
dense (Dense)               (None, 400)               468400
===============================================================
Total params: 468,400
Trainable params: 468,400
Non-trainable params: 0
_____
```

Let's add a few more identical dense layers:

```
uk_model.add(keras.layers.Dense(400, activation="relu"))
uk_model.add(keras.layers.Dense(400, activation="relu"))
uk_model.add(keras.layers.Dense(400, activation="relu"))
uk_model.add(keras.layers.Dense(400, activation="relu"))
```

Finally, we'll add an output layer designed to fit our output data. In most cases, the output layer of a classification ANN should have a number of neurons equal to the number of categories in our output, and use an activation function capable of producing the output we expect to see (we only want our ANN to make one guess per speech). In this case, that means we want an output layer with five neurons and a softmax activation function. The softmax activation function will estimate a probability for each of the political affiliation categories. All of the values across all of the categories will be non-negative, and they will sum to 1.

Let's add the output layer and run the `summary()` method again to see what our model looks like:

```
uk_model.add(keras.layers.Dense(5, activation='softmax'))
uk_model.summary()

Model: "sequential"

_____
Layer (type)                 Output Shape              Param #
=================================================================
dense (Dense)                (None, 400)               468400

dense_1 (Dense)              (None, 400)               160400

dense_2 (Dense)              (None, 400)               160400

dense_3 (Dense)              (None, 400)               160400

dense_4 (Dense)              (None, 400)               160400

dense_5 (Dense)              (None, 5)                 2005
=================================================================
Total params: 1,112,005
Trainable params: 1,112,005
Non-trainable params: 0
_____
```

And with that, our model is ready to be compiled!

Compiling a Keras ANN

Before a Keras model is ready to be trained, it must be compiled. Keras ANNs require you to provide them with a loss function and an optimizer. It's usually a good idea to include one or more metrics you'd like to have access to during training.

For this, our first ANN, we're going to use a standard line-up during compilation. Our loss function will be `sparse_categorical_crossentropy`, our optimizer will be `sgd` (stochastic gradient descent), and we'll use the `accuracy` metric:

```
uk_model.compile(
    loss=keras.losses.categorical_crossentropy,
    optimizer="sgd",
    metrics=["accuracy"]
)
```

Care, feeding, and training of your ANN

Everything is ready; we can begin training! A word to the wise: don't expect your neural network to perform well at first, and this neural network will be no exception. Observe the following:

```
history = uk_model.fit(X_train, y_train, epochs=50, validation_data = (X_valid,
    y_valid), verbose=0)
```

Normally, fitting a Keras model will produce a *lot* of output! Since we don't want to devote multiple pages to this output, we've used the `verbose=0` argument. If you run the code yourself, you can see it all in full. What does it mean?

On the left-hand side, our ANN lets us see how far along the model is in the training process. We asked the model to do 50 epochs of training; the current epoch is displayed at the top of the output. Below the epoch is a progress bar showing progress through the current epoch, alongside a constantly updating estimate of how long the epoch will take to finish (for the current epoch, at least; finished epochs display the total time they took instead).

After the progress outputs, you should see four metrics: `loss`, `accuracy`, `val_loss`, and `val_accuracy`. Here's what each of them means:

1   `loss` is simply the average value of the loss function across the entire epoch. The lower it is, the better our model is performing!
2   `accuracy` is a simple measure of how well our model is performing in practical terms. It measures the proportion of correct answers our model gave during that epoch.
3   `val_loss` is the same as loss, except that it's calculated for the 'validation' set of data, which our model isn't allowed to train on.
4   `val_accuracy` is the same as accuracy, except that it's calculated for the 'validation' set.

Now that we know what these labels mean, we can take a look at the values they contain. Let's start by plotting all four of them by epoch (Figure 23.1):

```
pd.DataFrame(history.history).plot(style=['*-','o-','^-'],
                                   linewidth=.5, markersize=3,
                                   figsize = (8, 8))
plt.grid(True)
plt.gca().set_ylim(0, 2)
plt.show()
```

Looking at our model's history, it started out with a modest accuracy rate of ~22% (specific numbers may vary from computer to computer), which – for a classification task with five labels – is about as good as randomly guessing. As our model trains, though, we can see it steadily improves until . . . Wow! There is more than 75% accuracy on the final epoch! That is an unreasonably high number. Is this cause for celebration?

Unfortunately, no. Recall that we care much more about our model's performance on the validation set. If we examine the progression of our `val_accuracy` score, we see no significant trend. Despite our ANN's ability to accurately predict three-quarters of the training data, its performance on the validation data reached ~45% after the third epoch and stayed nearly stationary from there on out, except for the occasional plunge down into the low 30s. Things get

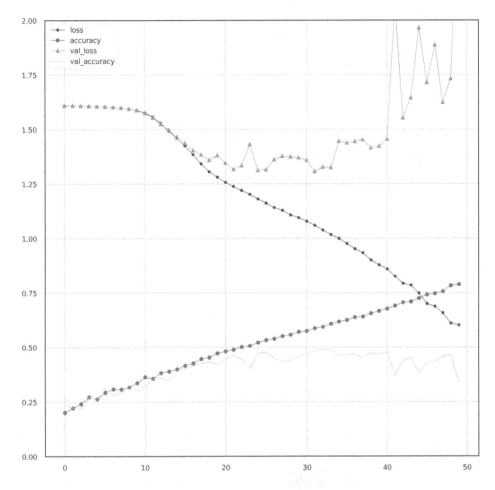

Figure 23.1 A plot with lines showing the loss and accuracy, for both the training and validation sets, of the neural network model as a function of training time

even worse when we examine our `val_loss` scores across the epochs: as our training set `loss` decreases (for loss, lower is better), our validation set `val_loss` shoots through the roof! The increasing loss indicates that our model is getting more and more confident in the incorrect predictions it is making on our validation set.

Why is this happening? The most plausible explanation – and the *usually* correct one in most cases – is overfitting.

Overfitting

One of the problems with ANNs is that you can provide them with enough data and memory capacity to perform nearly perfectly at the task performed on the training set, only to be utterly inept at tasks performed on the validation and testing sets. In other words, they are prone to overfitting. To successfully build and train neural networks, you have to walk a fine line. If you don't provide your ANN with enough neuron density and training data, it won't be able to effectively learn anything. If you provide it with too much, it'll become a near-perfect predictor of the training data, and – barring a fluke – will make negligible progress on the validation data.

To demonstrate the influence of model specification on overfitting, we'll train another neural network using a very similar approach, except instead of using five hidden dense layers with 400 neurons each, we're only going to use two hidden dense layers – one with 400 neurons and one with 10. We'll also take this opportunity to demonstrate a different way of specifying your Keras ANN model: rather than creating our layers one at a time by using the model.add() method, we can simply pass a list of layers as the first argument in our initial call to keras.models.Sequential():

```
uk_model_2 = keras.models.Sequential([
    keras.layers.InputLayer(words),
    keras.layers.Dense(400, activation="relu"),
    keras.layers.Dense(10, activation="relu"),
    keras.layers.Dense(5, activation="softmax"),
])
```

Now, let's compile and train our new model as before:

```
uk_model_2.compile(
    loss=keras.losses.categorical_crossentropy,
    optimizer="sgd",
    metrics=["accuracy"]
)
history2 = uk_model_2.fit(X_train, y_train, epochs=50, validation_data = (X_valid,
    y_valid), verbose=0)
```

Keep in mind that we're primarily interested in our val_accuracy and val_loss scores, and we're especially interested in making sure that they don't wildly jump around or trend for the worse during training. It might be a good idea to directly compare our models' performances – we'll do this by putting both of their history plots side by side (Figure 23.2):

```
lims = (0, 2)
fig, (ax1, ax2) = plt.subplots(2, 1, figsize=(8,16))
pd.DataFrame(history.history).plot(ax=ax1, style=['*-','o-','^-'],
                                   linewidth=.5, markersize=3,)
ax1.grid(True)
ax1.set_ylim(lims)
ax1.title.set_text("5-Layer Model")
pd.DataFrame(history2.history).plot(ax=ax2, style=['*-','o-','^-'],
                                    linewidth=.5, markersize=3,)
ax2.grid(True)
ax2.set_ylim(lims)
ax2.title.set_text("2-Layer Model")
plt.show()
```

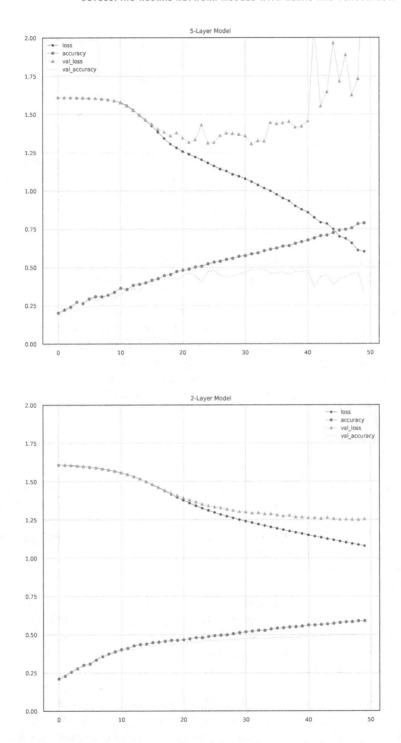

Figure 23.2 Two side-by-side plots, each with lines showing the loss and accuracy, for both the training and validation sets, of the neural network model as a function of training time. The left plot shows the results from the five-layer model, whereas the right-hand plot shows the results from the two-layer model

When we compare the two plots, we can see that our `val_loss` and `val_accuracy` scores for the two-layer model outperform those from the five-layer model, both in terms of stability and trending in positive directions. The difference between them is slight but made especially salient when one recalls that the better model is *far less complex* than its counterpart!

Reducing complexity isn't the only way to stave off overfitting; a variety of other techniques, such as 'dropouts', can be used. We're not going to fit any model with dropouts in this chapter, but it's useful to know what the term means: instead of using all connections between all neurons for every training iteration, dropout forces your model to perform without a randomly selected subset of connections between neurons. The group of dropped connections changes periodically, meaning that your network can't become too reliant on a comparatively small number of features; in essence, dropout uses a different approach to achieve the same end of preventing your model from simply learning the data.

There are two lessons to take away from the above examples:

1   When it comes to training neural networks, less is often more.
2   Your neural network is only as good as the training data it has access to.

We've already talked at length about how adding more parameters to a model can degrade its performance on validation data, but we haven't discussed the second point yet. We mentioned when creating the training and validation sets that we chose to represent the text of the speeches in a very simple way. We just counted all of the words in a given speech and fed that information into our neural network (after some minor processing to use TF-IDF and remove stop words). There are far better ways to process text – this book has already covered various approaches to doing so.

Confusion matrices

Throughout this chapter, we used 'accuracy' (alongside the categorical cross entropy loss function) as a means of assessing our models' performances. Accuracy may be the most easily understood metric, but as discussed in Chapter 22, it doesn't provide a particularly complete picture of what the model is getting right and what it's getting wrong. Rather than use one of those numerical assessments, I will introduce you to a graphical technique for classification tasks, regardless of the number of categories involved: the confusion matrix.

Confusion matrices are a simple way of assessing the balance between false positives and false negatives. In a 2 × 2 format, the first row of a confusion matrix shows the model predictions for the positive class, with *n* correct predictions in the first cell and *n* incorrect predictions in the second cell. The second row does the same for the negative class. The matrix diagonal (row 1 column 1 and row 2 column 2) then shows the number of correct predictions, and the other two off-diagonal cells show the number of incorrect predictions. Some confusion matrices will be larger than the simple 2 × 2 tables, but the columns still represent 'ground truth' and the rows represent predictions. Since more categories result in larger confusion matrices, it can be helpful to visualize the matrix as a heat map. The same premise applies to classification tasks with more than two categories: cells down the diagonal of the matrix are correct predictions, and anything off-diagonal is an incorrect prediction.

Confusion matrices help us put criteria other than overall accuracy in the foreground when evaluating machine learning models. Of course, the ratio of false positives and false negatives is one part of the larger concept of accuracy; accurate models should have relatively low numbers of both. But by shifting the focus from a single accuracy score to this balance of errors, we can think about evaluating and improving our models with other criteria in the foreground, such as reducing the risk of potentially harmful Type I and /or Type II errors.

Let's take a look at the confusion matrix from our two-layer model after 50 epochs of training. We'll use a heat map from the Seaborn package to make it easier to see what's going on. The results are shown in Figure 23.3.

```
y_pred = np.argmax(
    uk_model_2.predict(
        convert_sparse_matrix_to_sparse_tensor(X_test)),
    axis=1)

y_true = np.argmax(y_test, axis=1)

conf_mat = tf.math.confusion_matrix(y_true, y_pred)
plt.figure()

## GRAYSCALE FOR PRINTING
cmap = sns.cubehelix_palette(50, hue=0.05, rot=0, light=0.9, dark=0, as_cmap=True)

sns.heatmap(
    np.array(conf_mat).T,
    xticklabels=affiliation_encoder.classes_,
    yticklabels=affiliation_encoder.classes_,
    annot=True,
    fmt='g',
    cmap=cmap
)

plt.xlabel("Observed")
plt.xticks(rotation=45)
plt.yticks(rotation=45)
plt.ylabel("Predicted")
plt.show()
```

Along the x-axis, we have the 'observed' classes; along the y-axis, we have the 'predicted' classes. Each of the columns sums to 300 observations (but the rows don't, necessarily). All things considered, our simple model didn't fare too badly! It was especially proficient at making accurate predictions about speeches delivered by the centre-right party (Conservatives), and the 'other' parties. In the centre-left (Labour) and national (SNP) categories, it's a bit more of a mixed bag: less than 50% correct. The real blemish here is in the 'centre' category (Liberal Democrat): less than one-third of the predictions were correct. Our model was especially keen on misclassifying Liberal Democrats' speeches as belonging to Labour or the Conservatives.

At this point, you might be wondering why I have any praise at all for a model that barely managed to clear a 50% accuracy rate in two categories, didn't manage to clear 50% in another two, and completely botched the final one. I think there are a few reasons to look on the bright side here:

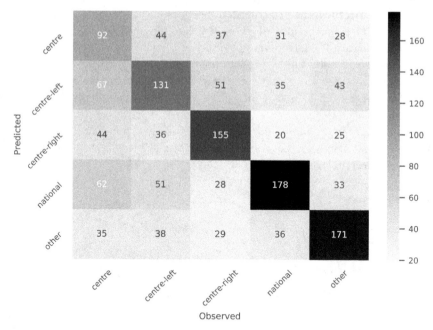

Figure 23.3 A heat map of the confusion matrix for our trained two-layer model; correct predictions are on the diagonal, incorrect predictions are off-diagonal

1   This model managed to achieve fairly good results using complex, nuanced speech that was almost entirely unprocessed. As I've said elsewhere, we did about as little as possible to the speeches before feeding them to the model: anything less would have been embarrassing. There's a *lot* of room for improvement here before we even create the neural network.

2   A nearly 50% accuracy rate might be abysmal for a two-label classification task, but it's a bit more impressive when you consider that there were five labels competing for our model's attention. If our model were simply guessing randomly, we'd only expect it to be right 20% of the time. Viewed in that light, getting validation accuracy up to around 50% isn't bad at all for such a basic ANN trained on minimally processed data.

3   The model we developed here was about as simple as neural networks come. Later in the book, we're going to start discussing more complicated neural network architectures, such as transformers and recurrent neural networks, which have *way* more parameters than what you've seen in this chapter.

The fact that a very basic ANN was able to make measurable gains after a relatively short training period should be all the proof you need that they represent a powerful arsenal of inferential tools. But for all the reasons we've already discussed, it is *very* important to understand them, to know their limitations, and to use them correctly in contexts where they are appropriate (and to avoid them entirely when they are not).

================ **Further Reading** ================

Now that you've had an introduction to some very simple neural network models, you may want to start learning about more complex ones. To that end, I recommend the sections on neural network modelling in Géron (2019), as well as Francois Chollet's (2018) *Deep Learning with Python*. These are more advanced materials, but now you've got a foundation to build on!

23.6 CONCLUSION

The key points in this chapter are as follows:

- Neural networks are a vast, heterogeneous group of models, but even simple instantiations of a deep neural network can achieve impressive results.
- Overfitting is a constant concern with neural network modelling, and great pains should be taken to diagnose and correct for overfitting. Many techniques for accomplishing this exist, but even using a simpler model can be sufficient.
- Accuracy and loss metrics alone aren't reliable measures of your model's power; it is often better to evaluate your model with other metrics and visualization techniques (e.g. confusion matrices and heat maps).

Visit the website at https://study.sagepub.com/mclevey for additional resources

PART V
BAYESIAN DATA ANALYSIS AND GENERATIVE MODELLING WITH PROBABILISTIC PROGRAMMING

24

STATISTICAL MACHINE LEARNING AND GENERATIVE MODELS

24.1 Learning Objectives

By the end of this chapter, you should be able to do the following:

- Compare statistical and machine learning models in terms of their underlying goals, for example prediction versus inference
- Explain why it can be helpful to use both statistical and machine learning models in a research project
- Compare the Frequentist and Bayesian paradigms given differences in their interpretations of the meaning of probability
- Compare discriminative and generative models

24.2 Learning Materials

You can find the online learning materials for this chapter in `doing_computational_social_science/Chapter_24`. cd into the directory and launch your Jupyter server.

24.3 Introduction

Our discussion of machine learning so far has focused on a selection of models that are central to the symbolic and connectionist paradigms, specifically linear and logistic regression models and tree-based methods such as decision trees, random forests, and gradient-boosted machines, and finally connectionist neural network models. These models are data-driven and mathematically inductive but can be put to good use in a wide variety of research designs, regardless of whether your goals are primarily inductive or deductive, theory-building or theory-testing, basic or applied.

This is another high-level chapter that transitions us into new set of methods and models, generally referred to as 'probabilistic programming', Bayesian data analysis or computational Bayesian statistics/machine learning, or generative modelling. (If you don't know what any of that means, you will soon!) The goals for this chapter are to deepen your understanding of the relationship between statistics and machine learning in general, to clarify the differences between Frequentist and Bayesian interpretations of probability, and to compare 'discriminative' and 'generative' models. In the next chapter, we will introduce some essential knowledge of probability theory. Together, these two chapters are the foundation upon which a series of chapters on generative modelling with structured, network/relational, and text data build.

24.4 Statistics, Machine Learning, and Statistical Machine Learning: Where Are the Boundaries and What Do They Bind?

Historically, statistics and machine learning have been fairly distinct fields, with computer scientists being the main developers of machine learning methods and, well, statisticians being the main developers of statistical methods. For some time, the computer scientists were sceptical of statistical methodologies and statisticians were sceptical of machine learning methodologies, in part because they were working towards different types of goals. For the most part, computer scientists were primarily interested in developing machine learning models that excelled at prediction tasks on large datasets, whereas statisticians were primarily interested in developing interpretable models with the goal of facilitating *inference* under uncertainty. While this distinction is still true *in general* (most statisticians are not doing machine learning, for example), the boundaries between the fields have become much more porous over time. Many of these changes have been ongoing since the early 1990s.

To help make sense of all of this, it's useful to distinguish between

1 specific methods and models and
2 the ends these methods and models serve, chiefly prediction and inference.

For a long time now, statistics and machine learning have made use of a lot of common methods and models. Linear and logistic regression models, principal component analysis, factor analysis, and data clustering methods such as k-means are all widely used in *both* statistics and machine learning. There are many other examples, some of which are featured heavily in chapters to come, but the point is this: trying to accurately discern the boundaries between machine learning and applied statistics based on specific methods and models that 'belong' to each is pointless. I suggest you think instead about what a method or model is being *used for* in any given situation. This is a better way of making sense of the many methods and models are learning. The same methods and models can be used in both machine learning and applied statistics, but to very different ends. It is very important to understand this if you are to make good modelling choices.

Prediction and inference are related but distinct goals that we might pursue when developing models, and each can guide us in different directions when iteratively critiquing and revising models (Box's loop). When our goal is prediction, for example, we critique and refine our models until the predictions they make are as accurate and reliable as possible. In doing so, we often make decisions that sacrifice understanding of the underlying processes and causal mechanisms involved. This is one reason why models that are optimized for prediction often rely on complex mathematical functions, or include a staggering number of parameters; the additional complexity can bring about (usually modest) improvements in prediction, but this complexity typically comes at the cost of interpretability. Inference, on the other hand, is a goal that typically guides us to make modelling decisions that prioritize interpretability, *understanding*, and *explanation*. To do so, we develop models of the processes that we think might underlie the *generation* of the data we observe – *how did this data come to be?* – and which deepen our understanding of the relationships between specific variables. Some models (usually the simpler ones) are well-suited for both inference and prediction, but more complex models tend to provide one whilst eschewing the other.

If you are trying to understand whether and how variables such as age or gender identity relate to some other variable of interest, such as preferred music genres, then your goal is inference. If, on the other hand, you are trying to use information about age, gender identity, and other variables to make many accurate guesses about whether someone will like a given music genre, then your goal is prediction. Clearly, the two are related; if you manage to construct a model that perfectly infers the relationship between some variables for a given population, you could use that model to make predictions about previously unobserved individuals within that population. This is an idea we will return to frequently in the coming chapters on generative modelling.

Traditionally, statistical models are developed with the goal of making interpretable inference and machine learning models are developed with the goal of making accurate and reliable predictions. Although we usually think of *the future* when we think of prediction, in practice, predicting 'the future' is usually just making predictions about data we haven't seen before; 'the future' is just out-of-sample data, and 'predicting the future' is just using a model to make predictions about the values that out-of-sample data take for a variable we are interested in. Unsurprisingly, given the history of the two fields of study, traditional statistics lend themselves better to datasets with a (relatively) smaller number of observations and variables, while machine learning is better suited to the huge quantities of data readily available in the digital age.

Statistics is built on a foundation of using theory to inform decisions about constructing models to assess hypotheses. We might construct a statistical model to test hypotheses about the effects of education on political identity while controlling for the usual suspects such as class, occupation/profession, age, ethnicity, and so on. Statistics has generally assumed a deductive orientation. We know, *based on theory* and other empirical research, what might be important to consider when we investigate the relationships between specific variables.

In machine learning, it is common (but by no means necessary) to make considerably less use of theory and focus instead on uncovering and interpreting patterns in the data itself. We could, for example, pass an entire dataset through an algorithm to determine which combination of variables best predicts an outcome we are interested in. When used in this way, data-driven and mathematically inductive machine learning models are well-suited to inductive and exploratory research. That said, there are many ways to develop more theory-oriented machine learning models.

I'll give away the plot here and tell you that most of what you will learn in the coming chapters obliterates these distinctions and thrives at the intersection of statistics, machine learning, and applied data analysis. Statistical and machine learning modelling are not mutually exclusive of each other, and it can be useful to make use of both. Most of the best contemporary work blends them in exciting ways!

One of the major moments in the evolving relationship between machine learning and statistics happened in 2001, when Leo Breiman (2001) published a now-classic treatise proposing that academic statisticians make space in their work for algorithmic (e.g. machine learning) models. Nowadays, it's difficult to imagine that such a plea was necessary, but at the time, algorithmic models were much more prevalent outside of academic statistics.

The original article is worth reading, but in short, Breiman (2001) points out that some algorithmic models, such as random forests, are more accurate predictors than classical statistical models. (Don't forget this was 2001, when the state-of-the-art in machine learning and statistics was very different.) Breiman (2001) also argued that decision trees are just as interpretable as traditional statistical models but still good predictors, even if less accurate than random forests. Finally, he showed that there is often more information available about the relationship between variables than just the reason they're related. For example, algorithmic models can give a more accurate sense of which variables are most *important* and *under which conditions*. As always, decisions about the type of information to look for, how to find it, and how to interpret it are all research design decisions that can be made well or poorly.

Many classic machine learning models are optimized for prediction to such an extent that humans are incapable of accurately interpreting and drawing inferences from them. Even when we constrain the models to prevent them from becoming too complex, understanding *why* they produce specific results can still be beyond us. Yet, with experience and expertise, we can use them to learn things that are very difficult to learn from classical statistical models, and we can learn even more by using *both* statistical and machine learning models, or by venturing into the exciting hybrid world of *Bayesian data analysis*, *generative modelling*, and *probabilistic programming*. There are lots of different names for what happens in this fascinating hybrid world, and it's evolving at a breakneck pace. The community is moving increasingly towards the inclusive label of 'probabilistic programming', so I'll use that term often, but I'll switch to 'Bayesian data analysis' and 'generative modelling' or 'probabilistic modelling' when it makes more sense in the specific context. In general, I use these terms interchangeably.

Before we get into the details of developing various kinds of probabilistic models, we need to take a step back and talk about something much more fundamental: the meaning of probability itself.

What is probability? Two interpretations, two paradigms

What *exactly* is probability? In a basic (and wholly inadequate) sense, it refers to the chance that an event will occur. While the mathematical foundations of probability theory are the same no matter who you ask, the interpretation of what probability *means* and where it applies can vary from statistician to statistician. In this part of the chapter, we will compare the two most influential philosophical perspectives on probability, the classical or 'Frequentist' paradigm and the Bayesian paradigm.

If you're a social science student, I'd wager that your quantitative methods classes have been wholly Frequentist. While Frequentist approaches certainly have their merits, everything that follows is Bayesian. While Bayesian methods certainly have their limitations, I'm going to be promoting them with enthusiasm. I hope that, like me, you find the Bayesian approach liberating, powerful, intuitive, humbling, and beautiful, but it's fine if you don't. Understanding Bayesian approaches can also help you become a better Frequentist.

On that note, a final disclaimer. In much of what follows, I'll be contrasting the philosophical foundations of Frequentist and Bayesian thinking. In doing so, I'll be contrasting a 'strict' Frequentist view with a Bayesian view. This 'strict' view is not necessarily one that most Frequentists think much about in day-to-day practice, and when presented with it in philosophical form may find that they do not agree with it. Regardless of whether any individual Frequentist agrees with the strict philosophical interpretation or thinks about it very much at all, Frequentist statistical methodology, including null hypothesis significance testing (NHST), is wholly premised on it (McShane et al., 2019; Szucs and Ioannidis, 2017). Bayesian thinking offers a good alternative to Frequentist statistical methodology that is better suited to certain types of problems, which happens to include just about anything of interest in the social and biomedical sciences, and likely many other fields as well. For this reason, you will find absolutely no NHST in what follows. What you'll find are Bayesian alternatives. Finally, in laying out these philosophical differences, I have emphasized their strict interpretations. This is mainly for pedagogical reasons, as I assume that like most social science students, you've probably had limited exposure to multiple statistical paradigms. It's easier to learn the differences by focusing on the big picture stuff first. Over time, you'll start to notice more of the philosophical complexities and will be capable of reasoning in the grey zone between the statistical paradigms.

With that said, let's compare interpretations of the meaning of probability!

The frequentist paradigm and the 'rigid view' of probability

Although this may be your first time encountering the term, the vast majority of statistical analyses are currently conducted within the 'Frequentist' paradigm. Anytime you've witnessed someone evoke 'statistical significance', 'confidence intervals', 'p values', or those little stars that show up next to regression tables, that person is almost certainly using Frequentist techniques and concepts.

For Frequentists, probability is understood to be the long-run relative frequency of an event across repeated trials. As these trials are repeated over and over, the frequency of the event in question (relative to other possible outcomes) will trend towards the 'true value'. Imagine performing an experiment, such as flipping a 'fair' coin, many times over. Even though the ratio of heads to tails would differ in small ways from the expected value of 1:1 (or 50% heads, 50% tails), its long-run value would approach the 'true' value of the coin.

At risk of grotesque oversimplification, the Frequentist paradigm holds that *all phenomena that can be repeatedly sampled from under nearly ideal and identical conditions* will produce certain results with a certain frequency. This is the concept that motivates Frequentists' interpretation of probability, and probability is meaningless without it. As such, a strict Frequentist would tell you that the concept of probability *can only be applied in two contexts*:

1   Experiments that can be performed repeatedly in 'nearly ideal' conditions, and whose outcomes across trials vary despite (nearly) identical conditions for each trial
2   Populations of sufficient size such that a *practically* limitless number of samples can be randomly drawn therefrom

That's it. From a strict Frequentist perspective, the concept of probability cannot be applied under any conditions other than these. As a result, I will refer to the Frequentist interpretation of probability as 'rigid'.

Despite these self-imposed strictures, or perhaps because of them, the Frequentist paradigm has proven itself capable of covering a whole lot of ground. Almost any experiment from fields such as physics or chemistry could be considered repeatable (after all, unrepeatable experiments are generally of little scientific value) and is thus fertile ground for Frequentist analysis. Much of population science (i.e. demography) also lends itself reasonably well to the Frequentist paradigm as it would be practically impossible to completely exhaust the ability to randomly sample from a population of even modest size.

The strict Frequentist approach isn't such a good fit for some types of scientific enquiry. For example, what happens when a Frequentist wants to develop a model to predict the outcome of a specific election that hasn't happened yet? A *strict* Frequentist would tell you that it can't be done. A presidential election between two candidates in a given year, for example, is a one-off event and cannot be sampled from or repeated under experimental conditions. As such, it would be improper to apply probability to the outcome.

Fortunately, the vast majority of the Frequentists alive today are not nearly so rigid in their interpretation of probability as the statisticians who invented the most widely used Frequentist techniques. They would generally be willing to say that it's possible to think of a presidential election as driven by a dizzyingly large set of plausible end states (in the form of electoral college results, district-level voting trends, or even individual voters' decisions), and that there's no good reason why we can't think of all these possibilities as stemming from a nearly infinite set of hypothetical elections that we can sample from in search of the outcome we care about (in this case, who wins the election).

A willingness to bend the rules can help, but can't always rescue Frequentism from contexts where its mathematical underpinnings really struggle. Cases such as these generally require analysts to further relax their criteria about what is, and is not, a valid target for probabilistic description. Speaking of which . . .

The Bayesian paradigm and the 'flexible view' of probability

If you're interested in computational social science or data science (if you are reading this book, I hope you are!), you've likely encountered the term *Bayesian* before, and may even have a vague sense of what it means. I'm going to proceed on the assumption that you know next to nothing about it.

The Bayesian paradigm is premised on the notion that probability can and should be used to describe states of knowledge. This might sound like a fairly mundane and uncontroversial idea, but the consequences that stem from it are substantial. For example, one implication of this view is that data itself is not inherently stochastic (as the Frequentists would have it), but rather that *our perception of and knowledge about a phenomenon is always imprecise, faulty, and incomplete.* As such, Bayesians use 'randomness' to describe the 'uncertainty' inherent to our understanding of a process, not of the process itself. See the difference?

Consider the simple coin flip yet again. For a Frequentist, a coin flip is a prototypical example of a simple random process, and you can determine the probability of heads by repeatedly flipping a coin and tallying the outcomes. A Bayesian, on the other hand, might argue that coin flips are not *really* random processes at all, they just seem random to us. Whether the coin lands on heads or tails is actually determined by a *huge* number of deterministic physical factors that are beyond our ability to observe and reason about, such as the coin's initial orientation, initial distance from the surface it will land on, the exact location and magnitude of the force imparted on it, ambient air pressure, wind, altitude, and so on. If we had endless time, energy, and resources, we could probably create a deterministic description of coin flip mechanics, capable of making perfect predictions provided we have perfect and complete knowledge of all the relevant factors.

This is a really important point, so here it is again, put a slightly different way: from a Bayesian point of view, the problem is not that the things we are trying to understand are inherently uncertain and random. If it were possible to know everything about every relevant factor completely and perfectly, we would find that things that seem random are not random at all. They simply *seem* random because we have imperfect and incomplete knowledge. It is our selective perception, cognitive biases, flawed beliefs, limited knowledge, and so on that are the sources of uncertainty. Therefore, we should approach the task of inference with these limitations in mind; when we iteratively design, develop, and improve models, we should do so while accounting for uncertainty in our knowledge rather than approaching inference on the assumption that 'randomness' is inherent in the things we want to understand.

You could say that the Bayesian *paradigm* is characterized by a certain amount of intellectual humility and appreciation for the staggering complexity of the world; all knowledge is provisional, incomplete, and imperfect. The rich intellectual world that has developed around Bayesian statistics and machine learning, and which continues to evolve, is explicitly organized around doing research in these ways and places a great emphasis on combining information from different sources, embracing uncertainty and heterogeneity, and integrating theory and data in iteratively developed bespoke statistical models that are well-matched for different problems. OK – enough with the unhinged admiration for Bayesian statistics. Let's move on.

If perfectly complete and objective knowledge about the world is not possible, then the Bayesian notion of using probabilities to quantify the degree of certainty for some state of knowledge becomes *extremely* useful and powerful. Bayesians work within an intellectual framework where differing states of knowledge (or hypotheses, in a scientific setting) can be rigorously evaluated and compared in light of observed empirical data. Unlike (strict) Frequentist inference, where new evidence cannot be incorporated on-the-fly, Bayesian contributions to knowledge are *always open to revision given new evidence*.

By this point, you might already be thinking something along the lines of 'Wait a second. Are you telling me that as a result of the Bayesian paradigm using probability to describe beliefs and states of knowledge, you can assign a probability to anything?' Well, no. But yes, sort of.

Bayesians think that questions of knowledge and 'belief' are the only domains in which one may legitimately apply probability theory, which means that technically one cannot assign a probability to just anything. But since literally *everything* we humans know and reason about is by definition a form of knowledge or belief, you would be hard pressed to find something that could not be assigned some sort of probability within the Bayesian paradigm. Anything a human brain can perceive and reason about falls under the purview of Bayesian probability. That's a pretty broad scope, and it's why I have opted to describe the Bayesian paradigm as having a 'flexible view' of probability.

Bayesian analysis has historically been the underdog in academic statistics but has thrived in applied settings, including government and industry. Sharon McGrayne (2011) provides an interesting historical account of how Bayesian analysis has thrived in applied settings in *The Theory That Would Not Die: How Bayes' Rule Cracked the Enigma Code, Hunted Down Russian Submarines, and Emerged Triumphant from Two Centuries of Controversy*, if you are interested. There is no question that Bayesian statistics is now well within the mainstream of academic statistics and has long been used in fields such as sociology, political science, and public policy (e.g. for sociology, see Lynch and Bartlett, 2019; Western, 1999), but in 2021, it is still the case that most researchers are trained in, and continue to work within, the Frequentist paradigm.

Why? It's a bit odd when considered in light of the fact that the Bayesian paradigm has proven capable of deftly tackling the most difficult of statistical problems in an intuitive fashion. While there are ongoing debates about the philosophical underpinnings of the Bayesian paradigm (e.g. Gelman and Robert, 2013a, 2013b; Johnson, 2013; Mayo, 2013), most commentators would argue that Bayesian approaches tend to perform well in cases where Frequentist approaches typically stumble, and in other cases they tend to produce similar types of estimates as do Frequentist approaches, only with more information about the uncertainty involved in those estimates. What gives?

One explanation is that some of the most powerful founding figures of modern statistics, such as Ronald Fisher, were diehard Frequentists who sought to sink Bayesian statistics with intense fervour, some of which was intellectual and some of which was nasty personal politics and messing with people's careers. McGrayne's (2011) book on the history of Bayesian methods is in part the story of brilliant mathematicians, computer scientists, and statisticians working using Bayesian reasoning in secret because of the hegemonic influence of the towering statistical giants and gatekeepers of the time.

But this is certainly not the only reason. The other, which is much less political, is the computational complexity inherent in the Bayesian paradigm. We won't spend very much time on these specifics as the problem of computational complexity in Bayesian analysis is largely obsolete, but the oversimplified answer is this: in many cases, *analytical* Bayesian inference requires the use of some truly intimidating integral calculus that sometimes fails to produce a closed-form solution even with a dizzying array of clever mathematical tricks. In bygone eras when computers were rare, slow, and expensive (or non-existent, as they were in the days of Reverend Thomas Bayes himself and the two great mathematicians Richard Price and Pierre-Simon Laplace, both of whom are largely responsible for what we now call Bayes' theorem, discussed at length in the next chapter), Bayesian inference was dually limited: it was, at best, the sole domain of inspired mathematicians, and there were some forms of inference it simply couldn't tackle. Fortunately, this is no longer the case, and the Bayesian paradigm is undergoing a renaissance. The renaissance is inherently computational.

Everyone's wrong, but sometimes we're wrong in useful ways

Time for a controversial claim: the Bayesian interpretation of probability comes relatively naturally to us, and the Frequentist view does not. When we evoke probability to describe something (e.g. 'I think there's a 70% chance the professor is going to be late to class today', or 'I think there's roughly a 55% chance Biden takes Pennsylvania in the 2020 American presidential election'), we're applying probabilities to 'beliefs' or knowledge. In that sense, many of us are 'natural' Bayesians.

This is unfortunate for many reasons, one being that Bayesian analyses are generally more intuitive than Frequentist analyses, and Bayesian techniques expose (rather than obscure) more of the assumptions, decision-making, and analytic procedures involved in modelling than do Frequentist techniques. More generally, Frequentists view 'subjectivity' and ironically any kind of human influence on inference as an inconvenience at best, and a fatal scientific flaw at worst. Bayesians would counter that science, statistics, and inference *are all human endeavours*. To pretend otherwise is folly. Rather than strive in vain to eliminate any form of situated knowledge, Bayesians prefer to put it all out in the open: make your knowledge visible; strive to uncover your biases and assumptions; and make them all explicit, visible, and open to critique in your models. If there is uncertainty in our knowledge, *make those uncertainties explicit*.

To be clear, there are very few truly doctrinaire Frequentists alive today, and similarly there are few dyed-in-the-wool Bayesians. In their quest for intelligible insights, most contemporary statisticians, data scientists, and computational scientists draw from both the Bayesian and Frequentist paradigms. Truly competent statisticians and researchers are comfortable with both and are intimately familiar with their relative merits, shortcomings, and idiosyncrasies. I won't bother trying to hide my strong preference for the Bayesian view in what follows (really, there would be no point), but that's not intended to be an indictment of the Frequentist paradigm, although it is, perhaps, an indictment of uncritically held institutional preferences for Frequentist approaches. Different statistical philosophies are useful in different intellectual and applied contexts.

Now that we've contrasted these two competing interpretations of probability and the statistical paradigms those interpretations are embedded in, let's turn to one final high-level distinction before we get into the guts of probability itself: generative versus discriminative modelling.

24.5 Generative Versus Discriminative Models

The famed physicist Richard Feynman once remarked, 'What I cannot create, I do not understand.' This is something of an informal motto for generative modellers across many disciplines. What does it mean, why does it matter, and what is a generative model?

The supervised learning models we have discussed in this book are all 'discriminative': they learn mathematical functions that use labelled data to map some input to an output. Put another way, we develop 'discriminative models' when we are trying to solve regression and classification problems (by which I mean continuous or categorical outcomes) in the context of *supervised learning*. For example, we can train a discriminative model to classify a speech according to the political party of the politician who gave it as a function of the words used in the speech. To do this, we would provide the model with the feature matrix **X** containing data on word usage, and we would provide the labelled vector *y* indicating the party of the speaker. We would then train a supervised learning model to *discriminate* between political parties based on the content of the speeches. Linear and logistic regressions, *k*-nearest neighbours, support vector machines, decision trees, random forests, and gradient-boosted machines are all examples of discriminative models. Provided the starting conditions don't change, discriminative models are *usually* deterministic, in that they calculate some sort of value based on an algorithmic process. If neither the inputs nor the initial conditions change between runs, then the value doesn't either – no matter how many times you run it.

We use discriminative models when we face discriminative problems, and supervised learning is all about discriminative problems. *Is this a speech from a Conservative or a Labour MP?* When provided with enough data, discriminative models can uncover hidden mathematical regularities that enable many different types of predictions, and because we always have the labelled values *y*, we can compute a wide variety of evaluation measures to assess the quality of those predictions; the evaluation metrics we discussed in Chapter 23 are all examples. Much of the hype about 'superhuman performance' in machine learning comes from the dramatic improvements in supervised learning on these measures, none more so than accuracy.

In sum, discriminative models are, ultimately, just models used for prediction problems in a supervised learning framework. Consequently, some people use the two terms interchangeably, but I find this creates some confusion. Supervised learning is more than just the specific models;

it's a larger process and framework that has evolved to develop high-quality discriminative models. Supervised learning is the goal, the general framework, and the process; discriminative models are the actual learning algorithms at the core of that learning process. We train the discriminative models with labelled data. The model learns how to map **X** to **y** such that it can make discriminative predictions about new observations (out-of-sample data). The machine learns from the training data *iteratively*, by correcting its prediction mistakes.

Generative models are completely different. Rather than attempting to learn how to discriminate between observations given a learnt mathematical function that maps **X** to **y**, generative models are concerned with *the underlying processes* that result in us seeing the data we are seeing. There are different kinds of generative models. For example, the contagion models we developed in Chapters 16 and 17 are generative models that are anchored not only in theoretical ideas developed within network analysis but also in complex systems theory more generally, and in agent-based modelling. Some generative models attempt to learn processes from data. With others, we develop generative models by thinking through generative mechanisms ourselves, and then iteratively critique and revise those models (Box's loop).

One way we know we have a good generative model is when it can generate data that looks a lot like the data we observe from the real world. For example, if we train models to generate images of seascapes, mountain ranges, and so on, the best models would produce realistic-looking images, and the bad ones will produce fake images (or complete nonsense). We could also train a model to generate sentences; the best ones could plausibly be strung together by a human, whereas bad ones would contain obvious mistakes and things that don't make sense. Consider models that learn generative processes, as opposed to models where we encode the generative mechanisms ourselves. If the model can generate new speeches or new images of seascapes, mountain ranges, and so on that *sound and look real*, then the model has learnt the underlying rules that govern what makes a speech sound authentic and an image look authentic; we know it knows these rules because it can use them to create realistic new speeches and images that have never existed in the world.

Generative models, then, are about modelling processes that generate the data we observe, and a *good* generative model is one that can successfully generate new data that is as close as possible to the original data. When we have successfully developed a model such as this, we can learn a lot *from the model*.

Generative models have long been popular in computational social science, from the early roots of agent-based models (see Macy and Flache 2009) to the current state of the field, where agent-based models continue to be used alongside the rapidly ascending generative approaches to network and text analysis. Generative models are at the core of computational social science regardless of how and where you draw boundaries around the field, or whether you consider the pre-2000s era dominated by agent-based models or the post-2000s era when the field expanded and broadened.

Generative models are thoroughly probabilistic, and depending on the type of model you are using and how you are specifying it, the results they produce include random noise and can produce slightly different results on different runs, which may or may not be noticeable. The key assumption they make is that there are a variety of probability distributions that govern what we see in the data, and the goal is to learn the parameters of these distributions. Discriminative models also make use of probability theory (e.g. a binary logistic regression outputs the probability that an observation belongs to class A or class B), *but they are not trying to learn the parameters of underlying probability distributions that cause observations to belong to one class or the other*. In other words, discriminative models try to learn the boundaries, hard or soft, that separate classes of observations, whereas generative models are focused on the processes and underlying probability distributions that give rise to the observations we observe. There's a large area of overlap between the precepts of generative modelling and the kinds of models typically used in the Bayesian paradigm. As you'll soon see, the generative properties inherent to most Bayesian models will be of great use to us, if we can unlock their potential. The next step is to ensure you have some understanding of the basics of probability theory. While not the most inherently exciting part of computational social science, a little knowledge goes a *very* long way.

Further Reading

Murphy's (2012) *Machine Learning: A Probabilistic Perspective* provides a deep and very comprehensive dive into probabilistic machine learning. Daphne Koller and Nir Friedman's (2009) *Probabilistic Graphical Models: Principles and Techniques*, Judea Pearl and Dana Mackenzie's (2018) *The Book of Why: The New Science of Cause and Effect*, and Pearl's (2009) *Causality* provide fascinating introductions to probabilistic graphical models, Bayesian networks, and Bayesian causal inference (all topics in probabilistic modelling that, regrettably, I did not have space to cover in this book).

24.6 Conclusion

The key points discussed in this chapter are as follows:

We compared:

- statistical models with machine learning models with an emphasis on the goals of inference and prediction;
- the Frequentist paradigm with the Bayesian paradigm, primarily with respect to their views on probability ('rigid' and 'flexible', respectively); and
- generative models with discriminative models.

Visit the website at https://study.sagepub.com/mclevey for additional resources

25

PROBABILITY: A PRIMER

25.1 Learning Objectives

By the end of this chapter, you should be able to do the following:

- Explain the meaning of key concepts in probability theory, including:
  - random variable
  - sample space
- Differentiate between (1) discrete probability distributions and probability mass functions (PMFs) and (2) continuous probability distributions and probability density functions (PDFs)
- Learn how to select probability distributions for modelling by thinking through their assumptions and learning about the parameters they take
- Explain the differences between marginal, joint, and conditional probabilities, and the notation used to express these probabilities
- Understand Bayes' theorem and its component parts

25.2 Learning Materials

You can find the online learning materials for this chapter in `doing_computational_social_science/Chapter_25`. `cd` into the directory and launch your Jupyter server.

25.3 Introduction

In the previous chapter, I explained how the Frequentist paradigm and Bayesian paradigms differ in their interpretation of probability, but we didn't actually discuss the mathematics of probability. The mathematics of probability are the same regardless of your philosophical persuasion, or the role that probabilities play in the models you develop.

This chapter is a basic primer on probability theory. Unlike other introductions to probability, we won't be getting into any mathematical proofs; there are plenty of those available elsewhere. Instead, we will clarify some foundational concepts and aim to build a bit of intuition about how different types of probability distributions work through simple simulations. Though not especially broad or deep, this introduction will provide enough knowledge of probability theory that you will be able to understand, develop, critique, interpret, and revise generative models for structured, network/relational, and text data.

Imports

```
import math
import numpy as np
np.random.seed(42)
import pandas as pd
pd.set_option("display.notebook_repr_html", False)
from collections import Counter

import seaborn as sns
import matplotlib.pyplot as plt
from dcss.plotting import custom_seaborn
custom_seaborn()
```

25.4 Foundational Concepts in Probability Theory

Frequentists and Bayesians differ in their philosophies but not in their mathematics. Both paradigms are built on a solid mathematical foundation of probability distributions that define the relative probability of *all* potential events that could result from some predefined system, experiment, or trial.

The starting point for probability theory is the sample space, sometimes referred to using the symbol S. The sample space is simply an exhaustive list of all the possible events (or outcomes) that could result from some trial or experiment. The sample space for a coin toss, for example, consists of heads and tails, but not 42 or a bag of catnip. Once we have defined the sample space, we assign probabilities to every possible event.

Probability distributions are just sample spaces where every possible event has an associated probability. They are governed by three axioms:

1. The probability of any event occurring is equal to or greater than 0. There can be no negative probabilities.
2. The probability of the entire sample space is 1. If the probability distribution is discrete (i.e. distinct events that can be individually counted, like the result of a coin flip), then the sum of those probabilities must equal 1. If the probability distribution is continuous (i.e. you can't count the distinct events because they are uncountably infinite), then the probabilities of each event must add up to 1 using an infinite sum operation.
3. If events A and B are mutually exclusive (a coin can't land both heads and tails), or disjoint, then the probability of either event occurring is equal to the probability of A + B.

This third axiom, the 'additivity axiom', is often expressed using notation from set theory. You may see it expressed in one of two forms, one that is common in more mathematical discussions of probability:

$$\text{if } P(A \cap B) = \emptyset, \text{ then } P(A \cup B) = P(A) + P(B)$$

and one that is more common in the statistical discussions of probability:

$$\cap P(A_i) = \emptyset, \text{ then } \cup P(A_i) = P(A_1) + P(A_2) + \cdots + P(A_n)$$

These two expressions are saying the same thing. The $\cup$ represents the set theoretic concept of the union of two events and the $\cap$ symbol represents their intersection. Consider the simple Venn diagram in Figure 25.1.

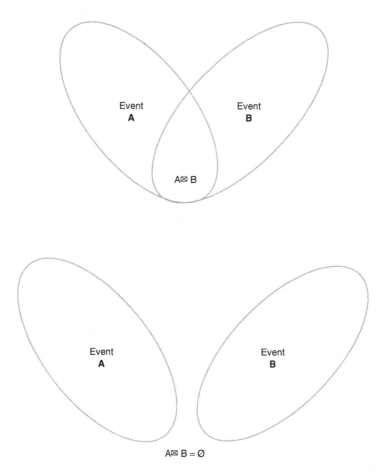

Figure 25.1 Two Venn diagrams: the top diagram depicts the intersection of A and B, the bottom diagram depicts a scenario where the intersection of A and B is an empty set

Two events, A and B, intersect in the top of the figure. The point at which they intersect is the portion of the Venn diagram where the two events overlap one another. This intersection is represented by the symbol $\cap$. If the two events do *not* intersect, as in the bottom of the figure, then the intersection ($\cap$) of the two sets is empty. We represent this emptiness with the symbol $\emptyset$. In essence, all the third axiom is saying is that if two events are disjoint, then the probability of either of those two events happening is the probability of the first event plus the probability of the second event. That's it.

These iron-clad rules are paraphrased versions of the original trio, known as 'Kolmogorov axioms' after the mathematician Andrey Kolmogorov. Together, they produce a number of useful features that we'll explore and exploit throughout the rest of this book.

Another essential concept in probability theory is that of a 'random variable'. Consider the example of a coin flip once again. There is no inherent numerical value for the outcome of a coin flip. When we flip it, it will either land heads-up or tails-up. The trouble is that neither 'heads' nor 'tails' has any inherent mathematical meaning, so it's up to us to create something that allows two worlds (the world of the coin and the world of statistics) to come together.

One way to do this is to say that there is a 'random variable' with values 0 and 1 that represent the outcomes of the coin flip; heads-up = 1, tails-up = 0. At this point, writing X = heads means the same thing as $X = 1$, and writing X = tails means the same thing as $X = 0$. What's more, we can use probability distributions to describe the probability of the coin flip taking on each value it is capable of producing. Random variables may take on more than two values; you might use one to describe income, occupation, or height. In short, random variables are what enable us to connect the tangible worlds of coin tosses, income inequality, and so on, with the mathematical world of probability and statistical inference.

Now, let's start learning about the properties of some specific probability distributions. While most of this is not inherently interesting to applied researchers, a bit of knowledge here goes a *very* long way. In the chapters that follow, I will assume you know the contents of this chapter in particular, even though you might be flipping back to it from time to time to remind yourself of the details. That's perfectly fine!

Finally, as with other chapters in this book, we'll be discussing some equations. These equations are not meant to carry the full explanatory weight here. If you are used to seeing and thinking about equations, great. If not, that's OK too. You still need to understand how the distributions work and what kinds of parameters they take, but it's possible to gain that knowledge from the simulations instead of the formulae. Ideally, the simulations will help you understand the equations, and the two can work together.

25.5 Probability Distributions and Likelihood Functions

The mathematics of probability vary depending on whether we are working with discrete or continuous distributions, and then there are further differences based on the specific discrete or continuous distributions. To help you understand some of the differences and build some intuition, we'll walk through a few examples of widely used distributions. We'll start with discrete distributions and 'probability mass functions', which represents the probability that a discrete random variable for a probability distribution is a specific value. Then we'll move on to continuous distributions and 'probability density functions'.

Discrete distributions, probability mass functions

Discrete distributions are used when we have a limited number of distinct countable outcomes. For example, we can flip heads or tails on a coin, but nothing in between. Similarly, we can roll a 3 or a 4 on a regular die, but we can't roll a 3.5. Below, we will learn a bit about three discrete probability distributions that are commonly used in models: the uniform, Bernoulli, and binomial distributions.

Everything is equally likely: the uniform distribution

The uniform distribution is probably familiar to you in practice, if not by name. *A uniform probability distribution describes a collection of possible outcomes for a random process where each outcome is equally (uniformly) likely.* To compute the probability of an event occurring given the assumption that all events are equally likely, we simply divide by the number of possible events,

$$P(x) = \frac{1}{n}$$

where x is the event whose probability we want to know, and n is the number of possible events. This simple equation, which applies *only* to uniform distributions, is an example of a probability mass function (PMF). If we want to know the probability that a random variable is some specific value, and we assume uniform probability, we can use the PMF for the uniform distribution. All we need to know is the number of possible events (n), and that x is one of those possible events.

For example, if we wish to know the probability of rolling a 7 on a die, we need only to know how many sides are on the die (n), and be sure that 7 (x) is on one of those sides. If we are rolling a classic six-sided die, our distribution is defined only for values 1 through 6: you cannot roll a 7. However, if we are rolling a 10-sided die, and 7 is on one of those sides, we can plug those numbers into the above PMF to see that

$$P(7) = \frac{1}{10} = 0.1$$

Since the uniform distribution assigns the same probability to all events, all events are equally likely. If we assign values to each event, then the expected value is simply the weighted average value of that distribution. It is calculated as follows:

$$E[X] = \sum_{i=1}^{n} x_i p_i$$

where $E[X]$ represents the expected value of X, i is an iterator, n is the number of different values X can take on, x_i is the value of one of the events represented by X, and p_i is the probability of that event. In this case, because we're using the uniform distribution, the weights p_i will all be identical, and $E[X]$ will just be the average value of X.

Let's use NumPy's random number generators to simulate a uniform distribution with different sample sizes and ranges and then visualize the differences. We'll simulate rolling a six-sided die 10,000 times by generating an array of 10,000 random integers between 1 and 6 (the number of possible events). If you set the same seed I did (42, in the imports), you should draw the same numbers. If you don't set a seed, or you set it to something different, your results will be slightly different.

```
n_possible_events = 6
samples = np.random.randint(1, n_possible_events+1, 10_000)
Counter(samples)
```

```
Counter({4: 1672, 5: 1689, 3: 1625, 2: 1692, 6: 1657, 1: 1665})
```

Good! That's exactly what we would expect to see (1 / n_possible_events * 10_000 = 1666.666) when drawing so many samples (rolling the die) from a uniform distribution. But what if we had drawn a smaller number of samples? Let's do few more simulations and visualize the results (Figure 25.2). We will add a red line showing *E*[*X*], the expected value.

```python
uniform_sim_1 = np.random.randint(1, n_possible_events+1, 6)
uniform_sim_2 = np.random.randint(1, n_possible_events+1, 100)
uniform_sim_3 = np.random.randint(1, n_possible_events+1, 1_000)
uniform_sim_4 = np.random.randint(1, n_possible_events+1, 10_000)


def get_percentages(simulation_array, n_samples):
    s = pd.Series(simulation_array).value_counts().div(n_samples)
    return s


fig, ax = plt.subplots(2, 2, sharex=True, sharey=True)


sns.barplot(x=get_percentages(uniform_sim_1, 6).index,
            y=get_percentages(uniform_sim_1, 6), ax=ax[0, 0], color='gray')
ax[0,0].axhline(1 / 6, color='crimson')
ax[0,0].set(title='6 samples')


sns.barplot(x=get_percentages(uniform_sim_2, 100).index,
            y=get_percentages(uniform_sim_2, 100), ax=ax[0, 1], color='gray')
ax[0,1].axhline(1 / 6, color='crimson')
ax[0,1].set(title='100 samples')


sns.barplot(x=get_percentages(uniform_sim_3, 1_000).index,
            y=get_percentages(uniform_sim_3, 1_000), ax=ax[1, 0], color='gray')
ax[1,0].axhline(1 / 6, color='crimson')
ax[1,0].set(title='1,000 samples')


sns.barplot(x=get_percentages(uniform_sim_4, 10_000).index,
            y=get_percentages(uniform_sim_4, 10_000), ax=ax[1, 1], color='gray')
ax[1,1].axhline(1 / 6, color='crimson')
ax[1,1].set(title='10,000 samples')


sns.despine()
plt.tight_layout()
plt.show()
```

These four simple simulations show that we get closer and closer to the expected value the more samples we draw. Go ahead and vary the number of samples and rerun the code. You'll find that the red line is always on the same *y*-value. Given a uniform distribution and in the case where the number of possible events is 6, the probability of any specific outcome of rolling our die is ~0.1666 . . ., or ~16.67%.

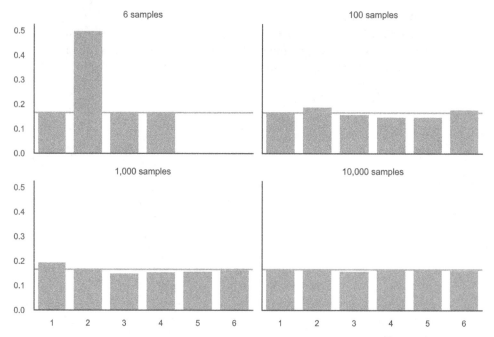

Figure 25.2   A set of four plots that represent samples from a standard six-sided die roll where each face of the die is equally likely to land face up on any given roll; the red horizontal line represents the expected value for each outcome. As the number of samples increases (from upper left to lower right), the outcome proportions of the simulated rolls approach the expected value line

The Bernoulli and binomial distributions

The Bernoulli distribution is a bit different from the other distributions we examine in this chapter. It's actually a special case of the binomial distribution, which we will discuss in a moment. The Bernoulli distribution describes an experiment *with only a single sample*, where the outcome of the experiment is binary (e.g. 0 or 1, yes or no, heads or tails, tested positive for COVID-19 [coronavirus disease 2019] or not), and described by a single probability *p*. Since we only have two possible outcomes, we only need to know the probability of *one* of those outcomes because the sum of the probabilities of all outcomes must equal 1. Necessarily, if the probability of testing positive for COVID-19 is 20%, the probability of testing negative is 80%.

The binomial distribution is the extended case of the Bernoulli distribution. The binomial distribution models observing certain events over some kind of interval. Specifically, the events are Bernoulli trials: events with binary outcomes with a probability *p* describing one outcome and *q* describing the other. The interval is a discrete range of number of trials.

The PMF for the binomial distribution models the number of events corresponding to probability *p* observed over *n* trials. The formula is

$$P(x) = \binom{n}{x} p^x q^{n-x}$$

where

- *x* represents observing a specific number of outcomes corresponding to the probability *p*
- *n* is the number of trials
- *p* is the probability of observing the chosen outcome
- *q* is the probability of observing the other outcome and is equal to $1 - p$

To make this more concrete, let's return to the somewhat tiresome, but useful, example of flipping fair coins. Since this is a binomial distribution, it's composed of a series of Bernoulli trials. If we flip the coin 10 times, we are conducting 10 Bernoulli trials ($n = 10$). Across all 10 trials, what's the probability of seeing heads *x* times?

Since we have decided to select heads as our success condition, we shall set the probability of observing heads equal to *p*. Given that we have a fair coin, both sides are equally likely, so we know that $p = 0.5$, and by extension the probability of tails is $1 - p = 0.5$. We also know that the number of Bernoulli trials is $n = 10$ because we are flipping the coin 10 times.

As with the other PMFs, we can get the probability of seeing heads *x* times by plugging the value for *x* into the formula. If we wanted to determine the probability of getting heads 3 times out of the 10 flips:

$$P(3) = \binom{10}{3} 0.5^3 0.5^{10-3}$$

$$P(3) = \binom{10}{3} 0.5^3 0.5^7$$

$$P(3) = 0.1171875$$

If we flip a fair coin 10 times, we should expect to get exactly 3 heads approximately 12% of the time.

Again, let's use simulations to deepen our understanding. We'll need to provide the number of Bernoulli trials we would like to run. Since we can calculate the one probability using the other, we only need the probability of the 'success' outcome, *p*, of our Bernoulli trial. We also provide the number of random samples we draw from the binomial distribution.

It is worth stressing the difference between the number of Bernoulli trials and the number of samples we draw. In the above example, *n* is the number of Bernoulli trials, or coin flips. The number of samples we draw does not feature in the equation: each time we draw a sample, we are essentially flipping 10 coins and tallying the results.

Before running the simulations, consider what you would *expect* to see given different values for the probability of the success condition, *p*. If *p* were 0.8, for example, what do you think you might see with an *n* of 40? How do you think the distribution would change with different values for *n* and *p*?

The results are shown in Figure 25.3.

```
binomial_sim_1 = np.random.binomial(20, 0.5, 10_000)
binomial_sim_2 = np.random.binomial(20, 0.8, 10_000)
binomial_sim_3 = np.random.binomial(10, 0.5, 10_000)
binomial_sim_4 = np.random.binomial(10, 0.8, 10_000)
```

```
binomial_simulations = pd.DataFrame(
    [binomial_sim_1, binomial_sim_2, binomial_sim_3, binomial_sim_4]).T

fig, ax = plt.subplots(2, 2,figsize=(8, 6))

t = list(range(1, 21))

sns.countplot(x=binomial_simulations[0], ax=ax[0, 0], color='gray', order=t)
ax[0, 0].set(xlabel="", title = r'$n=20$ and $p=0.5$', )
sns.countplot(x=binomial_simulations[1], ax=ax[0, 1], color='gray', order=t)
ax[0, 1].set(xlabel="", ylabel="", title = r'$n=20$ and $p=0.8$', xticks=range(0,
20))
sns.countplot(x=binomial_simulations[2], ax=ax[1, 0], color='gray', order=t)
ax[1, 0].set(xlabel="", title = r'$n=10$ and $p=0.5$')
sns.countplot(x=binomial_simulations[3], ax=ax[1, 1], color='gray', order=t)
ax[1, 1].set(xlabel="", ylabel="", title = r'$n=10$ and $p=0.8$')

sns.despine()
plt.show()
```

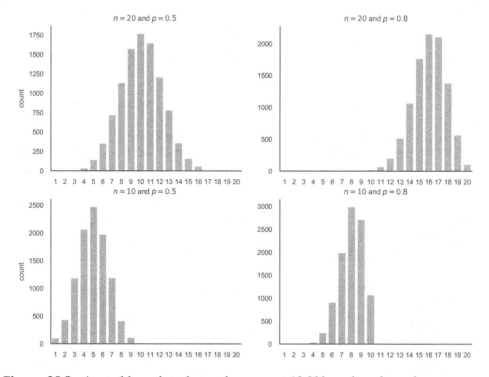

Figure 25.3 A set of four plots that each represent 10,000 random draws from a binomial distribution. The top row uses n=20, the bottom row uses n=10, the left column uses p=0.5, and the right column uses p=0.8

There are, of course, other discrete probability distributions that are commonly used in probabilistic models. There is little to no point in trying to introduce them all here, and there are many fine introductions that go into considerable technical depth. But now you should have a pretty good understanding of the basic concepts and ideas, and you should know to expect unfamiliar distributions to have (1) some set of assumptions that make them more or less appropriate to use given the nature of what you are trying to model and (2) some set of parameters that govern the distribution, and which can be used to compute probabilities for different samples.

25.6 Continuous Distributions, Probability Density Functions

Things work a bit differently when it comes to continuous distributions, as there are an uncountably infinite number of different values a continuous distribution can take on. Counter-intuitively, this means that the probability of any *specific* value in any continuous distribution (e.g. 8.985452) is 0; instead, we must describe the probability present across a *range* of values. Instead of using PMFs to compute probabilities, we use probability density functions (PDFs). Let's see how this works by focusing on the ubiquitous Gaussian/normal distribution.

The Gaussian/normal distribution

The normal distribution (often called the 'Gaussian' distribution, after the German mathematician Karl Friedrich Gauss) is foundational to traditional statistics. It describes a process that trends towards some mean value (μ) with data evenly spread around it in proportions that diminish the further away from the mean they are. We use the term 'standard deviation' (σ) to describe how quickly the data diminishes; you might also encounter publications and software that describe it as 'width' or 'scale'. The PDF for the normal distribution is this monstrosity:

$$P(x) = \frac{1}{\sigma\sqrt{2\pi}} e^{-\frac{1}{2}\left(\frac{x-\mu}{\sigma}\right)^2}$$

where

- μ is the mean of the distribution
- σ is the standard deviation
- e is the mathematical constant Euler's number ($\approx 2.71828...$)
- π is the mathematical constant pi ($\approx 3.14159...$)

A standard deviation of 0 indicates that every observation is the same as the mean value. The larger the standard deviation, the further away from the mean the average observation will be.

We'll use NumPy's `random.normal()` to perform four simulations, each pulling 10,000 samples from normal distributions with slightly different parameters. The first two arguments indicate the mean (μ) and standard deviation (σ) for the normal distribution, and the third indicates the number of samples we'll draw. Results are shown in Figure 25.4.

```python
normal_sim_1 = np.random.normal(0, 0.1, 10_000)
normal_sim_2 = np.random.normal(0, 0.2, 10_000)
normal_sim_3 = np.random.normal(0, 0.3, 10_000)
normal_sim_4 = np.random.normal(0.5, 0.2, 10_000)


b = np.linspace(-1, 1, 30)


fig, ax = plt.subplots(2,2, sharex=True, sharey=True,
                       figsize=(6,4))
sns.histplot(normal_sim_1, ax = ax[0,0], kde=True, bins=b)
ax[0,0].set_title(r'$\mu$ = 0 and $\sigma$ = 0.1')

sns.histplot(normal_sim_2, ax = ax[0,1], kde=True, bins=b)
ax[0,1].set_title(r'$\mu$ = 0 and $\sigma$ = 0.2')

sns.histplot(normal_sim_3, ax = ax[1,0], kde=True, bins=b)
ax[1,0].set_title(r'$\mu$ = 0 and $\sigma$ = 0.3')

sns.histplot(normal_sim_4, ax = ax[1,1], kde=True, bins=b)
ax[1,1].set_title(r'$\mu$ = 0.5 and $\sigma$ = 0.2')


sns.despine(left=True)
plt.tight_layout()
plt.show()
```

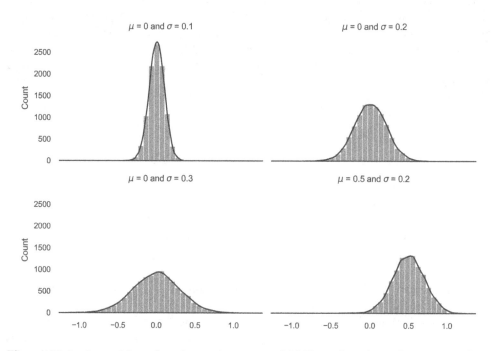

Figure 25.4 A set of four plots that each represent 10,000 random draws from a normal distribution. Each plot uses a different combination of mu (μ) and sigma (σ) parameter values

As usual, deepen your understanding of how the normal distribution behaves by experimenting with different values of mu (μ) and sigma (σ).

The exponential distribution

Another important continuous distribution is the exponential distribution. Among other things, the exponential distribution is often used to model the half-life of radionuclide decay, which describes the amount of time it takes for half of a given mass of radioactive atoms to decay into other atoms. Like the other distributions we've considered so far, we'll be using it a few times in the chapters that follow.

The PDF of the exponential distribution is normally given as

$$P(x) = \lambda e^{\lambda x}$$

where

- λ is the rate parameter of the events, and must be greater than 0
- e is Euler's number (~2.71828...)
- x is the time until the next event

Although 'rate parameter of the events' is a precise definition, it isn't a particularly intuitive one. You might be more familiar with λ representing 'rate of decay' or 'half-life'.

Note that what we presented above is not the *only* formulation of the exponential distribution PDF. These functions can be written in many ways, and for various reasons like interpretability or ease of calculation, some people prefer one over another. This is relevant because we will be drawing samples using NumPy's exponential distribution function, which uses the scale parameter $\beta = \frac{1}{\lambda}$ rather than λ.

This gives the following PDF:

$$P(x) = \frac{1}{\beta} e^{-\frac{x}{\beta}}$$

Let's jump right into the simulations. Results are shown in Figure 25.5.

```
exponential_sim_1 = np.random.exponential(1, 10000)
exponential_sim_2 = np.random.exponential(2, 10000)


fig, ax = plt.subplots()
sns.histplot(exponential_sim_1, color='crimson', label=r'$\beta = 1$')
sns.histplot(exponential_sim_2, color='lightgray', label=r'$\beta = 2$')
sns.despine()
plt.legend()
plt.show()
```

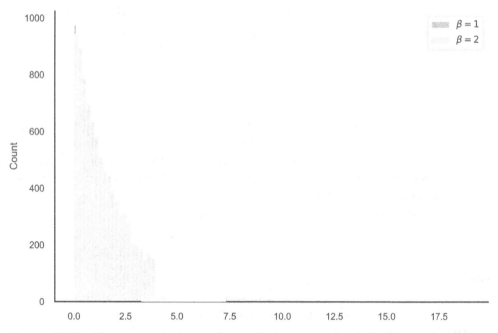

Figure 25.5 A histogram depicting the results from two sets of 10,000 random draws each from an exponential distribution, overlaid upon one another. The crimson bins used `beta=1`, whereas the grey bins used `beta=2`

As you can see from the simulations above, the exponential distribution always assigns the greatest probability density to values closest to 0, with a long tail to the right. The value of β or λ influences how much of the probability density is in the tail.

The exponential distribution always assigns a probability of 0 to any events that are less than 0. This is a useful property for us, as it allows us to use an exponential distribution to describe processes that cannot have negative values.

25.7 Joint and Conditional Probabilities

Joint probabilities

Up to this point, we've been primarily focused on *marginal probabilities*, though we haven't called them that. Marginal probabilities describe events that are unconditional on other events (which is why you'll also see us use unconditional probability to refer to the same kind of thing – the two terms are interchangeable). Joint probabilities, on the other hand, describe two or more events occurring together. Let us consider some simple examples.

Think of a standard deck of cards without jokers: 52 cards with two colours (red and black) divided into four suits (Clubs, Diamonds, Hearts, Spades), each with 13 cards having values of Ace through 10, Jack, Queen, and King. If we wanted to know the probability of randomly drawing a single Jack of any suit from the deck, then we are talking about a *marginal* probability, because the probability of drawing a Jack is independent of other events in this scenario. As there are 4 Jacks in the 52 cards, we can express this probability with the following:

$$P(\text{Jack}) = \frac{\text{Number of Jacks}}{\text{Number of cards}}$$

$$P(\text{Jack}) = \frac{4}{52} = \frac{1}{13}$$

If we wanted to know the marginal probability of drawing a Diamond:

$$P(\text{Diamond}) = \frac{\text{Number of Diamonds}}{\text{Number of cards}}$$

$$P(\text{Diamond}) = \frac{13}{52} = \frac{1}{4}$$

Sometimes we want to know the probability of two independent events occurring simultaneously, which again is known as a *joint probability*. When we want to represent the joint probability of two independent events which we will arbitrarily call A and B, we use $P(A \cap B)$, which represents the *intersection* of these two events. To get joint probabilities, we multiply the marginal probability of one event by the marginal probability of the other event, which can be expressed as follows:

$$P(A \cap B) = P(A) \times P(B)$$

Now consider the probability of drawing the Jack of Diamonds. The event we are interested in can be expressed as two events occurring: drawing a Jack and drawing a Diamond; in order to be both a Jack and a Diamond, our card must be the Jack of Diamonds, of which there is only one in the deck. We know there are 4 Jacks and 13 Diamonds in the 52 cards.

$$P(\text{Jack} \cap \text{Diamond}) = P(\text{Jack}) \times P(\text{Diamond})$$

$$P(\text{Jack} \cap \text{Diamond}) = \frac{\text{Number of Jacks}}{\text{Number of cards}} \times \frac{\text{Number of Diamonds}}{\text{Number of cards}}$$

$$P(\text{Jack} \cap \text{Diamond}) = \frac{4}{52} \times \frac{13}{52} = \frac{1}{52}$$

Finally, we have been representing joint probabilities here with the $\cap$ symbol. You may also see joint probabilities represented with commas, such as P(Jack, Diamond). There are no differences between the two; they mean the same thing.

Conditional probability

Whereas marginal probabilities represent the probability of an event independent of other events and joint probabilities represent the probability of two or more events occurring together, conditional probabilities represent the probability of an event occurring *given that another has already occurred*. You'll often see this relationship expressed using a statement like 'the probability of A conditional upon B' or 'the probability of A given B'.

Once again we'll think of drawing the Jack of Diamonds from a deck of 52 cards, but under slightly different circumstances. Imagine this time that someone has already drawn a card and informed us that it's a Diamond, and we would like to know the probability that the card in their hand is the *Jack* of Diamonds. We'll assume our friend is honest and the card they've removed is indeed a Diamond, which means that P(Diamond) = 1. Now we need to update our probabilities to account for this new certainty. Since that we know we're dealing with Diamonds only, there is only one Jack that we could have drawn. But it could only have been drawn from the pool of 13 Diamonds.

To represent the probability of an event, say A, *given that another event, say B, has occurred*, we use the notation P(A | B). You can read the | as 'given'; in this case, the probability of observing a specific value for A given a specific value for B that you have already observed. Knowing these new pieces of information, we can adjust our previous probabilities to the following:

$$P(\text{Jack}\,|\,\text{Diamond}) = \frac{\text{Number of Jacks that are Diamonds}}{\text{Number of cards that are Diamonds}}$$

$$P(\text{Jack}\,|\,\text{Diamond}) = \frac{1}{13}$$

We've used an easy case here. Other data can be much more complicated, making the above process more complicated to puzzle through. Fortunately, there is a more formal and generalizable definition we can use. We won't discuss the proof here, but know that

$$P(\text{Jack}\,|\,\text{Diamond}) = \frac{P(\text{Jack}\cap\text{Diamond})}{P(\text{Diamond})}$$

Recalling that $P(\text{Jack}\cap\text{Diamond}) = \frac{1}{52}$ and $P(\text{Diamond}) = \frac{1}{4}$, we can plug these probabilities we found earlier into this equation and get the same result as above:

$$P(\text{Jack}\,|\,\text{Diamond}) = \frac{\frac{1}{52}}{\frac{1}{4}} = \frac{1}{13}$$

25.8 Bayesian Inference

So far, we've played around with the nuts and bolts of a few discrete and continuous probability distributions to better understand how they work. But all of this is, of course, just a means to an end. We want to understand how these distributions work *because we want to use them to develop models!* To develop models that are more interesting than the distributions we've considered to this point, we need to introduce one more piece of probability theory: Bayes' theorem.

Bayes' theorem

The term 'Bayesian' is derived from the surname of Reverend Thomas Bayes – a British mathematician and Presbyterian minister of the first half of the eighteenth century. He's primarily famous for two things:

1   Articulating a special-case solution for finding the probability of an unobserved random variable
2   His use of probability to describe not just frequencies but also uncertainty in states of knowledge and belief

Of the two, the latter is more distinctly 'Bayesian', and is largely responsible for the move to associate his surname with the Bayesian statistical paradigm. What we now call Bayes' theorem was originally proposed by Bayes to compute what he called 'inverse probability', a term that has since fallen out of favour. The modern form of the theorem is used for finding the probability of an unknown variable, $P(A \mid B)$, given three known variables: $P(A)$, $P(B)$, and $P(B \mid A)$. It has a very impressive mathematical lineage. Though initially proposed by Bayes, the modern version of the theorem we know and love owes quite a lot to the Welsh mathematician and philosopher Richard Price and the French polymath Pierre-Simon Laplace. Really, it should be probably be named the Bayes–Price–Laplace theorem, but anyway.

If you're reading this book, you've probably encountered Bayes' theorem at some point:

$$P(A \mid B) = \frac{P(B \mid A) \times P(A)}{P(B)}$$

You can read this as 'The probability of A conditional on B is equal to the probability of B conditional upon A, times the marginal probability of A, all divided by the marginal probability of B'.

With the theorem introduced, I have some potentially surprising news to share. There's nothing uniquely – or even distinctly – Bayesian about using Bayes' theorem! Using it doesn't make you a Bayesian. Much of what we cover in later chapters will use Bayes' theorem in some capacity, *but the same would be true if you were using Frequentist methods*! Understanding Bayes' theorem is an important and necessary stepping stone along the path to working with a more flexible view of probability (which *is* a distinct feature of Bayesian analysis), but it is not a sufficient one. Not by itself, at least.

Now that I've spilled 'The Big Dirty Secret of Bayes' Theorem', the natural next step is to explain what, exactly, we need to do to make Bayes' theorem 'Bayesian'.

How to make Bayes' theorem Bayesian

Simply put, the best way to make Bayes' theorem Bayesian is to apply it to a hypothesis or a state of knowledge. In other words, we assign a probability to a hypothesis and then use Bayes' theorem to determine the probability of that hypothesis given the data we've observed. Isn't that a beautiful idea?

In the Bayesian paradigm, Bayes' theorem can be applied to hypotheses and data. In other words, just as we might use Bayes' theorem to compute $P(\text{Jack} \mid \text{Diamond})$, we can compute $P(\text{Hypothesis} \mid \text{Data})$, or expressed another way, $P(\text{Hypothesis} \mid \text{Evidence})$.

In order to introduce a little more clarity into our equations, you'll often find a slightly different form of notation used for the hypothesis-based version of Bayes' theorem. Below, we use the symbols θ or H to represent a hypothesis. We represent data with D, or evidence with E.

$$P(\theta \mid D) = \frac{P(D \mid \theta) \times P(\theta)}{P(D)}$$

Another equivalent rendition:

$$P(H \mid E) = \frac{P(E \mid H) \times P(H)}{P(E)}$$

You can read either of these versions of the theorem in a very similar way as the form we described earlier. In this case, one might read, 'the probability of a specific hypothesis conditional upon the data/evidence is equal to the probability of that data conditioned upon the hypothesis, times the unconditional probability of the hypothesis divided by the unconditional probability of the data'. Whew! That was a mouthful.

We're going to be referring back to the first of these forms of Bayes' theorem a whole lot (equation 12.17, with θ and D), so it might be a good idea to jot it down in your notes or take a picture of it. To reiterate, the reason why this particular form of Bayes' theorem can be considered 'Bayesian' is because we're using it to assess the probability of hypotheses.

This hypothesis form of Bayes' theorem has several components, each of which has a specific name that you'll need to know if you want to be conversant in Bayesian inference and data analysis, and to think deeply and systematically about probabilistic/generative modelling. We'll cover each of them shortly, but first, an apology: the terminology we must cover now is, for lack of a better word, *tragic*. Among other things, it will involve drawing a distinction between two words that are near-perfect synonyms in colloquial English. The distinction between them only matters in the specialized setting we currently operate within, and the differences in their meanings are confusing and oblique. I'll do my best to differentiate between them clearly, as the distinction is vitally important, but I'm sorry to have to ruin two perfectly good words for you. These words are 'probability' and 'likelihood'.

The components of Bayes' theorem

In this final part of the chapter, I'm going to walk through each of the components of Bayes' theorem – specifically:

1   the prior probability, or 'priors';
2   the likelihood; and
3   the normalizing constant.

Together, these three components are used to compute something called the 'posterior probability'. *Everything we do is in search of understanding the posterior.*

When people think of the Bayesian paradigm, they generally think of two things: (1) Bayes' theorem (which, as we've established, isn't especially Bayesian) and (2) the use of prior probabilities. While it is certainly true that Bayesian methods make extensive use of priors, they aren't the *point* of Bayesian methods. Having the ability to manipulate priors can be useful, but you should think of them as the price that Bayesians pay in order to enjoy principled access to the complete distribution of posterior probabilities (which we will get to soon) as opposed to the point estimates and confidence intervals that Frequentists use. So when thinking about what makes something Bayesian, don't focus on the priors – they're just the cost of entry, and you can develop models that minimize their influence anyhow. Instead, focus on the posteriors. Since you can't really make much sense of posteriors before understanding the other components, we'll save them for last.

Prior probability, or 'priors'

A 'prior probability' is a probability that Bayesians place on any unobserved variable. In the strictest sense, Bayesian priors are intended to serve as a quantified representation of an individual's 'state of belief' about a hypothesis under examination.

=== **Further Reading** ===

'Belief' is a widely used term here, but many Bayesians (myself included) think the term is a bit misleading while still being technically accurate. It's probably at least partly responsible for the persistent but outdated and inaccurate characterization of Bayesian models as 'subjective'. A better way of thinking about priors, which I encountered via Andrew Gelman's widely read blog 'Statistical Modeling, Causal Inference, and Social Science', is to think of priors as 'an expression of *information*' that is relevant to the modelling task. As far as I know, this better represents how most statisticians and scientists who would call themselves Bayesian think about the role of priors in modelling. When the word 'belief' is thrown around in relation to Bayesian models, it does not refer to just any old opinion you might have, it's a tentatively held 'belief' about what you think is going on in any given modelling context; it's a hypothesis *grounded in relevant information*. While this *could* have a 'subjective' source, it's really a way of leveraging theory and other kinds of knowledge, such as from previous empirical research.

Imagine you've got some coins in an opaque jar. Some are fair coins, others are trick coins, weighted so that they tend to land heads-up far more frequently than a fair coin (a fact that only becomes obvious once one starts flipping the trick coins). In this rather contrived scenario, you're going to select a coin from the jar and make as good a guess as possible about the probability that the coin – when flipped – would land heads-up.

If you didn't know there were some trick coins in the jar, then the best guess you could make is that any given coin has a 50% chance of landing heads-up. Think of this as a hypothesis; we 'believe' that there is a 50% chance of getting heads when we flip this coin.

$$P(\theta) = 0.5$$

If you knew about those trick coins, however, you might have a good reason to adjust your prior somewhat. You'd do this to account for the slim but non-zero chance that the coin you randomly grabbed from among all the coins in your jar would produce many more heads than tails. With that additional knowledge, maybe you hypothesize that the probability of getting heads is actually 0.65, for example.

Likelihood

Likelihood is, in many ways, the opposite of probability. For our purposes, likelihood describes the relative plausibility of some data *if we assume a given hypothesis is true*. All of the likelihoods we're going to consider are going to be *conditional* upon a hypothesis, which as a brief reminder is 'the probability of thing A in light of the fact that we know thing B has already occurred'.

In this case, we're not talking about conditioning on cards that we've observed, we're talking about conditioning data we've observed upon a hypothesis. In Bayes' theorem, it's this part:

$$P(D \mid \theta)$$

To briefly illustrate how likelihood operates, imagine we are testing the hypothesis that the coin we're flipping is biased such that it produces heads 80% of the time; *if we assume that's the case*, the likelihood of the coin landing heads-up is 0.8, and tails-up is 0.2.

$$P(D = \text{Heads} \mid \theta = 0.8) = 0.8$$

and, therefore,

$$P(D = \text{Tails} \mid \theta = 0.8) = 0.2$$

An important thing to keep in mind here is that likelihoods are useful in that they let us compare the *plausibility* of data given a hypothesis *relative to the same data given other hypotheses*. Likelihood is *not*, however, equivalent to probability. There are many implications that stem from this distinction, but one of the more salient ones is that likelihoods do not need to sum (or integrate) to 1; an individual likelihood can, in fact, be greater than 1! Even when multiplied by a prior (which is a probability), a likelihood isn't ready to be used as a probability just yet. For that, we need to add one more piece of the puzzle.

The normalizing constant

The normalizing constant is what converts the unstandardized 'Bayes numerator' – a term that refers to the product of the likelihood and the prior, or $P(D \mid \theta) \times P(\theta)$ – back into a standardized probability. If you recall, all probabilities must sum to 1, and the product of the prior and the likelihood very rarely do. In Bayes' theorem, the normalizing constant is $P(D)$, or $P(E)$, and is often referred to as the 'total probability'.

The normalizing constant is interesting because it's simultaneously the least important element in Bayes' theorem and the most difficult to calculate. It's the least important because Bayes' theorem is capable of working at nearly full power without it. $P(D \mid \theta) \times P(\theta)$ often won't sum (or integrate) to 1, so it can't be a probability, but it'll be exactly the same shape as the standardized posterior. From an inferential standpoint, they're *almost* identical. The normalizing constant is the most difficult to calculate because it is often unclear what the marginal probability of any given data was. What's more, even if one *knows* the marginal probability of the data, determining an exact analytical solution often involves performing some truly horrific multiple integrals, some of which have no closed-form solution (read: can't be solved exactly, and must be estimated).

Nevertheless, one of the great advantages offered by the Bayesian paradigm is the ability to take the result from one model (in the form of the posterior probability) and use it as the prior for another model (a process called Bayesian updating, which we'll introduce later). In order to do that, we must make use of the normalizing constant.

25.9 Posterior Probability

We've saved the best for last. The whole point of *all* of this is to compute the posterior probability, which represents our 'belief' in the hypothesis (θ) once we've considered it in light of the empirical evidence, our data. It is typically depicted like so:

$$P(\theta \mid D)$$

In the outputs of many models – including regression analysis – Frequentists will typically report two or three statistics designed to give you a rough idea of how the variables in your model are related. You'll commonly find a coefficient, the standard error associated with that coefficient, and the significance of that coefficient in light of its standard error (the significance is typically displayed using one or more stars next to the coefficient).

Bayesians don't skip immediately to summarizing model outputs like the Frequentists do; instead, Bayesian data analysis requires that you report the *entire posterior probability* of your model. In other words, we are not just interested in knowing what the 'best' estimate is and a bit about how much certainty to place in that estimate. We want to know the relative plausibility of *every* hypothesis in the form of a distribution. That's what working with Bayes gives us.

Once you have the posterior probability, you can easily calculate statistics that mimic what the Frequentists report directly – it's generally simple to calculate the mean or median value of an effect size, its variance, credible intervals (the Bayesian equivalent of confidence intervals), and so on. The important thing here is that a Bayesian has delivered the fullest and most complete answer they can once they've produced a posterior. Everything else is just designed to make the posterior easier to digest.

25.10 Conclusion

The key points in this chapter are as follows:

- The mathematics of probability are the same regardless of whether they are interpreted within the Frequentist or Bayesian paradigms.
- Probability distributions are key to statistical modelling. We used PMFs to compute the probability of events when dealing with discrete distributions, and PDFs to compute the probability of events when dealing with continuous distributions.
- Joint probabilities tell us the probability of two events occurring together, while conditional probabilities tell us the probability of one event conditional on another, or given that another has already occurred.
- Bayes' theorem is a foundational theorem in statistics, used by Bayesians and Frequentists alike. Using it does not make you a Bayesian, but it is commonly associated with the Bayesian paradigm. Bayesian's use the theorem to compute posterior probabilities based on a prior, likelihood, and total probability.

Visit the website at https://study.sagepub.com/mclevey for additional resources

26

APPROXIMATE POSTERIOR INFERENCE WITH STOCHASTIC SAMPLING AND MCMC

26.1 Learning Objectives

By the end of this chapter, you should be able to do the following:

- Understand the basic logic of developing a regression model within the Bayesian paradigm
- Differentiate between variables in a Bayesian model based on their 'origin'
- Develop a Bayesian model by repeatedly asking yourself 'what's that?'
- Explain how stochastic sampling methods enable us to fit Bayesian models that would otherwise be intractable
- Explain what a Markov chain is
- Explain how Metropolis–Hastings and Hamiltonian Monte Carlo allow us to efficiently explore posterior distributions

26.2 Learning Materials

You can find the online learning materials for this chapter in `doing_computational_social_science/Chapter_26`. `cd` into the directory and launch your Jupyter server.

26.3 Introduction

One of my PhD students, Pierson Browne, was once sitting in on a 'Mathematics for Statisticians' lecture at the University of Michigan when a professor of mathematics settled an in-class debate by boldly stating, 'there are many, many more functions then there are formulae'. He was trying to hammer home the idea that some numerical relationships are knowable, but cannot be readily described using a single algebraic equation. This might, at first, seem like a counter-intuitive claim because much of our mathematical instruction is focused on manipulating functions whose behaviour can be precisely expressed using an equation (most of which are defined for inputs along the real number line). It may come as a surprise, then, that there are many functions that cannot be accurately described using an equation. Form(ula) Follows Function.

In the previous chapter, we saw how the Bayesian paradigm uses statements of likelihood $P(D \mid \theta)$ and total probability $P(D)$ to condition a prior $P(\theta)$ on data, producing a posterior probability $P(\theta \mid D)$. The function that describes this process, however, is not often accompanied by a well-behaved formula. Consequently, for the majority of the twentieth century, the Bayesian paradigm required frequent use of daedal calculus and often produced algebraic dead ends, all of which severely hampered the development and adoption of Bayesian methods.

Fortunately, recent advances in computational Bayesian statistics and probabilistic programming have allowed the Bayesian paradigm to largely slip free from its intractable integrals by approximating the posterior. The two main ways of doing this are:

1 *stochastic sampling*, especially with the family of Markov chain Monte Carlo (MCMC) methods; and
2 *variational inference*, which approximates the posterior by using a simpler but very similar distribution as a proxy.

The primary purpose of this chapter is to demystify stochastic sampling with MCMC methods. We'll set variational inference aside until Chapter 30.

Understanding stochastic sampling with MCMC is our goal, but we won't actually *start* there. Instead, I'll start by setting up a scenario that demonstrates the practical utility of MCMC methods with a detailed work-through of a hypothetical Bayesian regression model based on principles established in previous chapters. This will also help you understand how Bayesians approach regression analysis (which will be the focus of the next two chapters). Then, I'll introduce MCMC methods with the goal of helping you develop an intuitive understanding of how they work.

In this chapter, I assume that you've been introduced to linear regression (beyond its brief appearance in Chapter 20), and more specifically, the classic Frequentist approach of ordinary least squares (OLS). A typical introductory quantitative methods class in the social sciences should suffice. If OLS is entirely new to you, it's worth taking a moment to familiarize yourself with the basic framework.

26.4 Bayesian Regression

If you haven't already noticed, one of the models you'll encounter *ad nauseum* in the social sciences is linear regression, often *ordinary least squares regression*. Linear regression is a workhorse in many fields and is notable for its ease of computation and interpretation (categorical variables make a lot of intuitive sense in OLS, and do not in many other models). We're going to use it to deepen your understanding of Bayesian data analysis.

Tackling linear regression from a Bayesian perspective still involves using data to condition priors and turn them into posteriors. In doing so, we're going to use a *continuous range* of hypotheses about the numerical relationship between two or more variables (including exactly one 'dependent' variable and some number of 'independent' variables). As a result, our 'hypotheses' are going to become significantly more complex. We might ask a question like 'how much does a 1000-dollar increase in yearly salary affect a person's life span?' This requires a numerical answer. We will consider an infinite number of such answers at the same time. That might sound impressive, but isn't: it's the natural consequence of using continuous variables to describe hypotheses.

As with other chapters in this book, my goal is to build intuition and understanding with practical examples. However, this means that from time to time I will have to hand-wave the specifics of how Bayes' theorem is being used. The basic logic is the same, but more complex, when we generalize it to multiple variables and higher dimensions. I don't think that it's necessary to have a deep understanding of the maths behind generalizing the theorem to these conditions, so when we get to places where there is a precise yet notationally baffling explanation for the logical leaps we're making, I'm just going to mention that it *Just Works*.

Playing the 'What's That?' game

When developing a Bayesian regression model, you can get pretty far by asking a bunch of annoying 'What's That?' questions. *Unleash your inner child!* I'll show you what I mean by walking through the development of a hypothetical regression model. This is not likely to be a *good* model; it's designed with pedagogical goals in mind, so there are some purposeful problems with the model.

Let's imagine we have a couple of thousand observations about individual-level wealth around the world. Since wealth is a continuous variable (or nearly enough so that we can treat it as such), and can hypothetically take on any value on the real number line, it can be expressed as a random variable drawn from the normal distribution. By doing this, we're effectively hypothesizing that individual wealth is distributed following a rough 'bell curve', with some mean (μ) and some standard deviation (σ). This is, of course, a very naive hypothesis (remember model criticism in the context of Box's loop, introduced in Chapter 7), but we'll proceed with it for now.

We can express the above using model notation, like this:

Wealth ~ Normal(μ,σ)

In one line, we've concisely defined the relationship between our three variables, Wealth, μ, and σ. The little squiggly line (called a tilde) separating Wealth from the rest of the model notation means 'is distributed as'. Using this notation, we're saying that 'Wealth has the same distribution as a normal distribution with mean μ and standard deviation σ.'

We don't yet have a complete model, though. For a Bayesian, you can't just conjure a variable out of thin air, it must have an origin of some sort. You should ask: *where did this variable come from?* There are, broadly speaking, three different types of origin for a variable:

1 *A variable can be observed:* In almost all cases, observed variables come from data we or someone else collected. Their origin is the real world, or perhaps a simulation.
2 *A variable can be calculated:* Its origin is a combination of other variables.
3 *A variable can be unobserved:* Unobserved variables are often referred to as latent or hidden variables, or parameters. If we haven't observed enough to know much about a variable, and the variable isn't calculated by mathematically combining other variables, then we must use our brains to produce a prior distribution for it (which serves as the origin).

This is not the place to belabour the point, but Bayesian statistics provides a powerful framework for working with unobserved variables in a wide variety of contexts. For now, we'll focus on regression problems and refer to 'parameters' since you're already acquiring a lot of new technical vocabulary very quickly, and discussing parameters in the context of regression modelling is likely more familiar than describing regression modelling in terms of latent or hidden variables.

The downside of this approach is that 'parameter' generally implies a single value that is estimated from some sort of model – a 'point estimate'. Whereas linear regression in the Frequentist paradigm produces point estimates with standard errors, Bayesian regression produces a full distribution. It is possible to produce a point estimate from that distribution (which is almost always the same as what you would get from a Frequentist point estimate).

In later chapters, we'll drop the language of parameters to speak more generally about 'latent' and 'hidden variables'. Mathematically and statistically, nothing will change; what we are calling 'parameters' in Chapters 26 to 28 *are the same thing as latent and hidden variables*. But once you have a slightly firmer grasp on the logic of Bayesian data analysis and inference, switching up our language a bit will help you get your head around the wider world of Bayesian latent variable models. We'll focus on drawing inferences about latent structure in social networks and latent thematic structure (topics) in large text datasets, but these two are also only a small subset of what's possible. Once you 'get' the bigger picture of latent variable modelling in a Bayesian framework, you're well on your way to developing high-quality bespoke probabilistic models for all kinds of really interesting research problems.

Our model has three variables. One is observed: Wealth. Both μ and σ are not calculated anywhere in our model specification, and we don't have data on them, so – by process of elimination – they are unobserved, and we must imbue them with a prior.

You can probably see the value of interrogating your models with the 'What's That?' game as you construct them. Every time you write down a variable, *make sure you ask yourself where it comes from*. If you can't identify a pre-existing origin, you must make one by supplying a prior. This will seem like a clunky and exhausting process at first, but it becomes second nature after a while.

Since both μ and σ are unobserved, we're going to have to come up with priors for them. Since μ simply represents the middle point of our normal distribution, we can probably come up with a sensible prior for it. If you take the total amount of wealth in the world, convert everything into USD, and divide the result by the number of humans on the planet, you get approximately 7000. You might be tempted to update your model specification like so:

$$\text{Wealth} \sim \text{Normal}(\mu, \sigma)$$

$$\mu = 7000$$

While that might be a prior (of a sort), it's not a very good one. In fact, *it's a very, very bad one*. Among other things, it's equivalent to saying that you are perfectly confident that the value of μ is *exactly* 7000 and will never change for any reason.

If we want our Bayesian model to be able to *update* our priors to produce the posteriors, we must inject some *uncertainty* into them. Rather than describing μ using an integer, we'll describe it using a full probability distribution. Since we know that μ represents the number of dollars per capita, and given that these dollars are the same unit (and thus follow the same rules) as our Wealth variable, we might as well use a normal distribution here, too. Since we're pretty sure of our mean value, we can afford to use a comparatively small value for the standard deviation of this distribution; if we use a value of 1000, we're saying that about 68% of the probability will lie between 6000 and 8000. If you're wondering why in the world it's permissible to pull numbers out of a hat like this, stay tuned: we'll cover the dark art of prior selection in more detail in the next chapter. If you're really concerned and can't wait, know that in most actual models with anything other than very small datasets, the evidence generally overwhelms the priors, and they have little effect.

We're going to have to go through the same process for σ as we did for μ. The standard deviation parameter in a normal distribution is a continuous variable that can take on any value from 0 to positive infinity. This means that we should be careful to assign a prior that can't produce negative values. There are many good candidates, but we'll use the exponential distribution, which covers the same domain (from 0 to positive infinity). The exponential distribution takes only one parameter – β. For simplicty's sake, let's assign a large value for β, which will help encode our lack of prior knowledge about the variability of wealth. When we put it all together, our model looks like this:

$$\text{Wealth} \sim \text{Normal}(\mu, \sigma) \qquad\qquad \text{[Likelihood]}$$

$$\mu \sim \text{Normal}(7000, 1000) \qquad\qquad [\mu \text{ Prior}]$$

$$\sigma \sim \text{Exponential}(4000) \qquad\qquad [\sigma \text{ Prior}]$$

At this point, we have a complete model. You can play the 'What's That?' game on any portion of it, and another part of the model definition will give you an answer. However, the model isn't very informative at this point. All we've done is lump all of our data into one big bin and described the shape of that bin by specifying where the middle is and how wide it is. If we had actual data, we could produce posterior probabilities for each of our priors and see how close our initial guesses were to the final answers. (Hint: they'd probably be *way, way off.*) For now, let's focus on two specific limitations with what we've done:

1. The model isn't even remotely interesting or informative.
2. It isn't yet a linear model. For that, we need an independent variable upon which wealth depends.

These two problems are related, and we'll attempt to solve them both in the subsequent section.

Introducing a predictor

In order to turn our normal model into a linear model, we're going to need to introduce another variable. Let's say you've been reading some international development and globalization research and learn there is a correlation between the absolute value of latitude and wealth per capita (*after* the Industrial Revolution). Whether you go north or south, per capita wealth is higher the further you get from the equator. How strong is this relationship? Maybe you want to know, for example, how much of a difference a 10° shift of latitude has on wealth. To show how we'd go about modelling this, let's rebuild our model, starting from the likelihood:

$$\text{Wealth}_i \sim \text{Normal}(\mu_i, \sigma) \qquad \text{[Likelihood]}$$

This looks almost exactly the same as the normal model we specified before! The only difference is that there are now subscripted 'i's after Wealth and μ – what gives?

The subscripted 'i' is a powerful clue. It means that rather than trying to find a single value for μ that applies to the entire dataset (which, in effect, gives us overall average wealth), we're going to be producing a different value of μ for each observation of Wealth in our dataset. Pay attention to subscripts (like 'i' or 'j') going forwards: their appearance in some part of the model indicates that we're going to be allowing that part of the model to take on many different values – usually, one value for each observation in the data.

In this case, rather than plunking a normal distribution somewhere along the real number line and trying to configure it to best account for all of the data we have, we're going to let it move about. Every time we calculate a μ value for one of the observations in the data, we'll plug it in as a parameter in our normal distribution, which will cause the distribution to scoot around the real number line in an attempt to get as close as possible to the observed data.

If we're serious about allowing our likelihood distribution to move, we can't put a prior directly on μ. Instead, we're going to recast μ as a statistic, and calculate it as a combination of other variables. This is where our linear model comes in!

$$\text{Wealth}_i \sim \text{Normal}(\mu_i, \sigma) \qquad \text{[Likelihood]}$$
$$\mu_i = \alpha + (\beta \times \text{Latitude}_i)$$

Note the new line uses = rather than ~. This indicates that the calculation of μ is now based on a *deterministic* combination of its constituent parts. This line is called the 'linear model', and it's how we tell our Bayesian model that we want to use a line to approximate the relationship between latitude and wealth. If you squint and blur your eyes a bit, you might even begin to recognize similarities between the linear model and the equation for a straight line:

$$y = mx + b$$

where m is the slope of the line and b is the intercept. We're doing the exact same thing here, except rearranging things, using α instead of b, and using β instead of m. It's a simple model, but simplicity is often a virtue in statistics. All we have to do to complete it is play the 'What's That?' game until we've covered all of our bases. Let's start from the top:

- We already know that Wealth is observed, and so it doesn't need to appear anywhere else in the model.
- We know that μ_i is unobserved, but unlike the previous model we made, it is now calculated from other variables in the model. As such, it doesn't need a prior – we already have a line telling us where it comes from. That line is a linear model.
- No such luck with σ; we're going to need a prior just like before.

- Similarly, we do not have information about α or β, and so they're both going to need priors.
- Latitude is observed, so we can leave it as is.

Consider what these terms might mean in the model, and then to try and extrapolate some sensible priors. Pay attention to what values the parameters *can* take. Recall that you can't have a negative standard error, and so it's vitally important that you assign a prior to σ that can't take on any negative values. Conversely, it's important to make sure that you don't artificially limit what values a variable can take. If you assign a probability of 0 to a value, you've made that particular value impossible; from that point onwards, it will never receive any probability from the model. If you ever assign any value a probability of 0, make sure that you've got *a really good reason for doing so* (a model predicting wealth using age probably shouldn't allow negative ages). If you think a particular value is unlikely *but still theoretically possible*, then it's far safer to use a distribution that will place a vanishingly small but still non-zero probability on those unlikely values.

Prior specification is a complex debate. Don't worry about it for now; until you're comfortable with Bayesian analysis, your focus should be on making sure that you don't unintentionally make the impossible possible, or vice versa. When you have lots of data and a simple model, the exact form of your priors won't matter because *they'll get overwhelmed by the evidence!* Even horrifically mis-specified priors will be 'washed out' and have next-to-no impact on inference.

When you've thought this through a bit, feel free to take a look at what I've selected. Got any criticisms? Good. That's a *vital* part of the process. Write them down.

$Wealth_i \sim Normal(\mu_i, \sigma)$	[Likelihood]
$\mu_i = \alpha + (\beta \times Latitude_i)$	[Linear Model]
$\alpha \sim Normal(4000, 2000)$	[α Prior]
$\beta \sim Normal(1000, 500)$	[β Prior]
$\sigma \sim Exponential(1000)$	[σ Prior]

Now that you've built a bivariate linear regression, you can easily extrapolate what you've learnt to add more variables to your model. Suppose we wanted to add another variable to the model we just finished specifying. We could do so by simply adding another term to the linear model equation and creating another prior for the coefficient!

$Wealth_i \sim Normal(\mu_i, \sigma)$	[Likelihood]
$\mu_i = \alpha + (\beta_1 \times Latitude_i) + (\beta_2 \times New\ Variable_i)$	[Linear Model]
$\alpha \sim Normal(4000, 2000)$	[α Prior]
$\beta_1 \sim Normal(1000, 500)$	[β_1 Prior]
$\beta_2 \sim Normal(-150, 100)$	[β_2 Prior]
$\sigma \sim Exponential(1000)$	[σ Prior]

And now, for the anticlimax: we don't have any data for this model, so we can't produce a posterior distribution. A shame, I know, but that wasn't the point. The point was to work through the process of developing a rudimentary Bayesian regression model using only hypotheticals to keep your focus as much as possible on the *structure* and *logic* of these regressions, including the use of a few priors that stretch credibility in order to emphasize the importance of *criticism* in model development.

As with all Bayesian models, our goal here is posterior inference. Rather than take a deep dive into the mathematics, we're going to skip to the cutting edge of Bayesian analysis and discuss the first of two computational approaches to approximating the posterior: stochastic sampling. Together with variational inference (introduced in Chapter 29), stochastic sampling has played a *major* role in the meteoric rise of Bayesian methods.

26.5 Stochastic Sampling Methods

Throughout the next few chapters, we're going to be making frequent use of stochastic sampling methods to produce posterior distributions for a variety of Bayesian models. Stochastic sampling methods represent the cutting edge of a remarkably adaptable approach to fitting otherwise difficult or impossible models. What they are *not* is a one-size-fits-all panacea. Unlike many other approaches, we can't simply feed our data and model specification into a sampler and reliably get an intelligible answer. You're going to have to know:

- how your sampler works,
- how to read and interpret the output it produces, and, most importantly,
- how to help a sampler that's fallen sick.

Fortunately, you don't need a rigorous understanding of the underlying maths in order to become a pretty good sampler medic; you will, however, need a strong intuitive understanding of how they work. In what follows, and over the course of the next two chapters, my goal is to help you build that essential intuition. Rather than wasting your time starting from first principles and working our way up to something interesting, I'm going to briefly introduce an especially important concept, Markov chains. Then we'll dive straight into the deep end with a grotesquely extended metaphor. We'll get into the details of diagnosing and fixing problems with samplers in the chapters to come. Let's begin.

Markov chains

At the root of everything we're going to cover in this section is the *Markov chain*. Named after Russian mathematician Andrei Markov, a Markov chain is a simple machine that transitions from one state to another based on some predefined set of interstate probabilities. Markov chain models are 'memoryless', which is a fancy way of saying that when they decide to switch states, they do so using information about the current state of the machine and nothing else. Figure 26.1 is a model that describes (pretty accurately) how my two cats, Dorothy and Lando Catrissian, spend their days.

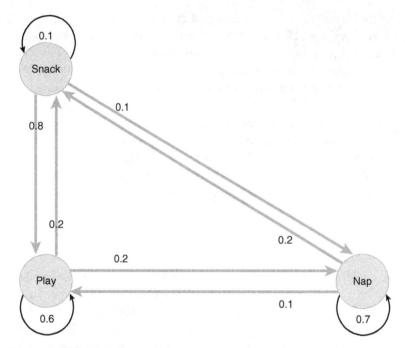

Figure 26.1 A Markov chain modelling my cats' behaviour on any given day; they'll transition between one of three states – play, nap, and snack – according to a predetermined set of probabilities

All we have to do is choose an initial state and some kind of looping time interval which governs when we check for a state transition. Let's say we start on the 'Play' node, jumping in boxes and pawing at strings. Every 5 minutes, we'll check to see if we transition to a different node. No matter which node we're on, there's a non-zero chance that we'll end up on any of the nodes (including the one we're currently on). From the Play node, there's a 60% chance that we'll stay exactly where we are, a 20% chance that we'll end up on the 'Nap' node, and a 20% chance of wandering over to the food bowl for a snack.

```
import numpy as np
np.random.seed(3)
np.random.choice(['Play', 'Snack', 'Nap'], p=[0.6, 0.2, 0.2])
```

```
'Play'
```

The choice is 'Play,' so we'll keep batting at strings. That was the most probable outcome (60% chance). After a further 5 minutes of wondering what you have to do to get a human to break out a laser pointer, we'll run the check once more:

```
np.random.seed(4)
np.random.choice(['Play', 'Snack', 'Nap'], p=[0.6, 0.2, 0.2])
```

```
'Nap'
```

Nap time! While on the Nap node, we're very likely to stay where we are: a 70% chance. Of the remaining probability, there's a 20% probability of getting up for another snack and a 10% chance of more play. Let's see what happens:

```
np.random.seed(5)
np.random.choice(['Play', 'Snack', 'Nap'], p=[0.1, 0.2, 0.7])
```

```
'Snack'
```

Sleeping is hard work! Time to reward all that effort with a well-deserved snack.

At this point, the pattern should be pretty clear: a Markov chain switches between some set of predefined states according to a set of probabilities that can be different for each of the nodes in the model. Crucially, Markov chain models converge, over long periods of time, to a calculable equilibrium state. This feature will come in handy in just a moment.

Markov chain Monte Carlo

As it happens, we can fruitfully apply Markov chains to probability distributions by replacing the bespoke probabilities we used in the previous section (Nap, Snack, Play) with probabilities computed on-the-fly based on a distribution. This is known as *Markov chain Monte Carlo*, and it is useful because it – much like the simpler Markov chains we already covered – converges with the probability distribution it is being asked to traverse. Very useful!

The issue with MCMC is that – while simple and elegant in theory – implementing it in practical settings involves a number of trade-offs. This has caused a plethora of specific implementations to emerge: one workhorse is the 'Metropolis–Hastings algorithm', which uses a proposal distribution to quasi-randomly walk around the parameter space. Instead of transitioning between abstract 'states', as in the case of the pure Markov chain above, we can imagine Metropolis–Hastings stepping between different parameter values. Let's say that we think a certain parameter in a model can only take on one of five discrete ordinal values (1 through 5), each of which might be more or less plausible. Metropolis–Hastings chooses a random parameter value to start with and then – for a predetermined number of iterations – starts stepping from value to value according to the following logic:

1   Randomly select an adjacent parameter value that's 1 higher or lower than the current parameter value. We'll call it the 'proposal'. If the proposal is outside the range of values (e.g. 0 or 6), wrap around to the other side of the value range.
2   Calculate the probability at the proposal, and compare it to the probability of the current parameter value. If the proposal has a higher probability, move to it immediately and return to Step 1. Otherwise, move to Step 3.
3   Since the proposal's probability is equal to or lower than the current node's, randomly choose from between the two with a probability proportional to the difference between them (e.g. if the proposal has half the probability of the current value, then there's a 1/3 chance that the algorithm will move to the proposal, and a 2/3 chance it will stay where it is).

That's it! Collectively, these rules ensure that the Metropolis–Hastings algorithm will trend towards the parameter values with the highest posterior probability, but won't entirely ignore the ones with lower probability.

Despite the Metropolis–Hastings algorithm not knowing about the shape of the distributions it is tasked with exploring, its stochastic meandering will eventually cause it to visit every portion of a probability distribution *in proportion to the probability density at that location*. Thinking back to the hypothetical Bayesian model we created in the first half of this chapter, using a sampling method like Metropolis–Hastings would allow us to create reliable estimates of the posterior distributions for all of our unobserved parameters (α, β, and σ), provided we had data to feed into our linear model/likelihood (which we don't).

Metropolis–Hastings 'Just Works', but sometimes it doesn't work quickly or efficiently enough for our purposes. It's not enough to employ an algorithm that will *eventually* provide us with a satisfactory approximation; we want to find one that will do so efficiently and in a reasonable amount of time, even when the shape of the posterior is irregular.

Rather than skipping straight to the answer, we're going to take a diversion into the realm of an extended thought experiment that will – with luck – provide you with an intuition for how one might go about efficiently exploring convoluted continuous parameter spaces. It's a bit of a weird thought experiment, but learning about stochastic sampling for the first time is a bit mind-bending anyway, so let's just have a bit of fun, shall we?

Mapping a skate bowl

Imagine we've made a bet with a friend that we can create a topographical map of the bottom of a skate bowl. The bowl is highly irregular in shape and depth, with several local minima scattered around, and there's no easy way to mathematically describe it. This poses a bit of a challenge already, but the *real* challenge is that the rules of the bet prevent us from ever seeing the skate park! All we know in advance is that there are several low areas scattered throughout the skate bowl (relative to their steeply sloping surroundings), and that our friend is more interested in the lower areas of the bowl than the steeply sloping sides of the bowl. They're entirely uninterested in the completely flat, high area surrounding the bowl. The 3D plots in Figure 26.2 offer three perspectives that are *similar*, but not the same, as the shape of the skate bowl we're trying to map in this example.

Figure 26.2   Three views of the same complex inverted probability distribution that we've been tasked with remotely mapping using only a physics-defying marble and a robot with a very limited repertoire of commands

This is already kind of a weird example, so let's just lean into the weird. Our friend has provided two unusual tools to help us: a frictionless, perfectly elastic marble which, once set into motion, will stop – dead – after a configurable length of time has elapsed. This marble is a marvel of modern engineering (and may potentially break several laws of physics), as it is capable of coming to an immediate and complete standstill whilst halfway up a slope that any other round object would immediately begin to roll down. What's more, the marble, once it has come to a complete stop, will send you an unnervingly accurate three-dimensional readout of its current position.

The other tool is a robot. We're allowed to program the robot to traverse the skate park, find the physics-defying marble, and move the marble either by picking it up and putting it down elsewhere, or by imparting some kind of force onto the marble. The robot is always aware (relative to its current position) of where the marble is, where the marble last came to a stop, and where the skate park's walls are – it is otherwise incapable of perceiving anything about its surroundings.

Our objective is to use the robot and the marble to 'map' the contours of the skate bowl (but none of the surrounding area) as efficiently as possible. How might we approach such a task? Let's think it through.

Gradient descent

Those of you who saw the 'efficiently as possible' qualifier above might have started thinking something akin to: 'why not just instruct the robot to repeatedly roll the marble over very small intervals until it descends into the skate bowl, and keep going until it reaches the bottom? We could use the resulting data as an approximation of best fit!' That would be very similar to the 'gradient descent' approach discussed in Chapter 22.

While this technique certainly gets top marks for ease of implementation, our friend wouldn't be sufficiently impressed to concede the bet. For starters, short of conducting several such throws, we'd have no way of knowing whether or not the marble had ended up in a 'local minima'; that is, one of the smaller sub-bowls in the diagram above that are quite a bit shallower than a nearby 'global minima', which is the actual lowest point in the skate bowl. What's more, recall that to win the bet our friend expects us to describe low points throughout the entire bowl, not just an approximation of the single lowest point.

Quadratic approximation

Since having a single point isn't good enough, we could use the data gathered as our marble slowly descended into the bowl (remember, it stopped frequently on the way down) to estimate the curve it followed as it descended. If you were thinking along these lines, it might be fair to say that you had hoped to employ a 'quadratic approximation' which involves using an analytically defined 'good-enough' parabolic curve to describe the shape of the bowl.

Since many statistical models make extensive use of the normal distribution, and given that the normal distribution can be fairly well-approximated using a parabola, quadratic approximation is commonly called upon to help provide useful approximations of posterior distributions in simple (and a few not-so-simple) Bayesian models. Unfortunately, based on the description of the bowl our friend provided us with (and the simulation of one possible bowl above), the skate bowl is not symmetric, has multiple 'lowest points' (multiple local minima), and undulates (not monotonic). Under such conditions, there's no easy way to produce an accurate quadratic approximation: the best-fitting curve will look nothing like the actual bowl.

Grid approximation

You may now be thinking 'okay, the quick-and-easy approach is out, so how about we double down on accuracy and try to systematically cover every inch of the skate park?' This is a method akin to 'grid approximation' or 'grid search', wherein we would systematically cover every part of the skate bowl by breaking the entire skate park into a regularly spaced grid, and then taking a sample at each intersection in that grid.

Using this approach, you'd be guaranteed to map the entire skate bowl. The problem here, though, is that you're going to spend a whole lot of time – a WHOLE lot – exploring areas of the skate bowl that aren't of any interest. Let's say the park is 100 metres by 100 metres. Even if you only take one measurement every 2 metres, you're going to have to take 2500 measurements to cover the entire park. If you double the resolution of your search to take one measurement every metre, the number of measurements balloons to 10,000. Further increases in resolution will result in exponentially larger numbers of required measurements.

If we were immortal, fine, grid search could be usefully applied to complex, continuous spaces. If, however, you want to settle this bet sometime between now and the eventual heat death of the universe, you're going to have to find a faster way.

Randomly whack the marble around

Those of you with a keen sense of irony may have seen something like this coming: rather than employing sophisticated mathematical approximations of our skate bowl, our best option overall involves instructing our robot to give the marble a good thump in a random direction with a random force, wait until it stops (after a fixed period of time), and then repeat the process from the marble's new location. This 'Randomly Whack the Marble Around' approach is known as 'Hamiltonian Monte Carlo' (HMC). The unusual thing about it is that – with the exception of a few edge cases – it is a reasonable, reliable, and comparatively efficient method for exploring the shape of a distribution, even if the distribution is very complex or has many different dimensions.

Providing any form of rigorous proof – mathematical or otherwise – of the effectiveness of HMC is *far* beyond the scope of this book. You'll have to take it for granted that this method 'Just Works'. You can get a good look under the hood with some of the recommended sources at the end of this chapter.

If you want to learn more about HMC, and it's use in regression analysis, I recommend McElreath's (2020) classic Bayesian statistics textbook *Statistical Rethinking*. Note, however, that you'll want to build up more of a foundation before jumping into that book, or others like it. Lambert (2018) and Kruschke (2014) are also excellent introductions to Bayesian statistics in the social and cognitive sciences that include discussions of various approaches to approximate and exact Bayesian inference.

Go see the marbles move

I've tried to make everything we've just covered as concrete and easy to picture as possible, but obviously all of this remains *very* abstract. This material can be incredibly difficult to grasp, especially if you're encountering it for the first time, and dually so when we try to extend the intuitions we've built in three dimensions to a higher number of dimensions. It is, sadly, impossible to imagine a marble rolling around in a 16-dimensional skate bowl.

It might be helpful to view an animated representation of what's happening. Since you're most likely reading this textbook on paper, I recommend reading Richard McElreath's (2017) blog post 'Build a Better Markov Chain', https://elevanth.org/blog/2017/11/28/build-a-better-markov-chain/. You can spend a bit of time observing and playing around with a few animated stochastic samplers to deepen your understanding.

In particular, I'd like to draw your attention to the section on the No-U-Turn-Sampler, or NUTS for short. NUTS is a sort of special case of HMC, wherein the marble is capable of intelligently detecting when it has pulled a U-turn and is headed back towards its starting location.

When you're all done watching the imaginary marbles zip around the imaginary skate bowls, we can move on to specifying some models in the next chapter.

26.6 Conclusion

The key points in this chapter are as follows:

- We learnt that all variables in a Bayesian model come from observed data, are calculated from other variables, or are hidden/latent.
- We learnt how to describe a Bayesian model using model notation.
- We learnt how Markov chains work, and the role they play in Markov chain Monte Carlo stochastic samplers for posterior inference.
- We used an extended metaphor to develop an intuitive understanding of how the HMC sampling algorithm works.

Visit the website at https://study.sagepub.com/mclevey for additional resources

PART VI

PROBABILISTIC PROGRAMMING AND BAYESIAN LATENT VARIABLE MODELS FOR STRUCTURED, RELATIONAL, AND TEXT DATA

27

BAYESIAN REGRESSION MODELS WITH PROBABILISTIC PROGRAMMING

27.1 Learning Objectives

By the end of this chapter, you should be able to do the following:

- Specify a Bayesian linear regression model with PyMC3
- Understand the logic of using Python's context management to develop models with PyMC3
- Use PyMC3 to conduct a prior predictive check to ensure that our model is not overly influenced by our priors
- Read a trace plot to assess the quality of a stochastic sampler
- Assess and interpret models by:
  - Constructing and interpreting credible intervals using the highest density interval method
  - Conducting posterior predictive checks
  - Plotting uncertainty

27.2 Learning Materials

You can find the online learning materials for this chapter in `doing_computational_social_science/Chapter_27`. `cd` into the directory and launch your Jupyter server.

27.3 Introduction

In this chapter, we'll actually develop some Bayesian regression models. We will slowly develop a simple linear model, explaining the ins and outs of the process using a package for probabilistic programming called PyMC3. Then we'll criticize the model (Box's loop) we've built and use those critiques to build a much better model in the next chapter.

Our example here, and in the next chapter, will be the influence of money on voting outcomes by state in the 2020 American General Election. Given that we would like data that is regionally representative and as numerous as possible, we're going to focus on the electoral contests that took place across 435 congressional districts.

It's almost a truism to state that money wins elections. In light of this fact, one of the most critical decisions a political party can make is where and how to allocate their funds. It's far from an easy problem to solve: every dollar spent on a race where the result is a foregone conclusion represents a dollar that might have helped shift the result in a more tightly contested district. In the USA, both the Democratic and Republican Parties are perpetually attempting to outdo each other by allocating their limited resources more efficiently, but their task is an asymmetric one: Republicans might, for instance, get better returns (measured in votes) on their investment in Alabama than Democrats would in the same state for the same amount. Of course, given that Alabama swings so heavily Republican, it might be a mistake for any party to invest funds there, given that the races in most of Alabama's districts were probably over before they began. Let's see what we can learn.

Imports

```
import pandas as pd
pd.set_option("display.notebook_repr_html", False)
import numpy as np
import seaborn as sns
import pymc3 as pm
import arviz as az

import matplotlib as mpl
from matplotlib import pyplot as plt

from dcss.plotting import custom_seaborn
custom_seaborn()

from dcss.bayes import plot_2020_election_diff, plot_2020_election_fit

import warnings
warnings.filterwarnings('ignore')
```

Data

The data we will use for this chapter is stored in a CSV file called `2020_election/2020_districts_combined.csv`. Rather than take you through the entire process of cleaning and preprocessing the data, we've done it for you this time; it's ready to go! It's worth noting, however, that the cleaning and preprocessing steps we've taken for this data (and the models we're going to fit in this chapter) are *very* similar to those that we've taken in previous chapters.

```
df = pd.read_csv('../data/2020_election/2020_districts_combined.csv')
df.head()
```

	vote	spend	state	districts	dem_inc	rep_inc	pvi
0	-110424	-1853145.17	Louisiana	5	0.0	0.0	-15
1	142997	844317.53	Vermont	0	1.0	0.0	15
2	87490	994256.62	Hawaii	2	0.0	0.0	19
3	80046	11428704.81	New York	17	0.0	0.0	7
4	65679	1634476.18	Texas	33	1.0	0.0	23

In this chapter, we're only going to be utilizing a small subset of the available variables: going forwards, I'm going to restrict my discussion to only those that are pertinent to this chapter (the rest will come into play in the subsequent chapter).

Checking and cleaning the data

We'll start by summarizing the variables we intend to use. Doing so helps us get a sense of what those variables look like, where on the number line they lie, and how they might best be modelled. We can do this by using Panda's `.describe()` method:

```
pd.options.display.float_format = "{:.2f}".format
df[['vote', 'spend', 'districts']].describe()
```

	vote	spend	districts
count	371.00	371.00	371.00
mean	-2408.57	70377.38	10.20
std	104536.61	2896688.38	10.57
min	-212953.00	-23465420.95	0.00
25%	-92659.00	-1058899.68	3.00
50%	-8376.00	386021.41	6.00
75%	79494.50	1373394.40	13.00
max	308869.00	11428704.81	52.00

The `state` and `districts` variables are straightforward: they represent the state and numerical identifier associated with the congressional district in question. The `vote` and `spend` columns are a little more involved. For the past 29 years, American federal elections have been an almost completely two-party affair. Almost all viable candidates at almost every level of government belong to either the Democratic or Republican Parties. There are some notable exceptions (e.g. the technically independent senators Bernie Sanders and Angus King), but almost all politically viable independent politicians in the USA are Democrats in all but name (they often even receive the official endorsement of the Democratic Party, and are not opposed by any member). Given the ubiquity of this political duopoly, we can simplify our data by focusing solely on the differential in votes and spending between the two major parties.

We've decided to treat Republicans as our 'negative' case and the Democrats as our 'positive' case. Casting the two in diametric opposition allows the `vote` and `spend` variables to represent the *differential* between the two parties: when `vote` is positive, it means the Democrats received more votes than the Republicans. A negative `vote` value means the Republicans received more votes than the Democrats. Ditto for `spend`.

Although this helps us simplify our model immensely, it also comes at a cost: we can only include districts where both Democrats and Republicans *officially* ran, spent campaign funds, and received votes. This limitation has reduced our data from 435 districts to 371; a steep cost, but not an altogether unwarranted one. More advanced models could incorporate and model the dropped data, but we're keeping it simple.

Now that the data is loaded, let's create a scatter plot so we can see how it is distributed (Figure 27.1).

```
plot_2020_election_diff(df)
```

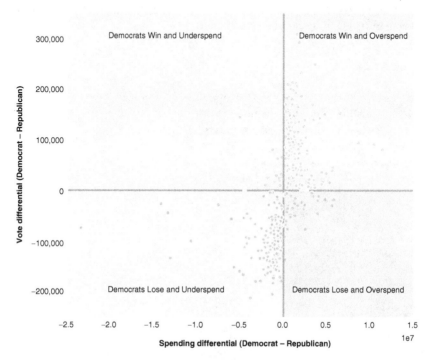

Figure 27.1 A scatter plot of each federal congressional district in the dataset (after filtering), by spending differential and vote differential; the quadrant labels represent the outcome for districts in that quadrant from the Democratic Party's perspective: the top two quadrants contain districts that Democrats won, the bottom two represent Democratic losses; the left-hand quadrants contain districts where the Democrats spent less money than the Republicans, the right-hand quadrants are where the Democrats spent more money than the Republicans

In the scatter plot shown in Figure 27.1, each point represents a single congressional district in one of the 50 states. The x-axis represents the Democrats' 'spending differential', which is just the amount of money the Democrats spent in a congressional race minus the amount the Republicans spent in the same. The y-axis, 'vote differential', is similar: it represents the amount of votes the Democrats received minus the amount the Republicans received.

I've broken the plot into four quadrants and labelled them. The upper left quadrant represents the best case scenario for the Democrats: districts here were won by Democratic candidates despite the fact that the Republicans spent more money on the race. The lower-right quadrant is the inverse; it represents the worst case scenario for the Democrats, wherein they outspent the Republicans yet still lost. You might notice that comparatively few districts fall into these two quadrants: this might imply that both parties are fairly adept at avoiding overspending in districts where they're unsure of victory.

The final two quadrants, upper right and lower left, contain the districts where the winning party spent more money than their opponents did (which, for the most part, is what we'd expect).

Standardize data, process categoricals

Generally speaking, it's a good idea to standardize any non-categorical data you plan to use in a modelling context. We do this by first shifting the numerical value so that its mean is 0. Then, we divide each observation by the standard deviation of the data, which converts the variable into a value whose units are 'standard deviations', or z-scores. We're also going to tackle our non-numerical categorical variable, state, which is currently a list of strings (the districts variable is also categorical, but it's already numerical and is thus good to go as is). We're going to use Pandas to convert state into an explicitly categorical object, extract numerical codes from it, and then use those codes to determine how many different states we're working with (remember, some may have been dropped when we cleansed our data of ~60 districts). The code cell below accomplishes all this; there are more efficient ways to accomplish our task, and we've even covered some of them elsewhere in the book. Nevertheless, we're going to do them manually here to help give you a better sense of what's going on.

```
spend_std = (df.spend - np.mean(df.spend))/ np.std(df.spend)
vote_std = (df.vote - np.mean(df.vote))/ np.std(df.vote)
state_cat =pd.Categorical(df.state)
state_idx = state_cat.codes
n_states = len(set(state_idx))
```

27.4 Developing Our Bayesian Model

Using the modelling language we established in the previous chapter, let's create a model that uses spending differential to predict vote differential in congressional districts:

$$vote_i \sim Normal(\mu_i, \sigma)$$
$$\mu_i = \alpha + (\beta \cdot spend_i)$$

Based on the hypothetical model we developed in the previous chapter, this format should look familiar: the top line is our likelihood, and the linear model on the second line determines where the mean of the likelihood function falls. Now that we have our likelihood and linear model specified, we can play the 'What's That?' game, which will see us through to the creation of a fully specified model. Let's look at our model definition again; we'll start with the data, which are the variables whose values we have observations of. They are as follows:

1   $vote_i$
2   $spend_i$

We have real, actual numerical values for both of the above, so we don't need to do any guessing about them. Next, let's turn our gaze to the statistics – the variables whose values are (at least in part) derived from other variables:

1   μ_i – mean parameter for likelihood function
2   α – the intercept
3   β – coefficient for spend
4   σ – standard deviation parameter for likelihood function

Since we don't have any strong reasons to think that any of these variables should take on any particular values, we can use *uninformative priors* for each. We have a large amount of data to work with, so as long as our priors are not unduly mis-specified, they will likely be overwhelmed by the weight of evidence and have no noticeable impact on our posterior distributions. Here's what I've elected to use (feel free to play around with different priors at your leisure). The text on the right (likelihood, linear model, etc.) is not necessary, but it's a nice reminder of what each line in the model represents.

$$\text{vote}_i \sim \text{Normal}(\mu_i, \sigma) \qquad \text{[Likelihood]}$$

$$\mu_i = \alpha + (\beta \cdot \text{spend}_i) \qquad \text{[Linear Model]}$$

$$\alpha \sim \text{Normal}(0, 2) \qquad \text{[alpha Prior]}$$

$$\beta \sim \text{Normal}(1, 2) \qquad \text{[beta Prior]}$$

$$\sigma \sim \text{Exponential}(2) \qquad \text{[sigma Prior]}$$

Making the model with PyMC3

Since we've already discussed how and why to use stochastic samples to approximate the posterior distribution in a Bayesian model (in the previous chapter), we'll go straight into using stochastic samplers using a package called PyMC3. PyMC3 is designed to facilitate the specification, fitting, and simulation of Bayesian models, and it includes state-of-the-art stochastic samplers. While far more sophisticated than anything we've described in this book thus far, PyMC3 is conceptually similar to – and based upon – the Markov chain and related techniques covered in the previous chapter.

PyMC3 is expansive and constantly evolving – any attempt to capture even a modest percentage of its contents would be futile. As with other packages discussed in this book, you will likely use a very small portion of it extensively, and the rest much more rarely. I encourage you to avail yourselves of PyMC3's extensive documentation and helpful tutorials. For now, we will focus on what you need to build your own Bayesian regression from scratch. I should also point out that this chapter was written using PyMC3 version 3.11. By the time you read this page, the package's functionality may be different from the way it was when I wrote this chapter. If you encounter issues in the code, try installing PyMC3 3.11.

Before we actually make the model, we have to introduce a bit of Python programming knowledge that we've *used* before but have not actually explained: context management.

Further Reading

Salvatier et al. (2016) provide a detailed introduction to PyMC3, and Martin (2018) provides an excellent in-depth introduction to statistical modelling and probabilistic programming with PyMC3. If you want to go beyond the Bayesian methods we discuss in this book, I especially recommend working through Martin (2018).

Context management for modelling with PyMC3

Although the PyMC3 package has a wide variety of use cases, we'll exclusively use it for modelling. PyMC3 uses an unusual (though convenient) convention to simplify the necessary syntax for modelling. To understand it, we first have to briefly cover what a 'context' is in Python.

Python contexts are immediately recognizable by their use of the with statement and are usually employed to manage system resources that are in limited supply. That's why you'll frequently see them used with I/O (input–output) operations, where files are being read from or written to disk. Rather than leaving those files open and available for further editing, the with block ensures that the files are opened and closed in perfect lockstep when they're needed. A typical I/O context might look like this:

```
with open("hello.txt", 'w') as file:
    file.write("hello")
```

PyMC3's approach to modelling seeks to simplify the syntax by requiring that their models be used within the bounds of a context. It looks something like this:

```
with pm.Model() as test_model:
    testPrior = pm.Normal("testPrior", 0, 1)
```

Anytime you want to create a model, add variables to a model, or specify any other aspect of the model or how you plan to fit it, you can do so using PyMC3's context management. In the code block above, we defined a new model and called it test_model. That object now persists in our global namespace, and we can call it directly, which will prompt PyMC3 to give us a (slightly confusing) printout of the model specification:

```
test_model
```

testPrior ~ Normal

We can also examine the individual variables, which also exist in the namespace by themselves:

```
testPrior
```

testPrior ~ Normal(*mu* = 0.0, *sigma* = 1.0)

Finally, we can also call the model directly with the with statement to add more variables (or do whatever else we please):

```
with test_model:
    anotherTest = pm.Normal("anotherTest", 2.5, 10)
test_model
```

testPrior ~ Normal
anotherTest ~ Normal

Specifying the model in PyMC3

Now, we can start describing our model. We're going to do this in chunks, starting with the priors:

```
with pm.Model() as pool_model:
    # Priors
    alpha = pm.Normal("alpha", mu=1, sigma=2)
    beta = pm.Normal("beta", mu=1, sigma=2)
    sigma = pm.Exponential("sigma", lam=2)
```

We used one line per prior to define a distribution for each. The distributions themselves were drawn from PyMC3's library of distributions, which contains all of the distributions we discussed in Chapter 25 and other well-known distributions.

Each call to pm.Normal in the code above included three arguments, the first of which is always a string representation of the variable's name. It's up to you how you name your variables. If at all possible, I prefer to name them so that they're a one-to-one match with their Python counterparts. Doing so makes it much easier to read model output without cross-referencing against your model specification. The second and third arguments were passed as keyword arguments (they don't need to be, but we wanted to make it explicit here); these are the μ and σ we know and love, and they represent the mean and standard deviation for each of the normal distributions we used.

There's only one exception to the pattern above, which comes in the form of the pm.Exponential distribution we used for the standard deviation of the outcome. It still took in a name as its first argument, but we provided a lam argument, which represents the distribution's 'rate' (and, conveniently, is also the inverse of its mean value).

Now, let's make another call to our model to add the line which represents the linear model – the part that's responsible for combining all of the observed variables and priors we specified above:

```
with pool_model:
    # Linear Model
    mu = alpha + beta * spend_std
```

The line we used to specify the linear model should look very familiar to you – it's nearly a dead ringer for the line we've been using in the formal model specification! The major difference is that we used spend_std, rather than spend – the former is the standardized version of the latter, and PyMC3 almost always prefers standardized variables. At this point, all that remains is to add the likelihood:

```
with pool_model:
    # Likelihood
    votes = pm.Normal("votes", mu=mu, sigma=sigma, observed=vote_std)
```

Our specification of the likelihood should appear as a straightforward representation of what we had built earlier, but with one major addition: the 'observed' parameter. When we pass data to this parameter, *PyMC3 knows to treat this variable as a likelihood as opposed to a prior*. Notice that if we were to remove the observed=vote_std argument, we would be supplying something that's functionally identical to the priors we added in the first step.

And that's it – we now have a fully specified PyMC3 model! All we need to do to get it to run is to add one more line, which we'll do in the following major section. But before we do, we're going to take a brief detour to make sure that our model isn't totally off base.

Prior predictive check

One of the most oft-repeated criticisms of the Bayesian paradigm is the use of potentially inde-fensible prior distributions. Yeah, sounds bad. Is it?

I've mentioned previously – and statisticians with far more expertise than I have have demon-strated elsewhere – that most models are simple enough and are conditioned on large enough volumes of data that *any* combination of priors, regardless of how off base they are, will be over-whelmed by the likelihood of the evidence, leaving inference more or less unaffected. The only really important exception here is an entirely off base prior that assigns probabilities of 0 to important parts of the parameter space. Hopefully, this is some cause for comfort, but the fact that our models are usually 'safe' from prior-based bias does *not* mean that we can become complacent.

One of the rituals we use to stave off complacency is the prior predictive check. As we learnt in previous chapters, one model's prior is another model's posterior; from a mathematical (but *not inferential*) standpoint, posteriors and priors are largely identical. This is convenient for us, because it means that we can draw samples from our model's prior distribution in much the same way as we'd draw samples from any other distribution. In so doing, we can give ourselves a picture of what our model thinks is likely to occur *before it has seen any data*.

PyMC3 has built-in functionality for sampling from the prior (which simply draws sample values from the distributions we've already defined). We'll reuse the model context to achieve this and save the results in a new variable:

```
with pool_model:
    prior_predictive = pm.sample_prior_predictive(
        samples=50, var_names=['alpha', 'beta', 'sigma', 'votes'], random_seed=42)
prior_predictive.keys()

dict_keys(['beta', 'votes', 'sigma', 'alpha'])

prior_predictive['votes'].shape

(50, 371)
```

The `prior_predictive` object that we just created is a simple Python dictionary – nothing special about it. We used the `.keys()` method to print out the keys it has, which you can access using simple subscripting. Each of the keys corresponds to either a parameter value (α, β, or σ) or an observed variable (votes). It could also include calculated statistics, such as μ. If we had recorded the value of μ by wrapping the line containing our linear model in the `pm.Determinstic()` function, the result would have been identical, but we could directly draw samples of μ values.

Take some time to flip through the values in the `prior_predictive` dictionary, and you'll notice that they're all NumPy arrays. If you use the `.shape` method on any of the values, you'll see that there are 50 items in each of them (the number of samples we asked for), except for votes. The votes array is a different story: it has a shape of (50, 371), with the '371' cor-responding to the number of observations we have in our dataset. You can think of this as representing how the Bayesian paradigm attempts to preserve uncertainty: we use priors (α, β) to articulate our uncertainty about parameter values (μ, σ), which, in turn, express our degree of uncertainty about the data our model is designed to replicate.

Now that that's done, we can just plug the parameter samples into a simple reproduction of our linear model.

Results are shown in Figure 27.2.

```
spend_grid = np.linspace(-20, 20, 50)

plt.xlim((-10, 10))
plt.ylim((-10, 10))

for a, b in zip(prior_predictive["alpha"], prior_predictive['beta']):
    # This is the same linear model that appeared in our PyMC3 definition above
    vote_sim = a + b * spend_grid
    plt.plot(spend_grid, vote_sim, c="k", alpha=0.4)

plt.axhspan(-2, 2, facecolor='black', alpha=0.2)
plt.axvspan(-2, 2, facecolor='black', alpha=0.2)
plt.xlabel("Expenditure differential (standard deviations)")
plt.ylabel("Vote differential (standard deviations)")
plt.show()
```

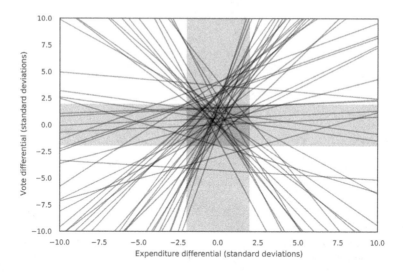

Figure 27.2 A plot of the regression lines from the first prior predictive; the dark grey area formed by the overlapping grey spans represent the area containing ~95% of the observed data

The plot shown in Figure 27.2 contains 50 different regression lines drawn from our model's prior distributions – a quick glance shows that our priors leave a whole lot of room for improvement. Here's how you can tell: the intersecting grey areas in the plot represent two standard deviations on both of our variables, which means that roughly 95% of our data points will fall somewhere within the darker grey area of overlap. We can see that the majority of the regression lines we sampled from our model cross through the darker grey area from the lower left quadrant to the upper right quadrant, albeit at slightly too sharp an angle. A great many of the lines, though, only barely skim the edges or corners of the box; some fail to cross it altogether. If your model produces one or two highly suspect regression lines, that's not a cause for concern. When your model produces a great many (as is the case with ours), it might be time to consider making your priors a little more informative.

Take a look at what we can do by tightening our priors a little. The results are shown in Figure 27.3.

```
with pm.Model() as regularized_model:

    # Priors
    alpha = pm.Normal("alpha", mu=0, sigma=0.5)
    beta = pm.Normal("beta", mu=0.5, sigma=1)
    sigma = pm.Exponential("sigma", lam=1)

    # Linear Model
    mu = alpha + beta * spend_std

    # Likelihood
    votes = pm.Normal("votes", mu=mu, sigma=sigma, observed=vote_std)

    reg_prior_pred = pm.sample_prior_predictive(
        samples=50, var_names=['alpha', 'beta', 'sigma', 'votes'], random_seed=42)

spend_grid = np.linspace(-20, 20, 50)

plt.xlim((-10, 10))
plt.ylim((-10, 10))

for a, b in zip(reg_prior_pred["alpha"], reg_prior_pred['beta']):
    # This is the same linear model that appeared in our PyMC3 definition above
    vote_sim = a + b * spend_grid
    plt.plot(spend_grid, vote_sim, c="k", alpha=0.4)

plt.axhspan(-2, 2, facecolor='black', alpha=0.2)
plt.axvspan(-2, 2, facecolor='black', alpha=0.2)

plt.xlabel("Expenditure differential (standard deviations)")
plt.ylabel("Vote differential (standard deviations)")
plt.show()
```

Based on the plot shown in Figure 27.3, we can see that our new regularized model has a very strong preference for regression lines that hem closely to the origin (0 on both axes), and feature a moderately positive relationship between spend_std and vote_std (most regression lines have a positive slope). There's still quite a bit of variability in the predictions: owing to their steeper incline, some of the regression lines travel through a limited span of the middle area. Others are more or less flat (predicting no relationship between spending and votes), and our model even permits a few of the lines to reverse the trend entirely and predict that increased spending is correlated with *fewer* votes received. All said, *MUCH better!*

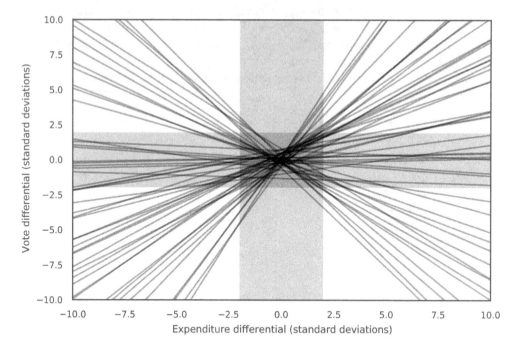

Figure 27.3 A plot of the regression lines from the second prior predictive; the dark grey area formed by the overlapping grey spans represents the area containing ~95% of the observed data. The priors, having been made slightly more informative, produce a more tightly clustered set of regression lines

When selecting priors for a model, I like to use two simple heuristics:

1 Priors shouldn't make the impossible possible.
2 Priors shouldn't make the possible impossible.

The process of setting good priors involves more than simply following these two heuristics of course, but this is a good starting point. Once you've gotten the hang of setting priors following basic guidelines, you should feel free to descend into the particulars at your leisure. A good place to start doing so is this guide from the developers of another probabilistic programming tool for Bayesian data analysis called STAN (Gelman, 2020).

Now that we've created a better model using more sensible priors, we're going to abandon it and forge ahead using the worse one. *Why?* I've got two didactic reasons:

1 By proceeding with the worse model, we'll be able to see how even modest amounts of evidence can overwhelm poorly specified priors with ease.
2 It won't happen until the next chapter, but we'll see how models with poorly specified priors can do ruinous things to more complex models.

Running our model

Our model is ready to run – all we need to do is to add one more line to get it started! This is where we tell PyMC3 to sample our model and produce a prior distribution (which, in

PyMC3-speak, is contained in a 'trace' object). By default, PyMC3 draws 2000 samples for each of the four traces, resulting in a grand total of 8000 samples. The first 1000 samples in each trace will be 'tuning' samples, used to get our proverbial marble into the right ballpark before we start drawing samples that we'll incorporate into the posterior. In terms of the skate bowl metaphor from the previous chapter, you can think of each of the different traces as representing a different marble–robot pair. Each of these four pairs will repeat the 'randomly whack the marble' process 1000 times, and the result of all of the marble whacks in aggregate will form our posterior. Let's get a-whackin'!

```
with pool_model:
    # Run Sample Traces
    trace_pool = pm.sample()


Auto-assigning NUTS sampler...
Initializing NUTS using jitter+adapt_diag...
Multiprocess sampling (4 chains in 4 jobs)
NUTS: [sigma, beta, alpha]

<style>
    /* Turns off some styling */
    progress {
        /* gets rid of default border in Firefox and Opera. */
        border: none;
        /* Needs to be in here for Safari polyfill so background images work as
        expected. */
        background-size: auto;
    }
    .progress-bar-interrupted, .progress-bar-interrupted::-webkit-progress-bar {
        background: #F44336;
    }
</style>
```

100.00% [8000/8000 00:02<00:00 Sampling 4 chains, 0 divergences]

```
Sampling 4 chains for 1_000 tune and 1_000 draw iterations (4_000 + 4_000 draws total)
    took 3 seconds.
```

If everything's working correctly, our PyMC3 model should spit out a collection of preliminary text followed by a progress bar that should fill up in relatively short order. Running this last line of code hasn't actually done anything to our model proper, but it has produced a 'trace' object that contains all the information we need to see how our model performed under sampling. First, let's use the trace variable to produce a summary (for which we'll use the ArviZ package, which is a companion module to the PyMC3 package, and which facilitates diagnosis and inference). The standard `az.summary` printout provides an overwhelming amount of data, so we're going to artificially limit what it shows us for now. We'll get to the other important variables a little later:

```
with pool_model:
    summary = az.summary(trace_pool, round_to=2)

summary[['mean', 'sd', 'r_hat']]
```

	mean	sd	r_hat
alpha	0.00	0.05	1.00
beta	0.44	0.05	1.00
sigma	0.90	0.03	1.00

Each of the rows in the dataframe above are dimensions of our posterior distribution, and the three columns represent different summary statistics ArviZ has calculated for us. The three statistics we care about right now are the mean, the standard deviation, and the 'r_hat' (or $\hat{r}$) of each dimension.

If you've fitted and interpreted regression models before, you might find the mean and sd variables familiar: they simply represent the centre and width of the posterior distribution for that particular dimension. In a Frequentist regression, we would be implicitly comparing each of these hypotheses (one for each covariate) to the assumed 'null hypothesis' and deciding whether or not to reject the null hypothesis based on the strength of the evidence. You would usually look for a series of little stars to rapidly assess the statistical significance of each alternative hypothesis. Since this is a Bayesian regression, you'll find no such machinery here: the numbers we've printed here are just a summary of the full answer we've tasked ourselves with providing, *which is always the full shape of the entire posterior distribution*. A good Bayesian is obsessed with retaining as much information and uncertainty as possible throughout the modelling process.

If you are not familiar with it, the r_hat statistic is a purely diagnostic statistic and is not normally interpreted. If all is well with your model, you would expect to see all of the r_hat values to be 1.00, or very close to. Anything higher than that (even 1.02 or greater) is a sign that something has gone wrong in your model.

Checking the trace plot

One of the most important steps in any Bayesian regression model involves checking your model's 'traces' to ensure that nothing went awry behind the scenes. ArviZ has some really nice built-in tools for this, shown for our trace pool model in Figure 27.4.

```
with pool_model:
    az.plot_trace(trace_pool, ['alpha', 'beta', 'sigma'], compact=True)
```

Each row in the grid of plots shown in Figure 27.4 corresponds to a row in the dataframe summary we produced above. The left column of plots presents you with the shape of the posterior distribution corresponding to one variable in the model (or, equivalently, one dimension of the posterior distribution). The right column of plots shows you the 'trace' of the PyMC3 sampler as it attempted to fit your model. You can think of each line in each trace plot representing a single marble being swatted around a high-dimensional skate bowl, and each row of the figure (there's one per parameter) is one of those dimensions. This might seem a bit unintuitive at first, but the x-axis in each of the plots on the left represents the exact same thing as the y-axis of their counterpart in the same row on the right! They both represent the

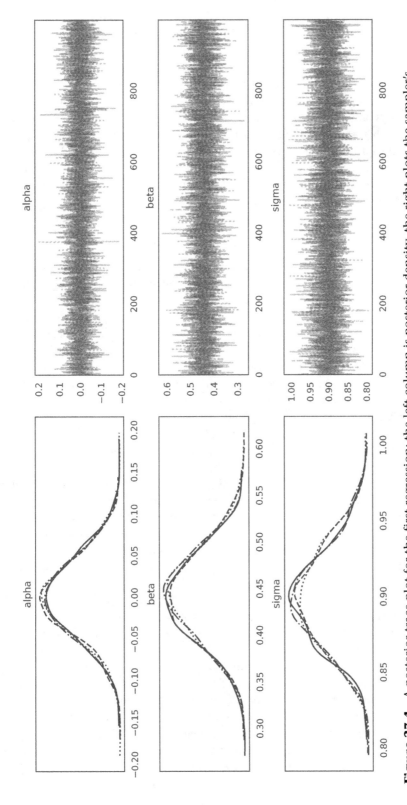

Figure 27.4 A posterior trace plot for the first regression; the left column is posterior density, the right plots the sampler's movement through parameter values (y-axis) as a function of sample step (x-axis). Each row corresponds to one parameter/latent variable in the model

parameter's value: the left is showing you the estimated posterior distribution of the parameter, and the right is showing you how the marbles moved to produce it (the x-axis for each plot on the right is the 'sample number'; you can think of the marbles as moving from left to right within each plot).

Another thing you might notice is that all of our parameters look normally distributed now; that isn't much of a surprise for α and β, but what about σ? Since we used the exponential distribution as its prior, shouldn't we expect its posterior to be exponentially distributed, too? Not at all; the only reason we were using the exponential distribution was to prevent our model from making the mistake of using negative numbers as potential parameter values for our normal distribution's σ parameter (which is undefined for all numbers below 0). Even if you use a non-normal distribution for a prior, you'll often find that your posterior distribution for that parameter is normal. Nothing to worry about.

What you *should* be worried about is the shape of your traces. There are three things we want to see in a 'good' trace:

1   We want to make sure that the algorithm is stationary, meaning that it has located the area of highest posterior probability and is spending all of its time bouncing around near it. When chains wander around and never settle in one region of the parameter space, it's a bad sign. To spot a non-stationary trace, look for lines that spend a good amount of time in one part of the posterior and then suddenly switch to another area and stay there for an extended period.

2   We want to make sure that our samplers are exploring the posterior space rapidly and efficiently, which is called 'good mixing'. When a chain is mixing well, it will appear to be darting around from one side of the posterior distribution to the other rapidly. Chains that aren't mixing well might be stationary in the long run but take a long time to move back and forth. To spot a poorly mixed trace, look for lines that slowly and gradually move around (as opposed to the frenetic, zippy movement of the healthy lines we see above).

3   We want to make sure that each of the various chains we use have converged, meaning they all spent most of their time in the same region of the posterior; if three chains are stationary in one area of the posterior, but the fourth chain is spending all of its time a good distance away, there's a problem afoot. It's often easier to spot non-stationary traces on the left-hand side of the trace plot, where it's easy to notice if one of the traces' distributions differ significantly from the others. The small amount of wiggliness we see in the σ plot above is no big deal at all.

The trace plots we've produced here are all ideal. Later on, we'll show you some that are *far* from ideal. If you can't wait to find out what bad trace plots look like, you can find lots of detail at this blog post: https://jpreszler.rbind.io/post/2019-09-28-bad-traceplots/. It features a bunch of examples that are more extreme than anything we're going to see in this book, but it is worth taking a look at nonetheless!

Let's return to those nice-looking distributions on the left-hand side of the diagram again. You might notice that there are a few different lines in each plot – each of the four different chains we used to fit our model is separately represented, each with a different line pattern. In fact, these four separate lines appear in the trace plots on the right-hand side, too; they're just much harder to see individually (which is a good thing – that means our marbles were well-behaved).

Since each of the four lines in each of our distribution plots are in broad agreement (they differ slightly, but not even remotely enough to indicate any problems), we can use these distributions to get an accurate idea of where our model thinks the parameter values are most likely to fall.

Establishing credible intervals

Now, let's dig into each of our variables in a bit more detail; we can do so using ArviZ's `plot_posterior` function. Our focus will be on something called the 'HDI', which stands for the 'highest density interval'. The HDI is the closest thing you're going to see to the Frequentist '95% confidence interval' (or similar) in Bayesian data analysis. Statistically, the HDI represents the shortest possible interval in one dimension of the posterior distribution which contains a predetermined amount of probability. We use the HDI interval to provide a sense of the area in the distribution that we're confident (to a predetermined extent) contains the best-fitting parameter value.

It's up to us to determine how much of the posterior probability we want to appear inside our HDI. In his classic Bayesian text, Richard McElreath (2020) uses an abundance of cheek when suggesting that Bayesians should employ a prime number for no other reason than the fact that it is prime. He portrays this as a way of subtly jabbing Frequentists for their automatic use of an arbitrarily set significance threshold of –.05, whose progenitor specifically indicated should not be adopted as a default. Hilarious! (Though, to be fair, many Frequentists are themselves trying to get other Frequentists to stop doing that.)

We'll follow in McElreath's (2020) footsteps and use 0.89, but there's no good reason why we couldn't use something like 0.83 or 0.79. The default for most ArviZ plots is 94%; having made our point, we'll leave the HDI intervals at their defaults from here on out. The results are shown in Figure 27.5.

```
with pool_model:
    fig, axs = plt.subplots(3, 1, sharex=True, sharey=True, figsize=(6, 6))
    az.plot_posterior(trace_pool,
                      ax=axs,
                      var_names=['alpha', 'beta', 'sigma'],
                      hdi_prob=0.89)
    fig.tight_layout()
```

In Figure 27.5, we decided to force PyMC3 and ArviZ to plot all three posterior distributions (and their HDIs) on the same unified axis so you could directly compare their positions and widths. The black bars under each of the plotted distributions represent the span of our chosen HDI. The numbers that appear to the left and right of the black bar represent the HDI's upper and lower bounds – this gives us a precise numerical range within which our chosen probability density can be found.

Remember that unlike the Frequentist paradigm, the Bayesian paradigm allows us to apply probability and probabilistic statements to hypotheses. That's exactly what we're doing when we create a credible interval! The credible interval represents the region of the posterior probability within which we expect the underlying parameter value to fall, conditional on a predetermined amount of uncertainty. The lower we set our HDI interval, the tighter it becomes, but the less certain of it we are. In our example above, we used an 89% interval; had we set that interval to, say, 79%, it would

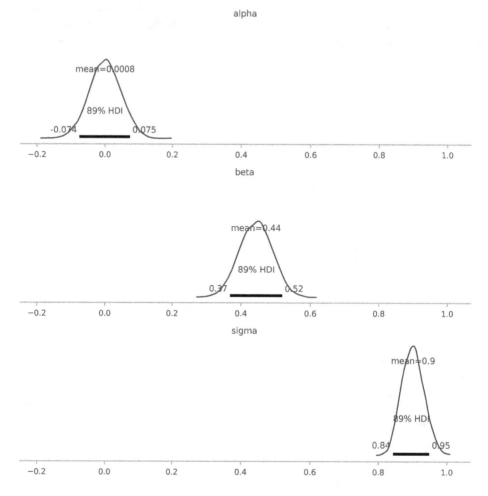

Figure 27.5 A three-part posterior plot from the first regression; each of the plots represents the posterior density of a different parameter/latent variable in the model; they share the same scale on the *x*-axis and *y*-axis, so their means and widths can be compared directly

occupy a smaller proportion of the number line, but we would also have less confidence that the interval contains the 'true' parameter value (if such a thing can be said to exist).

The more certain we are of a parameter's value (as a result of having a posterior distribution with a smaller standard deviation), the more narrow and concentrated our HDI becomes. But even if we had nearly limitless data to feed into our Bayesian machine, we'd never reach perfect certainty about a parameter value, at least not while using a continuous range of hypotheses. If you think back to our probability primer in Chapter 25, this is because our probability density is an integrated value, and the value of any integral on a span of 0 length is 0: thus, the probability of any single hypothesis (e.g. $\beta = 1$) will also be 0. We can only ever speak of probability as accumulating within a *range* of hypotheses.

The HDI is a common and well-understood method of constructing a credible interval. It is not, however, the only means of doing so. We don't have the time to cover them in detail, but it's worth weighing the merits of HDI against other techniques for developing a credible interval. Some place more emphasis on ensuring that the credible interval has the same amount of probability on either side of it, ensuring that it is in the 'middle' of the posterior distribution. Others mimic the HDI, but allow it to split in the middle so as to cover a two-humped posterior. Good options abound, many of which can be found in the details of the ArviZ's plot_posterior documentation.

Posterior predictive Checks

Just in case you hadn't yet seen enough plots of roughly normal-looking distributions, we're going to do one more. In much the same way as we drew samples from our model's prior distribution to perform a prior predictive check, we can draw samples from our model's posterior distribution to perform a posterior predictive check. While the purpose of the prior predictive was to ensure that our model wasn't out to lunch, the posterior predictive is designed to see how well it performs at retrodicting the evidence we fed to it.

Just as with the prior predictive, we start by drawing samples from our model:

```
with pool_model:
    ppc = pm.sample_posterior_predictive(trace_pool, var_names=['votes', 'alpha', '
    beta', 'sigma'])

<style>
    /* Turns off some styling */
    progress {
        /* gets rid of default border in Firefox and Opera. */
        border: none;
        /* Needs to be in here for Safari polyfill so background images work as
    expected. */
        background-size: auto;
    }
    .progress-bar-interrupted, .progress-bar-interrupted::-webkit-progress-bar {
        background: #F44336;
    }
</style>
```

100.00% [4000/4000 00:05<00:00]

If you inspect it, you'll find that the resulting ppc dictionary is eerily similar to the dictionary we received when sampling our prior distribution. Functionally, they're identical, but practically, they represent very different sets of samples. Fortunately for us, we can feed our posterior samples directly into a set of handy functions from the ArviZ package. In the code cell below, the inner function az.from_pymc3 simply extracts an ArviZ-specific object from our sample set, and the az.plot_ppc function produces a plot of our posterior predictive (Figure 27.6):

```
az.plot_ppc(
    az.from_pymc3(
        posterior_predictive=ppc,
```

```
        model=pool_model),
    num_pp_samples = 100,
        legend=False
)
plt.show()
```

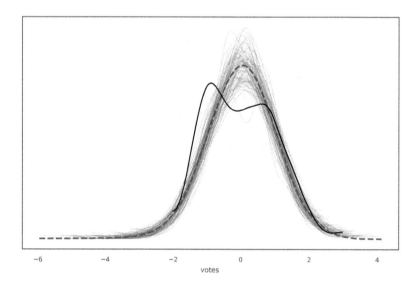

Figure 27.6   A plot of the posterior predictive samples, used to assess how effectively our model can retrodict the observed data. The thick solid line is the observed data, the small transparent lines represent the predictions derived from one of the 100 samples drawn from the posterior distribution, and the thick dashed line represents the mean value of the sampled prediction

In the plot shown in Figure 27.6, observations from our outcome variable (the standard deviation of vote differential) is arranged along the x-axis, and the frequency (or density) of an observation of that value is tracked along the y-axis. The light wispy lines represent all of the retrodictions made by one set of posterior parameter values (of which we sampled 100); the dashed line represents the overall average of each sample. The solid black line represents the observed data.

Ideally, we'd want to see our model adhere more closely to the observed data: as it stands, our model tends to under-predict the number of congressional districts that the Republicans won by a single standard deviation and greatly over-predicts the number of extremely close races (in and around the origin).

Plotting uncertainty

I know I've said it quite a lot already, but one of the reasons why we use Bayesian methods in the first place is because we want to preserve uncertainty to the greatest extent possible throughout the entire modelling process. You'll often find that other approaches to regression analysis produce a 'line of best fit' (as discusssed in earlier chapters of the book), a 'predictor line', or something similar. In Bayesian analysis, we instead produce a *range* of such lines, each of which is probabilistically drawn from our posterior distribution, and each of which differs from the others. Since it's difficult to appreciate information at this scale directly, Bayesian regression leans heavily on visualization techniques to provide intuitive guides to inference. Here, we're going to draw samples of predicted outcomes and parameter values from our posterior distribution (using a PyMC3 function designed for just such a task), feed those sampled values through our linear model, and plot the 94% HDI range of the results (Figure 27.7).

```
plot_2020_election_fit(spend_std, vote_std, trace_pool, ppc)
```

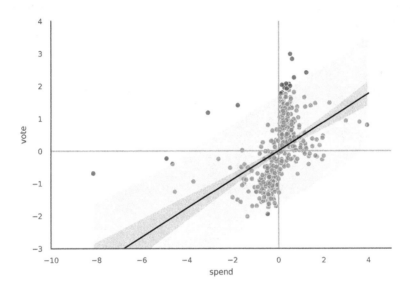

Figure 27.7 A scatter plot of each federal congressional district in the dataset (after filtering), by spending differential and vote differential; the average predictor (solid black line), 94% credible interval for the predictor (dark grey band around the average predictor), and the band containing 94% of the observed data (light grey band) are overlaid

In the plot shown in Figure 27.7, the black line represents the mean (or average) predictor line. Its value was produced by averaging thousands of such lines, 94% of which fall entirely within the smaller, darker band around the black line; that band represents our model's uncertainty in the regressor. Our model *also* models predictive uncertainty – or, in simpler terms, the width of the band within which it expects 94% of the data to fall (which is controlled by our model's sigma parameter, which we also have some uncertainty about). It's uncertainty piled upon uncertainty (and so on *ad infinitum*), but it produces a set of results and visualizations that are remarkably intuitive to read and interpret.

Nevertheless, we can now produce a preliminary interpretation of what our model is telling us: using the posterior predictive plot and the various parameters' summaries from earlier, our model is indicating an increase of 1 standard deviation in spending differential tends to correlate with a roughly 0.45 standard deviation increase in vote differential.

There's just one catch, which you may or may not have noticed by looking at the plot. This model is terrible. We can do better. That's what the next chapter is all about.

27.5 Conclusion

The key points in this chapter are as follows:

- We learnt how to specify and fit Bayesian models with PyMC3.
- Bayesian regression is a powerful, flexible approach to regression analysis.
- Just because simple Bayesian regression models with plenty of data aren't all that sensitive to the priors placed on their latent variables doesn't mean that you should be complacent about setting priors: a prior predictive check can be helpful in this regard.
- Bayesian regression emphasizes preserving and visualizing uncertainty whenever and however possible.

Visit the website at https://study.sagepub.com/mclevey for additional resources

28

BAYESIAN HIERARCHICAL REGRESSION MODELLING

28.1 Learning Objectives

By the end of this chapter, you should be able to do the following:

- Explain what a hierarchical linear regression model is
- Specify a hierarchical linear regression model using mathematical notation
- Specify a hierarchical linear regression model using PyMC3 code
- Explain what 'pooling' is in a hierarchical linear regression
- Differentiate between no pooling, partial pooling, and complete pooling
- Use informative priors to fix a problematic sampler
- Assess how well a hierarchical model fits the data
- Interpret the results of a hierarchical model

28.2 Learning Materials

You can find the online learning materials for this chapter in `doing_computational_social_science/Chapter_28`. `cd` into the directory and launch your Jupyter server.

28.3 Introduction

Generally speaking, most introductory and intermediate quantitative methods classes for social science students do not teach hierarchical linear regression models except as a special case of 'default' linear regression models. This is probably due to the fact that simple linear models are much easier to teach than complex ones, and because of the wise notion that, where possible, we should favour simple models over complex models. And so, hierarchical linear models are banished to 'advanced' electives that you *might* get to after years of learning ANOVA-like statistical tests (now with 300+ flavours!). This is all a bit silly given the philosophical gymnastics required of 'simple' statistical tests and linear models in the Frequentist tradition. We need a new normal in which our 'default' regressions are hierarchical. I'm going to assume that you, like me, were not taught statistics this way and that you may not even know what a hierarchical regression is. Let's change that.

Imports

```
import pandas as pd
pd.set_option("display.notebook_repr_html", False)
import numpy as np
import seaborn as sns
import pymc3 as pm
import arviz as az

import matplotlib as mpl
from matplotlib import pyplot as plt
from dcss.plotting import custom_seaborn
custom_seaborn()

from dcss.bayes import plot_2020_no_pool, plot_2020_partial_pool

import warnings
warnings.filterwarnings('ignore')
```

28.4 So, What's a Hierarchical Model?

Linear regression models of any variety can justifiably be called 'hierarchical' if they use data at different 'levels' to estimate parameters and make predictions. I'll come back to 'data at different levels' in a moment, but first, I want to acknowledge a very common source of confusion. For no good reason, hierarchical models go by a wide variety of different names, including 'random effects', 'mixed effects', and 'multilevel'. There are many others as well. The terminology here is hopelessly and inextricably muddled. In some fields, the various terms have specific meanings; in others, they don't. Sometimes the specific meanings are at odds with one another.

Thankfully, none of that really matters for our purposes here. Most of the time, I'll stick with hierarchical, but when I don't, I mean the same thing. Since you have now been introduced to two different languages for describing your models with precision, namely code and mathematical notation, a description of your model using either of these two languages is enough to banish any ambiguity about the type of model you're working with.

What do I mean when I say 'data at different levels'? Good question. Anytime I mention something along these lines (including references to 'pools', 'clusters', etc.), I'm referring to data where observations can be reasonably grouped together because they share some sort of context. (You might remember my alluding to this type of model when I introduced relational thinking in Chapter 13, where I compared network analysis to multilevel analysis.) The model we were working with in the previous chapter – the one that investigated if you could predict a Democratic candidate's margin of victory (or loss) from the amount by which the Democrats outspent (or were outspent by) the Republicans – used clustered data: each of the observations was drawn from one of the USA's 435 federal congressional districts, and each of those districts belonged to one of the 50 states. In this way, the state variable could have acted as a 'cluster', in the sense that two congressional districts from within the same state are more likely to share similarities with one another than two congressional districts chosen at random from the entire dataset.

The real power of a hierarchical model stems from its ability to balance the influence of individual-level observations (individual congressional districts) with the influence of whole clusters (each individual state). Bayesian hierarchical models permit this trade-off between countervailing influences by permitting the slopes and intercepts of each cluster to vary from one another, while still forcing all of the slopes and intercepts to be drawn from a simultaneously estimated prior. This is all getting a little too abstract, so let's get practical.

28.5 Goldilocks and the Three Pools

Whilst working your way through the previous chapter, you might have noticed the word 'pool' showing up in our model. I didn't explain it at the time, but the nomenclature was indicative of the modelling strategy we were using. In a regression model, the 'pooling' you use determines how the various categorical variables in your model can influence one another. The election data we used had one categorical variable – state – that indicated which of the 50 US states each congressional district belonged to. It might not have seemed so at the time, but our decision to omit the state variable by excluding it from the model entirely was an intentional choice: by preventing our model from accessing the information contained therein, it was forced to treat every congressional district from every state as if they had all come from one giant state (or, equivalently, no state at all). Doing so might have *seemed* like the 'default' option, but the only reason we went that route was for the sake of simplicity.

Now that we've seen a full example of developing a simple Bayesian regression model, it's time to take our categorical data more seriously. The idea here, which I am taking from McElreath's (2020) classic *Statistical Rethinking*, is that our modelling choices should reflect serious consideration of the options provided to us by the information available to us in our datasets. In this case, we should be asking ourselves: '*How should we handle the various US states that appear in this dataset?*' Let's discuss three primary options.

Option 1, Complete Pooling: All 50 US states are identical.

This is the approach we took in the previous chapter, treating all congressional districts from all states as if there was no meaningful difference between them. This approach is known as 'complete pooling', because it puts all of the observations into one big 'pool' and estimates parameters therefrom (now you know where all those 'pool' references come from). This is a simple approach, which is nice, but it's rarely the best one. It can be overly simplistic, obliterates differences between clusters, and is prone to underfitting. It is highly unlikely, for instance, that increased Democratic election spending will do anything to sway voters in the overwhelmingly Republican state of Wyoming. Ditto for Hawaii, where most voters are already committed Democrats. Best to avoid any impulse to artificially impose homogeneity.

Option 2, No Pooling: All 50 US states are utterly unique.

This approach – called 'no pooling' – would allow each state to have its own intercept (α) and slope (β), completely free from any other influences. This would mean that there would be practically no statistical commonalities between them, aside from the (very weak) regularizing influence of our priors. Going this route ensures that nothing our model learns about one state (or all of the states as a whole) can tell us anything about any of the others as individuals. Since the model is now free to create the best fit for each state based on the data available, this approach is very susceptible to overfitting.

Option 3, Partial Pooling: The US states differ from one another, but there are commonalities about them that we can infer and apply productively.

This approach – which we'll call 'partial pooling' – allows states to differ from one another, but it places limitations on how they may differ. Rather than giving each state free rein over its own parameters, this approach allows the model to simultaneously learn about each state's parameters from the data, as well as overall trends for the states in general by way of shared priors.

Logically and statistically, this approach usually makes the most sense: each state differs, but all are political entities within the USA, carrying all of the shared norms, values, and traditions incumbent upon belonging to the Union. This is the approach we primarily will use as we dive into hierarchical modelling. Before we do, though, let's take a brief detour to examine what a 'no pooling' model might look like.

Load data

Since our exploration of Bayesian hierarchical linear models builds off of the model we developed in the previous chapter, we're going to reuse the same 2020 House of Representatives Election dataset. We'll start by loading, standardizing, and previewing the data:

```
df = pd.read_csv('../data/2020_election/2020_districts_combined.csv')

spend_std = (df.spend - np.mean(df.spend))/ np.std(df.spend)
vote_std = (df.vote - np.mean(df.vote))/ np.std(df.vote)
state_cat = pd.Categorical(df.state)
state_idx = state_cat.codes
n_states = len(set(state_idx))
dem_inc = df.dem_inc
rep_inc = df.rep_inc
pvi_std = (df.pvi - np.mean(df.pvi))/np.std(df.pvi)

df.head()
```

	vote	spend	state	districts	dem_inc	rep_inc	pvi
0	-110424	-1853145.17	Louisiana	5	0.0	0.0	-15
1	142997	844317.53	Vermont	0	1.0	0.0	15
2	87490	994256.62	Hawaii	2	0.0	0.0	19
3	80046	11428704.81	New York	17	0.0	0.0	7
4	65679	1634476.18	Texas	33	1.0	0.0	23

Part of our objective in this chapter is to incorporate more of the available data into our model – as you may recall, we only utilized the vote and spend variables in the previous chapter. Now, we're going to expand our model to incorporate information from the state, dem_inc, rep_inc, and pvi variables. Before proceeding, let's take a moment to summarize each of the new variables and consider what they represent:

```
df[['dem_inc', 'rep_inc', 'pvi']].describe()
```

```
            dem_inc      rep_inc         pvi
count  371.000000  371.000000  371.000000
mean     0.490566    0.415094   -1.285714
std      0.500586    0.493404   14.937321
min      0.000000    0.000000  -33.000000
25%      0.000000    0.000000  -12.000000
50%      0.000000    0.000000   -4.000000
75%      1.000000    1.000000    8.000000
max      1.000000    1.000000   43.000000
```

The three new variables in our line-up, from left to right in the table above, represent Democratic Incumbent, Republican Incumbent, and Cook Partisan Voting Index, respectively.

The two incumbency variables are straightforward: both are binary categorical variables (whose only possible values are 1 or 0), and they represent which of the parties (if either) has an incumbent in the race. We can't really combine them in the same way we did with vote and spend, because some districts have no incumbent at all, and it's not yet clear that the effect of incumbency is the same for Republicans and Democrats alike. We'll have to keep them separate for now. The 'Cook Partisan Voting Index' (pvi) measures how strongly a given congressional district tends to lean towards one of the two major US political parties. It's based on voting data gathered from the two previous presidential elections, and – for this election – ranges from a minimum of –33 (the deep-red Texas Panhandle) to 43 (the true-blue Bronx).

Without looking at any regression results, I'd expect all three of these variables to play a strong role in our model: collectively, they speak volumes about how each congressional district has voted in the past. In fact, I'd be willing to bet that their collective influence on the model, regardless of its final form, will be stronger than the spend variable's will be, but that's fine: the purpose of our model is to tell us what the spend variable's influence is whilst controlling for things like statewide preferences and historical trends. If, after the control variables are added, our model finds that spend isn't that important, that's a perfectly valid result.

Of course, we're not yet certain how things are going to turn out; there's a lot of modelling to be done between now and then! As a prelude, let's take a moment to remind ourselves about the fully pooled model (i.e. 'All 50 states are identical') we used in the last chapter:

$$\text{vote}_i \sim \text{Normal}(\mu_i, \sigma) \qquad\qquad \text{[Likelihood]}$$

$$\mu_i = \alpha + (\beta \cdot \text{spend}_i) \qquad\qquad \text{[Linear Model]}$$

$$\alpha \sim \text{Normal}(0, 2) \qquad\qquad \text{[alpha Prior]}$$

$$\beta \sim \text{Normal}(1, 2) \qquad\qquad \text{[beta Prior]}$$

$$\sigma \sim \text{Exponential}(2) \qquad\qquad \text{[sigma Prior]}$$

The above model only uses a single value for α and a single value for β, which means that every observation (regardless of which state they come from) must use the same slope and intercept. When we build *hierarchical* models, we allow the slope and intercept to vary by state. Consequently, we're going to have to rebuild our model such that it is capable of accommodating multiple slopes and multiple intercepts. Rather than use 'dummy' variables for each state (as would be the standard Frequentist practice), we're going to use an unordered categorical 'index variable'. We can write it like so:

$$\mu_i = \alpha_{state[i]} + (\beta_{state[i]} \cdot spend_i)$$

Translated into plain English, the above line is saying that 'the value of μ_i for a given observation i is equal to the α for that observation's state plus the product of the β for that observation's state and that observation's spend value'. This makes it explicit that our model will now accommodate as many different values for α and β as there are states in the dataset (48, in our case, since 2 were dropped).

Now let's update the rest of the model:

$$vote_i \sim \text{Normal}(\mu_i, \sigma)$$

$$\mu_i = \alpha_{state[i]} + (\beta_{state[i]} \cdot spend_i)$$

$$\alpha_{state[i]} \sim \text{Normal}(0, 2) \qquad \text{for state } [i] = 0...47$$

$$\beta_{state[i]} \sim \text{Normal}(1, 2) \qquad \text{for state } [i] = 0...47$$

$$\sigma \sim \text{Exponential}(2)$$

Even though each of the 48 α and β parameters are completely separate and will have no influence on one another, *they all share the same respective priors*. I'm particularly fond of the state$_{[i]}$ nomenclature, because it very closely mirrors how a Python object would behave. What we're saying in the model definition above is that state is a mapping that accepts an integer, i (which can range from 0 to 370), and outputs an integer between 0 and 47. In so doing, it has mapped the observation number (0–370) into a state number (0–47).

We can replicate this behaviour using variables we've already defined:

```
district_3_state = state_idx[3]
print(district_3_state)
print(state_cat.categories[district_3_state])
```

```
30
New York
```

Feel free to go and check what state the corresponding row in the dataset belongs to; you should see that it's a perfect match!

Now that we've specified our model mathematically, let's feed it into PyMC3.

No pooling model

We'll start by specifying the full model. We won't go through it step by step, though, as we're tight on space and we've only made a few changes from the model in the previous chapter. These changes are as follows:

- We added a `shape=n_states` parameter to our α and β priors.
- We added `[state_idx]` to the α and β parameters in the linear model.

As a result of these changes, the α and β parameters are no longer one-dimensional scalars. Instead, they are each vectors of length 48 – one for each of the states in the dataset. Secondly, during fitting, our model will now seek out the α and β parameters that correspond to the *i*th district's state. Here's what it looks like in action:

```
with pm.Model() as no_pool_model:
    # Priors
    alpha = pm.Normal("alpha", mu=0, sigma=2, shape=n_states)
    beta = pm.Normal("beta", mu=1, sigma=2, shape=n_states)
    sigma = pm.Exponential("sigma", 2)

    # Linear Model
    mu = alpha[state_idx] + beta[state_idx] * spend_std

    # Likelihood
    votes = pm.Normal("votes", mu=mu, sigma=sigma, observed=vote_std)

    # Run Sample Traces
    trace_no_pool = pm.sample()
```

```
Auto-assigning NUTS sampler...
Initializing NUTS using jitter+adapt_diag...
Multiprocess sampling (4 chains in 4 jobs)
NUTS: [sigma, beta, alpha]
```

```
<style>
    /* Turns off some styling */
    progress {
      /* gets rid of default border in Firefox and Opera. */
      border: none;
      /* Needs to be in here for Safari polyfill so background images work as
      expected. */
        background-size: auto;
    }
    .progress-bar-interrupted, .progress-bar-interrupted::-webkit-progress-bar .{
        background: #F44336;
    }
</style>
```

100.00% [8000/8000 00:07<00:00 Sampling 4 chains, 0 divergences]

```
Sampling 4 chains for 1_000 tune and 1_000 draw iterations (4_000 + 4_000 draws total)
    took 9 seconds.
```

Rather than fitting a single parameter to all of the states, our unpooled model fit a number of intercept and slope parameters equal to the number of states left in the dataset. As a result, our trace plots are going to be either absurdly busy (more than 48 lines in a single row) or absurdly long (more than 90 rows). We'll show you the compact version in Figure 28.1, but don't expect to get that much information from the α or β rows:

```
with no_pool_model:
    az.plot_trace(trace_no_pool, ['alpha', 'beta', 'sigma'], compact=True)
```

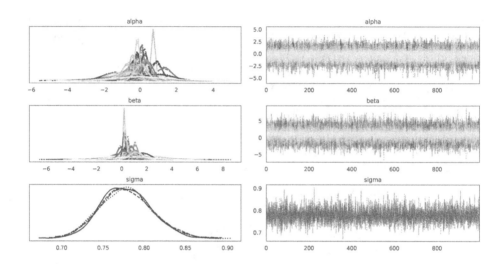

Figure 28.1 A posterior trace plot for the `no_pool_model` regression; the left column is posterior density, the right plots the sampler's movement through parameter values (*y*-axis) as a function of sample step (*x*-axis). Each row corresponds to one parameter/latent variable in the model. Because there are 48 different parameters condensed into the alpha and beta rows, the trace plot is very crowded and difficult to read; it should only be skimmed for glaring anomalies

Even though we can't tell for certain, a quick glance at our traces seems to indicate that everything is well and good. This assumption is backed up by the fact that the PyMC3 sampler didn't have any grievances to air. Operating under the assumption that our model was well-sampled, let's proceed with our examination of the results (Figure 28.2):

```
with no_pool_model:
        ppc = pm.sample_posterior_predictive(trace_no_pool, var_names=['votes',
        'alpha', 'beta', 'sigma',])

<style>
    /* Turns off some styling */
    progress {
        /* gets rid of default border in Firefox and Opera. */
        border: none;
        /* Needs to be in here for Safari polyfill so background images  work as
    expected. */
```

```
        background-size: auto;
    }
    .progress-bar-interrupted, .progress-bar-interrupted::-webkit-progress-bar {
        background: #F44336;
    }
</style>
```

100.00% [4000/4000 00:06<00:00]
```
plot_2020_no_pool(
    no_pool_model,
    trace_no_pool,
    n_states,
    state_idx,
    spend_std,
    vote_std,
    ppc,
    state_cat
)
```

Each state in the model has a different average regression line, and all of them seem to be doing a good job of fitting the data. While most of the states still show a positive relationship between spending differential and vote differential, not all do: Maine, Alabama, Massachusetts, and New Mexico have completely reversed the trend. Our model has determined that Democrats who outspend Republicans in these states tend to do worse than their colleagues who don't. According to our model, the only thing the Democrats would have to do to sweep Alabama is stop spending any money there! Though hilarious, this is clearly not a reasonable conclusion for the model to draw. Such is the peril of allowing a model to fit the data as closely as it can.

If you squint and look closely, you might be able to see some small bands around each of the regression lines, covering the interval that we have data for. It might come as little surprise, then, that those little bands are the exact same as the bands we used to surround our regression line from the previous chapter. As a brief refresher, the bands represent the model's uncertainty about the best fit regression line (inner band, 94% highest density interval [HDI]) and its uncertainty about where the data points themselves lay in relation to the regression line (outer band, 94% HDI; paramaterized as 'σ' in our model's likelihood, aka the standard deviation of the normal distribution in our likelihood).

We're not going to dwell too much on the specifics here: the important takeaway is that our unpooled model has allowed the data for each state to completely determine its own intercept and slope parameters, even when there are only a small number of observations. The only regularizing forces present are the relatively uninformative (and, therefore, weak) priors that we established for this model in the previous chapters (they haven't changed between now and then). With nothing stopping the model from rushing straight for the best possible fit, we've allowed it to descend into the dread valley of overfitting. Damn! Our model does an excellent job at fitting the data we have, but it is, in effect, painting a bullseye around an arrow that had already lodged itself into a wall. In order to curb these tendencies in a principled way, we're going to turn to the regularizing properties of the hierarchical linear model.

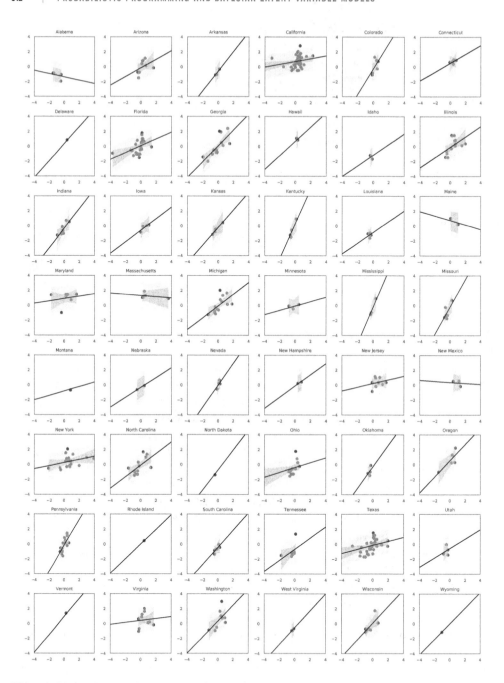

Figure 28.2 A grid of 48 scatter plots – one for each state in the filtered data – by spending differential and vote differential. Each contains that state's average predictor (solid black line), 94% credible interval for the predictor (dark grey band around the average predictor), and the band containing 94% of the observed data (light grey band) for the no_pool_model

Partially pooled model

Our objective for the hierarchical election model we are developing here is to permit slopes and intercepts to vary between states, but to ensure that each is being drawn from a set of higher-level distributions that encode our model's knowledge of the states *in general*. This means that we're going to have to do away with the numbers (μ and σ) we've been using thus far to specify our α and β priors and replace them with parameters. Let's do that now, even though the result will be incomplete:

$$\text{vote}_i \sim \text{Normal}(\mu_i, \sigma)$$

$$\mu_i = \alpha_{\text{state}[i]} + (\beta_{\text{state}[i]} \cdot \text{spend}_i)$$

$$\alpha_{\text{state}[i]} \sim \text{Normal}(\alpha_\mu, \alpha_\sigma)$$

$$\beta_{\text{state}[i]} \sim \text{Normal}(\beta_\mu, \beta_\sigma)$$

$$\sigma \sim \text{Exponential}(2)$$

Okay, great! We've now configured our αs and βs so that they'll be drawn from a common, higher-level distribution. This gives us four new variables to play the 'What's That?' game with. Since all are unobserved, they're going to need priors. You might be thinking to yourself 'aren't α and β *already* priors? Does this mean we're going to be giving priors to our priors?'

- α_μ
- α_σ
- β_μ
- β_σ

Yes! Exactly! In order to keep things as conceptually clear as possible, a 'prior for a prior' has a special name: 'Hyperprior'. Let's fill those in now, using similar numerical values as in earlier models. I've included line breaks to help clarify which type of prior is which.

$$\text{vote}_i \sim \text{Normal}(\mu_i, \sigma)$$

$$\mu_i = \alpha_{\text{state}[i]} + (\beta_{\text{state}[i]} \cdot \text{spend}_i)$$

$$\alpha_{\text{state}[i]} \sim \text{Normal}(\alpha_\mu, \alpha_\sigma)$$

$$\beta_{\text{state}[i]} \sim \text{Normal}(\beta_\mu, \beta_\sigma)$$

$$\sigma \sim \text{Exponential}(2)$$

$$\alpha_\mu \sim Normal(1, 2)$$

$$\beta_\mu \sim Normal(1, 2)$$

$$\alpha_\sigma \sim \text{Exponential}(1)$$

$$\beta_\sigma \sim \text{Exponential}(1)$$

Now that we have priors, and that our priors have priors (most of them, anyways; good ol' sigma remains untouched), let's translate everything into PyMC3:

```python
with pm.Model() as partial_pool_model:

    # Hyperpriors
    alpha_mu = pm.Normal("alpha_mu", mu=1, sigma=2)
    beta_mu = pm.Normal("beta_mu", mu=1, sigma=2)
    alpha_sigma = pm.Exponential("alpha_sigma", 1)
    beta_sigma = pm.Exponential("beta_sigma", 1)

    # Priors
    alpha = pm.Normal("alpha", mu=alpha_mu, sigma=alpha_sigma, shape=n_states)
    beta = pm.Normal("beta", mu=beta_mu, sigma=beta_sigma, shape=n_states)
    sigma = pm.Exponential("sigma", 2)

    # Linear Model
    mu = alpha[state_idx] + (beta[state_idx]*spend_std)

    # Likelihood
    votes = pm.Normal("votes", mu=mu, sigma=sigma, observed=vote_std)
```

Looking good! Surely, nothing will go wrong when we attempt to fit this model?

```python
with partial_pool_model:
    trace_partial_pool = pm.sample(random_seed=42)
```

```
Auto-assigning NUTS sampler...
Initializing NUTS using jitter+adapt_diag...
Multiprocess sampling (4 chains in 4 jobs)
NUTS: [sigma, beta, alpha, beta_sigma, alpha_sigma, beta_mu, alpha_mu]
```

```css
<style>
    /* Turns off some styling */
    progress {
        /* gets rid of default border in Firefox and Opera. */
        border: none;
        /* Needs to be in here for Safari polyfill so background images work as
    expected. */
        background-size: auto;
    }
    .progress-bar-interrupted, .progress-bar-interrupted::-webkit-progress-bar {
        background: #F44336;
    }
</style>
```

100.00% [8000/8000 00:08<00:00 Sampling 4 chains, 4 divergences]

```
Sampling 4 chains for 1_000 tune and 1_000 draw iterations (4_000 + 4_000 draws total)
    took 9 seconds.
There was 1 divergence after tuning. Increase `target_accept` or reparameterize.
There were 3 divergences after tuning. Increase `target_accept` or reparameterize.
The number of effective samples is smaller than 10% for some parameters.
```

Something went wrong when we attempted to fit this model.

The peril is in the priors

Roughly translated, the series of warnings we received can be interpreted as 'The sampling process didn't go well.' One of the benefits of working with PyMC3's default sampler is that it is *very* noisy. It will loudly complain whenever anything goes wrong. As annoying as it can be sometimes, you would do well to view this behaviour as a good thing: whenever your sampler is having trouble with your model, it means there's probably something wrong with your model.

Our largest cause for concern is the number of 'divergences' that the sampling process returned. The sampler records a divergence whenever the proverbial marble in the idiomatic skate bowl ends up somewhere that shouldn't be physically possible: it has ended up buried beneath the terrain, or bounced completely clear of the skate park and is zipping around the city causing chaos.

Let's examine our trace plot (Figure 28.3) to see the extent of the damage:

```python
with partial_pool_model:
    az.plot_trace(trace_partial_pool, ['alpha_mu', 'beta_mu', 'alpha_sigma', '
    beta_sigma', 'sigma'], compact=True)
```

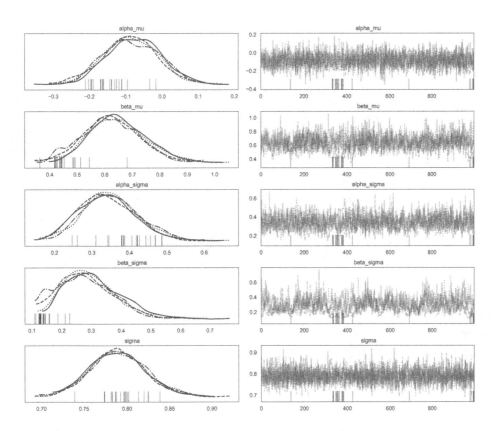

Figure 28.3 A posterior trace plot for the partially pooled regression; the left column is posterior density, the right plots the sampler's movement through parameter values (*y*-axis) as a function of sample step (*x*-axis). Each row corresponds to one parameter/latent variable in the model. The sampling process for this model was plagued by divergences that harm the model's inferential reliability; the effect of these divergent transitions can be seen in the undesirable behaviour in all of the traces except for `sigma`

This isn't a completely unmitigated disaster, but the problems are apparent enough that we should go through them in detail. The first thing you might notice here is that our traces don't meet the criteria we laid out in the previous chapter:

1   The chains are not stationary: some of the traces in `beta_mu` and `beta_sigma` seem to occasionally meander away from the overall mean and then get stuck in a local minima for long periods of time.
2   The chains are not mixing well: some of the traces alternate between rapidly zipping from one extreme to another (which is fine) and slowly moving in a single direction for 50 samples at a time or more (which is not fine).
3   The chains have not converged: the lower end of `beta_sigma` has some real issues.

Despite everything, the overall state of this posterior sampling trace isn't too bad; if you went ahead with the model as is, you would probably draw inferences that are pretty close to what you would have gotten from a better-behaved trace. I wouldn't be in a hurry to submit this to any peer-reviewed journal, though. The bottom line is this: we can do better. To do so, we're going to have to find a less chaotic way of throwing our marble around this 101-dimensional skate bowl.

Informative priors: a spoonful of information makes the sampler calm down

There are many ways to tame a rebellious model. I don't have the space here to cover some of the better ones (re parameterization is the usual go-to), but I want to show that informative priors can be used to improve sampling.

In order to keep things simple, we've specified each of our spend–vote models thus far using only two different distributions:

1   The normal distribution, which we've used for parameters that could, theoretically, take on any value on the real number line.
2   The exponential distribution, which we've used as priors for our standard deviation parameters, which must fall somewhere between 0 and positive infinity.

Our strategy for calming down our out-of-control model is going to involve tightening up our normal distributions and swapping our exponential distributions for gamma distributions (a distribution we did not explicitly discuss in Chapter 25, but which you now know how to learn about).

First, 'tightening our normals'. All I mean by this is that instead of using the wide, nearly flat priors we've been using thus far, we're going to shrink them down to cover a much smaller part of the real number line. You can see what I mean by looking at the priors for the model specified below.

The switch from an exponential distribution to a gamma distribution for our standard deviation parameters needs a bit more explanation. The gamma distribution is similar to the exponential in the sense that both can only take on values from 0 to positive infinity (a property we need for our standard deviations), and that they tend to peak early and have long tails. In the interests of avoiding technical jargon, the gamma distribution will let us 'scoop' a bit of the probability density away from 0, which is likely the cause of our woes here.

A quick note: the priors we're using here are designed to demonstrate how information can be used to combat model degeneracy. As such, they're a little more strongly informative than you might expect to see in the published literature, but not by that much. With these informative priors in place (and no other changes), let's examine how our model behaves:

```python
with pm.Model() as partial_pool_model_regularized:

    # Hyperpriors
    alpha_mu = pm.Normal("alpha_mu", mu=.1, sigma=.3)
    beta_mu = pm.Normal("beta_mu", mu=.1, sigma=.3)
    alpha_sigma = pm.Gamma("alpha_sigma", alpha=4, beta=0.10)
    beta_sigma = pm.Gamma("beta_sigma", alpha=4, beta=0.10)

    # Priors
    alpha = pm.Normal("alpha", mu=alpha_mu, sigma=alpha_sigma, shape=n_states)
    beta = pm.Normal("beta", mu=beta_mu, sigma=beta_sigma, shape=n_states)
    sigma = pm.Gamma("sigma", alpha=4, beta=0.10)

    # Linear Model
    mu = pm.Deterministic("mu", alpha[state_idx] + (beta[state_idx]*spend_std))

    # Likelihood
    votes = pm.Normal("votes", mu=mu, sigma=sigma, observed=vote_std)

    # Run Sample Traces
    trace_partial_pool_regularized = pm.sample(
        random_seed=42
    )


Auto-assigning NUTS sampler...
Initializing NUTS using jitter+adapt_diag...
Multiprocess sampling (4 chains in 4 jobs)
NUTS: [sigma, beta, alpha, beta_sigma, alpha_sigma, beta_mu, alpha_mu]

<style>
    /* Turns off some styling */
    progress {
      /* gets rid of default border in Firefox and Opera. */
      border: none;
      /* Needs to be in here for Safari polyfill so background images work as
    expected. */
      background-size: auto;
    }
    .progress-bar-interrupted, .progress-bar-interrupted::-webkit-progress-bar {
        background: #F44336;
    }
</style>

100.00% [8000/8000 00:09<00:00 Sampling 4 chains, 0 divergences]

Sampling 4 chains for 1_000 tune and 1_000 draw iterations (4_000 + 4_000 draws total)
    took 10 seconds.
The number of effective samples is smaller than 25% for some parameters.
```

Boom! No more divergences! (At least for us. If you use a different random seed or you're using a different version of PyMC3, your results may vary. Adjusting priors helps to combat divergences, but it isn't the best way. We don't have the room to get into any of the better ways, I'm afraid.) The sampler still had a few grievances to air (at least one of our parameters was sampled very inefficiently), but we should interpret the lack of divergences as permission to manually examine our trace plots (Figure 28.4):

```
with partial_pool_model_regularized:
    az.plot_trace(trace_partial_pool_regularized, ['alpha_mu', 'beta_mu', 'alpha_sigma
    ', 'beta_sigma', 'sigma'], compact=True)
```

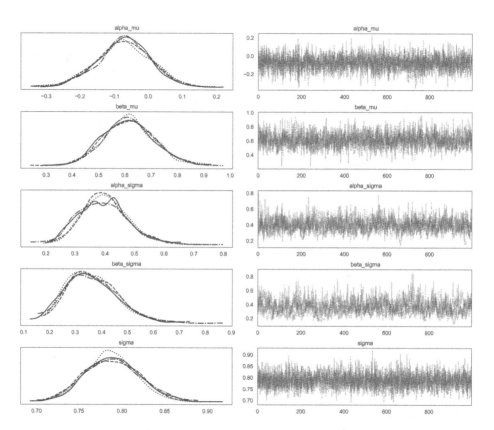

Figure 28.4 A posterior trace plot for the regularized partially pooled regression; the left column is posterior density, the right plots the sampler's movement through parameter values (*y*-axis) as a function of sample step (*x*-axis). Each row corresponds to one parameter/latent variable in the model. Tightening the model's prior distributions eliminated divergences

There are a couple of hiccups, and the `alpha_sigma` traces are verging on non-convergence, but there's nothing to be too concerned about.

```
with partial_pool_model_regularized:
    ppc = pm.sample_posterior_predictive(trace_partial_pool_regularized
                                , var_names=['votes', 'alpha_mu', 'beta_mu',
```

```
'alpha_sigma', 'beta_sigma', 'alpha', 'beta', 'sigma', 'mu'])
<style>
    /* Turns off some styling */
    progress {
        /* gets rid of default border in Firefox and Opera. */
        border: none;
        /* Needs to be in here for Safari polyfill so background images work as
        expected. */
            background-size: auto;
    }
        .progress-bar-interrupted, .progress-bar-interrupted::-webkit-progress-bar {
            background: #F44336;

    }
</style>
```

100.00% [4000/4000 00:05<00:00]

We won't include the α or β parameters in our ArviZ summary because there are 96 of them in total. No sense reading them all. Instead, we'll focus on our hyperpriors:

```
with partial_pool_model_regularized:
    summary = az.summary(trace_partial_pool_regularized, round_to=2, var_names=['
    alpha_mu', 'beta_mu', 'alpha_sigma', 'beta_sigma', 'sigma'])
summary[['mean', 'sd', 'r_hat']]
```

	mean	sd	r_hat
alpha_mu	-0.07	0.08	1.00
beta_mu	0.62	0.10	1.00
alpha_sigma	0.40	0.08	1.00
beta_sigma	0.36	0.10	1.01
sigma	0.79	0.03	1.00

It appears that there was a bit of an issue with alpha_sigma and beta_sigma; our assessment of alpha_sigma is backed by the r_hat value of 1.01 (anything noticeably greater than 1.00 indicates something's amiss). It's not high enough to be a true cause for concern, but it's worth pointing out.

Now that we've fit our hierarchical model, let's visualize the results (Figure 28.5):

```
plot_2020_partial_pool(
    partial_pool_model_regularized,
    trace_partial_pool_regularized,
    trace_no_pool,
    n_states,
    state_idx,
    spend_std,
    vote_std,
    ppc,
    state_cat
)
```

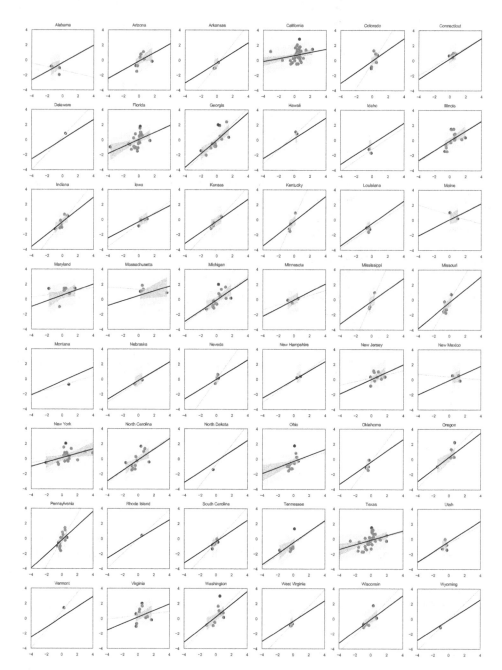

Figure 28.5 A grid of 48 scatter plots – one for each state in the filtered data – by spending differential and vote differential. Each contains that state's average predictor (solid black line), 94% credible interval for the predictor (dark grey band around the average predictor), and the band containing 94% of the observed data (light grey band) from the regularized partially pooled model, and the average predictor from the no_pool_model (solid grey line). The juxtaposition of the average predictor lines from the partially pooled and unpooled models evinces shrinkage.

The above plots should look familiar: they're very similar to the ones we used to investigate the results from our unpooled model above. All of the elements they share in common are the same, only for our latest model:

- each of the points represents a single congressional district,
- the black line represents the regression line from our partially pooled model, and
- the small and large bands around the lines represent the 94% HDI of posterior probability for the regressor and the predictions, respectively.

There's one additional element here, though. The grey lines represent the regression lines from the unpooled model; I included them here to facilitate comparison between the partially pooled and unpooled models.

Shrinkage

Let's dig into these lines a little. First of all, a cursory glance at the previous model's more outlandish conclusions shows that things have been calmed down considerably. Each of the states with downward-sloping regression lines (predicting worse voting outcomes in districts where Democrats spent more) – such as Alabama, Maine, and New Mexico – have been pulled back from the brink. In the opposite direction, some of the more steeply positive states (e.g. Kentucky, where the unpooled model predicted that a single standard deviation increase in relative spending for the Democrats would net 2 standard deviations' worth of votes) have been reined in.

Another thing you might notice is that each of the single-district states (Wyoming, Vermont, Rhode Island, etc.) have had their regression lines change from perfect fits (where the grey line travels straight through the sole point of data) to more 'standard' fits (where the black line misses the point, often by a good margin). That's not to claim that all of their black lines are identical: they're not (compare Rhode Island with Montana). Instead, what the model is telling us is that the posterior distribution for each of these individual states isn't all that much different from the distribution all states are drawing from.

What's happening here is that all of the states that have had their regression lines 'calmed down' by the model are being regularized by the impact of our model's prior. Unlike a single-level model, however, *we didn't choose this prior: the model learnt it from the data!*

This is the power of the hierarchical model; it adaptively learns how to straddle the line between underfitting and overfitting, leveraging regularizing probability distributions to calm down overeager predictions. The net effect is that our partially pooled model, at least compared with the unpooled model, has 'shrunk' the posterior distribution, causing the model's predictions to crowd more tightly around a more conservative predictor. This phenomenon is known as 'shrinkage'.

A final parting thought on this topic: you may have noticed that the larger states such as Texas, New York, and California – all of which already had fairly reasonable regression lines – barely changed at all. Each of them were endowed with enough observations that they could largely overwhelm the regularizing influence of the priors.

Note that many of these states aren't actually single-district states, but rather only have one valid district in the dataset because of the filtering we had to do.

Does the model fit? Posterior predictive plots

Adding variables to a model can be an excellent way to explore relationships that simply couldn't be tackled without some form of multivariate regression. It is unfortunate, then, that adding even a small handful of variables results in a model that the human brain can no longer perceive visually. A regression with just a predictor and an outcome variable is simple: you can capture everything in a two-dimensional scatter plot, with the predictor on the horizontal axis and the outcome on the vertical. A regression with two independent variables (say, a predictor and a control) and one outcome variable is less simple, but doable: you'll occasionally see them visualized as a three-dimensional plot with the two independents on the horizontal axes, and with a plane representing the regressor. Anything more than this is practically impossible, as the 'line' of best fit becomes a hyperplane that our brains are incapable of visualizing.

In this sad state of affairs, we're forced to turn to plots that collapse high-dimensional space back down into a two-dimensional plane that allows us to see the distance between our model's predictions and the true value of the observations. The resulting plot is called a 'posterior predictive plot', and is useful for assessing how well our model has fit the data. The main strength of this method is that it scales well into an arbitrarily large number of dimensions: we can picture all of the observations using a single plot. The downside is that we lose some of the nuance that we'd get from other visualizations. Here's how to make one (results shown in Figure 28.6):

```
mu_hpd = az.hdi(ppc["mu"], 0.89)
D_sim = ppc["votes"].mean(axis=0)

fig, ax = plt.subplots(figsize=(6, 6))

plt.errorbar(
    vote_std,
    ppc["votes"].mean(0),
    yerr=np.abs(ppc["votes"].mean(0) - mu_hpd.T),
    fmt="C0o",
)

ax = sns.scatterplot(vote_std, D_sim, s=1, color='darkgray')

min_x, max_x = vote_std.min(), vote_std.max()
ax.plot([min_x, max_x], [min_x, max_x], "k--")

ax.set_ylabel("Predicted vote differential")
ax.set_xlabel("Observed votes differential")

sns.despine()
plt.show()
```

Each of the points is an observation from our dataset. They're arranged along the horizontal axis according to their observed (actual) value, and along the vertical axis according to where our model thinks they should be. The vertical lines around each point indicates the range that contains 94% of the posterior probability for that particular observation (remember, in a Bayesian model, *everything comes with a healthy dose of uncertainty*).

Examining the plot below, we can see that our model does a passable job of retrodicting the voting data using nothing but the 'state' and 'spend' variables. We can, however, see some real problems at the far-right side of the plot: not only is our model incorrect about almost every

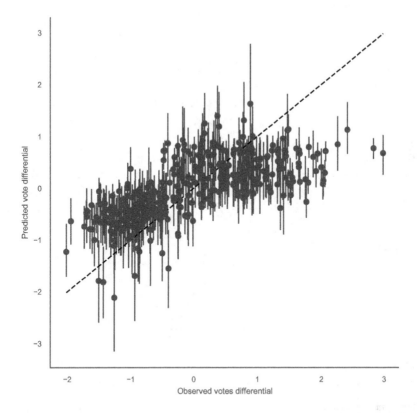

Figure 28.6 A posterior predictive plot for the regularized partially pooled model, showing the model's ability to retrodict the data. The model does not do a good job of retrodicting the data, especially on the right-hand side of the plot (high observed vote differential)

district which lays more than ~1.5 standard deviations above the mean, but also it is *confidently* incorrect about them. In the next section, we're going to see if we can do better.

28.6 The Best Model Our Data Can Buy

Now that we have established a hierarchical baseline and introduced a method for visualizing results from models whose regression 'lines' are in higher dimensions (and, thus, aren't lines any longer, but rather hyperplanes), we can start to add variables in an effort to improve model fit. Unfortunately, we don't have the room here to report all the proper checks every time we add a variable. Instead, I'll run you through how to add each of the remaining variables in the dataset and then present the finished model.

```
with pm.Model() as full_hierarchical_model:

    # Hyperpriors
    alpha_mu_state = pm.Normal("alpha_mu_state", mu=.1, sigma=.3)
    alpha_sigma_state = pm.Gamma("alpha_sigma_state", alpha=4, beta=0.10)
```

```python
    beta_mu_spend = pm.Normal("beta_mu_spend", mu=.1, sigma=.3)
    beta_sigma_spend = pm.Gamma("beta_sigma_spend", alpha=4, beta=0.10)

    # Priors from Hyperpriors
    alpha_state = pm.Normal("alpha_state", mu=alpha_mu_state, sigma=alpha_sigma_state,
        shape=n_states)
    beta_spend = pm.Normal("beta_spend", mu=beta_mu_spend, sigma=beta_sigma_spend,
        shape=n_states)

    # Priors
    beta_pvi = pm.Normal("beta_pvi", mu=1, sigma=0.3)
    beta_rep_inc = pm.Normal("beta_rep_inc", mu=-0.5, sigma=0.2)
    beta_dem_inc = pm.Normal("beta_dem_inc", mu=0.5, sigma=0.2)
    sigma = pm.Gamma("sigma", alpha=4, beta=0.10)

    # Linear Model
    mu = pm.Deterministic("mu",
                        alpha_state[state_idx] +
                        beta_spend[state_idx] * spend_std +
                        beta_pvi * pvi_std +
                        beta_rep_inc * rep_inc +
                        beta_dem_inc * dem_inc
                        )

    # Likelihood
    votes = pm.Normal("votes", mu=mu, sigma=sigma, observed=vote_std)

    # Run Sample Traces
    trace_full_hierarchical_model = pm.sample(
        target_accept=0.97,
        random_seed=42
    )


Auto-assigning NUTS sampler...
Initializing NUTS using jitter+adapt_diag...
Multiprocess sampling (4 chains in 4 jobs)
NUTS: [sigma, beta_dem_inc, beta_rep_inc, beta_pvi, beta_spend, alpha_state,
    beta_sigma_spend, beta_mu_spend, alpha_sigma_state, alpha_mu_state]

<style>
    /* Turns off some styling */
    progress {
        /* gets rid of default border in Firefox and Opera. */
        border: none;
        /* Needs to be in here for Safari polyfill so background images work as
     expected. */
        background-size: auto;
    }
    .progress-bar-interrupted, .progress-bar-interrupted::-webkit-progress-bar {
        background: #F44336;
    }
</style>
```

100.00% [8000/8000 00:23<00:00 Sampling 4 chains, 0 divergences]

```
Sampling 4 chains for 1_000 tune and 1_000 draw iterations (4_000 + 4_000 draws total)
    took 24 seconds.
The number of effective samples is smaller than 10% for some parameters.
```

Let's produce the trace plots for our `full_hierarchical_model` (Figure 28.7):

```
with full_hierarchical_model:
    az.plot_trace(trace_full_hierarchical_model,
                [
                    'alpha_mu_state',
                    'alpha_sigma_state',
                    'beta_mu_spend',
                    'beta_sigma_spend',
                    'beta_pvi',
                    'beta_rep_inc',
                    'beta_dem_inc',
                    'sigma',
                ], compact=True)
```

There are a few worrying signs here (the `alpha_mu_state` isn't sampling as efficiently as we would prefer), but nothing serious enough to call the model into question entirely! Time to take a peek at our model fit (Figure 28.8):

```
with full_hierarchical_model:
    ppc = pm.sample_posterior_predictive(trace_full_hierarchical_model, var_names=['
    votes', 'mu'])

mu_hpd = az.hdi(ppc["mu"], 0.89)
D_sim = ppc["votes"].mean(axis=0)

fig, ax = plt.subplots(figsize=(6, 6))

plt.errorbar(
    vote_std,
    ppc["votes"].mean(0),
    yerr=np.abs(ppc["votes"].mean(0) - mu_hpd.T),
    fmt="C0o",
)

ax = sns.scatterplot(vote_std, D_sim, s=1, color='darkgray')

min_x, max_x = vote_std.min(), vote_std.max()
ax.plot([min_x, max_x], [min_x, max_x], "k--")

ax.set_ylabel("Predicted vote differential")
ax.set_xlabel("Observed votes differential")

sns.despine()

plt.show()
```

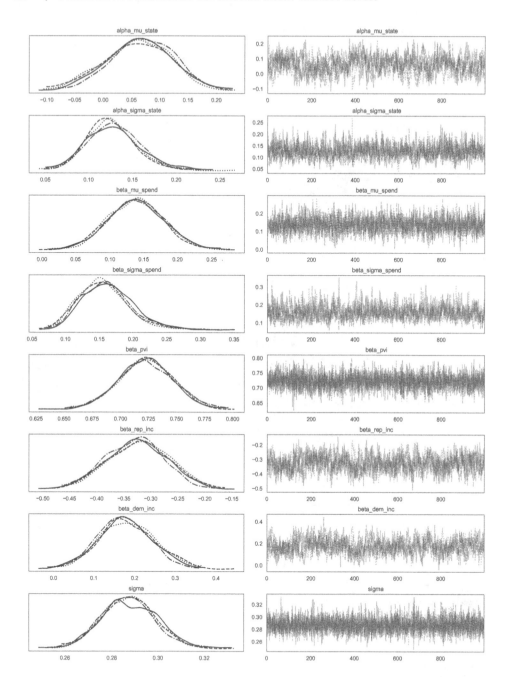

Figure 28.7 A posterior trace plot for the full hierarchical regression model; the left column is posterior density, the right plots the sampler's movement through parameter values (*y*-axis) as a function of sample step (*x*-axis). Each row corresponds to one parameter/latent variable in the model

```
<style>
    /* Turns off some styling */
    progress {
        /* gets rid of default border in Firefox and Opera. */
        border: none;
        /* Needs to be in here for Safari polyfill so background images work as
     expected. */
        background-size: auto;
    }
    .progress-bar-interrupted, .progress-bar-interrupted::-webkit-progress-bar {
        background: #F44336;
    }
</style>
```

100.00% [4000/4000 00:06<00:00]

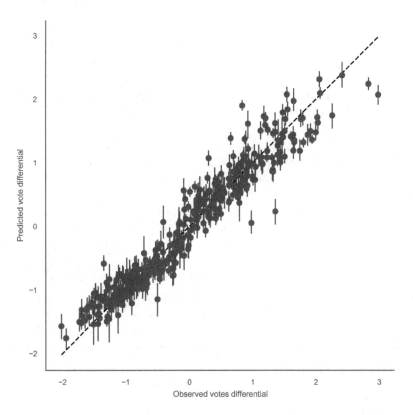

Figure 28.8 A posterior predictive plot for the full hierarchical regression model, showing the model's ability to retrodict the data. As a result of the additional predictor variables, the model does a good job of retrodicting the data

Much, much better. The addition of two categorical variables (Democratic and Republican incumbency), and one continuous variable (the Cook Partisan Voting Index), has allowed our model's predictions to fall closer to the observed values across the board.

Even though the above plot does a good job of showing us how well our model fits the data in general, it tells us nothing about the parameters of interest! For that, we're going to need to turn to a form of plot that can condense large amounts of coefficient information into a relatively small space (we have 51 to examine, after all). It's called a forest plot. Figure 28.9 is the forest plot for our model.

```
sns.set_style('whitegrid')
ax = az.plot_forest(trace_full_hierarchical_model,
                var_names=['beta_pvi', 'beta_dem_inc', 'beta_rep_inc', 'beta_spend'],
                combined=True,
                quartiles=False)

labels = np.append(np.array(list(reversed(state_cat.categories))),
                ('Republican Incumbency', 'Democratic Incumbency', 'PVI'))

_ = ax[0].set_yticklabels(labels)
_ = ax[0].set_title(
    "coefficients for spending differentials, incumbency, and PVI")

sns.despine(left=False, bottom=False, top=False, right=False)
plt.show()
```

After all that, we can finally settle down to the task of interpreting our handiwork.

Looking at the forest plot below, you might be struck by two countervailing trends. The first is that two out of the three variables we added in this latest model have a strong impact on its predictions. It should come as no surprise that the Partisan Voting Index is strongly positively correlated with vote differential, and that Republican incumbency has a predictably negative effect, showing the impact of Republicans' prior experience in helping them win their races.

The other trend that you might notice is that most of the rest of the model's claims are relatively tepid. Starting at the top, Democratic incumbency has a positive impact on the Democrats' vote margins, but it isn't as significant a boost as was the case for their Republican counterparts – a little under half. Finally, the 94% HDI for most of the states' spending coefficients shows only a weak effect, if any at all. Most of the coefficient estimates are above zero, but a good portion of their HDI ranges straddle 0, meaning that our model hasn't really ruled out the idea that spending has no (or even a negative) effect on Democratic margins of victory. Of all the states under consideration, only in Georgia, Maryland, Michigan, North Carolina, Oregon, and Wisconsin does our model see *unambiguous* evidence of a positive effect from Democrats outspending Republicans.

One interpretation of these results is that Democratic spending advantages don't often translate into vote advantages. An equally valid interpretation, and one which takes into account the specific historical context, is that Democrats did a good job of funnelling their resources towards close races in states whose districts were ripe for a Democratic breakthrough. They didn't succeed in all cases, but were able to translate their funding advantage in North Carolina and Georgia into a total of three seats flipped in their favour (the Democrats neither gained nor lost seats in any of the other states mentioned above).

Is this enough? Should we, at this point, be satisfied?

No.

coefficients for spending differentials, incumbency, and PVI

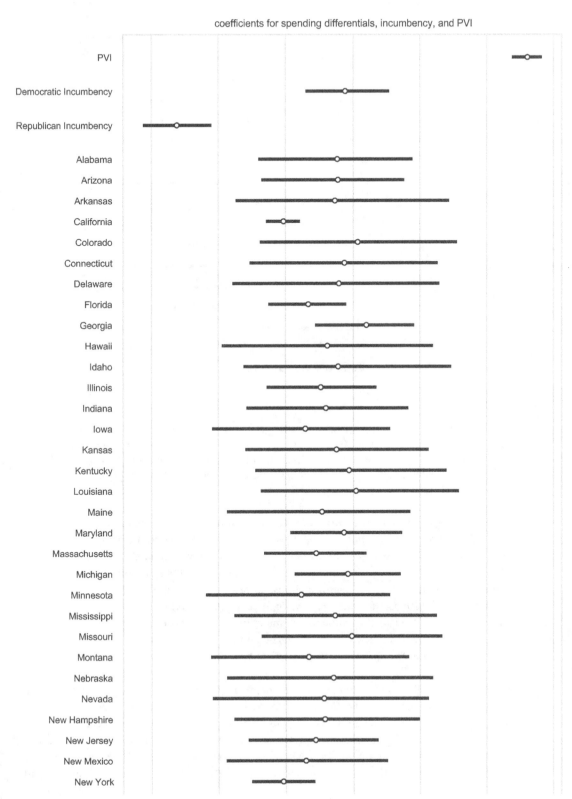

(Continued)

Figure 28.9 *(Continued)*

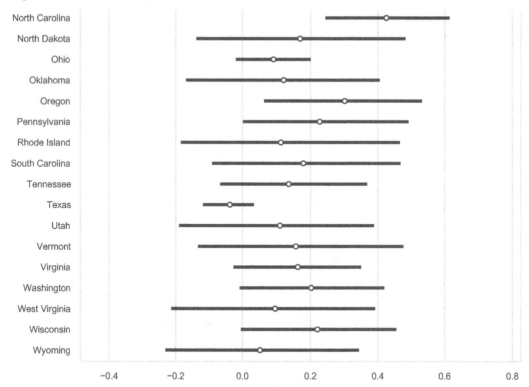

Figure 28.9 A forest plot showing a selection of the full hierarchical regression model's posterior parameter distributions. The hollow points represent the mean value of each parameter's posterior, and the dark bands represent the 94% HDI. Many of the coefficients – such as each of the alpha parameters – were omitted for space

Anytime we create a model with more than two variables, it is incumbent upon us to think through the causal implications of what we have done. To once again paraphrase Richard McElreath (2020), whose *Statistical Rethinking* has had a major influence on our discussion of Bayesian regression, a regression model is implicitly asking a set of questions about each of its variables simultaneously: that question almost always boils down to something like '*how much predictive information does this variable contain, once the effect of all the other variables is known?*' Since we're interested in the influence of spending differentials on vote differentials across different states, we're implicitly using our regression model to ask: '*what is the value of knowing the effect of the spending differential once the effects from incumbency and the Partisan Voting Index are already known?*'

Here's a plausible explanation for what's happening here. The negative effect that we're seeing in Texas might be indicative of a concerted Democratic push to try and flip histori- cally Republican-leaning districts. If you paid attention to the 2020 US election, you might know that Democrats generally underperformed in the 2020 House races, and, as such, our model may be picking up on an effect wherein Democrats funnelled cash into break-even or Republican-leaning districts, only to be rebuffed. To do this, they would have presumably had to move cash away from safer Democratic-leaning districts in metro Houston and Austin. Under such circumstances, it might be entirely plausible that, *once we control for all the other variables in the model*, Democrats were more likely to lose ridings they overspent on, and win those they underspent on.

Another problem is that our model is helpless to tell us if the presumed causal relationship underpinning the whole shebang (namely, that money helps win elections) is justifiable. It'd be just as easy to claim that our predictor (money spent) and outcome (votes received) variables share no direct causal link and instead share 'political popularity' as a common cause. The logic here being that popular candidates might be more likely to attract donations *and* votes. Modelling can't help us here. The best regression model in the world, be it Bayesian or Frequentist, wouldn't be able to help you determine if there's any validity to your assumptions of causality. If you're interested, computational social science is in the midst of a causal inference renaissance (such as Judea Pearl's work on structural causal models), and that renaissance is largely Bayesian. Unfortunately, this is another area of computational social science that I simply don't have the space to introduce in this book.

There is, in fact, a lot more we *could* get into here, but my hands are tied by space constraints and by the fact that this book is not a Bayesian regression textbook. Hopefully you've seen that it is possible, and even fun, to build an interesting, functional, and sophisticated statistical model from scratch. Its imperfections represent room for improvement, not something to be feared or ashamed of. Remember, Box's loop!

28.7 The Fault in Our (Lack of) Stars

Somewhere, someone in the world is saying something like 'Hold up, John. This is a chapter on regression analysis! Where are the hypothesis tests!? Where are the little stars that tell me if I can publish my findings or not?'

As these chapters have probably made abundantly clear, that's not what we're doing here. The Bayesian statistical paradigm is capable of comparing hypotheses in the way Frequentists think of such things, but are generally loath to do so. This is because we already have access to a very broad *range* of hypotheses defined by a posterior probability distribution, and that distribution already contains all of the information we can possibly derive from our model for a given set of data. Anything else we do – plotting, calculating HDI, hypothesis testing – is simply a summarization of that posterior distribution.

If you feel like comparing hypotheses in the style of a Frequentist, go for it. All of the Bayesian regression models we fit today contain infinite hypotheses (in multiple dimensions!) and the probability of any individual from among them (say, $\beta = 3$) being 'true' (whatever that means) is 0. We've already covered why that's the case.

You could compare ranges of hypotheses against a 'null' of sorts, but the Bayesian paradigm ensures that a simple posterior plot is all that is needed to quickly ascertain whether or not most of the posterior probability for any given parameter is credibly distant from 0, which is all null hypothesis significance testing does really anyhow.

Instead of using null hypothesis significance testing, consider treating each model as its own 'hypothesis' of sorts. Gelman and Shalizi (2013) advocate a paradigm wherein whole models are judged by how well they fit data (both in-sample and out-of-sample). Accepted models are used until their flaws become too egregious to ignore, at which point new, better models are developed using insights from the failings of the previous one. It's a different way of doing science than you might be used to, but it's worth knowing about: the winds of change are blowing decisively away from the traditional null hypothesis testing paradigm.

 **Further Reading**

As I mentioned in several previous chapters, there are a number of outstanding resources to which you can now turn to continue your journey into Bayesian regression analysis. I especially recommend McElreath (2020), Lambert (2018), Kruschke (2014), and Martin (2018). Finally, Lynch and Bartlett (2019) offer a literature review of the use of Bayesian statistics in sociology.

28.8 Conclusion

The key points in this chapter are as follows:

- When it comes to regression analysis, any dataset that features at least one clustering variable should be modelled, by default, using partially pooled hierarchical regression; any simpler models should only be used if justified.
- Wide, uninformative priors can cause a large number of divergences during sampling using a HMC sampler; using tighter, more informative priors can help ameliorate this.
- Higher-dimensional regression models (those with more than two variables) are difficult (if not impossible) to fully visualize – we can instead turn to specialized visualizations to assess model fit (via retrodiction) and model parameters (via forest plots).
- The first rule of Bayes Club is that we don't do *p* values, stars, or null hypothesis significance testing (exceptions apply).

Visit the website at https://study.sagepub.com/mclevey for additional resources

29

VARIATIONAL BAYES AND THE CRAFT OF GENERATIVE TOPIC MODELLING

29.1 Learning Objectives

By the end of this chapter, you should be able to do the following:

- Explain how variational inference differs from Hamiltonian Monte Carlo sampling, conceptually
- Explain the value of graphical models in developing generative models
- Describe *the distinction between deterministic and stochastic/generative topic models*
- Explain *what latent Dirichlet allocation is and how it works*
- Explore *the use of semantic coherence as an evaluation metric for topic models*

29.2 Learning Materials

You can find the online learning materials for this chapter in `doing_computational_social_science/Chapter_29`. `cd` into the directory and launch your Jupyter server.

29.3 Introduction

This chapter serves three purposes: (1) to introduce you to generative topic modelling and Bayesian latent variable modelling more generally; (2) to explain the role that graphical models can play in developing purpose-made generative models; and (3) to introduce you to another computational approach for approximating the posterior called 'variational inference' (VI).

We'll start by introducing the logic behind generative topic modelling. Then, we will discuss the technical details of one of the most widely used topic models: latent Dirichlet allocation (LDA). Then, we'll cover the basics of approximating the posterior using an alternative to Hamiltonian Monte Carlo (HMC) called variational inference. In the second section, we'll start developing LDA topic models with Gensim, discuss quantitative measures of coherence, and show how to visualize topic models.

29.4 Generative Topic Models

You've likely noticed that 'latent' is a not-so-latent theme in this book. Recall Chapter 8. Sometimes our data has highly correlated variables because they arise from a shared *latent* factor or process. That may even be *by design*, like when we collect data on low-level *indicators* of an abstract and unobservable concept that we want to measure. We later extended that idea to text analysis by discussing latent semantic analysis (LSA), which used deterministic matrix factorization methods (truncated SVD [singular value decomposition]) to construct a set of latent thematic dimensions in text data. In other chapters, we've touched on 'latent' variables in a variety of different ways, including regression models and latent network structure.

Latent variables are central to Bayesian thinking. When we develop models in the Bayesian framework, we define *joint* probability distributions with both latent and observed variables, and then we use an inference algorithm such as HMC or VI (introduced below) to approximate the posterior distribution of each latent variable conditional on the evidence provided by the observed variables. This is an extremely flexible and mathematically principled way of working with latent variables that you can use to develop probabilistic models for just about any research. So, what exactly would a Bayesian approach to modelling latent thematic structure – *topics* – in text data look like?

Generative topic models got their start when the computer scientists David Blei, Andrew Ng, and Michael Jordan (2003) published a classic paper proposing the model we will focus on in this chapter. This model and many variants of it are widely used in the social sciences and digital humanities, with some variants developed by social scientists (e.g. Roberts et al., 2013, 2014). Broadly speaking, generative topic models are a family of Bayesian models that assume, like LSA, that documents are collections of thematically linked words. Rather than using matrix factorization methods to understand latent themes, most generative topic models approach this as just another latent variable problem.

Although applicable in many contexts, we should be *especially* open to using generative topics models if:

1 we have data in the form of many text documents;
2 we know that each document contains words that represent different themes, or topics, in various proportions;
3 we want to infer the distribution of latent topics across documents given the words we observe in them; and
4 we have a plausible mechanism, or a 'simple generative story', of the relationship between our latent and observed variables that will help us accomplish Step 3: documents and their specific combinations of words are 'generated from' a mixtures of latent themes, which are themselves mixtures of words.

In the case of text data, posing a generative mechanism means thinking through the reasons why some words co-occur in documents while others tend not to. *Something* influences those relationships; our word choices are not random. What might lead a politician making a speech, or a scientist writing journal articles, to select some combination of words but not others? Why does elephant floral own snowstorm aghast the rock cat? (See what I did there?)

Many generative mechanisms have been posited and tested by different types of topic models, including some that are designed to take information about speakers/authors into account in a regression model-like framework (e.g. Roberts et al., 2013, 2014; Rosen-Zvi et al., 2012) or to account for the ordering/sequence of words (e.g. Blei and Lafferty, 2006; Wang et al., 2012), but the foundational generative mechanism that unites all topic models is that the particular mixture of words that show up in documents are related to an unobservable set of underlying themes, that is, latent topics. The probability of selecting one word over another depends in large part on the topic(s) we are discussing.

We learn about the underlying latent topics by constructing a probabilistic model and then using an inference algorithm to approximate the posterior. We will construct an LDA topic model (a subtype within the more general class of mixed membership models), which revolutionized natural language processing and probabilistic machine learning in the early 2000s. It remains a widely used model, alongside many variations.

The goal of approximating the posterior with an LDA topic model is learning about the distribution of latent topics over (1) documents and (2) words. Say we have a journal article about social movements focused on energy transitions. There are likely quite a few latent topics in this article, but it's safe to say that the dominant ones are probably 'social movements' and 'energy transitions'. Of course, the model doesn't actually know what 'social movements' and 'energy transitions' are, so it might tell us that the article in question is 17% 'topic 11', 12% 'topic 2', and then many other topics in much smaller proportions. *Note that these are mixtures;* documents always consist of multiple topics, though one may be dominant.

Every word in our document has a different probability of appearing in each of the topics we find. The words 'movement', 'mobilization', 'collective', and 'protest' may have a high probability of appearing in topic 11 (which we interpret as 'social movements'). The words 'environmental', 'transition', 'energy', 'oil', 'renewable', and 'pipeline' may have a high probability of appearing in 'energy transitions and politics', 'topic 2', but a relatively low probability of appearing in social movements topics. Other words, such as 'medical', and 'healthcare', will have a low probability of appearing in either topic (assuming they appear at all), but they might have a high probability of appearing in a topic about 'health' (which itself has a low probability of appearing in the article).

This notion that words have different probabilities of appearing in each topic makes it possible for the same word to have a high probability of appearing in more than one topic depending on its use (we discuss this more in the next chapter). For example, the word 'policy' might have a high probability of appearing in both topics. This turns out to be a major benefit of generative topic models. As prominent sociologists of culture have pointed out, this brings the topic modelling framework close to relational theories of language and meaning that have been influential in the social sciences for quite some time (e.g. DiMaggio et al., 2013; Mohr and Bogdanov, 2013).

Now that we've built a bit of intuition about what a generative topic model might look like, let's get into some of the technical modelling details. Then we'll use these models to analyse latent topics in 1,893,372 speeches made in Parliament by Canadian politicians over a 30-year period (1990–2020).

Latent Dirichlet allocation

LDA as a graphical model

In previous chapters, we developed and described our Bayesian models using statistical model notation, and we *briefly* saw graphical models as an alternative in the context of regression modelling. Graphical models are a powerful tool for developing, critiquing, and communicating our probabilistic models in part because they make three key things explicit:

1. The origin of every variable in our model as either observed or latent (we're always playing the 'What's That?' game introduced in Chapter 26)
2. Our assumptions about the structure of statistical dependencies between all the variables in our model
3. Our assumptions about the generative processes that give rise to the data we observe

Graphical models are a favoured tool in probabilistic machine learning in particular (Jordan, 2003, 2004; Koller and Friedman, 2009; McElreath, 2020; Pearl and Mackenzie, 2018), and you'll see them everywhere in the generative topic modelling literature. Though they can be a little confusing at first, they are transparent once you know how to read them. Let's break down the graphical representation of a vanilla LDA topic model, shown in Figure 29.1.

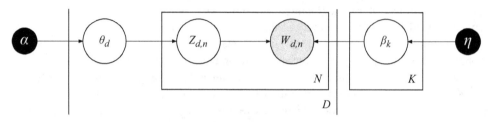

Figure 29.1 Latent Dirichlet allocation, depicted as a graphical model. The grey node represents the observed data, the white nodes are latent variables, and the black nodes represent hyperparameters. Plate notation is used to indicate how many instances of the objects contained within are present in the model (i.e. 'replicates')

> It is possible to produce graphical models like this automatically using PyMC3. Doing so can be very useful if you want to examine how your Bayesian models are structured. Consult the PyMC3 documentation if you want to learn more!

Now, what does it mean?

First, each node in the graph represents a random variable, with observed variables shaded and latent variables unshaded. The black nodes are model hyperparameters. Each arrow in the graph represents a statistical dependency or, to be precise, conditional independence. The boxes (called plates) represent repetition over some set of items (replicates), like words or documents. Plates notation is *very* useful for condensing your graphical models. For example, without it, you would need a node for each document in a text analysis. We will soon analyse 1,893,372 political speeches. Now, imagine how many nodes we would need for the $W_{d,n}$ node.

Let's break down this specific graphical model starting with the plates. The large outer plate with the D in the bottom right corner represents all of the documents in our document collection. When we get to our model for political speeches, D will equal 1,893,372. Everything inside the document plate is repeated for each individual document in the document collection. In other words, it pertains to D_i, where the index i represents any given document in the dataset.

The small inner plate with N in the bottom right represents the specific words and their position in the probability distribution for each topic. We'll come back to this momentarily. The third plate, with K in the bottom right, represents the latent topics whose distributions we are computing. If we model 100 topics, then β_k would be 100 probability distributions over terms.

Every document in our dataset is composed of a *mixture* of topics, with each topic being a probability distribution over words. Inside the document plate, then, θ_d represents the topic proportions *for each document*. Picture a matrix with documents in the rows and latent topics (represented by arbitrary numerical IDs) in the columns. Each document in our collection is made up of words. The grey node $W_{d,n}$ represents each observed word n for each document k, while $Z_{d,n}$ represents the topic assignments for each word in each document for each topic. In other words, each word in each document has a probability associating it with each topic. Imagine a matrix of probabilities with words in the rows and latent topics in the columns. β_k represents the topics themselves, with k being the number of latent topics to model. The value of k is selected by the researcher; we'll discuss that process shortly.

That leaves the black nodes α and η. These are priors for the parameters of the Dirichlet distribution, and we'll discuss the options for these below. α is the 'proportions parameter' and represents text–topic density. Think of this as the prior probability that a document will be associated with a topic. If we set α to a high value – say close to 1 – the probability of texts being associated with topics increases, and when α is set to a low value – say 0.1 – the probability decreases. η, on the other hand, represents topic–word density. It's known as the 'topic' parameter. When η is set to a high value, the probability of a word being associated with a topic increases. When it is set low, the probability decreases.

Putting this all in one convenient place, then,

- β_k represents the latent topics themselves;
- θ_d, inside the document plate, represents the latent topic proportions for each document;
- $z_{d,n}$ represents the latent topic assignments for each word n in each document d;
- $w_{d,n}$ represents each observed word n in each document d;
- α represents the portions' hyperparameter (the prior probability that a document is associated with a topic); and
- η represents the topic hyperparameter (the prior probability that a word is associated with a topic).

We are representing a three-level hierarchical Bayesian latent variable model with each document in a document collection modelled as a finite mixture of hidden topics in varying proportions, and with each topic modelled as an infinite mixture of words in varying proportions. It posits a generative relationship between these variables in which meaningful patterns of co-occurring words arise from the specific mixtures of latent themes. Altogether, it describes the *joint* probability distribution for (1) the latent topics, (2) their distribution over documents, and (3) their distribution of words, or

$$P(\beta, \theta, Z, W)$$

But, we *want* to know the posterior, which is the probability of the topics, their distribution over documents, their distribution of words *conditional* on the observed words, or

$$P(\beta, \theta, Z|W)$$

As with other Bayesian models, we can't derive the posterior from the joint distribution analytically because of the intractable denominator in Bayes' theorem, and because the number of potential latent topical structures is exponentially large, so we turn to approximate posterior inference. That's where VI comes in.

The Dirichlet in latent Dirichlet allocation

Like the probabilistic models we've developed in previous chapters, generative topic models are built out of probability distributions! The 'Dirichlet' portion in latent Dirichlet allocation, often written as Dir(α), is just another probability distribution of the kind discussed in Chapter 25. It's a generalization of the idea of a triangle (called the simplex), only it can have an arbitrary number of sides . . . What?

These kinds of descriptions (generalization of a triangle) are useful for those already deeply familiar with mathematical geometry or multidimensional probability distributions, but they're unlikely to get the rest of us very far. That said, with a little scaffolding, this will quickly make sense. In the probability primer chapter, we established that some probability distributions only cover some parts of the real number line; the exponential distribution, for instance, only supports positive values. The 'beta distribution' takes this idea a bit further: it only supports values from 0 to 1, inclusive. It takes two parameters, α and β, which jointly control the shape of the curve. You can think of the two as representing inversely correlated axes, both trying to pull more of the probability density towards the side of the distribution that they're more positive in (so α pulls to the right, towards 1, β pulls to the left, towards 0). Here's an example of one where β is doing more of the pushing (Figure 29.2):

The beta distribution is remarkably flexible: you should look up some examples of the shapes it can take!

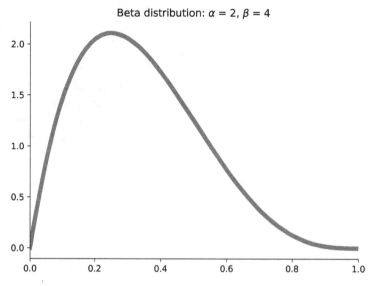

Figure 29.2   A plot showing the probability density function of a beta distribution with parameter settings $\alpha = 2$ and $\beta = 4$

Since the beta distribution only supports values from 0 to 1, what would it look like if we tacked on a second dimension to this distribution? See for yourself, in Figure 29.3.

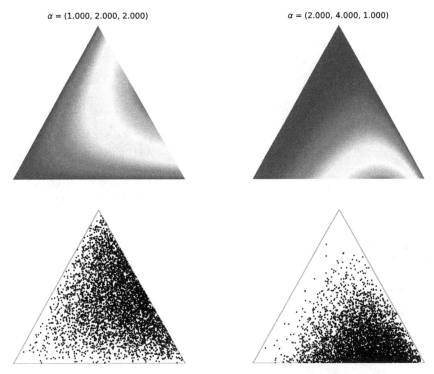

$\alpha = (1.000, 2.000, 2.000)$ $\alpha = (2.000, 4.000, 1.000)$

Figure 29.3 Two Dirichlet distributions (both visualized as 'two-simplexes' or, equivalently, triangles), both with three parameters. The black dots each represent one of 500 samples drawn from their respective distributions

Behold the Dirichlet distribution! The Dirichlet is a multidimensional generalization of the beta distribution. In Figure 29.3, instead of two parameters (α and β) having a tug of war along a real number line, we have three parameters having a three-way tug of war (the probability is concentrated in areas closer to the red end of the colour spectrum). The shape they're battling over is a *simplex* in two dimensions (which is just a triangle). If we add a third dimension, then our triangle becomes a pyramid (a three-dimensional simplex), and we'll have four parameters duking it out in a four-way tug of war. Remember that because the Dirichlet distribution is a probability distribution, its density must integrate to 1; this makes the Dirichlet very useful for describing probability across a large number of mutually exclusive categorical events.

Like the other Bayesian models we've seen, LDA topic models require priors. The α and η hyperparameters inform the generation of the Dirichlet distribution, and understanding them gives you much greater control over your model. If this discussion of priors reminds you of the chapters on Bayesian regression, good! LDA models function in a very similar framework. In fact, we can present LDA in a similar format to those chapters!

A few notes first. We're going to include a long list of variables, including what each of them mean. Normally, we don't do this kind of thing, because the variables in linear regression models are usually self-evident. In the case of LDA, most of the 'data' variables we're using are calculated using some aspect of the corpus and beg explanation. The first three sections that follow (Data, Hyperparameters, and Latent Variables) are all simple descriptions. They all come together in the four-line Model section at the end.

Data

V :	integer	[Number of Unique Terms in Vocabulary]
D :	integer	[Number of Documents]
d :	integer, values [min: 1, max: D]	[Document ID]
N :	integer	[Total Word Instances]
n :	integer, values [min: 1,max: N]	[Word Instance]
K :	integer	[Number of Topics]
k :	integer, values [min: 1, max: K]	[Topic]

Hyperparameters

α : vector of real numbers, length K [Topic – in – Document Prior Hyperparameter]

η : vector of real numbers, length V [Term – in – Topic Prior Hyperparameter]

Latent Variables

θ_d: K – simplex, Dirichlet – disturbed   [Topic Distribution for Documentd]

β_k: V – simplex, Dirichlet – disturbed   [Word Distribution for Topick]

Model

$\theta_d \sim \text{Dirichlet}(\alpha)$	for d in 1...D	[Topic – in – Document Prior]
$\beta_k \sim \text{Dirichlet}(\eta)$	for k in 1...K	[Term – in – Topic Prior]
$z_{d,n} \sim \text{Categorial}(\theta_d)$	for d in 1...D, n in 1...N	[Document – Topic Probability]
$w_{d,n} \sim \text{Categorial}(\beta_{z[d,n]})$	for d in 1...D, n in 1...N	[Likelihood]

Whew, that's a lot of variables! We've already discussed what some of them are (and how they function), but some remain enigmatic. Let's discuss them in the abstract here.

Understanding the α hyperparameter

The α parameter can be a relatively naive setting, or more informed. If it's a simple scalar (i.e. single value) it will be propagated into a matrix of *expected* topic probabilities for each document. In all cases, this matrix has a shape of n_topics × n_documents. When a single value is used for all of the topic, this is a symmetric prior. As you will soon see, this 'a priori' assumption actually matters, even though the LDA model will modify these values *a lot*. A symmetric prior essentially tells the model 'I expect the probability of each topic being a topic in each document to be the same, and you will have to work very hard to tell me otherwise'. There are times when this assumption might actually be helpful for the model. In most cases, though, we want to use LDA to tell us something we *don't* know about a corpus, with an unknown distribution of topics. In this case, an asymmetric prior is essential (Syed and Spruit, 2018; Wallach, Mimno, and McCallum, 2009). In the example from Hoffman et al. (2010), this value is set at 1/num_topics, but they mention that this is for simplicity, and reference (Wallach, Mimno, and McCallum, 2009) that asymmetric priors can also be used.

An asymmetric prior tells the LDA model that the probability of each topic in a given document is expected to be different, and that it should work on determining what those differences are. Unlike the symmetric prior, there is a lot of flexibility in the α hyperparameter for an asymmetric prior in Gensim. If a scalar is given, the model will incorporate the values from 1 to num_topics when it generates the prior. This means that each document has an array of topic probabilities that are all different, although *each document will have the same array*. Rather than a single scalar value, it's also possible to pass an α array of expected probabilities that is informed by prior knowledge. This could be domain knowledge, but then we would again be left wondering whether we want to learn something or just confirm what we already know. Perhaps the most exciting option here, then, is to *use Bayes to inform Bayes*. A crucial part about the use of asymmetric priors for the α hyperparameter is that the LDA model becomes a lot less sensitive to the number of topics specified. This decreased sensitivity means we should be able to trust the assignment of topics by the model regardless of how much choice we give it.

Of course, there's more than one way to do this. Gensim implements an automatic hyperparameter tuning method, based on work by Ypma (1995), where the model priors are updated at regular intervals during iterations of model training. This is convenient for a number of reasons, but in particular, we can train an LDA model on a random sample of the data, setting the model to update the priors as frequently and for as many iterations as we have time for. Then, the updated α prior can be used to model the entire corpus. As you will read about in the next chapter, this is a form of transfer learning, and it comes with many advantages.

The posterior results, theta, will be these priors fitted to the corpus, with which we can estimate unique topic probabilities for *each* document.

Understanding the η hyperparameter

The η hyperparameter functions quite similarly to α in terms of technical implementation, but it has very different assumptions and conceptual implications. The prior constructed from η is the expected probability for *each word* being a part of each topic. This can, again, be initialized in a relatively simple way by providing a single value – Hoffman et al. (2010) again use 1/num_topics. This time, the single value is used to populate an array of shape n_topics x n_words. This again results in a symmetric prior, but the conceptual implication is actually what we want – if we told the model that the probability of each word's topic contribution should be different from the beginning, we would be directing the model to prefer some words over others. This could bias words away from contributing to topics that they should, or towards topics that they shouldn't. This issue would tend to smooth out with a large amount of training data, but it's safer to just start this parameter with uniform word probabilities. In reality, the words we use are versatile and many of them are very likely to be used in *all* topics. So conceptually, this prior should actually be a symmetric one, and we'll look at some evidence for this shortly (Wallach, Mimno, and McCallum, 2009).

Nonetheless, there are also asymmetric options for η, although they're very similar to α, so we won't spend too much time rehashing the technical details. We can provide an array of probabilities for each word that will be their prior expected probabilities for each topic, or a matrix of shape `num_topics` × `n_words` to make the expected word probabilities specific to each word. The last option is to use the same prior update method introduced above for the α prior. We will demonstrate below that the latter method indicates that η becomes fairly symmetrical after model training, suggesting that a simple symmetrical prior is the most efficient choice and will not result in a loss of accuracy.

The posterior results, β, will be these η priors fitted to the corpus, which can be used to calculate unique topic probabilities for *each* word, as well as the top probabilities of words forming each topic.

Variational inference

We have just described the structure of our generative model. The structure is independent of the inference algorithm that we use to approximate the posterior probabilities for β, θ, and Z. We've seen this kind of thing before; in the chapters on Bayesian linear regression, we defined our models using priors, likelihood, and a linear model, and then sampled from those models' posteriors to produce final posterior distributions. We used PyMC3's HMC-like sampler to accomplish this (it's an easy, efficient, general-purpose approach), but we *could* have used any number of other techniques, such as a Gibbs sampler, grid approximation, quadratic approximation, and so on. Our models would have remained the same regardless of approximation techniques.

In this section, I'll introduce variational inference, which is another approach to approximating the posterior of a Bayesian model (Blei et al., 2003). The goal of VI is identical to that of HMC; both seek to efficiently approximate an entire posterior distribution for some set of latent variables. However, whereas HMC is based on the idea that we can learn about posterior distributions by *sampling* from them, VI attempts to approximate posteriors by using a parametric distribution (or some combination thereof) that gets as close as possible. For this brief introduction, the point is that we will still be approximating the posterior, but without imaginary robots hurling imaginary marbles around an unfathomably large sample space. Sampling methods like HMC construct an approximation of the posterior by keeping a 'tally' of where the marble ends up in space, building a jagged pyramid of sorts, and then sanding down the edges and filling in the gaps to produce the smooth posterior curves you saw in the model outputs of Chapters 27 and 28.

VI, to use another metaphor, approaches the problem by doing the rough equivalent of taking a bendy piece of wire and trying to warp it so that it closely matches the posterior. The key here is that VI provides us with an as-close-as-possible approximation of posterior distributions using a distribution that we can describe mathematically. Remember, from the beginning of Chapter 26, the fact that there are 'more functions than formulae'? The results that we get from a sampling-based approach to approximating the posterior (HMC, MCMC [Markov chain Monte Carlo], Gibbs) gives us the equivalent of a function *without a formula*. We know what those posteriors look like and the values they take on, but we can't use a mathematical formula to describe them. VI, on the other hand, *gives us a function with a formula*. It's not a perfect analogy, but it should help you grasp the difference between the two.

The major breakthroughs in generative topic modelling are due, in part, to VI. It provides a proxy which we can use to calculate an *exact* analytical solution for the (still approximate) posterior distribution of the latent variables $p(Z \mid X)$. To do that, we posit a family of distributions with variational parameters over the latent variables in our model, each of which is indexed by the parameter v. It's written like this:

$$q(Z, v)$$

We pick some initial value for v and then gradually modify it until we find parameter settings that make the distribution as close to the posterior $p(Z \mid X)$ as possible. We assess closeness by measuring the distance between the two distrubutions using a measure from information theory called Kullback–Leibler (KL) divergence. Once we know these parameter settings, we can use $q(Z, v)$ as a proxy for the posterior.

This is represented in Figure 29.4, which is adapted from Blei (2017). We represent the family of distributions $q(Z, v)$ as an ellipse, and every position within that ellipse represents a specific instantiation of the variational family, indexed by v. The squiggly grey line represents different realizations along the way to finding the parameterized distribution that is closest to the posterior, measured with KL divergence.

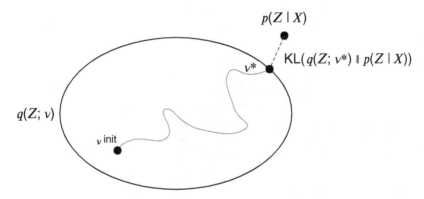

Figure 29.4 A conceptual visualization of variational inference, adapted from Blei (2017)

Remember that, as with HMC, we are *approximating* the posterior. Only instead of approximating it by drawing samples, we approximate it by finding another *very similar but not identical* distribution that can serve as an exact analytical proxy for the posterior. The general process works as I've described above, but the specifics are a thriving area of research in machine learning. Discussions of VI in the technical literature involve a healthy dose of dense mathematics, but most of the technical specifics are not really necessary to understand as an applied researcher. It 'Just Works'. It is especially useful when working with very large datasets, as we do in text analysis, and it's a good bit faster than HMC in cases like these, but is just as accurate.

I have just covered the basic goals and ideas behind LDA topic models and the importance of thinking through the generative mechanisms. You should also understand generative topics models using graphical models with plate notation, and the basics of how VI works. There's one final issue left to address: selecting the number of topics. Here, once again, the emphasis is on iterative multi-method workflows that leverage as much information and careful interpretive and critical work as possible.

Further Reading

If you want another friendly introduction to LDA topic models, I recommend Blei (2012). If you are looking to develop a deeper understanding of VI aside from its specific application in LDA topic models, I would recommend Chapters 21 and 22 of Murphy's (2012) comprehensive *Machine Learning: A Probabilistic Perspective*.

Selecting the number of topics

With LDA topic models, we need to specify the number of topics, K, in advance. In doing so, we are defining a random variable whose values we will infer from the posterior. Selecting the number of topics in a generative topic model is a bit of a dark art; due to the nature of the problem, there is no 'correct' number of topics, although some solutions are certainly better than others. If we tell our topic model to identify 12 topics, it will. It will model the probability distribution of those topics over a set of documents and a probability distribution of words for each of the 12 topics. So how do we know how many topics to look for, and what are the consequences of selecting a number that is too large or too small?

Let's explore a comparison. Imagine using a simple clustering method like k-means as a rudimentary topic model: you want to identify groups of documents that are thematically similar, so you create a bag-of-words representation of the documents, perform some dimensionality reduction with truncated SVD, and then conduct a k-means cluster analysis to find clusters of thematically related documents. With k-means, each observation (i.e. document) can only be assigned to a single cluster, and if clusters are thematically distinct, then they can only be assigned to a single theme. Continuing with our previous example, a hypothetical article about social movements focused on energy transitions would have to be assigned a single topic (either social movements, energy transitions, or a single topic capturing both of these things), which makes it *very* likely that documents will be assigned to clusters that don't fit them very well. There is no 'correct' value for k, but solutions that set the value of k too high or too low will result in clusters containing many documents that have no business being there.

Though topic models also require the researcher to choose the number of topics, the consequences of using a suboptimally calibrated topic model are different from clustering methods like k-means. To reiterate: in generative topic modelling, documents are always conceptualized as a *mixture* of topics. If the number of topics that we specify is too small, our model will return extremely general and heterogeneous topics. To a human reader, these topics often appear incoherent. On the other hand, if we set the number of topics too high, then the model will return extremely specific topics. This can seem like taking one topic and splitting it into two topics that are differentiated by things that don't really matter. It's the topic modelling version of the narcissism of minor differences. We don't want that either.

Let's continue with our hypothetical example for a bit longer. Say we pick a large number of topics and the result is that we split our social movement topic into multiple social movement topics. Is this a good thing or a bad thing? The short answer is 'it depends'. If we are lucky, that split may make some sense, such as separating content on resource mobilization theory (McCarthy and Zald, 1977) from other theoretical perspectives in social movement research, such as frame analysis (Benford, 1993; Benford and Snow, 2000; Snow et al., 2014), political process theory (Caren, 2007; McAdam, 2010), multi-institutionalism (Armstrong and Bernstein,

2008), or strategic adaptation (McCammon, 2009, 2012; McCammon et al., 2007). Or perhaps, it would differentiate between cultural approaches and structural approaches (Smith and Fetner, 2009). In reality, we may not find topics that align so neatly with theory or our own mental models, but the take-home message here is that general (fewer topics) and specific (more topics) solutions can both be good *or* bad; the 'best' solution depends on what we are trying to learn.

Looking for fine distinctions with a small number of topics is like trying to compare pedestrians' gaits while standing on the rooftop patio of an extremely tall building. It's not 'wrong' but if you really want to analyse gait, you would be better off getting a little closer to the action. On the other hand, if you were looking for a more general perspective on the flow of foot traffic in the neighbourhood, the top of a tall building is a perfectly fine place to be. The key thing to realize here is that *your goal makes one vantage point better or worse than the other.*

Luckily, the same research that found LDA results to be greatly improved by an asymmetric prior also found that the artificial splitting of topics was greatly diminished. This means that, in general, we're better off choosing too many topics than choosing too few, so long as we're using an asymmetrical prior. On the other hand, if you're using LDA on a corpus where you actually do expect a homogeneous set of topics to be equally likely in the documents, you might want to use a symmetric prior, in which case you will also want to experiment more with the number of topics. However, if you know enough about the data to determine this is the prior you need, then you probably also have a ballpark idea about how many topics to expect! The two a priori assumptions go hand in hand.

In short, we *can* make bad decisions when topic modelling, and these bad decisions can have major implications for what we find. But the risks are different from they are for methods like *k*-means clustering because documents are always a mix of topics. Most of the time, the risk of a bad topic solution is that we will be either too zoomed in or zoomed out to learn what we want to learn. The best course of action here is to develop many different models with different numbers of topics. And the best way to do this is in an iterative framework like Box's loop, or in this case a framework like computational grounded theory (discussed in Chapter 10) that is designed specifically for multi-method text analysis.

29.5 Topic Modelling With Gensim

There are a number of options for developing topic models with Python. In this chapter, we'll use Gensim because it's mature, well-maintained, and has good documentation. It offers some really nice implementations of widely used models, is computationally efficient, and scales well to large datasets.

```
import pandas as pd
import numpy as np
import seaborn as sns
import matplotlib as mpl
import matplotlib.pyplot as plt
pd.set_option("display.notebook_repr_html", False)
from dcss.plotting import custom_seaborn
custom_seaborn()

from dcss.text import preprocess, bow_to_df
```

```
from gensim import corpora
from pprint import pprint
from gensim.models import LdaModel
from gensim.models.ldamulticore import LdaMulticore
from gensim.models.coherencemodel import CoherenceModel
import pickle


df = pd.read_csv('../data/canadian_hansards/lipad/canadian_hansards.csv',
    low_memory= False)


df.info()


<class 'pandas.core.frame.DataFrame'>
RangeIndex: 946686 entries, 0 to 946685
Data columns (total 16 columns):
 #   Column          Non-Null Count    Dtype
---  ------          --------------    -----
 0   index           946686 non-null   int64
 1   basepk          946686 non-null   int64
 2   hid             946686 non-null   object
 3   speechdate      946686 non-null   object
 4   pid             824111 non-null   object
 5   opid            787761 non-null   object
 6   speakeroldname  787032 non-null   object
 7   speakerposition 202294 non-null   object
 8   maintopic       932207 non-null   object
 9   subtopic        926996 non-null   object
 10  subsubtopic     163963 non-null   object
 11  speechtext      946686 non-null   object
 12  speakerparty    787692 non-null   object
 13  speakerriding   686495 non-null   object
 14  speakername     923416 non-null   object
 15  speakerurl      763264 non-null   object
dtypes: int64(2), object(14)
memory usage: 115.6+ MB
```

The text data is stored in the `speechtext` series. We'll use the `dcss preprocess()` function to perform the same preprocessing steps that we've used in previous chapters on text analysis. As a reminder, this function passes each document through spaCy's `nlp` pipeline and returns a list of tokens for each document, each token being a lemmatized noun, proper noun, or adjective that is longer than a single character. The function also strips out English-language stop words.

```
texts = df['speechtext'].tolist()
processed_text = preprocess(texts, bigrams=False, detokenize=False, n_process = 32)


len(processed_text)


1893372
```

Since preprocessing 1.8 million speeches takes a good amount of time, we'll pickle the results. Then we can easily reload them again later rather than needlessly waiting around.

```
with open('../data/pickles/preprocessed_speeches_canadian_hansards_no_bigrams.pkl', '
    wb') as handle:
    pickle.dump(processed_text, handle, protocol=pickle.HIGHEST_PROTOCOL)

processed_text = pickle.load( open( '../data/pickles/
    preprocessed_speeches_canadian_hansards_no_bigrams.pkl', 'rb'))
```

Creating a bag of words with Gensim

To topic-model our data with Gensim, we need to provide our list of tokenized texts to the `Dictionary()` class. Gensim uses this to construct a corpus vocabulary that assigns each unique token in the dataset to an integer. If you run `dict(vocab)` after creating the `vocab` object, you'll see this is just a Python dictionary that stores a key–value pairing of the integer representation (the key) of each token (the value).

We'll also create a corpus object using the `doc2bow` method of the `Dictionary` class. The resulting object stores information about the specific tokens and token frequencies in each document. If you print the corpus object, you will see a *lot* of numbers. The corpus object itself is just a list, and each element of the list represents an individual document. Nested inside each document are tuples (e.g. `147, 3`) that represent (1) the unique integer ID for the token (stored in our `vocab` object) and (2) the number of times the token appears in the document.

We're going to filter the vocabulary to keep tokens that only appear in 20 or more speeches, as well as tokens that don't appear in more than 95% of speeches. This is a fairly inclusive filter but still reduces ~160,000 words to ~36,000 words. You will want to experiment with this, but one obvious advantage is that a lot of non-words from parts of the text data that are low quality should end up removed, as will non-differentiating words that would probably crowd the topic space.

```
vocab = corpora.Dictionary(processed_text) # id2word
vocab.save('../models/lda_vocab.dict')
```

The file saved above is easy to reload, so you can experiment with different filter parameters at will.

```
vocab = corpora.Dictionary.load('../models/lda_vocab.dict')
vocab.filter_extremes(no_below=20, no_above=0.95)
corpus = [vocab.doc2bow(text) for text in processed_text]

len(vocab)
```

```
36585
```

Note that we're not using term frequency–inverse document frequency (TF-IDF) weights in our LDA models, whereas we did use them in the context of LSA. While TF-IDF weights are appropriate in some cases (e.g. LSA), they are not in LDA models (Blei and Lafferty,

(Continued)

(Continued)

2009). The reason is because of LDA's generative nature. It makes sense to say that word frequencies are generated from a distribution, as LDA posits, but it does not make sense to say that TF-IDF weights are generated from that distribution. Consequently, using TF-IDF weights in a generative topic model generally worsens the results. In general, TF-IDF weights work well in deterministic contexts but less so in generative ones.

Running the topic model

We are now ready to fit the topic model to our data. We will do so using Gensim's `LdaModel` first, rather than `LdaMulticore` which is designed to speed up computation by using multiprocessing. They do almost the same things, though with one key difference that we'll discuss shortly.

The code block below estimates a model for 100 topics, which is an initial value that I selected arbitrarily. Later we will discuss other ways of selecting a number of topics. We're going to start with a random sample from the corpus and the processed list of text, because even with Gensim's efficiency and using algorithms designed to perform well on large datasets, this can take a while to run, and this will not be our final model.

```
import random
random.seed(100)

sample_corpus, sample_text = zip(*random.sample(list(zip(corpus,processed_text))
    ,100000))

ldamod_s = LdaModel(corpus=sample_corpus,
                    id2word=vocab,
                    num_topics=100,
                    random_state=100,
                    eval_every=1,
                    chunksize=2000,
                    alpha='auto',
                    eta='auto',
                    passes=2,
                    update_every=1,
                    iterations=400
            )
```

We'll pickle the results to easily load them later without having to wait for our code to run again:

```
with open('../data/pickles/lda_model_sample.pkl', 'wb') as handle:
    pickle.dump(ldamod_s, handle, protocol=pickle.HIGHEST_PROTOCOL)

ldamod_s = pickle.load(open( '../data/pickles/lda_model_sample.pkl', 'rb'))
```

Gensim provides a number of useful functions to simplify working with the results of our LDA model. The ones you'll likely turn to right away are:

- `.show_topic()`, which takes an integer topic ID and returns a list of the words most strongly associated with that topic, and
- `.get_term_topics()`, which takes a word and, if it's in the corpus vocabulary, returns the word's probability for each topic.

As you can see below, we can find the topics that a word is associated with:

```
ldamod_s.get_term_topics('freedom')
```

```
[(53, 0.02927819)]
```

Gensim provides the weights associated with each of the top words for each topic. The higher the weight, the more strongly associated with the topic the word is. The words in this case make quite a lot of intuitive sense – freedom has to do with the law, rights, principles, society, and is a fundamental concept:

```
ldamod_s.show_topic(53)
```

```
[('right', 0.15800211),
 ('human', 0.04227337),
 ('freedom', 0.029263439),
 ('law', 0.022657597),
 ('Canadians', 0.018386548),
 ('canadian', 0.018030208),
 ('citizen', 0.017851433),
 ('society', 0.015541217),
 ('fundamental', 0.014947715),
 ('principle', 0.013568851)]
```

When we look at how parliament talks about criminals, we can see that the associated words are pretty intuitive, although we might have to dig a bit further into the terms to find more particular term associations:

```
ldamod_s.get_term_topics('criminal')
```

```
[(20, 0.059014548)]
```

```
ldamod_s.show_topic(20)
```

```
[('crime', 0.07494005),
 ('criminal', 0.058972023),
 ('victim', 0.055283513),
 ('justice', 0.047199916),
 ('offence', 0.03621511),
 ('law', 0.03601918),
 ('offender', 0.03377842),
 ('sentence', 0.032146234),
 ('system', 0.022435088),
 ('person', 0.020964943)]
```

Let's look a little closer at something that's a bit more controversial, like 'marriage':

```
ldamod_s.get_term_topics('marriage')
```

```
[(28, 0.042418264)]
```

We can specify the return of a few more terms for a topic by adding an argument for topn. You can see that when marriage is discussed in parliament, it's around concepts such as equality, gender, tradition, and even abuse:

```
ldamod_s.show_topic(28, topn=30)
```

```
[('woman', 0.26727995),
 ('man', 0.069456935),
 ('violence', 0.06529136),
 ('marriage', 0.04248659),
 ('girl', 0.023184145),
 ('Women', 0.02255594),
 ('equality', 0.021070031),
 ('Canada', 0.019696228),
 ('society', 0.018637668),
 ('gender', 0.01841013),
 ('abuse', 0.015813459),
 ('issue', 0.015377659),
 ('action', 0.012950255),
 ('practice', 0.01211937),
 ('female', 0.011507524),
 ('equal', 0.011195933),
 ('Status', 0.011139394),
 ('medicare', 0.011124585),
 ('group', 0.010348747),
 ('physical', 0.008267313),
 ('psychological', 0.0075966706),
 ('prescription', 0.0070270123),
 ('traditional', 0.006817099),
 ('Speaker', 0.0067508616),
 ('killing', 0.006746756),
 ('status', 0.006714445),
 ('sexual', 0.0065426086),
 ('victim', 0.0060332483),
 ('government', 0.005900839),
 ('country', 0.0058119465)]
```

Evaluating the quality of topic models by measuring semantic coherence

The model we just estimated found 100 topics *because we told it to*. Was 100 a good number? How do we pick a good number of topics, at least as a starting point? Again, my advice here is that you develop your model iteratively, by zooming in and zooming out, each time learning a little more about your data. You should supplement this by reading samples of documents from the corpus. All of this will help you develop a better model.

You can also supplement this with quantitative measures. The ideal number of topics ultimately comes down to interpretability and usefulness for the task at hand. Strange as it might seem, there are quantitative approaches to estimating human readability – in this case using a measure called 'semantic coherence'. These readability measures can be used to help guide our decisions about how many topics to search for in our topic model. The higher the topic coherence, the more human-readable the topics in our model should be. Note that quantitative measures of semantic coherence should *help* you make a decision, not make it for you. You still want to be a human 'in the loop', reading things and thinking deeply about them.

Most semantic coherence measures work by segmenting the corpus into topics, taking the top words in a topic, putting them in pairs, computing their similarity in vector space, and then aggregating those scores to produce an overall summary of the semantic coherence in your model.[i] There is a growing technical literature on computing semantic coherence (for a good introduction to measures used in some Python implementations see Röder et al., 2015). Higher coherence means that the words in a topic are closer to one another in vector space. The closer they are, the more coherent the topic. The general idea here is that words in a topic are likely to come from similar positions in the vector space. (I'm being a bit hand-wavy here because these ideas are covered extensively in the coming chapters.)

Models with high semantic coherence will tend to have a smaller number of junk topics, but ironically, this sometimes comes with a reduction of the *quality* of the topics in your model. In other words, we can avoid having any really bad topics but the ones we are left with might themselves be middling. Imagine two models. In the first, you have 40 topics, 37 of which seem good, and three of which seem like junk. You can ignore the junk topics and focus on the good ones. In the second, you have 33 topics and end up with a higher coherence score. There are no junk topics in this model, but the 33 topics you got are not really as informative as the 37 good topics from your 40-topic model. Which do you prefer? Can you tolerate a few junk topics or not? Personally, I prefer the solution with more interpretable topics and a few junk topics, but again, there is no absolutely correct answer.

Human qualitative evaluation is labour-intensive and, yes, inevitably subjective. Quantitative methods for selecting the number of topics sometimes produce models that seem worse, and – like human qualitative evaluation methods – there may not be agreement that the results are more informative even if the model overall has better semantic coherence. What's the value of eliminating human judgement from a process that is intended to help you iteratively learn things you didn't know before? Besides, the whole point of Bayesian analysis is to provide principled ways of integrating information from multiple sources. This includes qualitative interpretation *and criticism* of the model. Semantic coherence measures are very useful when it comes to making what might seem like arbitrary decisions in developing your topic model, but ultimately you need to use your human abilities and make informed judgements. This is integral to Box's loop, as I've emphasized throughout the book. It's better to produce many models and look at them all, interpreting, thinking, critiquing. The more you learn, the better! Finally, to repeat a point I have now made many times, *you absolutely must read*. There's no getting around it.

Some alternative approaches are based on computations of conditional probabilities for pairs of words.

Gensim makes it fairly straightforward to compute coherence measures for topic models. There are numerous coherence measures available 'out of the box', each of which works slightly differently. The measure we will use below – C_v – was shown by Röder et al. (2015) to be the most highly correlated with all available data on human interpretation of the output of topic models.

There are four steps involved in computing the C_v measure. First, it selects the top (i.e. most probable) n words within any given topic. Secondly, it computes the probability of single top words and the joint probability of pairs of co-occurring top words by counting the number of texts in which the word or word pair occurs, and dividing by the total number of texts. Thirdly, it vectorizes this data using a measure called normalized pointwise mutual information, which tells us whether a pair of words W_i and W_j co-occur more than they would if they were independent of one another. Finally, C_v computes the cosine similarity for all vectors. The final coherence score for a topic model is the mean of all of these cosine similarity scores.

The c_v measure is already implemented in Gensim, so we can compute it with very little code. To start, let's compute the 'coherence' of our 100-topic model. Note that for c_v, coherence scores range from 0 for complete incoherence to 1 for complete coherence. Values above 0.5 are fairly good, while we can't expect to find values much above 0.8 in real-world text data.

```
coherence_model_s = CoherenceModel(model=ldamod_s,
                                    texts=sample_text,
                                    dictionary=vocab,
                                    coherence='c_v')
coherence_lda_s = coherence_model_s.get_coherence()
print('Coherence Score: ', coherence_lda_s)

Coherence Score:  0.3882056267381639

with open('../data/pickles/coherence_model_sample.pkl', 'wb') as handle:
    pickle.dump(coherence_model_s, handle, protocol=pickle.HIGHEST_PROTOCOL)

coherence_model_s = pickle.load( open( '../data/pickles/coherence_model_sample.pkl', '
    rb'))
```

Now that we can calculate C_v scores, we can gauge topic solutions. But what if 21, 37, 42, or n other number of topics would be better? As discussed earlier, we've used an asymmetric, trained prior, so even if we selected too many topics, the quality of the best ones should still be pretty good. Let's take a look at their coherence scores in a dataframe, sorted highest to lowest on coherence, and lowest to highest on standard deviation (although the latter will only have an effect if we have any identical coherence scores):

```
topic_coherence_s = coherence_model_s.get_coherence_per_topic(with_std = True)
topic_coherence_df = pd.DataFrame(topic_coherence_s, columns = ['coherence','std'])
topic_coherence_df = topic_coherence_df.sort_values(['coherence', 'std'], ascending=[
    False,True])
```

The top 10 most coherent topics actually have fairly high scores!

```
topic_coherence_df.head(10).mean()
```

```
coherence 0.640070
std        0.233939
dtype: float64
```

```
topic_coherence_df.tail(10).mean()
```

```
coherence 0.213738
std        0.182295
dtype: float64
```

Further Reading

Wallach, Murray, et al. (2009) and Mimno et al. (2011) offer useful guidelines for evaluating topic models using semantic coherence.

Going further with better priors

As promised, let's examine selecting a few different α and η hyperparameters. We'll use the same data as before, but rather than a sample, let's use the whole corpus. For the most part, you can probably feel safe using the 'auto' setting for both since your priors will be informed by the data rather than being arbitrary. Unfortunately, with the amount of data in the full corpus, you want to use LdaMulticore rather than the base LdaModel, but the 'auto' option is not implemented for α in the *much* faster multicore option. Your built-in options are either a uniform scalar probability for each topic, or 'asymmetrical'. The code block below shows how an asymmetrical α is constructed, as well as the simple scalar value for η used in the article that informs Gensim's LDA implementation (Hoffman et al., 2010):

```
alpha_asym = np.fromiter(
                (1.0 / (i + np.sqrt(100)) for i in range(100)),
                dtype=np.float16, count=100,
                )
eta_sym = 1/100
```

But we can also use the automatically updated α and η hyperparameters from our earlier model on the sample of the corpus as long as we plan to use the same number of topics. Because we ran LdaModel with (1) frequent model perplexity evaluations, (2) frequent hyperparameter updates, and (3) two full passes over the sample data along with 400 iterations per document, we can expect the α prior to have a lot of fine-grained nuance. There are more complex ways to sample the data in order to produce trained asymmetric priors, such as the Bayesian slice sampling detailed in Syed and Spruit (2018), but they are outside the scope of this chapter. Taking the output from one Bayesian model to use in another is a lot like the transfer learning methods that are covered in the final chapters of this book.

```
alpha_t = ldamod_s.alpha
eta_t = ldamod_s.eta
```

Let's get a sense of the difference between the options we've discussed for priors by calculating the average of the probabilities as well as the amount of variance they have:

```
print("Trained alpha variance: " + str(np.round(np.var(alpha_t), 4)))
print("Asymmetric alpha variance: " + str(np.round(np.var(alpha_asym), 4)))
print("Trained alpha avg: " + str(np.round(alpha_t.sum()/len(alpha_t), 4)))
print("Asymmetric alpha avg: " + str(np.round(alpha_asym.sum()/len(alpha_asym), 4)))

print("Trained eta variance: " + str(np.round(np.var(eta_t), 4)))
print("Symmetric eta variance: " + str(np.round(np.var(eta_sym), 4)))
print("Trained eta avg: " + str(np.round(eta_t.sum()/len(eta_t),4)))
print("Symmetric eta avg: " + str(np.round(eta_sym, 4)))
Trained alpha variance: 0.0006
Asymmetric alpha variance: 0.0004
Trained alpha avg: 0.0304
Asymmetric alpha avg: 0.0244
Trained eta variance: 0.0003
Symmetric eta variance: 0.0
Trained eta avg: 0.0098
Symmetric eta avg: 0.01
```

As you can see, the trained α prior has around 1.5× the variance of the simpler asymmetric version and around 1.25× the average topic probability. The trained η priors, on the other hand, end up with only half the variance of the trained alpha, and the average word probability is *very* close to the simple 1/100 symmetrical prior. Although the automatic updates for priors add only linear computation complexity, it's always nice to trim computation time wherever possible, so you might find that it's just as good to use a simple scalar for the η hyperparameter.

```
ldamod_f = LdaMulticore(corpus=corpus,
                id2word=vocab,
                num_topics=100,
                random_state=100,
                chunksize=2000,
                alpha=alpha_t,
                eta=eta_t,
                passes=1,
                iterations=10,
                workers=15,
                per_word_topics=True)

with open('../data/pickles/lda_model_full.pkl', 'wb') as handle:
    pickle.dump(ldamod_f, handle, protocol=pickle.HIGHEST_PROTOCOL)
```

```
ldamod_f = pickle.load( open( '../data/pickles/lda_model_full.pkl', 'rb'))


coherence_model_full = CoherenceModel(model=ldamod_f,
                                      texts=processed_text,
                                      dictionary=vocab,
                                      coherence='c_v')
coherence_full = coherence_model_full.get_coherence()

with open('../data/pickles/coherence_model_full.pkl', 'wb') as handle:
    pickle.dump(coherence_model_full, handle, protocol=pickle.HIGHEST_PROTOCOL)

coherence_model_full = pickle.load( open( '../data/pickles/coherence_model_full.pkl',
    'rb'))
```

We have actually gained a slight amount of topic coherence after training on 1.8 million documents rather than 100,000!

```
coherence_full
```

```
0.3943192191621368
```

Let's look at per-topic results in a dataframe to compare to the results from the sample corpus. First, we'll compare the average coherence scores for the top 30 and bottom 30 topics:

```
topic_coherence_f = coherence_model_full.get_coherence_per_topic(with_std = True)
topic_coherence_f_df=pd.DataFrame(topic_coherence_f,columns=['coherence','std'])
topic_coherence_f_df = topic_coherence_f_df.sort_values(['coherence', 'std'],
    ascending=[False,True])


print("Full model average coherence top 30 topics: " + str(topic_coherence_f_df['
    coherence'].head(30).mean()))
print("Sample model average coherence top 30 topics: " + str(topic_coherence_df['
    coherence'].head(30).mean()))
print("Full model average coherence bottom 30 topics: " + str(topic_coherence_f_df['
    coherence'].tail(30).mean()))
print("Sample model average coherence bottom 30 topics: " + str(topic_coherence_df['
    coherence'].tail(30).mean()))
```

```
Full model average coherence top 30 topics: 0.4943150877317519
Sample model average coherence top 30 topics: 0.550659531826426
Full model average coherence bottom 30 topics: 0.2952359669399737
Sample model average coherence bottom 30 topics: 0.2517402193295241
```

We've actually lost a bit of coherence in the top 30 topics, while gaining some in the bottom 30. One thing to keep in mind is that coherence scores are a convenient way to assess a topic model, but they are *not* a substitute for carefully inspecting the topics themselves! Below we can see that topic 20 remains the most coherent, while a few others also remain in the top 10 but at different positions:

```
topic_coherence_f_df.head(10)
```

	coherence	std
20	0.604434	0.331337
77	0.565511	0.242574
90	0.545323	0.344012
55	0.534403	0.306397
73	0.530510	0.295568
88	0.523907	0.287610
10	0.521217	0.340641
89	0.521041	0.333885
54	0.519937	0.309211
75	0.515672	0.339481

```
topic_coherence_df.head(10)
```

	coherence	std
20	0.721814	0.228599
65	0.676778	0.116802
12	0.657578	0.283031
55	0.640755	0.331486
74	0.632465	0.197373
42	0.630215	0.211954
17	0.626714	0.253870
80	0.609308	0.241425
4	0.607440	0.215214
75	0.597635	0.259641

Now that we have run through all of these models, let's actually examine the topics with some visualization of the most coherent ones!

Further Reading

Wallach, Mimno, and McCallum (2009) provide some useful advice on thinking through the use of priors in LDA topic models.

Visualizing topic model output with pyLDAvis

One way to explore a topic model is to use the pyLDAvis package to interact with dynamic browser-based visualizations. This package is designed to hook into Gensim's data structures seamlessly. We will provide pyLDAvis with (1) the name of the object storing our LDA model, (2) the corpus object, and (3) the vocab. We will then write the results to an HTML file that you can open in your browser and explore interactively. This can take a while to run, so if you just want to explore the results seen below, you can find the HTML file in the ../data/misc directory.

```
import pyLDAvis.gensim_models as gensimvis
from pyLDAvis import save_html

vis = gensimvis.prepare(ldamod_f, corpus, vocab)

save_html(vis, '../data/misc/ldavis_full_model.html')
```

Of course, I can't show the interactive results here on the printed page, but what you will see in your browser will be something like the graph shown in Figure 29.5. These maps contain a *lot* of information, so it's worth taking your time to explore them fully.

How do you read this? On the left, we have a two-dimensional representation of the distances between topics. The distances between topics are computed with Jensen–Shannon divergence (which is a way of measuring the distance between two probability distributions; Lin, 1991), and then a PCA is performed on the results. The interactive graph says the map is produced 'via multidimensional scaling' (MDS) because MDS is a *general* class of analysis and PCA is a *specific* method. Topics that are closer together in the map are more similar. Topics that are further away from one another are dissimilar. *However*, recall that we don't know how much variance in the data is actually accounted for with these two dimensions, so we should assume that, like other text analyses, the first two principal components don't actually account for much variance. Accordingly, we should interpret the spatial relationships between topics with a *healthy dose* of scepticism. Finally, the size of the topic in this map is related to how common it is. Bigger topics are more common. Smaller topics are rare. Sizing points like this is generally not considered best data visualization practice, but we are not focused on comparing topics on their size, so it's generally okay.

On the right of the graph, we have horizontal bar graphs that update as you mouse over a topic. These are the words that are most useful for interpreting what a given topic is about. The red shows you how common the word is in the topic, and the blue shows you how common it is in the rest of the corpus. So topics with a lot of red but not a lot of blue are more exclusive to the topic. If you mouse over the words in the bar graphs, the MDS map changes to show you the conditional distribution over topics on the MDS map.

Finally, you can change the meaning of 'words that are most useful for interpreting what a given topic is about' by changing the value of the λ parameter. You do this moving the slider. If $\lambda = 1$, then the words provided are ranked in order of their probability of appearing in that specific topic. Setting them at 0 reorders the words displayed by their 'lift' score, which is defined as the ratio of their probability within the topic to its marginal probability across the corpus. The idea, sort of like with TF-IDF, is that words that have a high probability of occurring across the whole corpus are not helpful in interpreting individual topics. You want to find some sort of balance that helps you understand what the topics are about. If you are following along with the code, take some time exploring the results in your browser.

29.6 Conclusion

The key points in this chapter are as follows:

- Generative topic models are Bayesian models used to understand latent themes in documents containing thematically linked words.

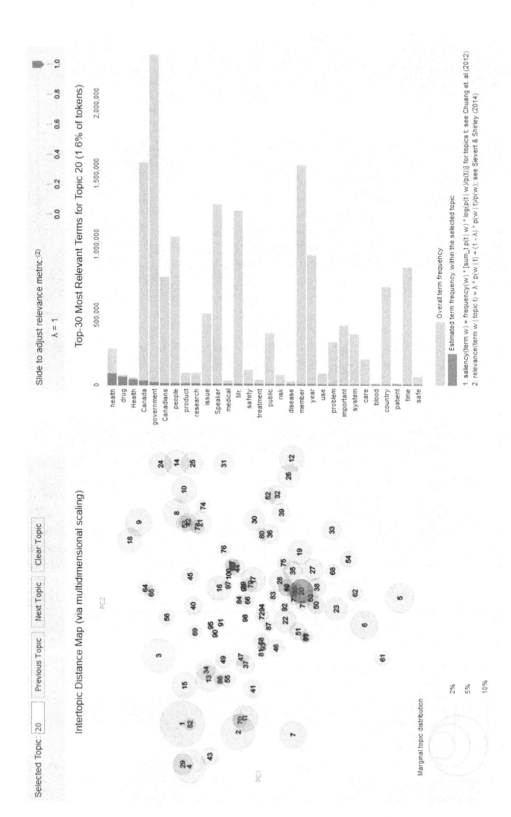

Figure 29.5 A still frame taken from the pyLDAvis package's interactive interface

- We developed LDA models using Gensim.
- VI is an alternative to HMC that provides a *function* with an analytical solution for the approximate posterior distribution.
- We evaluated topic coherence using quantitative measures.
- We visualized topic models with pyLDAvis.

Visit the website at https://study.sagepub.com/mclevey for additional resources

30

GENERATIVE NETWORK ANALYSIS WITH BAYESIAN STOCHASTIC BLOCK MODELS

30.1 Learning Objectives

By the end of this chapter, you should be able to do the following:

- Explain how stochastic equivalence builds upon, yet is distinct from, structural equivalence
- Describe the Bayesian logic of stochastic block models (SBMs) and how they aggregate nodes into stochastically equivalent blocks
- Use `graph-tool` to produce posterior distributions of nodes in hierarchically nested blocks
- Understand how TopSBM unifies SBMs and latent Dirichlet allocation models

30.2 Learning Materials

You can find the online learning materials for this chapter in `doing_computational_social_science/Chapter_30`. `cd` into the directory and launch your Jupyter server.

30.3 Introduction

In the previous chapter, we used Bayesian generative models to identify latent topic structure in text data. In this chapter, we use the same underlying Bayesian logic to tackle some difficult problems in network analysis. Just as latent Dirichlet allocation (LDA) addresses topic modelling as a latent variable problem using generative models, the models we introduce here – stochastic block models (SBMs) – approach network structure in a similar way. Whereas LDA assumes that documents contain a mixture of latent topics that are made up of words, SBMs assume that networks have latent modular structure, and the goal is to figure out how to partition a network according to these low-level building blocks.

I'll start by briefly introducing some new theoretical ideas about 'equivalence' and structural positions in networks. Then, I'll emphasize the theoretical and the generative logic of SBMs and their hierarchical Bayesian design. Then, I'll discuss the role of Bayesian inference in SBMs, following a similar explanatory process as in the previous chapter.

In the second half of the chapter, we'll focus on three related things. First, I'll introduce the Python package graph-tool. Secondly, we will fit a series of SBMs to an email communication network of Enron employees involved in the legal proceedings of the Enron scandal. Thirdly and finally, we will return to the comparison of LDA and SBM. I'll emphasize the shared conceptual logic of the problems of topic modelling and community detection. Then, I'll introduce TopSBMs as a shared modelling framework for both tasks. This combination marks the end of our journey through Bayesian generative modelling and probabilistic programming.

Latent network structure: connected communities and structural positions

Generally speaking, network researchers think about the structure of social networks in one of two ways, each of which posits different social mechanisms to produce an outcome of interest (e.g. whether someone adopts a belief or behaviour), or give rise to different kinds of patterns in network structure. Both perspectives subsume a wide variety of specific methods, measures, and models.

The first of these two perspectives focuses mainly on issues related to connection, cohesion, and network flow. We work within this general perspective anytime we are thinking through the processes by which ties and cohesive subgroups form and dissolve, or when concerned with the role of networks in facilitating or mitigating the *spread* of a contagion or the creation of opportunities from one's direct ties or the structure of ties in their neighbourhood. Everything we have discussed in relation to networks to this point in the book has assumed this general perspective. Because of the role of direct connection and walk structure, research that adopts this perspective measures and models *specific* relationships between *specific* nodes.

By contrast, positional approaches are premised on the notion that we can reduce the complexity of networks that represent specific relationships between specific nodes to a smaller set of connections between blocks (i.e. groups) of nodes that are judged to be 'equivalent' in some meaningful way. In other words, each 'block' in a network consists of a group of structurally interchangeable nodes, each of which share a common structural position in the network. The research goals here focus on understanding the *general* relationships between *general structural positions* rather than understanding the specific connections between specific people.

Why would we care to do this in the first place? It depends on whom you ask, but a common motivation for working with this positional approach is generalization: we want to abstract away the concrete details of specific connections between specific people to focus on understanding *the big picture, in general*. As we will soon see, this way of thinking lends itself well to probabilistic models of network structure, and it is more robust to problems that arise from the imprecise and imperfect observation and measurement of relational data.

Let's imagine a simple scenario. Imagine two professors, each principal investigators of research labs at a university but in completely different departments and with no overlap in their research agendas or lab members. Let's also assume that both labs have a fairly hierarchical organizational structure, as is historically typical of many sciences. In both cases, the professors have a group of students and lab technicians who report directly to them. Regardless of how we measure relevant network ties (e.g. communication, collaboration, advice giving), the community detection methods we discussed in Chapter 14 would place both professors into different communities. From a connection, community, and flow perspective, these two professors and their labs are completely distinct, with the only relationships between them being indirect connections along the walk structure of the network. By contrast, the models we're going to discuss in the rest of this chapter would identify the two professors as being equivalent despite the fact that they are not connected to one another and they have no connections in common. This is because the focus is on *general* patterns of *aggregate* relations between *categories* of nodes (Prell, 2012; Scott, 2013).

Nodes that occupy the same structural positions in a network tend to have behavioural similarities even when they are not connected to one another. Structurally equivalent nodes may behave in similar ways because they are conforming, to varying degrees, to the expectations associated with their position and social roles. Professors do what professors do, grad students do what grad students do, undergrad students do what undergrad students do, and so on. Another mechanistic explanation is that equivalent nodes have to negotiate similar types of problems, situations, and institutional environments, and they exhibit behavioural similarities due to these common experiences and contexts rather than the influence of their direct social ties (bringing us back to that idea of *shared institutional environments* and the connection to hierarchical models first introduced in Chapter 28).

Finally, people who occupy the same structural positions in networks might look to mirror the behaviours of other people who share their structural positions. For example, if they are uncertain about how to behave, or what is needed for success, they may model their behaviour on someone who is in the same position and seems to be thriving (similarly, they may observe behaviours and outcomes they want to *avoid*). Returning to our hypothetical example, it doesn't stretch credibility to claim that a professor is more likely to make decisions about running their research lab based on observations of how similar professors run their labs than the interpersonal influence of their friends and family (who are not professors running research labs).

The first thing we need to do in any positional analysis is specify exactly what we mean by 'equivalence'. We need an operational definition.

Equivalence

Lorrain and White (1971) theorized that nodes in a network could be considered structurally equivalent if they connected to the rest of a network in *identical* ways. In this definition, equivalent nodes are literally substitutable for one another, which was the initial inspiration behind the move to aggregate nodes into abstract blocks that reveal an underlying structure of generic positions and social roles.

It is exceedingly rare to find nodes that meet this strict definition of equivalence when analysing real social networks. As a result, we typically use some measure of *approximate equivalence* instead. Since Lorrain and White's (1971) classic article, researchers have proposed many different ways of conceptualizing equivalence executing positional analyses, one of the most influential of which was White and Reitz's (1983) regular equivalence. To be 'regularly equivalent', nodes must have similar connection profiles to other regular equivalence classes, rather than the identical connection profile of structural equivalence.

Structural and regular equivalence are both deterministic. Probability offers us yet another way of operationalizing the idea of equivalence, and one that is well-aligned with Bayesian probabilistic modelling. Nodes are stochastically equivalent if they have the same probabilities of connecting with other nodes. In other words, nodes are grouped into the same blocks if they are statistically indistinguishable from one another due to sharing similar probabilities of connecting with other nodes according to their stochastically equivalent blocks.

Further Reading

Like the deterministic conception of equivalence, this stochastic conception was initially developed in the social sciences and statistics (see Holland et al., 1983; Nowicki and Snijders, 2001; Snijders and Nowicki, 1997; Wang and Wong, 1987), but over the same time period were developing in other sciences (a textbook example of 'multiple discovery'); it is now very much an interdisciplinary affair at the cutting edge of network science (see Peixoto, 2019).

Block models

Once we've adopted some operational definition of equivalence, the second step is to use that definition to cluster nodes into different equivalence classes. As previously mentioned, these classes represent generic positions and are typically referred to as 'blocks'. The process of identifying these blocks is called 'block modelling', and there are a number of different ways it can be done (see Doreian et al., 2002, 2005; Ferligoj et al., 2011; Peixoto, 2019; Snijders and Nowicki, 1997). The most important distinction is between deterministic block models and SBMs. Unsurprisingly, deterministic block models are used alongside deterministic understandings of equivalence, and SBMs are used alongside stochastic understandings of equivalence.

The results of deterministic block models are fully determined by (1) the parameters of the model, such as the number of blocks to look for, and (2) the input data itself. Given the same parameter values and the same input data, the models will always produce the same results. Typically, this is done by constructing a similarity or distance matrix from an adjacency matrix, and then performing some form of cluster analysis, such as hierarchical clustering, on that matrix. There have been many specific algorithms for block modelling introduced since Harrison White and his students first introduced the idea of structural equivalence and block modelling in the 1970s, the most famous of which are CONCOR and REGE. A discussion of these and other deterministic block models is beyond the scope of this chapter, but they are described in most social network analysis methods texts.

By contrast, the block models we will discuss in the rest of this chapter are *stochastic* and are based on notions of *stochastic equivalence*. Let's shift the discussion to them now.

Bayesian hierarchical stochastic block models

Unlike their deterministic counterparts, Bayesian SBMs conceptualize network structure as a latent variable problem to be addressed with a generative model. Just as LDA assumes that specific combinations of words observed in documents are *generated* from shared latent themes, SBMs assume that specific patterns of ties between nodes in social networks are *generated* from some latent network structure that influences the formation and dissolution of relationships. The types of latent structure that we are interested in varies, and we can develop models for specific types of structure.

Having a probabilistic model of how this works, grounded in plausible generative mechanisms, is an important part of developing models that don't under- or overfit our data. It helps us differentiate structure from random noise in the process of moving from concrete connections between concrete nodes to general connections between categories of nodes. This allows us to overcome some of the limitations of deterministic approaches, which can be tripped up by structure that is caused by random fluctuations rather than some meaningful network-driven social process.

Tiago Peixoto (2019) summarizes the Bayesian response to this problem in one pithy paragraph:

> The remedy to this problem is to think probabilistically. We need to ascribe to each possible explanation of the data a probability that it is correct, which takes into account modeling assumptions, the statistical evidence available in the data, as well as any source of prior information we may have. Imbued in the whole procedure must be the principle of parsimony – or Occam's razor – where a simpler model is preferred if the evidence is not sufficient to justify a more complicated one. (p. 291)

As with LDA, the underlying logic of developing a Bayesian generative model here is the same as in other contexts. To continue drilling that underlying logic:

1. we have observed data (connections between nodes in a network) and unobserved latent variables (block or community membership),
2. we want to infer the distributions of the latent variables (i.e. the assignment of nodes into latent blocks) conditional on the observed data, and
3. to do so, we construct a joint probability distribution of every possible combination of values for our latent and observed variables (i.e. the numerator in Bayes' theorem) and then perform approximate posterior inference to determine the probabilities of different distributions on the latent variables conditional on the observed data.

We are after the posterior probabilities of many different partitions of the network conditioned on the connections we observe. In other words, we want to know the conditional probability that some node partition b could have plausibly generated an observed network G,

$$P(b \mid G)$$

As with all Bayesian models, we need to play the 'What's That' game, providing priors for all latent variables. The natural tendency here is to prefer uniform priors. If you recall from Chapter 27, using a uniform distribution for our priors means assigning an equal probability to every possible value of the latent variable. Peixoto (2019) has shown, however, that this strategy often results in suboptimal results with network models, as it has an a priori preference for solutions with number of blocks comparable to the number of nodes in the network. Who wants that? Nobody. Instead, Peixoto (2019) proposes a three-level hierarchical Bayesian approach where we sample (1) the number of blocks, (2) the size of each block, and the (3) the partition of the observed network into those blocks.

This hierarchical model is much less likely to overfit our data, and it does so without requiring us to determine the number of groups in advance, or indeed making any assumptions about the higher-order structure of the networks we are interested in. We will use this model exclusively below. It's known as a nested stochastic block model. Peixoto (2014) describes a number of interesting variations on inference algorithms for this hierarchical model. One *very* important thing to know about the SBM implementation in graph-tool is that rather than strictly considering equivalence, it also considers the probability of nodes connecting to other nodes in the more standard sense of network models we've looked at previously (the connection and cohesion approach). This means that the network partitions from graph-tool will be based on a mixture of assortative community structure (as we've seen in Chapter 14 with Louvain and Leiden) along with disassortative (structural equivalence). Incorporating edge weights into the SBM estimation tends to push the balance in the results towards the assortative side, which makes some intuitive sense – a highly weighted connection between two nodes could drown out the latent influence of structural equivalence. We will examine this shortly.

This has all been very abstract. Let's get our hands dirty with some code.

30.4 Block Modelling with Graph-Tool

When it comes to the fitting Bayesian SBMs, there's no beating Tiago Peixoto's graph-tool, in Python or otherwise. It has astonishing performance in terms of both speed and memory, and as a result it can handle exceptionally large networks efficiently. This performance is achieved by offloading most of the heavy lifting to C++ on the back end. The cost of these performance improvements, however, is that using graph-tool is less 'Pythonic' than you might be used to by this point in the book. The graph-tool package is considerably more complex than the network analysis packages we've seen so far (NetworkX and NDlib).

The additional overhead and less Pythonic nature that gives graph-tool its superior performance capabilities also means that I have to spend more time upfront describing how things work. It is entirely possible some of this won't really 'sink in' until you start working with graph-tool. That's OK! Once you get your hands dirty with some models and have built up a bit of intuition, you can always come back to this content to deepen your understanding.

Installing graph-tool

The easiest way to get up and running with graph-tool is to install it via `conda-forge` with the following command. Because of its numerous dependencies, I strongly recommend that you do this inside a `conda` environment (e.g. the `dcss` environment, if you've been following along with the supplementary learning materials). As a reminder, `conda` environments were introduced in Chapter 1.

```
conda install -c conda-forge graph-tool
```

If you haven't been using an environment already, you can also install graph-tool inside a `conda` environment designed specifically for graph-tool. You can use that environment the same way you use any other `conda` environment. To download and activate the graph-tool environment, simply execute the following from the command line:

```
conda create --name gt -c conda-forge graph-tool
```

When `conda` prompts you for permission to download and install the required packages, agree. When it's finished, activate the environment with

```
conda activate gt
```

When you do so, you should see your command prompt change; it will now start with `(gt)` (as opposed to `dcss` if you've been using the `conda` environment for this book). If you are using Jupyter, note that you'll have to launch your Jupyter Notebook server inside that environment to access the packages inside the environment.

Understanding property maps

The most important graph-tool concept to understand is how its array-like 'property maps' work. Rather than attaching information about a node (e.g. its ID/label or degree centrality) to the node itself, each node in the network is assigned a unique index. That same index is contained in a property map, and whenever we want to know some information about a node, we use the node index to find the relevant information in the property map. There's a bit of extra friction here, though: because of the C++ back end, each property map object contains *only one type of data,* which you have to declare in advance. This is a pain, but it's what allows us to enjoy some pretty remarkable performance improvements.

Because graph-tool makes such heavy use of these array-like property maps, it's easiest to think of a network in graph-tool as a collection of *associated arrays.* For example, in a network with three nodes – `['Lebron James', 'Anthony Davis', 'Kentavious Caldwell-Pope']` – and an associated property map of colours – `[Red, Green, Blue]` – Lebron James would be `Red`, Anthony Davis would be `Green`, and `Kentavious Caldwell-Pope` would be `Blue`. We can encode just about anything in a property map, including vectors of values. For example, the `[Red, Green, Blue]` property map could also be stored as RGB values, `[[255,0,0], [0,128,0], [0,0,255]]`, which would associate `[255,0,0]` with Lebron James.

It's also very important to note that:

1 graph-tool does not automatically label nodes, and
2 it is possible for multiple nodes to have the same label.

This can result in some unwelcome surprises. For example, if your edge list contains strings as opposed to numbers – such as

```
[
    ('Karamo', 'Tan'),
    ('Karamo', 'Tan')
]
```

then graph-tool will create four different nodes and two edges rather than creating two nodes and aggregating the edges into a weight of 2 for the tie between Karamo and Tan.

You might recall from Chapter 13 that different disciplines tend to use different words to refer to nodes and edges. In graph-tool, nodes are referred to as vertices. They are *exactly* the same. When we create a new vertex in graph-tool – `v = g.add_vertex()` – `v` becomes a `vertex` class object, which we can refer to as a vertex descriptor. Vertex descriptors are alternative to node indices and can be used to access information about a node from a property map. If we assigned our [Red, Green, Blue] property map to an object called `colour_map`, we could retrieve the information for node v with `colour_map[v]`.

Edge property maps, which can contain useful information such as edge weight, behave somewhat differently. They are accessed using edge descriptors, which can be obtained from the source and target nodes. For example, we might obtain and store an edge descriptor between nodes Karamo and Tan with e = g.edge('Karamo','Tan') or e = g.edge(1, 2) if you've assigned Karamo and Tan integer IDs to benefit from faster compute times.

Finally, entire networks can themselves have property maps. These network-level property maps can be accessed by passing the graph object itself. For example, if we have a network object called g and a property map called `graph_property_map`, we could access the properties with `graph_property_map[g]`.

This might sound like a lot of additional overhead to worry about when conducting a network analysis, but you'll likely find the impact fairly minimal once you get used to things. As with other network analysis packages, it makes it relatively easy to do a large amount of data processing outside of the package itself. For example, you can do a lot of work with the data that will eventually be stored as property maps using Pandas and NumPy. My main advice here is *take great care that all of the data in your lists and arrays is in the same order, and of equal lengths.*

Now, let's model.

Imports

```
from graph_tool.all import *
import pandas as pd
pd.set_option("display.notebook_repr_html", False)
import matplotlib
import numpy as np
import math
import pickle
from dcss.networks import label_radial_blockmodel, get_block_membership
```

Data

As usual, I suggest refreshing yourself on the data we are using here by returning to the overview of datasets from the Preface. In brief, the Enron email data is provided as two CSV files, one with the edges between employees who have exchanged emails with one another, and one with the organizational position of Enron employees.

When developing a block model, we typically do so without having some external set of positions or roles that we want to approximate; the goal here is not supervised learning. However, for learning purposes, our goal will be to develop a block model using relational data that mirrors job titles. The purpose of doing things this way is to illustrate the power of this approach to network analysis, as well as make the discussion of 'positions' a bit less abstract. So, remember that when we talk about 'positions' and 'roles', we don't always (or even often) mean *official* positions or roles such as job titles.

The two datasets below contain the relational data from employee email communications and information about the job title each employee held in the organization:

```
edges_df = pd.read_csv('../data/enron/enron_full_edge_list.csv')
edges_df.head()
```

	source	target
0	press.release@enron.com	all.worldwide@enron.com
1	office.chairman@enron.com	all.downtown@enron.com
2	office.chairman@enron.com	all.enron-worldwide@enron.com
3	press.release@enron.com	all.worldwide@enron.com
4	office.chairman@enron.com	all_enron_north.america@enron.com

As you can see, our edge list has two columns, `source` and `target`. We don't have any edge weights (though we will compute them below) or other edge attributes.

```
employee_df = pd.read_csv('../data/enron/enron_employees_updated.csv')
employee_df.head()
```

	id	position
0	liz.taylor@enron.com	Administrative Assistant
1	michelle.lokay@enron.com	Administrative Assistant
2	holden.salisbury@enron.com	Analyst
3	kam.keiser@enron.com	Analyst
4	matthew.lenhart@enron.com	Analyst

The information about each employee's *official* position in the organization is provided in a column called `'position'`. Let's count the number of employees in each role:

```
employee_df['position'].value_counts()
```

```
Trader                     35
Vice President             26
Director                   17
Manager                    15
In House Lawyer            11
Senior Specialist           8
Specialist                  6
Managing Director           6
Analyst                     5
Employee                    5
President                   4
CEO                         4
Administrative Assistant    2
Associate                   2
Senior Manager              1
COO                         1
CFO                         1
Name: position, dtype: int64
```

Constructing the communication network

To create our network, let's construct a weighted communication network between core employees using the edge list and node attribute files above. First, we'll aggregate and count edges to compute a weight. We'll ignore any nodes that are not in the employee_df dataframe, narrowing our focus to core employees only. The 'core employees' are those who were involved in the legal proceedings following the Enron scandal.

Since this is a directed communication network, i,j ties are different from j,i ties, so we can simply aggregate our edges dataframe by the combination of 'source' and 'target' columns and treat the count of their occurrences as our edge weight. We'll also filter the resulting dataframe so that it only includes nodes that are part of the core employee subset.

```
edges_df = edges_df.value_counts(['source', 'target']).reset_index(name='count').copy
        ()
core_employees = set(employee_df['id'].tolist())
core_edges_df = edges_df[edges_df['source'].isin(core_employees) &
                    edges_df['target'].isin(core_employees)]
```

With our weighted directed edge list created, we can initialize a directed network:

```
eG = Graph(directed = True)
```

We can add the core employees to this network as nodes, add their job titles to a property map, and add the edge data (weights) to a property map. We'll do this in three steps:

1   Get the information into lists
2   Initialize the property maps and tell graph-tool what type of data we are going to provide
3   Loop over our two lists to add the employees to the networks and their node and edge attributes (job titles, edge weights) to property maps

First, we'll create the lists:

```
employee_list = employee_df['id'].tolist()
title_list = employee_df['position'].tolist()
```

Secondly, we'll initialize the property maps. Note that in addition to the property maps themselves, we are creating a dictionary called vertex_lookup. As mentioned earlier in the chapter, we can use this dictionary to simplify the 'lookup' process to select nodes using string values that carry some meaning about the node, rather than the integer identifier used by graph-tool.

Since we are going to use email addresses as node labels, we'll initialize a property map called labels and tell graph-tool to expect strings (because email addresses are strings). Similarly we will initialize a property map for job titles, called titles, and also containing strings. Finally, we will create an edge_weight property map. Since edge weights are integers in this case, we will tell graph-tool to expect integers:

```
vertex_lookup = {}

label = eG.new_vertex_property('string')
title = eG.new_vertex_property('string')
edge_weight = eG.new_edge_property('int')
```

Now we're ready to add information to the property maps! Let's zip up our employee_list and title_list and then iterate over it. For each pairing of elements from the two lists, we'll add the core employees to the network as nodes, their email addresses to the `labels` property map, and their job titles to the `titles` property map. Finally, we will add the information about the node index to the `vertex_lookup` dictionary we created above.

```
for vertex in zip(employee_list, title_list):
    # create a new vertex instance
    v = eG.add_vertex()

    # add attributes to the property maps in the index position of the vertex
    label[v] = vertex[0]
    title[v] = vertex[1]

    # add the vertex to the lookup dictionary, converting it to an integer
    vertex_lookup[vertex[0]] = int(v)
```

As you probably anticipated, the next thing we need to do is process the edges between nodes. We can do that by using lists pulled from the edges dataframe, but remember we *also* need to consult `vertex_lookup` to ensure we are assigning the right edges between the right nodes!

```
source_list = core_edges_df['source'].tolist()
target_list = core_edges_df['target'].tolist()
weight_list = core_edges_df['count'].tolist()

for nodes in zip(source_list, target_list, weight_list):
    from_idx = vertex_lookup[nodes[0]]
    to_idx = vertex_lookup[nodes[1]]

    # Let's ignore self-loops
    if from_idx != to_idx:
        edge = eG.add_edge(from_idx, to_idx)
        edge_weight[edge] = nodes[2]
```

We've now reached the very final bit of preparation. We'll make each of the property maps we've just initialized and populated with information *internal to the graph* and save the graph in `graph-tool`'s own format. That way we don't need to recreate the network again later, we can just load up the network with all the relevant property maps already defined.

```
eG.vertex_properties['label'] = label
eG.vertex_properties['title'] = title
eG.edge_properties['edge_weight'] = edge_weight

lookup = eG.new_graph_property('object')
lookup[eG] = vertex_lookup
eG.graph_properties['vertex_lookup'] = lookup
```

And with that, we're ready to start developing SBMs!

Developing stochastic block models

In the introduction, we discussed how there are some properties that SBMs share with LDA. One of these properties is the process for developing, critiquing, improving, and eventually selecting the best model in an iterative fashion: Box's loop. For example, in this case, after approximating the posterior distribution of the latent variables, we can test the fit of that posterior on the data, and repeat the process using the insight gained about what is and isn't working in the model. In theory, enough iterations would produce the best model possible in terms of representing the data (*not* in terms of the usefulness of the results). In practice, we have to make a choice about when we're satisfied with the results, because there's no good way to know how many iterations it would take to produce the best model you can, given the data you have.

As I mentioned earlier, our goal here is to develop a block model that will partition our network into a set of positions that mirror the job titles that the core employees held within Enron. The catch, of course, is that we want to do this using only information from the relational data itself.

graph-tool has a very handy function, `minimize_nested_blockmodel_dl()`, that takes care of all the hard work for us. It's fast to run and tends to produce good results right out of the box. `minimize_nested_blockmodel_dl()` attempts to minimize something called the 'description length' of a nested block model. Let's break this down, starting with the nested part. As you hopefully recall from earlier in this chapter, a *nested* SBM is a hierarchical Bayesian model. In other words, it embeds blocks inside other blocks in a multilevel hierarchy. Doing things this way makes it easier to find small blocks in a network that may contain a small number of nodes.

The `minimize` and `dl` parts of `minimize_nested_blockmodel_dl()` are a shorthand for minimize the description length. Minimum description length is an operationalization of Occam's razor; it suggests that the best model is one that can represent all of the data with the least amount of information required. It helps us select a model that fully explains the data but is as simple as possible given the observed data.

Finally, the block model we will fit here is also degree-corrected (Karrer and Newman, 2011). A standard baseline SBM assumes that nodes within any given block tend to have very similar, if not identical, degrees. Since this is *extremely unrealistic* in real-world networks, it is almost always better to use the degree-corrected implementation:

```
state = minimize_nested_blockmodel_dl(eG, deg_corr = True)
```

With that one line of code, we've executed our three-level hierarchical Bayesian SBM!

The function we just executed created something called a blockstate, which is an object containing the results of partitioning the network running our block model. We can print a summary of the blockstate for our nested degree-corrected description-length-minimized block model to find out:

* the number of blocks that nodes were assigned to,
* the number of levels in the nested hierarchy, and
* the number of 'meta-blocks' at each of those levels (blocks within blocks in the nested hierarchy).

```
state.print_summary()
```

```
l: 0, N: 149, B: 13
l: 1, N: 13, B: 4
l: 2, N: 4, B: 1
```

Remember that the model we just ran is a *stochastic generative model,* so the number of blocks will vary for each run of the model, but it typically finds 12 to 14 blocks at the bottom level. Remember, this is a nested variant where the 'bottom level' consists of all the individual nodes, while the upper levels of the hierarchy are aggregate blocks found by creating a new network where each block is a node and estimating a block model based on that network. After some consideration, 12 to 14 blocks seem fairly reasonable. We have 17 job titles in the data but if we combined 'Manager + Senior Manager', 'Senior Specialist + Specialist', 'Administrative Assistant + Employee', and 'CEO + CFO + COO', we'd have 12 titles. This kind of combination would not impact the computation of the model at all and can be left until it's time for interpretation.

Finally, we can get a quick sense of how things went by visualizing the block model (Figure 30.1). I'm limited to a narrow colour palette in print, but you can access a full-resolution colour version of the image (and others like it) in the supplementary online materials. I recommend looking at the colour versions of these images, as colour is used very effectively in these block model visualizations.

```
state.draw(
    layout = "sfdp",
    vertex_text = eG.vertex_properties['title'],
    eorder = eG.edge_properties['edge_weight'],
    vertex_text_position = 315,
    bg_color=[255,255,255,1],
    output_size=[4024,4024],
    output='../figures/core_enron_blockmodel_sfdp.pdf'
    )
```

In Figure 30.1, each node is represented by an individual point (as in other network visualizations), only the nodes are organized into blocks. The squares are points where blocks converge up the hierarchy to form the nested structure – the structure of email exchanges between blocks will decide whether a block should be grouped with another one. For example, if you look at the group of six blocks in the top left of the image, you might notice that there are only two traders present, but there are a lot of lawyers and vice presidents, as well as a CEO.

This first attempt is already looking pretty good. We have three of the four CEOs in the same block near the right-hand side, along with three presidents. Note for later: the remaining CEO isn't in the same meta-block – one level up the hierarchy – as the other CEOs.

As with other generative models, *we need to think through generative mechanisms here.* If you recall from Chapter 24, all this really means is that we need to think through simple social and interactional processes that may have resulted in (i.e. generated) the patterns we see in our data. *What's a plausible story of how this data was generated?*

Remember that we are dealing with *email communications* between employees within an organization. There are many ways to imagine the social mechanisms that best predict structure in a network like this. In this case, it could be that emails between the core employees predict the relationship between those employees, or it could be that the emails

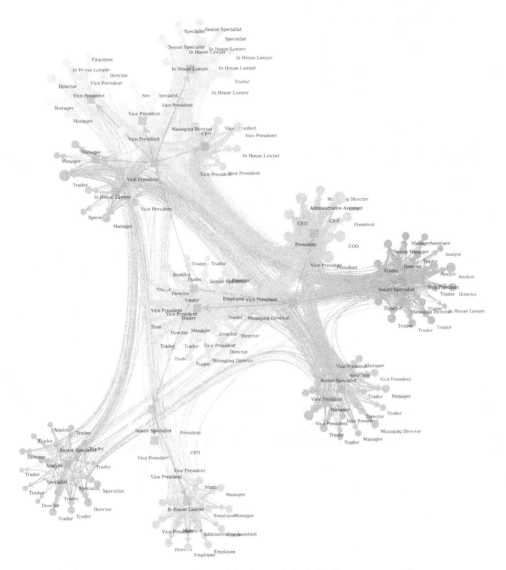

Figure 30.1 A hierarchical stochastic block model of the Enron network

they send *to other non-core employee Enron email addresses* are more predictive. This is an exploratory process that can't fit reasonably in this chapter, but you can see a bit of it in the online supplement.

Let's see what the outcome is with different block model estimation criteria. SBMs in graph-tool are able to incorporate edge weights into the estimation:

```
state_w = minimize_nested_blockmodel_dl(eG, deg_corr = True,
    state_args = dict(
        recs = [eG.edge_properties['edge_weight']],
        rec_types=["discrete-binomial"]))
```

```
state_w.print_summary()
```

```
l: 0, N: 149, B: 67
l: 1, N: 67, B: 10
l: 2, N: 10, B: 2
l: 3, N: 2, B: 1
```

We can see already that we end up with far too many blocks to be useful here! There's no need to visualize this graph, but we have another option – let's try setting the number of blocks to be the same as it was for the unweighted model, then see what the weights do for the results:

```
state_w2 = minimize_nested_blockmodel_dl(eG, deg_corr = True,
    B_min = 12, B_max = 12, state_args = dict(recs=[
        eG.edge_properties['edge_weight']], rec_types=["discrete-binomial"]))
```

```
state_w2.print_summary()
```

```
l: 0, N: 149, B: 12
l: 1, N: 12, B: 3
l: 2, N: 3, B: 2
l: 3, N: 2, B: 1
```

At first glance (Figure 30.2), incorporating edge weight seems as though it produces more tightly knit, smaller blocks, and only two distinct groups of blocks one level up the hierarchy where we had four with the first model. The larger blocks are also more heterogeneous, with CEOs grouped alongside many traders and even 'employees'.

```
state_w2.draw(
    layout = "sfdp",
    vertex_text = eG.vertex_properties['title'],
    eorder = eG.edge_properties['edge_weight'],
    vertex_text_position = 315,
    bg_color=[255,255,255,1],
    output_size=[4024,4024],
    output='../figures/core_enron_blockmodel_sfdpw.pdf'
    )
```

The use of edge weights in a block model is a theoretical consideration more than it is a technical one, so it takes some careful thought and experimenting to see what the impact is. In our case, we have people with quite different roles in the company, so their email volume will be quite different. If we don't use edge weights, we stick to a stricter definition of equivalence, closer to structural, and here this produces the most intuitive results. Nonetheless, we should have a way to compare the results beyond just looking at a graph – these graphs won't be very helpful for huge networks. We can use the get_block_membership utility from the dcss package to add block assignment information to the employee dataframe:

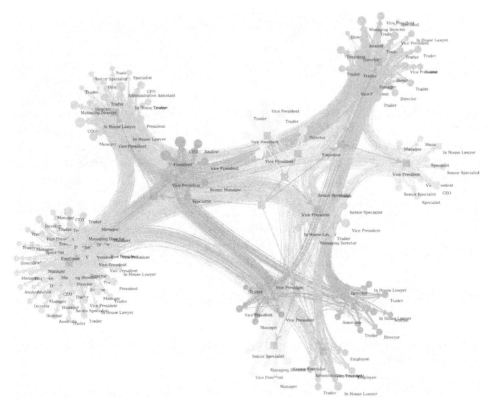

Figure 30.2 A hierarchical stochastic block model of the Enron network, incorporating edge weights

```
employee_blocks_df = get_block_membership(state, eG, employee_df,
                                          'model_uw_1')
employee_blocks_df = get_block_membership(state_w2, eG, employee_blocks_df,
                                          'model_w_2')
```

Let's take a look at some of the job titles that one would expect to be more well-defined:

```
df_by_position = employee_blocks_df.groupby('position').agg(list)
df_by_position[df_by_position.index.isin(['CEO','President', 'In House Lawyer'])].head
    ()
```

```
                                                                  id \
position
CEO                     [david.w.delainey@enron.com, jeff.skilling@enr...
In House Lawyer         [bill.rapp@enron.com, carol.clair@enron.com, d...
President               [greg.whalley@enron.com, jeffrey.a.shankman@en...
                                          model_uw_1_block_id \
position
CEO                                          [5, 5, 0, 0]
In House Lawyer              [1, 9, 10, 10, 9, 7, 5, 3, 9, 9, 3]
President                                    [5, 5, 0, 12]
```

```
                                      model_w_2_block_id
position
CEO                                            [0, 5, 1, 5]
In House Lawyer          [9, 9, 0, 8, 2, 8, 3, 5, 6, 1, 6]
President                                      [2, 2, 1, 5]
```

You might be able to get a sense of things from some of the smaller lists here. For example, in the model_uw_1_block_id column, we can see that one block has three of the four CEOs, as well as three of the four presidents, while another has the remaining CEO and president. Six of the lawyers also tend to end up in the same block on this run (again, this is stochastic so results might vary a little bit). With the weighted model, only two of the CEOs end up in the same block, although they are joined by a president and a lawyer.

Alternatively, we can count the number of unique block assignments by role (job title) and calculate the average, based on the number of people with those roles. A lower value here would be a loose indicator of accuracy, with two caveats: a 0.5 value for CEO would be the same if the four CEOs were divided equally into two blocks, rather than three in one block and one in another. This block assignment difference is conceptually significant, so a more robust metric might be desirable. Job titles that apply to only one employee will also, necessarily, have a perfectly poor score of 1.0 every time.

```
employee_blocks_df.groupby(['position'])['model_uw_1_block_id'].agg(lambda x: x.
    nunique()/x.count())
```

```
position
Administrative Assistant       1.000000
Analyst                        0.400000
Associate                      1.000000
CEO                            0.500000
CFO                            1.000000
COO                            1.000000
Director                       0.411765
Employee                       0.600000
In House Lawyer                0.545455
Manager                        0.466667
Managing Director              0.666667
President                      0.750000
Senior Manager                 1.000000
Senior Specialist              0.875000
Specialist                     0.500000
Trader                         0.200000
Vice President                 0.423077
Name: model_uw_1_block_id, dtype: float64
```

```
print(employee_blocks_df.groupby(['position'])['model_uw_1_block_id'].agg(lambda x: x.
    nunique()/x.count()).sum())
print(employee_blocks_df.groupby(['position'])['model_w_2_block_id'].agg(lambda x: x.
    nunique()/x.count()).sum())
```

```
11.338629507747154
11.916386064915477
```

We can do the exact inverse to roughly assess the homogeneity of the blocks, by reversing the columns in the `groupby` operation:

```
employee_blocks_df.groupby(['model_uw_1_block_id'])['position'].agg(lambda x: x.
    nunique()/x.count())
```

```
model_uw_1_block_id
0             0.750000
1             0.583333
2             0.277778
3             0.476190
4             0.555556
5             0.416667
6             0.230769
7             0.625000
8             0.714286
9             0.400000
10            0.666667
11            0.500000
12            0.666667
Name: position, dtype: float64
```

```
print(employee_blocks_df.groupby(['model_uw_1_block_id'])['position'].agg(lambda x: x.
    nunique()/x.count()).sum())
print(employee_blocks_df.groupby(['model_w_2_block_id'])['position'].agg(lambda x: x.
    nunique()/x.count()).sum())
```

```
6.862912087912089
7.970732305329079
```

This loose evaluation suggests that the unweighted model might be preferred, but we can do better with this evaluation. Sci-kit learn provides *many* classification evaluation metrics, and the problem we're solving here is essentially a clustering classification. There are metrics within Sklearn's clustering section that provide the above evaluations but with more nuance (remember the equivalent 0.5 score if the CEOs were clustered with different proportions but with the same number of blocks). A `homogeneity_score` evaluates, you guessed it, the homogeneity of the detected clusters, so if clusters contain more of the same type of job title, the results will score higher. Scores here are on a scale from 0 to 1, with 1 being the best.

```
from sklearn.metrics import homogeneity_score, completeness_score,
    adjusted_mutual_info_score
```

Let's compare homogeneity scores for the unweighted network and then the weighted one. As with the rough evaluation above, the unweighted model has a better score.

```
homogeneity_score(employee_blocks_df['position'], employee_blocks_df['
    model_uw_1_block_id'])
```

```
0.353428152904928
homogeneity_score(employee_blocks_df['position'], employee_blocks_df['
    model_w_2_block_id'])
```

```
0.25528558562493037
```

The `completeness_score` inverts the previous score, instead assessing the homogeneity of block assignments for each job title, so the degree to which nodes are assigned to blocks with other nodes that have the same title. The result is actually very similar in this case!

```
completeness_score(employee_blocks_df['position'], employee_blocks_df['
    model_uw_1_block_id'])
```

```
0.3435558493343224
```

```
completeness_score(employee_blocks_df['position'], employee_blocks_df['
    model_w_2_block_id'])
```

```
0.2771316517440044
```

Finally, we can also do both of the above in a unified score, `adjusted_mutual_info_score`, where homogeneity and completeness are considered together and the position of the ground truth and predicted labels doesn't matter. This can also be used to calculate agreement between two labelling methods when there is no known ground truth, but unfortunately our block assignment classifications will not be the same between models – `block 1` in one model is not necessarily the same as `block 1` in the next, or even in repeat runs of the same model. Note that this method is a version of `normalized_mutual_info_score` that is adjusted to account for chance, because the standard mutual information score tends to overestimate the shared information between models that have a larger number of clusters.

For this score, the maximum is 1 but it is possible to have a negative score if the predicted clusters are nonsensical enough. We can see that the adjusted mutual info score below is roughly half of the individual scores above, for the unweighted network. For the weighted network, the score is *much* lower. If we compare the two block assignments together, they actually have more agreement with each other than the weighted model has with the ground truth job titles.

```
adjusted_mutual_info_score(employee_blocks_df['position'], employee_blocks_df['
    model_uw_1_block_id'])
```

```
0.15309516996415473
```

```
adjusted_mutual_info_score(employee_blocks_df['position'], employee_blocks_df['
    model_w_2_block_id'])
```

```
0.0756412457785869
```

```
adjusted_mutual_info_score(employee_blocks_df['model_w_2_block_id'],
    employee_blocks_df['model_uw_1_block_id'])
```

```
0.15563023649762936
```

With this information in mind, let's continue with the unweighted network to see if we can optimize it more, then examine the end result.

Model selection and optimization

Given the stochastic nature of these models, it is always advisable to run them a number of times and then select the model with the least entropy. (Higher entropy is not *inherently* bad. For example, a compressed JPEG image with only two colours will have a lot less entropy than one with a thousand colours.) In the case of SBMs, entropy returns the minimum description length, which is the amount of information the model needs to recreate the entire network. The goal of reducing entropy is fundamental to these models, with the assumption that minimizing entropy results in simpler models that do a better job of uncovering latent similarities in the data without overfitting. Remember, Occam's razor!

Below, we'll execute 10 runs of `minimize_nested_blockmodel_dl` and print the entropy for each:

```
states = [minimize_nested_blockmodel_dl(eG, deg_corr=True)
         for n in range(10)]
for s in states:
    print(s.entropy())
```

```
6162.281933127059
6187.135324492942
6168.918484063684
6161.190122173799
6163.517013260514
6162.876759036053
6178.052196472743
6154.1481501809185
6166.798460034726
6154.869718381805
```

We can automatically grab the lowest entropy state using `np.argmin`:

```
state = states[np.argmin([s.entropy() for s in states])]
```

More Markov chain Monte Carlo

At the expense of increased runtime, we can also follow up the above model selection process by sampling from the posterior distribution and running `mcmc_equilibrate`, which performs random changes in the block assignments of the nodes, automatically handles the entropy calculations, and chooses the optimum values at the end. This step is also required to collect the block assignment posterior marginals, which tell us the likelihood (if any) that a node belongs to each block, based on the assignments it was given during the iterations. More iterations here will always improve the model, but runtimes will increase and improvements will eventually diminish.

First, we will use the object `S1`, defined below, to keep track of the original entropy score to see how much we improved the model:

```
S1 = state.entropy()
S1
```

```
6154.1481501809185
```

To collect marginal probabilities with Markov chain Monte Carlo (MCMC), the blockstate needs to have been prepared for sampling, rather than for minimizing description length, which we can achieve by copying the blockstate and setting sampling to `True`. At the same time, we will add an additional four empty levels to the nested hierarchy so that the model has a chance to assign more levels. If these hierarchy levels don't improve the model, the equilibration method will collapse them.

```
state = state.copy(bs=state.get_bs() + [np.zeros(1)] * 4, sampling = True)
```

We're going to perform many iterations of the `mcmc_equilibrate` function, where nodes are moved between different blocks. Importantly, the MCMC method used in graph-tool doesn't perform fully random moves. By taking advantage of the assumption that networks are made up of heavily interdependent observations, the MCMC estimation only has to randomly sample from probable block assignment moves – to the blocks that a node's alters are members of.

We create a `callback` function to pass to `mcmc_equilibrate` so that we can collect a set of block assignment choices from each iteration. The bs values can be thought of as votes for block reassignment, and constitute the posterior marginal probability of each node's assignment to each block.

```
bs = []
## OUR CALLBACK FUNCTION THAT APPENDS EACH ESTIMATED BLOCKSTATE TO THE ARRAY
def collect_partitions(s):
    global bs
    bs.append(s.get_bs())
```

```
mcmc_equilibrate(state, force_niter=10000, mcmc_args=dict(niter=10), callback=
    collect_partitions)
```

```
(6159.927069603201, 37378153, 4808499)
```

Note that this will sometimes result in higher entropy for the block model solution! That's because we need to select the best partition from the ones added to the bs list by the `callback` function.

```
state.entropy() - S1
```

```
5.778919422760737
```

The `PartitionModeState` function takes our set of labelled partitions and tries to align them into a single set of common group labels. We can then use the `get_marginal()` method of the returned object to create a vertex property map of marginal probabilities for our original network graph. This property map can be used for calculations as well as for visualization of probable block memberships.

```
pmode = PartitionModeState(bs, nested=True, converge=True)
```

```
pv = pmode.get_marginal(eG)
eG.vertex_properties['pv'] = pv
```

Finally, the convenience function `get_max_nested()` returns the most likely block assignment for each node as a single final blockstate, which will group nodes in proximity to each other in our visualization based on their most likely membership. We apply this result back to our original blockstate object by providing it to the `copy()` method of the state object. Note that our entropy has improved a bit more here!

```
bs = pmode.get_max_nested()
state = state.copy(bs=bs)
state.entropy()
```

```
6153.278269237107
```

Let's recalculate the same mutual information scores we used earlier to see if things have improved on those criteria:

```
employee_blocks_df = get_block_membership(state, eG, employee_blocks_df, '
    model_uw_mcmc')
homogeneity_score(employee_blocks_df['position'], employee_blocks_df['
    model_uw_mcmc_block_id'])
```

```
0.38131989351325507
```

```
completeness_score(employee_blocks_df['position'], employee_blocks_df['
    model_uw_mcmc_block_id'])
```

```
0.3526819549124348
```

Homogeneity improves from 0.35 to almost 0.39, while completeness only improves a small amount.

```
adjusted_mutual_info_score(employee_blocks_df['position'], employee_blocks_df['
    model_uw_mcmc_block_id'])
```

```
0.1561547346951431
```

The adjusted mutual info score above is actually slightly worse than it was before! This doesn't necessarily mean the results are worse, though. We'll take a look at a different layout for the block model below and discuss some potential explanations for this.

Visualizing block connections as a radial tree

While the sfdp layout does a nice job of positioning nodes (and blocks) in spatial relation to each other, the radial tree layout can be very helpful for getting a sense of the connection patterns between the blocks and also keeps nodes together in a way that makes individual blocks very easy to distinguish. Since it is the default layout for printing a blockstate, we can easily obtain a simple representation using the `.draw()` method (see Figure 30.3):

```
state.draw()
```

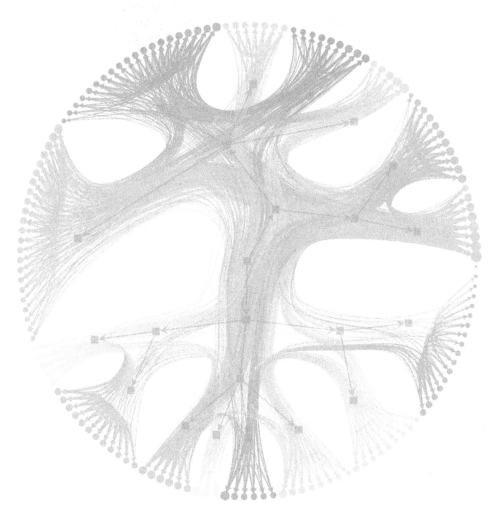

Figure 30.3 A hierarchical stochastic block model of the Enron network, visualized as a radial tree

As is often the case, there are a few preparation steps we can do to improve the visualization of edges, as well as to add node labels to our figure. This process is a bit complex and is an adaptation of one that was devised by the author of graph-tool. The details aren't particularly important, so we can use the utility function `label_radial_blockmodel` from the dcss package to take care of most of it:

```
eG = label_radial_blockmodel(eG, state)
```

The resulting figure is much improved (Figure 30.4) and clearly shows the relations between blocks, while also making it easier to examine which job titles were assigned to each block.

```
state.draw(
    vertex_text = eG.vertex_properties['title'],
    eorder = eG.edge_properties['edge_weight'],
    vertex_shape='pie',
    vertex_pie_fractions=eG.vertex_properties['pv'],
    edge_control_points = eG.edge_properties['cts'],
    pos=eG.vertex_properties['pos'],
    vertex_size=10,
    edge_pen_width = 0.2,
    bg_color=[255,255,255,1],
    vertex_text_rotation=eG.vertex_properties['text_rot'],
    vertex_text_position=0,
    output='../figures/core_state_radial_tree_labels.pdf'
    )
```

You'll notice that some of the nodes are broken up into pie fractions – these indicate their probability of being assigned to a different block. In the full-colour version, these fractions are coloured the same as the alternative block that the node might have been assigned to. You'll also notice that the blocks have become significantly more heterogeneous! Traders are in blocks with other traders, most lawyers are in a block that two other lawyers had some probability of being assigned to, and the CEOs are in fairly exclusive blocks. Although we no longer have three CEOs in one block with the COO, the block that one of the CEOs was moved to contains the other CEO, and their two respective blocks form a single block one level up the hierarchy! Earlier I mentioned that there are possible explanations for a decreased adjusted mutual information score and this is one example – that score doesn't incorporate the higher levels of the hierarchy. Even though it's probably actually a better model to have the four CEOs split evenly among two blocks, then put those two blocks together at the next hierarchy level, this would still negatively impact the mutual info score compared to the model where three CEOs were in one block.

It's quite clear from the results of these SBMs that there's some very powerful estimation going on, and that the Bayesian aspects of it allow a great deal of nuance. The versatility of the modelling that drives graph-tool has led to a collaborative extension for topic modelling. Given the relational nature of words in text, topics can be discovered by applying stochastic block models to text data to great effect. We'll explore this method in the section that follows.

TopSBM: a unified Bayesian approach to latent variable modelling for text and networks

At the start of this chapter, I noted that there is a deep underlying similarity between SBMs and LDA. Both are hierarchical Bayesian models developed to overcome the limitations of widely used deterministic methods. Recently, Gerlach et al. (2018) have generalized SBMs to text data as an alternative to LDA, and in doing so they have addressed some of the limitations inherent in the baseline LDA models we discussed in the previous chapter. Specifically, TopSBM, as the generalization is known, makes use of the full set of additional inferential techniques described above that enable it to:

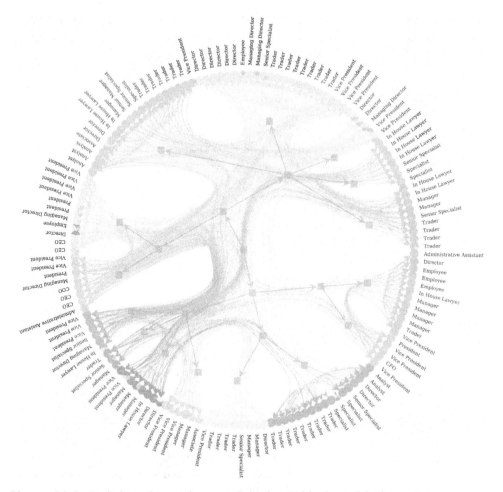

Figure 30.4 Radial tree layout for nested stochastic block model of core Enron employees, with nodes labelled by job title. Nodes are divided into pie fractions that reflect their posterior probability of being assigned to other blocks

- explore a broader variety of topic mixtures by avoiding the use of a Dirichlet prior;
- remove the need to select a number of topics in advance due to the specific hierarchical design of the model, and the use of hyperpriors;
- use efficient MCMC posterior inference rather than variational inference, which means that the model can handle large-scale data without relying on an optimization strategy.

The TopSBM approach models text datasets as a bipartite network, which is a network that has two types of nodes, and where connections are only allowed across types. In this case, the two types of nodes are words and documents, where we assign an edge between words and documents if a word appears in a document, but we do *not* assign edges from word to word, or document to document.

One of the deep conceptual similarities here is that the matrix form of a bipartite network is directly analogous to a document-term matrix. In fact, when the nodes in the bipartite network are words and documents, as they are here, *the matrices are identical*. The identical underlying data structures and the conceptual similarity of the goals of recovering latent topics in text data and latent blocks in network data (or communities, for that matter) allows us to easily develop SBM models for text data. In doing so, we benefit from the additional inferential techniques that have been developed for SBMs.

A full discussion of TopSBM is beyond the scope of this chapter, and sadly so is developing a model. A full example of developing a TopSBM is available in the supplementary online material. Once you've looked it over, I strongly encourage you to put your developing skills to use and try your hand at developing your own. Meanwhile, if you want to learn more about the theory and mathematics behind TopSBM, or better understand the relationship between topic modelling and block modelling and community detection, I recommend reading Gerlach et al. (2018). If you just want to take a look at some results, there is a pickle available in the ../data/ pickles directory, and a few example topics in a dataframe below. This model was run on a 100,000 random sample of the Canadian Hansards (and took quite a long time to complete).

```
topSBM_model = pickle.load( open( '../data/pickles/can_hansard_100k_sample_topSBM.pkl'
    , 'rb'))


topic_dict = topSBM_model.topics(l=1,n=20)


df_list = []
for topic in [76,91,200,228,104,126]:
    df = pd.DataFrame.from_records(topic_dict[topic], columns = ['words_' + str(topic)
    , 'scores_' + str(topic)])
    df_list.append(df)
topic_df = pd.concat(df_list, axis=1)
topic_df.head(20)
```

	words_76	scores_76	words_91	scores_91	words_200	scores_200 \
0	gas	0.184736	regime	0.206437	infrastructure	0.259398
1	climate	0.141000	violation	0.109540	municipality	0.131606
2	carbon	0.101561	Iran	0.064138	road	0.109510
3	emission	0.088723	torture	0.049770	building	0.093287
4	clean	0.075559	protest	0.032759	municipal	0.077184
5	greenhouse	0.069086	iranian	0.029655	construction	0.059265
6	fuel	0.065223	Cuba	0.026782	transit	0.058902
7	pollution	0.048523	activist	0.023678	mayor	0.042920
8	green	0.046075	brutal	0.019885	bus	0.026273
9	ethanol	0.013056	Egypt	0.018966	design	0.018221
10	heating	0.012566	dictator	0.017126	stream	0.013742
11	warming	0.012185	systematic	0.015632	councillor	0.011926
12	fossil	0.012131	Venezuela	0.014253	Municipalities	0.011320
13	temperature	0.011913	Khadr	0.013448	sewer	0.008112
14	Climate	0.009846	execution	0.012644	Mayor	0.007022
15	polluter	0.009248	embargo	0.011494	pass	0.006659
16	Change	0.009084	Omar	0.011034	upgrade	0.004903
17	pollutant	0.006582	Amnesty	0.010920	shovel	0.004480

18	dioxide	0.006473	Burma	0.010575	subway	0.003753
19	diesel	0.006093	Myanmar	0.009195	Road	0.003753

	words_228	scores_228	words_104	scores_104	words_126 \
0	emergency	0.360683	social	0.351863	society
1	vaccine	0.064984	poverty	0.166007	principle
2	virus	0.054231	poor	0.128998	value
3	outbreak	0.047920	rich	0.067926	institution
4	SARS	0.046517	living	0.055031	fundamental
5	pandemic	0.040673	welfare	0.051680	basic
6	spread	0.040673	wealth	0.038989	equal
7	epidemic	0.039037	decent	0.020104	voice
8	preparedness	0.031791	inequality	0.016753	concept
9	Ebola	0.030856	disadvantaged	0.016347	powerful
10	dose	0.023142	load	0.012793	ideal
11	H1N1	0.022207	hungry	0.008529	characteristic
12	flu	0.021272	disparity	0.007869	like
13	influenza	0.020570	needy	0.006650	cornerstone
14	quarantine	0.020103	steady	0.005584	noble
15	infectious	0.018700	kitchen	0.005026	Coalition
16	kit	0.014960	pie	0.005026	institutional
17	mask	0.014493	clothe	0.005026	philosophical
18	containment	0.013558	tory	0.004366	motivated
19	avian	0.012856	soup	0.002741	hallmark

	scores_126
0	0.191839
1	0.164089
2	0.145013
3	0.115906
4	0.085317
5	0.066920
6	0.052844
7	0.048091
8	0.043677
9	0.016174
10	0.008890
11	0.008581
12	0.007964
13	0.007007
14	0.005772
15	0.005062
16	0.004784
17	0.003519
18	0.002469
19	0.002346

As you can see, these topics end up being pretty coherent! There were 267 topics found from this run, and the majority of them are intuitive enough that they seem a bit obvious. This is a good thing.

30.5 Conclusion

The key points in this chapter are as follows:

- Hierarchical SBMs are remarkably powerful models that provide a nearly unparalleled degree of insight into the structure of a network and nodes' roles within it.
- SBMs build on the Bayesian intuitions established earlier in this book; they employ a similar approach of using latent variables and prior distributions to model unknown/unobserved variables.
- TopSBM helps clarify the deep similarities between detecting latent topic structure in text data with LDA topic models and latent block structure in networks using stochastic block models.

Visit the website at https://study.sagepub.com/mclevey for additional resources

PART VII

EMBEDDINGS, TRANSFORMER MODELS, AND NAMED ENTITY RECOGNITION

31

CAN WE MODEL MEANING? CONTEXTUAL REPRESENTATION AND NEURAL WORD EMBEDDINGS

31.1 Learning Objectives

By the end of this chapter, you should be able to do the following:

- Learn what word embeddings models are and what they can be used for
- Learn what Word2vec is and how the continuous bag-of-words and skip-gram architectures differ
- Understand why we should not trust intuitions about complex high-dimensional vector spaces

31.2 Learning Materials

You can find the online learning materials for this chapter in `doing_computational_social_science/Chapter_31`. `cd` into the directory and launch your Jupyter server.

31.3 Introduction

The text analysis models we've been working with to this point in the book have primarily been focused on fairly traditional content-analytic tasks, such as describing and comparing the thematic content contained in a collection of text documents. Nearly all of these models have been based on long and sparse vector representations of text data, otherwise known as a 'bag-of-words'. In this chapter, we will learn how to represent text data with short dense vectors, otherwise known as word embeddings. Embeddings have interesting implications if used to understand how different words are used in similar contexts, giving us insights into patterns of language use. There is a tendency to think of embeddings as proxies for meaning, but for reasons that will become clear in this chapter, we should practise a bit of scepticism here.

In what follows, we'll discuss some of the challenges involved with modelling meaning in general, followed by an introduction to using neural word embedding models. As always, we'll break the models down to better understand how they work. Then we'll spend a bit of time working with pretrained embeddings to deepen your understanding of embeddings and to get a feel for vector space. We'll emphasize fairly simple vector maths operations with these embeddings to help you understand why we need to be very careful when interpreting the results of analyses that bundle together many vector operations to construct larger 'dimensions' of cultural meaning. Finally, I'll close the chapter by showing you how to train your own word embedding models, including how to train multiple models in a way that facilitates valid cross-sectional comparisons and historical/temporal analysis.

31.4 What Words Mean

Word embeddings have received a lot of interest as quantitative representations of what words 'mean'. It's an astoundingly complex problem, and we need to tread very carefully. So, before we get into the specifics of the models, let's take a moment to briefly consider some of the relevant theoretical background here.

Questions about *meaning* and its consequences for social science enquiry have been at the centre of some of the biggest theoretical and methodological debates and divides in sociology and other social sciences since at least the early twentieth century (for a fascinating discussion in the context of contemporary cultural sociology, see Mohr et al., 2020). Researchers primarily concerned with understanding meaning have tended to prefer more qualitative and interpretivist approaches. Historically, this complexity has led many quantitatively minded researchers to concede serious efforts to understand meaning to interpretivists and to focus instead on describing and comparing *content*.

Despite this long-standing paradigmatic and methodological fault line, these have never been the only two options for social science text analysis. For example, relational sociologists working at the intersection of cultural sociology and social network analysis have developed a wide variety of formal and mathematical models of the cultural–cognitive dimensions of institutions and for inductively exploring and modelling 'meaning structures' (Edelmann and Mohr, 2018; Mohr, 1998; Mohr and Bogdanov, 2013; Mohr et al., 2015). Much of the theoretical and methodological considerations guiding text-analytic work in 'relational sociology' have evolved in lockstep with network analysis (see Crossley, 2010; Emirbayer, 1997; Mische, 2011), and in particular with the evolution of network-analytic methods that are focused on understanding relational identities, the cultural–cognitive dimensions of institutions, and the dynamics of socio-semantic networks (which combine network analysis with various kinds of natural language processing). These developments are interesting in part because much of network analysis in the era of the 1970s and 1980s energetically eschewed all questions of culture and meaning, considered intractable and unscientific, in pursuit of establishing a thoroughly *structural* paradigm. But from the 1990s onwards, even the most fervent structuralists were taking culture and meaning seriously (e.g. White, 1992), in search of a deeper understanding of the co-constitution of social structure (networks) and culture (meanings, practices, identities, etc.). Much has happened since then.

As part of this larger effort to integrate relational theory and methods, we've seen a proliferation of new methodological tools and approaches for text analysis – some developed 'in-house', others imported – that try to avoid counterproductive dichotomies (e.g. quantitative and qualitative, inductive and deductive, exploratory and confirmatory). The embedding methods I introduce in this chapter and the next can be seen as another contribution to efforts to measure and model meaning structures. They have opened up new discussions in computational research on culture, knowledge, and ideology (Kozlowski et al., 2019; Linzhuo et al., 2020; McLevey et al., 2022; Rheault and Cochrane, 2020; Stoltz and Taylor, 2019; Taylor and Stoltz, 2020), including deeply embedded cultural stereotypes and collective biases (Bolukbasi et al., 2016; Garg et al., 2018; Jones et al., 2020; Papakyriakopoulos et al., 2020). There are also ongoing efforts to develop new methodological tools for using word embeddings to conduct research, informed by intersectionality theory (Collins, 2015; Collins and Bilge, 2020; Crenshaw, 1989), on the social categories and institutions that intersect to create and maintain social inequality and systems of oppression (e.g. Nelson, 2021). We will briefly discuss these and other applications below.

Of course, sociologists and other social scientists are not the only ones who've struggled long and hard with the problem of measuring and modelling meaning. The dominant way of modelling meaning in the field of computational linguistics has deep affinities with social science paradigms. The branch of linguistics concerned with meaning is called semantics, and in many respects, its starting point is the failure of dictionary-based approaches for defining the meaning of words. Paul Elbourne's (2011) book *Meaning: A Slim Guide to Semantics* starts with a thorough debunking of the dictionary approach to meaning, showing the limitations of everyday dictionary definitions when applied to the laborious work done by philosophers over thousands of years to define the meaning of specific words like 'knowledge'. Many social scientists who gripe about the lack of broadly shared definitions of core concepts in our field – for example, culture, network, field, habitus, system, identity, class, gender, and so on – will be comforted to know that similar concerns are raised in other sciences and in engineering, like metallurgists being unable to reach a consensus on an acceptable definition of metal (Elbourne, 2011: 9).

We are used to the idea that dictionaries are an authority on meaning, but of course, dictionary definitions change over time in response to how language is used. For example, *Merriam-Webster* recently added 'they' as a personal pronoun, reflecting large-scale social changes in how we think and talk about gender identities. Other new words, phrases, and concepts from popular culture have also been added, such as the Bechdel test, swole, on point, page view, screen time, cyber safety, bottle episode, go cup, gig economy, and climate change denial. Culture and language evolve.

Elbourne (2011) provides many examples of the 'mind-boggling complexity' involved in giving adequate definitions to the meanings of words. His larger point is that any definition-based approach to assigning meanings to words (including dictionaries) will *always* be unsatisfactory. A serious theory or approach to modelling meaning needs much more than definitions. His comparison of different cognitive and linguistic theories is well worth reading but is beyond the scope of this chapter, but one of the key takeaways is that meanings are *not definitions* and they are not determined by the characteristics of the things they refer to. Instead, meanings are concepts that reside in our heads and are generally attached to low-level units like words, which are strongly modified by the contexts in which they're used and scale up to higher-level units like sentences. These meanings are shared but not universal. When it comes to any given thing – say the word 'populist' – the concept in my head is not *identical* to the concept in your head, but communication does not break down because our concepts are qualitatively similar.

We might not mean *exactly* the same thing by the word populist, but our concepts overlap sufficiently enough that we can have a meaningful conversation and our interactions don't descend into conceptual chaos.

The core sociological idea here is grounded in a critique of two extremes. Traditional philosophical approaches to cognition and meaning have been overly focused on individual thinking and meaning. Conversely, neuroscience primarily focuses on processes presumed to be more or less universal, such as understanding the biological and chemical mechanisms that enable thought *in general* rather than explaining specific thoughts. But as Karen Cerulo and many others have pointed out, even if the cognitive *processes* are universal, cognitive *products* are not (Cerulo, 2002, 2010; Ignatow, 2009; Lizardo et al., 2019). There is variation in how groups of people – societies, subcultures, whatever – perceive the world, draw boundaries, employ metaphors and analogies, and so on (Brekhus and Ignatow, 2019; DiMaggio, 1997). These meaning structures are not reducible to concepts in individual people's heads; they are embedded in different cultural systems that are external to any individual person and are *shared but not universal*. Given this variability and the staggering complexity of meaning *in general*, we can best understand *meaning* by observing and comparing how groups of people use language in context.

The idea that we could best understand shared but not universal meanings by studying how groups of people use language was, surprisingly, a revolutionary idea as recently as the 1950s. It was most famously posited by the famed philosopher Ludwig Wittgenstein (1953), whose argument that 'meaning resides in use' was the inspiration behind the *specific* linguistic hypothesis that informs embedding models and is a common theme underlying many of the recent breakthroughs in natural language processing: the distributional hypothesis.

The distributional hypothesis

Wittgenstein's (1953) proposal that empirical observations of how people actually use language could reveal far more about meaning than formal rules derived through logical analysis was taken up by a group of linguists in the 1950s (especially Firth, 1957; Harris, 1954; Joos, 1950) who first proposed the distributional hypothesis, which has informed approaches to measuring and modelling meaning in language data ever since.

According to the distributional hypothesis, words that appear in similar semantic contexts, or 'environments', will tend to have similar meanings. In one of the foundational statements of the idea, Zellig Harris (1954) defined a word's context in terms of the other words that it *co-occurs* with, given some boundary such as a phrase or a sentence. For example, we can infer that 'physician' and 'doctor' mean similar things if we see that they tend to be used interchangeably in sentences like 'Alondra is looking for a [physician, doctor, ...] specializing in pain management'. Across many texts, we might also learn that 'doctor' and 'professor' are also more or less interchangeable but in different types of contexts. While the former pair of words might co-occur in contexts shared with words such as 'pain', 'medicine', 'nurse', and 'injury', the latter pair may co-occur in contexts shared with words like 'university', 'students', 'research', 'teaching', and 'knowledge'. 'Professor' and 'physician' may also co-occur, but more rarely. In any instance, the meaning of the words depends on the other words surrounding it. Words that have identical or nearly identical contexts are synonyms. In fact, the distributional hypothesis bears a striking resemblance to the idea of structural equivalence in social network analysis, which was introduced in Chapter 29. (Like synonyms, people who are structurally similar tend to be connected to the same alters.)

Distributionalists like Harris and Firth believe that formal theories of language should be kept to a minimum and knowledge should be produced by rigorous analysis of empirical data on language use. Given enough data on natural language use (e.g. in everyday interactions, in email messages and social media posts, in news stories and scientific publications, etc.), we can learn an enormous amount about the contextual relationships between words *as they are actually used*. In practice, this idea is operationalized in terms of vector semantics, and it is the foundation of all modern natural language processing that is concerned with understanding *meaning* (Jurafsky and Hand, 2009).

With that briefest of context introduced, let's turn our attention to word embeddings.

31.5 What Are Neural Word Embeddings?

In previous chapters, we used bag-of-word models to represent individual documents as *long* and *sparse* vectors, and document collections as *wide, sparse* matrices (i.e. document-term matrices [DTMs]). These matrices are wide because each feature represents a unique word in the vocabulary, and they are sparse because most words do not appear in most documents, which means that most cells (which represent presence/absence, frequency, or some sort of weight such as TF-IDF) have values of 0. Bag-of-word models can be very powerful for modelling latent distributions of topical content, but it seems that we can gain more insight into what words 'mean' by using shorter, denser vector representations, generally referred to as word embeddings. Words are just the beginning, though. In recent years, computational social scientists have been developing methods for using embeddings to explore and model meaning and larger cultural systems in ways that were not possible just a short time ago (e.g. Kozlowski et al., 2019; McLevey et al., 2022; Nelson 2021; Linzhuo et al. 2020; Stoltz and Taylor, 2019; Taylor and Stoltz, 2020).

In bag-of-word models, we represent *documents* with long sparse vectors indicating the presence or absence, frequency, or weight of a word in each document. Embeddings differ in that they represent *words* with short dense vectors that capture information about the local semantic contexts within which words are used. Figure 31.1 illustrates this idea of local semantic contexts using a window of five words that slides over each word in sentence from Neblo et al. (2018). This sliding window approach gives us much deeper insight into how words relate to other words, but it comes at the cost of fine-grained information about how each word relates to the documents in which they appeared.

In addition to (1) assigning vectors to words instead of documents, (2) observing co-occurrences within small local contexts rather than entire documents, and (3) using short dense vectors instead of long sparse vectors, embeddings are also different in that (4) the vector representation for any given word is *learnt* by a neural network trained on positive and negative examples of co-occurrence data. (In fact, we could have extracted embeddings from the neural networks we trained in Chapter 23!) Words that tend to appear in the same contexts, but rarely with one another, tend to share meanings. The learnt word embeddings put words with similar meanings close to one another in vector space.

Learning embeddings with Word2vec

Now that we have some context for understanding embeddings, let's discuss one of the most important recent breakthroughs in *learning* word embeddings from text data – Word2vec.

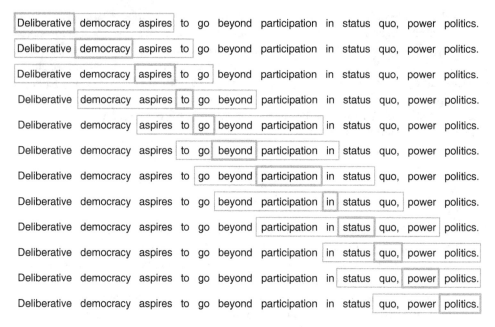

Figure 31.1 An example showing how a sliding window moves over a snippet of text

As with previous chapters, the goal here is mainly to clarify the way the models work at a relatively high level.

The development of Word2vec by Tomas Mikolov and a team of researchers at Google (Mikolov, Chen, et al., 2013; Mikolov, Sutskever, et al., 2013) was a transformative development in natural language processing. As we've already discussed, word embedding models in general are focused on the local semantic contexts that words are used in rather than the documents they appear in; they *learn* these short dense representations from the data rather than relying on count-based features. Let's break down the modelling process.

Word2vec has two different architectures: continuous bag-of-words (CBOW) and skip-gram. Both use word co-occurrence data generated from local semantic contexts, such as a moving window of five words around a focal word as shown in the example in Figure 31.1. However, CBOW and skip-gram use this co-occurrence data differently: CBOW uses the *context words* (within each thin crimson box) in a shallow neural network model trained to predict the target word (in each thick crimson box), whereas skip-gram uses the target word to predict the context words. The interesting thing about the neural network model used in these two architectures is that *we don't actually care about their predictions*. What we care about are the feature weights that the neural networks learn in the context of figuring out how to make their predictions well. *Those feature weights are our word embeddings, which are sometimes simply referred to as word 'vectors'.* We only train the neural network models to obtain the embeddings. That's their *raison d'être*.

The shallow neural network models that Word2vec uses to learn the embeddings, illustrated in Figure 31.1 (which is adapted from Mikolov, Sutskever, et al., 2013), have a few clever modifications. In CBOW, the *non-linear* hidden layer is replaced by a much simpler *linear* projection. For each token in the dataset, the neural network model takes the average of the vectors of the token's context words (or in some cases the sum of those vectors) and then attempts to predict the target word. After the neural network makes its prediction, the resulting probabilities are used to update the vectors for both the target token *and* the vectors of the context tokens that were averaged (or summed). Once training is done, each word is represented with a single, dense vector – its embedding. For skip-gram, the neural network attempts to predict context words using the target word, and the outputs of the prediction task are a set of error vectors for each context word, which are them summed and used to update the embeddings.

The second Word2vec innovation is that the functions used to make predictions in the output layer differ from those that are typically used in neural network models. The skip-gram architecture replaces the traditional softmax classifier with a much more efficient hierarchical softmax variant,[1] while the CBOW architecture replaces it with a binary logistic regression classifier. This is an especially valuable innovation for CBOW, as using the traditional softmax classifier to make and evaluate predictions would require updating the vectors for every word in the vocabulary every time the model makes a prediction for every token in the corpus! Instead, Word2vec uses a clever innovation called negative sampling, in which the target word is evaluated as either co-occurring with the context words from the moving window or not, which enables the use of binary logistic regression in the output layer. In Figure 31.2, *T* represents the target word, and the indices represent word position in relation to the target word.

If you're thinking *'hold up, won't the context words all have a score of 1?'*, you're right! To deal with this problem, the model randomly selects the required number of negative samples from the rest of the corpus (i.e. not from the local semantic context) and assigns them all 0s for that particular batch. As a result, the embeddings only need to be slightly increased for the target and context words and slightly decreased for the words from the negative sample.

The CBOW architecture is a variant of bag-of-words in that word sequence *within the local semantic context* does not have an impact on the prediction task described above, but the similarities end there. Rather than creating one large static matrix, the 'continuous' part of CBOW refers to how the sliding window moves through the whole corpus, creating and then discarding a small bag-of-words for each target word. Since the embeddings for each of the context words are averaged (or summed) for the prediction task, the semantic context is flattened to a single vector regardless of the number of words in the semantic context. For this reason, it's better to keep the semantic contexts fairly small. Otherwise the averaging (or summing) of embeddings can result in a nondescript vector soup, with the subtleties of each word increasingly diminished by the inclusion of more distant words. The authors of Word2vec report that a window size of 4 on each side of the target word produced the best results for them.

Recall that in the skip-gram architecture, the input and prediction tasks are basically the inverse of CBOW. Rather than using the average (or sum) of the embeddings of context words to try to predict the target word, skip-gram uses the target word to try to predict the context words. There is no averaging or summing of vectors before training, and since the training process focuses on the relationship between the target word and many different context words,

---

[1] A discussion of the hierarchical softmax variant is beyond the scope of this chapter, but the simplified version is that words and their outputs are arranged in a tree-like pattern, such that many words (leaves) are often connected to the same output and their embeddings can all be updated from a single calculation. The more important thing to know is that hierarchical softmax tends to perform better on infrequent words, whereas negative sampling performs better on frequent words. Either of these classifiers can be used for both the CBOW and skip-gram options, and can actually be used at the same time.

embeddings learnt by skip-gram tend to be more subtle and lossless than those learnt by CBOW. Skip-gram has a much longer training time, though, because each word under consideration is used to predict multiple context words before updating the embeddings for those context words. As with CBOW, we can improve the training runtime by using negative sampling.

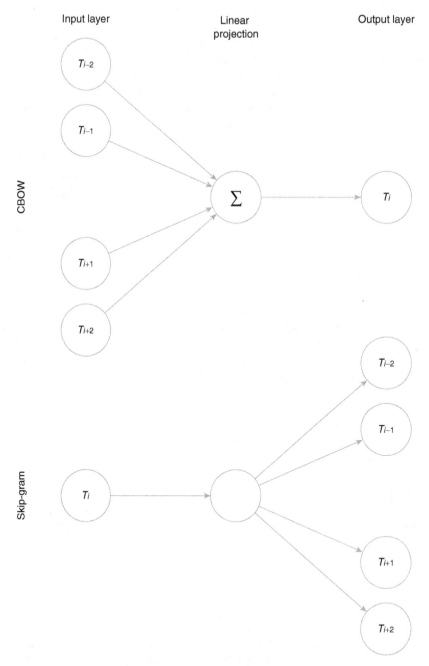

Figure 31.2 A diagram comparing how the continuous bag-of-words architecture differs from the skip-gram architecture

Unlike CBOW, where the averaging or summing of embeddings prior to prediction can result in a less informative vector soup if the semantic contexts are too large, skip-gram actually *benefits* from larger window sizes (at the expense of increased runtime). One benefit is that the lack of averaging or summing means any updates to the weights are specific to that word and are therefore more precise. Secondly, there are far more updates to the embeddings, as each word is used in far more model predictions than would be the case in CBOW. Finally, skip-gram models do consider word ordering *a bit*, in that they weight relationships between the target word and context words based on how far away they are within the semantic context, so a window of 10, for example, is a pretty good balance.

Both model architectures, then, have their strengths and weaknesses. The CBOW architecture is a bit better at learning syntactic relationships, so it is likely to produce embeddings where word pairs like 'neuron' and 'neurons' or 'broken' and 'broke' will be very similar. CBOW also tends to better represent frequently appearing words and is faster to train, so it is well-suited to large corpuses. Skip-gram models produce more precise word embeddings in general, and especially for rare words, and is very good at finding words that are near-synonyms. The cost of these improvements is increases in runtime, but in cases where that is less of a concern (e.g. working with smaller datasets), the improvements can certainly be worth the wait. The differences between these architectures are less significant given the specific model parameters used and given enough iterations.

31.6 Cultural Cartography: Getting a Feel for Vector Space

Word embeddings are very powerful for many applications, and sometimes the results are astonishing. But there are some very important caveats to keep in mind when using Word2vec-style embeddings. I'll illustrate some of these caveats with perhaps the most iconic and oft-referenced example of word embedding 'analogies': 'King − Man + Woman = Queen'.

King − Man + Woman ≠ Queen

Mikolov, Wen-tau Yih, et al. (2013) famously found that if you take the word embedding vector for 'king', add it to the vector for 'woman', and then subtract the vector for 'man', the resulting vector is 'very close' to the vector for 'queen'. This example has been referenced countless times, including in package documentation and papers that aim to measure and compare complex cultural concepts.

We will use the very convenient `whatlies` package to plot the iconic word embedding example:

```
from whatlies import Embedding
from whatlies.embeddingset import EmbeddingSet
from whatlies.language import SpacyLanguage
lang = SpacyLanguage('en_core_web_md')

import pandas as pd
pd.set_option("display.notebook_repr_html", False)
from dcss.utils import list_files, IterSents, mp_disk
from dcss.text import bigram_process
```

```
import gensim
from multiprocessing import Process, Manager
from gensim.utils import simple_preprocess

import matplotlib.pyplot as plt
from dcss.plotting import custom_seaborn
custom_seaborn()
```

Using the `plot()` function, we can plot either a single word vector, or some mathematical combination of vectors enclosed in brackets (as shown in Figure 31.3). If you call `plot()` multiple times in the same cell, all of the requested vectors will show up in the figure:

```
(lang['queen'] - lang['king']).plot(kind='arrow', color='lightgray', show_ops=True)
(lang['king'] + lang['woman'] - lang['man']).plot(kind='arrow', color='lightgray',
    show_ops=True)

lang['man'].plot(kind='arrow', color='crimson')
lang['woman'].plot(kind='arrow', color='crimson')

lang['king'].plot(kind='arrow', color='black')
lang['queen'].plot(kind='arrow', color='black')

plt.axis('off');
plt.show()
```

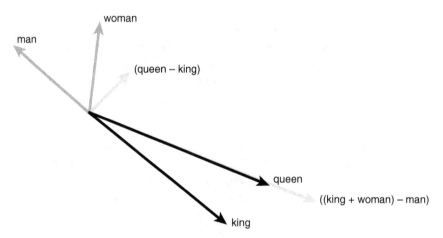

Figure 31.3 A plot of the now-famous '((king + woman) – man) = queen' 'finding', using word embeddings and vector algebra to find regularities in the embedding space

The combination vector appears to be virtually identical to the vector for 'queen'. But there is more to this than meets the eye. Let's look at a few comparisons between the vectors with some useful vector combination and comparison functions built-in to whatlies.

```
print("Queen and King: " + str(lang['queen'].distance(lang['king'])))
print("Man and Woman: " + str(lang['man'].distance(lang['woman'])))
print("Man and King: " + str(lang['man'].distance(lang['king'])))
print("Woman and King: " + str(lang['woman'].distance(lang['king'])))
```

```
Queen and King: 0.27473903
Man and Woman: 0.2598256
Man and King: 0.59115386
Woman and King: 0.7344341
```

Take note that 'queen' and 'king', and 'man' and 'woman', aren't very distant from each other (this is cosine distance). This is because they actually *share* a lot of the same semantic contexts; that is, they are used, conversationally, in very similar ways. Let's do the vector maths:

```
king_woman_no_man = lang['king'] + lang['woman'] - lang['man']
print("King and combo-vector:" + str(lang['king'].distance(king_woman_no_man)))
print("Queen and combo-vector: " + str(lang['queen'].distance(king_woman_no_man)))
```

```
King and combo-vector:0.19757414
Queen and combo-vector: 0.21191555
```

The combined vector *that should be almost the same as 'queen'* is actually still closer to the vector for 'king'. Given the plot above, in which the combined vector appears to be much closer to 'queen', how is this possible? This is the first caveat: word embedding vectors are *high-dimensional* spaces – in this case, we are dealing with a 300-dimensional space – and at most we can visualize the relationships between words in three dimensions. The plots we have used here are two-dimensional. In short, there is a *lot* of data reduction happening in visualizations such as these, and we need to be properly sceptical of what we (think we) see.

Let's get a different perspective on things by using `plot_interactive()` (a screenshot of which is shown in Figure 31.4). First, we add the vectors to an `EmbeddingSet()` class instance. Then it's as simple as adding `.plot_interactive()` to that object, along with a few parameters, including the distance metric to use for the axes (cosine distance):

```
## RENAME THE COMBINATION VECTOR BECAUSE THE ORIGINAL ('MAN') WOULD BE USED FOR THE
    PLOT
king_woman_no_man.orig = king_woman_no_man.name
king_queen_man_woman_plus = EmbeddingSet(lang['king'], lang['queen'],
                                lang['man'], lang['woman'], king_woman_no_man
    )
king_queen_man_woman_plus.plot_interactive(x_axis=lang["king"],
                                y_axis=lang["queen"],
                                axis_metric = 'cosine_similarity')
```

This helps put things into perspective. The combination vector is nearly equidistant (0.8) from both 'king' and 'queen'! Recall the point I made earlier about how these words, which you might be tempted to consider opposites, actually *share a lot of semantic contexts*. Their embeddings are all wrapped up with each other. When you subtract the vector for 'man' from the vector for 'woman', you are actually taking some defining details away from the vector for 'woman' because you've removed parts of the contexts that they share! Here's an illustrative example:

```
print("Woman and Queen: " + str(lang['woman'].distance(lang['queen'])))
print("Woman and Queen without man: " + str((lang['woman']-lang['man']).distance(lang[
    'queen'])))
```

Woman and Queen: 0.5933935

Woman and Queen without man: 0.7745669

The distance between 'woman' and 'queen' actually increases by about 18% if you subtract the vector for 'man'!

Hopefully you can see why we need to be *extremely* careful and methodical in any research that relies on complex combinations of word vectors, and in fact you might want to avoid such complex combinations entirely. If you find yourself in a situation where one term is more central to the concept you're examining than others, for example, bundling together a series of vector operations often results in less important words outweighing the vector for the important word.

Since embeddings are just arrays, it is possible to weight the entire array to change the contribution of each individual word vector to the combined vector. For example, we can access the raw vectors for 'woman' and 'man', multiply the vector for 'man' by 0.5 to remove only half of the vector for 'man', and then create a new Embedding class object:

```
print("Woman and Queen without man: " + str(Embedding('halfway', lang['woman'].vector-
    lang['man'].vector*0.5).distance(lang['queen']))
```

Woman and Queen without man: 0.61308193

As you can see, removing only half of the vector for 'man' dramatically reduces the amount of extra distance between 'woman' and 'queen'.

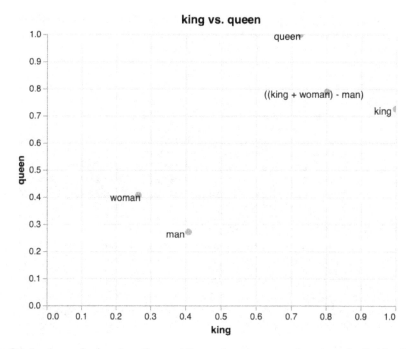

Figure 31.4 A graph showing the positions of various word vectors (individual and arithmetic combinations) as measured by their cosine distance from 'queen' and 'king', respectively

Despite these issues, you will find that in some implementations of Word2vec, 'queen' will be returned as the 'most similar' word to the combined vector. Typically, when you use an in-built function to combine words and then return the most similar words, the results returned will *not* include the constituent words! If they didn't, those functions would always return the word itself as the top similar word! This is understandable for a convenience function, but it is also important to be aware of when using embeddings for research. This issue has been noted and discussed in more detail previously, with some heavy caution about the use of word analogy tasks for any serious research purposes (Nissim et al., 2020). The authors also reference the introductory paper for transformer models, which we'll introduce in the next chapter, noting that they've completely eliminated the concept of analogy as either a training task, or model evaluation method. And though more complex, transformer models can be used to better accomplish some of the tasks that word embeddings are currently being used for (McLevey et al., 2022).

In short, word embeddings are a major advance in NLP and can offer deep insights in how language is used. When trained and interpreted with care, they are useful but imperfect proxies for meaning, but we should be very careful, and properly sceptical, when jumping from vector operations with individual words to complex combinations of vector operations involving many words at once.

31.7 Learning Embeddings with Gensim

So far, we've worked with pretrained embeddings. In the rest of this chapter, I'll show you how to train your own Word2vec embedding models, including for temporal/historical and comparative research.

Data

We'll train our Word2vec models using the Canadian Hansards dataset:

```
datasets = list_files("../data/canadian_hansards/lipad/", 'csv')
len(datasets)
```

3401

Training good word embeddings requires a lot of text, and we want to avoid loading all that text into memory at once. Gensim's algorithm expects only a single sentence at a time, so a clever way to avoid consuming a lot of memory is to store each sentence from the data on its own line in a text file, and then read that enormous text file into memory one line at a time, passing the sentence to Gensim. That way, we never have to hold all of our data in memory at the same time.

This requires some preprocessing. The Canadian Hansards data is provided as a large collection of CSV files, each containing a single Series with full text for a given speech. We want to get each sentence from each speech in each dataset, while working as efficiently as possible and minimizing the amount of data held in memory.

The function below is one way to do this. It will take some time to run, but perhaps not as long as you would think given how much data we are working with here, and given that we can use the mp_disk utility for multiprocessing to take advantage of available CPU (central processing unit) cores. A less general version of the mp utility, mp_disk, accepts an iterable (e.g.

a list) of the data that needs processing, the function you'll use to process it, a filename to write the results to, and any other arguments that the processing function needs.

You may notice the unexplained q object at the end of this function call. Although a full discussion of the ins and outs of multiprocessing is beyond the scope of this chapter, it is useful to know a little bit about what is going on here. The q and the m objects are specific instances of general classes in Python's multiprocessing module that allow us to write to a text file from multiple parallel processes without having to worry about file access locks or file corruption. The iterable with the data in it will also be divided into multiple lists, so that each CPU core can work on its own subset, so it's important that the function is prepared to deal with a list of data and also return that data in a list.

The next block of text iterates over each of the dataframes in the batch, adding the speeches from each to a list. The batch of speeches is sent to our bigram_process function, which as you may recall expects a flat list of documents, segments each into sentences, and then creates the flat list of sentences that Gensim expects for bigram model training. The utility function returns a list of untokenized sentences, with bigram pairs of words joined by _.

To cap off the process, we send each batch of results to the multiprocessing Queue object so that each sentence can be written onto a new line of the file speeches.txt. Before sending the sentences to the file writing Queue, we join them into a single string with a new line character in between, because this is much faster than having the multiprocessing Queue write each line to the output file individually.

Whew! Let's do it:

```
def get_sentences(dataset):
    dfs = [pd.read_csv(df) for df in dataset]
    speeches = []

    for df in dfs:
        speeches.extend(df['speechtext'].tolist())
    speeches = [str(s).replace('\n|\r', ' ') for s in speeches]
    _, sentences = bigram_process(speeches, n_process = 1)
    sentences = '\n'.join(sentences)

    q.put(sentences)
```

Below, we use the above get_sentences() function to process the data in our datasets object, writing the results out to speeches.txt, with each sentence from each speech getting its own line in the file. It will take some time to run, but perhaps not as long as you would think given how much data we are working with here.

```
m = Manager()
q = m.Queue()
mp_disk(datasets, get_sentences, '../data/txt_files/can_hansard_speeches.txt', q)
```

Let's do a quick count to see how many words our dataset contains:

```
with open('../data/txt_files/can_hansard_speeches.txt') as file:
    data = file.read()
    words = data.split()
    print(len(words))
    179910997
```

This file has roughly 180 million words after processing.

With our data reorganized in `speeches.txt`, we can iterate over the file to train a CBOW or skip-gram classification model while using as little memory as possible. We will use a custom class called `IterSents()` that does the iteration for us, yielding one sentence at a time, which we can then pass into `gensim.models.Word2Vec()`. Once again, you can expect this process to take some time, but it'll be sped up by setting the `workers` parameter to the number of CPU cores you have:

```
sentences = IterSents('../data/txt_files/can_hansard_speeches.txt')

model = gensim.models.Word2Vec(sentences, size = 300, window = 4, iter = 5,
                               sg = 0, min_count = 10, negative = 5, workers = 4)
```

And with that, we've learnt our embeddings from a dataset of roughly 180 million words! We don't want to have to relearn these embeddings needlessly (who has time for that?), so we'll write the model vocabulary to a text file called `model_vocabulary.txt` and then save the model itself to disk. That way, we can reload our vocabulary and trained model, rather than wasting time and energy retraining.

```
vocabulary = sorted(list(model.wv.vocab))

with open('../models/model_vocabulary.txt', 'w') as f:
    for v in vocabulary:
        f.write(v)
        f.write('\n')

model.save('../models/word2vec.model')
```

The model can be reloaded anytime, and if we don't have to update it anymore, we can keep just the word vectors themselves, which is a leaner object.

```
model = gensim.models.Word2Vec.load('../models/word2vec.model')
model = model.wv
```

We can use these newly trained embeddings just as we did the pretrained embeddings earlier in the chapter. Go ahead and experiment with some vector maths!

31.8 Comparing Embeddings

Everything we've done so far can also be done comparatively, which makes things much more interesting from a social science perspective. The trouble with these sorts of extensions is that the word embedding training process is stochastic, so we can't just learn embeddings for various different datasets and directly compare them. In fact, there's no guarantee that two models trained on the exact same data will end up looking even remotely similar! While the relations between the words in vector space should be more or less consistent across models (in the sense that the angle between them will be similar), their individual embeddings will often be completely different due in large part to differences in their random starting positions within the vector space. To do anything comparative, cross-sectional or over time, we need our vector spaces to be aligned.

There have been a number of solutions proposed to solve this problem (e.g. Artetxe et al., 2016; Di Carlo et al., 2019; Mogadala and Rettinger, 2016; Ruder et al., 2019), but we will focus on the 'compass' approach developed by Di Carlo et al. (2019) because it's well-implemented, efficient, and has Gensim at its core. It's designed with temporal data in mind, but we can handle cross-sectional comparisons in the exact same way. Below, I'll walk you through training a word embedding model 'anchor' (the compass) as a basis for comparison, and then we'll spend a bit of time working through a few temporal and cross-sectional comparisons.

The compass functionality is available in the Python package TWEC, which must be installed manually from the source code provided on GitHub. As the authors of the package note, TWEC requires a customized version of Gensim, so it's advisable to make a virtual environment specifically for working with this package. As a reminder, you can do so with the following steps, all from the command line:

- Clone the GitHub repository at https://github.com/valedica/twec.git
- Create a new conda virtual environment with `conda create -n twec_training`
- Activate your new conda environment with `conda activate twec_training`
- `pip install cython`
- Install the author's custom version of Gensim, `pip install git+https://github.com/valedica/gensim.git`
- `cd` into the TWEC repository
- `pip install --user .`

If you end up having a lot of trouble getting TWEC up and running, you can use any version of Gensim to load the models that have been pretrained for this chapter. You can read more about our pretrained models in the online supplementary materials.

Imports

Since we are working in a new virtual environment (details provided in the box in section 31.8) with a fresh new Python kernel, we'll continue to work with the Canadian Hansards data.

```
from twec.twec import TWEC
from gensim.models.word2vec import Word2Vec
import pandas as pd
from dcss.utils import list_files, mp_disk

from tok import Tokenizer
from gensim.utils import simple_preprocess
from multiprocessing import Process, Manager
import re
```

Aligning your vector spaces!

The general process of using the TWEC approach to train a series of embedding models *that are aligned from the start* is as follows:

1 Train a Word2vec model on the entire dataset in one go, retaining the position layer of the neural network model. This layer is called the compass. It computes a set of baseline embeddings that a series of embedding models (trained in Step 2) trained on every subset of the data (e.g. temporal slices) can use as a common starting point, like a kind of 'reference model'.

2 Train a Word2vec model for each subset of the data using the compass layer from Step 1 as the starting point. This ensures the vector spaces are properly aligned and lets the vector coordinates move around according to the embeddings of words in that subset of data.

Once the reference model has been trained, the series of models trained in the next step can all be trained with a *common* starting point (as opposed to a random one). Since the embeddings from each of the non reference models diverge from a common origin (given by the reference model), similarities and differences between word vectors learnt by different models can be interpreted as meaningful. Di Carlo et al. (2019) provide plenty of technical details on how TWEC works, if you are interested in going beyond what I introduce here.

Let's perform both steps. We'll use the compass (i.e. reference model) trained instep 1 for a series of temporal and cross-sectional comparisons later in the chapter.

Step 1: Train the compass

To train the compass, TWEC expects a text file where each sentence in our dataset is provided on a new line. Since we prepared this exact file in the previous chapter, we'll reuse it here. It's stored in speeches.txt:

```
compass_path = '../data/txt_files/can_hansard_speeches.txt'
```

Because TWEC uses a custom version of Gensim, it doesn't automatically receive the many updates that Gensim has had in recent years. One of the package dependencies has been updated since the Di Carlo et al. (2019) paper was published and now produces a warning about a function that will eventually be deprecated. To keep things a bit cleaner, we'll tell Python to suppress those warnings:

```
import warnings
warnings.filterwarnings("ignore")
```

Now we can initialize a TWEC class object, providing the parameters to pass to Gensim for training (note that the negative= argument for negative sampling is replaced by ns= here). We'll use this object to create the compass and when training the aligned temporal slices.

The results are automatically saved to a model/ folder in the current working directory. This process will take the same amount of time as it took to train the Word2vec model above, so it's best to set 'overwrite' to False so we don't accidentally lose all of that processing time. Remember to set the number of workers to the number of cores you want to use – most personal computers have four cores. If you ever need to pick things back up after a restart (or a kernel crash), running the cell again will simply reload the trained compass.

```
aligner = TWEC(size = 300, siter = 5, diter = 5, window = 10, sg = 0, min_count = 10,
    ns = 5, workers = 4)
aligner.train_compass(compass_path, overwrite=False)
```

Step 2: Train a series of aligned embedding models

Now that our reference model has been trained and stored in the `aligner` object, we can proceed with training a series of embedding models on various subsets of our data. In the examples that follow, we will train a series of models to show change over time, followed by a series of models to compare speeches by different political parties. We will use the same `aligner` object as the reference model for both.

Research on cultural change with temporal embeddings

Regardless of whether our comparison is cross-sectional or temporal, we need to subset our data *prior* to training any additional models. Since we are starting using embeddings to compare change over time, let's divide our data into different temporal slices. We'll be training a Gensim Word2vec model with each subset, so we will prepare the data with one sentence-per-line file for model training.

In this case, the CSV files in the Canadian Hansard dataset are organized into folders by year. We can use that to our advantage here. First, we'll load up the CSV files and create some lists to store the file paths for each decade:

```
datasets = list_files("../data/canadian_hansards/lipad/", 'csv')
len(datasets)

canadian_1990s = []
canadian_2000s = []
canadian_2010s = []

for i in range(1990,1999):
    year_data = '../data/canadian_hansards/lipad/' + str(i) + '/'
    datasets_1990s = list_files(year_data, 'csv')
    canadian_1990s.extend(datasets_1990s)

for i in range(2000,2009):
    year_data = '../data/canadian_hansards/lipad/' + str(i) + '/'
    datasets_2000s = list_files(year_data, 'csv')
    canadian_2000s.extend(datasets_2000s)

for i in range(2010,2019):
    year_data = '../data/canadian_hansards/lipad/' + str(i) + '/'
    datasets_2010s = list_files(year_data, 'csv')
    canadian_2010s.extend(datasets_2010s)
```

Now that we have our data organized into temporal slices, we need to create our sentence-per-line files. To do that with multiprocessing, we'll reuse the `get_sentences()` function we used in the previous chapter:

```
m = Manager()
q = m.Queue()
mp_disk(canadian_1990s, get_sentences, '../data/txt_files/1990s_speeches.txt', q)

m = Manager()
q = m.Queue()
mp_disk(canadian_2000s, get_sentences, '../data/txt_files/2000s_speeches.txt', q)

m = Manager()
q = m.Queue()
mp_disk(canadian_2010s, get_sentences, '../data/txt_files/2010s_speeches.txt', q)
```

Finally, we can train individual models on the slices using the `aligner` object. As you may have guessed, this can take a bit of time and you probably want to process each in its own cell, setting 'save' to `True` so that the model will be output to the `model/` directory, with a filename matching the name of the text file provided:

```
model_1990s = aligner.train_slice('../data/txt_files/1990s_speeches.txt', save=True)

model_2000s = aligner.train_slice('../data/txt_files/2000s_speeches.txt', save=True)

model_2010s = aligner.train_slice('../data/txt_files/2010s_speeches.txt', save=True)
```

At this point, we don't need the compass model anymore, but it's a good idea to keep it around. The contextual models we've trained for each temporal slice are good to go and, unlike the compass model, can simply be loaded into Gensim for analysis. Note that although I used `sg=0` above because skip-gram takes a long time to train compared to CBOW, the models you can load below were trained with skip-gram:

```
model_1990s = Word2Vec.load('../models/1990s_speeches.model')
model_2000s = Word2Vec.load('../models/2000s_speeches.model')
model_2010s = Word2Vec.load('../models/2010s_speeches.model')
```

Now that we've trained our aligned temporal embedding models, we can do all kinds of interesting and useful things, such as comparing the embeddings of terms in different decades. As a simple example, let's look at the most similar words to 'climate_change' across each decade. We should expect to see tokens such as 'global_warming' showing up, *but that's what we want;* our model (which doesn't actually know what words mean) is doing what it's supposed to do. Below we can see that the similarity between these terms starts to decline a bit in the 2010s, when 'climate_change' became the preferred term:

```
model_1990s.wv.most_similar(positive = 'climate_change', topn = 10)

[('global_warming', 0.6837976574897766),
 ('ozone_depletion', 0.6168003082275391),
 ('greenhouse_gases', 0.5897352695465088),
 ('greenhouse_gas', 0.5879524946212769),
 ('warming', 0.5868030190467834),
```

```
('climatic', 0.5418505072593689),
('ozone_layer', 0.5390327572822571),
('authoritative_confirmation', 0.5330763459205627),
('greenhouse', 0.5314763784408569),
('persistent_organic', 0.5246102809906006)]
```

```
model_2000s.wv.most_similar(positive = 'climate_change', topn = 10)
```

```
[('global_warming', 0.7735908031463623),
('greenhouse_gases', 0.672980546951294),
('kyoto', 0.6418241262435913),
('greenhouse_gas', 0.629040002822876),
('kyoto_protocol', 0.6282004714012146),
('climate', 0.6164438724517822),
('warming', 0.5926787853240967),
('themissions', 0.5906884670257568),
('pollution', 0.568431556224823),
('environmental', 0.5578656792640686)]
```

```
model_2010s.wv.most_similar(positive = 'climate_change', topn = 10)
```

```
[('climate', 0.6681504249572754),
('greenhouse_gases', 0.6233293414115906),
('warming', 0.6029214262962341),
('greenhouse_gas', 0.5946380496025085),
('global_warming', 0.5818494558334351),
('pollution', 0.5526135563850403),
('themissions', 0.5510997772216797),
('adaptation', 0.5503489375114441),
('ipcc', 0.5492062568664551),
('anthropogenic', 0.548987865447998)]
```

Cross-sectional comparisons: political parties on climate change

Sometimes our research goals are to compare culture and meaning across subgroups in a population, rather than change over time. For example, continuing with the examples we've used in this chapter so far, we might be more interested in comparing how different political parties talk about climate change than how political discussions of climate change in general have evolved over time.

To make these comparisons, we need to organize our data by political party rather than by decade. To keep things relatively simple, we'll focus on the three major political parties, namely the Liberals, the New Democratic Party, and the Conservatives, keeping in mind that the latter is a relatively recent merger of the former Canadian Alliance, Progressive Conservative, and Reform Parties. In this case, slicing the data isn't quite as straightforward, so we'll create a modified version of get_sentences() that will accept lists of terms to mask (filter) the dataframes with:

```
liberal = ['Liberal']
conservative = ['Conservative', 'Canadian Alliance', 'Progressive Conservative', '
    Reform']
```

```
ndp = ['New Democratic Party']

def get_sentences_by_party(dataset, filter_terms):

    dfs_unfiltered = [pd.read_csv(df) for df in dataset]
    dfs = []

    for df in dfs_unfiltered:
        temp_df = df.dropna(subset = ['speakerparty'])
        mask = temp_df['speakerparty'].apply(lambda x: any(party for party in
    filter_terms if party in x))
        temp_df2 = temp_df[mask]
        if len(temp_df2) > 0:
            dfs.append(temp_df2)

    speeches = []

    for df in dfs:
        speeches.extend(df['speechtext'].tolist())
    speeches = [str(s).replace('\n|\r', ' ') for s in speeches] # make sure
     everything is a lowercase string, remove newlines
     _, sentences = u.bigram_process(speeches)
    sentences = '\n'.join(sentences) # join the batch of sentences with newlines into
     1 string

q.put(sentences)
m = Manager()
q = m.Queue()

mp_disk(datasets, get_sentences_by_party, '../data/txt_files/liberal_speeches.txt', q,
     liberal)

m = Manager()
q = m.Queue()

mp_disk(datasets, get_sentences_by_party, '../data/txt_files/conservative_speeches.txt
    ', q, conservative)

m = Manager()
q = m.Queue()
mp_disk(datasets, get_sentences_by_party, '../data/txt_files/ndp_speeches.txt', q, ndp
    )
```

Now we can train an aligned model for each of the three parties, using the same `aligner` object we used earlier (trained on the full corpus):

```
model_liberal = aligner.train_slice('../data/txt_files/liberal_speeches.txt', save=
    True)

model_conservative = aligner.train_slice('../data/txt_files/conservative_speeches.txt'
    , save=True)
```

```
model_ndp = aligner.train_slice('../data/txt_files/ndp_speeches.txt', save=True)
```

With our three aligned models, we can now compare how each of the three major parties talk about climate change. Remember that this is for *all* party-specific talk from 1990 onwards. We *could* train more models to disaggregate things even further (e.g. each party in each decade), but we'll keep things simple here.

```
model_liberal = Word2Vec.load('../models/liberal_speeches.model')
model_conservative = Word2Vec.load('../models/conservative_speeches.model')
model_ndp = Word2Vec.load('../models/ndp_speeches.model')
```

```
model_liberal.wv.most_similar(positive = 'climate_change', topn = 10)
```

```
[('global_warming', 0.7236964702606201),
 ('greenhouse_gas', 0.691413938999176),
 ('greenhouse_gases', 0.6698545217514038),
 ('kyoto_protocol', 0.6651817560195923),
 ('kyoto', 0.6485368609428406),
 ('climate', 0.6196231842041016),
 ('themissions', 0.5910802483558655),
 ('warming', 0.5807555913925171),
 ('carbon', 0.5598022937774658),
 ('ozone_depletion', 0.5564819574356079)]
```

```
model_conservative.wv.most_similar(positive = 'climate_change', topn = 10)
```

```
[('global_warming', 0.6451274156570435),
 ('climate', 0.635093092918396),
 ('greenhouse_gas', 0.6260195970535278),
 ('greenhouse_gases', 0.6220650672912598),
 ('adaptation', 0.6139771342277527),
 ('kyoto', 0.6091358065605164),
 ('themissions', 0.6083964109420776),
 ('gas_themissions', 0.5831836462020874),
 ('kyoto_protocol', 0.5714175701141357),
 ('continentally', 0.5591344833374023)]
```

```
model_ndp.wv.most_similar(positive = 'climate_change', topn = 10)
```

```
[('global_warming', 0.6599026918411255),
 ('climate', 0.6140391826629639),
 ('greenhouse_gas', 0.6137247681617737),
 ('greenhouse_gases', 0.5791583061218262),
 ('themissions', 0.5666577219963074),
 ('kyoto', 0.5609204769134521),
 ('kyoto_protocol', 0.5440766215324402),
 ('warming', 0.529146134853363),
 ('pollution', 0.5277700424194336),
 ('copenhagen', 0.5228224396705627)]
```

Of course, everything we did previously with the pretrained embeddings can be applied and generalized with the models we've trained here. Give it a shot!

Further Reading

Adji Dieng et al. (2020) have developed a really interesting probabilistic topic model that uses embeddings to represent text rather than the DTM representations used in latent Dirichlet allocation topic models. They also generalize this model for dynamic data in Dieng et al. (2019). If you are interested in the relationship between topic models and word embeddings, I recommend reading their articles.

31.9 Conclusion

The key points in this chapter are as follows:

- Word embeddings represent words with short dense vectors that describe the word's local semantic contexts.
- Embeddings as a whole depict patterns of word usage and language structure.
- Embeddings are *not* a straightforward proxy for 'meaning', and we should not trust intuitions built on low-dimensional representations of high-dimensional vector space.
- We trained a variety of embedding models using Gensim, and a series of aligned embedding models (to facilitate temporal/historical and comparative research) with TWEC.

Visit the website at https://study.sagepub.com/mclevey for additional resources

32

NAMED ENTITY RECOGNITION, TRANSFER LEARNING, AND TRANSFORMER MODELS

32.1 Learning Objectives

By the end of this chapter, you should be able to do the following:

- Learn what named entity recognition (NER) is and what it's used for
- Use spaCy to train an out-of-the-box NER model
- Know what transfer learning is and how it applies to machine learning
- Learn what transformer models are and what makes them so efficient
- Use transformer models for NER and sentiment analysis
- Combine multiple methods and models from this book to identify named entities, assess sentiment, construct a network, and interpret it

32.2 Learning Materials

You can find the online learning materials for this chapter in `doing_computational_social_science/Chapter_32`. `cd` into the directory and launch your Jupyter server.

32.3 Introduction

In this final chapter, we'll turn our attention to another set of text analysis tools. We'll begin with named entity recognition (NER), which tries to identify and classify references to named 'things' in unstructured text data into predetermined categories. We'll use spaCy's 'out-of-the-box' models to conduct some simple NER. Following the general iterative logic of Box's loop, we'll critique that model and consider how to improve it by updating spaCy's model by teaching it with our own data, which is an example of transfer learning.

In the second part, we wander into the world of large language models, more specifically transformer models, which are right at the cutting edge of contemporary NLP. Following a conceptual introduction, we return to the task of NER, this time using data from the Canadian Hansards and transformer models. We'll finish by working through an example of combining multiple methods and models in one analysis by constructing a network of co-occurring named entities from speeches made by former party leaders of the three major Canadian political parties. We'll use a transformer model to predict the positive or negative sentiment of the semantic contexts the named entities occur in and then fit a stochastic block model (SBM). This extended example is meant to show how various different types of models can be productively combined, and is hence more open-ended and exploratory than your own research work may be.

32.4 Named Entity Recognition

Named entity recognition (also referred to as entity identification, chunking, or extraction) is the task of sifting through unstructured text data to identify real-world entities that have, or could have, proper names. Consider this three-paragraph excerpt from a story in the *Guardian* (Cadwalladr, 2019) about the Cambridge Analytica scandal and whistle-blower Christopher Wylie a year after the initial story broke. I have manually emphasized some 'named entities'.

> **Wylie** became a public figure overnight. And the story triggered what, in many ways, looked like a year of reckoning for the tech industry. **Damian Collins**, the chair of the **Department of Culture, Media and Sport**'s 18-month-long fake news inquiry, which delivered last month's report, described the story's publication as a 'pivotal moment' when 'public attitudes and government policy towards the tech companies started to change'.

> Last week, on the 30th anniversary of the worldwide web, its creator **Tim Berners-Lee** urged people to stop the 'downward plunge' to 'a dysfunctional future' that the **Cambridge Analytica** scandal had helped expose. It was, **Berners-Lee** said, the moment people realised that 'elections had been manipulated using data that they contributed'.

> The problem is that while the tech companies have been called to account, they haven't actually been held accountable. In November, after **Zuckerberg** refused to comply with a summons to **parliament** to answer questions about **Facebook**'s role in the scandal, **Collins** convened an international committee of nine parliaments. **Zuckerberg** refused to come to that too.

Before going further, let's briefly re-examine the three preceding block quotes. The excerpts contain the full and partial names for a number of people (Christopher Wylie, Damian Collins, Tim Berners-Lee, Mark Zuckerberg) as well as references to specific organizations (Cambridge Analytica, Facebook). They also contain some more ambiguous entities, such as 'parliament' (which here does refer to a specific parliament) and 'chair of the Department of Culture, Media and Sport', which refers to a specific person (Damian Collins) while also containing a reference to a specific real-world organization (the Department of Culture, Media and Sports). We used our human cognitive abilities to identify these named entities in the original text. How does a computer do it? And can we use computers to extract more complex types of entities, such as events?

Initially, NER might seem pretty straightforward, but perhaps you've already noticed potential challenges. Indeed, it has proven very difficult for computational linguists to develop accurate NER models. The latest models from spaCy (version 3) are 89.48% accurate for the state-of-the-art transformer models (discussed below) and 85.5% for the large English model (a convolutional neural network). That is very good, but you should expect false positives and false negatives if you don't update these models on your own data.

In this example, most of the named entities are proper nouns, which in English are typically capitalized. It turns out that capitalization and a word's part-of-speech go a very long way towards identifying named entities, but they are imperfect guides. If NER only had to identify capitalized nouns, it would be a relatively simple task with consistently high levels of accuracy. However, not all proper nouns are capitalized (macOS) and not all capitalized nouns are proper. Furthermore, some entities are unambiguous, clearly refer to a single entity (the name of a person: Angela Merkel), while others are ambiguous and may refer to one of many possible entities (the name of a position that a person holds: Chancellor of Germany). The former (unambiguous) are referred to as 'rigid designators' and the latter (ambiguous) are 'flaccid designators' (Squire, 2016). As you might guess, identifying the former is significantly easier than identifying the latter. In NER, there is a tension between the many 'easy' cases and the few 'hard' cases that always drag accuracy rates down. Any given approach to NER should get the easy cases right, and any advancements will come in the form of small improvements to coping with the hard cases.

One approach to tackling hard cases involves using a list of 'seed' entities. If we already have access to a list of entities – such as politicians, co-operatives, cities, or countries – we can instruct our model to search the corpus for those entities and learn underlying patterns associated with the type of entity we are looking for. Then the model can use what it learnt to uncover references to additional entities that we previously didn't know about. This process can also work if we don't already have a list of entities. In that scenario, we would select a reasonable sample of documents and manually identify and annotate the named entities, and they become our initial seed list. This process could be repeated several times, each time expanding and refining the seed list.

This approach to NER is called bootstrapping. The idea is to use supervised learning to train a model to predict an outcome we care about, like classifying a word as the name of an organization or not. Once we run the model, we select those instances (here, words) that were classified with a high degree of confidence and move them into our training data (the seed list). The classifiers are then run again, following the same process of moving highly accurate classifications into the seed list. This process is repeated multiple times, growing the training data with each repetition. This bootstrapping approach to NER is powerful but – like other approaches – imperfect.

When we do our own NER classification later in the chapter, we will once again use spaCy because of its relative ease of use and its highly advanced NER models. It is extremely important to remember that the accuracy of these pretrained models depends in large part on the data they were trained on, and how similar that data is to the your own data. If you are working with highly specialized text data – say, text from journal articles in biomedical science or transcripts of YouTube videos about cryptocurrencies – you will likely get better results by training your own NER models on a comparable dataset that you manually annotated.

It's possible to do this on your own, of course, but if possible, it is better to have multiple annotators and to compute inter-rater reliability scores for annotations. While many people crowdsource this work using platforms like Amazon's Mechanical Turk, CrowdFlower, or

Productive Academic, the best annotation jobs are likely to be done by people with extensive domain knowledge, and is therefore likely best done in-house. An interesting example of training custom models that require domain expertise is scispaCy, which uses a spaCy pipeline custom built by Allen AI for doing natural language processing (NLP), including NER, on biomedical publications and scientific documents more generally. In cases where no domain expertise is needed to perform annotations, pretrained models are likely an appropriate choice.

The spaCy documentation provides a fairly detailed explanation of how to train an NER model on your own data. Remember, you need to construct the training data yourself by manually annotating your data. You should also know that you will likely need access to a fairly powerful computer to be able to train your own model. Depending on the resources available to you, this may be expensive and/or time-consuming, but if you annotate enough data, the results in your domain-specific application will be greatly improved. If you decide to train your own NER model, *put care into data annotation*. It will pay dividends later.

At present, spaCy (version 3) can recognize 18 different types of entities: people's names, nationalities or religious or political groups, infrastructure, organization, geopolitical entities, locations, products, events, works of art, documents made into laws, languages, dates, times, percentages, money, quantitative measurements, ordinal ranks, and other numerals (i.e. cardinal). As with part-of-speech tagging, we can use `spacy.explain()` to get a description of each type of entity. For example, `spacy.explain('GPE')` returns `'Countries, cities, states'`.

Let's compare our manual annotation of the excerpt from the story about Christopher Wylie and Cambridge Analytica against spaCy's NER analysis of the same text to see what it looks like, and what kinds of entities it identifies (Figure 32.1).

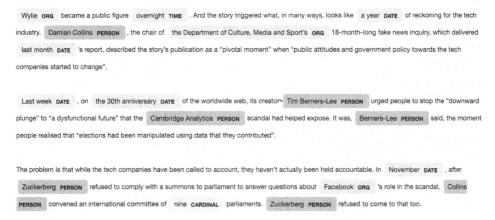

Figure 32.1 The results of spaCy NER on the same excerpt of text that we manually annotated

spaCy picked up on all of the entities we tagged, but it mistakenly classified 'Wylie' as an organization. It also identified several other types of entities – dates, times, and cardinals – that we did not manually annotate.

Let's make all of this a little less abstract by working through an NER example using the full article text rather than just an excerpt. First, we will load the full article text, which is stored in a text file in the `data/misc` directory. Then we simply process it using spaCy's `nlp()` pipeline, without disabling any modules like we did previously.

NER, out of the box

Imports

```
from dcss.text import *
from dcss.networks import *
from dcss.utils import list_files
from dcss.plotting import draw_ner_blockmodel_sfdp
import spacy
from graph_tool.all import *
import math
import pandas as pd
pd.set_option("display.notebook_repr_html", False)
from collections import Counter
nlp = spacy.load('en_core_web_sm')

with open('../data/txt_files/ca_story.txt', 'r') as f:
    full_text = [line.strip() for line in f]
    full_text = " ".join(full_text)

doc = nlp(full_text)
```

Once spaCy has processed our text, we can retrieve information about the named entities from the Doc object. The code block below constructs a list of the named entity types discovered in this story. spaCy finds more than 250 unique entities in the news story, depending on your version of the language model, most of which are organizations, people, and geopolitical entities.

```
ent_types = [ent.label_ for ent in doc.ents]
print('Found {} named entities'.format(len(ent_types)))
Counter(ent_types).most_common()
```

```
Found 268 named entities

[('PERSON', 67),
 ('ORG', 51),
 ('GPE', 49),
 ('DATE', 39),
 ('CARDINAL', 18),
 ('NORP', 14),
 ('TIME', 9),
 ('ORDINAL', 9),
 ('MONEY', 6),
 ('LOC', 4),
 ('EVENT', 1),
 ('PRODUCT', 1)]
```

We can filter for all entities of a certain type with .label_, such as the geopolitical entities:

```
Counter([str(ent) for ent in doc.ents if ent.label_ == "GPE"])

Counter({'Cambridge': 15,
         'UK': 2,
```

```
        'Britain': 4,
        'Analytica': 1,
        'US': 4,
        'Media': 1,
        'Washington': 1,
        'New York': 3,
        'London': 3,
        'New Jersey': 1,
        'Israel': 1,
        'Afghanistan': 1,
        'Nigeria': 1,
        'Cambridge Analytica': 1,
        'Stockholm': 1,
        'South Africa': 1,
        'France': 1,
        'Charlottesville': 1,
        'Virginia': 1,
        'New Zealand': 1,
        'Russia': 1,
        'Hollywood': 1,
        'the British Empire': 1,
        'Wylie': 1})
```

This list is mostly cities, countries, and states, but it also includes 'the British Empire', 'Cambridge', 'Analytica', 'Cambridge Analytica', and even 'Wylie' once. The 'PERSON' and 'ORG' tags are, in some ways, more interesting, because they reveal the challenges that models have in differentiating how we talk about people and how we talk about organizations. This isn't surprising, given that in many places, organizations *are* spoken about like people and even have some of the same rights. The code block below will print all entities identified as people in the article:

```
Counter([str(ent) for ent in doc.ents if ent.label_ == 'PERSON']).most_common(10)
```

```
[('Wylie', 23),
 ('Analytica', 6),
 ('Brexit', 4),
 ('Zuckerberg', 3),
 ('Cambridge Analytica', 3),
 ('Analytica Files', 2),
 ('Alexander Nix', 2),
 ('Trump', 1),
 ('Christopher Wylie', 1),
 ('Mark Zuckerberg', 1)]
```

```
Counter([str(ent) for ent in doc.ents if ent.label_ == 'ORG']).most_common(10)
```

```
[('FBI', 4),
 ('Congress', 3),
 ('Cambridge Analytica', 2),
 ('Collins's', 2),
```

```
('the Department of Justice', 2),
('FTC', 2),
('H&M', 2),
('BBC', 2),
('the Independent Group', 1),
('Observer', 1)]
```

In the full article, spaCy's small model realizes that 'Wylie' refers to a person most of the time, but also identified 'Cambridge Analytica' and 'Analytica' as people. If we look for 'ORG' instead, the most frequent is the FBI (more than Cambridge Analytica), and we also have Congress, Collins's (who is a person), and two instances of Cambridge Analytica. This is a good time to mention that the entity attribute, if detected, is assigned *per token* – this is why the model can label 'Wylie' as both a person and a geopolitical entity.

The rest of the organizations seem pretty valid (the Department of Justice, BBC, H&M, FTC, etc.), but obvious ones like Facebook are missing. For reference, 'Cambridge Analytica' appears in the article 22 times and 'Facebook' 26 times. Depending on your research question, you may opt to combine the results of the 'PERSON' and 'ORG' labels. There are alternatives, though, such as updating the spaCy model as we will do below, or even training an entirely new one.

Customizing spaCy's pretrained named entity recognition

One of the ways we can get better results with NER is to update the pretrained NER model in spaCy using our own data. We'll do this by creating a dictionary of example 'texts' that are actually just sentences from the article that have been annotated with NER labels. The expected format is a list of texts, where each text is a tuple of (doc, label). The doc is a doc object from the string of text that's being labelled, and each label is a dictionary with a key that specifies the attribute to update (in this case, 'entities') and a value that is a tuple of (span start, span end, entity label). You might recall that spans refer to the index of the beginning and end of a text, but remember that they behave like the range function in Python – the character at the span end index will *not* be included.

```
import random
random.seed(7)
from spacy.training import Example
```

Here are some pre-crafted entity annotation training sentences, with 'Cambridge Analytica', 'Facebook', and 'Wylie' annotated. As you can see, creating more than a few of these manually would be pretty mind-numbing.

```
update_list = [
    ('It was a report that drew on hours of testimony from Cambridge Analytica
    directors, Facebook executives and dozens of expert witnesses',
    {
        'entities': [(53, 72, 'ORG'), (84, 92, 'ORG')]
    }),
    ('Cambridge Analytica rode it out, initially, but finally called in the
    administrators in May',
     {
```

```
                'entities': [(0, 19, 'ORG')]
        }),
    ('In April Facebook admitted it wasn't 50 million users who had had their profiles
        mined',
        {
                'entities': [(9, 17, 'ORG')]
        }),
    ('Facebook published a statement saying that it had banned both Cambridge
        Analytica and Wylie from its platform.',
        {
                'entities': [(0, 8, 'ORG'), (62, 81, 'ORG'), (86, 91, 'PERSON')]
        })
]
```

This seems like a pretty small list to expect it to have much impact. However, remember *this is not a string-matching rule list*. What we are doing here is teaching spaCy how to make better predictions based in part on semantic context, so we need not supply an *exhaustive* list of annotations. In this case our training set is very small, so we'll iterate it a number of times to give the model time to learn. We will use a drop rate (i.e. forgetting) of 0.6 so that the model has to see things more times before it remembers them, and will shuffle the list of texts between iterations so that it has to 'think' instead of just memorize. Different drop rates and numbers of training iterations will bring quite different results with such a small training set, so it takes some fiddling to see improvements. With more training data and less iterations required, this becomes more reliable.

```
nlp = spacy.load('en_core_web_sm')

for i in range(10):
    random.shuffle(update_list)
    examples = []
    for text, label_spans in update_list:
        doc = nlp.make_doc(text)
        examples.append(Example.from_dict(doc, label_spans))
    nlp.update(examples, drop = 0.6)

trained_doc = nlp(full_text)
```

Now let's see what kind of improvements we made!

```
Counter([str(ent) for ent in trained_doc.ents if ent.label_ == "GPE"])

Counter({'UK': 2,
        'Britain': 2,
        'US': 4,
        'Washington': 1,
        'New York': 3,
        'London': 3,
        'New Jersey': 1,
        'Israel': 1,
        'Afghanistan': 1,
```

```
    'Nigeria': 1,
    'France': 1,
    'Charlottesville': 1,
    'Virginia': 1,
    'New Zealand': 1,
    'Russia': 1,
    'Hollywood': 1,
    'the British Empire': 1})
```

Impressively, 'Cambridge' no longer appears as a geopolitical entity, even though in other contexts it could be and we didn't annotate that word without 'Analytica'. The word 'Media' is also gone but we do lose a few valid entries such as 'Stockholm' and 'South Africa'. Let's see how well the model can recognize specific people:

```
Counter([str(ent) for ent in trained_doc.ents if ent.label_ == 'PERSON']).most_common
    (10)
```

```
[('Wylie', 16),
 ('Brexit', 4),
 ('Zuckerberg', 2),
 ('Alexander Nix', 2),
 ('Christopher Wylie', 1),
 ('Mark Zuckerberg', 1),
 ('Damian Collins', 1),
 ('Tim Berners-Lee', 1),
 ('Jason Kint', 1),
 ('George Soros', 1)]
```

The results for recognizing people are also mixed: all of the 'Cambridge Analytica' related entries are gone, but Brexit is still there and we've lost some instances of Wylie. Let's look at the organizations:

```
Counter([str(ent) for ent in trained_doc.ents if ent.label_ == 'ORG']).most_common(10)
```

```
[('Cambridge Analytica', 17),
 ('Facebook', 4),
 ('FBI', 4),
 ('Congress', 3),
 ('Wylie's', 3),
 ('Observer', 2),
 ('the Cambridge Analytica Files', 2),
 ('Trump', 2),
 ('Britain's', 2),
 ('Cambridge Analytica's', 2)]
```

Likewise, the number of 'Cambridge Analytica' ORG tags is greatly improved (17/21) and 'Facebook' finally makes an appearance (11/26), but so does 'Wylie's' and 'Trump'. Let's see what happens if we update the model with the full text, annotating the full text with the three entities of interest, instead of a few lines. This would be pretty time-consuming to do manually, so we'll use a function called `create_examples` (from the dcss package) to take care of some of the annotation:

```
## RELOAD A FRESH VERSION OF THE PRE-TRAINED MODEL
nlp = spacy.load('en_core_web_sm')


examples = create_examples(full_text)

for i in range(10):
    random.shuffle(examples)
    nlp.update(examples, drop = 0.6)

trained_doc = nlp(full_text)
```

This gives us a perfect Wylie detection count of 27 with his full name included. Unfortunately, 'Brexit' is still detected as a person and only one of two 'Trump' appearances are corrected.

```
Counter([str(ent) for ent in trained_doc.ents if ent.label_ == 'PERSON']).most_common
    (10)

[('Wylie', 26),
 ('Brexit', 4),
 ('Zuckerberg', 3),
 ('Trump', 1),
 ('Christopher Wylie', 1),
 ('Mark Zuckerberg', 1),
 ('Damian Collins', 1),
 ('Collins', 1),
 ('George Soros', 1),
 ('Jamie Bartlett', 1)]
```

The organization detection is also improved but not perfectly. There are two cases of 'Cambridge Analytica' missing and nine cases of 'Facebook'.

```
Counter([str(ent) for ent in trained_doc.ents if ent.label_ == 'ORG']).most_common(10)

[('Cambridge Analytica', 17),
 ('Facebook', 10),
 ('FBI', 4),
 ('Congress', 3),
 ('Cambridge Analytica's', 2),
 ('the Department of Justice', 2),
 ('FTC', 2),
 ('BBC', 2),
 ('the Independent Group', 1),
 ('the Department of Culture', 1)]
```

There's another simple option that's useful in many cases. If you know that you'll always want a certain word to be identified as a specific type of entity, you can add the `EntityRuler` pipeline component. For example, it will always be safe to add 'Facebook' and 'Cambridge Analytica' as organizations but not 'Wylie', because outside of this article, it could refer to many unknown entities.

```
ent_labels = [
    {'label': 'ORG', 'pattern': 'Facebook'},
    {'label': 'ORG', 'pattern': 'Cambridge Analytica'}
]

ent_ruler = nlp.add_pipe('entity_ruler', config = {'overwrite_ents': True})
ent_ruler.add_patterns(ent_labels)

ruled_doc = nlp(full_text)
Counter([str(ent) for ent in ruled_doc.ents if ent.label_ == 'ORG']).most_common(10)

[('Facebook', 26),
 ('Cambridge Analytica', 21),
 ('FBI', 4),
 ('Congress', 3),
 ('the Department of Justice', 2),
 ('FTC', 2),
 ('BBC', 2),
 ('the Independent Group', 1),
 ('the Department of Culture', 1),
 ('Washington', 1)]
```

Of course, we now have perfect accuracy for the two entities that we know are key to the article. But these methods will not work quite as well if you have a large corpus with a wide range of topics, or even a midsized corpus that you don't know much about, or if you just don't have the time or resources to iteratively craft a combination of training data and rules until you get accurate results. Thankfully, others have trained numerous models on more text than a single person will ever annotate, and there are ways to use what those models have learned as a baseline that you can update with your own data. This is a form of transfer learning.

NER with transfer learning

Although it isn't a new concept in machine learning, transfer learning has gained considerable attention in recent years, perhaps most visibly in the recent rise of transformer neural network models, like Google's BERT. We will discuss transformer models shortly, but first I'll introduce the general idea behind transfer learning.

Transfer learning is predominantly used in neural network modelling, where a model is trained for some task or data and then used for a different, but related, task or data. When you use a pretrained model of any sort – one of spaCy's models, for example – you're using transfer learning. Recall that in Word2vec, we train a neural network model but we don't actually care about its predictions. We discard the output layer entirely but extract the word embeddings the model learnt while performing those predictions. Those embeddings can then be used in *other* unrelated tasks, such as calculating the similarity between two words. This is transfer learning.

Much has been said about the opportunities offered by the enormous amount of textual data available in the digital age, but not everyone has the computing resources or time to train a model on millions or billions of texts. Pretrained models save time and resources for everyone while making the accuracy benefits of working with training data of that scale more widely accessible. And as we've already seen, pretrained models (such as embedding models or NER models) can be updated with domain-specific data, or fine-tuned for a specific research task. If a pretrained model has enough features and has seen enough contexts, it will have a pretty good sense of what to do with your training data already – these things are either shared across domains, or in recent years with transformer models, the model has more or less covered all domains.

32.5 Transformer Models

While transfer learning and most of the now-prevalent neural network architectures were introduced before the 1990s, transformers are only a few years old (Vaswani et al., 2017). Consider recurrent neural networks (RNNs), which are commonly used to analyse text data. When we read texts, meaning can be composed of complex references that can also change over time, and the more abstract you go, the more likely that the meaning of a word is dependent on a complex combination of words from other places in the sentence, or even the whole document! Based on this intuition, RNNs are designed to process input data sequentially; the calculations performed on a given word are performed using results from processing the previous word. While this has some benefits, it also means that the dependency between any two words is impacted by the words that appear between them, regardless of whether it should be, and this impact can unduly magnify the importance of proximity.

RNNs used for language modelling typically take word embeddings as their input, with the sequential component of the RNN introducing the ordering of the words in their local context to the calculation. Importantly, each word in an embedding model is given only one embedding, so the word 'mean' has the same embedding even though its meaning differs greatly between the contexts of 'mean grade', 'mean grader', and 'what does this grade even mean?' An additional limitation is that words at the beginning of a sequence are increasingly unlikely to be associated with words at the end of the sequence. To address this, attention mechanisms are added on top of RNNs, so that dependencies will be considered between all words in a sequence regardless of their proximity, and these calculations are performed on the entire sequence using matrix manipulation.

Training an RNN is computationally expensive – even more so with an attention mechanism added to it – making it especially difficult to train a model that could be transferred to a different context with reasonable accuracy. To this end, Google researchers decided to skip the RNN entirely and focus instead on the attention mechanism itself (Vaswani et al., 2017), which might remind you of how other Google researchers discarded the output from the RNN learning objective of the Word2vec model. This led to the creation of transformer models.

Transformers replaced the functionality of RNNs in two ways: (1) by adding positional encodings to the input embeddings so that sequence order would be retained and (2) with multi-headed attention mechanisms that pay attention to parts of the text independently of each other, rather than sequentially building from previous learning. The key innovation of transformers over attention-based RNNs is not so much a conceptual improvement, but rather an enormous performance improvement brought from parallel calculations and reduced computational complexity. To accurately differentiate between two contexts that a word appears in, a model needs to have seen both contexts enough times to consider them distinct, but also needs to know when those contexts aren't different, despite the surrounding words being different. Unlike a lot of other modelling situations, more training data means that an attention model learns more of these nuances with a limit that has yet to be reached, and transformers can be trained on enormous amounts of data in far less time.

Like all neural networks, transformers can be fine-tuned for virtually any task you can craft that conforms to the training input required by the neural network implementation. Transformer models often handle tasks like question answering, machine translation, sentence completion, or sentiment analysis (which we will get into later in this chapter).

HuggingFace + spaCy

There is an important and perhaps obvious caveat to the accessibility of recent state-of-the art NLP developments: accessibility is relative. The first transformer models were trained on eight Tesla P100 graphics processing units (GPUs) designed by Nvidia for scientific and research applications – at a cost. A few years later, many researchers – especially social scientists – wouldn't have access to the equivalent of one Tesla P100, never mind eight of them. The top performing of the first transformer models took 3.5 days to train on 8 GPUs (Vaswani et al., 2017). The follow-up and now-ubiquitous BERT family of transformer models was trained on the 800 million words in the Google Books corpus and 2.5 billion words from English-language Wikipedia (Devlin et al., 2018). While many of the early NLP models were for applied purposes, such as topic modelling for information retrieval, the motivation behind NLP development in recent years has taken an undeniable commercial turn. These models are developed towards benchmarks for tasks like automated question answering, machine translation, text generation, and search (including 'next sentence prediction'). The automated assistant greeting you from the website of your cell phone provider could very well be a transformer model, likely fine-tuned but probably not trained from scratch. How these models are trained, and the data they are trained on, matter a great deal for their applications in other contexts.

One of the more recent high-performing transformer models, Open AI's `GPT-3`, was developed with an eye towards skipping fine-tuning steps by training a model with 175 billion parameters (Brown et al., 2020). That number of parameters, unfortunately, points to the bottom line: you probably can't run many of the cutting-edge transformer models you read about in papers by computational linguists and NLP researchers. It's more or less necessary to use a GPU to apply the marquee pretrained models, such as BERT, whereas fine-tuning them often requires that you have a GPU with 12 GB of memory or more. Thankfully, there are ongoing efforts to change this, such as the development of MobileBERT, which runs on a smartphone (Sun et al., 2020).

Once you've solved your computing requirements, you should probably make your way to the `transformers` package, developed by HuggingFace as a Python architecture for any transformer model. HuggingFace supports an ambitious number of transformer models under one roof while providing access to thousands more via a widely used community repository. Aside from the core transformer models and their pared-down variants, HuggingFace offers models that have been fine-tuned for different types of domains, and in some cases models that have been modified more substantially. For example, the company Allen AI's `Longformer` builds on Facebook's offering, `RoBERTa`, by replacing the attention mechanism with one that handles sequences longer than 512. Recall that an attention mechanism is able to consider dependencies between any two points in a sequence – a sequence much longer than 512 might be useful if you have long documents about homogeneous topics.

If you want to explore the depth of transformer models, HuggingFace is probably the best place to start. Training a fine-tuning layer on top of a model will be tricky enough to be instructive. For an API that might be a bit more familiar at this point in the book, the latest version of spaCy now offers full interoperability with models that are available through HuggingFace. RoBERTa is officially distributed by spaCy and can be simply downloaded and dropped-in to improve the performance of all of the spaCy pipelines that you're already familiar with. The others just need an additional import step.

There are a few additional things to consider, however. Keep in mind that inference (applying the model) is slower with transformer models, so it's worth carefully considering what you need. One of these considerations should be whether you really need to use a transformer at all, or if you would be better off putting a bit of work into fine-tuning a more basic pretrained language model. In other words, the model might not need to know the entirety of Wikipedia and the content of every book indexed by Google to tell us whether Mark Zuckerberg is a person or an organization.

Let's get our hands on some transformers. spaCy makes this as easy as loading up any standard model. We'll load `'en_core_web_trf'`, which is Facebook's `roberta-base` under the hood. It's actually smaller than the largest standard model, but unfortunately the smaller size doesn't mean that it's as fast to process large amounts of text, especially without using a GPU.

Let's load up the model and apply it to the full text!

```
nlpt = spacy.load('en_core_web_trf', exclude=['tagger','lemmatizer'])
doct = nlpt(full_text)
```

```
Counter([str(ent) for ent in doct.ents if ent.label_ == 'ORG']).most_common(10)
```

```
[('Facebook', 25),
 ('Cambridge Analytica', 17),
 ('Observer', 5),
 ('FBI', 4),
 ('Congress', 3),
 ('H&M', 3),
 ('Cambridge Analytica's', 2),
 ('the Department of Justice', 2),
 ('FTC', 2),
 ('BBC', 2)]
```

```
Counter([str(ent) for ent in doct.ents if ent.label_ == 'PERSON']).most_common(10)
```

```
[('Wylie', 25),
 ('Zuckerberg', 3),
 ('Collins', 3),
 ('Nix', 3),
 ('Trump', 2),
 ('Damian Collins', 2),
 ('Alexander Nix', 2),
 ('Christopher Wylie', 1),
 ('Mark Zuckerberg', 1),
 ('Tim Berners-Lee', 1)]
```

As you can see, the accuracy right out of the gate is better than the standard model or the trained standard model, and acceptably close enough to the rule-based one. There is also an impressive set of improvements for entities that weren't detected – 'Observer' ends up with perfect accuracy, 'Trump' is no longer mistaken for an organization, and 'Brexit' is no longer a person.

The training data for the `roberta-base` model we've used here was actually unlabelled, which makes the context-based, self-supervised results all the more impressive. The training data includes both Wikipedia and a crawl of news articles, which was conducted before the *Guardian* article we analysed above but after the Cambridge Analytica scandal itself, so it's well-suited for this particular text data. An often fascinating part of contextually supervised models is that their 'errors' can sometimes be informative about the cultural use of a term. We can investigate a bit using some of spaCy's convenient approaches to NLP. Let's look at how the word 'Brexit' and the entities in the sentences it appears in have been handled now:

```
for ent in doct.ents:
    if ent.text == "Brexit":
        print(ent.label_)
        print(ent.sent.text)
        for ent2 in ent.sent.ents:
            print(ent2.text + ': ' + ent2.label_)
```

```
GPE
The account of a whistleblower from inside the data analytics firm that had worked in
    different capacities – the details are still disputed – on the two pivotal
    campaigns of 2016 that gave us Brexit and Trump.
two: CARDINAL
2016: DATE
Brexit: GPE
Trump: PERSON
```

Although one out of four 'Brexit' appearances is now labelled as a geopolitical entity, this could be because the term is used in some contexts as a stand-in for 'Britain without the EU'. We can look at all sentences that contained the word 'Brexit' to see what might have distinguished them:

```
for token in doct:
    if token.text == "Brexit":
        print(token.sent.text)
```

```
The account of a whistleblower from inside the data analytics firm that had worked in
    different capacities – the details are still disputed – on the two pivotal
    campaigns of 2016 that gave us Brexit and Trump.
It goes from Trump to Brexit to Russian espionage to military operations in
    Afghanistan to hacking the president of Nigeria.
 "When you look at how, for example, the NCA [National Crime Agency] has just sat on
    blatant evidence of Russian interference in Brexit," Wylie says. "
The Brexit angle of the Cambridge Analytica Files, the explosive revelations of a
    second whistleblower, Shahmir Sanni, fell inexplicably flat.
```

It does seem as though it's only the first sentence where the term could be replaced by 'Britain without the EU'. Notice also that nothing in the sentence in question points to 'Brexit' and 'Trump' being different types of entity – that's the pretraining of the model. Let's see how much data the model needs to make this distinction. First we'll pass a sentence through the transformer model, then we'll pass the full paragraph that the sentences comes from:

```
sentence = nlpt("The account of a whistleblower from inside the data analytics firm
     that had worked in different capacities "
               "- the details are still disputed - on the two pivotal campaigns of
     2016 that gave us Brexit and Trump.")

for ent in sentence.ents:
        print(ent.text + ": " + ent.label_)

two: CARDINAL
2016: DATE
Trump: PERSON
```

As we can see, when considering just this sentence, the transformer model did not assign an entity type for Brexit. Let's apply the model to the full paragraph and see what happens:

```
sentence = nlpt("It was a year ago this weekend that the Observer published the first
     in a series of stories, known as the Cambridge Analytica Files, "
               "that led to parliament grappling with these questions. The account of
     a whistleblower from inside the data analytics firm that had "
               "worked in different capacities - the details are still disputed - on
     the two pivotal campaigns of 2016 that gave us Brexit and the Trump
     administration.")

for ent in sentence.ents:
        print(ent.text + ": " + ent.label_)

a year ago this weekend: DATE
Observer: ORG
first: ORDINAL
the Cambridge Analytica Files: WORK_OF_ART
two: CARDINAL
2016: DATE
Brexit: ORG
Trump: PERSON
```

As you can see, it isn't until the full paragraph is processed that Brexit is detected as an organization rather than a geopolitical entity. Remember that transformers can analyse dependencies between fairly distant tokens, so it may be that the word 'parliament' is being tied to 'campaign' here, indicating that the model considers that incidence of 'Brexit' to be a government (i.e. political organization). What this example demonstrates is that a transformer model considers a wide context not just for training, *but also when it's applied to a piece of text.*

It is also a bit amusing that the Cambridge Analytica files were detected as a work of art. Read the article in full and reflect on why the model might be making such a judgement!

Sentiment analysis and named entities in context

Now that we have a pretty dependable way of detecting entities in text, there is quite a lot we can do. For example, we can gain more qualitative knowledge about those entities by going *back* to the original text to see how any given entity is being discussed, balancing more qualitative reading of original documents with more computational methods within an integrated multi-method framework like computational grounded theory (Nelson, 2017). Remember Firth's (1957) quote, 'You will know a word by the company it keeps.' Context here is everything, and when we rip entities from the contexts they are discussed in, it becomes harder to know what they actually mean, or why they were together in the sentence. In what follows, we'll use a combination of sentiment analysis and network analysis to demonstrate one way of learning more about the contexts that named entities are referenced in.

It's entirely possible to fine-tune transformer models to focus on a specific task to give us the context we want, but that process could be a chapter on its own and would require a lot more system resources than you likely have easy access to. Thankfully, there are hundreds of models that have been fine-tuned for downstream tasks and made available in the HuggingFace repository – by developers, research labs, or the wider NLP community. Many of those tasks are optimizations for benchmarks that assess model performance for applications that are commercially oriented and are of limited applicability to social science research, such as automated question answering and translation (although there are probably some clever ways that someone could make use of those). Others are of greater interest to social scientists, such as sentiment analysis.

Briefly, sentiment analysis is an NLP method for identifying and assessing positive and negative *evaluations* in text. Sentiment analysis can be fine-grained with multiple categories, or it can be simply a positive or negative score. If you want to go fine-grained, you need to take care that the training used to tweak the objective is well-crafted enough to justify the complexity of the sentiment categories.

Further Reading

To learn more about sentiment analysis, I recommend Taboada (2016), Prabowo and Thelwall (2009), Hutto and Gilbert (2014), Mohammad (2016), and McLevey and Crick (2022).

spaCy has never been particularly focused on sentiment analysis, and so it doesn't have functionality to handle the heavy lifting. In this case, you're better off taking advantage of the pipelines built-in to HuggingFace's `transformers` library. Normally, even using a fine-tuned model takes a bit of work to apply, as the text you want to analyse needs to be preprocessed using the tokenizer that the base model expects and there are a number of moving pieces and decisions to make. With the built-in pipeline, `transformers` will handle virtually all of this, from downloading and caching the model to creating a classifier object that provides formatted results that are easy to work with.

Start by importing the `pipeline` class and instantiating a sentiment analysis classifier. This is when the model will be downloaded and cached. The default model is `distilbert` with fine-tuning for the Stanford Sentiment Treebank benchmark.

```
from transformers import pipeline

sentiment = pipeline('sentiment-analysis')

sentiment('"When you look at how, for example, the NCA [National Crime Agency] has
    just sat on blatant evidence of Russian interference in Brexit," Wylie says.'
        '"The Brexit angle of the Cambridge Analytica Files, the explosive
    revelations of a second whistleblower, Shahmir Sanni, fell inexplicably flat.')

[{'label': 'NEGATIVE', 'score': 0.9997309446334839}]
```

The returned score is the probability that the classification is accurate.

Notice that the input was technically two sentences. There is no reason why we have to process our text a sentence at a time; we can process and classify text of arbitrary lengths. However, one thing to keep in mind with transformers is that most have an inherent maximum sequence length (BERT is 512), including fine-tuned pretrained models, which will often have their own sequence length configured (the model we're using is 128). These limits are set because of the resource requirements inherent to the attention mechanisms used by the transformers. As previously mentioned, there are some options for processing longer text input, such as `Longformer`, which replaces the self-attention mechanism in RoBERTa with one that combines local windowed attention with task-specific global attention. It's also important to know that *sequence* length does not translate into a maximum *word* length. Most transformers, including BERT, use sub-word tokenization, as well as their own special tokens that you won't necessarily see, but are part of the sequence length. There are many different ways to address this limitation, but these are more or less model-specific, so here we will just play it safe by processing a single sentence at a time.

With the HuggingFace library, we can classify a batch of sentences at once. We simply pass a list of raw sentences. In return, we get a list of dictionaries containing the labels and scores (i.e. the probability that the score is correct):

```
scores = sentiment(['"When you look at how, for example, the NCA [National Crime
    Agency] has '
                    'just sat on blatant evidence of Russian interference in Brexit,"
    Wylie says.',
                    '"The Brexit angle of the Cambridge Analytica Files, the explosive
    revelations '
                    'of a second whistleblower, Shahmir Sanni, fell inexplicably flat."'
    ])
print(scores)

[{'label': 'NEGATIVE', 'score': 0.9984580874443054}, {'label': 'NEGATIVE', 'score':
    0.9997546076774597}]
```

We can return to our spaCy doc object to keep this process simple:

```
sentences = [sent.text for sent in doct.sents]
```

```
scores = sentiment(sentences)
```

Let's make the results into a dataframe so we can take a better look at them. We'll print the positive sentences with the highest and the lowest probability, and the same for negative sentences:

```
label, score = [x['label'] for x in scores], [x['score'] for x in scores]

df = pd.DataFrame()
df['sentence'], df['label'], df['score'] = sentences, label, score

top_pos = df[df['label'] == 'POSITIVE']['score'].idxmax()
bot_pos = df[df['label'] == 'POSITIVE']['score'].idxmin()
top_neg = df[df['label'] == 'NEGATIVE']['score'].idxmax()
bot_neg = df[df['label'] == 'NEGATIVE']['score'].idxmin()

for pos in [top_pos, bot_pos, top_neg, bot_neg]:
    print('Value: ' + str(df['score'].iloc[pos]) + '\nSentence: ' + df['sentence']
    .iloc[pos], '\n')
```

```
Value: 0.9997883439064026
Sentence: And this change in political tone is hugely significant."

Value: 0.5255212187767029
Sentence: But the scandal that followed seems to reveal something far more shocking.

Value: 0.9997935891151428
Sentence: " If it wasn't so tragic, it would be funny to Wylie that one of the
    biggest takeaways of the story – which was generating 34,000 news stories a day
    at its height and cost one of the biggest companies on Earth billions – is how it
    failed.
Value: 0.5627380013465881
Sentence: My overriding impression of the months before publication, I tell him, when
    we were working with lawyers on how to break his non-disclosure agreement and
    trying to prove the public interest case, and dealing with other news
    organisations, is of this long and dark and scary winter.
```

The first two exerpts are the most and least confident positive predictions, and the latter two are the most and least confident negative predictions. The latter three results make some sense, but the high certainty of the top positive result is a bit mysterious. The sentence seems fairly ambiguous on its own, as a political tone can change for better or for worse. But the classification and its high score are less ambiguous when you look at the sentence in context:

'But especially Facebook', says Bartlett. 'Just yesterday, the Democrat presidential hopeful Elizabeth Warren said she wants Facebook broken up. She wouldn't have said this without the Cambridge Analytica story. And this change in political tone is hugely significant.'

It's difficult to determine how the model made this decision. The article itself is highly positive about the Cambridge Analytica *story* but is implicitly negative about Cambridge Analytica *the organization*. It could be informative to see the sentiment in all of the sentences where Cambridge Analytica is recognized as an entity.

Below, we'll use the `entity_sentiment()` function from the `dcss` package to process each speech and then expand them out into a dataframe of sentences, with the leader who spoke them, their sentiment label, sentiment score, and the entities detected in the sentence. This convenience function simply chains together several methods you've seen in this chapter (and a few others).

```
sent_df = entity_sentiment(doct, sentiment, ['Cambridge Analytica'])

sent_df['sent_signed'] = sent_df['sentiment_score']
sent_df.loc[sent_df['sentiment'] == 'NEGATIVE', 'sent_signed'] *= -1

sent_df['sent_signed'].mean()

-0.4811149269592862
```

The average sentiment score for sentences that make explicit reference to Cambridge Analytica is pretty negative. To save space, we won't print all of these sentences, but if you look at them, you will notice that two high-probability *positive* sentences are about the story itself, rather than the organization.

We can be pretty confident that the sentiment analysis of the fine-tuned `distilbert` model is sensible enough to try applying it to a larger corpus and integrate the results into a larger analysis. Let's explore the speeches made by recent long-term leaders of the three largest national parties in the Canadian House of Commons.

Translating transformer insight into human insight

We'll load the speech data into a dataframe the same way that we have in previous chapters.

```
datasets = list_files("../data/canadian_hansards/lipad/", 'csv')
dfs = [pd.read_csv(df, low_memory=False) for df in datasets]
df = pd.concat(dfs)
```

Next, filter for the three Canadian political party leaders who were the heads of their parties for fairly long periods of time. I selected Jack Layton in particular because he led the New Democratic Party (NDP) during a time when they were the official opposition – party leaders who are neither in power nor the official opposition have far less speaking opportunities in the House of Commons. Even still, Jack Layton was in this position for a much shorter time than the other two leaders, and this is reflected in the number of speeches he has in the data.

```
leaders = ['Stephen Harper', 'Jack Layton', 'Jean Chrétien']
df_filt = df[df['speakername'].isin(leaders)]
df_filt.speakername.value_counts()

Stephen Harper    11394
Jean Chrétien     11060
Jack Layton        3334
Name: speakername, dtype: int64
```

To shorten the processing time, we'll disable the tagger, parser, and lemmatizer in spaCy's pipeline, but we'll enable the rule-based sentencizer. You will find that processing a modest corpus of less than 30,000 documents in spaCy with the transformer model is still quite slow if you don't use a GPU. As an alternative, you can simply skip the next couple of cells and load the provided pickle with all of the processing completed already:

```
nlp = spacy.load('en_core_web_trf', exclude=['tagger', 'parser', 'lemmatizer'])
nlp.add_pipe('sentencizer')
```

```
<spacy.pipeline.sentencizer.Sentencizer at 0x7f6718ebf5c0>
```

The following `process_speeches_sentiment()` function will also produce the same thing as the pickle below it, after some time:

```
sentiment_df = process_speeches_sentiment(df_filt, nlp, sentiment)
```

```
sentiment_df.to_pickle('../data/pickles/can_hansard_sentiment.pkl')
```

```
## RUN THIS CELL TO LOAD THE DATA WITH EVERYTHING ABOVE ANALYSED ALREADY
sentiment_df = pd.read_pickle('../data/pickles/can_hansard_sentiment.pkl')
```

We'll create a new column with negative sentiment scores negated, in order to simplify using them in any calculations:

```
sentiment_df['sent_signed'] = sentiment_df['sentiment_score']
sentiment_df.loc[sentiment_df['sentiment'] == 'NEGATIVE', 'sent_signed'] *= -1
```

As you can see, Jack Layton has a much larger proportion of sentences with negative sentiment than the other leaders, even though he was often considered to be a relatively positive figure, as far as politicians go. This is also likely an artefact of him only ever being the official opposition and never in power. The role of the official opposition is to challenge the government in power, while governments in power want to maintain the impression that life is mostly okay.

```
sentiment_df.value_counts(subset=['speaker', 'sentiment'], sort=False)
```

```
speaker           sentiment
Jack Layton       NEGATIVE    2765
                  POSITIVE    1715
Jean Chrétien     NEGATIVE    4560
                  POSITIVE    6209
Stephen Harper    NEGATIVE    7412
                  POSITIVE    6492
dtype: int64
```

If we group the dataframe by speaker and then take the average of their sentiment score probabilities, we end up with a sort of metric that better accounts for the cases where the sentiment model wasn't as confident about its assessment. Another way of thinking of this is that sentences aren't 100% positive or negative all the time and can instead express a mixture of the two.

```
sentiment_df.groupby('speaker')['sent_signed'].mean()
```

```
speaker
Jack Layton         -0.228365
Jean Chrétien        0.152638
Stephen Harper      -0.062230
Name: sent_signed, dtype: float64
```

We'll move onto the final step of incorporating a network analysis shortly, but first let's use the `create_speaker_edge_df()` function in the `dcss` package to create a dataframe that conveniently doubles as a way to look at the sentiment in sentences containing specific entities. Then, we'll group and sort the dataframes to see the pairings of entities with the highest and the lowest sentiments.

```
chretien_df = create_speaker_edge_df(sentiment_df, 'Jean Chrétien')
layton_df = create_speaker_edge_df(sentiment_df, 'Jack Layton')
harper_df = create_speaker_edge_df(sentiment_df, 'Stephen Harper')
```

Let's take a look at some results for Jean Chrétien:

```
chretien_df.groupby(['source','target'])['weight'].mean().reset_index().sort_values(by
    ='weight', ascending = False)
```

	source	target	weight
1107	David Pelletier	Jamie Sale	0.999883
1091	Daniel Wesley	Karolina Wisniewska	0.999870
1811	Karolina Wisniewska	Lauren Woolstencroft	0.999870
458	Brian McKeever	Lauren Woolstencroft	0.999870
457	Brian McKeever	Karolina Wisniewska	0.999870
...	...	...	...
2775	Speaker	the Globe and Mail	-0.999705
122	Amman	British Columbia	-0.999717
125	Amman	Speaker	-0.999717
1523	House	NHL	-0.999755
429	Bouchard	the Province of Quebec	-0.999758

```
[3101 rows x 3 columns]
```

For Chrétien, we can clearly see negative sentiment expressed in contexts where Quebec and the leader of their national party at the time, Lucien Bouchard, are mentioned together. If you know much about Canadian politics, this should not come as a surprise; Chrétien was quite open about not being a fan of Bouchard.

On the flip side, one of the highest sentiment combinations for Jack Layton (see the code below) is Quebec and their government. Layton's NDP became official opposition largely because of an unexpected sweep of seats in Quebec that had never voted NDP party members into office before. Layton's sentiment towards the province could be a contribution to that sweep, gratitude for it, or likely some combination. Also high on the list, unsurprisingly, is Olivia Chow, who was also a member of parliament in the NDP and Jack Layton's partner. Finally, the low sentiment combinations involving HST (Harmonized Sales Tax) reflect Layton's open opposition to a new method of taxation that was being introduced at the time.

```
layton_df.groupby(['source','target'])['weight'].mean().reset_index().sort_values(by='
    weight', ascending = False)
```

	source	target \
1316	Longueuil	Pierre-Boucher
1615	Quebec	the Government of Quebec
462	Canada	June
1386	Mike	Olivia Chow
1531	Olivia Chow	Sarah
...	...	...
1409	Molson	The Bay
342	Bruce Fitzpatrick	the Peterborough Federal Conservative Riding A...
341	Bruce Fitzpatrick	HST
987	HST	the Peterborough Federal Conservative Riding A...
3	ATI Technologies	Abitibi

	weight
1316	0.999855
1615	0.999850
462	0.999843
1386	0.999830
1531	0.999830
...	...
1409	-0.999782
342	-0.999785
341	-0.999785
987	-0.999785
3	-0.999791

[1864 rows x 3 columns]

Like Jack Layton, Stephen Harper (see the code below) also spent some time courting votes in Quebec, with the pairing to Canada reflecting his strategy of appealing to the somewhat nationalist side of Quebec's population; he referred to the province as the 'foundation of Canada'. As a final example, the low sentiment of the combination of the Liberal Party and the Canadian Senate – a level of government with appointed rather than elected members – likely reflects his frustrations with the Senate as an institution in general, and particularly one that had a strong majority of Liberal appointees.

```
harper_df.groupby(['source','target'])['weight'].mean().reset_index().sort_values(by='
    weight', ascending = False)
```

	source	target	weight
1787	Grant	Robert	0.999878
927	Canada	Peterborough	0.999873
3631	Veterans Affairs	Walt Natynczyk	0.999870
935	Canada	Québec	0.999863
2293	John Paul II	the Catholic Church	0.999863
...	...	...	...
2083	Hussein	the United Nations	-0.999770
854	Canada	Hussein	-0.999770
2384	La Presse	Pierre Gravel	-0.999788
3892	the Liberal Party	the Senate of Canada	-0.999788
2889	Obama	the Liberal Party	-0.999790

[3928 rows x 3 columns]

There are many, many other ways that one could look in great detail at the results of this entity co-occurrence sentiment analysis, but we will now move on to a technique for analysing whether there are latent structural configurations discernible from the entities mentioned together in these speeches. We'll do this with the SBMs that were introduced in much more detail in Chapter 30.

Analysing co-occurring named entities with stochastic block models

One of the main goals of NER is to extract *structured* pieces of data, such as the name of an event or a person from *unstructured* text. Squire (2016) likens this to sifting for gold, separating the gold (the names of the entities) from the dirt (the rest of the text). Sometimes the analysis we want to do is on the entities themselves, such as counting the most frequently occurring organizations, or looking at networks of co-occurrences of named entities within sentences or paragraphs.

In this exploratory analysis, we'll use a function from `dcss – create_speaker_edge_df()` – that accepts the sentiment and entity dataframe we created above and returns an edge list dataframe for the designated speaker. We assign an undirected edge between two entities if they are both referenced in the same sentence, and we'll use the sentiment score for that sentence as an attribute of the edge. Then we'll analyse the data by fitting an SBM.

```
chretien_df = create_speaker_edge_df(sentiment_df, 'Jean Chrétien')
layton_df = create_speaker_edge_df(sentiment_df, 'Jack Layton')
harper_df = create_speaker_edge_df(sentiment_df, 'Stephen Harper')
```

As mentioned above, we can start this process with the same dataframes we used to take a quick look at sentiment towards co-occurring entities. By sending these dataframes to the `shrink_small_df` utility from the `dcss` package, we end up with a dataframe that has been grouped so that all of the edges between the same two entities are aggregated, with the number of edges added as an edge weight:

```
chretien_small_df = shrink_sent_df(chretien_df)
layton_small_df = shrink_sent_df(layton_df)
harper_small_df = shrink_sent_df(harper_df)
```

We can provide the grouped dataframes to the `blockmodel_from_edge_df` function from the `dcss` package to construct the network and estimate the SBM. The function provides the option to produce a filter mask for the graph, so that it can be filtered later (or anytime) in order to produce a block model graph with `n_edges` from highest weight to lowest weight. Note that the block model is estimated with all edges and nodes – the filter is only meant to help create cleaner visualizations. Finally, there is an optional parameter `use_weights` in the utility function that can be set to `True` in order to incorporate whatever values are in the 'weight' column of the dataframe, as a covariate for block model estimation. This option is not used here because it can *dramatically* increase processing time (even on the lab server I am using here, which has 32 CPU cores available).

So, let's estimate those block models! We'll set `n_edges` to 200, as mentioned, for visual clarity:

```
chretien_small_G, chretien_small_blocks = blockmodel_from_edge_df(chretien_small_df,
    n_edges = 200)
```

```
layton_small_G, layton_small_blocks = blockmodel_from_edge_df(layton_small_df, n_edges
    = 200)
harper_small_G, harper_small_blocks = blockmodel_from_edge_df(harper_small_df, n_edges
    = 200)
```

Before we start interpreting the results of the block model partitioning, let's create a block model graph for each of the leaders. Once again, there is a utility function for this available from dcss, called draw_ner_blockmodel_sfdp. This function expects the first argument to be the network graph and the second to be the block model. It also accepts an optional filename to output an image to the given filename (which can be a full filepath, not just the name of the the the file). If a filename is not provided, the block model graph will be displayed in the notebook instead.

The code below produces all three of the images, which are Figures 32.2–32.4.

```
draw_ner_blockmodel_sfdp(chretien_small_G, chretien_small_blocks, filename = '../
    figures/chretien_blockmodel_top200_unweighted_sfdp.pdf')
draw_ner_blockmodel_sfdp(layton_small_G, layton_small_blocks, filename = '../figures/
    layton_blockmodel_top200_unweighted_sfdp.pdf')
draw_ner_blockmodel_sfdp(harper_small_G, harper_small_blocks, filename = '../figures/
    harper_blockmodel_top200_unweighted_sfdp.pdf')
```

As with the earlier sentiment dataframes, there's too much information here to exhaustively interpret. But in Chrétien's graph (Figure 32.2), for a start, we can clearly see certain countries

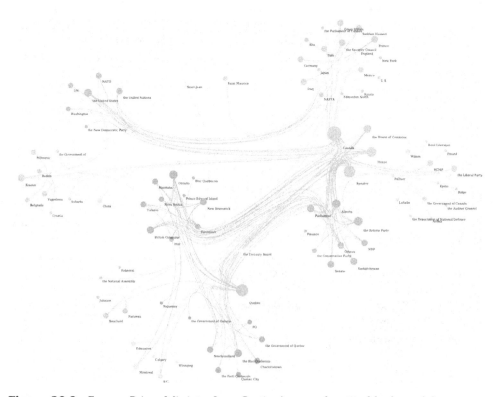

Figure 32.2 Former Prime Minister Jean Cretien's named entity block model

together in one partition, while others are in another. Similarly, a number of Canadian provinces that had uneasy relationships with Chrétien (Quebec, Alberta, and Newfoundland & Labrador) are in one block while the rest of the provinces are in another.

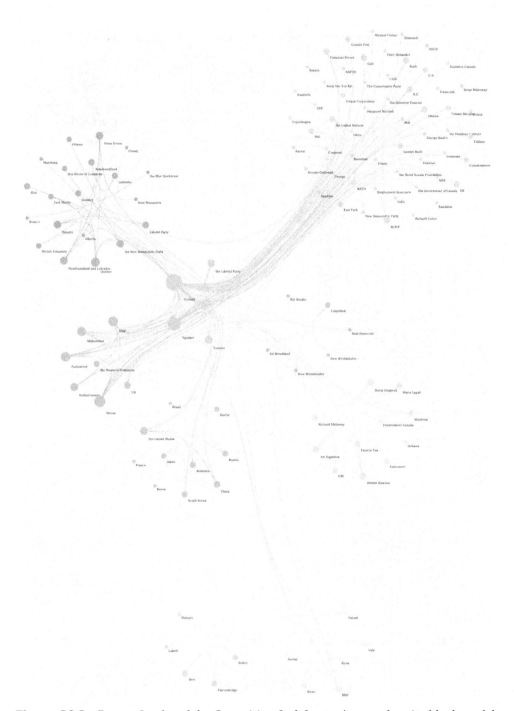

Figure 32.3 Former Leader of the Opposition Jack Layton's named entity block model

The results for Jack Layton are a bit of a mixed bag. Some blocks make sense, such as a block containing countries other than Canada, and another containing provices and the Bloc Quebecois Party as the lone government entity. However, there's also a very populated block with a wide range of entities that are tough to see an intuitive common ground for. This block model (Figure 32.3) might call for some iterative development (Box's loop) to produce more well-defined partitions out of the very large group, or it might be the case that the way Layton talked about each of these various entities was less patterned and predictable than his political colleagues.

Finally, for Stephen Harper, the entities are partitioned in a fairly intuitively way. One block consists of provinces with fairly small populations, while his home province of Alberta shares a block with the two provinces that house more than half of Canada's population (Figure 32.4). Meanwhile, another three blocks seem to be made up of entities related to three different international conflicts – in Syria, Afghanistan, and Iraq. China, India, and Japan are also grouped together. What do think is going on there?

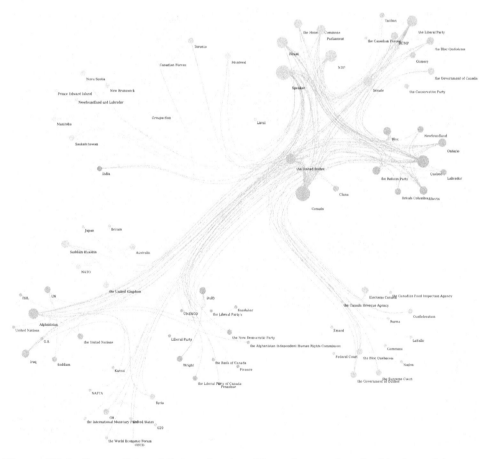

Figure 32.4 Former Prime Minister Stephen Harper's named entity block model

The `get_sentiment_blocks_df` function from `dcss` returns a dataframe with the block assignment for every entity in the graph. We pass it the graph object first and then the block model:

```
chretien_results = get_sentiment_blocks_df(chretien_small_G, chretien_small_blocks)
layton_results = get_sentiment_blocks_df(layton_small_G, layton_small_blocks)
harper_results = get_sentiment_blocks_df(harper_small_G, harper_small_blocks)

chretien_results.head()
```

```
              entity        block
0             Canada            0
1             Quebec            1
2            Speaker            0
3   the United States          2
4              House            0
```

Finally, `calculate_avg_block_sentiment`, also from the `dcss` package, produces a dataframe where each row is a block, the entities column has a list of the names of each block member, and there's an average sentiment score for sentiment pairwise between each member of the block. This means the speaker expressed that average sentiment when speaking of those entities together. Take note that this will not necessarily reflect the block assignment structure – these sentiment weights were not factored into the block model estimation. These can take a bit of time to run, so preprocessed pickles are available, as usual:

```
chretien_block_sentiment_df = calculate_avg_block_sentiment(chretien_results,
    chretien_df)
chretien_block_sentiment_df.to_pickle('../data/pickles/
    chretien_blockmodel_sent_analysis.pkl')

## RUN TO LOAD THE PICKLED DATAFRAME
chretien_block_sentiment_df = pd.read_pickle('../data/pickles/
    chretien_blockmodel_sent_analysis.pkl')

chretien_block_sentiment_df.head(30)
```

```
    block                                   entities  avg_sentiments
0       0  [Canada, Speaker, House, the House of Commons,...       -0.068260
1       1  [Quebec, the Bloc Quebecois, New Brunswick, Ne...       -0.270369
2       2  [the United States, France, Great Britain, Ger...        0.204894
3       3  [Ontario, Manitoba, Saskatchewan, Charlottetow...        0.261303
4       4  [the Parti Quebecois, Mexico, PQ, Johnson, Par...        0.091311
5       5  [the Reform Party, Parliament, Alberta, RCMP, ...        0.063778
6       6           [NATO, Kosovo, the United Nations, UN]        0.655119
7       7  [the Security Council, Saddam Hussein, Blix, I...        0.138377
8       8  [Senate, Bloc, the Conservative Party, Airbus,...        0.145302
9       9  [China, India, Pakistan, Indonesia, the Soviet...        0.783205
10     10  [Milosevic, Bosnia, Croatia, the Government of...        0.227347
11     11  [Saint-Maurice, Esquimalt, Juan de Fuca, Nanai...        0.488620
12     12  [Saint-Jean, Kingston, Afghanistan, the Canada...        0.265714
13     13  [Roberval, UNSCOM, Israel, Palestine, Saddam, ...        0.340711
14     14  [Antonine Maillet, Gabrielle Roy, Margo Kane, ...        0.965706
15     15  [The Arthritis Society, the Calgary Catholic I...       -0.998867
```

If you cross-reference the members of these blocks with the block model graphs (Figures 32.2–32.4), you'll be able to see who's in each block and who they are connected to, but with a better sense of the sentiment from the speaker when speaking about each pair of entities.

```
layton_block_sentiment_df = calculate_avg_block_sentiment(layton_results, layton_df)
layton_block_sentiment_df.to_pickle('../data/pickles/layton_blockmodel_sent_analysis.
    pkl')
```

```
## RUN TO LOAD THE PICKLED DATAFRAME
layton_block_sentiment_df.to_pickle('../data/pickles/layton_blockmodel_sent_analysis.
    pkl')
```

```
layton_block_sentiment_df.head(30)
```

```
    block                                entities avg_sentiments
0       0              [Canada, Speaker, House, Parliament]      -0.444194
1       1   [Afghanistan, NDP, Quebec, UN, Ontario, the Li...      -0.300015
2       2   [the United States, Darfur, China, Japan, Sout...      -0.061132
3       3   [NATO, U.S., Bush, the House of Commons, the N...      -0.024512
4       4   [British Columbia, Coquitlam, New Westminster,...      -0.171941
5       5   [Montreal, Toronto, Ottawa, Nortel, the Bloc Q...      -0.234125
6       6   [Vancouver, GM, Oshawa, Margaret Mitchell, Gat...       0.067261
7       7   [Falconbridge, Inco, Alcan, Alcoa, Stelco, Dof...      -0.995202
8       8   [Vale, BHP, Potash, Georgia-Pacific, Vale Inco...      -0.863167
9       9   [David Dingwall, Richard Mahoney, Art Eggleton...      -0.668836
10     10   [Bill Blaikie, Ed Broadbent, Frank Rainville, ...       0.823316
```

Remember that, in this case, the visualization of the block model graph is filtered to the top 200 edges. Any nodes that weren't part of those connections won't be on the graph. In a huge network, it becomes pretty difficult to discern nodes anyway and edges even more. But with a high-quality image and reliable layout, you can look at the block members in a dataframe and see where they'd be situated if they *were* on the graph.

```
harper_block_sentiment_df = calculate_avg_block_sentiment(harper_results, harper_df)
harper_block_sentiment_df.to_pickle('../data/pickles/harper_blockmodel_sent_analysis.
    pkl')
```

```
## RUN TO LOAD THE PICKLED DATAFRAME
harper_block_sentiment_df.to_pickle('../data/pickles/harper_blockmodel_sent_analysis.
    pkl')
```

```
harper_block_sentiment_df.head(30)
```

```
    block                                entities avg_sentiments
0       0   [NDP, Speaker, the Liberal Party, House, Parli...       0.058924
1       1               [Canada, the United States, China]      -0.000844
2       2   [Quebec, Bloc, Senate, the Conservative Party,...      -0.167042
3       3   [Duffy, Wright, UNESCO, Gomery, the Liberal Pa...      -0.036970
```

```
4     4  [Ontario, the Bloc Quebecois, Labrador, Newfou...     -0.058601
5     5  [Afghanistan, the Canadian Forces, Taliban, NA...      0.172953
6     6  [Iraq, the United Nations, U.S., UN, ISIL, Syr...     -0.158887
7     7  [Saddam Hussein, Australia, the United Kingdom...      0.508794
8     8  [Elections Canada, LaSalle, Émard, Penashue, t...     -0.010631
9     9  [Laval, the Conseil du patronat du Québec, the...      0.997304
10    10 [OECD, G8, the International Monetary Fund, th...       0.284104
11    11 [India, Mexico, Mulroney, Laurier, Trudeau, Ky...     -0.325267
12    12 [Groupaction, Canadian Forces, the Department ...      -0.314922
13    13 [the Federation of Canadian Municipalities, th...      0.999614
14    14 [Calgary, Edmonton, CFB Calgary, CFB Edmonton,...      0.526361
```

32.6 Conclusion

The key points in this chapter are as follows:

- We iteratively developed several NER models using spaCy, starting from out of the box and then tuning it.
- Transfer learning is using machine learning models in contexts for which they were not originally trained.
- Transformer models are incredibly powerful, incredibly efficient, and can make use of data and computing power in incredible ways.
- We combined many different concepts, methods, and models from this book into a single exploratory data analysis.

Visit the website at https://study.sagepub.com/mclevey for additional resources

REFERENCES

adams, j. (2020) *Gathering Social Network Data*. Thousand Oaks, CA: Sage.

Ananny, M. and Crawford, K. (2018) 'Seeing without knowing: limitations of the transparency ideal and its application to algorithmic accountability'. *New Media & Society*, 20 (3): 973–89.

Angwin, J., Larson, J., Mattu, S. and Kirchner, L. (2016, 23 May) 'Machine bias'. *ProPublica*.

Armstrong, E. and Bernstein, M. (2008) 'Culture, power, and institutions: a multi-institutional politics approach to social movements'. *Sociological Theory*, 26 (1): 74–99.

Artetxe, M., Labaka, G. and Agirre, E. (2016) 'Learning principled bilingual mappings of word embeddings while preserving monolingual invariance'. In *Proceedings of the 2016 Conference on Empirical Methods in Natural Language Processing*, 2289–94.

Ball, P. (2016) *Principled Data Processing*. New York: Data & Society.

Barabási, A.-L. and Albert, R. (1999) 'Emergence of scaling in random networks', *Science*, 286 (5439): 509–12.

Barton, A. (1968) 'Bringing society back in survey research and macro-methodology'. *The American Behavioral Scientist*, 12 (2): 1–9.

Bearman, P., Moody, J. and Stovel, K. (2004) 'Chains of affection: the structure of adolescent romantic and sexual networks'. *American Journal of Sociology*, 110 (1): 44–91.

Benford, R. (1993) 'Frame disputes within the nuclear disarmament movement'. *Social Forces*, 71 (3): 677–701.

Benford, R. and Snow, D. (2000) 'Framing processes and social movements: an overview and assessment'. *Annual Review of Sociology*, 26 (1): 611–39.

Beninger, K. (2017) 'Social media users' views on the ethics of social media research', in L. Sloan and A. Quan-Haase (eds), *The SAGE Handbook of Social Media Research Methods*. London: Sage. pp. 57–73.

Benjamin, R. (2019) *Race After Technology: Abolitionist Tools for the New Jim Code*. Cambridge: Polity Press.

Berelson, B. (1952) *Content Analysis in Communication Research*. Glencoe, IL: Free Press.

Biernacki, R. (2009) 'After quantitative cultural sociology: interpretive science as a calling', in I. Reed and J.C. Alexander (eds), *Meaning and Method*. London: Routledge. pp. 125–213.

Biernacki, R. (2012) *Reinventing Evidence in Social Inquiry: Decoding Facts and Variables*. New York: Springer.

Biernacki, R. (2015) 'How to do things with historical texts'. *American Journal of Cultural Sociology*, 3 (3): 311–52.

Birhane, A. and Cummins, F. (2019) 'Algorithmic injustices: towards a relational ethics'. *Sociology, Computer Science. arXiv Preprint arXiv:1912.07376*.

Blei, D. (2012) 'Probabilistic topic models'. *Communications of the ACM*, 55 (4): 77–84.

Blei, D. (2017, 1 May) 'Variational inference: foundations and innovations'. *Computational Challenges in Machine Learning*. Berkeley, CA: Simons Institute.

Blei, D. and Lafferty, J. (2006) 'Dynamic topic models'. In *Proceedings of the 23rd International Conference on Machine Learning*, pp. 113–20.

Blei, D. and Lafferty, J. (2009) 'Topic models', in A.N. Srivastave and M. Sahami (eds), *Text Mining: Classification, Clustering, and Applications*. Boca Raton, FL: CRC Press. pp. 71–94.

Blei, D., Ng, A. and Jordan, M.I. (2003) 'Latent Dirichlet allocation'. *Journal of Machine Learning Research*, 3: 993–1022.

Bolukbasi, T., Chang, K.-W., Zou, J., Saligrama, V. and Kalai, A. (2016) 'Man is to computer programmer as woman is to homemaker? Debiasing word embeddings'. *arXiv Preprint arXiv:1607.06520*.

Bonacich, P. (1987) 'Power and centrality: a family of measures'. *American Journal of Sociology*, 92 (5): 1170–82.

Bonikowski, B. (2017) 'Ethno-nationalist populism and the mobilization of collective resentment'. *British Journal of Sociology*, 68: S181–213.

Bonikowski, B. and Gidron, N. (2016) 'The populist style in American politics: presidential campaign discourse, 1952–1996'. *Social Forces*, 94 (4): 1593–1621.

Borgatti, S. and Everett, M. (2020) *Three Perspectives on Centrality*. R. Light and J. Moody (eds). Oxford: Oxford University Press.

Borgatti, S., Everett, M. and Johnson, J. (2018) *Analyzing Social Networks*. Thousand Oaks, CA: Sage.

Brailly, J., Favre, G., Chatellet, J. and Lazega, E. (2016) 'Embeddedness as a multilevel problem: a case study in economic sociology'. *Social Networks*, 44: 319–33.

Brandes, U. and Fleischer, D. (2005) 'Centrality measures based on current flow'. In *Annual Symposium on Theoretical Aspects of Computer Science*. New York: Springer. pp. 533–44.

Breiger, R. (1974) 'The duality of persons and groups'. *Social Forces*, 53 (2): 181–90.

Breiman, L. (2001) 'Statistical modeling: the two cultures'. *Statistical Science*, 16 (3): 199–231.

Brekhus, W. and Ignatow, G. (2019) *The Oxford Handbook of Cognitive Sociology*. New York: Oxford University Press.

Brienza, J., Kung, F., Santos, H., Bobocel, R. and Grossmann, I. (2018) 'Wisdom, bias, and balance: toward a process-sensitive measurement of wisdom-related cognition'. *Journal of Personality and Social Psychology*, 115 (6): 1093–1126.

Brown, P., Roediger, H. and McDaniel, M. (2014) *Make it Stick: The Science of Successful Learning*. Cambridge, MA: Harvard University Press.

Brown, T., Mann, B., Ryder, N., Subbiah, M., Kaplan, J., Dhariwal, P., et al. (2020) 'Language models are few-shot learners'. *arXiv Preprint arXiv:2005.14165*.

Bruch, E. and Atwell, J. (2015) 'Agent-based models in empirical social research'. *Sociological Methods & Research*, 44 (2): 186–221.

Buhari-Gulmez, D. (2010) 'Stanford school on sociological institutionalism: a global cultural approach'. *International Political Sociology*, 4 (3): 253–70.

Buolamwini, J. and Gebru, T. (2018) 'Gender shades: intersectional accuracy disparities in commercial gender classification'. In *Conference on Fairness, Accountability and Transparency*. PMLR. pp. 77–91.

Cadwalladr, C. (2019, 17 March) 'Cambridge Analytica a year on: a lesson in institutional failure'. *Guardian*.

The Canadian Parliament (2021) 'The Canadian Commons Hansard'.

Caren, N. (2007) 'Political process theory', in G. Ritzer (ed.), *The Blackwell Encyclopedia of Sociology*. Malden, MA: Blackwell.

Centola, D. (2018) *How Behavior Spreads: The Science of Complex Contagions*. Princeton, NJ: Princeton University Press.

Centola, D. (2021) *Change: How to Make Big Things Happen*. New York: Little, Brown Spark.

Centola, D. and Macy, M. (2007) 'Complex contagions and the weakness of long ties'. *American Journal of Sociology*, 113 (3): 702–34.

Cerulo, K. (2002) *Culture in Mind: Toward a Sociology of Culture and Cognition*. London: Psychology Press.

Cerulo, K.A. (2010) 'Mining the intersections of cognitive sociology and neuroscience'. *Poetics*, 38 (2): 115–32.

Charmaz, K. (2006) *Constructing Grounded Theory: A Practical Guide Through Qualitative Analysis*. Thousand Oaks, CA: Sage.

Chollet, F. (2018) *Deep Learning with Python* (Vol. 361). New York: Manning.

Collins, H., Evans, R., Durant, D. and Weinel, M. (2020) *Experts and the Will of the People*. Cham, Switzerland: Palgrave Macmillan.

Collins, P. (2015) 'Intersectionality's definitional dilemmas'. *Annual Review of Sociology*, 41: 1–20.

Collins, P. and Bilge, S. (2020) *Intersectionality*. New York: Wiley.

Coppedge, M., Gerring, J., Glynn, A., Knutsen, C.H., Lindberg, S., Pemstein, D., et al. (2020) *Varieties of Democracy: Measuring Two Centuries of Political Change*. Cambridge: Cambridge University Press.

Coppedge, M., Gerring, J., Knutsen, C., Lindberg, S., Teorell, J., Altman, D., et al. (2021) 'V-Dem Codebook v11.1'. Varieties of Democracy (V-Dem) Project.

Crawford, K. and Paglen, T. (2019) 'Excavating AI: the politics of images in machine learning training sets'. https://excavating.ai/

Crenshaw, K. (1989) 'Demarginalizing the intersection of race and sex: a black feminist critique of antidiscrimination doctrine, feminist theory and antiracist politics'. *University of Chicago Legal Forum*, 139.

Crossley, N. (2010) *Towards Relational Sociology*. London: Routledge.

Crossley, N., Bellotti, E., Edwards, G., Everett, M.G., Koskinen, J. and Tranmer, M. (2015) *Social Network Analysis for Ego-Nets: Social Network Analysis for Actor-Centred Networks*. Thousand Oaks, CA: Sage.

Davis, J.A. and Leinhardt, S. (1967) *The Structure of Positive Interpersonal Relations in Small Groups*. Chicago, IL: National Opinion Research Center.

Deerwester, S., Dumais, S., Furnas, G., Landauer, T. and Harshman, R. (1990) 'Indexing by latent semantic analysis'. *Journal of the American Society for Information Science*, 41 (6): 391–407.

Denton, E., Hanna, A., Amironesei, R., Smart, A., Nicole, H. and Scheuerman, M.K. (2020) 'Bringing the people back in: contesting benchmark machine learning datasets'. *arXiv Preprint arXiv:2007.07399*.

Devlin, J., Chang, M.-W., Lee, K. and Toutanova, K. (2018) 'BERT: pre-training of deep bidirectional transformers for language understanding'. *arXiv Preprint arXiv:1810.04805*.

Di Carlo, V., Bianchi, F. and Palmonari, M. (2019) 'Training temporal word embeddings with a compass'. In *Proceedings of the AAAI Conference on Artificial Intelligence*, 33 (01): 6326–34.

Diakopoulos, N. (2017) 'Enabling accountability of algorithmic media: transparency as a constructive and critical lens', in T. Cerquitelli, D. Quercia and F. Pasquale (eds), *Transparent Data Mining for Big and Small Data*. New York: Springer. pp. 25–43.

Diakopoulos, N. (2020) 'Transparency', in M.D. Dubber, F. Pasquale and S. Das (eds), *The Oxford Handbook of Ethics of AI*. Oxford: Oxford University Press.

Dieng, A., Ruiz, F. and Blei, D. (2019) 'The dynamic embedded topic model'. *arXiv Preprint arXiv:1907.05545*.

Dieng, A.B., Ruiz, F.J.R. and Blei, D.M. (2020) 'Topic modeling in embedding spaces'. *Transactions of the Association for Computational Linguistics*, 8: 439–53.

Dietz, K. and Heesterbeek, J.A.P. (2002) 'Daniel Bernoulli's epidemiological model revisited'. *Mathematical Biosciences*, 180 (1–2): 1–21.

DiMaggio, P. (1997) 'Culture and cognition'. *Annual Review of Sociology*, 23 (1): 263–87.

DiMaggio, P., Nag, M. and Blei, D. (2013) 'Exploiting affinities between topic modeling and the sociological perspective on culture: application to newspaper coverage of US government arts funding'. *Poetics*, 41 (6): 570–606.

DiPrete, T. and Eirich, G. (2006) 'Cumulative advantage as a mechanism for inequality: a review of theoretical and empirical developments'. *Annual Review of Sociology*, 32: 271–97.

Domingos, P. (2015) *The Master Algorithm: How the Quest for the Ultimate Learning Machine Will Remake Our World*. New York: Basic Books.

Doreian, P., Batagelj, V. and Ferligoj, A. (2002) *Positional Analyses of Sociometric Data*. Ljubljana, Slovania: University of Ljubljana, Institute of Mathematics, Physics and Mechanics.

Doreian, P., Batagelj, V. and Ferligoj, A. (2005) *Generalized Blockmodeling* (Vol. 25). Cambridge: Cambridge University Press.

Douglas, H. (2009) *Science, Policy, and the Value-Free Ideal*. Pittsburgh, PA: University of Pittsburgh.

Doyle, T. and Zakrajsek, T. (2018) *The New Science of Learning: How to Learn in Harmony with Your Brain*. Sterling, VA: Stylus.

Duckett, J. (2011) *HTML & CSS: Design and Build Websites* (Vol. 15). Indianapolis, IN: Wiley.

Dumais, S. (2004) 'Latent semantic analysis'. *Annual Review of Information Science and Technology*, 38 (1): 188–230.

Edelmann, A. and Mohr, J. (2018) 'Formal studies of culture: issues, challenges, and current trends'. *Poetics*, 68: 1–9.

Elbourne, P. (2011) *Meaning: A Slim Guide to Semantics*. Oxford: Oxford University Press.

Emirbayer, M. (1997) 'Manifesto for a relational sociology'. *American Journal of Sociology*, 103 (2): 281–317.

Epstein, J. (2006) *Generative Social Science: Studies in Agent-Based Computational Modeling*. Princeton, NJ: Princeton University Press.

Ericsson, A.K. and Poole, R. (2016) *Peak: How to Master Almost Anything*. Toronto: Penguin Random House.

Eubanks, V. (2018) *Automating Inequality: How High-Tech Tools Profile, Police, and Punish the Poor*. New York: St. Martin's Press.

European Values Study. (2017) 'European Values Study 2017: Integrated Dataset (EVS 2017)'.

Evans, J.A. and Aceves, P. (2016) 'Machine translation: mining text for social theory'. *Annual Review of Sociology*, 42: 21–50.

Feld, S. (1991) 'Why your friends have more friends than you do'. *American Journal of Sociology*, 96 (6): 1464–77.

Ferligoj, A., Doreian, P. and Batagelj, V. (2011) 'Positions and roles', in J. Scott and P.J. Carrington (eds), *The SAGE Handbook of Social Network Analysis*. Thousand Oaks, CA: Sage. pp. 434–46.

Field, A., Miles, J. and Field, Z. (2012) *Discovering Statistics Using R*. Thousand Oaks, CA: Sage.

Firth, J. (1957) 'A synopsis of linguistic theory, 1930-1955', in *Studies in Linguistic Analysis*. Oxford: Blackwell.

Fontes, R. (2020) 'US Election 2020'.

Franzosi, R. (2004) *From Words to Numbers: Narrative, Data, and Social Science*. Cambridge: Cambridge University Press.

Freedom House. (2020) 'Freedom on the Net'. Washington, DC: Freedom House.

Freeman, L. (2004) *The Development of Social Network Analysis: A Study in the Sociology of Science*. Vancouver, Canada: Empirical Press.

Freelon, D. (2018) 'Computational Research in the Post-API Age'. *Political Communication*, 35 (4): 665–668.

Garg, N., Schiebinger, L., Jurafsky, D. and Zou, J. (2018) 'Word embeddings quantify 100 years of gender and ethnic stereotypes'. *Proceedings of the National Academy of Sciences*, 115 (16): E3635–44.

Gebru, T. (2018) 'How to stop artificial intelligence from marginalizing communities?' https://www.youtube.com/watch?v=PWCtoVt1CJM

Gebru, T. (2020) 'Race and gender', in M.D. Dubber, F. Pasquale and S. Das (eds), *The Oxford Handbook of Ethics of AI*. Oxford: Oxford University Press. pp. 251–69.

Gebru, T., Morgenstern, J., Vecchione, B., Vaughan, J.W., Wallach, H., Daumé, H. III, et al. (2018) 'Data sheets for datasets'. *arXiv Preprint arXiv:1803.09010*.

Gelman, A. (2004) 'Exploratory data analysis for complex models'. *Journal of Computational and Graphical Statistics*, 13 (4): 755–79.

Gelman, A. (2015, 15 July) 'Statistical modelling, causal inference, and social science' [Blog].

Gelman, A. (2020) Prior choice recommendations. https://github.com/stan-dev/stan/wiki/Prior-Choice-Recommendations

Gelman, A. and Robert, C. (2013a) '"Not only defended but also applied": the perceived absurdity of Bayesian inference'. *The American Statistician*, 67 (1): 1–5.

Gelman, A. and Robert, C.P. (2013b) 'Rejoinder: the anti-Bayesian moment and its passing'. *The American Statistician*, 67 (1): 16–17.

Gelman, A. and Shalizi, C.R. (2013) 'Philosophy and the practice of Bayesian statistics'. *British Journal of Mathematical and Statistical Psychology*, 66 (1): 8–38.

Gerlach, M., Peixoto, T. and Altmann, E. (2018) 'A network approach to topic models'. *Science Advances*, 4 (7): eaaq 1360.

Géron, A. (2019) *Hands-on Machine Learning with Scikit-Learn, Keras, and Tenso Flow: Concepts, Tools, and Techniques to Build Intelligent Systems*. Sebastopol, CA: O'Reilly Media.

Glaser, B. and Strauss, A. (1999) *Discovery of Grounded Theory: Strategies for Qualitative Research*. Piscataway, NJ: Aldine Transaction.

Goel, V. (2014, August 12) 'As data overflows online, researchers grapple with ethics'. *New York Times*, p. 12.

Gonen, H. and Goldberg, Y. (2019) 'Lipstick on a pig: debiasing methods cover up systematic gender biases in word embeddings but do not remove them'. *arXiv Preprint arXiv:1903.03862*.

Granovetter, M. (1973) 'The strength of weak ties'. *American Journal of Sociology*, 78 (6): 1360–80.

Granovetter, M. (1978) 'Threshold models of collective behavior'. *American Journal of Sociology*, 83 (6): 1420–43.

Green, B. (2021) 'Data science as political action: grounding data science in a politics of justice'. Working Paper.

Grimmelmann, J. (2015, May 7) 'The law and ethics of experiments on social media users'. *Colorado Technology Law Journal*, 13: 219.

Guilbeault, D., Becker, J. and Centola, D. (2018) 'Complex contagions: a decade in review', in S. Lehmann and Y. Ahn (eds), *Complex Spreading Phenomena in Social Systems*. London: Springer Nature. pp. 3–25.

Hamidi, F., Scheuerman, M.K. and Branham, S. (2018) 'Gender recognition or gender reductionism? The social implications of embedded gender recognition systems'. In *Proceedings of the 2018 Chi Conference on Human Factors in Computing Systems*, pp. 1–13.

Handcock, M., Hunter, D., Butts, C., Goodreau, S. and Morris, M. (2003) 'Statnet: Software Tools for the Statistical Modeling of Network Data' (version 2). Seattle, WA: University of Washington.

Hanna, A., Denton, E., Smart, A. and Smith-Loud, J. (2020) 'Towards a critical race methodology in algorithmic fairness'. In *Proceedings of the 2020 Conference on Fairness, Accountability, and Transparency*, pp. 501–12.

Hanneman, R. and Riddle, M. (2005) *Introduction to Social Network Methods*. Riverside, CA: University of California.

Harrigan, N., Labianca, G. and Agneessens, F. (2020) 'Negative ties and signed graphs research: stimulating research on dissociative forces in social networks'. *Social Networks*, 60: 1–10.

Harris, Z.S. (1954) 'Distributional structure'. *Word*, 10 (2–3): 146–62.

Healy, K. (2013) 'Using metadata to find Paul Revere'. https://kieranhealy.org/blog/archives/20 13/06/09/using-metadata-to-find-paul-revere/

Healy, K. (2018a) *Data Visualization: A Practical Introduction*. Princeton, NJ: Princeton University Press.

Healy, K. (2018b) 'The plain person's guide to plain text social science' [Blog post].

Healy, K. and Moody, J. (2014) 'Data visualization in sociology'. *Annual Review of Sociology*, 40: 105–28.

Hoffman, M., Bach, F. and Blei, D. (2010) 'Online learning for latent Dirichlet allocation'. In *Proceedings of the 23rd International Conference on Neural Information Processing Systems*, pp. 856–64.

Hogan, B. (2018) 'Social *Media Giveth, Social Media Taketh Away*: Facebook, friendships, and APIs'. *International Journal of Communication*, 12: 592–611.

Hogan, B. (2021) 'Networks area lens for power: a commentary on the recent advances in the ethics of social networks special issue'. *Social Networks*.

Holland, P., Laskey, K.B. and Leinhardt, S. (1983) 'Stochastic blockmodels: first steps'. *Social Networks*, 5 (2): 109–37.

Holland, S., Hosny, A., Newman, S., Joseph, J. and Chmielinski, K. (2020) 'The dataset nutrition label', in D. Hallinan, R. Leenes, S. Gutwirth and P. De Hert (eds), *Data Protection and Privacy: Data Protection and Democracy*. London: Hart. pp. 1–26.

Hutto, C. and Gilbert, E. (2014) 'VADER: a parsimonious rule-based model for sentiment analysis of social media text'. In *Proceedings of the Eighth International AAAI Conference on Weblogs and Social Media*, p. 1.

Ignatow, G. (2009) 'Culture and embodied cognition: moral discourses in internet support groups for overeaters'. *Social Forces*, 88 (2): 643–69.

Ignatow, G. and Mihalcea, R. (2016) *Text Mining: A Guidebook for the Social Sciences*. Thousand Oaks, CA: Sage.

Johnson, W. (2013) 'Comment: Bayesian statistics in the twenty first century'. *The American Statistician*, 67 (1): 9–11.

Jones, J., Amin, M.R., Kim, J. and Skiena, S. (2020) 'Stereotypical gender associations in language have decreased over time'. *Sociological Science*, 7: 1–35.

Joos, M. (1950) 'Description of language design'. *Journal of the Acoustical Society of America*, 22 (6): 701–7.

Jordan, M. (2003) *An Introduction to Probabilistic Graphical Models*. Cambridge, MA: MIT Press.

Jordan, M. (2004) 'Graphical models'. *Statistical Science*, 19 (1): 140–55.

Jünger, J. (2021) 'A brief history of APIs: *Limitations and opportunities for online research'*, in U. Engle and A. Quan-Haase (eds),. *Handbook of Computational Social Science* Abingdon: Routledge.

Jurafsky, D. and Hand, M. (2009) *Speech & Language Processing* (2nd edn). Hoboken, NJ: Pearson Prentice Hall.

Karrer, B. and Newman, M. (2011) 'Stochastic blockmodels and community structure in networks'. *Physical Review E*, 83 (1): 016107.

Kermack, W.O. and McKendrick, A. (1927) 'A contribution to the mathematical theory of epidemics'. *Proceedings of the Royal Society of London. Series A, Containing Papers of a Mathematical and Physical Character*, 115 (772): 700–721.

Kitts, J. (2014) 'Beyond networks in structural theories of exchange: promises from computational social science'. In *Advances in Group Processes* (Vol. 31). Bingley: Emerald Group. pp. 263–98.

Kitts, J. and Quintane, E. (2020) 'Rethinking social networks in the era of computational social science', in R. Light and J. Moody (eds), *The Oxford Handbook of Social Network Analysis*. Oxford: Oxford University Press. pp. 71–97.

Koller, D. and Friedman, N. (2009) *Probabilistic Graphical Models: Principles and Techniques*. Cambridge, MA: MIT Press.

Kozlowski, A., Taddy, M. and Evans, J. (2019) 'The geometry of culture: analyzing the meanings of class through word embeddings'. *American Sociological Review*, 84 (5): 905–49.

Krippendorff, K. (2019) *Content Analysis: An Introduction to its Methodology*. Thousand Oaks, CA: Sage.

Kruschke, J. (2014) *Doing Bayesian Data Analysis: A Tutorial with R, JAGS, and Stan*. Cambridge, MA: Academic Press.

Kusner, M. and Loftus, J. (2020) *The Long Road to Fairer Algorithms*. London: Springer Nature.

Lambert, B. (2018) *A Student's Guide to Bayesian Statistics*. Thousand Oaks, CA: Sage.

Lasswell, H. (1927) *Propaganda Technique in the World War*. Eastford, CT: Martino Fine Books.

Lazega, E. and Snijders, T. (2015) *Multilevel Network Analysis for the Social Sciences: Theory, Methods and Applications* (Vol. 12). New York: Springer.

Lee, M. and Martin, J.L. (2015a) 'Coding, counting and cultural cartography'. *American Journal of Cultural Sociology*, 3 (1): 1–33.

Lee, M. and Martin, J.L. (2015b) 'Response to Biernacki, Reed, and Spillman'. *American Journal of Cultural Sociology*, 3 (3): 380–415.

Lewis, K., Kaufman, J., Gonzalez, M., Wimmer, A. and Christakis, N. (2008) 'Tastes, ties, and time: a new social network dataset using Facebook. com'. *Social Networks*, 30 (4): 330–42.

Lin, J. (1991) 'Divergence measures based on the Shannon entropy'. *IEEE Transactions on Information Theory*, 37 (1): 145–51.

Linzhuo, L., Lingfei, W. and James, E. (2020) 'Social centralization and semantic collapse: hyperbolic embeddings of networks and text'. *Poetics*, 78: 101428.

Lizardo, O., Sepulvado, B., Stoltz, D.S. and Taylor, M.A. (2019) 'What can cognitive neuroscience do for cultural sociology?' *American Journal of Cultural Sociology*, 1–26.

Lorrain, F. and White, H.C. (1971) 'Structural equivalence of individuals in social networks'. *Journal of Mathematical Sociology*, 1 (1): 49–80.

Lusher, D., Koskinen, J. and Robins, G. (2013) *Exponential Random Graph Models for Social Networks: Theory, Methods, and Applications* (Vol. 35). Cambridge: Cambridge University Press.

Lynch, S. and Bartlett, B. (2019) 'Bayesian statistics in sociology: past, present, and future'. *Annual Review of Sociology*, 45: 47–68.

Ma, E. (2021) *Data Science Bootstrap: A Practical Guide to Getting Organized for Your Best Data Science Work*. Victoria, British Columbia: LeanPub.

Macy, M. and Flache, A. (2009) 'Social dynamics from the bottom up: agent-based models of social interaction', in P. Bearman and P. Hedström (eds), *The Oxford Handbook of Analytical Sociology*. Oxford: Oxford University Press. pp. 245–68.

Macy, M.W. and Willer, W. (2002) 'From factors to actors: computational sociology and agent-based modeling'. *Annual Review of Sociology*, 28 (1): 143–66.

Martin, O. (2018) *Bayesian Analysis with Python: Introduction to Statistical Modeling and Probabilistic Programming Using PyMC3 and ArviZ*. Birmingham: Packt.

Mastrandrea, R., Fournet, J. and Barrat, A. (2015) 'Contact patterns in a high school: a comparison between data collected using wearable sensors, contact diaries and friendship surveys'. *PLOS One*, 10 (9): e0136497.

Mayo, D. (2013) 'Discussion: Bayesian methods applied? Yes. Philosophical defense? In flux'. *The American Statistician*, 67 (1): 11–15.

McAdam, D. (2010) *Political Process and the Development of Black Insurgency, 1930-1970*. Chicago, IL: University of Chicago Press.

McCammon, H. (2009) 'Beyond frame resonance: the argumentative structure and persuasive capacity of twentieth-century US women's jury-rights frames'. *Mobilization: An International Quarterly*, 14 (1): 45–64.

McCammon, H. (2012) *The US Women's Jury Movements and Strategic Adaptation: A More Just Verdict*. Cambridge: Cambridge University Press.

McCammon, H.J., Muse, C.S., Newman, H.D. and Terrell, T.M. (2007) 'Movement framing and discursive opportunity structures: the political successes of the US women's jury movements'. *American Sociological Review*, 72 (5): 725–49.

McCarthy, J.D. and Zald, M.N. (1977) 'Resource mobilization and social movements: a partial theory'. *American Journal of Sociology*, 82 (6): 1212–41.

McElreath, R. (2017, 28 November) 'Markov chains: why walk when you can flow?' [Blog post]. https://elevanth.org/blog/2017/11/28/build-a-better-markov-chain/

McElreath, R. (2020) *Statistical Rethinking: A Bayesian Course with Examples in R and Stan*. Boca Raton, FL: CRC Press.

McGrayne, S.B. (2011) *The Theory That Would Not Die: How Bayes' Rule Cracked the Enigma Code, Hunted Down Russian Submarines & Emerged Triumphant from Two Centuries of Controversy*. New Haven, CT: Yale University Press.

McLevey, J., Browne, P. and Crick, T. (2021) 'Reproducibility and principled data processing', in U. Engel, A. Quan-Haase, S.X. Liu and L.E. Lyberg (eds), *Handbook of Computational Social Science*. London: Routledge.

McLevey, J. and Crick, T. (2022) Machine learning and neural network language modelling for sentiment analysis', in L. Sloan and A. Quan-Haase (eds) *The SAGE Handbook of Social Media Research*. London: Sage.

McLevey, J., Crick, T., Browne, P. and Durant, D. (2022) 'Word embeddings and the structural and cultural dimensions of democracy and autocracy, 1900-2020'. *Canadian Review of Sociology*. Forthcoming.

McShane, B., Gal, D., Gelman, A., Robert, C. and Tackett, J. (2019) 'Abandon statistical significance'. *The American Statistician*, 73 (suppl. 1): 235–45.

Merton, R.K. (1968) 'The Matthew effect in science: the reward and communication systems of science are considered'. *Science*, 159 (3810): 56–63.

Meyer, J.W., Krücken, G. and Drori, G. (2009) *World Society: The Writings of John W. Meyer*. Oxford: Oxford University Press.

Mikolov, T., Chen, K., Corrado, G. and Dean, J. (2013) 'Efficient estimation of word representations in vector space'. *arXiv Preprint arXiv:1301.3781*.

Mikolov, T., Sutskever, I., Chen, K., Corrado, G.S. and Dean, J. (2013) 'Distributed representations of words and phrases and their compositionality'. In *Proceedings of the 26th International Conference on Neural Information Processing Systems*, pp. 3111–19.

Mikolov, T., Yih, W.-t. and Zweig, G. (2013) 'Linguistic regularities in continuous space word representations'. In *Proceedings of the 2013 Conference of the North American Chapter of the Association for Computational Linguistics: Human Language Technologies*, pp. 746–51.

Mimno, D., Wallach, H., Talley, E., Leenders, M. and McCallum, A. (2011) 'Optimizing semantic coherence in topic models'. In *Proceedings of the 2011 Conference on Empirical Methods in Natural Language Processing*, pp. 262–72.

Mische, A. (2011) 'Relational sociology, culture, and agency', in J. Scott and P.J. Carrington (eds), *The SAGE Handbook of Social Network Analysis*. Thousand Oaks, CA: Sage. pp. 80–97.

Mitchell, M. (2019) *Artificial Intelligence: A Guide for Thinking Humans*. London: Penguin.

Mitchell, M., Wu, S., Zaldivar, A., Barnes, P., Vasserman, L., Hutchinson, B., et al. (2019) 'Model cards for model reporting'. In *Proceedings of the Conference on Fairness, Accountability, and Transparency*, pp. 220–9.

Mitchell, R. (2018) *Web Scraping with Python: Collecting More Data from the Modern Web*. Sebastopol, CA: O'Reilly Media.

Mogadala, A. and Rettinger, A. (2016) 'Bilingual word embeddings from parallel and non-parallel corpora for cross-language text classification'. In *Proceedings of the 2016 Conference of the North American Chapter of the Association for Computational Linguistics: Human Language Technologies*, pp. 692–702.

Mohammad, S.M. (2016) 'Sentiment analysis: detecting valence, emotions, and other affectual states from text'. *Emotion Measurement*, 201–37.

Mohr, J. (1998) 'Measuring meaning structures'. *Annual Review of Sociology*, 24 (1): 345–70.

Mohr, J., Bail, C., Frye, M., Lena, J., Lizardo, O., McDonnell, T., et al. (2020) *Measuring Culture*. New York: Columbia University Press.

Mohr, J. and Bogdanov, P. (2013) *Introduction – Topic Models: What They Are and Why They Matter*. Amsterdam: Elsevier.

Mohr, J., Wagner-Pacifici, R. and Breiger, R. (2015) 'Toward a computational hermeneutics'. *Big Data & Society*, 2 (2). doi: 10.1177/2053951715613809

Molina, M. and Garip, F. (2019) 'Machine learning for sociology'. *Annual Review of Sociology*, 45: 27–45.

Müller, A. and Guido, S. (2016) *Introduction to Machine Learning with Python: A Guide for Data Scientists*. Sebastopol, CA: O'Reilly Media.

Murphy, K. (2012) *Machine Learning: A Probabilistic Perspective*. Cambridge, MA: MIT Press.

Mützel, S. and Breiger, R. (2020) 'Duality beyond persons and groups', in R. Light and J. Moody (eds), *The Oxford Handbook of Social Networks*. Oxford: Oxford University Press. pp. 392–413.

Neblo, M., Esterling, K. and Lazer, D. (2018) *Politics with the People: Building a Directly Representative Democracy* (Vol. 555). Cambridge, MA: Cambridge University Press.

Nelson, L. (2015) 'Political logics as cultural memory: cognitive structures, local continuities, and women's organizations in Chicago and New York City'. *Working Paper*.

Nelson, L. (2017) 'Computational grounded theory: a methodological framework'. *Sociological Methods & Research*, 49 (1): 3–42.

Nelson, L. (2021) 'Leveraging the alignment between machine learning and intersectionality: using word embeddings to measure intersectional experiences of the nineteenth century US South'. *Poetics*, 101539.

Nelson, L. (2021) 'Cycles of conflict, a century of continuity: the impact of persistent place-based political logics on social movement strategy'. *American Journal of Sociology*, 127 (1): 1–59.

Nelson, L.K., Burk, D., Knudsen, M. and McCall, L. (2018) 'The future of coding: a comparison of hand-coding and three types of computer-assisted text analysis methods'. *Sociological Methods & Research*, 50 (1): 202–37.

Neuendorf, K.A. (2016) *The Content Analysis Guidebook*. Thousand Oaks, CA: Sage.

Nielse, A. (2021) *Practical Fairness: Achieving Fair and Secure Data Models*. Sebastopol, CA: O'Reilly Media.

Nissim, M., van Noord, R. and van der Goot, R. (2020) 'Fair is better than sensational: man is to doctor as woman is to doctor'. *Computational Linguistics*, 46 (2): 487–97.

Nivre, J. and Fang, C.-T. (2017) 'Universal dependency evaluation'. In *Proceedings of the NoDaLiDa 2017 Workshop on Universal Dependencies (UDW 2017)*, pp. 86–95.

Noble, S.U. (2018) *Algorithms of Oppression: How Search Engines Reinforce Racism*. New York: New York University Press.

Nowicki, K. and Snijders, T. (2001) 'Estimation and prediction for stochastic blockstructures'. *Journal of the American Statistical Association*, 96 (455): 1077–87.

O'Neil, C. (2016) *Weapons of Math Destruction: How Big Data Increases Inequality and Threatens Democracy*. New York: Crown.

Palla, G., Derényi, I., Farkas, I. and Vicsek, T. (2005) 'Uncovering the overlapping community structure of complex networks in nature and society'. *Nature*, 435 (7043): 814–18.

Papakyriakopoulos, O., Hegelich, S., Serrano, J.C.M. and Marco, F. (2020) 'Bias in word embeddings'. In *Proceedings of the 2020 Conference on Fairness, Accountability, and Transparency*, pp. 446–57.

Pearl, J. (2009) *Causality*. Cambridge: Cambridge University Press.

Pearl, J. and Mackenzie, D. (2018) *The Book of Why: The New Science of Cause and Effect*. New York: Basic Books.

Pearson, K. (1901) 'On lines and planes of closest fit to systems of points in space'. *The London, Edinburgh, and Dublin Philosophical Magazine and Journal of Science*, 2 (11): 559–72.

Peixoto, T. (2014) 'Hierarchical block structures and high-resolution model selection in large networks'. *Physical Review*, X 4 (1): Article 011047.

Peixoto, T.P. (2019) 'Bayesian stochastic blockmodeling', in P. Doreian, V. Batagelj and A. Ferligoj (eds), *Advances in Network Clustering and Blockmodeling*. New York, Wiley. pp. 289–332.

Perrin, A.J. and Vaisey, S. (2008) 'Parallel public spheres: distance and discourse in letters to the editor'. *American Journal of Sociology*, 114 (3): 781–810.

Perry, B., Pescosolido, B., Small, M. and McCranie, A. (2020) 'Introduction to the special issue on ego networks'. *Network Science*, 8 (2): 137–41.

Prabhu, V.U. and Birhane, A. (2020) 'Large image datasets: a pyrrhic win for computer vision?' *arXiv Preprint arXiv:2006.16923*.

Prabowo, R. and Thelwall, M. (2009) 'Sentiment analysis: a combined approach'. *Journal of Informetrics*, 3 (2): 143–57.

Prell, C. (2012) *Social Network Analysis: History, Theory and Methodology*. Thousand Oaks, CA: Sage.

Price, D.D.S. (1965) 'Networks of scientific papers'. *Science*, 149 (3683): 510–15.

Price, D.D.S. (1986) *Little Science, Big Science... and Beyond* (Vol. 480). New York: Columbia University Press.

Reed, I.A. (2015) 'Counting, interpreting and their potential interrelation in the human sciences'. *American Journal of Cultural Sociology*, 3 (3): 353–64.

Rheault, L. and Cochrane, C. (2020) 'Word embeddings for the analysis of ideological placement in parliamentary corpora'. *Political Analysis*, 28 (1): 112–33.

Roberts, M., Stewart, B., Tingley, D. and Airoldi, E. (2013) 'The structural topic model and applied social science'. *Advances in Neural Information Processing Systems Workshop on Topic Models: Computation, Application, and Evaluation*, 4: 1–20.

Roberts, M.E, Stewart, B.M., Tingley, D., Lucas, C., Leder-Luis, J., Gadarian, S.K., et al. (2014) 'Structural topic models for open-ended survey responses'. *American Journal of Political Science*, 58 (4): 1064–82.

Robins, G. (2015) *Doing Social Network Research: Network-Based Research Design for Social Scientists*. Thousand Oaks, CA: Sage.

Röder, M., Both, A. and Hinneburg, A. (2015) 'Exploring the space of topic coherence measures'. In *Proceedings of the Eighth ACM International Conference on Web Search and Data Mining*, pp. 399–408.

Rosenblatt, F. (1958) 'The perceptron: a probabilistic model for information storage and organization in the brain'. *Psychological Review*, 65 (6): 386–408.

Rosen-Zvi, M., Griffiths, T., Steyvers, M. and Smyth, P. (2012) 'The author-topic model for authors and documents'. *arXiv Preprint arXiv:1207.4169*.

Rossetti, G., Milli, L., Rinzivillo, S., Sirbu, A., Pedreschi, D. and Giannotti, F. (2017) 'NDlib: studying network diffusion dynamics'. In *2017 IEEE International Conference on Data Science and Advanced Analytics (DSAA)*, pp. 155–64.

Rossetti, G., Milli, L., Rinzivillo, S., Sirbu, A., Pedreschi, D. and Giannotti, F. (2018) 'NDlib: a Python library to model and analyze diffusion processes over complex networks'. *International Journal of Data Science and Analytics*, 5 (1): 61–79.

Ruder, S., Vulić, I. and Søgaard, A. (2019) 'A survey of cross-lingual word embedding models'. *Journal of Artificial Intelligence Research*, 65: 569–631.

Rudin, C. (2019) 'Stop explaining black box machine learning models for high stakes decisions and use interpretable models instead'. *Nature Machine Intelligence*, 1 (5): 206–15.

Ruhe, A.H. (2016) 'Enron data'. www.ahschulz.de/enron-email-data/

Rumelhart, D., Hinton, G. and Williams, R. (1986) 'Learning representations by back-propagating errors'. *Nature*, 323 (6088): 533–6.

Russell, M. and Klassen, M. (2019) *Mining the Social Web* (3rd edn). Sebastopol, CA: O'Reilly Media.

Salganik, M. (2019) *Bit by Bit: Social Research in the Digital Age*. Princeton, NJ: Princeton University Press.

Salvatier, J., Wiecki, T. and Fonnesbeck, C. (2016) 'Probabilistic programming in Python using PyMC3'. *PeerJ Computer Science*, 2: e55.

Sanh, V., Debut, L., Chaumond, J. and Wolf, T. (2019) 'DistilBERT, a distilled version of BERT: smaller, faster, cheaper and lighter'. *arXiv Preprint arXiv:1910.01108*.

Sapiezynski, P., Stopczynski, A., Lassen, D.D. and Lehmann, S. (2019). 'Interaction data from the Copenhagen Networks Study'. *Scientific Data*, 6 (1): 1–10.

Scott, J. (2013) *Social Network Analysis* (3rd edn). Thousand Oaks, CA: Sage.

Scott, J. (2017) *Social Network Analysis* (4th edn). Thousand Oaks, CA: Sage.

Severance, C.R. (2016) *Python for Everybody*. CreateSpace Independent Publishing Platform.

Shaw, L. (2015) 'Mechanics and dynamics of social construction: modeling the emergence of culture from individual mental representation'. *Poetics*, 52: 75–90.

Shaw, L. (2019) 'Charting the emergence of the cultural from the cognitive with agent-based modeling', in W. Brekhus and G. Ignatow (eds), *The Oxford Handbook of Cognitive Sociology*. New York: Oxford University Press. p. 403.

Shotts, W. (2019) *The Linux Command Line: A Complete Introduction*. San Francisco, CA: No Starch Press.

Sloan, L. and Quan-Haase, A. (2017a) 'A retrospective on state of the art social media research methods: ethical decisions, big-small data rivalries and the spectre of the 6Vs', in L. Sloan and A. Quan-Haase (eds), *The SAGE Handbook of Social Media Research Methods*. London: Sage.

Sloan, L. and Quan-Haase, A. (eds) (2017b) *The SAGE Handbook of Social Media Research Methods*. London: Sage.

Small, M. (2011) 'How to conduct a mixed methods study: recent trends in a rapidly growing literature'. *Annual Review of Sociology*, 37: 57–86.

Small, M., Perry, B., Pescosolido, B. and Smith, N. (eds) (2021) *Personal Networks: Classic Readings and New Directions in Ego-Centric Analysis*. Cambridge: Cambridge University Press.

Smith, J. and Fetner, T. (2009) 'Structural approaches in the sociology of social movements', in B. Klandermans and C. Roggeband (eds), *Handbook of Social Movements Across Disciplines*. New York: Springer. pp. 13–57.

Snijders, T. and Nowicki, K. (1997) 'Estimation and prediction for stochastic blockmodels for graphs with latent block structure'. *Journal of Classification*, 14 (1): 75–100.

Snow, D., Benford, R., McCammon, H., Hewitt, L. and Fitzgerald, S. (2014) 'The emergence, development, and future of the framing perspective: 25+ years since "Frame Alignment"'. *Mobilization: An International Quarterly*, 19 (1): 23–46.

Spillman, L. (2015) 'Ghosts of straw men: a reply to Lee and Martin'. *American Journal of Cultural Sociology*, 3 (3): 365–79.

Squire, M. (2016) *Mastering Data Mining with Python: Find Patterns Hidden in Your Data*. Birmingham: Packt.

Steed, R. and Caliskan, A. (2021) 'Image representations learned with unsupervised pre-training contain human-like biases'. In *Proceedings of the 2021 ACM Conference on Fairness, Accountability, and Transparency*, pp. 701–13.

Stoltz, D. and Taylor, M. (2019) 'Concept mover's distance: measuring concept engagement via word embeddings in texts'. *Journal of Computational Social Science*, 2 (2): 293–313.

Stopczynski, A., Sekara, V., Sapiezynski, P., Cuttone, A., Madsen, M.M., Larsen, J.E. and Lehmann, S. (2014) 'Measuring large-scale social networks with high resolution'. *PLOS One*, 9 (4): e95978.

Stovel, K. and Shaw, L. (2012) 'Brokerage'. *Annual Review of Sociology*, 38: 139–58.

Sun, Z., Yu, H., Song, X., Liu, R., Yang, Y. and Zhou, D. (2020) 'Mobilebert: a compact task-agnostic Bert for resource-limited devices'. *arXiv Preprint arXiv:2004.02984*.

Sweeney, L. (2002) 'K-Anonymity: a model for protecting privacy'. *International Journal of Uncertainty, Fuzziness and Knowledge-Based Systems*, 10 (05): 557–70.

Syed, S. and Spruit, M. (2018) 'Selecting priors for latent Dirichlet allocation'. In *2018 IEEE 12th International Conference on Semantic Computing (ICSC)*, pp. 194–202.

Szucs, D. and Ioannidis, J. (2017) 'When null hypothesis significance testing is unsuitable for research: a reassessment'. *Frontiers in Human Neuroscience*, 11: 390.

Tabachnick, B.G. and Fidell, L.S. (2007) *Using Multivariate Statistics* (Vol. 5). Boston, MA: Pearson.

Taboada, M. (2016) 'Sentiment analysis: an overview from linguistics'. *Annual Review of Linguistics*, 2 (1): 325–47.

Tatmam, R. (2020, 5 July) 'What I won't build'. Widening NLP Keynote.

Taylor, M. and Stoltz, D. (2020) 'Concept class analysis: a method for identifying cultural schemas in texts'. *Sociological Science*, 7: 544–69.

Tindall, D., McLevey, J., Koop-Monteiro, Y., and Graham, A. (2022) 'Big data, computational social science, and other recent innovations in social network analysis'. *Canadian Review of Sociology*. Forthcoming.

Traag, V.A., Waltman, L. and Van Eck, N.J. (2019) 'From Louvain to Leiden: guaranteeing well-connected communities'. *Scientific Reports*, 9 (1): 1–12.

Tubaro, P., Ryan, L., Casilli, A. and D'angelo, A. (2020) 'Social network analysis: new ethical approaches through collective reflexivity. Introduction to the Special Issue of *Social Networks*'. *Social Networks*.

The UK Parliament. (2021) 'The UK Commons Hansard'.

Upsahl, K. (2013) 'Why metadata matters'. Electronic Frontier Foundation. https://www.eff.org/deeplinks/2013/06/why-metadata-matters

US Federal Election Commission. (2020) 'Individual contributions'.

VanderPlas, J. (2016) *Python Data Science Handbook: Essential Tools for Working with Data*. Sebastopol, CA: O'Reilly Media.

Vasiliev, Y. (2020) *Natural Language Processing with Python and SpaCy: A Practical Introduction*. San Francisco, CA: No Starch Press.

Vaswani, A., Shazeer, N., Parmar, N., Uszkoreit, J., Jones, L., Gomez, A.N., et al. (2017) 'Attention is all you need'. *arXiv Preprint arXiv:1706.03762*.

Vries, T.d., Misra, I., Wang, C. and van der Maaten, L. (2019) 'Does object recognition work for everyone?' In *Proceedings of the IEEE/CVF Conference on Computer Vision and Pattern Recognition Workshops*, pp. 52–59.

Wallach, H., Mimno, D. and McCallum, A. (2009) 'Rethinking LDA: why priors matter'. In *Proceedings of the 22nd International Conference on Neural Information Processing Systems*, pp. 1973–81.

Wallach, H., Murray, I., Salakhutdinov, R. and Mimno, D. (2009) 'Evaluation methods for topic models'. In *Proceedings of the 26th Annual International Conference on Machine Learning*, pp. 1105–12.

Wang, C., Blei, D. and Heckerman, D. (2012) 'Continuous time dynamic topic models'. *arXiv Preprint arXiv:1206.3298*.

Wang, Y. and Wong, G. (1987) 'Stochastic blockmodels for directed graphs'. *Journal of the American Statistical Association*, 82 (397): 8–19.

Ward, B. (2021) *How Linux Works: What Every Superuser Should Know* (3rd edn). San Francisco, CA: No Starch Press.

Ward, J. (2020) *The Student's Guide to Cognitive Neuroscience* (4th edn). London, Routledge.

Wasserman, D. and Flinn, A. (2020) 'Introducing the 2017 Cook Political Report Partisan Voter Index'.

Watts, D. and Strogatz, S. (1998) 'Collective dynamics of "small-world" networks'. *Nature*, 393 (6684): 440–42.

Weinstein, Y., Sumeracki, M. and Caviglioli, O. (2018) *Understanding How We Learn: A Visual Guide*. London: Routledge.

West, S.M., Whittaker, M. and Crawford, K. (2019) *Discriminating Systems: Gender, Race, and Power in AI*. New York: AI Now Institute, New York University.

Western, B. (1999) 'Bayesian analysis for sociologists: an introduction'. *Sociological Methods & Research*, 28 (1): 7–34.

Weston, S.J., Ritchie, S.J., Rohrer, J.M. and Przybylski, A.K. (2019) 'Recommendations for increasing the transparency of analysis of preexisting data sets'. *Advances in Methods and Practices in Psychological Science*, 2 (3): 214–27.

White, D. and Reitz, K. (1983) 'Graph and semigroup homomorphisms on networks of relations'. *Social Networks*, 5 (2): 193–234.

White, H. (1992) *Identity and Control: How Social Formations Emerge*. Princeton, NJ: Princeton University Press.

Wittgenstein, L. (1953) *Philosophical Investigations: The English Text of the Third Edition*. New York: Macmillan.

Wolff, K.H. (1950) *The Sociology of Georg Simmel*. Glencoe, IL: Free Press.

Ypma, T.J. (1995) 'Historical development of the Newton–Raphson method'. *SIAM Review*, 37 (4): 531–51.

Zimmer, M. (2010) '"But the data is already public": on the ethics of research in Facebook'. *Ethics and Information Technology*, 12 (4): 313–25.

INDEX

Figures and Tables are indicated by page numbers in bold print.

CPSIA information can be obtained
at www.ICGtesting.com
Printed in the USA
JSHW041522190622
27055JS00002B/4

9 781526 468185